Acclaim for *The Knife Man:*

www.booksattransworld.co.uk

The Knife Man

Wendy Moore

BANTAM BOOKS

LONDON • TORONTO • SYDNEY • AUCKLAND • JOHANNESBURG

THE KNIFE MAN
A BANTAM BOOK : 9780553816181

Originally published in Great Britain by Bantam Press,
a division of Transworld Publishers

PRINTING HISTORY
Bantam Press edition published 2005
Bantam edition published 2006

5 7 9 10 8 6 4

Set in 11/13.5pt Sabon by
Falcon Oast Graphic Art Ltd.

Bantam Books are published by Transworld Publishers,
61–63 Uxbridge Road, London W5 5SA,
A Random House Group Company.

Addresses for Random House Group Ltd companies outside the UK
can be found at: www.randomhouse.co.uk
The Random House Group Ltd Reg. No. 954009.

Printed and bound in Great Britain by
CPI Antony Rowe, Chippenham, Wiltshire

The Random House Group Limited supports The Forest Stewardship
Council (FSC), the leading international forest certification organisation.
All our titles that are printed on Greenpeace approved FSC certified paper
carry the FSC logo. Our paper procurement policy can be found at:
www.rbooks.co.uk/environment.

For Peter, Sam and Susie

I have made candles of infants fat
The Sextons have been my slaves,
I have bottled babes unborn, and dried
Hearts and livers from rifled graves.

From 'The Surgeon's Warning',
Robert Southey, *Poems*, 1799

Contents

Acknowledgements

Without the assistance of a great many people who have given their time and expertise freely and generously, it would have been impossible to turn my ambition to write a biography of John Hunter into a reality. In particular, I am indebted to the patient encouragement and expert advice of Andrew Cunningham, Wellcome Trust senior research fellow in the history of medicine at Cambridge University, who has diligently read and commented on my manuscript and offered enthusiastic support throughout, helping me to appreciate 'the reasons of things'.

Numerous people at museums and libraries in England and Scotland have helped me enormously. Fil Dearie of the Hunter House museum in East Kilbride kept me going with his spirited enthusiasm, John McLeish of East Kilbride public library gave vital local history help, and Bill Niven, former provost (mayor) of East Kilbride, provided wonderful local history insights and a fascinating guided tour of Hunter sights. At the Royal College of Surgeons in London, former curator of the Hunterian Museum Liz Allen gave me essential early help, Simon Chaplin, the current curator, provided invaluable guidance and specialist advice, and head librarian Tina Craig met my seemingly endless demands for manuscripts with unerring patience. At the Wellcome Library for the History and Understanding of Medicine (one of my favourite places to spend a day), staff provided generous assistance and expert knowledge on an almost daily basis. I would also like to thank everybody at the Wellcome Trust Centre for the History of Medicine at University College London, especially Professor Hal Cook, for welcoming a mere journalist into their academic fold. My research was completed while I was an honorary research assistant with the centre. Many more staff at various libraries and museums have been instrumental in my research. In particular I wish to thank everybody who helped me at the Natural History Museum, the library of the Royal Society, the British Library, the Guildhall Library, the City of Westminster Archives Centre, London Metropolitan Archives, the library of the Royal Academy, the Royal Humane Society, the British Dental Association, Dr Johnson's House, the Society of Apothecaries and, at the University of Glasgow, the Special Collections Library, the Hunterian Museum and the Hunterian Art Gallery.

I have been extraordinarily lucky in enjoying the support of many individual experts who have advised me on specialist areas. Mick Crumplin, honorary consultant surgeon and honorary curator at the Royal College of Surgeons, kindly helped me appreciate eighteenth-century army conditions. Professor Harold Ellis, Professor Sir Peter Bell and Alan Scott helped elucidate aneurysm surgery today and in the eighteenth century. Malcolm Bishop provided generous advice on dental issues, Dr Michael Waugh gave me technical assistance on questions concerning sexual diseases, and Peter Baskett and John Zorab both helped me when researching resuscitation today and in the past. I am also particularly grateful to all the staff at the dissecting rooms of Guy's, King's and St Thomas' School of Biomedical Sciences, London, where I was privileged to be allowed to witness a contemporary dissecting class conducted with respect and dignity. Dr Colin Stolkin, senior lecturer in anatomy, has been encouraging from the beginning. Dr Alistair Hunter, academic manager of the dissecting rooms, helped me to understand the scientific compulsion that motivated John Hunter to explore the beauty of the human form and has answered my numerous and often strange anatomical queries with good humour and generosity throughout. I am grateful too to Dr James Munro, who kindly read my manuscript and provided vital medical insights.

On the publishing front, I was extremely fortunate to find my superb agent, Patrick Walsh, who helped me shape my ideas with a gentle but firm touch. And I am especially grateful to all the enthusiastic, warm and committed staff at Transworld, especially to my wonderful editor Brenda Kimber for her calm, supportive and creative guiding hand. Thanks also to Sheila Lee and Kate Brader who helped research and locate the pictures, and to Daniel Balado and Katrina Whone for skilful editing.

Finally, a big thank you is due to my family and friends – too many to mention individually, but they know who they are – who have steadfastly given me practical support and spiritual encouragement. My children, Sam and Susannah, deserve special praise for their forbearance and understanding (and my failure to attend numerous school trips). My mum and dad have also given loyal support. Most of all, this book would never have been begun, let alone completed, without the constant enthusiasm and encouragement of my partner, Peter Davies, who believed in this project, and in me, throughout.

Picture
Acknowledgements

COLOUR SECTIONS
Dorofield Hardy after Robert Home *John Hunter*, *c.*1770. © The Royal Society; Allan Ramsay *William Hunter*, 1765. Hunterian Art Gallery, University of Glasgow; L. P. Boitard *The Covent Garden Morning Frolick*, 1747. Guildhall Library and Art Gallery © Corporation of London

Engraving by J. H. Savigny of portable amputation and trepanning instruments from a book of engravings published in 1798; etching after Gillray *Breathing a Vein*, 1804; watercolour of St George's Hospital as reproduced in Jessé Foot's *Life of John Hunter*, 1822; Thomas Rowlandson *Transplanting of Teeth*, 1787; Thomas Rowlandson *The Amputation*, 1785. All Wellcome Library, London.

Engraving after William Hogarth *The Execution of the Idle Apprentice at Tyburn*, 1747; engraving by William Austin *The Anatomist Overtaken by the Watch in Carrying off Miss W—ts in a Hamper*, 1773; engraving by Thomas Rowlandson *The Resurrection Men*, 1775;

lithograph by Thomas Rowlandson *The Dissecting Room*, *c.*1770; engraving by William Hogarth *The Reward of Cruelty*, 1751. All Wellcome Library, London.

Illustration by Jan van Rymsdyk from John Hunter's *The Works, Atlas*, 1835; cock's comb implanted with a human tooth; illustration by Jan van Rymsdyk from John Hunter's *The natural history of human teeth*, 1771; illustration by Jan van Rymsdyk from William Hunter's *The Anatomy of the Human Gravid Uterus*, 1774; the coachman's leg bone. All reproduced by kind permission of the President and Council of the Royal College of Surgeons of England.

Etching by Charles Mosley *The Tar's Triumph, or Bawdy-House Battery*, 1749. Department of Prints and Drawings, British Museum, London; title page of John Hunter's *Treatise on the Venereal Disease*, 1786 and illustration from John Hunter's *The Works, Atlas*, 1835. Both reproduced by kind permission of the President and Council of the Royal College of Surgeons of England.

Portrait of John Hunter by Henry Bone after Sir Joshua Reynolds. Hunterian Museum; some of Hunter's pocket knives. Both reproduced by kind permission of the President and Council of the Royal College of Surgeons of England.

All specimens reproduced by kind permission of the President and Council of the Royal College of Surgeons of England.

Watercolour of John Hunter's house at Earls Court, from Jessé Foot's *The Life of John Hunter*, 1822. Wellcome Library, London; pencil drawing by Sawrey Gilpin *Mr Wright's Freemartin*, from John Hunter's drawing books. Reproduced by kind permission of the President and Council of the Royal College of Surgeons of England; John Stubbs *The Great Indian Rhinoceros*, commissioned by John Hunter. Hunterian Museum. Reproduced by kind permission of the President and Council of the Royal College of Surgeons of England; after William Byrne *An Animal found on the coast of New Holland called a Kanguroo*, c.1773. © National Maritime Museum; watercolour of a giraffe, possibly by John Hunter, from his drawing books. Reproduced by kind permission of the President and Council of the Royal College of Surgeons of England.

Lithograph after Sir Nathaniel Dance Holland *John Hunter*, 1793. Wellcome Library, London; John James Masquerier's portrait of Anne Hunter. Photo Royal College of Surgeons, reproduced by kind permission of the Jobson family; ground plan of Hunter's premises in Leicester Square; Wellcome Library, London; pastel portrait of Edward Jenner by John Raphael Smith. Wellcome Library, London; portrait by Benjamin West of Sir Joseph Banks in a Maori mantle. Lincolnshire County Council, Usher Gallery/www.bridgeman.co.uk; copy by Henry M. Allen of Sir Joshua Reynolds' portrait of John Hunter, 1785. Reproduced by kind permission of the President and Council of the Royal College of Surgeons of England; etching by John Kay of Charles Byrne, the Irish Giant, 1784. Mary Evans Picture Library; Byrne's skeleton. Reproduced by kind permission of the President and Council of the Royal College of Surgeons of England.

Watercolour by T. H. Shepherd of the Royal College of Surgeons Museum, *c*.1840. Reproduced by kind permission of the President and Council of the Royal College of Surgeons of England; mezzotint after John Opie of Jessé Foot from his *The Life of John Hunter*, 1822. Wellcome Library, London; engraving after William Beechey of Sir Everard Home *c*.1810. Wellcome Library, London; engraving of William Clift after a daguerreotype by Claudet, 1849. Reproduced by kind permission of the President and Council of the Royal College of Surgeons of England.

1

The Coach Driver's Knee

'I have seen a man die almost immediately upon the loss of a testicle . . . The loss of a limb above the knee, is more than man can bear . . .'

John Hunter[1]

St George's Hospital, Hyde Park Corner, London, December 1785

The patient faced an agonizing choice. Above the cries and moans of fellow sufferers on the fetid ward, he listened as the surgeon outlined the dilemma. If the large swelling at the back of his knee was left to continue growing, it would eventually burst, leading to certain and painful death. If, on the other hand, the leg was amputated above the knee, there was a slim chance he would survive the crude operation – provided he did not die of shock on the operating table, or bleed to death soon after, or succumb to infection on the filthy ward days later – but he would be permanently disabled.

For the forty-five-year-old hackney coach driver either option was unthinkable. Since he had first noticed the swelling in the hollow behind his knee three years ago, the lump had grown steadily until it was now the size of an orange; it throbbed continuously and had become so painful he could barely walk.[2] Extended on the hospital bed before him, the leg and foot were hideously swollen while the skin had turned an unsightly mottled brown. Once the coachman had gained admittance to St George's, having successfully persuaded the governors he was a deserving recipient of their charity, the surgeon on duty had lost no time in making a diagnosis. After examining the tell-tale lump, which was 'so large as to distend the two hamstrings laterally', he had no doubts about the verdict. The surgeon had seen popliteal aneurysms at exactly the same spot on numerous occasions and knew all too well the prognosis.

It was a common enough problem in the cab driver's line of work: popliteal aneurysms could happen to anyone – they could develop in arteries anywhere in the body either through injury or, more commonly, due to a medical condition as a result of which the artery walls lose their elasticity – but appeared to occur with unnatural frequency among coach drivers, postilions and others working in equestrian occupations in Georgian London. The problem may quite possibly have been exacerbated by the wearing of high leather riding boots which rubbed at the back of the knee.[3] Whatever the cause, the weakened section of artery would begin to bulge and develop into a sac which eventually became filled with clotted blood. When these occurred behind the knee, in the popliteal artery, they were not only extremely painful but made walking exceedingly difficult. The outcome was often an early death, if not from the condition itself then from the treatment generally meted out. To lose his leg, even supposing the coach driver survived such a drastic procedure in an era long before anaesthesia or antiseptics, would inevitably mean never being able to work again. But to carry on working, navigating his horse-drawn carriage over London's rutted and congested roads, would be plainly impossible if the lump was left to grow. Either way, the cabbie faced destitution and the workhouse.

But there was a third choice, the surgeon at his bedside now confided on that early December day, for a coach-man sufficiently willing or desperate. In his slow Scottish lilt, redolent of his humble Lowland farming origins, the surgeon laid out his scheme for a daring and novel operation. Surrounded by the poxed, maimed and diseased bodies of London's poorest, huddled in their beds on the draughty ward, the cabbie resolved to put his life in the hands of John Hunter.

Without a doubt, John Hunter's reputation would have been well known to the coach driver long before he limped through the portal of St George's, for he was generally acknowledged as one of the best-skilled surgeons in London, if not Europe, and was a favourite among the well-heeled and the unshod alike. As well as working for no recompense in St George's, patching up the poor most afternoons, he was in constant demand from the fee-paying patients who thronged each morning to his fashionable home in Leicester Square or called him out for consultations in the elegant drawing rooms of their West End mansions. For all his blunt manners, his coarse speech and his disdain for fashion – he currently sported an unkempt beard and tied his tawny-coloured hair back in preference to the customary wig – Hunter was firmly established in Georgian high society, visiting court as Surgeon Extraordinary to George III, dining with the society artist Sir Joshua Reynolds, and debating science with his close friend, the well-connected naturalist Sir Joseph Banks.

Now aged fifty-seven, with seventeen years' service on the staff of St George's under his belt, Hunter was approaching the peak of his career and success, and enjoyed fame and earning power in equal measures as reward. When the Scottish philosopher David Hume consulted a galaxy of doctors about his worsening health in 1776, it was Hunter – the only one of the medics physically to examine the patient – who diagnosed terminal cancer.[4] It was Hunter who gave first-aid to Dr Nevil Maskelyne, the ambitious astronomer royal, when he collapsed vomiting in a coffee-house after eating tripe in 1782.[5] And when the genial American diplomat Benjamin Franklin became crippled with pain from a bladder stone in the summer of 1785, it was Hunter he consulted.[6]

Aside from tackling the routine surgeons' fare of stanching stab-wounds from duels, removing lumps and limbs, and tending sundry abscesses, boils, pimples and running sores, Hunter was renowned for his pioneering operations. Only two months before the coach driver's admission he had skilfully cut away from the neck of a thirty-seven-year-old man a massive benign tumour that weighed more than four kilograms and measured roughly the size of an extra head. The grateful patient had walked away with only a long, neat scar as a souvenir of his ordeal.[7]

No doubt the coachman had also watched from his bed

as Hunter's medical students trooped devotedly after their teacher on his regular rounds of the surgical wards, for more pupils flocked to Hunter's side than to all the other surgeons at St George's put together.[8] Aspiring young surgeons travelled not only from the far reaches of the British Isles but even from across the Atlantic to 'walk the wards' at Hunter's side and to hear their hero expound his radical views in the private lectures he held at his home throughout the winter. Fired by his revolutionary ideas, they walked home to their lodgings through the dimly lit streets hotly debating the theories they had absorbed, and would quote their mentor, as one put it, with all the authority of Aristotle.[9] One zealous student reported Hunter's lectures as 'so far superior to every thing I had conceived or heard before, that there seemed no comparison between the mind of the man who delivered them, and all the individuals whether ancient or modern who had ever gone before him'. Another devotee called him simply 'the dear man'.[10]

But the cabbie would doubtless also have heard darker stories, whispered on the wards, insinuated in newspapers or muttered in taverns, coffee-houses and cockpits, for Hunter was not a popular man within the four walls of St George's. Although his pupils idolized their master, and patients were frequently thankful to the bluff but honest surgeon, Hunter's fiery temper and maverick views, coupled with his decidedly unorthodox methods, had earned him powerful enemies at the hospital and beyond. While aristocrats humbly bowed to his medical advice and denizens of the Royal Society – the engine room of eighteenth-century progress – hung on his every pronouncement, Hunter was isolated at St George's. To his fellow surgeons he was at best a laughing stock and at worst a reckless, ill-educated fool. Hunter had quarrelled too with several of the city's other leading practitioners, not least his own brother.

To the students, the explanation was straightforward: Hunter was simply so far ahead of his contemporaries that he stood alone. 'It was a comfortless precedence, for it deprived him of sympathy and social co-operation; and he felt that his labours and merits were not known, or fairly estimated,' said one.[11] But rival surgeons had other views. Colleagues at St George's decried Hunter's novel approach and his controversial methods, preferring rather to bleed, blister and purge their patients to early graves, in strict accordance with classical teaching stretching back to Ancient Greece, than to question any established modes of practice. They certainly concurred with, if not actively encouraged, Hunter's most vociferous enemy, a mediocre house surgeon at the nearby Middlesex Hospital called Jessé Foot, whom Hunter had once stung by summarily dismissing a surgical appliance the young man had invented. In Foot's view, Hunter was 'a very inferior, dangerous, and irregular practical surgeon' who was, furthermore, embroiled in 'continual war' at St George's.[12]

Aside from concerns at his unusual ways, the chief source of conflict at the hospital was Hunter's enduring campaign to create a medical school aimed at providing students with a rounded introduction to surgery along the lines of the model established earlier in 1785 at the London Hospital. But this idea had been peremptorily rejected by Hunter's contemporaries. Thwarted by his efforts to enhance medical education, Hunter had been staging lectures on surgery in his own home for more than a decade, and had even invited St George's pupils to his early courses for free.

But there were stranger stories still about the rebellious surgeon, which could hardly have escaped the coach driver's attention. Hunter, for instance, was well known to keep rare and exotic wild beasts – including a lion, a jackal, a dingo and two leopards – at his country home in the tranquil village of Earls Court, a few miles to the west of London. It was in this rural retreat that the surgeon performed countless experiments on animals both dead and alive. Innumerable research papers, presented to his friends in the Royal Society, detailed the bizarre experiments he had pioneered, such as grafting a cockerel's testicle into the belly of a hen – an early step towards transplanting body parts in humans – as well as the freezing of fish and rabbits' ears in a forlorn attempt to invent a scheme for human immortality. At this prototype research centre, Hunter dissected great carcasses, including whales washed up on the banks of the Thames, apes sent back from explorations into unmapped territories, and elephants donated by Queen Charlotte. Yet he was just as fascinated to study the tiniest of living forms, like the worms he discovered inside the whales' intestines and the bees he tended in observation hives in the conservatory. It was here too that he experimented on living animals, tying down squealing pigs, sheep and dogs for lengthy dissections designed to explore how healthy organs function and to test theories on ways to improve surgery for his numerous patients. Curious neighbours, by now inured to the sight of rare animals grazing his lawns, had nicknamed Hunter 'the cunning man', reputedly in reference to his reputation for knowledge rather than to anything more sinister.[13] Yet the villagers must still have gaped on occasions when the surgeon himself drove a cart pulled by three Asian buffaloes from Earls Court through the crowded West End streets to his Leicester Square townhouse, where a drawbridge could be swiftly lowered – and just as swiftly raised – to allow mysterious cargoes to trundle in and out.[14]

Naturally enough, the enterprising surgeon did not confine his zeal for research to the animal kingdom. Hunter had built up his surgical expertise through an unrivalled knowledge of human anatomy. Ever since arriving in London almost four decades earlier, Hunter had dissected human bodies in unprecedented numbers. Giving evidence as an expert witness at a recent murder trial, he had been asked, 'I presume you have dissected more than any man in Europe?' and agreed, 'I have dissected some thousands during these thirty-three years.'[15] It was through this relentless first-hand exploration of the human body, rather than by reading the dry works of the Ancient Greeks and Romans or passively watching over the shoulders of other medical men, that Hunter had become such a skilled operator. Although other surgeons of the day had become adept at certain procedures through the long experience of trial and error, many operations performed in London's charity hospitals were still risky gambles through comparative ignorance of anatomy and physiology. Whenever Hunter, by contrast, lifted his knife to begin an operation he knew precisely what lay beneath; he possessed a better knowledge of the human interior than any other surgeon in town. When Hunter cut, probed, sliced and sawed, he knew better than anyone else the exact whereabouts, the precise functions and the particular habits of every organ, muscle, blood vessel and tissue, healthy or diseased, that he was likely to encounter.

Yet while many of Hunter's patients, rich and poor, had good reason to give thanks for the surgeon's intimate knowledge of the human body, precious few would have given their approval to the sinister extremes to which he went to obtain his research material. Like all surgeons and anatomists of the time, Hunter had no lawful source for the majority of the bodies he daily dissected and he, like others, was forced to turn to underhand means to pursue his work. Although more enlightened families might give their consent to an autopsy on a relative who died on the operating table in order to discover the cause of death, most of the London populace still recoiled with horror at the notion of cutting up the body of a loved one. In consequence, surgeons had little option but to find alternative sources for the bodies they needed to hone their skills.

The gallows provided one steady stream of corpses for keen anatomists, both within the law – the Company of Surgeons in London was legally entitled to the bodies of six hanged murderers each year for public dissection – and outside the law, as surgeons flocked to Tyburn Tree on hanging days to beg, buy or steal the corpses of executed villains. But since even the steady flow of petty felons condemned to the gallows could not keep pace with the growing demands of anatomists, other more devious methods had evolved. Like other London anatomists, Hunter had turned to unscrupulous undertakers, shifty gravediggers and, above all, the gangs of professional body-snatchers who scoured London's churchyards by night unearthing fresh bodies to deliver to dissecting rooms before dawn. Hunter, however, had gone further than any other anatomist of his day in his connections with the Georgian underworld.

Since embarking on anatomy as an enthusiastic youth, Hunter had fostered the closest and friendliest of relations with the so-called Resurrectionists; he was renowned for offering the highest prices to ensure a regular supply of dissection material for himself and his students. In particular, he was notorious for paying above the odds for any kind of anatomical curiosity, whether rare human deformities or the results of a pioneering but ultimately fatal operation. Indeed, even as the coach driver pondered his dilemma, rumours were still circulating over the fate of the body of the towering Charles Byrne, better known as the 'Irish giant', who had begged on his deathbed in 1783 to be buried in a lead coffin at sea in an effort to keep out of John Hunter's clutches. Whether or not Byrne's skeleton would finally be unveiled in Hunter's remarkable museum, newly established in his Leicester Square house, alongside the dried limbs and pickled organs of unfortunate patients, the varnished bones of tropical beasts and the shrivelled bodies of unborn babies was still the subject of speculation.

So as the tortured coach driver stared anxiously from his hospital bed into Hunter's pale blue eyes, he would have been well aware that volunteering to go under the renowned surgeon's knife once, in the operating theatre at St George's, could very well mean going under his knife a second time – dead on the dissection table with his mutilated leg destined for the anatomist's museum. Nonetheless, clinging to the slim prospect of recovery now held out to him, he gave John Hunter his consent for the new operation.

For Hunter, the coach driver represented the perfect human guinea-pig for his experimental approach to surgery. Until now, he had attempted to save patients with popliteal aneurysms from either a premature death or a life-threatening amputation by performing an operation which was both highly risky and exceedingly painful. This procedure, which had been attempted by surgeons both in

Britain and on the Continent with various refinements for several centuries, meant cutting directly into the back of the knee, tying the damaged artery above and below the aneurysm, and scraping out the blood-filled sac. Based on his knowledge of anatomy and experiments performed in his Earls Court laboratory, Hunter hoped that once the blood was prevented from taking its usual route down the tied popliteal artery, the main blood vessel at the back of the leg, it would find alternative routes – or 'collateral circulation' – through the smaller blood vessels in the area. Almost without exception, the technique had failed; more often than not the already weakened blood vessel burst, haemorrhaging ensued and the patient died, making Hunter even more the butt of his colleagues' scorn.

Percivall Pott, a respected surgeon at St Bartholomew's Hospital and once Hunter's own teacher, insisted that amputation was the only viable remedy for popliteal aneurysms, even though he admitted the procedure was 'terrible to bear, horrid to see, and must leave the person on whom it has been performed in a mutilated imperfect state', and despite the fact that so many patients expired on the table.[16] Denouncing Hunter's method, he argued that the surrounding blood vessels in the leg were simply too few and too small to foster collateral circulation once the main artery was tied. Conversely, William Bromfield, the recently retired senior surgeon at St George's who had once been Hunter's examiner for his surgeon's diploma, argued that neither amputation nor 'Hunter's operation' were the slightest use in treating the condition. Mistakenly averring that a popliteal aneurysm indicated that a patient's entire arterial system was diseased, he claimed that there was simply no cure for the problem. It was an opinion that effectively dealt a death sentence to every poor coachman who ventured into his care.[17]

Never one to bow to authority or defer to his elders, Hunter was not prepared to give up hope and consign his patients to a lingering, agonizing death, while his aversion to drastic surgery except as a last resort and his firm belief in nature's healing powers made him equally unwilling to perform amputations. Refusing to be defeated, he resolved to apply his unique and controversial approach to the problem. Unlike the vast majority of surgeons operating in London homes and hospitals, who wielded their lancets and saws in imitation of long-dead past masters of the art and rarely considered any need for improvement, Hunter believed that surgery should be governed by scientific principles, based on sound reasoning, observation and experimentation. Much of this iconoclastic philosophy he owed to his unconventional training.

In general, eighteenth-century surgeons learned their practice through a system of apprenticeship, no different to that for barbers, carpenters or tailors, in which they slavishly followed in the footsteps of a senior surgeon and copied more or less exactly his methods of performing operations – with often lethal results – while rarely, if ever, questioning them. Techniques for most operations had changed little since medieval times, while treatment regimes still owed their theory largely to the Ancient Greeks. Although medical students usually learned some rudimentary anatomy, in private lessons, this was considered a useful but not vital adjunct to on-the-job experience. And when patients therefore died painful deaths on the operating table through ignorance and blundering, as they frequently did, few if any lessons were learned from the outcome.

Hunter, by contrast, had enjoyed a distinctly different preparation for the job, having spent a full twelve years studying anatomy in his brother's dissecting rooms and only a few short spells 'walking the wards', followed by a brief period as an army surgeon. As a consequence, he considered anatomy the foundation stone for all surgery. Only by minutely studying the human body, in order to understand the whereabouts and connections of every living part, did he believe that surgeons could possibly hope to improve their skills. Furthermore, his experience on the hospital wards had taught him principally, in ghastly and bloody detail, how primitive his profession really was. Inquisitive by nature, Hunter was never content simply to mimic in passive silence the lethal methods of others. Investigation and experimentation were the only way forward, in his view, if surgery was ever to make progress.

A few enlightened surgeons, such as Pott at St Bartholomew's, also saw the necessity of dragging surgery out of its medieval shackles and into a scientific age, but only Hunter systematically set out to question every established practice, develop hypotheses to advance better methods, and demonstrate whether these worked through rigorous observation, investigation and experiment. More often than not, Hunter tested out his theories on animals before attempting new procedures on humans, while the results of the handiwork he performed in the operating theatre were always carefully observed during the patient's subsequent recovery, or, if they died, in postmortem investigations. Lessons thus learned were diligently applied to modify his methods in a continuous research loop which would still stand up to scientific scrutiny more than two centuries later. Instilling the same approach in his loyal pupils Hunter summed up his doctrine in characteristically concise style when his favourite protégé, Edward Jenner, asked him for help in solving a problem. 'I think your solution is just,' responded his mentor, 'but why think, why not trie the Expt.'[18]

So, while Pott persisted in amputating limbs swollen by aneurysms, in the absence of any alternative, and Bromfield simply wrote off patients with aneurysms who arrived at hospital during his rota, Hunter set out to apply scientific method to the problem. Indeed, he had been studying aneurysms in the numerous bodies that ended up on his dissecting-room slab for at least twenty years. His few surviving case books record the dissection of a chairman – someone hired to carry a sedan chair – who died from an aneurysm in his thigh as far back as the winter of 1764–5.[19] Although the chairman was among Hunter's earliest patients, he even then believed that had the man's artery been tied, the blood circulation would have found alternative routes and his leg, and life, would have been saved. 'Here was a Case where something might have been done to save a patient's life', he lamented, but, wary of risking his early reputation, he added dolefully, 'it would have been trying experiments that the Cautious Ignorant are not fond of'.

Nevertheless, Hunter refused to let the problem alone, all too aware that 'This disease, if not attended to, is as dangerous as any that can affect the human body, because it is such as must always, even in the smallest arteries, kill.'[20] Convinced that aneurysms could be cured, he expounded his views to rapt students at his private lectures in typically robust manner.[21] First, describing Bromfield's objections while mischievously aping the elder surgeon's pompous style, Hunter recounted, 'he says, "I once saw this operation performed by a gentleman (that's me, gentlemen) upon a popliteal artery; but the difficulty of the operation and the embarrassment which the operator underwent (me again), will, I dare say, deter him from performing it again" '. But Hunter was 'not so soon deterred', he assured his pupils, declaring, 'Unfortunately, either for Mr Bromfield or myself, this is the very case from which I have formed favourable ideas of the success of further operations of a similar nature.'

Despite the fact that his usual method of operating on popliteal aneurysms by tying the artery at the point of the damage – behind the knee – had so far failed, he remained convinced that the basic theory of collateral circulation held good. An understanding of collateral circulation had been grasped even by the Romans, who tied small blood vessels when damaged and relied on alternative routes for the blood supply, as far back as the first century AD.[22] Yet Hunter's peers refused to believe that collateral circulation could provide an adequate blood supply to nourish an entire leg once the main artery was severed, or that it could develop sufficiently quickly before gangrene set in. Knowing his attempts to tie the artery behind the knee had failed, he now asked his students, 'Why not tie it up higher in the sound parts, where it is tied in amputation, and preserve the limb?' Tying the artery in the patient's thigh, where the blood vessel was healthy, might have more chance of holding firm, he theorized, while allowing the blood flow to create bypass routes around the diseased area lower down. And he summarily dismissed Bromfield's objections to such a scheme with the words, 'With respect to the objection from the disease being of the whole arterial system, unfortunately for Mr Bromfield, and fortunately for me and for mankind, this is not always the case.'

According to his usual scientific doctrine, Hunter first conducted experiments on animals to test out his hypothesis, choosing dogs as his substitute patients. In one such trial he instructed an assistant, his young brother-in-law Everard Home, to cut open the leg of a live dog and expose the artery.[23] Under Hunter's directions, Home carefully peeled away layer after layer of artery walls until the vessel was so thin that the blood could be seen as it pumped through. Home sewed up the dog's leg and after six weeks killed the animal, to discover that the artery had fully recovered its normal thickness. The results clearly suggested that the thinness of the artery walls did not account for the failure of the operations, confirming Hunter's belief that the section of artery close to the aneurysm must be otherwise damaged or diseased. He was now more certain than ever that tying the popliteal artery behind the knee, close to the aneurysm, was clinically doomed; the only chance of success was to tie the artery higher up in the leg, where it is called the femoral artery.

Hunter even tested his theory on a stag from the royal herd in Richmond Park with permission from George III, according to oral traditions handed down from one of Hunter's assistants to another.[24] Having caught the stag, Hunter cut into its neck and tied the carotid artery, which supplies blood to the antlers. Soon enough the half-grown antlers grew cold to the touch, as he expected. But a week or so later, upon checking the stag, he discovered that the antlers had not only regained their warmth but continued to grow. Ordering the deer to be slaughtered and sent to his dissecting room at Leicester Square, he opened the beast and injected its blood vessels with a coloured resin. Now he discovered that the stag's blood supply had found a new route through smaller blood vessels, bypassing the tied artery. The experiment provided further proof to support his belief in collateral circulation. It was now abundantly clear that blood could find alternative routes, and quickly too.

Yet despite his passion for experiment and experience in surgery, Hunter never approached an operation lightly. All too aware of the inadequacies of his own profession, as well as the dangers of infection and blood loss, he recommended extreme caution, advising his students against operating at all unless strictly necessary, with the admonition, 'No surgeon should approach the victim of his operation without a sacred dread and reluctance'.[25] In one instance he even went so far as to deter a patient whom he believed had been erroneously diagnosed with cancer by another surgeon and who was about to undergo a needless castration by describing the procedure in all too graphic detail. Relating the story to his pupils, he said, 'the Instruments were all ready and the Patient also and how to settle matters so as to save the Credit of the Surgeon, I was at a loss to know. I could not possibly think of letting the Poor Man loose his Testicle & therefore took advantage of the fear he express'd on account of the operation, painting it in the most horrid light to him, when he enquired of me what was to be done. This had the desir'd effect; for he declar'd he would not have it perform'd at any rate.' After being despatched with a relatively harmless potion, the patient soon recovered.[26]

Hunter was also firmly of the opinion that no surgeon should perform an operation he would not willingly have performed on himself under similar circumstances. 'I would have no one perform an operation that he is not clear about the propriety of himself, especially when it requires more anatomical skill than falls to the share of most practitioners,' he advised his pupils. And so, when outlining his plan for the new popliteal aneurysm operation, he declared, 'In this account, it may be supposed that I carry my notion too far; but it is to be understood that I only give my own feelings upon this subject, and I go no further in theory than I would perform in practice, if patients, being acquainted with the consequences of the disease, would submit to, or rather desire, the operation; nor do I go further than I now think I would have performed on myself were I in the same situation.'[27] Having therefore acquainted the coach driver with the likely consequences of his condition, and having advanced his opinion as to the most amenable remedy, Hunter left his patient in little doubt that the new operation was his best hope.

Just days later, on 12 December, the coachman was helped into the operating theatre – situated rather inconveniently directly above the hospital's boardroom – to begin his ordeal. Although minor operations were still sometimes carried out in patients' beds on the wards – and some beds were equipped with straps and handcuffs for the purpose – Hunter would have desired an audience of students and fellow surgeons for his radical experiment. Covering his normal day clothes with an apron, probably stiff with the dried blood of past patients, he would have worn neither gloves nor mask. With no understanding of how infection transferred from surgeon's begrimed fingers to patient's open wounds – this was almost a century before Joseph Lister pioneered antiseptics – Hunter would have had no cause to wash his hands or sterilize his instruments. Quite likely they were encrusted with the blood, pus and tissue of previous operations. As his personal set of knives lay ready and junior surgeons craned their necks to see, Hunter would have checked that his patient still consented to the operation. Then, grabbed by muscular assistants, the cabbie would have been held tightly on the narrow wooden operating table, his leg firmly secured. If he was lucky, he would have been offered a stiff shot of brandy or some laudanum – a heady mixture of alcohol and opium – to dull the coming pain, although it would be many decades before the introduction of effective anaesthesia. Held, observed, conscious and petrified, the coach driver tensed for the first cut. Well aware the experimental operation was still very much a gamble, he would have known that Hunter's whiskered face might be the last he would ever see.

Among the spellbound observers gathered in the theatre to watch the spectacle was a young Italian surgeon, Paolo Assalini, who was on a tour of Europe to further his medical education. He later wrote an eyewitness account of the whole operation:

John Hunter, having placed the patient in a convenient position, made an incision about five inches long in the skin of the inner, lower part of the thigh with a small knife; he exposed the artery, then grasped it in his finger-tips and separated it from the cellular membrane, the vein and the nerve for a distance of eight inches, making use only of the slender handle of his knife. This done, he passed under the artery a grooved probe, and ran along this a silver needle threaded with a thick ligature which he tied on the lower part of the artery to block it off. The pulsation in the tumour ceased immediately but the blood thumped with such force against the ligature that to diminish the knocking and the danger of the thing bursting he made another ligature two inches away from the first one and tied it less tightly. Above this second one he made a third, tied even more loosely, and then a fourth ... Then, after pulling the threads to the outside, and separating them, he closed the lips of the wound.[28]

Hunter then bound the two sides of the wound together with sticking plaster and bandages, leaving the ends of the threads hanging out to be removed later.[29] He had to work quickly to keep blood loss to a minimum and to reduce the risk of traumatic shock, so the whole process would have taken less than five minutes.

By the following day, the coachman's leg was already less swollen and the lump one-third smaller. By the fourth day, when the dressings were removed, the wound had sealed and the patient reported no pain. Although the wound bled a little some days later, after two weeks the silk threads fell away and the lump was significantly reduced. At the end of January 1786, six weeks after his operation, the coach driver walked out of St George's Hospital, and by July he was back in the driving seat of his hackney carriage, transporting passengers around London's chaotic streets. As word of the dramatic new operation spread, it was soon being copied in other London hospitals. Indeed, Hunter's operation rapidly became the standard procedure for aneurysms in various arteries, its details described extensively in the *London Medical Journal* of 1786. Almost as quickly, the technique was adopted in France and Italy. As the gleeful Assalini enthused, 'This operation, followed by such a happy outcome, excited the greatest wonder and awakened the attention of all the surgeons in Europe.'[30]

As with so many pioneering medical advances, progress was not, however, completely unhindered. After almost a year back at work, exposed to all the elements, the poor coach driver caught a fever – completely unconnected with either his aneurysm or the operation – and on 1 April 1787 he died. 'He had not made any complaint of the limb on which the operation had been performed from the time of his leaving the hospital,' insisted Hunter's brother-in-law Everard Home when later describing the operation. Seven days after his patient had died, and 'with some trouble and considerable expense', Hunter managed to obtain the cabbie's leg. Eagerly, he brought the limb back to his attic dissecting room, anxious to see for himself the results of his great experiment. Once more he wielded his knife and cut into the coach driver's leg. The aneurysm behind the knee was easy enough to find, still 'larger than a hen's egg', but the femoral artery above it had formed new routes through smaller blood vessels to bypass the diseased area and rejoin the artery further down, just as Hunter had predicted. The leg was otherwise perfectly healthy; there could be no doubt that the operation had been a success. Hunter went on to repeat his operation on at least four occasions, and although one of these patients died soon after, his fourth patient, another coach driver, recovered completely – after recuperating in the country-side at Hunter's expense – and went on to live for another fifty years.[31]

The operation first performed on the coach driver not only extended Hunter's reputation for daring and exper-imentation among Europe's surgeons while enhancing his prowess in the adoring eyes of his pupils, it would save countless lives, unroll a whole new era of operations and help to establish the foundations of scientific surgery. The procedure, which was a perfect example of the way Hunter applied scientific principles to every aspect of his work, would ensure his name lived on. The technique was henceforth called 'Hunter's operation', and the site of his knifework was ever after known as 'Hunter's canal'. This tribute alone might have been enough for any ambitious surgeon hoping to secure a place in the medical hall of fame, but it would never have satisfied the irrepressible John Hunter. He barely paused to acknowledge his advance, and never personally wrote about it, before plunging back into his daily round of ceaseless experiments. Hunter had far too many other medical interests, from artificial insemination to electrical stimulation of the heart, and far too broad a vision, spanning botany, geology, early biology and even the origins of life itself, ever to rest on his laurels.

Neither did the success of the remarkable operation do anything to stop the carping of his jealous colleagues at St George's, or the scorn flowing from Jessé Foot's barbed pen, both of which continued regardless. But it was not Hunter's style to build bridges or attempt to resolve conflicts amicably, for he had courted controversy from the moment he dismounted from his horse, a brash, ill-educated, rough-mannered country boy fresh down from Scotland, in the middle of London's vibrant Covent Garden in 1748.

2

The Dead Man's Arm

'Health is the basis of all happiness of this world's giving.'

Samuel Johnson[1]

Covent Garden, London, September 1748

The severed arm lay on the dissecting-room table, turning putrid. The bloodless flesh looked grotesquely pale but the hairs on the forearm and the nails on the fingers seemed as lifelike as ever they had when attached to a man's body. Keen to impress his brother William, ten years his senior, the twenty-year-old John Hunter picked up the knife set before him to begin his first human dissection.[2] Virtually strangers, the two brothers had not cast eyes on each other since William had left the family farm to make his future in London when John was only twelve years old. The intervening years, at least as far as William's critical eye would have assessed, had done little to improve the younger brother.

A shrewd and ambitious social climber, William had moved in ever more rarefied circles since leaving Glasgow University and arriving in his 'darling London' eight years previously.[3] Now thirty, he had already visited both Paris and Leiden to further his anatomy studies, obtained his surgeon's diploma in order to embark on a surgical career, and begun to build a fashionable practice attending the deliveries of the babies of the well-to-do. Although he had only just secured his first hospital post – as 'surgeon-man-midwife' at London's new Middlesex Hospital – and had but a few years' private practice to his name, William was steadily accruing both wealth and esteem. Already he had pretensions to leave his lowly surgical colleagues behind and join the elevated ranks of the physicians, who enjoyed the highest status in London's strict medical hierarchy.[4]

Yet for all William's self-assurance, climbing the greasy pole of Georgian English society was no easy ascent for a Scot of relatively humble beginnings with limited connections. The Jacobite uprising in 1745 and the British army's bloody victory at Culloden the following year were still fresh in Londoners' memories, so no matter that most Lowland and urban Scots had had no sympathy with the revolt, anti-Scots prejudice was rife. Accordingly, William had carefully smoothed his Scottish burr and anglicized his manners in order to blend in with polite London society. Elegantly dressed and wearing a full powdered wig, he dined with fellow Scottish intellectuals, including the novelist Tobias Smollett, the physician John Pringle and the painter Allan Ramsay, who had similarly gravitated to the metropolis as part of a collective migration of talent from Glasgow and Edinburgh universities. But William had astutely managed to penetrate English social circles too, forging connections with influential men such as the magistrate and writer Henry Fielding and the prolific diarist Horace Walpole. Between coffee-houses and theatres, dissecting rooms and salons, William skilfully bridged both the divergent Scots and English cultures and the contrasting worlds of science and the arts.

But William was not only a sophisticated socialite, he possessed a smart business brain – vital in the risky world of Georgian enterprise where commercial know-how mattered as much as knowing the right people. The anatomy school he had established in Covent Garden two years earlier had proved both a popular and a profitable venture. Aspiring young surgeons, attracted to London from throughout the British Isles and overseas to walk the wards of the capital's grim charity hospitals, had flocked to the school for expert tuition in dissection. Indeed, so successful had his classes become that William now desperately needed help to run the business, leaving him more free time to tend his demanding wealthy patients. With classes beginning in just two weeks' time, William was anxious that his younger brother should prove a competent and biddable assistant – especially when it came to taking over the more sinister side of his enterprise.

The prospects did not appear immediately promising. An awkward, uncultured and largely uneducated country lad, the slight youth with his shock of red hair had failed utterly to distinguish himself to date. Eschewing all scholarly pursuits, he had so far frittered away his days on the family farm without any obvious aim or ambition. After briefly toying with enlisting in the army, an apparent sudden impulse had prompted him to offer his assistance to William and make the arduous two-week journey on horseback from Lanarkshire down to London. Now he found himself in the full glare of his clever elder brother's attention, presented with the biggest challenge of his uneventful life so far: to dissect a rotting limb and tease out the various muscles under William's rigorous scrutiny. Surrounded by the human skeletons and skulls, the varnished bones hanging from rafters and the pickled organs ranged on shelves already prepared for the forth-coming students, any novice anatomist would have needed strong nerves to steel himself against the sight and stench of human remains in that room.

He would not have been the first to blanch at the experience. The Renaissance artist Leonardo da Vinci, who cut up more than thirty bodies which he stole from the scaffold in order to study the human form, cautioned, 'though you have a love for such things you will perhaps be hindered by your stomach, and, if that does not impede you, you will perhaps be impeded by the fear of living through the night hours in the company of quartered and flayed corpses fearful to behold'.[5] But as John Hunter made his first cut through the leathery skin of the man's arm set in front of him, he would have been careful not to flinch or to show his distaste to watchful William. He would have known that this was a crucial test, the most important moment in his life so far. At last he was being given a chance to prove his worth.

Born in deep mid-winter, the tenth child of a farming family struggling to make ends meet in the rugged countryside south of Glasgow, John Hunter had embraced controversy from his first cry. Although local folklore confidently attests to the exact whereabouts of his birth – in the bedroom above the kitchen of the family home in Long Calderwood near East Kilbride[6] – the actual date of his arrival remains obscure. The old parish register records his birth unambiguously on 13 February 1728, yet Hunter himself would always celebrate his birthday on 14 February. Even more perplexingly, the ancient family bible gives his date of birth as 7 February, while a commonplace book belonging to an uncle records the birth as 9 February.[7] Most likely, the exact time of birth of the tenth child in the middle of a cold night in a hushed room lit at best by candles simply went unremarked. With three children, including an earlier John, having already died, and their ageing father, also called John, constantly worried about finances for his large family as well as his own failing health, the arrival of another mouth to feed was not necessarily welcome. John Hunter senior, who was sixty-five years old by the time of his youngest son's birth, plainly neglected the newest member of the family in favour of his studious older boys, James and William, then thirteen and ten. It was left to John's mother, Agnes, and his four older sisters – Janet, Agnes, Dorothy and Isobel – to bestow attention on the youngest son.

Reputedly descended from an old Norman family, the Hunters of Hunterston in Ayrshire, John Hunter senior had married Agnes Paul, the daughter of a prosperous Glaswegian family, in 1707, the year of English and Scottish union. He was forty-four and she was twenty-two.[8] They baptized their first child, the original John, in 1708 and buried him fourteen years later. Their second child, Elizabeth, died at just one year, and a second son, Andrew, survived only to the age of three. Trading as a grain merchant in the market village of East Kilbride, John Hunter senior had also acquired some farm lands, and after the birth of four more children the family moved from their village home to a thatched stone house at Long

Calderwood, a mile to the north-east, making this farmstead the centre of their small world.[9]

Although relatively well off by the standards of most local people, who lived from hand to mouth in humble cottages, it was nevertheless a fairly comfortless existence for a large family, squeezed into a smoky two-bedroom cottage where a single peat fire provided the only source of heat and the children slept in box-beds which were pulled out of the walls like giant drawers every night.[10] While there were farmhands to help tend the crops and livestock, the winters were long and often severe and the Clyde valley soil was stony and poorly drained, so it was a relentless battle to eke out an existence for a growing family. As a consequence, a year after John Hunter was born his father was forced to sell a large parcel of land, probably to raise funds to send fourteen-year-old James to train as a lawyer in Edinburgh and William, a short while later, to Glasgow University to study theology for a career in the Scottish Kirk.

Ignored by his preoccupied father, indulged by his adoring mother and pampered by his older sisters, young 'Jock' or 'Johnny', as he was nicknamed, grew up a head-strong boy. While his mother found her wayward son difficult to control, his father appeared neither to know nor care how his youngest child spent his days. So although Johnny was despatched daily to trudge the mile-long walk to the village school where his brothers had distinguished themselves, whenever he had the chance he would skip lessons to go rambling through the woods and fields, stalking wild animals in the undergrowth, paddling the burns in pursuit of fish and scaling the hills to look down on the smoking chimneys of Glasgow. Despite his mother's encouragement, he detested both lessons and books with a vengeance, as he later recalled:

> When I was a boy it was a little reading and writing, a
> great deal of spelling and figures; geography which never
> got beyond the dullest statistics, and a little philosophy
> and chemistry as dry as sawdust, and as valuable for dead-
> ing [deadening] purposes. I wanted to know about the
> clouds and the grasses, why the leaves change colour in
> the autumn. I watched the ants, bees, birds, tadpoles, and
> caddis worms. I pestered people with questions about
> what nobody knew or cared anything about.[11]

His sister Dorothy, seven years his elder, remembered
that while dutiful William was of a 'diligent and careful
disposition, indefatigable in making himself master of
anything that he wished to know', young Johnny 'would
do nothing but what he liked and neither liked to be
taught reading nor writing nor any kind of learning'.[12] At
times, her little brother flew into tantrums or fits of crying while he 'remained obstinately impenetrable to
everything in the form of book-learning'. And although he
was 'by no means considered as a stupid boy', he made
such little advancement with his studies and rebelled so
furiously at any efforts to direct his education that
eventually the village schoolmaster gave up on him and at
thirteen he abandoned formal education.

At a time when Scotland prided itself on its Kirk-run
school system and the Scots boasted literacy levels well in
excess of their English neighbours, John's obstinacy
towards learning was a heart-felt family disappointment.
Indeed, his hatred of books was so intense that he probably suffered from some form of dyslexia, for not only did
he struggle with schooling throughout childhood, being

unable to read or write until his teens, he retained his distaste for all things academic throughout his life. Certainly he would be able to dash off a letter in a reasonably well-formed script as well as anyone, although his spelling was erratic even by eighteenth-century standards and his style often stilted or abrupt, but whenever possible, in later life, he would always prefer to employ assistants to take down his words and even to read books out loud to him.[13] He even revelled in his dislike of the printed word. Although in reality he built up quite a respectable book collection, publicly he liked to declare that he 'totally rejected books' and preferred to take up 'the volume of the animal body'.[14]

Not surprisingly, John Hunter's childhood aversion to formal education and lifelong avoidance of literary studies would provide powerful ammunition for later enemies, particularly the snobbish Jessé Foot, although he only dared publish his malevolent biography the year after Hunter's death. Seeking to equate Hunter's difficulties in reading with a lack of intelligence, Foot claimed that the surgeon 'was incapable of putting six lines together grammatically into English'.[15] As a result of this illiteracy, Foot alleged, Hunter had not personally written a single word of any of his publications, instead employing, among others, his friend the novelist Smollett as a ghost writer. It was this 'want of the polish of education' which Foot also blamed for Hunter's notoriously colourful language or 'vulgarity'. Certainly Hunter loved to damn and curse in an age when polite conversation was considered the mark of a gentleman; his pupils would later feel moved to excuse his bad language while nineteenth-century editors of his works deemed it necessary to excise his oaths. And he evidently did enjoy some editorial help with his writings. But the reams of written material Hunter produced, in scientific papers to the Royal Society, published works and letters sent around the world, more than demonstrated his ability to put pen to paper. Indeed, Foot, who peppered his haughty attacks with quotations in Latin and Greek to demonstrate his literary superiority, wanted to have it both ways: he also charged Hunter with concealing his reading prowess in order to plagiarize rivals without suspicion.

Yet it was precisely his frustration with books and academic learning that impelled the young John Hunter to develop his revolutionary mode of scientific inquiry. His early distrust of the written word would make him forever sceptical of classical teaching and the slavish repetition of ancient beliefs; he would always prefer to believe the evidence of his own eyes to the written words of others. Since books refused to yield anything of value to him, and country folk could not come up with the answers to his relentless queries about the natural world, he simply embarked on his own lines of inquiry. And so from his earliest years, roaming the countryside of Lanarkshire when he should have been poring over Latin primers at a school desk, he sought the solutions to the questions that puzzled him through painstaking observation and experiment.

There was ample opportunity on and around the family farm. The inquisitive Johnny would have witnessed count-less births and deaths among the horses, cattle and fowl and would have watched the farmers' attempts at crude veterinary care when their animals fell ill; maybe he even helped to nurse sickly youngsters back to life. He certainly studied the behaviour of the wildlife in the nearby hills and valleys, for he would remember some of these observations all his life. Possibly he was encouraged by his older sisters, since his closest sister in age, Isobel, was said to have enjoyed petting the 'Foles and Calfs' born on the farm. It was perhaps Isobel who made a misguided attempt to save some wild birds that had been numbed by the frost one winter by warming them in front of the cottage fire. The incident was remembered by Hunter many years later when he was asked for advice on how to revive people who had drowned. 'I observed, many years ago, in some of the colder parts of this island,' he recalled, 'that when intense cold had forced blackbirds or thrushes to take shelter in outhouses, such of them as had been caught, and were, from an ill-judged compassion, exposed to a considerable degree of warmth, died very soon.'[16]

It may even have been on the farm that Hunter attempted his first dissections, perhaps investigating the decaying corpses of wildlife he discovered in the hedgerows or beasts that had died in the farmyard, for he later remarked on the benefits of dissecting animals in open fields. Indeed, many of the questions that were obviously sparked by his earliest observations – such as pinpointing the exact moment when an embryo chick begins to form in a hen's egg, determining precisely what distinguishes a living, breathing creature from a lifeless carcass, and even puzzling over the origins of the human species itself – would occupy him all his life. As he would later comment, 'I love to be puzzled, for then I am sure I shall learn something valuable.'[17] Equally, his childish awe at the powers of nature would never leave him, as when he marvelled, 'No chemist on earth can make out of the earth a piece of sugar but a vegetable can do it', and, 'This production of Animals out of themselves, excites wonder, admiration, and curiosity'.[18]

But at the age of thirteen, leaving the village school in the same year that his embattled father died, the adolescent John Hunter was left with no more material purpose in life than to help his mother and sisters run the farm. Both of his older brothers had since changed their earlier plans and thrown in their lot with medicine, yet Johnny apparently felt no urge to follow suit. William left Glasgow University after five years without taking his degree in theology, having fallen under the spell of one of the founding figures of the Scottish Enlightenment, the philosopher Francis Hutcheson. Irish-born Hutcheson had been professor of moral philosophy at Glasgow since 1729 and there had influenced a generation of Scottish intellectuals, including the economist Adam Smith and the minister Alexander Carlyle.[19] His humane and compassionate approach to religion was manifestly at odds with the Scottish Kirk's literal take on the Bible; imbibing his views was clearly incompatible with William's planned career as a minister. His plans for the Church abandoned, William was taken under the wing of the family physician, the kindly and far-sighted William Cullen, who would become a towering force for scientific progress on the Scottish medical scene. Cullen trained William in basic medicine, sent him to Edinburgh University to learn a little anatomy, and in 1740 packed him off to London to learn the latest approach to childbirth, all with a view to setting up partnership together in neighbouring Hamilton, where Cullen practised. Eldest brother James, meanwhile, had discovered the law too dull, had briefly considered enlisting in the army, had dabbled in painting, had co-written a play with Smollett (although the drama has never come to light) and finally, after their father's death, followed William on the road to

London in a joint bid to make their names in medicine.[20]

Already death had claimed another of the family. John's sister Agnes died early in 1741 – not even surviving her father – at just twenty-five years old. Riding home with James one day she had complained of 'great sickness & cold feet' and was taken into a roadside house where the ever attentive Cullen rushed to her aid. There was little even the learned Cullen could do and the much-loved 'Nanie' expired in his arms to 'the most violent grief' of brother James. Her body was jolted home in a cart to the waiting family the next day.[21] Now her siblings followed in a tragic procession to the grave. The following summer it was Isobel whose health was worrying Cullen, prompting William in London to write to his mother, 'I'm heartily concerned for my little dear sister Tibbie'.[22] The mare's milk William recommended that she drink was powerless to prevent her death before the month was out, at the age of just seventeen. Finally it was James, the eldest surviving child and always the brightest star in the family's firmament, who was forced to return home from London through sickness, probably consumption. He quickly spiralled into decline and the seventeen-year-old John stood helplessly by his adored brother's bedside as he coughed up blood and died a painful death in the prime of life. His premature demise left William head of the family, with more necessity now than ever to make his London enterprises a success, while John still languished at home, with only his mother and two sisters Janet and Dorothy in an increasingly empty house.

So six of John Hunter's nine siblings, as well as his father, had now been carried along the narrow lane from the family's farmhouse to the little graveyard encircling East Kilbride parish church. Although the loss of those

closest to him through his teenage years must have left a
deep mental scar, such a death toll was by no means
unusual by Georgian standards. Life expectancy in
England in the middle of the eighteenth century, taken as
an average, was just thirty-seven years; it would have been
roughly similar in Scotland, although this stark figure
masks a disproportionately high death rate in childhood.[23]
Surviving infancy was life's biggest battle; having reached
adulthood there was a fair chance of attaining a ripe old
age. In London, where child death rates were at their
highest, almost half of the babies born between 1750 and
1769 never reached their second birthdays. Burials far
exceeded baptisms in the capital throughout most of the
century.[24] Nevertheless, London's population continued to
mushroom in spite of its thriving funeral business since
impoverished families arrived from the countryside looking for work faster than their predecessors expired.
Contagious diseases ran rampant in the city, thanks to
appalling poverty and malnutrition, overcrowding in slum
dwellings and filthy living conditions. While the carcasses
of dead animals lay rotting in the streets, open sewers
carried human excrement and animal offal down central
gutters. But prospects of health were little better in the
countryside, where poor harvests, lean years and disease
epidemics could equally lead to early death.

Although Georgian families no longer had to fear the
medieval scourges of plague and leprosy, there were plenty
more menaces to worry about. A child born into
eighteenth-century Britain required a tough constitution
and no small amount of luck to evade or defeat the
innumerable infectious diseases – diphtheria, measles,
mumps, scarlet fever, influenza and consumption (tuberculosis), to name but a few – he or she was likely to

encounter during the first years of life. Where disease failed to snare the youngster, malnutrition, neglect and misguided child-rearing often succeeded. With little appreciation of hygiene or nutrition, babies were force-fed with sugared and alcohol-laced pap from germ-ridden cups as soon as they could breathe, dosed with weak beer or neat gin to soothe their cries, and swaddled tightly in blankets that were rarely changed. Schooling was limited or non-existent for most children in England, so as soon as a child was considered fit for work – from the age of five or so – she or he was prone to workplace accidents and job-related diseases. The first occupational illness to be identified, by John Hunter's later rival Percivall Pott, was cancer of the scrotum in young chimney sweeps, caused by exposure to soot.[25] And throughout adolescence there were numerous deadly fevers and raging epidemics to battle, from the typhus fever that reigned in jails, hospitals and ships to the dreaded smallpox virus, which accounted for one in ten of all deaths, killing a fifth of those it struck and hideously disfiguring those who survived. Against such odds, parents might have been more prepared for their offspring to be snatched suddenly from them, but childhood illness still left many families bereft.

Surviving this obstacle course conferred lifelong immunity against a raft of infectious diseases, but negotiating adulthood was only a little less precarious, with the perils of accidents and illnesses lurking around every corner. Life hung on a slender string. With no modern antibiotics to fight bacteria, it was not uncommon for an apparently healthy adult to fall suddenly sick with a contagious fever and be dead within days. Both consumption and smallpox continued as ever-present threats throughout life. For women, childbirth was an exceptionally hazardous experience, with many dying during agonizing deliveries from complications, haemorrhaging and bungled midwifery; many more succumbed to sepsis days later, especially in the 'lying-in' hospitals which sprang up from the middle of the century and provided new breeding grounds for bacteria. Even for those adults who made it through to middle age there were still innumerable ailments and complaints, from gout to bladder stones, venereal disease to toothache, that could cause excruciating pain and discomfort, with little hope of cure or relief.

With so many risks to life and limb as well as numerous conditions that could make life almost insufferable, it is little wonder that the Georgians were fanatical in their pursuit of health. Letters, diaries, novels and newspapers reveal an almost unhealthy preoccupation with the workings of the human body. Whether conversing with family or friend, business associate or acquaintance, the Georgians revelled in reporting intimate details of their bodily functions and personal ailments, and few could resist recommending their favourite homespun remedies or precautionary measures. Samuel Johnson, who fretted constantly about his health after a sickly childhood, regularly proffered his advice. 'Give me leave, who have thought much on medicine,' he wrote to one dear friend, the spinster Hill Boothby, in 1755, 'to propose to you an easy and I think a very probable remedy for indigestion and lubricity of the bowels.'[26] Dried orange peel, finely powdered and mixed with warmed port, was Johnson's recipe for long life, though it did little to help Boothby, who died the following year. Others advocated much less palatable self-help remedies, including toxic potions, violent purges that acted as laxatives, emetics that induced vomiting, and the copious letting of blood, as well as seabathing, cold baths and daily blasts of wintry air.

Those who could afford the time and money were obsessed with the latest fads in treatment to the point of hypochondria. And there was no lack of variety; when it came to healthcare the Georgians were spoilt for choice. In the buoyant medical marketplace of the day, the health-conscious Hanoverians could pick any number of weird and wonderful therapies purveyed by a bewildering array of practitioners. With no reigning medical orthodoxy, no effective regulation or policing, and no consensus on diagnosis or therapy, a patient was equally likely to buy a noxious potion peddled by a travelling quack, a herbal con-coction stewed by the village wise woman or a traditional remedy prescribed by a learned physician – and sometimes all three. Medical treatment was based on a hotch-potch of superstition and folklore, and only a smattering of science.

It should have been a golden age for medicine. In the previous century the philosopher Francis Bacon had con-fidently predicted that scientific progress would bring nature firmly under control. In 1628 the English physician William Harvey had discredited prevailing medical beliefs, based on Ancient Greek ideology, when he proved that the heart, not the liver, propelled the blood around the body in a continuous circulation. Further anatomical dis-coveries served to reinforce the notion promulgated by the French scientist René Descartes, the driving force of the scientific revolution, that the body was more like a machine than a mysterious receptacle for the soul. A new spirit of optimism was in the air as the Royal Society, established with the blessing of Charles II in 1660, and in France the Académie Royale des Sciences ushered in a new

era of natural philosophy in which scientific experimentation was heralded as the stepping stone to a modern
society.[27]

So much for the theory; the reality was rather more
down to earth. The promise of the scientific revolution did
little, if anything, to render medicine safer or more
effective; healthcare still waited for its enlightenment and
the eighteenth century became a free-for-all for mounte-
banks, cranks and meddling medics. While learned
physicians, flourishing doctorates from Oxford,
Cambridge and universities across Europe, paid lip service
to scientific progress, in practice they clung like leeches to
their classical doctrines. Apart from a few notable
exceptions, most held firm to the teachings of the Greek
father of medicine Hippocrates, who taught in the fifth
century BC that all illness was due to an imbalance of the
four 'humours' of the body: blood, phlegm, black bile,
and choler or yellow bile. An excess of one humour or a
deficiency in another was diagnosed by establishing
patients' eating, sleeping and toiletary habits, by inspecting their urine and stools, and occasionally by feeling the
pulse, but rarely if ever by examining the site of the complaint. The remedies prescribed were designed to restore
the 'humoral balance', whether through medicinal concoctions of animal, mineral or vegetable matter in potions
and pills made up by apothecaries, 'clysters' – enemas –
injected by syringe, or copious bleeding.

Remedies were rarely anything less than drastic; that
way Georgian patients could at least feel they were getting
value for their money. Patients happily submitted to being
dosed with toxic elixirs, blistered by heated glass cups
applied to their backs, and bled to the point of unconsciousness. Despite Harvey's demonstration that the

theory behind bloodletting – to let out blood at a specific site in the body – was a nonsense since blood circulated through the entire body, phlebotomy only increased in popularity as a virtual cure-all for every ill. If not recommended by physicians it was often demanded by patients. Dr Johnson was doing no more than reflecting the culture of his times when he advised his friend Mrs Thrale on the care of her husband, 'Gentle purges, and slight phlebotomies are not my favourites, they are popgun batteries, which lose time and effect nothing.' He reminded her, 'It was by bleeding till he fainted that his life was saved'.[28] Bloodletting was not only practised routinely as a preventive measure against illness, it was administered for almost every condition, from ailments in young children to prolonged childbirth. As much as thirty ounces could be removed at one sitting, often disastrously weakening the body's natural defences against disease.

Yet while physicians prescribed bloodletting in every circumstance, their dread of touching the human body meant they never personally slit open a vein to let the blood flow. In the strict medical hierarchy that prevailed, all messy and distasteful jobs that involved touching or cutting flesh were left either to certified surgeons or to barbers and barber-surgeons, who offered bloodletting as a sideline to cutting hair and shaving beards. Far from being interlopers in the field of surgery, barbers were the first surgeons. The earliest organized medical care, in medieval times, was centred on monasteries, but the Church frowned on its devotees spilling blood so barbers, frequent visitors to the brethren in order to keep tonsures and beards in trim, began to assist the monks in their medical work by removing warts, cutting out abscesses and letting blood. The familiar red and white striped poles outside barbers' shops are left-over reminders of their erstwhile professions: originally they signified the bandaged and bloodied stick gripped by patients during minor surgical procedures.

Given the pomposity and ineptitude of most physicians and some of the higher-earning surgeons, they were easy targets for ridicule, and medical practitioners were roundly lampooned in novels and dramas, newspapers and cartoons. In 1735 the satirical artist William Hogarth depicted a gaggle of bewigged physicians tasting a patient's urine, in the same frame as three notorious quacks, under the collective title *The Company of Undertakers*.[29] Even Tobias Smollett, himself a trained surgeon as well as a friend of the Hunter brothers, could not resist a pop at the ignorance of the profession when his eponymous hero Roderick Random attempted to secure an apprenticeship with a master surgeon. 'Studied surgery! what? in books I suppose,' exclaimed his putative teacher. 'But let's hear no more of this stuff, – can you bleed and give a clyster, spread a plaister and prepare a potion? answer me to that.'[30]

Understandably distrustful of organized medicine, desperate patients turned to the folk remedies peddled by alternative healers – the so-called 'quacks' – which were no less likely to prove effective. In the month before John Hunter arrived in London, the *Gentleman's Magazine* published a list of more than two hundred nostrums available over the counter in druggists' stores, ranging from 'horseballs' for coughs to powders for piles.[31] While a correspondent to the magazine extolled the virtues of 'Tar Water' in curing cancer, readers were enthralled by reports of Bridget Bostock, a healer in Cheshire, who reputedly cured every ill with the simple remedy of applying her spit. Ailing Georgians also sought relief in electric shocks and hypnotism, even by inhaling the breath of young women. And like many infants of his day, in 1712 the toddling Samuel Johnson was lifted up by his hopeful parents to receive the 'Royal Touch' from Queen Anne in the forlorn hope of curing his scrofula, a form of tuberculosis.[32] He wore the gold 'touch-piece' the monarch gave him around his neck all his life. Yet these remedies were little crankier than the ingredients authorized by the country's elite medical men in the list of recommended medicines, the *Pharmacopoeia Londinensis*, published by the Royal College of Physicians in 1746.[33] In a spirit of modernization the newly revised formulary had jettisoned such 'preposterous Mixtures' as unicorn's horn and moss from human skulls but whole-heartedly endorsed oyster shells, crabs' eyes and ground woodlice among its 'speedy, safe and pleasant Cures'.

Interventions were not only radical and unpleasant, they were often downright harmful. Lavish dosing with mercury – the standard treatment for venereal disease – led to horrible side-effects including black saliva, loss of teeth and sometimes fatal poisoning. And it was not uncommon for cack-handed surgeons accidentally to damage an artery or introduce a fatal infection with their filthy knives when letting blood for some minor complaint. Indeed, of all the pills, potions and plasters in the practitioner's medicine bag, there was only one truly effective ingredient: cinchona, or Peruvian bark. Originally a native American remedy brought back from the New World by Jesuit missionaries in the seventeenth century, it contained quinine, which served as a valuable therapy for malaria, or 'ague', which was still prevalent in the British Isles in the eighteenth century. Another innovation, inoculation against smallpox using a minute amount of infectious pus taken from an afflicted person, had similarly been adopted from a folk remedy popular in Turkey. Initially opposed by the snooty physicians when it was introduced to Britain in 1721 by Lady Mary Wortley Montagu, the wife of the British ambassador in Constantinople, inoculation saved countless children from certain death, although it could also prove fatal in over-zealous hands. In addition, the ubiquitous consumption of opium, prescribed for a variety of ills as well as pain relief, could at least provide some welcome respite from the miseries of sickness. Beyond these few successes, which owed little to learned medicine, the rest was largely useless or worse.

In contrast to the physical harm often caused by university-educated physicians, some travelling quacks and folk-healers could boast widespread success for their efforts. Some even became quite proficient at pulling rotten teeth, setting bones and other minor surgery. The herbalist Joanna Stephens convinced the government to pay her £5,000 – a sizeable fortune – for the secret of her remedy for treating bladder stones, although it was later revealed to contain nothing more miraculous than eggshells, honey and soap.[34] Most notoriously, the eccentric Sarah Mapp, popularly known as 'Crazy Sally', achieved such acclaim for her skill in setting broken bones that in the 1730s she rode in a coach drawn by six horses to give weekly consultations at a London coffee-house. Although Percivall Pott, who considered himself somewhat adept at setting bones, condemned Mrs Mapp as an 'ignorant, illiberal, drunken, female savage', she was fêted in cartoons and on the stage. Certainly Sir Hans Sloane, the president of the Royal College of Physicians and head of the Royal

Society, turned to Crazy Sally rather than some bungling fellow physician to mend his niece's long-term back injury. The niece, by all accounts, was perfectly cured.[35]

Precisely what compelled the twenty-year-old John Hunter to enter this maelstrom of muddled, ignorant and incompetent medical practice remains unclear. Perhaps the loss of six siblings to the ravages of disease at such early ages inspired him to confront death head on. Rather than passively accepting the inevitability of premature death, as did most Georgians, the sight of his childhood playmates transformed into cold corpses made him all the more determined to fight for life. Perhaps, too, the misery of the severe winter of 1746–7 convinced him of the need finally to look for a form of diversion more profitable than farming, while the sight of retreating Jacobite rebels straggling through East Kilbride the previous Christmas may have suggested he seek that end elsewhere than in Scotland.

Certainly his mother, ever concerned for her favourite son's future, had attempted to find him alternative employment earlier in 1748. That summer he had gone to live briefly in Glasgow with his sister Janet, by then thirty-five, and her new husband, a wealthy but idle timber merchant with a penchant for carousing.[36] Already well known for the dexterity and neatness of his hands, it was in his brother-in-law's timber-yard that Johnny learned to handle knives and saws with expert precision by watching carpenters at work. Naturally enough, this short interlude, lasting at most a few months, would later provide Hunter's enemies with ammunition to dismiss the surgeon as an ignorant carpenter. 'A wheelwright or a carpenter he certainly was,' sneered Jessé Foot, before he decided to 'lay down the chissel, the rule, and the mallet; and take up the knife, the blow pipe, and the probe'.[37] But before the summer was over the timber-yard had closed, its owner bankrupt, and John Hunter was back home, kicking his heels once more.

After quickly dismissing an impulse to join the army, finally he took the plunge and wrote to William, asking to join him in London in a move that would not only transform John Hunter's life but alter the course of medicine for ever. Desperate for a new assistant, especially one who would be bound by family loyalty to keep the murky secrets of the dissecting room, William immediately assented. So early in September 1748, the farmer's son left his Scottish homeland for the first time, riding the four hundred miles to London with a family friend, Thomas Hamilton, to arrive in Covent Garden just two weeks before the anatomy school opened for the autumn term.

The contrast between rural Lanarkshire and bustling, chaotic London could not have been more startling. With a population of around 675,000, almost forty times the size of Glasgow, London was now the biggest city in Europe.[38] Approaching from the north-east, through the pleasant villages of Tottenham, Islington and Pentonville, the rough, rutted road became increasingly busy, while houses, shops and taverns wrestled for space along the way. As Hunter neared the city, the narrow, towering tenements, which housed whole families in single cellars and attic rooms, almost blocked out the sky. Negotiating the congested streets, where stage coaches and private carriages battled for passage with farm carts and live-stock, must have seemed hopelessly confusing; the sounds of horses' hooves, creaking wheels and complaining cattle were deafening. Mud, animal dung, refuse and human waste splashed pedestrians as they walked the pavements, trying to dodge the precariously swinging shop signs, the speeding sedan chair bearers and downpours of foul water from upper-storey windows. By late afternoon, oil lamps lit the smoky streets and candles illuminated shop windows displaying silk clothing, exquisite ornaments and ornate jewellery whose luxury formed a pantomime backdrop to the squalor of ragged children begging on the pavements.

In Hatton Garden, in Holborn, where John initially joined William in lodgings, the affluent residents could still enjoy the pastoral view north towards fields and market gardens.[39] But in Covent Garden, where William had rented rooms for his anatomy school, the once fashionable square had become a shambling market surrounded by a jumble of taverns, gin-houses and brothels. London's gentry had forsaken the elegant piazza, designed in the previous century by Inigo Jones, in a steady shift towards the cleaner air and pleasant squares of the West End. In their stead, the apartments beneath the arcades had been taken over by writers, artists, actors and pimps. By day, hawkers yelled out their wares to passers-by; by night, the neighbourhood was stalked by press-gangs, pickpockets, prostitutes and armed robbers. The view north from here, towards the desperately poor neighbourhood of St Giles, would provide Hogarth with inspiration for his famous *Gin Lane*, with its grotesque images of lives destroyed by the ubiquitous spirit.[40]

Well used by now to such extremes of wealth and poverty, William had been comfortably settled in Hatton Garden for a full five years. When he first arrived in London, in 1740, he had lodged with William Smellie, another Scottish exile, who was fast building a reputation as a teacher of midwifery at a time when the delivery room was almost exclusively the preserve of women. It was Smellie, brandishing his newly improved forceps, who began to make midwifery a respectable following for men and thereby triggered the dramatic shift which eventually pushed female practitioners out of childbirth. Advised all the while by his putative partner, the family physician Cullen, William dutifully accompanied Smellie to emergency deliveries through the night, while by day he attended private anatomy lectures.

But William shrewdly realized that the down-to-earth Smellie would never offer him the social advancement he craved. Within a year he had ingratiated himself with James Douglas, another Scot intent on muscling into the delivery room, but one who was making his advance with a rather more subtle and refined air, much more in keeping with young William's style. Before long, William had begged release from his partnership plans with Cullen – who reluctantly but magnanimously agreed – joined forces with Douglas, taken on the tuition of the Douglas son, secured an engagement to the Douglas daughter, and moved into the Douglas home, in Red Lion Square.

But the Douglases, too, failed to fulfil their allotted roles in William's grand scheme. No sooner had William joined the household than James Douglas died, putting a swift end to a promising partnership. Although William went ahead with a planned trip to Paris to study anatomy with Douglas junior in tow, the son proved a poor companion, more intent on gambling and drinking than absorbing the latest medical advances. On their return in 1743, William's marriage plans were scuppered too: his fiancée Martha had died in his absence, aged twenty-eight. It would be many years before William trusted himself to another professional partnership; he would never again allow himself to become romantically involved. Determined, nonetheless, to make his way in London, William persevered in establishing himself as a male-midwife, staying with the widowed Mrs Douglas when she moved to Hatton Garden, and forged ahead with plans to launch an anatomy school, renting for the purpose apartments belonging to the Society of Naval Surgeons.[41]

Amid the squalor, sexual scandal and violent crime that characterized Covent Garden, William's anatomy school was fast gaining its own notoriety. The first of its kind in Britain, offering young medical students daily hands-on tuition in human dissection, the school was a daring, even dangerous, venture. The study of anatomy still languished in its infancy in mid-eighteenth-century England, with inevitable ignorance about the workings of the human body among medical practitioners as a consequence. While would-be physicians spent years at university poring over ancient medical theories and aspiring surgeons blithely copied the disastrous errors of their tutors during long apprenticeships, the study of the human body remained a backwater of medical education. There had been some efforts to improve anatomical understanding, but these had been few and far between.

Some thirty years before William's enterprise, William Cheselden, the most famous surgeon of his day, had begun inviting medical students to private lectures on anatomy at his home in Cheapside. The young surgeons crowded around the celebrated Cheselden as he demonstrated parts of the body on a corpse dragged from the Tyburn gallows, which he cut up on his dining-room table. His anatomy dinners soon attracted the attentions of the Company of Barber-Surgeons and he was smartly disciplined in 1715 on the grounds that he 'did frequently procure the Dead bodies of Malefactors from the place of execution and dissected the same at his own house'.[42] The rebuke was less in response to Cheselden's domestic arrangements than to his timing: the demonstrations clashed with the company's own anatomy lectures.

Since its foundation by royal charter in 1540, the Company of Barber-Surgeons had secured the right to the bodies of four criminals hanged in London each year, later increased to six. The corpses were dissected in public demonstrations staged several times a year, in an arrangement designed as much to serve as the ultimate punishment for felons and a deterrent to others as for educational purposes. But by 1631 the company was also encountering some difficulties reconciling its anatomy duties with its catering facilities; minutes noted that 'the bodies have been a great annoyance to the tables, dresser boards and utensils in the upper kitchen by reason of the blood, filth and entrails of these anatomies'.[43] A purpose-built anatomy theatre was duly opened in 1638. But when the barbers and the surgeons agreed to part company in 1745, egged on by the aggrieved Cheselden, the resulting new Company of Surgeons was temporarily homeless and therefore devoid of an anatomy theatre in which to stage any demonstrations. This sorry situation would continue for almost a decade, until a new theatre was built in 1753, and while anatomy teaching in London did not stop completely it was certainly a significant backwards step.

Although the Company of Barber-Surgeons had stipulated that nobody should stage anatomy lectures without its approval, private anatomy classes had in fact flourished unchecked. Several practitioners, including James Douglas and Percivall Pott, ran lectures at their hospitals and in their own homes from time to time during the first half of the century. But these courses were relatively short, often sporadic and generally limited in their scope; there was no dedicated anatomy school in London – indeed there were no medical schools at all, in sharp contrast to the flourishing centres in major cities in Scotland, Ireland and continental Europe – and no notion of a proper syllabus. More importantly, the difficulties in obtaining human bodies – the six legally available corpses all being earmarked for the Company of Barber-Surgeons – meant such private lectures afforded little opportunity for students to attempt practical dissection. Private lecturers competed with one another, and with the beadles of the Company of Barber-Surgeons before its split, to seize the few extra bodies available from the gibbet. Consequently, students in crowded anatomy lessons were lucky to catch a glimpse of the inside of a single human body as it decayed over several weeks; when bodies were impossible to obtain an animal corpse was substituted. William Hunter, who had sampled anatomy lessons both in London and Edinburgh, described a typical class under Professor Alexander Monro at Edinburgh University: 'There I learned a good deal by my ears; but almost nothing by my eyes; and therefore, hardly anything to the purpose. The defect was, that the professor was obliged to demonstrate all the parts of the body, except the bones, nerves and vessels, upon one dead body. There was a foetus for the nerves and blood-vessels; and the operations of surgery were explained, to very little purpose indeed, upon a dog.'[44] He was equally unimpressed by his studies in London. The thirty-nine anatomy lectures presented by the physician Frank Nicholls which William had attended had been able to offer only two dead bodies for the entire course.[45]

William's experience of anatomy lessons in England and Scotland had taught him above all that such courses were hopelessly inadequate as a preparation for a career in medicine. But he had also witnessed anatomy lessons in Paris and Leiden, where more liberal laws allowed surgeons an abundant supply of bodies for research purposes, and he was in no doubt of the value of practical experience. His entrepreneurial nose immediately sniffed a gap in the market for a properly designated school offering comprehensive studies in anatomy in London. With the newly formed Company of Surgeons in disarray, unable even to police private anatomy classes let alone provide its own, it was forced to rescind the rule that dissections must be performed only under its auspices. William seized his opportunity. Setting up his lecture theatre and dissecting room in the rented Covent Garden apartment, he imported to London the continental approach, advertising his first course in the *London Evening Post* in September 1746 with the inducement: 'Gentlemen may have the opportunity of learning the Art of Dissecting during the whole winter session in the same manner as at Paris.'[46]

When it finally opened its doors on 13 October 1746, the new school was a revolutionary venture. With lectures running from 5 p.m. until 7.30 p.m. every evening except Sundays, each course spanned more than seventy lessons. The courses were repeated in two terms, lasting almost four months each, from October to early January and from late January until April, in a step-by-step programme designed as a complete introduction to the subject. Perched on his podium, William held the students' attention as he imparted up-to-the-minute knowledge on the human body in his eloquent and inspirational style. As the pupils took notes, bottles of pickled organs and dried specimens of muscle and bone were passed around for them to handle and inspect.

But the school offered more than just lively lectures and interesting visual aids: each student was also guaranteed hands-on experience. Adopting the 'Paris manner', as William so discreetly put it, meant quite simply that every student was guaranteed a corpse of his own on which to practise dissection and surgical methods. For the first time, students were able not only to learn the basics of anatomy from an expert teacher, they could see with their own eyes precisely how the different organs, tissues, muscles and bones interconnected; with their own hands they could feel the weight of a human heart, unravel the coils of the gut and trace the branches of the delicate air tubes in the lungs. Their waistcoats and breeches covered with aprons, they could spend hours delving inside a human carcass up to their elbows in blood and guts. The school was an overnight success. Young students rushed to enrol from every corner of the British Isles, and even from overseas. Fired by a new thirst for knowledge, eager to explore and discover for themselves, the pupils spared little thought for the revulsion ordinary members of the public might feel for their pursuits, and scant concern over the source of their teaching material.

At last William's finances were on a secure footing. And determined now to capitalize on the achievements of two years' success, William – the self-made man – was keen to recruit brother John – the self-taught youth – to his cause. With no time to lose before the students clamoured once more at his doors, he put the lad immediately to work, setting him the critical test of dissecting an arm. Stooped over the bench, John Hunter mustered all the skills he had learned in carpentry, applied all his inborn curiosity for nature, and meticulously picked the fat from the various muscles of the limb with a dexterity unknown in a novice. The neatness and delicacy of his workmanship exceeded even William's exacting standards. But still unconvinced, William set his brother an even harder task: to dissect a second arm in which the arteries had already been injected with coloured wax, separating the vivid blood vessels from the fleshy muscles. Once again John's performance surpassed all his brother's expectations; William even went so far as to prophesy that his young brother had the makings of an excellent anatomist who should never want for employment.[47]

This was high praise indeed from the fastidious elder brother. As far as William was concerned, it was plain that his stubborn, rough-edged, untutored brother – the wild child of the family – could be successfully moulded into the competent, compliant workhorse he needed to help run the school. With careful tutoring and wise guidance, William evidently believed that his young brother could become a skilled assistant, perhaps a well-groomed young man, even an able surgeon, leaving William free to increase his wealthy clientele and pursue his goal of becoming at last a physician and a true gentleman. Encouraging and ambitious for his new ward, William must have seemed to the younger brother like a true father figure – everything John's own father had not been – at least while he remained under William's influence and in his shadow.

So on the first day of the autumn term, John Hunter took his place in the lecture theatre alongside his fellow pupils as his brother rose to greet the new class. After detailing the purpose of anatomy, the history of the subject and the programme for the busy next three months, William outlined to the impressionable youngsters gathered in the room the stark choice that now lay before them: they could choose to idle away their days, skimp their studies and follow other diversions – of which Covent Garden offered many – and then they would forever struggle to find work, want for money and tread 'a low path in life'; or they could work hard, study diligently and pursue perfection, and then, he assured them, they would be respected, courted and satisfied with their lot. In the eighteenth-century can-do society, an ambitious young man with a will to work, a few connections and a mind to adopt the correct manners could truly take the world by storm, insisted William. Rising to his finale, he urged, 'and I firmly believe, that it is in your power not only to *chuse*, but to *have*, which rank you please in the world'.[48]

Nobody listened more attentively than his own younger brother. Almost overnight, the carefree youth became an industrious young man; the aimless boy found his lifelong passion; the diffident Johnny of the Scottish Lowland was transformed into the popular, companionable, fun-loving Jack who frequented the taverns, theatres and coffee-houses of Covent Garden. His days were fully employed: up at first light every morning preparing specimens for the students to peruse, demonstrating anatomy skills and the art of preserving body parts in the dissecting room all day, and listening beside his fellow pupils at William's lectures every evening. But even after that there was to be little rest. One more task fell to Jack Hunter, but this job could only take place under cover of darkness. While William built up his bank balance and his reputation, rapidly becoming London's most sought-after *accoucheur*, John was put in charge of the seamier side of his business: procuring the school's essential teaching material.

3

The Stout Man's Muscles

'... be upon your guard; and, out of doors, speak
with caution of what may be passing here, especially with
respect to dead bodies'.

William Hunter[1]

When baby John Race died in early December 1747, his
grieving parents laid his body in its tiny box in the frozen
ground of the paupers' graveyard at Whitechapel, east
London. But the two-year-old infant was not to be
allowed to rest in peace. Shortly after midnight on
Sunday, 6 December, shovels broke soundlessly through
the freshly dug soil, rough hands wrenched the coffin
from its shallow grave, and John's limp corpse was
dragged from its box, stripped of its shroud and shoved
into a sack.

For once, the Whitechapel burial ground was under
watch. James Thomas and Charles Pritty were caught in
the act of exhuming the infant's body and promptly

brought to justice. Ten days later the two men stood un-repentantly before a judge and jury at the Hick's Hall courthouse in the City of London. They were charged that they 'unlawfully did dig up' the dead body of John Race, removed the corpse from its coffin and carried it away 'to the evil example of all others'. The jury hearing the case lost no time in finding the pair guilty. Thomas and Pritty were each fined one shilling – a relatively paltry sum – but their sentence of six months' confinement in the dreaded Newgate prison would have provided ample opportunity for remorse.[2]

Placed in charge of procuring dead bodies for his brother's anatomy school at the tender age of twenty, less than one year after the gruesome Thomas and Pritty court case, John Hunter faced a formidable challenge. He had been left in no doubt that the school required a regular and abundant supply of human corpses in order to con-tinue its success. William had made clear his conviction that regular practical dissection was the surest way by which any aspiring medical man could properly learn his trade, telling his pupils, 'It is by Anatomy alone, that we know the true nature, and therefore the most proper cure of the greatest number of local diseases.'[3] Indeed, if future surgeons were denied the chance to practise their primitive operations on dead bodies, to make their blunders on unfeeling flesh, the only alternative was to practise on live bodies, with inevitably fatal results, he stressed. And as William made clear to the new students at the start of their autumn term in 1748, it was therefore necessary 'for giving a complete course of Anatomy, to provide a number of *fresh subjects*'.[4]

The emphasis was deliberate. William's promise that every one of his pupils would enjoy first-hand access to a corpse was the very *raison d'être* of his teaching; it was precisely what set his school apart from his rivals. The handful of other anatomists offering occasional courses in London presented little threat; William knew his main competition came from over the border back home in Scotland. It was there, at the highly respected medical school of Edinburgh University, that his own former tutor, Professor Alexander Monro, was attracting students from across Europe with rising success. And although William was careful to acknowledge the 'great reputation' of his former teacher when addressing his own pupils, he was a canny businessman at heart and could not resist adding that 'he might have been a much better anatomist . . . if he could have been better supplied with dead bodies'.[5]

Experienced anatomists such as Monro, working in a small city like Edinburgh, experienced considerable difficulties obtaining the corpses they needed for anatomical exploration; accordingly Monro had become adept at eking out just two bodies for an entire course of more than a hundred lectures.[6] But for William, working in a huge and anonymous city like London, rampant poverty and disease guaranteed a plentiful supply of teaching material. This was where he knew he had the edge. It was the main selling point of his anatomy course, and as the popularity of his lectures grew, so his requirement for supplies of bodies increased. In practice this meant that for every student who walked through William's front door, another corpse needed to be heaved in through the back. And since a dead body rarely lasted much more than a week before decomposing beyond use, even in winter, in effect the school needed a steady stream of cadavers hustled through the back entrance on an almost nightly basis in order to keep the pupils coming.

Quite plainly, these needed to be fresh bodies, laid out on the dissecting bench within a day or two of death. 'The dead body cannot be too fresh for dissection,' William told his class. 'Every hour that it is kept, it is losing something of its fitness for anatomical demonstrations.'[7] As he well knew, the process of natural decomposition would quickly cause the blood to seep out of the tissues and vessels, rendering the various parts one indistinguishable soupy mass, while all the while putrefaction advanced, turning the flesh flabby and indistinct, not to mention noxious in the extreme. But in addition to a regular stock of corpses he also needed bodies to order, ready to show particular parts of the anatomy, in men, women, children and fetuses, both healthy and diseased. As William observed, 'diseases frequently alter the state of the parts, so as to render them unfit for a demonstration of their natural condition. Thence it is that we are under a necessity of having, sometimes, several subjects to shew the bowels only.'

In short, the secret of William's success lay in bodies – abundant, regular, varied, fresh stocks of bodies. But with his polished manners, expensive finery and affluent clientele, William certainly did not regard himself as the appropriate person to ferret out corpses in the night. As his refined midwifery skills and charming bedside manner endeared him to the wives and daughters of London's nobility, so he grew more and more inclined to distance himself from the darker side of his business. To date the job of obtaining dissection material had fallen largely to his assistant, a surgeon called John Symons, who had attended William's first course in 1746 and stayed on to help in the dissecting room.[8] But Symons' tenure was coming to an end, so the job of ensuring a reliable supply of fresh corpses now fell to young John. His ungainly country ways, plain dress and the vulgar oaths he seemed unable or unwilling to suppress, would surely allow him to mix easily in the seedy taverns of the London underworld while William could continue supping claret with his distinguished associates. Plainly, John was the ideal person to take over Symons' job.

Completely dependent on William for his board and lodging, his job and even his pocket money, John Hunter was in no position to decline his allotted role. In any case, he was anxious to excel at the only work for which he had ever felt any interest. Bodies were needed and he was the man to make sure they were delivered. But accomplishing the job to William's demanding requirements was an organizational and logistical challenge of staggering proportions. Human cadavers on which to teach medical students the rudiments of anatomy were in exceedingly short supply in Georgian Britain; not one was available legally to private anatomists like William.

Since it was almost unheard of in the mid-eighteenth century for anyone to donate their body for dissection in the cause of aiding research into medical care, there were few opportunities for lawful post-mortems. In one rare exception, a certain James Brooke made a prior arrangement to sell his body after death to a surgeon in Salisbury in 1736, but his motivation was clearly financial rather than altruistic.[9] As the century advanced, the idea of requesting a post-mortem after death would gradually gain some acceptance. The socialite Lady Caroline Holland and the physician Messenger Monsey would both request that autopsies be performed on their dead bodies, in an effort to ascertain their causes of death.[10] But such enlightened views were still exceedingly uncommon in the middle of the eighteenth century.

At the same time, of course, the supply of bodies authorized by law for anatomical practice was both extremely limited and strictly circumscribed. Surgeons in Britain had begun lobbying for a legal right to bodies for dissection ever since the vogue for anatomy had filtered across the English Channel from Renaissance Europe in the fifteenth century. The earliest concession came in Scotland, where the Guild of Surgeons and Barbers was granted in 1506 the right annually to 'ane condampnit man after he be deid to mak anatomea of'.[11] It was not long before the English authorities allowed similar privileges. Henry VIII granted the Company of Barber-Surgeons the right in 1540 to 'have and take without contradiction foure persons condempned, adjudged, and put to death for feloni' and Elizabeth I extended the same allowance of four bodies to the Company of Physicians in 1565. When Charles II upped the barber-surgeons' annual quota to six bodies a year in 1663, Samuel Pepys was one of the first spectators to witness a public dissection at Surgeons' Hall. Frequently, such demonstrations spanned several days, with public lectures on different parts of the body, such as the muscles or the viscera, and a banquet to follow. After Pepys had listened to a lecture on the structure of the kidneys, demonstrated on the body of a recently hanged man in the elegant Inigo Jones theatre on 27 February 1663, he enjoyed a 'fine dinner' in the company's hall. Dinner over, he readily took up the invitation from some of the assembled surgeons to inspect the mutilated body in a private room, recording in his diary, 'I did touch the dead body with my bare hand; it felt cold, but methought it was a very unpleasant sight.'[12]

Almost a century later, when John Hunter was charged

with the job of obtaining bodies for William's school, legal provision remained unchanged. Although anatomists on mainland Europe enjoyed specific rights to plentiful supplies of bodies in order to conduct their essential work, throughout the English-speaking world, in Britain, Ireland and the American colonies, there was no legal source of corpses for anatomical training or research beyond the narrow allocation to the elite medieval guilds.[13] And with the new Company of Surgeons effectively moribund since the split with the barbers in 1745, even the legally endorsed demonstrations at Surgeons' Hall were drastically curtailed. Consequently, any teacher who wished to offer his students a practical foundation in anatomy, any anatomist who desired to enhance his understanding of the human body, any surgeon who wanted to hone his skills, was forced to break the law.

Yet if there were no corpses available legally for private anatomists in eighteenth-century London, there was certainly no shortage of dead bodies. And it did not take a great amount of ingenuity to work out where to find them. The first, and most obvious, source for a young man charged with obtaining corpses by underhand means in 1748 was the gallows. With hanging the penalty for nearly two hundred crimes, from pickpocketing a watch to highway robbery and murder, as many as fifty men, women and even children were executed at Tyburn in a single year.[14] Just as Leonardo da Vinci had stolen cadavers from the scaffold to make his anatomical sketches in Renaissance Italy, so eighteenth-century London anatomists turned for their research requirements to Tyburn Tree, the notorious triple-legged gibbet on the north-east corner of Hyde Park, at London's western fringe.[15] In the uproarious mêlée around the scaffold on hanging days, anatomists and their agents fought hand-to-hand battles with officials of the Company of Barber-Surgeons and relatives of the convicted in a desperate effort to wrest control of the hanged bodies. The crowd loved it; it was all part of the festival atmosphere on the public holidays which became known as 'Paddington fair day'.

Condemned prisoners were drawn in an open cart along the three-mile stretch from Newgate prison to Tyburn in a manic parade punctuated by halts for the convicted to imbibe large quantities of beer at taverns along the route. Finally arriving at the gallows, as many as twenty-three convicts on exceptional occasions were 'turned off' at once to the cheers of spectators squashed into the wooden stadium or perched on lamplighters' ladders precariously propped together for an unhindered view. The drop of the nooses was the signal for the ranked combatants to rush forwards. Friends and relatives of the executed leapt up to grab the dangling corpses' feet, in an effort to shorten the usually slow and painful death by strangulation which ensued and to claim the bodies for a decent burial. At the same time, the beadles of the Company of Barber-Surgeons tussled with the bereaved families to seize their legitimate booty for the dissecting table, while other surgeons and their assistants muscled in for a slice of the action. The novelist Samuel Richardson, author of the best-selling *Pamela*, was horrified by such a scene at Tyburn in 1740: 'As soon as the poor creatures were half-dead, I was much surprised before such a number of peace-officers, to see the populace fall to hauling and pulling the carcasses with so much earnestness, as to occasion several warm rencounters, and broken heads. These were the friends of the persons executed ... and some persons sent by private surgeons to obtain bodies for dissection. The contests between these were fierce and bloody, and frightful to look at.'[16]

Though the Company of Barber-Surgeons' right to six bodies annually from Tyburn was firmly endorsed by royal authority, it was by no means accepted by the Georgian populace. Consequently, the beadles appointed to bring the allotted bodies back to Surgeons' Hall in their waiting cart were reduced to using violence, bribery and sometimes legal redress to assert their rights. Frequently they were thwarted by the crowds, occasionally they were obstructed by the hangman – bribed either by surgeons or relatives to protect his victims – and once even the officers of the law were accused of 'siding with the mob'. Securing the executed bodies proved a costly ritual for the barber-surgeons: not only did they have to pay the hangman a regular fee for his compliance, they also on occasion had to grease the palms of the Sheriff of London's officers to provide protection. Even so, in 1712 a certain John Wooding was found guilty of taking from Tyburn a body designated for the surgeons, and in 1720 the company requested the assistance of the High Constable of St Giles parish to recover a body 'which had been taken from the Beadles by the Mobb'. Nine years later the company had to petition George II with a reminder of its time-honoured allocation, complaining that 'lately riotous persons had wrested the bodies from the Beadles'.[17]

Hanging days became a violent free-for-all, especially when some of the period's most notorious villains went to their deaths. When the infamous house-breaker Jack Sheppard was hanged in 1724, the surgeons tussled all day with the criminal's friends and well-wishers, anxious to provide their hero with a respectful burial; the mob prevailed and Sheppard was allowed to rest in peace.[18] But when Jonathan Wild, the self-styled 'Thief-Taker General' who governed all organized crime in London, was finally convicted and hanged the following year, the surgeons had their revenge: after the body was carefully buried by his devotees it was secretly dug up and smuggled away to Surgeons' Hall.[19] His skeleton remains at the Royal College of Surgeons to this day.

Popular feeling clearly ran high. The idea of being dissected after death, or allowing the body of a loved one to be dissected, provoked widespread horror and disgust; the practice offended deeply-held religious convictions and transgressed age-old beliefs in the sanctity of the grave.[20] With religious fervour intense and fear of eternal damnation real, it was sincerely believed that a dead body had to rest undisturbed in its burial place until the trumpets sounded on Judgement Day, signalling the reunion of body and soul. Most God-fearing Georgians were convinced that if their bodies were mutilated by anatomists and their remains scattered far afield or even fed to dogs, they would never be resurrected whole in Paradise. Typically heart-felt emotions were expressed by Vincent Davis, a butcher at Smithfield market who was sentenced to hang in 1725 for murdering his wife, when he declared, 'I have killed the best wife in the world, and I am certain of being hanged, but for God's sake, don't let me be anatomised!'[21] And the artist William Hogarth graphically reflected the fear of anatomy in *The Reward of Cruelty*, showing the feckless Tom Nero being carved up on the barber-surgeons' table with the Tyburn noose still tight around his neck, a grinning surgeon gouging out one eye and the dissecting-room dog nibbling at his discarded heart.[22]

But there was another, much more immediate, reason

why condemned Georgians feared the anatomist's knife. With the hangman's art still far from scientific, criminals executed at Tyburn usually died from slow asphyxiation rather than a swiftly broken neck. Consequently, it was not uncommon for hanged convicts to regain consciousness some time after being cut down from the scaffold, occasionally on a dissecting-room table. Several cases of people reviving after being hanged have been noted since records began; the phenomenon would evoke particular interest for John Hunter.

In possibly the first recorded case of revival after execution, in 1587 a hanged man taken to London's barber-surgeons' hall sprang to life on the dissecting table just as a knife was plunged into his chest, providing the gathered audience with more than the usual public spectacle.[23] He lived three days, prompting the barber-surgeons to stipulate that if future anatomy subjects should have the audacity to regain life then the guild should not be expected to foot the bill for their medical care. In the following century, the political economist William Petty helped to recovery an Oxford servant, Anne Greene, when she revived under his anatomy knife after being hanged for murder – apparently unjustly – in 1650.[24] Several more cases were recorded in the first half of the eighteenth century. Most recently, in 1740 a seventeen-year-old thief called William Duell had swung on the gallows for half an hour before he was delivered to the barber-surgeons. Just as the gathered surgeons were about to slice open his chest, the youth emitted a groan and sat up; having cheated death once, his sentence was commuted to transportation.

And so, on 28 October 1748, the first hanging day after William's school had opened its doors for the new term, there can be little doubt that John Hunter would have taken up a vantage point, standing in the shadow of the gallows, as nine men and one woman were strung up from Tyburn Tree. As the carts that had carried the condemned through the rowdy streets from Newgate prison lurched away from the gibbet, there were no last-minute reprieves for John Lancaster, John Armson, John Roberts, Thomas Atkins, Francis Andrews, Sam Chapman, Robert Cunningham, Thomas Thomson, William James or Sarah Kenningham, all condemned to die for assorted acts of burglary, smuggling, horse-stealing and highway robbery.[25] And the minute their jerking bodies swung loose above the heads of the crowd, John Hunter would have joined the brawl with the surgeons, relatives and spectators to grab a leg and hold on tight. Although of slender build, and at five feet two inches slightly less than average height for the time, he was broad-shouldered and strong, his muscles developed by years of labouring on the farm, and he could reasonably hold his own with any of the rough-necks and villains arrayed at Tyburn.

Whether John Hunter succeeded in securing any of the bodies that dangled from the hangman's rope that day is unknown, but certainly he would obtain corpses from Tyburn, whether by bribery, skulduggery or brute force, on a number of occasions. Although ordinarily careful never to divulge the sources of his dissection 'subjects', he would casually refer in one published work to an instance when two bodies at once were smuggled away from Tyburn, remarking, 'in the spring of 1753 there was an execution of eight men, two of whom I knew had at that time very severe gonorrheas. Their bodies being procured for this particular purpose, we were very accurate in our examination, but found no ulceration.'[26] Some few years later, when William was giving lectures on anatomy to a group of artists – probably the Society of Artists of Great Britain, a precursor to the Royal Academy – his young brother had apparently advanced considerably in his ability to procure hanged bodies, obtaining 'eight men at once from Tyburn in the month of April'. In notes that he scrawled in the margins of a biography on William, in his usual idiosyncratic spelling style, John explained:

> This society were acquainted with it and they were desired to come and chuse the best subject for such purpose. When they had fixed upon one he was immediately sent to their appartments. As all this was done in a few hours after death, and as they had not become stif Dr. Hunter conceived he might be first put into an atitude and alow'd to stifen in it which was done, and when he became stif we all set to work, and by next morning we had the external muscles all well exposed ready for making a mold from him, the cast of which is now in the Royal Academy.[27]

The bodies of those who were hanged were particularly valuable to the students at William's school: since the executed felons died suddenly, their corpses were generally free of the diseases that proved fatal to most people dying a natural death. The pupils could therefore study the human anatomy in its normal, healthy state. Yet the gibbet could not provide the school with women who were pregnant – a pet interest of William's given his growing obstetrics business – since the law prohibited pregnant women from being hanged. Indeed, huge numbers of women escaped the rope in the eighteenth century by 'pleading their bellies', making sure if they were not already pregnant before they were imprisoned that they got themselves pregnant in Newgate's lax environment by the time they came to be sentenced. Neither could Tyburn provide the pupils with the bodies of fetuses, babies or young children, which were likewise required, and obtained, for the students. Moreover, with only eight hanging days in a typical year and fierce competition for the corpses, Tyburn would never supply John Hunter with the regular stock of bodies he needed to satisfy William.

Ingenious alternatives were required. Accordingly, anatomists took to loitering at Newgate prison in the days leading up to execution, bartering to buy the bodies of condemned prisoners in advance of their deaths. In 1752, one William Signal was persuaded to sell his body to a surgeon solely so that he could buy decent clothes for his day of execution. Another common ruse was to bribe unscrupulous undertakers to sell bodies prior to burial; sometimes the stolen cadaver was replaced with paving stones or soil to simulate the weight of the corpse. Many a bereaved relative followed an empty coffin in a solemn funeral procession through Georgian London, while mourners often shed tears as coffins stashed with stones were lowered into graves. Indeed, in April 1748, only six months before John Hunter arrived in London, a night-watchman called John Walker was sentenced to transportation for seven years after being convicted at the Old Bailey of stealing a coffin containing the body of a hanged convict prior to burial. The theft was discovered by the family too late: the body was already on a surgeon's dissecting bench with its head sawn off.[28]

Resorting to ever more desperate measures, some anatomists even took to dissecting the bodies of their own relatives when no other corpses were available. William

Harvey had conducted post-mortems on his father and sister when they died, although he insisted that upon his own death his body should be wrapped in lead to thwart any fellow enthusiasts.[29] Ordinarily, however, surgeons went to extreme lengths to avoid either their own bodies or those of their families ending up on the dissecting table. None of these methods, however, could really help John Hunter fulfil his Herculean quest. For the serious anatomist determined to procure a reliable supply of human bodies for dissection in mid-eighteenth-century London there was really only one viable source: the grave.

Grave-robbing had occurred on occasion and in places across the British Isles since at least the seventeenth century; John Hunter would help transform it into an industry. When the raw, fresh-faced youth arrived in Covent Garden in 1748, body-snatching was in its infancy. There had been a number of cases of grave-robbing by surgeons, students and occasional down-beat ruffians such as Thomas and Pritty, and these in turn had provoked public outrage and sometimes legal redress. But in general grave-robbing was small-scale with few perpetrators and few victims, and therefore drew little notice. During the span of John Hunter's career, body-snatching would grow exponentially, spawning warring gangs of professional grave-robbers who stalked the city's churchyards night after night, to the horror and fury of the general public. By the end of the eighteenth century, John and William Hunter's disciples would have exported the practice to Ireland and America, stoking up mass protests in both countries, while the increasingly expert body-snatchers whom John Hunter patronized would send their merchandise as far afield as Bristol and Edinburgh. Eventually, the practice would reach such a scale – as London burial grounds had to be policed by armed vigilantes to thwart the thieves – that Parliament was forced in 1828 to investigate. Even then, it was only the discovery of murders committed by Burke and Hare in Scotland, and by similar but lesser known assassins in London, which ultimately compelled the government to legislate and end more than a century of body-snatching by introducing the Anatomy Act of 1832.[30]

Driven initially by his brother's demands, then compelled by his own zeal to extend knowledge of human physiology, John Hunter would dissect more bodies, and therefore require more bodies stolen from graves, than any other anatomist of the eighteenth century. He would develop closer relationships with the grave-robbers than any other surgeon – even, in all likelihood, joining their night-time expeditions – and he would ultimately pull off the most dramatic body-snatching ruse of all time.

In its earliest days, body-snatching had principally been carried out by a handful of surgeons and their students, visiting graveyards periodically by night to seek out dissection material for lessons the next day. Instances of grave-robbing were reported in Scotland, where the flourishing Edinburgh and Glasgow medical schools were forced to compete both for students and for corpses, as far back as 1711 when it was recorded that 'of late there has been a violation of sepulchres in the Grey-Friars Churchyard by some who most unchristianly have been stealing the bodies of the dead out of their graves'.[31] While Edinburgh's professors soon secured the services of professional body-snatchers, Glasgow's medical students would be forced to forage for their own corpses throughout the whole of the eighteenth century and into the next.[32] Medical students at Oxford organized similar night-time raids in the face of public protest. John Bellers, a prominent Quaker and philanthropist, reported that in 1714 'It was not easy for the students to get a body to dissect at Oxford, the mob being so mutinous to prevent their having one.'[33] And at Trinity College in Dublin, both anatomy and art students exhumed bodies from the city's public burial ground to furnish subjects for their respective classes on dissecting and life-drawing.

As anatomy classes grew and student numbers increased, demand for corpses escalated; as surgeons prospered and improved their status in society, they became less willing literally to get their hands dirty or to run the gauntlet of angry mobs following the all-too-obvious trail from empty tombs to dissecting rooms. Professional grave-robbers began supplying anatomists with corpses for dissection from the early 1700s. Concentrated mainly in London and Edinburgh, but also working in provincial English towns and later the American colonies, the body-snatchers developed unique methods of unearthing corpses with speed, stealth and efficiency. Strongly despised and universally feared, the rival packs of ruthless men were nicknamed the 'Resurrectionists', after their ability to raise vast numbers of dead from their graves, or the 'Sack 'Em Up Men', after their method of transporting their wares. Initially, the perpetrators were gravediggers and sextons bribed by surgeons to exhume the corpses they had only just helped to bury. One gravedigger who had been thus seduced was caught in 1736 lifting bodies from St Dunstan's churchyard in Stepney, east London, where he worked, and selling them to a surgeon for dissection. Sentenced to be publicly whipped, he received hundreds of lashes from the angry crowds that gathered in the churchyard to dole out his punishment.[34]

So not only were the grave-robbers now providing a regular supply of bodies to Scottish and English anatomists, they were also proving to be convenient scapegoats for outraged public opinion. By the time Pritty and Thomas were caught stealing John Race's corpse in 1747, the growing business in dead bodies was beginning to attract all manner of lawless desperadoes and petty crooks, greedy for rich pickings from the eager surgeons. Before long, body-snatching would become a carefully orchestrated, highly managed and increasingly lucrative industry. Rising public vigilance and widespread condemnation would only prompt the Resurrectionists to develop ever more sophisticated techniques.

Working on moonless nights throughout the winter, when the anatomy classes ran, the teams used wooden shovels to dig silently through the freshly turned soil of a new grave. By the discreet glow of covered lanterns, they would dig a narrow shaft at the head of a grave down to the top end of a coffin, exposing about one-third of the lid. Then, using crowbars or grappling hooks they pulled on the coffin lid, snapping the cheap, thin wood under the weight of the remaining soil, to reveal their quarry. It was then but an easy matter to sling a rope around the arms and drag the body from its dank hole. Quickly the gang stripped the corpse of its funeral shroud, working on the widely believed principle that while there was no law against stealing a body, taking clothes, a coffin or even a wedding ring could be punishable by hanging – though in practice this was not always the courts' view, as Pritty and Thomas had found to their cost. Then the naked and usually limp body – rigor mortis would normally have passed within a day or two of death – was bundled into a sack or hamper ready for delivery before dawn to the basement steps of a waiting anatomist.[35]

At the peak of their reign of terror, before the Anatomy Act ended the practice, professional gangs could unearth a body from a shallow grave in fifteen minutes flat, while a corpse buried in deeper, firmer earth could be exhumed within an hour.[36] A single team, well equipped and knowing the territory, could procure as many as ten bodies in a night's work or as many as three hundred in one year.[37] Paupers' graves were always the most popular: often poor people were buried in mass graves left uncovered until full or in shallow graves in easily accessible public burial grounds. Richer folk took care to protect their dead in locked vaults or lead coffins.

Gravediggers, church sextons and nightwatchmen employed to guard the graves were often in the pay of the body-snatchers, while meticulous care was taken to disguise the violation by carefully replacing soil, flowers and other mementoes in their original positions. The crimes were often so stealthy that a gang would sometimes burrow into a likely-looking new grave only to find it empty – their rivals had got there before them.[38] In such cases, when one team had 'trespassed' on the burial ground considered the territory of another, revenge was swift; there was no honour among body thieves. The crooks shopped one another to the authorities, raised a mob against their rivals, or left a trail of guilt, propping up coffins in their graves and leaving shrouds strewn on the ground.[39] Ultimately the reckless men became so adept at their trade, and demand from anatomists grew so constant, that London's churchyards were honeycombed with empty tombs. On several occasions when thefts were suspected, horrified relatives would frantically dig up grave after grave only to find every body gone.

Under the laws of the black market, rising demand meant rising prices. An adult body in the mid-eighteenth century could be bought by surgeons for about one guinea, but the price had doubled by the 1780s and leapt to as high as sixteen guineas over the next twenty to thirty years.[40] The bodies of children, known as 'smalls', were priced by the inch, while an unusual or rare medical condition could always command a premium. At a time when a merchant seaman earned less than £2 for a month's hard labour, the body-snatchers' nightly toil was a lucrative business, even if they were idle through the summer when bodies would not keep and anatomy classes were therefore forced to close.[41] Often surgeons connived with their suppliers, directing them to the grave of an unlucky patient whose condition they wished to investigate or whose diseased organ they wished to obtain. There was nowhere to hide, as Sir Astley Cooper, one of John Hunter's most fervent devotees, made clear when he looked the members of the 1828 parliamentary select committee in the eye and chillingly informed them, 'The law does not prevent our obtaining the body of an individual if we think proper; for there is no person, let his situation in life be what it may, whom, if I were disposed to dissect, I could not obtain.'[42]

Certainly the law seemed largely indifferent to the antics of the grave-robbers as well as the receivers of their stolen goods. While the Resurrectionists were sometimes caught and prosecuted – and there were other notable cases like that of Pritty and Thomas – often police officers looked the other way when they encountered the thieves at work. If the crooks were prosecuted the courts usually dealt out relatively lenient penalties, and even then their surgeon masters often paid their bail and supported their families while they were imprisoned. Only a handful of surgeons were ever brought to justice; John Hunter would never face legal action over his relentless trade. Likewise, government and Georgian high society turned a blind eye to the buoyant market in bodies; those in power knew that the army and navy were desperately short of skilled surgeons, they appreciated the need for anatomists to practise their art, and in any case the desecrated graves were rarely those of their relatives. But the practice was not without its risks: body-snatchers were often stoned, shot at and, in Ireland, even killed by outraged members of the public.[43]

Needless to say, the body-snatchers were scrupulously discreet about their craft. No first-hand accounts of their work in the eighteenth century survive, but a rare example describing a gang in action in the early nineteenth century is probably an accurate representation of the methods adopted by earlier miscreants. In *The Diary of a Resurrectionist*, an anonymous grave-robber, later identified as the notorious gang-leader Joshua Naples, outlined a typical January night in 1812: 'Got up at 3 in the morning, the whole party went to Guys and St Thomas, got 3 adults, 1 from Guy's and 2 from St Thomas's, took them to St Thomas, came home and met again, took one of the above to Guy's, settled for the Horse £24.'[44]

But in October 1748, when John Hunter began his quest, demand from anatomy teachers was still relatively modest and professional body-snatching a rarity. Grave-robbers were still in the main opportunistic down-and-outs such as Pritty and Thomas, who would by now have been released from Newgate, and the shifty sextons or gravediggers who needed just a little temptation to supplement their incomes. So at first, following the example of students in Glasgow and Dublin, the twenty-year-old John Hunter almost certainly set out himself under cover of darkness from the Covent Garden school, armed with a shovel and crowbar, to scour local burial grounds for freshly dug graves. Quite possibly he would already have learned of grave-robbing practices from William, when he had attended Monro's anatomy classes in Edinburgh; possibly too he had heard tales of the students' nocturnal raids in Glasgow when living only a few miles distant in East Kilbride. By the time he arrived at William's school he would have been exceptionally naive had he not already been prepared for the darker side of his new job. No doubt William's assistant, John Symons, made haste to initiate him.

Although John Hunter would never refer explicitly to the source of his anatomy material in his writings, an unusually indiscreet entry in his case books confirms that he did obtain bodies from London graveyards: 'Sept 1758. In this Autumn we got a stout Man for the Muscles from St George's ground.'[45] His ambivalent 'we' suggests he may well have been among the crew of students or jobbing body-snatchers who raided the burial ground – which was probably St George's churchyard in Bloomsbury although there were others similarly named in the city – not just the recipient of the stout man's corpse. Well-built men were always in demand: with the skin stripped off they could be used to display the muscles to best advantage. Hospital patients provided an obvious source of bodies, as another record in Hunter's case books recounts: 'In 1759, I stripped the bones of an old Woman that died in St George's Hospital.'[46] It is clear that the elderly woman was not one of Hunter's patients whose family had consented to a post-mortem from his adjoiner: 'I knew nothing of her history.'

It is highly likely, too, that the young John Hunter commandeered parties of William's students, just two or three years his junior and probably bolstered by several rounds of ale in a tavern beforehand, to help in his grisly undercover work. Certainly, even several decades later pupils at William's school would find themselves undertaking graveyard expeditions, according to a letter sent by one of them to his father on Christmas Day, 1777:

> I am affraid I shall not have much for my dissecting fee as bodies are not to be got and there are several before me. G. Reid has promised to get me one and John the servt who is a very necessary man to be great with, to whom G. Reid has introduced me and spoke for me has promised me the first that comes. The way I am to have it is this, if a body comes Mr Reid (who has told the pupils he is going out soon to lift one) is to say he got it and of consequence it belongs to him and he is to chuse me for his partner and then we pay the Body to the servt.[47]

The adventurous G. Reid planning to go out and 'lift' a body was George Reid, a pupil of William's and the son of Thomas Reid, then professor of anatomy at Glasgow University, who would obviously not have been surprised or dismayed by his son's night-time pursuits.

There was certainly no lack of local graveyards for John Hunter to choose from in the winter of 1748. From the windows of the Covent Garden dissecting room he would have been able to see the churchyard of St Paul's, facing the piazza. Within five minutes' stroll he could reach the churchyards of St Giles near Monmouth Street, St Mary in the Strand, St Clement's in Portugal Street and St Martin's in St Martin's Lane, as well as the burial grounds belonging to the workhouses of St James' and St Clement Dane's, and, of course, St George's burial ground, just north of the Foundling Hospital in Bloomsbury. Only a little further afield there were plenty of public burial grounds designated for the poor, including the fearful-sounding Cross Bones ground for 'low women' in Southwark, the Cripplegate ground in Warwick Place, and the Bethlem graveyard where the inmates of the dreaded Bethlem Hospital for the insane ended their tortured lives.

But above all, it was professional body-snatchers he turned to. From the day he started work in William's anatomy school, John Hunter embarked on a long and fruitful relationship with the Resurrectionists that would plunge him deep into London's criminal underworld. As procurer-in-chief of corpses for the school, he immediately sought out willing grave-robbers and probably recruited more to the job. It was his role to give the villains their orders for the night, haggle over the prices and keep a candle burning in the dissecting room waiting for the cumbrous sacks to arrive. But far from finding the job distasteful, as William clearly had and other anatomists certainly would, Jack Hunter – as he now liked to be known – soon acquired a reputation for relishing his task. His youthful liking for a drink, lack of social airs and colourful language evidently endeared him to his sinister suppliers. One early biographer, writing within living memory of the anatomist, called him 'a great favourite' with the body-snatchers.[48] A Victorian author described him 'hobnobbing with the resurrection-men'.[49]

Plainly, he was good at his job. William was a demanding taskmaster, requiring the corpses not just of random men, women and children, but also fetuses, babies and pregnant women, at various stages of gestation, for his own research purposes as well as for lectures and students' practice. His young brother supplied them all. The case books record: 'In the winter, 1749, a child was brought into the room used for dissection in Covent-garden.'[50] The lack of medical history betrays the obvious source of the unnamed child. And in page after page the vagueness of the descriptions of the bodies detailed in the case books points clearly to their origins. 'There was an Old Man dissected at our house' reads one entry, while another records, 'A Young Boy about four years was dissected.' Later, Hunter would also publish sketches of teeth and jaws he dissected during his years in Covent Garden from the mouths of fetuses, babies and children with similar uncertainty as to their ages, referring only to a fetus 'about seven or eight months old', a child 'of five or six years of age' and 'a youth about eleven or twelve years old'.[51]

Pregnant women were a recurrent requirement throughout the time he spent with William. Partly due to the difficulty in obtaining the corpses of pregnant women, the structure of the pregnant womb had been only rarely investigated by anatomists to date. Keenly aware that this was a field ripe for exploration and discovery, and eager to further his own professional interest, William devoted much of his life to investigating the pregnant womb. Needless to say, he did not dirty his own hands procuring the bodies. That, as usual, was left to his brother. Through the underground contacts he had established, John Hunter learned the whereabouts and acquired the bodies of women who had died at different stages of pregnancy, their bloated corpses being dragged from their coffins and shoved into sacks as usual. In William's later treatise on the pregnant womb, *The Anatomy of the Human Gravid Uterus*, an advertisement boasted that William had 'had more opportunities of examining this subject than any other anatomist'.[52] But it was John who had made most of those opportunities.

In all, during the twelve winters John Hunter would spend with his brother, he would later admit to having 'been present at the dissection of more than two thousand human bodies'.[53] The intense industry involved was later captured dramatically in a watercolour by Thomas Rowlandson entitled *The Dissecting Room*, which shows three naked corpses in the process of being cut open by a huddle of more than a dozen excited anatomists.[54] Prominent among the dissectors are William and John Hunter. Numerous other pictures and cartoons published throughout the eighteenth century depict the act of body-snatching in all its grotesque horror, with frequent references to the Hunter brothers. Given the scale of their operation, both in dissecting human bodies and acquiring the corpses, it was little wonder that William made sure to bind his pupils at the start of every term in an oath of silence: 'In a country where liberty disposes the people to licentiousness and outrage, and where Anatomists are not legally supplied with dead bodies, particular care should be taken, to avoid giving offence to the populace, or to the prejudices of our neighbours. Therefore it is to be hoped, that you will be upon your guard; and, out of doors, speak with caution of what may be passing here, especially with respect to dead bodies.'[55]

Out half the night scavenging in graveyards or waiting in the dissecting room for a muffled knock on the back door, John Hunter soon learned to survive on minimal rest; he would manage on little more than four or five hours' sleep a night for most of his life. But under William's demanding instruction his days were fully employed too. Up at sunrise, to catch the best light for dissection, he was kept busy preparing bodies, helping students with their practical dissection and making specimens until dusk, before attending William's lectures for close to two hours every evening. Although he would never settle to scholarly studies, he was evidently impressed by William's commanding lecture style – so different to the dry, dusty school lessons he had despised. Later he would observe that his brother had 'reduced the pompous oratorial mode of Lecturing to the simple and familiar discription which probably no man could excell'.[56] Witty, well-read and intelligent, William began each course with a simple explanation of the purpose of anatomy, followed by a scholarly account of the history of the subject since ancient times. The next two to three months were devoted to describing meticulously the known structure of the human body; surviving notes taken by his many students typically run to three volumes.[57] Indeed, William's lectures would eventually become so acclaimed that society intellectuals and aristo-cratic gentlemen clamoured to listen. The economist Adam Smith would attend a complete course along with his friend, the historian Edward Gibbon, in 1777; at the end of each lecture Gibbon would make a point of thank-ing William for his instruction.[58] But while John Hunter, listening in 1748, must have rejoiced that at last somebody was able to furnish some of the answers to his relentless questioning – he even managed to scribble a few notes himself – he would always prefer to trust the evidence before his own eyes to the discourse in his ears. And there would always be more questions.

Swiftly mastering the basic art of human dissection under William's expert guidance, it was not long before pupil began to outshine master. By the end of the spring course in 1749, William declared his protégé sufficiently accomplished to take over all the work in the dissecting room; now William could begin directing his brother to investigate the anatomical puzzles he knew could bring them lasting fame, while devoting his own time to furthering his obstetrics career.[59] With his deft fingers and sharp powers of observation, John excelled at preserving body parts as specimens – or 'preparations' as they were known – which could be passed around at lectures for the pupils' perusal. He spent long hours hunched over the dissecting bench, pickling organs and tissues in spirits, drying bones and muscles before varnishing, and injecting intricate systems of arteries and veins with vividly coloured wax. Some survive to this day, despite the handling of numerous students, their colours as bright as ever. Yet the vast majority of the innumerable specimens John prepared would end up in his brother's jealously guarded collection. William would always be adamant that all anatomical research produced under his roof belonged firmly to him.

What little time John Hunter had left each day was occupied principally in demonstrating anatomy skills to the students. Working shoulder to shoulder with other young enthusiasts in the dissecting room by day and debating anatomical questions of the moment into the night, he would forge lifelong friendships. Among such friends was Thomas Hamilton, the lad with whom he had travelled down from Scotland, who stayed as a fellow pupil in 1748–9, and with whom he would maintain a warm correspondence. Compared to William's sometimes austere and forbidding demeanour, John's easy-going, personable manner won him many devoted companions. Although there would be no shortage of people ready to testify to his outspokenness and quick temper – he never suffered fools – later pupils would assert that his manners were 'extremely companionable' and that he possessed 'a very considerable humour'.[60]

Despite the overwhelming demands on his time – even his venomous first biographer Jessé Foot would have to concede, 'That he was always of a turn to industry, is very clear'[61] – Jack Hunter still found time to enjoy the many social pleasures of Georgian London. Carousing with his fellow pupils, and sometimes with his new-found friends in the criminal underworld, he quickly familiarized himself with the drinking venues in Covent Garden and beyond. He enjoyed the local theatres too, at a time when David Garrick had just taken over management of the popular Drury Lane playhouse, and joined in the riotous barracking by audiences demanding their favourite scenes or actors.[62] As Foot put it, 'He had not at this time exacted those rigid severities of temperance to which he was observed to adhere at his later part of life. John Hunter at this time, and for some time after, was a companionable man: he associated in company, drank his bottle, told his story and laughed with others.'[63] Rakish Jack may even have sampled some of the other establishments so popular in Covent Garden, the epicentre of London's vibrant red-light district, as did so many men of his age and time. Several of his pupils and early biographers refer guardedly to his first few months of 'dissipation' in London. While one Victorian writer described 'that coarse species of enjoyment, in which, in company with the lowborn and illiterate, John Hunter occasionally found delight', another remarked that he 'joined in that sort of dissipation which men at his age, and freed from restraint, are but too apt to indulge in'. Hunter's future brother-in-law would similarly dismiss the period with the comment that he 'entered into youthful follies like others of the same age'.[64]

The first warm rays of spring sunshine brought the tireless John Hunter's six months' labour in the dissecting room to a necessary end: even the most hardened of anatomists could not stomach cutting up rotting corpses in summer heat. With warm days ahead and the coming harvest to consider, he might have expected to enjoy a well-deserved break back home on the farm. His eldest sister, Janet, had died that spring at the age of thirty-six, and his grieving mother was herself now sixty-four and in failing health; there is no doubt she would have wanted comfort from her favourite son.[65] But William had other plans for his young brother. Having honed his knife skills on dead bodies throughout the winter, John Hunter was now despatched to practise on the living.

4

The Pregnant Woman's Womb

'... some men who, whether they only imagined the fact might be true, or really found it to be so, would be very ready to assume all the merit of discovery to themselves.'

John Hunter[1]

The Royal Hospital Chelsea, London, spring 1749

Striding up the sweeping driveway leading from the Thames to the grand façade of the Royal Hospital in its pastoral setting at Chelsea, John Hunter could have been forgiven for lapsing into a relaxed frame of mind. Londoners had just celebrated the end of the War of the Austrian Succession – actually concluded six months previously – with a spectacular firework display and a concert by Handel in Hyde Park. The soldiers who had limped back from the battlefields across Europe could now nurse their wounds in the tranquillity of their riverside home at Chelsea. And the spring sunshine which was bringing out the blooms in the Chelsea gardens had brought an end to Hunter's first long winter in his brother's anatomy school. As the warmth seeped into his fingers, numbed by months of teasing apart tissues and fibres in the chilly dissecting room, he could take a deep breath of the country air and enjoy the scene in the stately hospital grounds.

Founded by Charles II and opened in 1692, the Royal Hospital and its gardens had been designed by Christopher Wren essentially as a retirement home for elderly or infirm soldiers.[2] For the nearly five hundred residents who lived there, the hospital provided a veritable haven. Walking through Wren's formal water gardens, the twenty-one-year-old John Hunter may well have doffed his cap to the elderly war heroes in their distinctive uniforms of scarlet jackets, blue breeches and black gold-edged hats, sunning themselves on benches along the front of the building. But as he approached the impressive front portal he turned abruptly left, through an archway into a second courtyard. And as he neared the low brick building, the hospital's little infirmary, on the south side of the quadrangle he doubtless felt some trepidation at the prospect of his first serious job. After a winter confined with the cold, silent corpses of the dissecting room, he was to spend the summer tending the ailing veterans at Chelsea under the watchful eye of the country's greatest surgeon.

Most likely he would have discovered William Cheselden at work in the infirmary, where the fresh spring air would have been instantly overpowered by the nauseous smells emanating from the communal toilet bucket and the blood-soaked sheets. He may well have found the surgeon at a soldier's bedside, inspecting the dressings of an old wound, or perhaps in his surgery in the middle of a bloody operation.

Although his post at Chelsea amounted to semi-retirement, Cheselden, the venerable surgeon who had once so infuriated the Company of Barber-Surgeons by staging rival dissections on his dining-room table, was still justifiably renowned.[3] Having taken charge of the newly formed Company of Surgeons in 1746, a year after he helped force the split from the barbers, the popular anatomy teacher was famous throughout Europe. His textbook *The Anatomy of the Humane Body* was the standard work for students, while his fabulous atlas of the human bones, *Osteographia*, was a collector's item. But although his talents with a pen were widely respected, it was Cheselden's skill with a knife that had made him the most celebrated surgeon of his age. Principally a man of action rather than words, he was best known for his pioneering operation to remove bladder stones.

Known as lithotomy, the operation to extract a bladder stone had been performed since ancient times; as with most surgery in the eighteenth century, methods had changed little since then.[4] Without anaesthesia or anti-septics, operations were generally crude, frequently agonizing and often deadly. Consequently it was only when the pain of a stone pressing inside the bladder became unbearable that a sufferer would submit to a lithotomy; surgery was always the treatment of last resort. Unfortunately, however, bladder stones were extremely common, even among children, in the eighteenth century and therefore many sufferers had little alternative but to endure the gruelling procedure, which was not only exceedingly risky but also highly humiliating. In order to allow the surgeon access to the necessary area, patients were trussed up like a chicken and placed flat on their backs with their ankles tied to their hands and their buttocks exposed. Usually the surgeon would insert a finger into the rectum, probe the stone so that it bulged outwards, then cut straight through the muscles of the perineum, between the genitals and the anus, and withdraw the stone from the bladder with forceps. Sometimes the surgeon would insert a metal probe into the patient's urethra, the tube carrying urine from the bladder, to help locate the stone, and sometimes he would withdraw it this way too.

The diarist Samuel Pepys underwent a lithotomy in 1658, probably of the first type, when he had a stone the size of a tennis ball cut out by a surgeon from St Thomas' Hospital. He kept the stone in a case and celebrated his survival on the first anniversary of the operation the following year.[5] Others were not so lucky. One in five patients died from the procedure in Holland in the eighteenth century; in Paris the death toll was two in five. Success rates were unlikely to have been much different in Britain. The wonder is mortality figures were not higher: without adequate anatomical knowledge inept surgeons could blunder about for up to an hour, slicing through vital parts, while their shrieking patient expired on the table through loss of blood. Unhygienic conditions in the home, where wealthy patients had their operations – sometimes on the kitchen table – but especially in hospitals, where the poor underwent surgery, frequently led to fatal infections. In the days before bacteriology was understood, surgeons were blissfully unaware that they themselves were often the cause of their patients' demise, by passing on deadly germs from their grimy hands and encrusted tools. But even survival was not without its risks, for many victims were rendered incontinent or otherwise permanently mutilated by a careless or ignorant slip of the knife.

With such poor chances of a reasonable recovery, patients understandably took the utmost care to find a skilled surgeon, and for lithotomies in mid-eighteenth-century England there was really only one name to conjure with. Cheselden had secured his fortune and his reputation through his prowess in removing bladder stones. Having initially practised the standard lithotomy method, he adapted his technique after learning of the successful work of a French travelling practitioner, Frère Jacques de Beaulieu – the Frère Jacques of the nursery rhyme – who traversed Europe at the end of the seventeenth century performing his 'lateral' operation. Rather than cutting through the middle of the perineum, as conventional surgeons did, Frère Jacques approached an inch or so to one side, providing safer access to the bladder while reducing injury to other organs. While orthodox surgeons pointedly ignored the example of someone they regarded as a blatant quack, Cheselden had no such scruples. He adopted Frère Jacques' operation in 1725 and with the anatomical expertise he had developed on his dining table he perfected the technique, to international acclaim.[6] After word of the new operation spread back across the Channel, the Académie Royale des Sciences – the French equivalent of the Royal Society – sent a surgeon to witness Cheselden's innovation. The envoy was powerfully impressed.

Cheselden routinely performed the lateral operation in less than a minute, on occasion in half a minute, dramatically reducing the risk of fatal bleeding or shock and thereby cutting death rates to less than one in ten. Out of

213 patients he 'cut for the stone' over several years working at St Thomas' Hospital, only twenty died.[7] And even this scale of fatalities Cheselden blamed on the fact that once news of his success had spread 'even the most aged and most miserable cases expected to be sav'd by it'. In fact almost half of the patients he treated at St Thomas' were children under ten, of whom only three died. As well as saving the poorest patients from almost certain death, the surgeon was in constant demand from private clients. He reputedly charged his paying patients up to £500 – equivalent to a modern surgeon charging £41,000 – for his services.

Although he had retired from most of his hospital duties in 1737, when he accepted the comfortable post of surgeon to the Royal Hospital Chelsea, Cheselden had continued a busy private practice and retained his position as Britain's elder statesman in surgery. At a time when physicians were unquestionably at the top of the rigid medical hierarchy, and when many of his surgical colleagues were blithely hacking and sawing with little inclination to change brutal methods, Cheselden was one of a tiny handful of surgeons who garnered any respect in early eighteenth-century society. It seemed only natural, then, that when William Hunter sought a teacher of surgery for his young brother John it was Cheselden to whom he turned.

Having mastered all his older brother could teach him on the dead body, John Hunter knew that if he was ever to employ his knowledge on the living, he needed some bedside training. William himself had 'walked the wards' as a surgical pupil at St George's Hospital in his early career and was anxious to obtain a similar position for John. As William presciently declared in his lectures, 'were I to place a man of proper talents, in the most direct road for becoming truely *great* in his profession, I would chuse a good practical Anatomist, and put him into a large hospital to attend the *Sick*, and dissect the dead'.[8] William had met Cheselden – and made a favourable impression on him – when he had worked as an assistant to James Douglas, his earlier mentor, who had been a close friend of the revered surgeon. Indeed, Cheselden had mentioned William's kindness in giving him two specimens in one of his anatomical texts.[9] So once the anatomy school closed its doors at the end of the spring term, William recalled the favour and secured John a coveted position shadowing the best surgeon of the age.[10] Arriving at the Royal Hospital in spring 1749 for his first taste of practical surgery, Hunter would have followed the surgeon on his ward rounds, attended his consultations with private clients, and assisted him in operations both at Chelsea and privately.

It was not the most regular route to a career in surgery. Most surgeons who enjoyed any training at all in the first half of the eighteenth century began learning their craft at the age of fourteen or fifteen, apprenticed to a master surgeon for up to seven years.[11] With large fees stumped up by their parents, these adolescent boys – girls were barred from this elite world – were bound by the strict rules of their indentures. They had to live in their master's house, work all hours without pay or holiday, and were forbidden from marrying, drinking, theatre-going or gambling. Only at the end of this arduous initiation were they likely to study any anatomy, if at all. If they were lucky and could afford it, young apprentices would spend a few months at anatomy lectures in Edinburgh or Paris; if not, they might attend one of the cursory courses offered in London. Only after this long apprenticeship with a smattering of anatomy would the typical trainee 'walk the wards' of a London hospital, enrolled as the pupil of an established surgeon for up to a year. Again a hefty fee was due for this privilege – as much as £50 for a pupillage at St Thomas' Hospital in 1750. At the end of this lengthy training, a would-be surgeon could take the examination at Surgeons' Hall to qualify for a diploma, allowing him officially to practise. Finally, he could start as a junior surgeon on the first rung of the hospital career ladder – a necessary prerequisite to building up a thriving private practice – provided he had the right connections. As in all realms of life in Georgian Britain, nepotism was the surest route to advancement in London's voluntary hospitals; the tradition of fathers recruiting sons, and uncles handing over to nephews, would persist throughout the century. Once set up in a hospital job it was a steady, if protracted, path to a lifelong position as a senior surgeon with a lucrative private clientele.

Inevitably, however, in the unregulated, shambolic medical world of the mid-eighteenth century, innumerable surgeons attained status and fortune despite bucking the system; John Hunter would be one of them. Many young men, and even a few women who stepped into a deceased husband's shoes, became successful surgeons with scant experience or training: they skipped the apprenticeship, forwent anatomy lessons, spent at most a few months walking the wards, and launched into practice without ever securing a diploma from the Company of Surgeons.[12] Indeed, for most of the first half of the century, although the Company of Surgeons admitted candidates for its oral examination only after they had completed a full apprenticeship and could demonstrate a knowledge of

Latin, there was no requirement to have studied anatomy or to have obtained any surgical experience. After 1745, the government was so desperate to recruit surgeons to the army and navy that anyone willing to try their hand as a surgeon's mate was allowed to take the examination before being let loose on the nation's unfortunate soldiers and sailors – and, once demobbed, the general public. The Hunter brothers' lifelong friend Tobias Smollett had served a five-year apprenticeship in surgery in Glasgow before taking his examination in 1740 in order to serve as a surgeon's second mate in the Royal Navy. Later abandoning surgical practice for writing, he ridiculed the farcical test when the hero of his semi-autobiographical novel *The Adventures of Roderick Random* trembled before the 'dozen grim faces' at Surgeons' Hall. Informed that Roderick had completed a mere three years' apprenticeship, one examiner 'fell into a violent passion' and 'swore it was a shame and a scandal to send such raw boys into the world as surgeons'.[13]

For all the pomposity, it mattered little how long a novice surgeon was apprenticed, where he walked the wards, or whether he obtained the Company's diploma, while their masters, teachers and examiners clung to medieval procedures based on the theories of the ancients with barely a nod towards anatomical research. In any case, the Company exerted its feeble influence only within the metropolis; elsewhere, launching a surgical career was even more of a free-for-all.

In John Hunter's case, time was firmly against his signing up as an apprentice at the mature age of twenty-one, and he would certainly have baulked at the strictures of typical indentures; his liking for carousing in the taverns and barracking at the theatre were plainly at odds with an apprentice's sedate lifestyle. Yet most of London's charitable hospitals would not accept anyone as a surgical pupil, no matter how able or skilled at anatomy, without the hard-won certificate of apprenticeship. Signing up with Cheselden was therefore a happy compromise. The elderly surgeon was willing to accept the industrious young anatomist without the requisite apprenticeship on a recommendation – and presumably a generous fee – from William. And though walking the wards at Chelsea would not offer Hunter the usual path to a surgical career, it would serve as a more than adequate introduction to the agony and brutality of Georgian surgery.

Scant records of Cheselden's practice at Chelsea have survived; John Hunter left no reference to his training with Cheselden. But without doubt the work Hunter helped Cheselden perform at Chelsea would have been much the standard fare for surgeons of the day: letting blood, lancing boils, dressing sores, treating venereal disease and tending to minor injuries.[14] As Cheselden's pupil, following him around the wards and working at his side in the surgery, Hunter would first have learned the Georgian surgeon's panacea for all ills: to slit open a vein in a patient's arm or foot with a lancet or 'fleam' and drain the leaking blood into a specially gradated bleeding bowl; some of the bowls were expressly designed with cut-out half-moons to fit a patient's arm. He would quickly have picked up other forms of torture too, routinely prescribed for various ailments, including producing blisters on a patient's back or neck. In this remedy, a glass cup was heated to create a vacuum and was then applied to the patient's flesh; as the trapped air cooled it raised a blister, which the surgeon often lanced. On other occasions, surgeons would lacerate a patient's skin with a 'scarificator', a tool containing as many as sixteen spring-loaded blades, while sometimes pieces of thread known as 'seatons' were inserted into these wounds to create 'laudable pus', regarded since Greek times as a requisite sign of healing.

Major operations were a rarity, given the risks and the anguish they entailed, and even those that were performed were usually constrained within realistic limits. Surgeons almost never attempted to open a patient's chest or abdominal cavity. Even if they had a clue as to what they were likely to encounter inside, and many did not, they knew enough to realize they could not combat the internal bleeding or post-operative infection that would almost certainly ensue. Consequently, surgery was usually restricted to the limbs, the head and the more accessible internal areas such as the bladder, breasts and testicles. Given Cheselden's reputation, there is no doubt that through the summer of 1749 John Hunter would have assisted in performing the most common operations of the day both on the pensioners at Chelsea and on members of Georgian high society. As a pupil, it would have been Hunter's job to help patients to the surgery, secure them to the wooden table, dose them with laudanum if they were lucky, and hand his master the knives, probes and saws for lithotomies, amputations, eye surgery, hernia operations and other brutal but necessary procedures. Standing at his side, Hunter must also have witnessed the understandable apprehension Cheselden experienced before embarking on any operation, for as the elder surgeon admitted, 'no one ever endured more anxiety and sickness before an operation, yet from the time I began to operate, all uneasiness ceased'.[15] While Hunter himself would never quail before an operation, he plainly adopted Cheselden's reluctance to wield the knife unless absolutely necessary.

Inevitably, Hunter would also have aided Cheselden with his trademark lithotomies, helping to truss up victims in the oven-ready position, assisting in the delicate procedure and dressing the wound afterwards. Hunter would doubtless have helped perform amputations too, removing limbs that had turned septic or had never healed after war injuries. As assistant, he would have helped hold down a struggling patient as Cheselden removed a leg in three swift actions. First he cut through the skin with a long, curved knife in a single motion circling the leg; then he cut through the fat and muscle in a second rapid movement down to the bone, tying major blood vessels to prevent haemorrhage; and finally he hacked through the bone with an amputation saw.[16] Having removed the leg, he pulled the skin over the bone and bandaged the stump.

No doubt Hunter also helped in the primitive operation of trepanning, which had undergone little change since first practised in neolithic times: just as in the Stone Age, Georgian surgeons drilled into a patient's head to remove portions of skull. Although brutal, it seemingly helped in some circumstances by removing blood clots and relieving pressure on the brain; certainly a surprising number of people, even in neolithic times, survived the ordeal. Cheselden performed trepanning on numerous occasions, including in one instance on a nine-year-old girl who had fractured her skull in an accident. After a recuperation period of five months, the young patient recovered.

Other operations in which Hunter must have assisted would have included tapping, in which large quantities of fluid were drained from the abdomen, chest or sometimes testicles using a metal spike fitted inside a tube. Cases of 'dropsy', as oedema or the collection of fluid in the tissues was known, were common in eighteenth-century Britain,

and before the introduction of effective diuretic medication tapping was the only known remedy. One woman
reportedly died in 1728 after being tapped sixty-six times
in sixty-seven months with a total of 240 gallons of liquid
removed.[17]

As with his lithotomy operation, Cheselden was never
averse to learning techniques from so-called quacks, an
open-mindedness John Hunter would also espouse. But in
a straight role reversal, one of the century's best-known
travelling healers, Chevalier Taylor, had earned widespread acclaim for his method of removing cataracts,
which he had initially copied from Cheselden. Like most
Georgian surgery, the operation of couching, which
entailed extracting or displacing a lens in which a cataract
had developed, had its roots in ancient times. Unlike most
Georgian surgery, it is still performed today according to
much the same principles – if with markedly better
success. As with lithotomy, Cheselden's expertise in
couching was well known. He restored sight in several
patients, including one man who afterwards could 'with
pleasure look round the House and walk the street' and
who could even read after Cheselden supplied him with
spectacles.[18]

Working at Chelsea with Cheselden, even in his
advanced years, was a unique opportunity for the young
John Hunter. Despite differences in age and background,
the pair were well matched. Cheselden's surgical dexterity,
based on decades of experience dissecting dead bodies,
would certainly have impressed Hunter, but the elder
surgeon must equally have noted his pupil's agile fingers
and anatomical know-how. More important, however,
than any manual skills he might have gleaned from the
experienced surgeon, Hunter clearly benefited from

Cheselden's approach to his craft, which was founded on humility at the fallibility of common methods and a willingness to learn new techniques. Almost any other surgeon of the time would have taught his pupil strict reverence for the ancient methods and theories handed down through centuries while firmly cautioning against any challenge to established ways. Cheselden, conversely, was open to change, eager to observe and experiment, reluctant to operate without a good chance of success, willing to learn from his anatomical pursuits and even from unqualified healers, and adaptable enough to amend his methods accordingly. Hunter would pursue this same creed throughout his career, systematically applying the lessons he learned in the dissecting room and operating theatre to future practice.

But time was running out for both of them. Cheselden would fall ill in 1751, after Hunter had spent another summer at his side, and died in 1752. For Hunter, the summer was fading, his days in the pleasant country air of Chelsea were over, and his attendance was required back in the dissecting room for the start of the autumn term.

In readiness for the influx of new pupils, in September 1749 the brothers moved from their lodgings in Hatton Garden to a large house at 1 Great Piazza, Covent Garden, providing for the first time permanent premises for the anatomy school as well as a shared home. The comfortable house, set back under the vaulted arcade in the north-west corner of the Italianate square, possessed a basement, a high-ceilinged ground floor, two upper storeys and an attic. The front door was a stone's throw from St Paul's Church, its churchyard a minute's night-time amble away. The brothers set up their dissecting room at the rear of the house, where stables and a garden backed on to Hart Street (now Floral Street) with a conveniently discreet entrance for nightly deliveries.[19] There was space for a lecture theatre and preparations room too. But the elegant home belied the squalor of the square, which echoed with the cries of street vendors and market stall holders by day and the carousing of sailors and other pleasure-seekers patronizing the brothels by night. With London's gin craze at its height, anyone crossing the square for a morning dish of coffee in Bedford's coffee-house or an evening's entertainment at Covent Garden Theatre was likely to stumble over men, women and children slumped in a drunken stupor among the rotting vegetables.

If not the most fashionable address in London, at least the spacious quarters allowed the brothers to take in resident pupils for the first time. The fresh-faced eighteen- and nineteen-year-olds who joined them not only provided a useful source of extra income but helped create a lively community of enthusiastic scholars, effectively forming the first medical school in the capital. Many stayed an entire winter to attend both the autumn and the spring courses by day and participate in animated debates on anatomy into the small hours, as well as forming graveyard exploration parties as required. Many would go on to become leading anatomists and medical practitioners in their own right. Thomas Hamilton would later become professor of anatomy at Glasgow University after riding down from Lanarkshire with John to attend lectures with him through the winter of 1748–9; John Smith, who studied with the brothers in 1750, would later be appointed reader in anatomy at Oxford University; and

Charles White, who attended an early course, would become one of the foremost obstetrics practitioners of the century, helping to found Manchester Infirmary.[20] John Hunter would remain firm friends with them all. He must also have found a kindred spirit in the bright young Erasmus Darwin, grandfather of Charles, who attended the school in 1753 before returning to the West Midlands to practise medicine and, in time, found the Lunar Club with fellow enthusiasts.[21] Whether they discussed fledgling ideas about the origins of life is unknown; certainly it would prove an abiding interest for them both.

As the pupils took their places in autumn 1749, the vital job of demonstrator and instructor now fell to John. The previous year's least experienced pupil was now master of the dissecting room, presiding over all the anatomical research of students just a few years his junior. From first light until dusk, in a cold, north-facing room, John Hunter could be found stooped over the dissecting bench, teasing apart blood vessels, nerves and fibres with nimble fingers as the acrid stench of the rotting cadavers invaded his nostrils. When the pupils crowded in for practical dissection, Hunter helped them tackle the delicate knife work they were expected to master on their individual corpses.

The pupils' dissection programme was dictated strictly by necessity, according to the process of decomposition.[22] Since the guts were the first parts to putrefy, the students would begin by slitting open the abdomen, folding back the flaps of skin and fat, and examining the parts of digestion: the stomach, the ten or more metres of intestines, and the smaller organs like the spleen, gall bladder and pancreas, packed tightly into the abdominal cavity. Next they would open the chest, sawing apart the ribcage to expose and remove the lungs, their lobes blackened by London's ubiquitous winter smogs; mastery of dissection demanded not only intricate skills with a knife but brute strength with a hacksaw. The lungs discarded, the pupils could examine the heart, which even the most novice anatomist now knew, having studied Harvey, to be the centre of the human physiological system. Hunter would then help the pupils with the tricky tasks of detaching and inspecting the other main organs – the liver, bladder, kidneys, reproductive parts, and the brain – encouraging them to probe the cavities with their fingers, disentangle the vessels with their knives and fingernails, and weigh the organs in the palms of their hands. Finally, they could work on the muscles, which decayed slowest, and the bones, which Hunter showed them how to wire together to create their own articulated skeletons.

But they would have to work fast. Even though the dissecting room faced north, which Hunter would later recommend as the ideal position for reducing the pace of putrefaction, exposure to air quickly dried the tissues, making them brittle and difficult to work with, while the decaying flesh would swell, discolour and generate foul odours.[23] The necessity of working mainly in winter was made indisputably clear by one example of a post-mortem in warm weather, recorded by Hunter in his case books: 'He was become extremely putrid: the air was so much let loose as almost ready to burst the Skin, (especially the belly.) The Scrotum was full, and the Penis almost erect with the air ... The kidneys were almost reduced to a pulp with the Putrifaction.'[24] But more commonly, when opening a body on an 'extremely cold day' with frost in the air and no fire in the grate he noted that 'the cellular membrane immediately under the Skin crackled upon pressure'.[25]

While the dissecting room inevitably acquired a permanent stench, so too would the hands and clothes of the pupils and their teachers. After handling human remains all day without wearing gloves – although they probably donned protective aprons and sleeve covers – the only washing facilities for their blood-stained hands, the fingernails clogged with putrid flesh, would be a bucket of cold water pumped directly from the foul Thames. Some of the students, combining anatomy instruction with a spell on the wards, would go on to pass deadly bacteria to their unfortunate patients. A later manual for anatomy students would offer welcome advice on dispelling some of the discomforts of a typical dissecting room: 'The student should endeavour to prevent the bad effects of sitting for hours in a cold dissecting room; the most effectual way is to put on an additional flannel jacket, and carpet shoes over his boots . . . never to sit in the dissecting room with the coat which he wears during the day, but to keep one for the purpose while he is there. A cap should be worn in preference to a hat, which is not only inconvenient, but also quickly acquires a bad smell . . .'[26]

Anatomy was invariably a sensory experience. As well as the all-pervading odour of decay, the crackle of the dried membranes and the need for intense visual inspection, students were urged to feel the textures of the different parts and even to taste the body fluids. Without sophisticated methods of scientific analysis, at a time when even microscopes were relatively primitive and visually unreliable, anatomists were forced to depend on their innate senses. Hunter frequently employed his sense of taste in dissection, and encouraged his pupils to do likewise, as he recorded matter-of-factly: 'The gastric juice is a fluid somewhat transparent, and a little saltish or brackish to the taste.' Another time he noted, 'The fine transparent mucus of the urethra is strongly impregnated with sea-salt, which is immediately known by the taste.' And he would even observe, 'The semen would appear, both from the smell and taste, to be a mawkish kind of substance; but when held some time in the mouth, it produces a warmth similar to spices, which lasts some time.'[27]

Yet no matter how competently an anatomist employed all five senses, his skills were wholly transitory without the ability to preserve his knife work, both for teaching and research purposes. Carefully executed preparations played a crucial role in eighteenth-century medical education; John Hunter excelled at the art. Specimens of bones and body tissues were vital not only for showing the pupils complicated or minute networks of blood vessels and other structures they were too inexperienced to distinguish for themselves, but also for displaying diseases or conditions which the future surgeons might encounter in the living. In an age when medical practitioners still commonly blamed ailments on an imbalance of humours, morbid anatomy – the study of diseased or damaged organs – was in its infancy. Linking the appearance of disease in the dead to symptoms of illness in the living, and thereby diagnosing medical conditions with accuracy, would be critical to later improvements in treatment. The Hunter brothers, and their future nephew Matthew Baillie, were fundamental in developing this approach.

In his usual succinct style, William summed up the importance of anatomical specimens to the pupils: 'Preparations serve two purposes chiefly, to wit, the preservation of uncommon things, and the preservation of such things as required considerable labour to anatomize them, so as to shew their structure distinctly.'[28] He counselled his students to collect as many as they could, recommending that they acquire not only a complete articulated skeleton but several skulls, preparations of blood vessels, two specimens of the trunks of children showing the abdominal organs from back and front, and 'as many preparations of the organs of sense and generation, and of the particular viscera as he can easily procure'. Moreover, while pupils should not rely solely on preparations, they were certainly convenient since 'the more they are used there will be less expense and trouble with fresh subjects'. More preparations meant fewer nocturnal outings.

Essentially, specimens could be divided into 'wet' or 'dry' preparations. The latter were relatively easy to make: stripped bones and sometimes muscles or organs were dried in the air, often by hanging from the rafters of dissecting rooms, then varnished to preserve them from decay. Care was needed to ensure the varnish reached all nooks and crannies otherwise, as John Hunter explained in notes detailing his techniques, insects would lay their eggs in the hollows and the hatching worms would eat the carefully tended specimen.[29] In summer, however, he would sometimes turn this natural process to his advantage: 'The quickest way of destroying the flesh without Boiling, is to put the Bones into a Tub, and cover it with some loose Cover, so as to let Flies get into them. They will fly blow them immediately, and in a fortnights Time there will not be a bit of flesh left.' Dry preparations were of limited value, however, since they often became shrivelled and discoloured in time. The anatomist's chief goal was to preserve his handiwork in such a way that the beauty of the human anatomy was retained in its natural supple form.

The seventeenth-century scientist Robert Boyle is credited with discovering the use of alcohol to preserve organic tissue; he reputedly preserved a linnet and a snake for four months without decay in spirit of wine.[30] Although gin, rum, brandy and whisky were later sometimes substituted, spirit of wine would remain the preservative of preference until superseded in 1893 by formaldehyde, which is still in use today. But the individual recipes anatomists cooked up for their potent alcoholic cocktails, particularly the preservatives they injected into arteries and other vessels to embalm soft tissues, were kept closely guarded secrets – much in the way medieval alchemists had vied in their futile quest to find the philosopher's stone.

The Dutch teacher Frederik Ruysch, who presided over anatomy demonstrations in Amsterdam's public theatre from 1666 to 1731, took this conspiracy to extremes. Notoriously proud of his secret embalming process, he created a vast collection of unique preparations in a bizarre museum.[31] A major tourist attraction for travellers, the collection included surreal tableaux of fetal and infant skeletons posed in landscapes fashioned from human and animal parts – 'trees' concocted from arterial branches and 'rocks' from bladder stones. The museum was later bought by Peter the Great, who found the embalmed features of one child so life-like that he kissed its face.[32] Although Ruysch took his secret recipes with him to the grave, his embalming fluid was later revealed to contain nothing more magical than spirit of wine with black pepper.

The techniques used in injecting blood vessels with preservative fluids and coloured resins were equally jealously contested, as preparations became not only a vital component in attracting students to lectures but also a valuable market commodity in the eighteenth century. William, who had learned the tricks of the trade during lessons with anatomist Frank Nicholls in the early 1740s, was the first to teach the art of making preparations in public lectures. From 1748 he added to his course lessons on producing specimens according to the Nicholls method, which he specifically advertised as a draw to potential pupils. Guided initially by his brother, John Hunter learned the basic techniques of preparing wet and dry specimens, but was soon surpassing William's prowess at both. Later, describing his techniques, he would advise that 'young and healthy subjects' were preferable when creating preparations of normal parts, as their vessels were easiest to inject.

A whole battalion of implements was required for the intricate processes involved. Aside from the normal dissecting equipment, the anatomists' toolbox required silver pipes, glass tubes, reeds and syringes for injecting the vessels; brass wires, bristles and silk threads for holding different parts in place; pots and kettles for mixing the preserving fluids; and specially crafted glass bottles and jars for displaying the finished results.

Injections were used to highlight vessels in vivid colour, demonstrating their paths and ramifications. The knack was to inject a liquid that was sufficiently viscous to fill an entire vascular system, including the tiniest vessels which were otherwise invisible to the naked eye, without bursting the fragile structures and leaking into other parts. The resin or wax was usually injected into the arteries and expected to return via the veins, but it was often a process of trial and error. Some parts, such as bladders or lungs, were first inflated with bellows or blowpipes to enlarge the vessels, as Hunter explained: 'When I was injecting the lungs of a man, the injection did not run freely; I then inflated them, and found that the injection immediately ran with freedom.'[33] Usually he would first inject the arteries with warm water to flush out the blood, drive out any air and warm the tissues. He then fitted a pipe into the open end of a vessel and fixed it with pins before injecting the fluid by syringe. Like Ruysch, Hunter developed a veritable cook book of recipes for the concoctions he used: they included oil compounds made from hog's lard, tallow or butter, and water-based solutions, mixed with glues or resins from plants or animals. Sometimes he used wax, heated until fluid for injection then allowed to cool to a solid state in the vessels, or mercury for its propensity to flow easily. Mercury was also useful in investigations: it could reveal vessels and connections that were otherwise impossible to distinguish.

Having prepared the injection fluid, brilliant hues were added to display the vessels clearly and show the handi-work to best advantage; Hunter used artists' pigments such as Vermilion, King's Yellow, Blue Verditer or Flake White. Sometimes bristles were employed to demonstrate where certain tubes began and ended. The hairs from a rhinoceros tail were ideal, Hunter advised; if these were in short supply, as they must have been for most of the century, goose quills would suffice.

Plainly, the art of making preparations was an expensive business. As well as artists' hues and rhinoceros bristles to buy, there were hefty government taxes on both spirit of wine and flint glass jars. At least the pig's bladder required to seal the jars, along with a layer of lead, could be cheaply obtained from a butcher. But the alcohol-based preservatives also had to be changed regularly: since they were not wholly effective, the continuing process of putrefaction would taint the liquid so that 'the Spirit acquires a very disagreeable smell'. The job of distilling these used fluids, during which 'the foul animal matter rises to the surface', must have been a particularly unpopular task, not least with the neighbours.

Many injected preparations were simply bottled in alcohol and displayed on the shelves of the school's preparations room to demonstrate particular structures or rare conditions. Others were submitted to a process of corrosion during which the organic flesh was destroyed to leave a cast of the wax-filled vessels. Usually this was achieved by lowering the injected part into a bucket of acid, which ate away the tissues to leave an intricate and often stunningly beautiful network of coloured vessels. A skilfully corroded preparation of the injected airways of the lungs, for example, would emerge as a delicate and brightly stained 'bronchial tree'.

Though the specimens were primarily intended to display anatomical features, aesthetics were always an essential aspect, of which Hunter was acutely aware. He recommended blood-red vermilion for run-of-the mill injections in dried preparations, but in an extremely vascular part, such as the inner surface of the stomach, the anatomist should simply 'chuse the Colour that pleases the Eye most'. By contrast, bones, which emerged as a 'dark or dirty brown', were not deemed pleasing, for their colour was 'a bad one', he declared. A particularly fine or rare preparation, expertly injected in vivid colour, could fetch a handsome price at auctions of anatomical parts, where amateur collectors competed for items with professional anatomists. Both Hunter brothers would become regular customers at auctions of preparations. But on one occasion, when Hunter found that no amount of money could secure a preparation he coveted from a fellow practitioner, he finally snapped, 'Well then, take care I don't meet you with it in some dark lane at night, for if I do, I'll murder you to get it.'[34] He was probably joking.

Most of the exquisite preparations John Hunter painstakingly created during his long hours in the Covent Garden dissecting room were made at William's behest. They were produced to illustrate the finer points of William's lectures, to display interesting anatomical details for his pupils, and to investigate areas of anatomical debate relevant to his research. Some were handled so enthusiastically at classes that they literally fell apart, but by far the majority would remain firmly in William's hands. Ever the astute businessman, William scrupulously asserted proprietary rights over handiwork generated under his roof; later assistants would find their specimens similarly claimed as his property. As far as William was concerned, he financed the work and therefore he owned it. Ultimately, most would end up in his collection, which he bequeathed to his alma mater Glasgow University.[35]

How many of the more than three thousand specimens that would eventually grace the shelves of William's collection at the Hunterian Museum in Glasgow were actually the work of John will never be known.[36] Only a handful can now be positively identified as John's handiwork, based on his later descriptions of his research, although hundreds more must certainly have sprung from his knife. A number did at least coax some form of tribute from William, if not perhaps as wholeheartedly as might have been deserved. But in one particular area, John's unrecognized contribution to William's rising career would rankle for decades to come. Like a stubborn sore festering for years on end, this wound would never heal.

The rift stemmed from an unprecedented opportunity in the winter of 1750, after John had returned from his second season with Cheselden, when an exceptional delivery arrived at the back door of the Covent Garden school.[37] The atmosphere in the dissecting room was tense as the sack was opened. The corpse belonged to a woman towards the end of her ninth month of pregnancy; on the verge of giving birth she had died suddenly, from an unknown cause, with her unborn child still intact within the womb. It was an almost unique chance. Since pregnant women were never hanged at Tyburn, and women of childbearing age were unlikely to die just prior to giving birth, anatomists rarely managed to dissect the body of a woman in the final stage of pregnancy. William had studied midwifery with two of the best-skilled male midwives of the time, yet he had never before seen a fully developed baby still in the womb. Until now, he had been forced to study full-term pregnancy in animal corpses. Almost unable to contain his excitement, he explained, 'A woman died suddenly, when very near the end of her pregnancy; the body was procured before any sensible putrefaction had begun; the season of the year was favourable to dissection; the injection of the blood-vessels proved successful; a very able painter, in this way, was found; every part was examined in the most public manner, and the truth was thereby well authenticated.'[38] In other words, circumstances could not have proved more perfect, and there was almost nothing William himself had to contribute to the event.

The body had been 'procured' – the euphemism for stolen – almost certainly by John from his underworld associates and it was most likely John who conducted most of the expert knife work required. William would later admit that he was 'assisted by his brother Mr John Hunter', adding rather grudgingly, 'whose accuracy in anatomical researches is so well known, that to omit this opportunity of thanking him for that assistance, would be in some measure to disregard the future reputation of the work itself'. Certainly John had vastly greater experience in dissection by this stage, having laboured at the dissecting bench throughout the daylight hours, seven days a week, for more than two winters, while his brother lectured, socialized and tended patients. Indeed, by July 1753, fewer than three years after the pregnant woman's corpse was obtained, when William was elected joint Master of Anatomy, with Pott, to the new Company of Surgeons, he was rebuked for insisting that his brother undertake the dissections while he expounded at a safe distance from a podium.[39] It seems unlikely, therefore, that William would have entrusted the tricky dissection of an exceedingly rare subject to anyone but the most experienced in his school – his brother. Likewise, the 'successful' injection of the blood vessels would doubtless have been performed by the anatomist with most experience of this difficult technique – again his brother. Finally, the services of a 'painter', as William somewhat perfunctorily termed him, were obtained in the form of the Dutch artist Jan van Rymsdyk. Although the commission would be the first of many anatomical projects for the young Dutchman, his expert artwork in Covent Garden would never be surpassed.[40]

Working together in the odorous dissecting room, Jan and John laboured over the critical task of opening the pregnant body and accurately depicting its contents. The job required extremely delicate knife work to unveil the uterus step by step without damaging the small body nestled inside. First, John made a cruciform cut in the woman's abdomen and peeled back the four corners of skin to reveal the bulging womb. Carefully, he injected the arteries and veins criss-crossing the surface in different coloured waxes, then he opened the uterus to expose the thick lining inside. William promptly named this lining the *decidua*, since it was shed after childbirth, while claiming for himself the discovery that it derives from the womb rather than from the fetus. Finally, John cut open the membrane sac to reveal the fully developed child, its plump, inverted body wedged tight, its fingers curled, its dark hair glistening wetly on its head, awaiting the very moment of a birth that would never happen.

At each stage, van Rymsdyk captured the revelations in ten stunning red-chalk drawings; simultaneously they evoke awe at the simple beauty of the baby that would never draw breath and shock at the butchered body of its mother who had breathed her last. Whereas previously anatomical pictures of babies in the womb had shown curiously adult-like figures floating in a shapeless void, for the first time van Rymsdyk portrayed the intimate relationship between mother and child in completely naturalistic style. Immediately, William recruited a team of engravers to convert the sketches into copper plates, sending the best two illustrations to Robert Strange, a fellow Scot, renowned as the best engraver of the day. The following October, William announced he would shortly be publishing the ten plates, and a year later, in October

1752, he sought subscriptions for publication. Meanwhile, the plates had already been circulated to students at the school and to fellow anatomists, while plaster of Paris casts of John's dissections had been made.

But before the plates had even been completed there was more excitement in the dissecting room. The corpses of two more women near the end of their pregnancies arrived at the back door and John and Jan were set to work again, dissecting and sketching under William's exacting supervision. The pair had to work especially quickly on the second 'subject', which arrived when 'the weather happened to be very unfavourable', presumably in the summer of 1751, but the third corpse 'occurred very opportunely, which cleared up some difficulties', William recorded. In all, a total of five pregnant bodies, and one of a woman who died two hours after giving birth, were delivered to the school between 1750 and 1754.[41] All were investigated and sketched. In one extraordinary drawing van Rymsdyk even included the image of a nine-paned window reflected in the membrane covering a five-month-old fetus – it must have been the very window that provided light for Jan and John to conduct their delicate tasks in the Covent Garden dissecting room.

At this point, however, it struck William that rather than publish ten pictures of a full-term pregnancy, spectacular as that would be, it would be far more dramatic if he could depict the pregnant womb at every stage, thus producing the first complete study of pregnancy from a tiny fetus to birth. Everything was in place: his young brother was adept at procuring and dissecting the corpses; his young artist was skilled at depicting the intricate anatomy. The project would take nearly a quarter of a century. It would be 1774 before William published his lifetime's goal, a huge atlas entitled *The Anatomy of the Human Gravid Uterus exhibited in figures*, which traces the development of the fetus backwards from the chubby full-term baby of 1750 to a three-month fetus, with its tiny fingers, features and ears still softened in development. The life-sized images and accompanying text accurately revealed and described for the first time both the *decidua* and the separate blood supplies of mother and fetus. The thirty-four plates of almost photographic detail, printed in massive 'elephant' folio dimensions at huge expense, were a triumph: the book would be acclaimed one of the greatest ever anatomical works, rivalling even the spectacular Renaissance atlases of Andreas Vesalius. The vision was William's, but the crucial value of the work was in the meticulous dissection carried out by John – and William's later assistants – and the splendid artwork of van Rymsdyk. In all, sixteen of the thirty-four plates depict dissections conducted between 1750 and 1754, almost certainly performed by John, while thirty-one of the plates are from drawings by Jan. Yet while William awarded some credit to his young brother for assistance in 'most of the dissections', he failed to mention van Rymsdyk at all, reserving his praise for the two plates engraved by Strange. And when William's posthumous portrait was painted by the society artist Sir Joshua Reynolds, a specimen of a uterus turned inside out, originally from the 1754 dissection prepared by John in the light of the nine-paned window, stood at his elbow.[42]

Oddly, after the flurry of activity poring over pregnant corpses between 1750 and 1754, no more were obtained for a further ten years. John's absence for the three latter years could explain the later gap, but an incident in 1754, which would test the brothers' partnership to breaking point, may well have been the reason for the research coming to a premature halt.

It was in May, rather late in the dissecting season, when Colin Mackenzie, an anatomy assistant working for William Smellie, burst into the Covent Garden school looking for John. Like the Hunters, Smellie and Mackenzie had obtained a full-term pregnant corpse to investigate the anatomy of the uterus. Mackenzie, who had become friendly with John, had dutifully injected the blood vessels in order to highlight the circulation within the placenta but the intricate pattern was still too complicated for him to interpret the results. Of all the anatomists working in London, it was John to whom he applied to help dispel the confusion. Together they rushed back to Smellie's dissecting room, where John carefully cut open the placenta to examine the injected arteries and veins. What he saw came as a revelation. Having tried for years to trace the minute vessels, at last the pattern was plain to see. 'After having considered these appearances,' John later enthused, 'it was not difficult for me to determine the real structure of the placenta and course of blood in these parts.'[43]

Suddenly it became clear that the maternal and fetal blood supplies were separate; although they come close enough together in the placenta to exchange nutrients and oxygen, they never actually connect. Preserving the dissected parts in spirit of wine, John returned home eager to tell William of his discovery. At first, William 'treated it and me with goodhumoured raillery', John later recalled, but after accompanying John to Smellie's dissecting room 'he was soon convinced of the fact'.

Indeed, William even managed to obtain certain of the preparations which he then began showing at his lectures, and, as John pointedly added, 'probably they still remain in his collection'.

The key to the gathering storm lay perhaps in that final comment, for William assumed ownership not only of John's dissection work but also his lovingly prepared specimens, and even, it seems, the discoveries he made. Later, in his *Gravid Uterus* as well as in his lectures, William claimed priority for discovering the circulation in the placenta, making no reference to the joint investigation by his brother and Mackenzie. It would be more than twenty years before John would seek to set the picture straight. On one score, however, John was certainly prescient: one of the preparations he and Mackenzie had jointly made in their 1754 investigations did indeed find its way to the shelves at William's Glasgow collection – along with many, many more.[44] Not only the specimens John created for William's satisfaction but others he now began to prepare as part of his own investigations into teeth, bone growth, animal life and, not surprisingly in the noisome dissecting room, the nerves of smell would remain William's property. Indeed, many of the specimens John would later use to illustrate his own first major work, on teeth, would be kept firmly in William's steely grip.[45] Only a handful of John's earliest endeavours would remain in his possession: just four of the items recorded in the first catalogue he drew up, in about 1764, can categorically be dated to his time in Covent Garden.[46] Somehow escaping William's clutches, eventually they would take their places in John's own museum, their delicate knife work perfectly preserved, their glorious colours as brilliant as ever they were when glowing on the Covent Garden dissecting bench.

His winters devoted to William's bidding in the dissecting room, John spent each summer in surgical tuition. When Cheselden fell ill in 1751, Hunter enrolled as an assistant to Percivall Pott, the up-and-coming staff surgeon at St Bartholomew's Hospital, next to Smithfield meat market in the City.[47] As Cheselden's star waned, so Pott's was rising. Having secured his diploma to practise surgery at twenty-two, following the requisite apprenticeship, Pott, now thirty-seven, was a keen anatomist as well as a cautious surgeon. Though he disliked performing amputations – he even managed to avoid having his own leg removed by appealing for conservative treatment when thrown from his horse – he could wield a knife with skill when occasion demanded. A 'very clever neat surgeon' is how one American pupil described Pott after watching him perform at Bart's.[48]

Britain's oldest hospital, having been founded in 1123 by a pious but wealthy jester in the court of Henry I, St Bartholomew's had been exempted from closure when Henry VIII dissolved the monasteries. In the new spirit of philanthropy which saw several hospitals founded in the first half of the eighteenth century, Bart's had been re-furbished by 1751 in a splendid new building comprising four elegant blocks around a spacious quadrangle.[49] But the beautiful setting offered little comfort to the patients in the bug-infested wards, where Hunter dutifully followed Pott through the summer; neither did it comfort the terrified patients, tied to the table of the operating theatre, where Hunter witnessed operations during the winter of 1751–2.

With the minimal experience he had received under Cheselden and Pott, and many years before he would receive his surgical diploma, but with the inestimable benefits of three winters poring over human anatomy, Hunter now began to treat his first patients.[50] Determined that each of these endeavours should be a learning experience, he recorded his observations and the outcomes of his work. Many of the patients he saw during those earliest years went unnamed and their interventions undated in his records; but the five volumes of case notes that survive from his forty-year career, now collected in the *Case Books*, reflect a vibrant cross-section of Georgian life. From soldiers to sailors, artists to housepainters, from lords, lawyers and politicians to servants, waifs and paupers, their fortunes and fates were recorded in John Hunter's slanting script.

Many of the case notes on those first patients have been lost, but it must have been in that winter of 1751–2 – Hunter later said 'about the year 1752'[51] – on the wards at St Bartholomew's that he treated his earliest recorded patient. He was an anonymous man of unknown age working in a typically Georgian trade, as a chimney sweep shinning up London's narrow, choking flues. Having contracted gonorrhoea, the sweep had developed a urethral stricture that made passing water painfully difficult. He was, remembered Hunter, 'the first patient I ever had with this disease'; indeed, he was one of the first patients he had had with any disease. But he brought to bear all of his natural scientific curiosity – embarking on the experimental approach to surgery that would characterize his whole life – on the chimney sweep lying in pain and frustration in his bed at Bart's.

Initially, Hunter attempted the classic approach to

unblocking a stricture, presumably learned from Pott, which entailed attempting to push a 'bougie' – a cylindrical bung made of wax or sometimes lead – into the urethra to force a way through the blockage. When this failed, characteristically he decided to experiment and, importantly, to record his results. Hunter conjectured that he might shift the blockage by burning a way through, using a caustic salve on the end of a bougie, and that when the resulting scab fell off this would create a free passage. The method, called 'escharotics', had been used before for other ailments but had fallen into disuse.

First he inserted a bougie loaded with 'red precipitate' – mercuric oxide – but this only caused severe in-flammation. So then he had a silver cannula – a hollow rod through which a probe could be pushed – specially made and used this to insert a second bougie impregnated with mercuric oxide. This served no better. Finally, with remarkable forbearance on the part of the chimney sweep, Hunter fastened a piece of 'lunar caustic' – silver nitrate – onto the end of the cannula and probed the urethra a third time. 'After doing this three times at two days interval, he came to me and told me that he had made water much better; and in applying the caustic a fourth time, my canula went through the stricture; a bougie was afterwards passed for some little time till he was perfectly well,' Hunter jubilantly recorded. It was a victory for experimental medicine. His approach – trying a traditional method, analysing his outcomes, forming a hypothesis aimed at improvement, and implementing his results – would become a standard practice throughout his career and would ultimately form the foundation for his scientific revolution of surgery.

Hunter's brief forays into London's hospitals – he spent

a further summer, in 1754, as a surgical pupil at St George's Hospital – would furnish him with plenty of areas ripe for investigation. Much of this experience, watching helplessly as patients died excruciating deaths on the wards and in the operating theatres, served only to reinforce his growing conviction that the surgery of the day was primitive and inept. For William, the blundering brutality of the operating theatre was just too much; although still licensed to practise as a surgeon, he increasingly avoided all involvement with surgery. As John put it, his brother 'hated operations, would often faint at an operation, even disliked to bleed'.[52] Whether from compassion, distaste or his status-conscious desire to become a physician, with its traditional hands-off approach, William now edged further and further away from the grisly surgical arena. He had even secured a medical degree, conferred on him by Glasgow University in recognition of his role as 'one of the most able Anatomists in Europe', in October 1750.[53] For John, by contrast, the grim scenes in operating theatres were a spur rather to shake surgery out of its medieval shackles than to walk away. Intense study of anatomy taught him profound respect for the human body; as a surgeon he determined to use his anatomical know-how to preserve that superlative design. For John, a lifetime's mission to transform surgical practice was just beginning.

So busy had the young surgeon's schedule now become that even when his mother had fallen ill with stomach cancer in 1751 her favourite son could not be spared to visit her bedside. It was William Cullen who wrote to William conveying his patient's increasingly pitiful requests for 'Johnie' to visit.[54] 'I wish you would send down Johnie as soon as you conveniently can,' he urged

William. But it was not convenient. Whether or not 'Johnie' wanted to interrupt his tuition and research to pay his last respects to his mother was immaterial; it was William who put his foot down and forbade the visit. Dismissing his mother's appeal as 'every way a bad scheme', William wrote back, 'I cannot consent this season to her request, for my brother's sake, for my own sake, and even for my mother's sake.' With John hard at work researching the pregnant womb, William was clearly reluctant to lose his trusted deputy; it was birth, not death, that was his priority. After their mother died in November 1751, and Cullen had taken their last remaining sibling, Dorothy, into his own home, William confessed that his refusal to let his mother enjoy a last visit from her youngest child had made him 'very unhappy' but reiterated sternly that the notion would have been 'impossible'. He concluded briskly, 'The past is unavoidable.'

It was not until the following summer, once the spring term was over in 1752, that John won leave to make the trek to Long Calderwood. Doubtless he visited his mother's grave, next to that of his father in the village churchyard, beside the school where he had so detested lessons. Returning to London in time for the autumn term, he brought Dorothy back with him, to share the brothers' Covent Garden home, leaving the family farmhouse, which had once resounded with the laughter of children, cold and empty. It would be his last visit to his home country. His future was now firmly settled in London.

5

The Professor's Testicle

'It has likewise been observed of anatomists, that they are all liable to the error of being *severe* on each other in their disputes . . . and for anything that we know, the passive submission of dead bodies, their common objects, may render them less able to bear contradiction.'

William Hunter[1]

Covent Garden, London, autumn 1755

The start of the autumn term was inevitably a fractious time as William and John prepared for the arrival of their new pupils at the Covent Garden school. But tensions were more strained than usual in October 1755, as the brothers watched a fellow young Scot slide into his seat for the first lecture. At twenty-two, Alexander Monro junior was older than many of the students packed into the lecture room, although considerably younger than John, now twenty-seven, and William, at thirty-seven. Yet

Monro *secundus*, as he was known, was already a prominent figure on the Scottish medical scene; he had qualified as a physician and had just been appointed joint professor of anatomy and surgery at Edinburgh University with his illustrious father, Alexander Monro I.[2]

The youngest son of Monro I, Alexander had been something of a child prodigy. While his older brother, Donald, was making his way as a physician in London, Alexander had shown an early aptitude for anatomy. By the age of eleven he was helping his father, who had been William's own anatomy tutor, to carve up corpses in the university dissecting room. At a time when family connections were vital to professional progress, Monro I was plainly grooming his youngest son to succeed him. If the Hunter brothers suspected that the young professor was somewhat over-qualified as an anatomy novice, they were right.

In truth, William's feelings were mixed. Having learned the rudiments of his craft at Monro I's feet, he was understandably flattered that his old master now judged him proficient enough to teach his own son. Appealing as this did to William's vanity, he reasoned that imparting his knowledge to Monro II could be judged 'a particular honour conferred on me'.[3] This was not an unlikely explanation. Preening himself as a newly qualified physician, William had begun using the title 'Dr' in 1755 and was about to renounce his membership of the Company of Surgeons in favour of the elite Royal College of Physicians, although he would have to content himself with being a licentiate, since his medical degree had been awarded by a Scottish university rather than Oxford or Cambridge, instead of a full fellow. At the same time, with the Covent Garden school now firmly established as a popular alternative to Edinburgh and the Continent, he regarded himself as a leading 'breeder' of anatomists. Accordingly, William extended a guarded welcome to Monro II, assuring him in rather superior tones that he was certain to see many interesting experiments and unusual preparations at the school since 'in London we have commonly a greater plenty of subjects than at Edinburgh'. That this flurry of research activity was abundantly John's dominion he made plain when he added, 'In the dissecting room you will find a great deal of that sort of work going on through the whole winter, under my brother's direction.' But much too wily to be totally seduced by a little flattery, William plainly had his doubts about the precocious new pupil, so eager to hear his lectures. And in the fiercely competitive world of eighteenth-century anatomy, William had every reason for concern.

On the treacherous high seas, British adventurers were risking their lives to claim uncharted territories for King and country, beating off European rivals in the struggle for global domination. Success brought not only immediate fortune but lasting fame: the victors' names would be forever commemorated in some remote river, mountain or coastal feature. The exploration of the human body was no different. Across Europe, anatomists vied to discover and name previously unmapped parts of the body, staking their claim to a piece of the human interior. Intrepid anatomists could be assured of immortality through the parts they described; if they did not themselves bestow their names on their discoveries they could be certain their disciples would arrange that honour. Thus in the sixteenth century the followers of Italian professor Gabriello Fallopio ensured his name would live for ever after he described the tubes to the uterus; his compatriot and contemporary Bartolomeo Eustachio likewise had his name commemorated in the tube running between the nose and the ear; and in the following century, striking back for England, the anatomist Thomas Willis left his name to the Circle of Willis, the loop of arteries at the base of the brain.[4]

But just as pioneering colonialists scrapped over important territory, so anatomists squabbled for priority in their discoveries. Often their claims and counter-claims could be exceedingly difficult to determine. The advent of printing and the development of high-quality plate engraving helped in allowing rival researchers to publish and display their findings, but in a period long before authoritative peer-reviewed scientific journals, and when anatomy books were beyond the pocket of many ordinary practitioners, anatomists also chose alternative ways of announcing their achievements. A skilfully prepared specimen was one way of demonstrating an anatomical discovery, while some might regard teaching a new idea in lectures as equivalent to publication. Whichever route they took, the potential for controversy was considerable.

Like any self-respecting eighteenth-century anatomist, William was determined to claim a piece of anatomical territory, and a place in history, for himself. Intelligent and well read, he knew precisely which areas of the human body were ripe for further exploration. During lectures he took pride in passing on his knowledge and views to the pupils, although by now he evidently preferred to direct his brother in the noxious business of practical dissection than to begrime his own elegant fingers. He was, after all, in John's words, 'genteel and delicate'.[5]

William's resolve to establish the school as a centre for

pioneering anatomical research, exactly as he had implied to Monro II, was as much a matter of financial security as professional pride; in the precarious free enterprise society that prevailed the brothers were entirely dependent on their own talents and resources to support themselves – and now their sister too. William's rising status as a physician, anatomy teacher and fashionable *accoucheur* had begun to bring in a substantial income. 'As his business in midwifery increased especially among the people of fashion, he found it necessary to fix his fee for attendance upon a labour at ten guineas,' John recalled.[6] But while William enjoyed the fine clothing, refined company and other small luxuries elevation to the nouveaux riches brought him, he was scrupulously careful with his money. Although he loaned cash to friends like Smollett, he maintained a tight rein on the family budget. Georgian dinner tables frequently groaned with a profusion of rich delicacies, but guests invited to dinner at the Hunters' home were rarely offered more than two dishes; when not entertaining, the family made do with one.[7] When dining out he was equally frugal. Alexander Carlyle, the minister and physician who had been a fellow student at Glasgow, remembered William's sparing repast at weekly gatherings of Scottish physicians in the British coffee-house: 'He had no dinner, but supped on a couple of eggs, and drank his glass of claret.'[8] And although his sister Dorothy, who would be dependent on William's funds for much of her life, described him as 'a steady and liberal benefactor', she admitted that 'through lacking frankness and generosity William did not freely win love'.[9] Since this parsimonious lifestyle left William with a sizeable income to secure, he had opened his first bank account in 1755 and was soon investing large sums in shares, coins and works of art.[10] Prudence was certainly William's byword, as John would later attest, remarking that 'whatever he was really attached to he was in the strictest sense a miser'.[11]

Labouring under William's harsh financial regime and working to his demanding research programme, John was beginning to strain at the leash; by now he had developed his own anatomical interests to pursue as well as his own ideas about his future. He had fallen in obligingly with his brother's schemes to date, performing his dirty work in the graveyards, doing his bidding in the dissecting room and serving his time on the wards, but in the summer of 1755 he finally rebelled when William packed him off to Oxford University, presumably with the notion of fitting him for a career as a physician.[12] Nothing could have been less suited to John's enquiring mind than the stultified atmosphere at Oxford where his compatriot, Adam Smith, complained that the tutors had abandoned 'even the faintest pretence of learning'.[13] Enrolled as a 'gentle-man-commoner' – an undergraduate without a scholarship – at St Mary Hall within Oriel College he survived two months before storming back home. Later he would hotly declaim, 'They wanted to make an old woman of me; or that I should stuff Latin and Greek at the University,' before jabbing his thumbnail emphatically on the table and adding, 'but these schemes I cracked like so many vermin as they came before me'.[14] His reference to making an 'old woman' of him suggests William had aspirations to train John as a male-midwife; John's deprecatory term for the role made plain his disdain for William's chosen career.

In a further step towards independence, John had taken over some of William's lectures, initially when his brother fell ill in spring 1753 and routinely from the following year as his brother's wealthy patients called him away.[15] But it was clear that John would never match William's poise at the podium: when he stood before the pupils with William's lecture notes in front of him he became tongue-tied and stumbling, although he recovered his usual liveliness when it came to answering the students' questions after lessons. Public speaking would always be a strain, as his future brother-in-law later explained: 'Giving lectures was always very unpleasant to him; so that the desire of submitting his opinions to the world, and learning their general estimation, were scarcely sufficient to overcome his natural dislike to speaking in public.'[16] Yet he was popular with the pupils, who liked his approachable manner, good-humoured company and passion for staying up late to debate anatomy topics of the moment.

There was much to discuss. In the two thousand years since anatomists had begun exploring the human body many secrets of its structure and functions had been unlocked but much remained unexplored or unexplained. The earliest known anatomical explorations had taken place in Ancient Greece – the term 'anatomy' derived from the Greek to 'cut' or 'dissect' – but moral objections to invading the human body restricted investigations to animals.[17] Some puzzling ideas about the human body would result. The first reported human dissections were conducted in Alexandria by two enterprising physicians, Herophilus and Erasistratus, in the third century BC. Not only did they dissect human bodies in public, they were also reputed to have experimented on live victims, most probably condemned criminals. Whatever their ethical approach, the Alexandrian pair at least overturned some

At one with nature. John Hunter as a young man, petting his wolf-dog hybrid, originally painted by his future brother-in-law Robert Home, *c*.1770.

A shrewd and sophisticated entrepreneur, William Hunter is portrayed in full grey wig by his fellow Scot Allan Ramsay, *c*.1764–5.

Drunkenness and debauchery were regular scenes in mid-eighteenth-century Covent Garden. This 1747 cartoon shows the Hunter brothers' home and anatomy school, 1 Great Piazza (the first building fronted by an arched colonnade on the right-hand side), only a short stroll from St Paul's churchyard across the square.

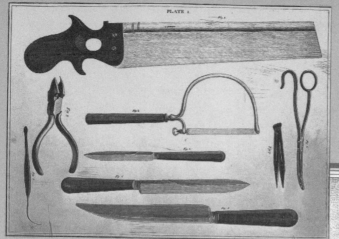

PLATE I.

(*Above*) Knives, saws and other surgical instruments of the kind used by Hunter.

(*Right*) Despite this victim's apparent apprehension, blood-letting – or 'breathing a vein' was as popular with patients as with medical practitioners and was regarded as a panacea by all.

Founded on a wave of eighteenth-century philanthropy, St George's Hospital (*below*) was the setting for interminable conflict and professional rivalry.

Breathing a vein.

A young chimney sweep has a healthy tooth extracted for transplantation into the waiting jaws of a wealthy elderly woman in Thomas Rowlandson's 1790 cartoon *The Transplanting of Teeth*.

Without anaesthetics or pain relief, surgery was a brutal experience. The journey from the operating room to the dissecting bench could be short, as Rowlandson gruesomely depicts in his 1785 cartoon.

(*Above*) Crowds crane for a glimpse as the condemned 'Idle Apprentice' is escorted to Tyburn in Hogarth's series *Industry and Idleness*.

In the final scene of his series *The Four Stages of Cruelty* (*opposite, bottom*), Hogarth's executed felon is dissected with obvious relish at Surgeons' Hall while his heart is eaten by the dissecting-room dog.

From the tomb to the dissecting room … (*left*) Two body-snatchers bundle a shrouded woman's corpse into a sack destined for one of London's anatomy schools in Rowlandson's cartoon *The Resurrection Men*. (*Below*) Another grave-robber is apprehended by the watch, as an anatomist (probably William Hunter) escapes unpunished in this 1773 engraving.

(*Opposite, top*) Three grimacing corpses are carved up by a group of enthusiastic anatomists in *The Dissecting Room*, thought to depict the Hunter brothers with some of their pupils. William Hunter is standing centre left, while John is at his left elbow.

THE REWARD OF CRUELTY.

Behold the Villain's dire disgrace!   Torn from the Root, that wicked Tongue,   His Heart expos'd to prying Eyes,
Not Death itself can end.   Which daily swore and curst!   To Pity has no Claim;
He finds no peaceful Burial-Place;   Those Eyeballs from their Sockets wrung,   But dreadful! from his Bones shall rise,
His breathless Corse, no friend.   That glow'd with lawless Lust!   His Monument of Shame.

Published according to Act of Parliament Feb.1.1751.

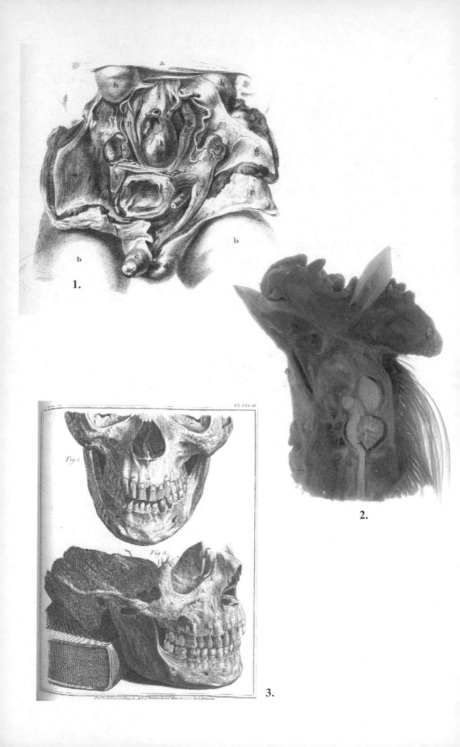

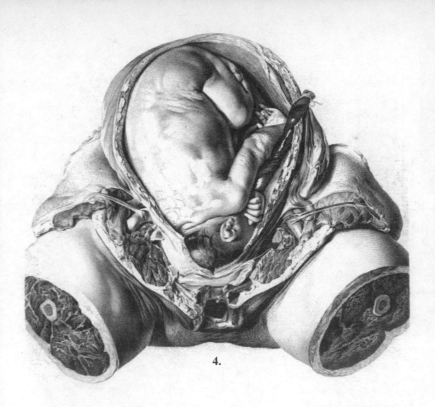

4.

Hunter's expert knife work is preserved for posterity in his exquisite preparations and the skilled drawings of his artists.

1. The testes of a six-month-old foetus before their descent, showing what Hunter called the 'gubernacula or ligaments of the testis'.
2. A cross-section of a rooster's head in which Hunter had transplanted a human tooth.
3. Specimens of human jaws, sketched by Jan van Rymsdyk.
4. A full-term child forever poised on the point of birth, dissected by John Hunter and depicted by van Rymsdyk, for William Hunter's *Anatomy of the Human Gravid Uterus*.
5. The leg of the fourth coachman operated on by Hunter for a popliteal aneurysm.

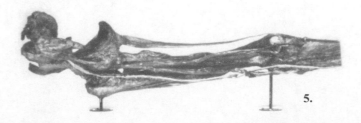

5.

The scourge of venereal disease was almost ubiquitous in eighteenth-century London. In *The Tar's Triumph* (*above*), based on an actual incident in 1749, sailors take their revenge on a brothel in the Strand, where they claim to have been robbed, by throwing from the windows the prostitutes' wares, including a drawer full of condoms. Hunter illustrated his 1786 *Treatise on the Venereal Disease* with a graphic depiction of a penis split open to show the internal structure (*right*).

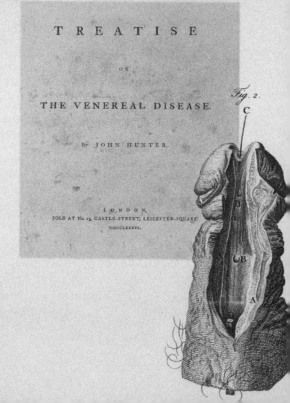

TREATISE

ON

THE VENEREAL DISEASE.

BY JOHN HUNTER.

LONDON,
SOLD AT No. 13, CASTLE-STREET, LEICESTER-SQUARE.
MDCCLXXXVI.

of their forerunners' animal-based errors, accurately describing several structures of the human body.

After Alexandrian pre-eminence, human dissection fell into decline as moral and religious taboos prevailed again. Under Roman rule, the study of anatomy was further set back by Claudius Galen, a flamboyant surgeon to the Roman gladiators in the second century AD. Born in the Greek-speaking empire, trained in Alexandria and appointed surgeon to a series of Roman emperors, Galen was a learned scholar and a competent practitioner, but he was also a bombastic and arrogant self-publicist who likened his achievements in medicine to the engineering works of Roman bridge and road builders. Sadly, though his prolific theories would match Roman engineering for endurance, his accuracy was far inferior. Galen popularized the doctrine of Hippocrates, the Greek father of medicine, that all illness stemmed from an imbalance of bodily 'humours', but unlike his Greek ancestor he advocated copious and routine bloodletting as a panacea for every ill, launching the dangerous fashion that would remain in vogue well into the nineteenth century.

His views on anatomy were equally influential and equally wrong-headed. Like so many anatomists down the centuries, Galen was an irrepressible showman. His favourite public stunt was to cut the throat of a pig then dramatically silence its squeals by severing the nerves to its vocal cords. Although he laid down a groundwork in anatomy, he based his research entirely on animals, thus promulgating errors that would be accepted unquestioningly for more than a millennium. Having never seen the inside of a human body, he mistakenly described the human liver as possessing five lobes, just like those of the pigs he opened. The sheer weight of his works – he wrote sixteen books on the pulse alone – was sufficient to silence any critics as effectively as he had the pigs.

After the Dark Ages, Galen's flawed writings formed the syllabus of the first medical schools, founded in Italy from the twelfth century onwards. Human dissection did not revive until the fourteenth century, when limited public dissections were staged in purpose-built theatres; beginning in Italy, these spread across continental Europe. For the first time, onlookers could perceive the truth about the human form for themselves – if only they were willing to look. Such revelations, if made, were rarely voiced, however, since learned professors generally read aloud from Galen's works while an assistant pointed out the relevant, and irrelevant, parts of the human corpse on the table.

The revival of all things classical during the Italian Renaissance gave renewed impetus to Galen's seemingly indestructible works so that while human dissections continued so did the blind repetition of ancient misconceptions. But at last the Flemish anatomist Andreas Vesalius dared to speak the unspeakable. After taking the chair in anatomy at Padua University with a brief to preach the customary Galenic creed, his investigations led him to realize that his erstwhile hero had never opened a human body. Determined to establish the facts for himself, Vesalius embarked on a relentless programme of human dissection; the results, published in 1543 in the seven books of his sumptuously illustrated work *On the Fabric of the Human Body*, set out the first systematic map of human anatomy. Even if he introduced misconceptions of his own, at least Vesalius established the principle of direct observation of the human body as a way of furthering scientific understanding. Finally, anatomists began to take autopsy – literally 'to see with one's own eyes' – at face value.

With Galen's errors exposed, new discoveries came fast and furious as enthusiasts carved up the body with gusto. Fallopio, Eustachio and their contemporaries staked their claims to parts they discovered, while Realdo Colombo showed how the blood moved from the right to the left side of the heart via the lungs, and Hieronymus Fabricius discovered the one-way valves inside veins, although he could not discern their purpose. Arguably it was but a small step to the landmark discovery of the circulation of the blood by William Harvey, published in 1628. Educated at Cambridge and then Padua, Harvey became royal physician to James I and later Charles I. His dissections of live animals and experiments on human beings convinced him that blood was pumped around the body and returned to the heart in a continuous circulation, finally despatching any lingering ideas that blood was made in the liver.

After Harvey's momentous revelation, it might have seemed to the young anatomists gathered in William's lecture theatre that little of great significance was left to uncover. Indeed, most anatomists after Harvey had focused their energies on the minutest aspects of the body, using the recently invented microscope to discover the capillaries linking arteries and veins, the red corpuscles of the blood and even spermatozoa in semen – all invisible to the naked eye. Not William; he still anticipated discovery on a grand scale, seeking nothing less than the description of an entire system of the human body equivalent to, if not more significant than, Harvey's circulation of the blood. This trophy, just waiting to be plucked, was the exploration of the lymphatic vessels. It was this prize

William hoped to claim for his own, and it was precisely for this reason that he eyed young Monro with mistrust.

Now that most major organs of the body had been named, the circulation of blood outlined and the nervous system described, explaining the lymphatic vessels was the next big peak for anatomists to scale. Some of the earliest dissectors had spotted the vessels in various parts of the body, notably the intestines; they seemed similar to veins but contained a transparent or white fluid.[18] Yet since the minutely fine vessels were exceedingly difficult to trace, anatomists were still unable to chart their geography; many assumed they were simply extensions of the veins. Likewise their purpose remained an enigma.

William, however, was convinced he had all but unlocked the secrets of the lymphatic vessels and that acclaim for their proper discovery lay just within his grasp. Ever since 1746 he had expounded in lectures his theory that the lymphatic vessels formed a complete and independent system existing throughout the body – the lacteal vessels that could easily be discerned in the stomach were simply one part of this complex network – while their function was to absorb fluids all over the body. Here was an entire new bodily system revealed, compared to which the discovery of a single organ or a new muscle was 'trifling', insisted William. Yet although he had broadcast his theory in lectures for nearly ten years and had promptly set John to work investigating the lymphatic vessels, he had never published his views nor provided any proof for his beliefs. With rival anatomists working equally frantically to explain the lymphatic vessels, he knew the race would be close. So when young Monro had written in the summer of 1755 asking to attend the brothers' lectures that autumn, William was naturally suspicious some subterfuge was afoot. When he read the graduation thesis Monro sent with his letter, his fears were confirmed.

William was horrified. In his thesis, the twenty-two-year-old professor declared emphatically that the lymphatic vessels formed a complete system which absorbed fluids throughout the body, exactly repeating the doctrine William had taught in lectures. 'Valvular lymphatic vessels, in all parts of the body, are absorbent veins; they do not emanate from arterial twigs, as is generally believed,' remarked Monro, though without any apparent justification.[19] Monro claimed to have come to this dramatic conclusion in 1753, when he was still a medical student of twenty, coincidentally making two other discoveries William regarded as his: finding the tear ducts and injecting the structure of the testes. With leaden sarcasm, William would later remark, 'Shall we call the year 1753, *fortunate* or *unfortunate* for Alexander Monro, jun. Professor? Surely it was a *remarkable* year. He was then a *student* of anatomy, and in *that one year* made *three discoveries* . . . If he goes on at the same rate, he will become a prodigy.'[20] William was convinced Monro had stolen his landmark theory on the lymphatic system from his lectures, after either hearing reports or reading notes from past pupils. Pupils' lecture notes, he knew, were often circulated among their friends, while there was a regular traffic of students between London and Edinburgh. Unsurprisingly, he was furious that the young professor had seemingly plagiarized his work and deeply suspicious that he had now enrolled at the school to commit further academic theft. Yet for all his jealous rage it was not William's glory the young Monro sought to steal, but John's.

Whether John shared his brother's fury is unknown; he was probably far too engrossed in his solo voyage of discovery among the corpses in the dissecting room to bother about academic squabbles. For if William hankered after a place as the latest in the line of anatomical pioneers stretching back to antiquity, John saw himself rather as the first in a completely new breed of anatomists. With his lifelong distaste for academic study, John had scant idea of the discoveries of his predecessors, beyond what he had gleaned from his brother's lectures, and little interest in emulating their small triumphs by naming a new organ or muscle. Rather than seeking to build on the ancient knowledge of others, John approached the human body with the same spirit of discovery he had applied while roaming the Lanarkshire countryside – he simply set out to establish the facts for himself. Instead of puzzling out queries with pen and paper or turning to classic works as William might do, John took his knife and tweezers to the human body and teased out each mystery he encountered there. It was, as he would often stress, bodies not books that he preferred to read. Just as in childhood, there were always so many questions to answer. How do bones grow – from the middle or the outside edges? Was the substance of teeth alive or dead? How could blood regenerate itself?

Bent over the dissecting bench in his blood-spattered apron throughout each winter, John traced every vessel, probed every cavity and followed every fibre in a systematic exploration of the human corpse. Driven by tireless curiosity and a compulsion to improve the surgery he had witnessed in hospitals, he set out to create his own map of the human interior. Comparing organs, bones, muscles and tissues in diseased and healthy states in hundreds of bodies, he examined how the different parts worked when healthy and what happened when they went wrong. It was a relentless journey. Compared to the limited number of bodies Monro II must have dissected over his short career – two or three a year according to William's experience in Edinburgh – John had the benefit of a ceaseless supply of cadavers dumped at the back door by the body-snatchers. Given the sheer number of hours he spent poring over an endless stream of corpses, he had had more opportunities to study the human interior than any other anatomist in Britain at the time.

But even the darkest mysteries of the human body were not sufficient to absorb all of his attention. Wherever aspects of the human anatomy proved too intricate or complex to determine, he turned to animals, whose simpler structures could often provide clearer explanations, conducting experiments on living creatures bought from markets, animal dealers and private menageries to understand how different body parts function. One thing led to another. Investigating the human stomach led him to compare it with the digestive systems of other mammals, then fish – from the fishmonger – birds and even insects; making a preparation of a human kidney prompted him to study the kidneys of other animals he could find. Initially this comprised mainly dogs, horses, donkeys, fowl and other domestic beasts easily obtainable in the markets and shops of teeming Georgian London. But soon his tastes became more exotic and he had to search further afield to satisfy his growing obsession, applying to circuses and travelling showmen for the corpses of performing animals when they died. He even managed at some point in the 1750s to arrange a deal with the keeper of the royal menagerie at the Tower of London to receive the corpses of all the rare beasts that died there.[21] Before long the bodies of a seal, a monkey, a leopard, an opossum, a mongoose, two crocodiles and assorted other creatures rarely seen within British shores had fallen into his hands.[22] Painstakingly, he dissected their bodies and lovingly preserved parts of their anatomy during moments stolen from William's busy schedule.

William rather despised the investigation of what he regarded as lesser species, collecting 'very few preparations in comparative anatomy, having always objected strongly against them', but for John, animal anatomy was a consuming passion. Hour after hour he stood at the dissecting bench comparing human organs, bones, muscles and structures with the same parts in simpler life-forms; their differences, and more importantly their similarities, would prompt almost unthinkable questions about the development of life on earth. There were no such awkward questions for William: despite rejecting a theological career he had no doubts that the spectacular design of the human form was unequivocally God's work. For John it was always nature, supreme and omnipotent, which deserved worship for the wondrous design of the human anatomy. Precisely how nature had performed this fantastic trick was the question that absorbed him more and more as he studied the human and animal form. This was no random interest in a particular species or a single system of the human body; it was nothing less than a complete exploration of all organic life. As one of his pupils would explain:

Mr Hunter was the first in this country, who studied Comparative Anatomy and Physiology extensively, in order to perfect the knowledge of our animal economy.[23]

So John had embarked on a remarkable series of investigations and experiments leading to a trail of discoveries for which, often, William would simply adopt the credit. Sometimes John's lack of academic study meant he unknowingly repeated experiments previously done by others. Earlier in 1755 he had kept a dog breathing artificially by cutting its windpipe and inserting the muzzle of a pair of double bellows into the hole; as one motion pumped in fresh air, the next sucked it out. 'While this artificial breathing was going on I took off the sternum of the dog, and exposed the lungs and heart,' he recorded; 'the heart continued to act as before, only the frequency of its action was considerably increased.'[24] Unknown to Hunter, the same experiment had been performed as far back as 1664 by the indefatigable Robert Hooke for the benefit of the Royal Society.[25]

At other times, however, John would purposely repeat experiments when he doubted the conclusions of other anatomists. Having heard William outline research on the development of chick embryos by the Swiss anatomist Albrecht von Haller, John determined to try these for himself.[26] Anatomists had argued since the days of Aristotle over how an embryo developed into a living being; by the eighteenth century embryo research was a highly controversial topic. Most anatomists believed, as Aristotle had and Haller still did, that every living being was perfectly formed in miniature in its earliest embryonic stage and thereafter simply grew in size. In his epic tale *The Life and Opinions of Tristram Shandy*, Laurence Sterne would comically capture the idea of a perfect tiny human being, sometimes called the 'homunculus', or 'little man', who 'consists as we do, of skin, hair, fat, flesh, veins, arteries, ligaments, nerves, cartilages, bones, marrow, brains, glands, genitals, humours and articulations'.[27] To John this notion was indeed laughable; accordingly he began his own experiments in autumn 1755.

First he tried to watch a chick embryo develop from conception to hatching by incubating an opened egg in warm water, but the embryo always died after a few hours. Instead, like Haller, he gathered eggs from hens' broods and opened them at intervals to observe the development of the chick in stages. For sufficient numbers of fertilized eggs to be readily to hand, he must have kept hens in the backyard at Covent Garden; while William ate his dainty supper of two eggs at coffee-house gatherings, John squandered dozens of them at home. Since he also needed to view the embryos at frequent intervals in their earliest stages, he had to work day and night, creeping down to the yard in the dark to steal the warm eggs from the clucking hens.

Studying the chicks growing inside their shells required meticulous care, as he later described in handwritten notes. Each egg should be gently cracked open near its top, then a portion of shell about 'the breadth of a shilling' detached, before removing the shell completely to expose the insides.[28] Now the membrane covering the embryo chick had to be peeled away gingerly with a pair of forceps and examined while still alive in a bowl of warm water. After this scrutiny, the membrane containing the embryo should be cut away, preserved in spirits, and placed on a piece of 'black ivory' – presumably ebony – to distinguish the minuscule parts. 'In this way I have been able to bring parts distinctly to view that before appeared to be involved in a cloud,' he wrote, adding that a microscope helped to reveal aspects otherwise too small to see.

As well as making careful notes of his observations, he enlisted the trusty van Rymsdyk to sketch the specimens, recording every stage over nearly three weeks until the moment of hatching. Just prior to the point when the fully developed chick emerged, he noted, 'we can hear it pip and chirp in the egg'. Employing all his senses as usual, he also observed, 'whenever an egg was hatched, the yolk . . . was always perfectly sweet to the very last'.[29]

Straining to see the minute changes through a primitive microscope, Hunter noted the development first of the chick's brain and spinal cord, then its major organs and limbs, and finally its features, including the eyelids and the eyetooth it would use to break out of the shell; he even observed the tiny blood islands before they developed into connected arteries and veins. More significantly, he noticed the striking similarities between the early stages of the embryos of both chicks and humans; the fact that these similar early organic forms could evolve into such different beings struck him as remarkable. And it was manifestly clear, to Hunter's trained eye, that the chick's various parts were transformed from simple structures into more complex ones in the egg; plainly it did not develop from a perfectly formed miniature creature. Although he could not discern the very first beginnings of life – the minuscule bundle of simple cells – he correctly surmised that these parts were simply too small to detect. Though he would not publish his findings until much later in the century, by which time a German anatomist, Caspar Wolff, had published the same, correct, conclusions detailing embryonic development, he had clearly understood the process in 1755. These remarkable experiments, which he would repeat on various animals, were the start of a remorseless campaign to pinpoint the first moments of life and explain the awe-inspiring process of generation. The puzzle would absorb him throughout his career.

At the same time as he wrestled with controversies of the moment, Hunter was following his own individual lines of inquiry. In the summer of 1754 he had become engrossed in tracing the paths of the twelve pairs of nerves leading from the brain.[30] Assisted by Dr John Smith, one of William's former pupils, and unusually working during the heat of summer, Hunter sawed the head from a corpse in an effort to determine the endpoint of the delicate nerves emanating from the skull. 'I steeped the head in a weakened acid of sea-salt till the bones were rendered soft,' he noted, 'and that the parts might be as firm as possible, and at the same time free from any tendency to putrefaction (it being summer), the acid was not diluted with water, but with spirit.' While Smith took notes, Hunter deployed his knife, gently teasing apart the fibres to follow the first pair of nerves to their destination in the nose. Anxious to record this first discovery of the nerves of smell, he employed van Rymsdyk's skills once more to depict his handiwork, while pickling the parts in spirit of wine. William promptly announced the discovery and presented the specimen in his lectures, but for once John managed to hang on to his preparation. It would become the earliest known specimen in his own fledgling collection.[31]

Another pet subject was the teeth, a vastly neglected area of anatomy despite the widespread incidence of dental problems among the sugar-loving Georgians. Intrigued by the development of first teeth in babies and the growth of the second teeth ranked in orderly file underneath, Hunter dissected jaws in fetuses, children and adults. Most of the investigations for what would form his first major research work were performed in the winters before 1755 in Covent Garden. His preparations, and the sketches he commissioned van Rymsdyk to produce, were as usual 'constantly demonstrated' by William from the autumn of 1755. Many of his specimens inevitably found their way into William's collection.[32]

Other investigations by John were directed by William, their results invariably deemed William's property. A typical case concerned the injection of the internal structure of the testes – one of the experiments the young Monro claimed to have done in the summer of 1753. Back in November 1752, nearly a full year before Monro's supposed achievement, William had managed to inject mercury through the vas deferens, the duct that carries sperm from the epididymis, where newly formed sperm mature, towards the urethra. He showed his preparation to pupils in lectures the next day. But while still fairly handy with a knife at this stage, William did not trust himself to undertake the next crucial step – to cut open the injected testicle and reveal the intricate labyrinth of minute tubes, the seminiferous tubules that manufacture sperm, lying inside. This was a job for the best-skilled anatomist he knew, and sure enough he 'desired my brother to lose no opportunity of making the trial'.[33] Within a fortnight, John had accomplished the formidable task and rushed to show William his handiwork. 'He shewed me the Testis opened, and the tubular internal substance very generally filled with mercury,' recorded William, who was so delighted at the success that he displayed the preparation at his lecture that very evening, and in every ensuing course. More importantly, as far as their rival Monro was concerned, William had six witnesses, all former pupils, prepared to sign an oath confirming that they too had seen John's preparation in 1752.[34] The young Monro, however, was one step ahead. Although he did not complete the same injection until the following summer, and never reached John's important next stage of showing the internal structure, he had published details of his accomplishment in an Edinburgh medical journal in 1754, later expanded in his thesis. On this basis he claimed priority for the work.

Crucially, it was while injecting a testicle that Monro claimed to have reached his climactic conclusions about the lymphatic system. Lacking John's dexterity, Monro had pushed his syringe rather too energetically; the delicate epididymis tube burst and Monro watched helplessly as the leaking mercury filled the nearby lymphatic vessels. It was from this unfortunate accident that Monro had apparently jumped to the conclusion that the lymphatic vessels formed an absorbent system. But by the time Monro's thesis had come off the press, the brothers had already taken another vital step in the exploration of the lymphatic system.

Although the first of these explorations was evidently directed by William, very soon John was following his own trails of inquiry, now just as intent as William on solving the biggest anatomical enigma of the age. At some point in 1753 or 1754 – William was later unsure of the exact year – John had succeeded in injecting some lymph glands with mercury, along with the vessels coming from the glands. His method, watched by the fascinated pupils, entailed inflating the vessels carefully with a blowpipe before blowing mercury into them; John could demonstrate the lymphatic vessels in the testicles by the same method, a trick he commonly performed on the male organs of dead dogs, and horses too. Having found 'so easy a method', John now determined to trace the lymphatic vessels throughout the whole body and to publish the first 'complete description and figure of the whole absorbing system'.[35] So, once the 'hurry of dissections' was over – by the spring of 1753 or 1754 presumably – John embarked on his campaign to trace the lymphatic network. By the time Monro arrived for the start of the autumn term in 1755, John was itching to pick up his investigations where he had left off.

So far, Monro had seemingly outwitted them. Whether or not he had appropriated his theory on the lymphatic system after hearing William's students gossiping in Edinburgh, as the brothers suspected, they would give him the benefit of the doubt. William therefore introduced Monro to his fellow scribes and even mentioned his dubious thesis 'favourably' in lectures. John returned to his dissecting bench. That winter he duly produced a handsome preparation displaying the lymph vessels running from the thigh up to the thoracic duct 'all finely filled with mercury'; the following spring van Rymsdyk sketched his work. It was that same spring, of 1756, that Monro left the school, having scrupulously noted William's lectures and observed John's preparations, for a study tour of Europe. The brothers seemingly forgot his potential threat to their reputations and continued with their own pursuits.

In May, John secured his first proper hospital job, as a house surgeon – a junior doctor on the first rung of the medical career ladder – at St George's, where he had already served time as a pupil.[36] Founded by philanthropists in 1734, St George's was based in a former stately home at Hyde Park Corner, on the edge of the capital's growing urban sprawl.[37] Like the several other London hospitals founded at the time, St George's was established specifically to treat the 'deserving' poor, partly in a genuine spirit of charity and partly on the more mercenary principle that returning honest labourers to a working life as quickly as possible benefited the nation as a whole. With the so-called voluntary hospitals notoriously filthy and ill run, anyone who could afford medical fees opted for treatment in their own home; those who were so destitute they were not deemed fit for charitable aid were thrown on the mercy of family and friends. Funded by subscriptions from donors, who thereby earned a place on the governing board, the voluntary hospitals offered free medical care to those found eligible, while their medical staff worked for nothing: the opportunity for a physician or surgeon to enhance his reputation through charitable work while practising his rudimentary skills on the uncomplaining poor was considered sufficient recompense for his occasional attendance. But for a patient to gain admission to a voluntary hospital could be almost as hard as obtaining an audience with royalty. As well as having to prove their merit for charitable care to the satisfaction of the governors, prospective patients had to convince the board their condition was neither infectious nor incurable. Since infectious diseases were rampant in poverty-stricken London, and since medical practitioners were incapable of curing most illnesses, it was virtually impossible to comply with such stringent conditions. Indeed, patients recorded as admitted to St George's had a variety of contagious diseases, including scarlet fever, whooping cough and chicken pox, as well as conditions from which they were distinctly unlikely to recover. Once a patient had wheedled his way through the doorway, regulations were equally strict, with bans on smoking, gambling, drinking gin, bringing in food and swearing, though the observance of these rules was just as lax as it was on admission: in 1750 the governors lamented the fact that 'not only victuals, but also spiritous liquors, are too often introduced into the wards'.

Having secured the post of most junior surgeon at St George's at the relatively advanced age of twenty-eight, John Hunter began to employ his considerable experience in anatomy on the patients who turned up at its doors with limbs mangled in traffic accidents, skulls fractured in falls, bites from mad dogs, and assorted tumours, abscesses and sexual diseases. Among his duties, it was the junior surgeon's job to treat any casualties admitted when the staff surgeons were absent, prepare patients for operations in the first-floor theatre and bandage post-operative wounds on the draughty wards.[38] For this privilege, he had to pay for his board and lodging, living in a little cottage within the grounds.

But as well as the valuable experience of hands-on surgery, the job brought something else of particular use to John Hunter – the keys to the 'dead house', or mortuary, where the least fortunate patients of St George's awaited interment in the nearby burial ground. Often their wait would be cut short. As well as recording operations at St George's, Hunter's case books detail numerous autopsies he conducted on patients in the late 1750s. While some of these may have been approved by families – it was certainly not a legal requirement – many more were plainly performed on bodies purloined from the dead house or the graveyard.

One such post-mortem was performed on twenty-six-year-old Ann Miller, who died at St George's in 1756 from a condition of the pancreas probably connected with heavy drinking; Ann may well have been one of the last victims of the gin-drinking mania. Finding her pancreatic duct filled with a large number of stones 'like small pieces of white Coral', John preserved the specimen for William's collection.[39] Another autopsy concerned an eight-month-old baby, listed in the case books simply as 'J. Burn', who had died at St George's in November 1755 of 'a Watery Head' – hydrocephalus, a condition in which fluid collects around the brain. After taking measurements and making sketches, Hunter found the brain 'at some places was as thin as a shilling: at others an inch thick', while one of its cavities 'contained eight Ale-house pints'.[40]

By rights, Hunter's job should have gone to another aspiring surgeon, John Gunning, who had already completed a full three years' pupillage at the hospital. No doubt William, who numbered several governors of St George's among his influential friends, had pulled a few strings. But at the same time, John's growing reputation as an accomplished anatomist, as well as his patent appetite for industry, probably helped determine the choice; the rough-mannered, beer-swilling, brash Hunter plainly had something about him that impressed the board. It was a slight, however, that Gunning would remember all his life, never forgiving his youthful rival. In the event, Hunter spent only five months in the job instead of the typical spell of between one and two years, whereupon Gunning nimbly stepped into his shoes. Inevitably, the pompous Foot, Hunter's venomous biographer, would use the brevity of this training as supposed evidence of Hunter's inadequacies, commenting, 'to my own knowledge I can speak it that the period of five months' duration at hospital in the office of house-surgeon is the shortest which can be found in the unerring journals of hospitals'.[41]

The fact was that with winter steadily approaching, Hunter had to abandon the living for the dead once more and return to his duties in Covent Garden, where an empty house now awaited him as well as further controversy. During the summer, William had joined the fashionable migration to the West End, setting up home with Dorothy in a smart townhouse in Jermyn Street; their new abode was not only more in keeping with William's status as a physician but safely distant from the stench and distasteful activities of the dissecting room.[42] Living alone in the Great Piazza, awaiting the next influx of pupils, John had become something of a minor celebrity among London's growing community of medical students. As a record class of around a hundred pupils crowded into the lecture room for the autumn course, his latest research was the buzz of the town.[43]

As part of his study of the male reproductive system during the previous winter, John had investigated how the testes descend in babies while in the womb. The task had initially been set by William, prompted by another research paper from the busy Haller published in 1755. In this, Haller had concluded that the testicles suddenly dropped at the moment of birth as a result of the baby taking its first breath. John, however, had realized from dissections of fetuses at different stages that the testes underwent a gradual descent from high in the abdomen to the scrotum as the fetus developed; by the time of birth they had generally already descended. Since he was almost certainly working on stolen bodies, or fetuses that had miscarried, charting this progress precisely was not easy.

'It is the more difficult to ascertain the exact time of this motion, as we hardly ever know the exact age of our subject,' he frankly admitted.[44] Yet he correctly assessed that the descent was normally complete by about the eighth month. Furthermore, he found that the process of descent sometimes resulted in a congenital hernia, where a portion of gut protrudes through the abdominal wall and into the scrotum because a section of the baby's intestines has been pulled down with the descending testicle. While William had initially suggested this hypothesis too, it was John, as always, who obtained the proof.

William had already given a brief outline of his brother's conclusions on the descent of the testes and congenital hernia at the end of the spring course in 1756, when John first made his discoveries; that autumn, John confirmed his findings. It was William, assuming proprietorship of his brother's deftness as usual, who broadcast John's findings to the pupils crammed in the lecture room. And as John proudly handed round his delicate preparations displaying the progressive stages of descent and the congenital hernia, the students were suitably impressed. No sooner had they seen for themselves this exciting anatomical discovery than they passed on the details to their fellow students and teachers on the London wards. Before long, the school was besieged by fellow anatomists eager for a peek. 'The discovery was become the novelty of the time among students in London, and other inquirers after anatomical improvements,' William noted, 'and many gentlemen of my acquaintance desired to see the preparations which my brother had made.'[45]

Among the first visitors was Percivall Pott, John's

former tutor at Bart's, who arrived one autumn morning unannounced at the Covent Garden house. Having first enquired after William, who was generally present now only for evening lectures, Pott was invited in by John, who was more than willing to describe his findings. Pott's interest in the topic was no surprise: he had himself published a book on different types of hernias, *A Treatise on Ruptures*, just a few months earlier. John immediately countered Pott's view, like Haller's, that the testes descended only as the baby took its first breath; he duly showed Pott his preparations to prove his point. John recalled, 'I went with him into the preparation-room, and we examined them together ... and after we had examined and talked of these matters, Mr Pott came into the parlour with me, and sat with me some time longer.'[46] Pott's friendly interest could not have appeared more convivial.

So as the new year of 1757 dawned, prospects for the Hunter brothers seemed rosy. The reputation of their school as a focus for pioneering research had been firmly established and the discoveries the brothers had magnanimously shared with fellow anatomists seemed to place them at the centre of a vibrant and mutually beneficial intellectual community. But it was not to last: before the year was out the heady atmosphere of co-operative interaction would be shattered by venomous rows which split the anatomical world apart. In bitter slanging matches, even by the standards of typically acrimonious eighteenth-century polemics, the brothers quarrelled first with Pott and then with Monro II.

As with Monro, William gained an early hint of possible deceit when Pott announced his intention to publish a treatise on congenital hernias shortly after his friendly parlour chat with John. When the new publication, *An account of a particular kind of rupture frequently attendant upon new-born children*, hit the streets in March 1757, William was apoplectic.[47] Pott plainly stated that congenital hernias were an accidental by-product of the descent of the testes in the fetus, just as John had explained to him, although he erroneously repeated Haller's notion that they only fully descended after birth. 'It hardly contained one new idea,' William fumed. 'It was what any of my pupils might have written . . . and yet neither my brother's name, nor mine was mentioned.'

Fortunately, as always, William had friends in high places, or at least a loyal chum with the power of the press in his grasp. The trusty Smollett, indebted to William for his elastic loans, leapt to his benefactor's defence in the March issue of the *Critical Review*, which the novelist had founded a year earlier. Reviewing Pott's book, Smollett roundly accused its author of plagiarizing the findings of both Haller and the Hunters. It was the beginning of what William – who automatically defended his brother's discoveries as if they were his own – would call a 'paper war'. Pott returned fire robustly in the *Review* insisting he had arrived at his conclusions solely through his own inquiries, having neither read Haller's work nor heard of John's discovery. But his initial denial that he had ever visited the Hunters' school was a mistake. Two of the pupils wrote to confirm that John had indeed shown the surgeon several preparations, described his view on the descent of the testes and outlined his proof on congenital hernias. Pott was cornered, and he knew it. He recovered his memory sufficiently to claim grudgingly that John had shown him 'a single preparation' while still denying ever discussing hernias; he also asserted that he had never intended to cheat the Hunters of their rightful claim and vowed never to speak on the subject again.[48] William appeared willing to accept this olive branch, although he could not resist repeating the argument in 1762 in a pompous pamphlet devoted to his quarrels with Pott and Monro.[49] It was in that same pamphlet that John's discoveries on the descent of the testes would be detailed. It was his first published paper, comprising a ten-page outline with three plate engravings, in which John even named a new anatomical part – the 'gubernaculum', Latin for 'steering oar' or 'rudder', after the fact that it 'steers' the route of the descending testicle.

Yet if William was prepared to excuse Pott, he was not about to let young Monro off the hook so lightly. The brothers may have forgiven Monro's earlier trespass on their territory, but they would not excuse his next transgression. Having spent his intervening years studying anatomy abroad, the ambitious Monro published a major work on the lymphatic vessels in Berlin in the summer of 1757. Expanding his earlier thesis, Monro repeated the view that the lymph vessels form a complete circulatory system designed to absorb fluids from the tissues and return them to the blood, reiterating the description of his supposed injection of the testicles. Once again, Smollett leapt to the brothers' defence, denouncing Monro's pamphlet in the September issue of the *Critical Review* as a blatant theft of William's views, which had been 'publicly made by Dr Hunter to his pupils, for the space of eleven years'.

But the powerful Monro family was not as easy as Pott to subdue. First, Monro senior responded to the attack with a letter to Smollett's magazine, insisting that his son had written his student thesis 'in absolute ignorance of Dr Hunter's having any particular opinion concerning lymphatics' and had been 'surprised' on attending the Covent Garden lectures to hear William teach the same view. William immediately countered with the support of six witnesses, all now esteemed lecturers or surgeons in their own right, confirming he had taught his doctrine in lectures since 1746 and that notes of the lectures had circulated in Edinburgh for several years. Then, in December, big brother Donald Monro, about to take up a post as physician at St George's Hospital, weighed in with his support. Finally, young Monro, now safely back home in Edinburgh, joined the affray with a highly abusive sixty-nine-page pamphlet attacking the Hunters.

It was a provocation too far. When in 1762 William responded with his own pamphlet, *Medical Commentaries, containing a plain and direct answer to Professor Monro jun*, he countered Monro's claims in impeccable court-room style. Accusing Monro of 'the open violation of truth and candour', William proved his priority with incontrovertible evidence, publishing two damning letters from the chemist Joseph Black. Black confirmed that Monro II had shown him his unpublished student thesis back in 1755, whereupon he had immediately warned him that the theory on the lymphatic system had already been expounded by William Hunter; Black had even accused Monro of filching his views from reports of William's lectures circulating in Edinburgh. There was no question but that Monro II had been aware of William's theory before he published his thesis, and quite possibly had simply appropriated it from the gossip of fellow students.

Though the rift between the two Scottish families would never be healed – and Donald would avenge the fraternal slur by joining later attacks against John at St George's – it did neither side much harm either. Monro II went on to teach anatomy to increasing acclaim at Edinburgh, eventually retiring at the age of seventy-five in favour of his son, known, of course, as Alexander Monro *tertius*; in all, the Monro dynasty would hold the Edinburgh anatomy chair for a total of 126 years. The Hunters would continue their dynamic relationship too, with William delivering his pithy lectures every afternoon and John overseeing every other aspect of the school, with mounting success – although John declined to formalize the partnership when William finally made him the offer in 1758 'on account of his aversion to public speaking, and his extreme diffidence of his own abilities and skill'.[50] William would later dismiss the whole nasty episode involving Pott and the Monros with the casual comment, 'Anatomists have ever been engaged in contention'. He would certainly do his utmost to make sure that state of affairs continued, going on to squabble with numerous colleagues, not least his own brother. In fact, as so often in such anatomical wrangles, really neither camp deserved full credit for the discovery of the lymphatic system. An earlier British anatomist, Francis Glisson, had actually suggested a century earlier that the lymphatic vessels formed a system to recycle fluids, although his theory had languished in obscurity.[51] And it would be many more years before the other vital roles of the lymphatic system, filtering bacteria and fighting infection, were understood.

Throughout the unseemly public wrangles William had taken the lead in defending the Hunters' corner, ranting and blustering in an effort to present himself as the intrepid discoverer, even though it was often John who proved his theories. Always in this partnership it was sophisticated, suave William who was the visionary; down-to-earth, practical John the man of action. While John may have been happy to accept his supporting role to William's star performance at first, he would later remark that William had not 'done justice to my Experiments'.[52] In particular, he would feel aggrieved that William assumed credit for discovering the true function of the lymphatic vessels. Although he was always careful to award William merit for devising the theory on absorption, it was John who provided the irrefutable evidence to prove the doctrine true.

That proof of William's long-vaunted theory involved a dramatic set of experiments, controversial even then, on living animals in the winter of 1758. By this stage John had not only dissected large numbers of dead animals but was performing regular experiments on living creatures, as William reported: 'At this time my brother was deeply engaged in physiological enquiries, in making experiments on living animals, and in prosecuting comparative anatomy, with great accuracy and application. It is well known that I speak of him with moderation, when I say so.'[53] In what Benjamin Franklin would call the 'age of experiments', it was common practice to invite parties of fellow professionals, students and interested amateurs to observe and verify significant scientific events. The artist Joseph Wright would powerfully record such a scene in his *An Experiment on a Bird in the Air Pump*, which depicts a group of adults and children watching in mixed fascination and horror as a cockatoo is suffocated in a vacuum.[54] As Wright's painting suggests, such experiments, while shocking, shed light to dispel the darkness of human ignorance; without the technology of sophisticated visual aids, such events often provided a dynamic forum for education and debate. And so, when John Hunter tied a yelping dog to his dissecting table on 3 November 1758, a crowd of onlookers had been invited to Covent Garden for the show. The party included three physicians and four surgeons, as well as several of the brothers' pupils.

John's aim in this showpiece experiment was to prove once and for all his brother's theory that only the lymphatic vessels – in this case the lacteals in the intestines – and not the veins were capable of absorbing fats. The question was still open to debate since Monro II, for one, had declared himself unconvinced that the veins were not involved in absorbing fluids. As his observers craned to watch, John slit open the dog's belly, whereupon 'The intestines rushed out immediately'. While the bleeding animal writhed and squealed, he made a hole in its upper intestines then poured warm milk through a funnel into the gap. As the guests peered forwards, he proudly demonstrated the lacteals turning white as they conveyed fat from the gut, while the veins remained filled with blood. But this was not conclusive enough for his purposes so John made a second cut lower down in the tortured animal's intestines and repeated the milk test. Again he made sure all his guests could see for themselves the fruits of his labours, recording:

> In both these experiments we could not observe that the least white fluid had got into the veins. After attending to these appearances a little while, I put all the bowels into the abdomen for some time, that the natural absorption might be assisted by the natural warmth; then took out and examined attentively the two parts of the gut and mesentery upon which the experiments had been made:

but the lacteals were still filled with milk and there was not the least appearance of a white fluid in the veins.

In all, Hunter performed a total of four experiments on the unfortunate mongrel until 'the gut at last burst' and the animal died. John went on to conduct similar experiments, before similar parties of guests, using milk, dyed blue starch, and warm water mixed with musk, on four more living animals – three sheep and an ass – from November through to August of the following year. The notion, proposed a century earlier, that lymphatic vessels alone absorb fats and fluids had been proved beyond all doubt. But if the evidence of Hunter's experiments was now broadly accepted, the morality of such apparently barbaric acts on innocent living creatures was certainly not.

Hunter was by no means alone in performing numerous acts of vivisection at the time: throughout Europe enthusiasts conducted experiments on creatures of every description. In the Age of Enlightenment often the only way in which anatomists could enlighten themselves on how the living human body functioned was by dissecting living animals. At a time when brutal deeds were daily inflicted on all manner of creatures in London's popular cockpits and bull-baiting rings, animal experiments were broadly condoned, but not by all. In the very year that Hunter tortured his dog, three sheep and an ass, such practices had provoked a passionate assault by no less a figure than Samuel Johnson. Writing in a London journal, *The Idler*, in August 1758, Johnson launched a ferocious tirade against acts of vivisection by unnamed anatomists: 'Among the inferior professors of medical knowledge is a race of wretches, whose lives are only varied by varieties of cruelty; whose favourite amusement is to nail dogs to tables and open them alive; to try how long life may be continued in various degrees of humiliation, or with the excision or laceration of the vital parts,' stormed the formidable animal lover.[55] The article continued in similar vein, arguing that such 'acts of torture' were designed more for their perpetrators' amusement than to extend scientific knowledge. 'I know not,' he declared, 'that by living dissections any discovery has been made by which a single malady is more easily cured.'

Although Johnson nowhere identified the target of his attack, it is easy to believe that he had in mind John Hunter, who was by now renowned for his anatomical experiments, especially since Johnson added the jibe that 'he surely buys knowledge dear, who learns the use of the lacteals at the expense of his humanity'. However, Johnson wrote his article three months before John began his famous round of experiments on the lacteals. The likelihood is he was looking further afield and that Haller, the indefatigable Swiss, who was conducting more experiments on living animals than probably any anatomist in Europe, was the real source of Johnson's ire.[56] Indeed, Hunter himself would condemn the practice of endlessly performing similar experiments, for as he would later comment, 'I think we may set it down as an axiom, that experiments should not be often repeated which tend merely to establish a principle already known and admitted; but that the next step should be, the application of that principle to useful purposes.'[57]

Whether or not Hunter was in Johnson's sights at the end of the 1750s, his reputation had certainly captured interest far and wide. When William Shippen, a prominent physician in Philadelphia, decided on furthering his young son's medical education in 1758, it was to Britain, and to John Hunter, he naturally turned. Having already served a four-year apprenticeship with Dad, young 'Billey' was to cross the Atlantic and spend the winter in London walking the wards and studying the human body 'with the finest Anatomist for Dissections, Injections, etc in England'.[58] Shippen arrived in the winter of 1758 and set out to enjoy all the pleasures 'dirty London' could afford, which he carefully recorded in his animated diary. But his social life came to an abrupt end on 2 October when he 'moved my trunk to Mr. Hunter's', becoming a resident pupil in John's Covent Garden house for the brothers' autumn course. From now on, Shippen's packed schedule left little time for social activities. On one typical day, 9 October, Shippen recorded, 'Rose at 6, operated till 8, breakfasted till 9, dissected till 2, dined till 3, dissected till 5. Lecture till 7, operated till 9, sup'd till 10 then bed.'[59] On other evenings he would sit up debating the latest turns in anatomy with John, so that daily entries commonly ended, 'chatted till 10 with Mr. Hunter upon anatomical points'. As their friendship grew, Shippen spent more time at Hunter's shoulder in the dissecting room, plainly in awe of the charismatic teacher who seemingly had a knack of inspiring young pupils with a fascination for anatomy.

When he returned to Philadelphia in 1762, after also studying medicine at Edinburgh University, Shippen imported wholesale the Hunterian approach. In November that year he established the first anatomical lectures delivered in America in which he not only promoted the Hunter brothers' hands-on model of dissection but copied their reliance on body-snatchers for research material. Shippen's school would face attack by outraged crowds on several occasions; at one point its proprietor narrowly escaped with his life.[60] Three years later he co-founded America's first medical school, initially called the College of Philadelphia and later the University of Pennsylvania, along with a fellow former pupil from the Hunters' school, John Morgan, who studied under John, staying in his Covent Garden house, and attended William's lectures in the autumn of 1760. Together, Shippen and Morgan established Pennsylvania as the cradle of modern American surgery, but it was the Hunter brothers who were its inspirational parents.

That autumn course of 1760 was the last in which the two brothers worked side by side. After twelve winters of tireless labour in the rank atmosphere of the dissecting room, the strain had begun to take its toll on John's health and he had taken to his bed in early 1760.[61] It is unclear precisely what ailed him, and in any case eighteenth-century diagnostic skills were always vague, but early biographers suggested he had contracted pneumonia, while William recorded that his brother suffered a 'very indifferent state of health, the effect of too much application to anatomy, which obliged him to be much in the country'. Hunter himself would later record that 'I left anatomical pursuits in the beginning of the Summer 1760,' without explaining why; yet he was not so ill that he could not be tempted to undertake post-mortems in both May and June, and to treat a patient at St George's in July. He was obviously back living in Covent Garden by the autumn, when Morgan stayed, for Hunter would later hint that Morgan had pinched a research idea from him while lodging in his house.

That same autumn, John reached a momentous decision – to part company with William and chart his own course in the medical world. For some time he had been straining at the leash in William's strict domain; he must have been desperate to be master of his own destiny, not to mention finances. The wild, unkempt country lad of twelve years earlier had grown into a self-assured, spirited young man, ambitious to make his own way in society. Having dissected, by his own reckoning, some thousand human corpses in his years at the school, he was without doubt the most experienced anatomist in Britain, if not Europe, yet his limited training in surgery and lack of formal qualifications severely restricted his chances of securing a permanent hospital job or setting up private practice in highly competitive London. That left him with one obvious place to pursue his talents – the battlefield. Like so many aspiring surgeons before him, John Hunter signed up as a surgeon with the army in October 1760 and awaited orders through the winter.

Without the help of his brother, William taught his last complete course that autumn then gave up the lease on the Covent Garden house for a solitary existence in Jermyn Street; Dorothy had earlier married and returned to Scotland. At last the house in the Great Piazza, the scene for more than a decade of countless human dissections, live animal experiments, heated anatomical debates, cosy parlour chats and secretive night-time deliveries, was empty and quiet, its neighbours' peace finally restored. And in March 1761, the thirty-three-year-old John Hunter set sail from Portsmouth to face the muskets and cannon of the French troops.

6

The Lizard's Tails

'It will also be immediately necessary on the field to replace many parts that would destroy the patient if their restoration was delayed, such as the bowels or lungs protruding out of their cavities, or to remove large bodies, such as a piece of shell sticking in the flesh.'

John Hunter[1]

Spithead, off Portsmouth, March 1761

Commodore Augustus Keppel surveyed the men crammed on board the squadron of almost 130 ships anchored at Spithead with dismay. Dishevelled, ill disciplined and decidedly unfit, many were plainly sick or lame and one whole regiment was clothed entirely in rags.[2] Already he had proposed leaving the two worst regiments behind. But this, he knew, was impractical, for Keppel had been handed his 'Secret Instructions' from the newly crowned George III only days earlier. The orders were clear: his mission, impossible as it might seem, was to capture the French island of Belle-Ile.

Having been at war with France and its allies for five years, Britain had already won important campaigns under its popular war secretary William Pitt.[3] The struggle for overseas supremacy, which would later become known as the Seven Years War – effectively the first world war – had begun badly. But after early setbacks, Pitt's audacious strategies had helped Britain seize control in key territories so that by the end of 1760 there was little doubt that France had been pushed to the brink of defeat. All Pitt needed was one more push to secure the victory he knew was within grasp: the conquest of Belle-Ile, in its strategic position eight miles south of Brittany, was the goal he believed would win the war. With eight thousand troops commanded by Major-General Studholme Hodgson, under the escort of a powerful fleet supervised by Keppel, Pitt was determined his daring joint-forces expedition would prove a success. And on 29 March 1761, just four days after the commodore had received his secret orders, the British force set sail for the coast of France.

Crossing into French waters on board the hospital ship *Betty*, innocently unaware of his intended destination, John Hunter was already hard at work tending the assorted ailments that were an inevitable fact of life in the cramped and unhygienic conditions at sea; bribed or press-ganged into action, many soldiers and sailors were in poor shape before they ever engaged battle. But Hunter had joined the army because he was 'anxious for a more enlarged field of observation', and his role in the expedition to Belle-Ile would certainly provide him with that.[4] The Greek father of medicine Hippocrates had counselled, 'he who wishes to be a surgeon should go to war', and centuries later the battlefield still provided the perfect training ground for would-be surgeons.[5] Indeed, a spell as a surgeon in the services bestowed the automatic right to practise in civilian life. Not only did wartime present surgeons with the opportunity, indeed the necessity, to brandish their knives fully and freely on parts of the body they never normally encountered, the inevitable failures this engendered provided numerous chances for instructive autopsies. Desperate for more experience in both fields, and despite a complete lack of formal qualifications, Hunter had secured a commission as an army staff surgeon on 30 October 1760, most likely through William's influence with Robert Adair, the army's deputy surgeon-general.[6] Having initially embarked for an earlier, abandoned expedition that same month, he had then waited in London all winter until finally ordered back to Portsmouth to join the *Betty*.[7] Now flagging with sea-sickness as the vast fleet lurched into the tempestuous Bay of Biscay, while struggling to patch up sores and old wounds in the tiny sick bay swaying below deck, he may well have regretted his urge to broaden his horizons.[8]

No doubt his friend Smollett, who had worked as a surgeon's second mate in the navy during the previous war with France, had warned him of the conditions he could expect.[9] Describing his sea-going experiences in his first novel, *The Adventures of Roderick Random*, Smollett's eponymous hero had found that 'The sick and wounded were squeezed into certain vessels, which thence obtained the name of hospital ships ... and the space between decks was so confined, that the miserable patients had not room to sit upright in their beds. Their wounds and stumps being neglected, contracted filth and putrefaction, and millions of maggots were hatched amid the corruption of their sores.'[10]

Even allowing for a little artistic licence on Smollett's part, Hunter's discomfort must have been compounded when the floating army arrived on 6 April within sight of its target and the anxious troops stared at the soaring cliffs and fortified battlements defending Belle-Ile. Surveying the jagged coastline merely confirmed what Keppel and Hodgson had already surmised: the island appeared to be impregnable. Nevertheless, the commanders attempted a landing two days later, at a tiny inlet on the southern end of the island. After the fleet knocked out the large guns defending the bay, more than three thousand soldiers were rowed through the smoke in flat-bottomed boats to storm the French positions. Although some of the redcoats succeeded in landing, and a hardy band of about sixty grenadiers – the army's crack troops – even mounted the cliffs, they were speedily mown down by the French muskets above, while their fellows flailed helplessly in the surf below. The assault was hastily abandoned but not before hundreds of troops had been shot or taken prisoner by the French or drowned in the storms that then blew up.

Fearfully reporting the disastrous defeat back to England, Hodgson estimated that five hundred soldiers had been killed, wounded or taken prisoner during the assault. 'Purcell is killed, and Maclean had his arm broke with a musket shot, and is taken prisoner,' he wrote. 'My secretary, who was at the poop, on board the *Dragon*, looking through a glass to satisfy his curiosity, has got a shot in his forehead.'[11] There could have been little hope for Hodgson's inquisitive secretary, but those soldiers who could be rescued from the lashing waves were hauled on board the *Betty*, waiting their turn with the sailors injured by cannon fire and splintered timbers, to be patched up by Hunter and his fellow surgeons. While the storm tossed and dispersed the wooden ships, Hunter battled to save the wounded, bleeding and dying men in his primitive surgery.

Nothing in his experience of performing operations in London's hospitals had prepared him for this. As men lay groaning in the long straggle waiting for treatment, he worked at full speed, sawing off smashed limbs, digging out musket balls, prising free shards of wood and splintered bone, and bandaging ragged wounds. With his traditional officer's red jacket conveniently concealing the blood stains, or more likely thrown off in the heat of the cockpit surgery below decks, his urgent appeals for more supplies would have been lost in the tumult of the raging storm and the frenzied shrieks of his patients. A naval surgeon, Edward Ward, described operating under similar circumstances some years later: '. . . at the very instant when I was amputating the limb of one of our wounded seamen, I met with an almost continual interruption from the rest of his companions, who were in the like distressed circumstances; some pouring forth the most piercing cries to be taken care of, while others seized my arm in their earnestness of being relieved, even at the time when I was passing the needle for suturing the divided blood vessels by a ligature.'[12] With no anaesthesia to numb the pain, many patients would have died of shock as the amputation knife cut through their flesh, or bled to death while the surgeons probed around in their wounds to extract debris; their bodies were given hurried burials at sea. Others would join them days later as sepsis took hold in their wounds while they lay in the hammocks of the foul-smelling sick bay. No doubt, like Smollett's hero, Hunter must have been 'much less surprised to find people die on board, than astonished to find any body recover'.[13]

As two weeks of gales prevented any further attempt on the island, Pitt sent reinforcements for a renewed assault, launched on 22 April. This time a battalion of men succeeded in scrambling up the rocky slopes on the southern coast where they overpowered the French forces at the summit. By nightfall, British troops had control of the surrounding area, the French had beat a retreat to the island's fortified capital of Le Palais, and the conquest of Belle-Ile was declared a triumph. British casualties had been few – a total of fifteen soldiers killed and twenty-nine wounded. One of the officers, Captain Patterson, had lost an arm, Hodgson reported. There were also several wounded French prisoners needing treatment.[14] As soon as the remaining troops could be landed and supplies unloaded onto the beach, the surgeons and surgeons' mates set up basic first-aid stations in cottages and chapels abandoned by the retreating French, where they again set to amputating limbs and probing gunshot wounds. 'Poor Faulkener has had a dangerous wound in his head with a grape-shot,' Hodgson wrote home. 'He has been trepanned; and the surgeons have hopes for him. He is a brave lad.'[15] Although Faulkener's fate under the trepanning saw is unknown, the surgeons' optimism may well have been misplaced, for Hunter later wrote of his battlefield experiences, 'Very little can be done to relieve the brain in such a situation.'[16]

Treating the injured in the makeshift field hospitals, Hunter quickly discovered that there was little he could do to relieve many of Faulkener's fellows either. Where the poor grenadiers or their French opponents had been shot

at pointblank range or bayoneted in the chest or
abdomen, their chances of survival were slim; even if the
surgeons could stitch their slashed organs together and
stanch the bleeding, which was unlikely, the internal infection that inevitably followed would lead to almost
certain death. That did not stop them making valiant
efforts, however, even performing crude emergency
surgery right on the field of battle. But given the conditions Hunter was forced to work under, it was hardly
surprising that 'Such cases will seldom or ever do well.'[17]
In addition to the casualties of the successful assault, there
were still the victims of the earlier attack who were now
carried gingerly ashore and laid on straw mattresses in
their rough shelters.

While Hunter and his colleagues struggled to save who
they could, the army advanced on Le Palais, forcing the
three thousand inhabitants and the troops defending them
to take refuge in the city's fortress, the Citadel, where they
were bombarded mercilessly for six weeks. Now on
standby for further British casualties, Hunter rushed to
the aid of Brigadier Thomas Desaguliers, who was con-
cussed by a bursting shell; he recovered sufficiently for
Hunter to attend him nineteen years later on his
deathbed.[18] Finally, the weakened islanders surrendered.
Their resilience having won them the respect of the British
victors, they were escorted safely to the French mainland.

The long siege had brought the final toll of British killed
or wounded to more than seven hundred – official reports
home rarely bothered to differentiate between the dead
and the nearly dead – but just as the rudimentary
hospitals were overflowing with surgical cases, an out-
break of 'severe fever and flux' now attacked those troops
who had not already been injured by the French artillery.[19]

Having full possession of the island now, the army medical department set up a general hospital in Le Palais itself where both the wounded and the infected were laid side by side on the straw palliasses. Contagious diseases swept through the troops so that the soldiers who survived the primitive operations performed in dirty surroundings frequently succumbed to the sickness raging all around them. In the overcrowded, dirty conditions of typical army camps, where sewage overflowed from pits, linen went unwashed for months and water was rarely clean, infectious diseases such as dysentery, typhus, malaria and smallpox spread out of control. The army physician Richard Brocklesby, who had served in Germany during earlier campaigns, reckoned that typhus – or 'camp fever' – commonly claimed eight times as many lives as enemy action.[20]

Despite the fact that fevers and infections dominated the military sick list, army surgeons always vastly outnumbered army physicians. There was logic in this, since any competent surgeon could liberally dose a soldier with a concoction of the usual ineffective medications while few physicians knew how to wield an amputation saw, even if they deigned to stoop to such base levels. Only one physician, Edward Blythe, had accompanied the huge expedition to Belle-Ile, and even then he scurried away immediately after the siege despite the sickness being at its height. Meanwhile, half a dozen surgeons laboured together in the general hospital at Le Palais, assisted by twelve nurses and twenty surgeons' mates.[21] The usual strict division of labour was not an option. 'I am obliged to be Physician and everything here,' John Hunter complained to William in one of six letters he sent to his brother from Belle-Ile, adding with typical brio, 'and I think I do as well as the best of them'.[22] Naturally enough, the haughty physicians commanded a significantly higher salary – double the daily rate of ten shillings awarded to army surgeons, who were only on a par with the apothecaries and even had to fork out from their own pockets to purchase medicines and other supplies.[23] Since practice in treating the fevered patients varied little from the standard care back home – letting blood, administering noxious purges or enemas, and prescribing unpalatable medications – differences in outcome were rarely noted. In the absence of any effective antibiotics, and with only the most basic ideas about hygiene, there was little the beleaguered surgeons could do to combat internal diseases apart from doling out the usual remedies and hoping for the best.

Hurrying between the sweating and vomiting soldiers laid out on their foul mattresses as flies buzzed around the wards in the sweltering mid-summer heat, John Hunter could offer his patients no more than the typical contents of the army medicine chest, although he was at least liberal with the opium to relieve the worst of their discomfort while also advocating restraint in bloodletting. When it came to surgery, however, he was not prepared to conform to age-old methods simply through convention. Although he was new to the army, devoid of qualifications and with no previous knowledge of battlefield surgery, it was never in Hunter's temperament meekly to kowtow to authority without demonstrable reason. With the self-confidence that stemmed from his twelve years' investigations of the human body and his experience working with Cheselden and Pott, he developed his own maverick style of treating war wounds which quickly attracted the scornful attention of his colleagues. Writing

home to William in September not long after the successful siege, he told him 'my practice in Gunshot wounds has
been in a great Mesure different from all others, so that I
have had the eyes of all the surgeons upon me, both on
account of my suppos'd knowledge, and method of treatment'. Plainly, his departure from orthodoxy had not won
him friends, judging from his subsequent comment: 'My
fellow creatures of the Hospital are a damn'd disagreeable
set. The two Heads are as unfit for the employment, as the
devil was to reigne in heaven.'[24]

If Hunter's unconventional methods aroused the wrath
of his fellow surgeons, he was simply practising the
scientific approach to surgery he would advocate all his
life. When first the casualties poured in from the initial
failed assault on the island, Hunter had closely observed
his colleagues' treatment of gunshot wounds. Conventional practice dictated that army surgeons open up a
gunshot wound – a technique known as 'dilatation' or
enlargement – prise out the musket ball or shot with
forceps, or more often with their fingers, then clean away
any debris before dressing the wound.[25] The principle of
dilatation stemmed from a belief that gunpowder was
poisonous, dating back to its first use in European warfare
in the thirteenth century. In the sixteenth century the
French army surgeon Ambroise Paré had at least put
a stop to the practice of branding gunshot wounds with a
red-hot iron or scalding oil as a supposed antidote to the
poison, but methods in both British and French armies
had continued relatively unchanged since then.[26]

In theory, and in ideal circumstances, Hunter's
colleagues were right in most cases to excise a missile, and
especially to remove any debris such as timber shards or
fragments of a soldier's filthy clothing embedded in a

wound, in order to prevent sepsis; often it was the debris pulled in by bullets which led to fatal deep-wound infection. In practice, however, since the circumstances they worked in were far from ideal, their doctrine probably increased the death and suffering, as Hunter evidently noted. Not only was the act of incising flesh within a wound exceedingly painful and traumatic before the advent of anaesthesia, causing huge shock and loss of blood, it frequently introduced fatal infection, since the military surgeons often treated their casualties on muddy, manure-ridden battlefields, digging around in their patients' wounds with dirty, blood-smeared knives, forceps and fingers. Surviving surgery was no guarantee of success; often deadly bacteria were passed from bed to bed when pus-soaked dressings were changed. Indeed, cross-infection was so common that surgeons simply regarded it as a normal stage in recovery, or decline.

Ever a passionate believer in the healing powers of nature, and always adamant that surgeons should intervene as little as possible, Hunter realized that conservative treatment – what he called 'being very quiet' – was the most effective remedy for gunshot injuries. Observing that meddling with the wound generally led to a worse outcome than leaving the injury alone, he believed the wounded soldiers and sailors had a better chance of survival by letting nature take its course, even to the extent of leaving bullets embedded permanently in their wounds. In his later *Treatise on the Blood, Inflammation and Gun-shot Wounds*, published thirty years later from notes made on the island, he would explain, 'It is contrary to all the rules of surgery founded on our knowledge of the animal oeconomy to enlarge wounds simply as wounds. No wound, let it be ever so small, should be made larger, excepting when preparatory to something else.'[27] Like his colleagues, he was well aware that infection frequently followed battlefield injuries. But while his contemporaries viewed infection as a necessary, even beneficial, stage in healing, Hunter rightly regarded it as a failure of treatment. 'Suppuration may be considered a resolution but it is a mode of resolution which we mainly wish to avoid,' he would later write.[28] Not until 1867, when Joseph Lister published his successful trials using antiseptics to fight infection, would Hunter's radical view finally be accepted.

Always determined to act on the facts rather than bow to superstition, Hunter soon found the evidence he needed for his controversial beliefs in a chance incident that stands as a prototype controlled experiment. On the day the British landed, five French soldiers had been shot in the exchange of fire but had managed to hide out in an empty farmhouse where they lay low until discovered four days later. One had been hit in the thigh by two musket balls, one of which was still lodged in his thigh bone; a second had been shot in the chest and was spitting blood; the third had been hit in the knee; the fourth had been hit in an arm; and the fifth was only slightly wounded.[29] Neglected through accident rather than design, their injuries had healed significantly better than those of their British counterparts who had been subjected to the surgeon's knife. 'The first four men had nothing done to their Wounds; indeed very little was done to the men themselves; for they lay in an uninhabited house for more than four days, with hardly any subsistance,' Hunter noted. 'The wounds were never dilated, nor were they dressed all this time, excepting once by one of our Surgeons. All of them healed as well, and as soon (if not sooner) as the like accidents do in others who have all the care that possibly can be given of them: indeed they did surprisingly well, for the man that was shot through and through the breast, recovered perfectly: as also did the others.' Further proof of his beliefs arrived in the shape of a British grenadier who had been shot in the arm and taken prisoner by the French during the first attack; he too had received only superficial care. Having escaped a fortnight later, he surprised his surgeons by revealing his wounds healed and his elbow only a little stiff.[30]

While his colleagues dismissed these examples as mere curiosities, Hunter adapted his methods to suit his observations in his first systematic application of scientific evidence to practice. He was not dogmatic. He still advocated opening a wound in certain circumstances – to tie severed arteries or extract pieces of smashed bone, for example – and he adopted this doctrine when treating an officer wounded by a musket ball that shattered his cheek, recording that 'with a pair of small forceps I extracted all I could of the loose pieces of bone'.[31] Despite the infection that inevitably followed, the officer got well. But when a second officer arrived at the hospital with a musket ball lodged in the same place and Hunter perceived no splinters of bone, he recommended leaving the wound to mend of its own accord, noting, 'my advice was complied with, and the wound did well, and rather better than the former, by healing sooner'. Even if his methods were raising eyebrows, he was obviously not being opposed. Hunter's novel ways might be making him enemies, but he had the cool self-assurance, bolstered by his renowned anatomical knowledge, to silence even more experienced surgeons.

Just as he approached gunshot wounds with caution, Hunter advised similar restraint in the army surgeon's other main stock in trade – amputations. Customarily, military surgeons would hack off mangled arms and legs right beside the field of battle, often labouring under fire as they cowered behind a hedge rather than risk causing further damage by moving injured soldiers to a first-aid tent. But Hunter observed of such patients that 'few did well'.[32] This was scarcely surprising considering the trauma such operations involved as well as the desperately unhygienic operating conditions. Even fifty years later, George Guthrie, a surgeon on the Duke of Wellington's campaigns, would graphically describe such a battlefield scene: 'A military surgeon should never be taught to expect any convenience; his field pannicr for a seat for the patient, and a dry piece of ground to spread his dressings and instruments upon, are all that are required.'[33] Having witnessed such brutal and bloody procedures amid the fury of battle at first hand, Hunter declared, 'Nothing can be more improper than this practice, for the following reasons; in such a situation it is almost impossible for a surgeon in many instances to make himself sufficiently master of the case, so as to perform so capital an operation with propriety . . .' Weighing up the outcomes of different practices as usual, he concluded, 'it has been found, I say that few did well who had their limbs cut off on the field of battle; while a much greater proportion have done well, in similar cases, who were allowed to go on till the first inflammation was over, and underwent amputation afterwards'.[34] As a consequence, he recommended delaying surgery until the patient could be transported to more comfortable surroundings and their condition was stable, in order not to 'run the risk of producing death by an operation'.[35] Again his doctrine suited the unsavoury circumstances he worked in; only under more sanitary conditions would early amputations generally increase survival chances. Certainly many soldiers would have been saved from bleeding to death or fatal infection from battlefield amputations at Hunter's hands; some may well not even have needed such drastic surgery in the cold light of day.[36]

Despite Hunter's unorthodox regimens, he won the respect of his superiors. When William Young, the director of the hospitals on Belle-Ile – and with Blythe one of the two heads whom Hunter had deemed 'unfit for employment' – returned to England in early 1762, Hunter was appointed to take his place, becoming chief surgeon and director of all medical operations on the island. Writing with obvious pride to William in March he announced, 'my titles and business are at present many, I am called the Surgeon-general, Deputy Purveyor, and Inspector and Director of the Regimental Hospitals'. And he added, with blatant designs on gaining further advancement, 'I could wish that you would give a hint of this to Mr Adair who I hope is my friend.'[37]

In truth, by this point there was not a great deal of medical care to superintend on Belle-Ile, since Hodgson had departed with many of the troops while most of the soldiers left behind to defend the island had little to do but drink, gamble and guess where they were destined for next. Hunter hoped it would not be the West Indies, as widely rumoured, recalling from his choppy voyage across the Bay of Biscay that 'the Sea plays the Devil with me'.[38] Much preoccupied, as in all his letters, with the state of his earnings – which were being deposited with William in London for safekeeping – he preferred to stay on the island and remain in charge of the hospital. This would guarantee that his daily pay stayed at the double rate of twenty shillings and, equally importantly, would double his half-pay once he returned to civilian life. But since five shillings of his daily rate went to his surgeon's mate, and he had to keep a horse in order to inspect the first-aid camps stationed around the island, he was not much better off in the short term at least.

With his prospects hanging in the balance and talk of a new campaign to Portugal in the air, John petitioned William relentlessly to secure him promotion in his next assignment, wherever that should be. 'There is nothing here talkd of but Portugal,' he wrote home in April 1762. 'Mr Smith our apothecary is appointed as one there; but no accounts of my going. If I am to leave this place I should like to go there, but should chuse to stay here, if an Hospital was to be keept, as I suppose that I shall loose my ten shilling by going (but that as it may be).'[39] Having heard that Young and Blythe were appointed to run medical operations in Portugal, he added, 'God help the Hospital when directed by such two.'

Though Hunter was angling to remain in Belle-Ile, he was also clearly homesick: successive letters implored William to tell him 'how anatomy is to go on this winter' and to send news of Dorothy and her new husband the Reverend James Baillie, who were now living in Scotland. At one point he remarked forlornly, 'we seem to be a people almost distinct from the rest of [the] world'.[40] If William was somewhat tardy in his replies he could perhaps be forgiven, for when Queen Charlotte, the new King's bride, had fallen pregnant at the end of 1761 it was to William that her care had been entrusted. Renowned for his conservative management, William presided over her delivery the following August, waiting decorously in an ante-chamber while a female midwife described the progress of the birth of the new prince, the future George IV. William was made Physician in Extraordinary to Queen Charlotte the following month; he would attend the deliveries of all fifteen of the royal couple's children.[41]

Away from the buzz of royal births and court appointments on his solitary rocky island, John found time after the initial rush of casualties to put down his knife and pick up a pen, not only writing lively letters to William but compiling notes on the soldiers and sailors he had been treating as part of his early case books.[42] Many of them owed him their lives. Thomas Thruber, who had received a four-inch wound in his loins after being stabbed by a bayonet, recovered with no lasting effects after Hunter dressed him with 'Cloths dipped in Vinegar'. Another patient was Lieutenant Robert Home, himself a surgeon with General Burgoyne's regiment of light dragoons, who was treated by Hunter for a swollen eyelid caused by blowing his nose too hard. At first the lieutenant had been seen by another surgeon, who had adopted the inevitable practice of taking large amounts of blood from the officer and had then applied a poultice to his eyelid. Called in for a second opinion three hours later, Hunter characteristically decided to let nature run its course. 'I took off all the applications and desired him to avoid blowing his nose till the swelling could subside, and it got well in a few days,' he noted. Lieutenant Home plainly appreciated Hunter's no-nonsense care, and he liked the intelligent and energetic young surgeon too; he would remember him with particular favour when back in London.

By spring 1762, with many of the troops having left Belle-Ile to pursue British war interests elsewhere, island life slowly began to return to normal; seabirds settled back on their nests in the sheer cliffs, and lizards basked on the rocks edging the white beaches. Effectively a captive on the rugged island, where Alexandre Dumas would later maroon two of his musketeers in *The Man in the Iron Mask*,[43] Hunter spent his leisure hours riding across the moors and clifftops or walking along the shores and creeks, searching for local wildlife. He had already snatched moments between battles to haul fish from the sea and cut open their bellies on deck to test how their blood coagulated. He had also netted conger eels, having seen a 'vast number' in the seas around the island, and dissected them in the forlorn hope of discovering their spawn.[44] During the winter he had captured hibernating lizards and force-fed them with worms and pieces of meat, then sliced them open in an effort to understand how their digestion shut down during their long sleep. At a time when fellow naturalists were still struggling in vain to understand basic principles of life, this suspended animation proved a consuming subject. Hunter would always be keen to explore the boundaries where life seemed to merge with death.

The lizards he kept captive in his quarters offered an even more remarkable peculiarity which Hunter dis-covered to his amazement one day when picking one up by its tail: the tail came off in his fingers and the stumpy creature promptly ran away. He tried the same trick on others and realized their tails were expressly designed to detach at a certain point when caught by predators. 'The separation is so easily effected,' he noted, 'that if a lizard be caught by the tail, it will leave it in your hand by the strength of the animal only.'[45] Watching the severed tail on his temporary dissecting bench he saw that 'the tail continues to move and writhe for some time, and when these motions have ceased, as it were from fatigue, they recommence when the tail is pricked or otherwise irritated'.[46]

With his customary zeal, he began experimenting in earnest on the island's lizard population, catching more reptiles in order to break or cut off their tails, dissecting the animals to discover how their tails became so easily detached, and then pickling some of the mutilated animals in alcohol to take back home. What astounded him even more was that the tails of his amputated lizards regrew; some even generated double tails where the first had broken off. Both these peculiarities would afford him fertile new territories for future research: the ability of lizard tails to regrow would lead him to conduct controversial experiments attempting to stimulate regeneration in humans; the double-tailed lizards provided him with a classic example of nature deviating from the norm which started him pondering on the ways in which organic life might have developed on earth.

John Hunter's peaceful springtime pursuits on Belle-Ile were short-lived, however, for May brought the new orders he had been waiting for: he was bound for Portugal with a contingent of troops sent to defend Britain's oldest ally against its neighbour, Spain, which had just joined the war. In the early summer of 1762, a force of seven thousand soldiers was despatched for Lisbon from Belle-Ile and Ireland under the command of Lord Loudoun, a stalwart of campaigns in North America. Hunter followed with some of the island's remaining troops in July, on board the good ship *Betty* once more, now restocked with fresh supplies from England; with him he brought some of the last casualties as well as the remaining medical team.[47] In a return of the sick, which he sent to Loudoun shortly before leaving, Hunter pronounced seventeen of the soldiers still too ill to leave the island, while fifty-five – variously diagnosed with rheumatism, consumption, lameness, short-sightedness, 'old age' and 'infirmity' – were to be conveyed with him on the *Betty*.[48] The medical team that helped him tend to the patients' needs on the ten-day voyage comprised the apothecary Hugh Smith, four surgeons' mates, one matron and four nurses.[49] Evidently they had some effect, or at least the malingerers were weeded out, for as the *Betty* neared Lisbon Hunter reported that a total of nineteen patients were now sufficiently healthy to take up arms once more, while only fifteen still needed medical care for complaints ranging from venereal disease to a sore foot.[50]

The conditions his patients would discover on arriving at their hospital beds in Lisbon, however, were not conducive to their recovery. The medical staff who had been sent ahead by Loudoun from Portsmouth had already established a 'general hospital' in Lisbon but this grand title hardly described the four assorted buildings – three large houses and a fort – which had been pressed into use for the purpose.[51] The fort was considered 'much the worst Hospital', with its small rooms, situated a quarter of a mile from the other buildings. Already, before hostilities had even commenced, more than two hundred sick soldiers were squeezed into the scattered and inadequate quarters – with ensuing chaos. Weak and wounded as they were, the patients had such little regard for order that regulations were drawn up forbidding them from leaving their hospital beds without permission from the medical staff; the penalty for disobeying orders was to be clapped in irons or slung in the 'black hole' where they would be restricted to a diet of bread and water.[52] Guards even had to be posted at the gates to prevent patients leaving their beds and picking fights with the local inhabitants in the city's 'Tipling houses'.

Arriving in the middle of this administrative nightmare in mid-July, Hunter stepped off the *Betty* with his medicine chest and his stock of bottled lizards confidently expecting to slip into the second most senior position in the medical division. As far as he was concerned, the job of deputy purveyor, second in line to the director of all medical activities in the Portugal campaign, was in the bag, since William, his faithful fixer as usual, had supposedly settled the business in London with the new Secretary of War, Charles Townshend. But in the confusion of wartime communications, news of his appointment had failed to reach Lisbon, as John informed his brother in a long and grumbling letter shortly after his arrival at the end of July.[53]

At first, as he explained, events had seemed to favour him. William Young, who had previously been John's boss as director of the hospital in Belle-Ile, had promised him the position in Portugal. To assist Young, the War Office had appointed two physicians, including Blythe from Belle-Ile, two further surgeons – William Maddox and Francis Tomkins – as well as Hunter, a second apothecary to support Smith, and sixteen hospital mates.[54] In addition, each of the regiments had its own attached surgeons and surgeons' mates, who accompanied them to the front line. And although Hunter had already caused ructions with his unorthodox surgical methods, when he rolled up his sleeves to begin work in the Lisbon hospitals Young immediately welcomed him as his deputy.

At that point, William Maddox stepped smartly forward with a warrant for the same job sanctioned by

Loudoun himself. Hunter was livid; not only would he be effectively demoted from his previous status in Belle-Ile, he would also lose half of the twenty-shilling daily pay to which he had become accustomed. He implored Young and Maddox to sort matters out; generously, both agreed. Young, previously condemned by Hunter as 'unfit for employment' but now his 'stance [staunch] friend', wrote immediately to Loudoun supporting John's case, while Maddox obligingly sent Loudoun a letter giving up his claim to the job on the grounds that it had only been promised to him if Hunter had stayed on Belle-Ile.[55] Even Loudoun appeared content for the post to go to Hunter, although he was clearly reluctant to override any decision that had been taken in London. Urging his brother to dash along to the War Office and confirm his appointment, John ended the letter plaintively: 'I wish I could get it as it makes a vast difference with me here.' But despite William's interest and his colleagues' support, the wrangle was never resolved and ultimately nobody was appointed deputy director. Indeed, while Maddox had to return to England almost immediately to accompany a sick general and Tomkins ingratiated himself sufficiently with his superior officers to bypass most of the action, it was Hunter who was packed off straight away to the front line with thousands of troops heading straight for the Spanish guns.

In the event, there would be scarcely any battle casualties among the British forces in Portugal. The campaign was little more than a side-show at the tail-end of a costly war of which all sides had wearied. The Spanish invaders were always half-hearted about their advance – after all, the Queen of Portugal was the sister of the King of Spain. Consequently, the campaign proved short and relatively painless, involving only two major battles, in August and October, in which Loudoun's redcoats forced the Spanish back across the eastern border. Thereafter activities were focused on maintaining the defence of Portuguese territories against any further incursions.

Although John Hunter worked close to the front line throughout the campaign, he would not, after all, get the chance to practise his novel treatment regimen on a significant number of further battle casualties. His case books record only one patient treated for gunshot wounds in Portugal, a soldier called John Murray who was wounded in the leg by three bullets during the recapture of Valencia de Alcantára in August; Hunter did little for the first two wounds, where the bullets had passed straight through muscle, but he extracted the third musket ball since it had lodged in the soldier's shin bone.[56] For the few other battle casualties he treated he adhered to his customary practice, recording in the case books that he never dilated any gunshot wound in Portugal, 'except I found the Bone injured'.

But the lack of action by no means allowed the surgeons to rest idle; indeed, Hunter and his colleagues were kept far busier in Portugal than ever they had been during the thick of battle on Belle-Ile. There they had only the French artillery to contend with; in Portugal they were swamped by the far more deadly invasion of infectious diseases which spread uncontrollably among the weakened soldiers in the blistering heat and squalid conditions. Marching at the height of summer in temperatures that could reach forty degrees in open countryside, sleeping in makeshift camps without proper sanitary facilities, fresh food or water, and lacking basic medical supplies, the soldiers quickly succumbed to virulent fevers, 'fluxes' (probably dysentery), malaria and other contagious diseases.

The movement of troops towards the front line, which Hunter joined within weeks of arriving in Lisbon, was a classic example. As soon as British forces arrived in Lisbon, Loudoun despatched the regiments up the River Tejo as far as the little port of Muge. From here they had to march the ten miles or so across wild countryside to the hilltop town of Santarèm, a strategic point of defence near the front line. Although the distance was relatively short and the soldiers marched slowly under their heavy burdens, one of the regiments – the Third Regiment of Foot, known as the Buffs – lost eleven men on the gruelling journey, probably from heatstroke. They had set off at 6 a.m., but the sun had quickly become so hot and water so scarce that the men fell down 'choked with heat and dust', according to their commanding officer, Major Biddulph.[57] Continuing their march through deep sand, 'the men fell down sick so fast that there were not sufficient well men left to attend them'. Stopping would have been 'useless and dangerous', explained Biddulph, and he therefore had no option but to urge his men on in the 'burning Sun and Sand' until at last he found a shady olive grove. With half the regiment having fallen by the wayside, Biddulph sent an officer on horseback to drive the stragglers forward, and the troops finally arrived at the bottom of the hill leading up to the town. Biddulph later reported, 'It was with difficulty the men got up a steep hill that leads into the higher town of Santarem – Having marched thro' the upper town, on the hill that overlooks the lower town seven men died. One died on the Parade immediately after we came in and 3 died behind among the Sands above mentioned. In all Eleven.'

Whether Hunter accompanied the Buffs on their disastrous march is unknown; their own regimental surgeon, Peter Bernard, later blamed the death toll on the 'extreme heat of the weather'.[58] But Hunter was certainly with the regiment shortly after, for it was he who pronounced Bernard himself unfit to continue duty, recommending that he return home to England, after he had fallen violently ill with a fever within days of their hard march.[59]

There was to be no such reprieve for Hunter, however. Barely given time to rest at Santarèm, where the army established a second 'general hospital' in August, Hunter was given the job of setting up 'flying hospitals' close to the front line to receive the worst of the sick and wounded sent back from the fighting by the regimental surgeons. Essentially very basic emergency posts, the flying hospitals were set up in requisitioned houses and farm buildings and staffed by battalion surgeons and surgeons' mates, who tended the men as best they could before sending them on again, usually by boat down-river, to the general hospitals at Santarèm or Lisbon. The hospital conditions Hunter encountered when first he stopped at Santarèm were bad enough. His colleague, the apothecary Hugh Smith, reported that ninety-three invalids were being nursed in one cramped building with 'very near half' of the patients lying on bare ground.[60] By the end of August a further two buildings had been sequestered in Santarèm, but patient numbers had now swelled to four hundred and the desperately sick soldiers were still without mattresses.[61]

If conditions for the soldiers in the general hospitals were barely sufferable, life for their miserable fellows in the flying hospitals was worse. Housed in tumbledown farmhouses and outbuildings, they lacked sufficient food or medical supplies, let alone clean straw for bedding. Riding or travelling by carriage large distances cross-country between these scattered hovels, it was Hunter's task to supervise the mates, report on the sick and attempt to wheedle supplies from the inhospitable locals. This was no easy task, as one of the military surgeons revealed when he complained that 'This morning I sent a corporal and two men . . . to get sheep for the sick, instead of getting them he was threatened by the peasants and a Portuguese Dragoon would have killed him if he had not had a stick to defend himself.'[62] Faced with similar obstacles, Hunter appealed to his superiors for mules and horses 'to transport our Mates, medicines, and Instruments', pointing out that 'many of them have fallen sick from the Fatigue and want of these Conveniencys, as also many of the Medicines and Instruments have been obliged to be left behind'.[63]

The labour was relentless. At the end of August, Hunter was despatched to Tancos, a small settlement close to the defence line, where 130 desperately ill men were squeezed into quarters which the mates sent 'a very bad account of', according to Young.[64] But almost immediately, with further action feared at any moment, he was ordered to 'break up the hospital' at Tancos and send its invalids down-river to Santarèm, then to join the front-line troops to help the beleaguered regimental surgeons. By the time the evacuated patients arrived at Santarèm it was scarcely surprising that, as Young reported, several were 'brought just dead out of the boats'.[65] Struggling to cope with almost seven hundred diseased and delirious soldiers in accommodation considered adequate for four hundred, Young was unable to spare any of his four mates to help Hunter near the front.

As fevers raged through the troops in September, even the medical staff were being struck down. Back in Lisbon, one of the army physicians and one of the three mates were sick, in Santarèm a mate was dangerously ill, while Hunter himself, exhausted from his travels and labour, was in danger of joining the sick list.[66] Stuck at the village of Tomar in early September waiting for a carriage to take him northwards, he had written to Young, who promptly relayed to Loudoun, 'He does not downright say he is sick but that he is allmost knock'd up. He has had much to do. He says he is stopp'd at Tomar for want of a Carriage, but hopes to set out soon.'[67]

The carriage eventually arrived and Hunter pressed on regardless, for ten days later he was writing to Loudoun himself from the city of Coimbra, a further forty-five miles north, where troops were defending a bridge securing lines of communication upcountry. It was at Coimbra, while receiving and evacuating the sick, that Hunter showed he was no easy push-over for the troops. One soldier with General Lambert's regiment had recovered from a fever and was 'got pretty strong' but mysteriously developed a sudden attack of bleeding from his mouth and nose. Various remedies failed to stem the unexplained complaint until finally Hunter discovered a leech, probably filched from the medicine chest, at the back of the soldier's throat. He noted in his case books, 'at last a leech came into the fauces [back of the mouth], which he spit out, which immediately shewed us the cause of the bleeding'.[68] He added, 'All the time of the disease I suspected some trick, and ordered some persons to watch him; for it is very common for Soldiers to try schemes to avoid duty.'

By October hostilities were all but over and heavy rains drove the Spanish back across their border, yet the sick troops continued to flood in unabated to the flying hospitals and Hunter was allowed no rest. Having returned southwards, he recorded sixty-seven patients at one base in early October; three days later he sent a scrap of paper – even paper was in short supply – recording forty-five invalids at another hospital only a few miles away.[69] Even his fellow surgeon Francis Tomkins, who had kept well away from the line of fire treating the least sick patients at Lisbon for most of the campaign, was now sent to the front to help Hunter manage the flying hospitals; they wrote together from one of the bases in October. But the trials of tending the sick and dying without respite for so long had taken its toll on the medical staff: one hospital mate died at the end of September, while William Cadogan, the physician who had been ailing at Lisbon since the start of the campaign, appealed in October for leave to return home.[70]

It was the chance Hunter had been waiting for. Still disappointed in his campaign for the deputy directorship, he now set his sights on the post of physician, a promotion that would have afforded him an important hike up the medical hierarchy on his return home. Never one to hide his light under a bushel, he wrote to Loudoun to push his claim, arguing that he had worked in the medical division longer than any of the other surgeons – although in truth Tomkins had ten years' more experience with the army – and urged that 'my education in Phisick', by which he meant lack of education, should 'be no objection to me'.[71] In November he wrote excitedly to William, 'I am now applying for Phisician, if I get that I shall be a Dr. as well as the best of you.'[72] However, Loudoun could ill afford to lose a capable surgeon and instead the post went to a qualified physician who had accompanied Loudoun on previous campaigns, sent out for the purpose from England.

By now thoroughly fed up with his Herculean labours for scant reward, Hunter was desperate to return home himself. On hearing from William that he planned to restart his anatomy lectures that autumn after a break of two years, he wrote, 'Nothing could give me more pleasure than seeing your advertisement in the papers, excepting a peace.' Given such intolerable working conditions, and the relentless hours the surgeons were forced to endure, it was hardly surprising that sometimes tempers, as well as health, suffered. Hunter could be brusque with people who crossed him at the best of times and he was plainly uncompromising over his controversial methods. So when rows flared up between him and his fellow surgeon Tomkins it might be easy to blame the disputes on Hunter and his fiery temper. According to the mischievous Jessé Foot, Hunter provoked Tomkins to such an extent that the older and more experienced surgeon at one point drew his sword on him. No sooner had Hunter arrived in Portugal, Foot claimed, than he 'excited an uneasiness among the faculty, which their situations had never experienced before'.[73]

Yet Foot had plainly gleaned his version of events wholesale from Tomkins himself, since he proposed that anyone doubting the facts should visit the 'manly veteran' at his London home to verify the story. In all likelihood it was Tomkins, not Hunter, who played the aggressor in the army disputes. Having joined the army initially in 1751 as a regimental surgeon, probably with little practical experience, Tomkins had quarrelled with almost all of the medical staff in Portugal.[74] And far from being the protagonist, Hunter had been requested by Loudoun to step in and smooth over one of these rows. The incident occurred in early November, long after the fighting had died down, when Tomkins imprisoned Samuel Hayes, a surgeon's mate stationed at a flying hospital near the frontier, in his own room for three days on the charge of incorrectly dispensing some drugs. Hunter, who witnessed the incident, was promptly asked by Loudoun to set Hayes free. Later writing to Loudoun to explain the circumstances, Hayes maintained that his real crime had been to criticize Tomkins for stealing Hayes' bedding. Indignant at this complaint, Tomkins had flown 'into a great passion' and threatened to knock him down with 'a Quart Bottle from the Table'. According to Hayes, Tomkins 'had quarrell'd in almost the same manner with the whole Hospital, viz, Dr Cadogan, the two Apothecarys, Mr Hamilton and Mr Smith, and since he joyned the Army with Mr. Hunter very seriously several times'.[75]

Presumably one of these times was the occasion on which Tomkins pulled his sword on Hunter. Seemingly, Hunter had accused Tomkins of cowardice – probably the most serious charge a fellow officer could level against another – for having wheedled his way into remaining in Lisbon, as far from enemy action as possible, for most of the campaign while Hunter had been criss-crossing the unfriendly countryside near the front line in a super-human effort to manage the flying hospitals. Tomkins himself referred to 'Hunters Differences and mine' in a letter to a superior officer in December, saying that 'it only proceeded from a jealousy of my having made interest with his Lordship to stay behind; which upon my honour I never did and that you well know'. Yet this is exactly what Tomkins had done in another letter only the previous day to the same officer, with whom he was plainly chummy, when he had written, 'I would willingly, between friends, when I evacuate this hospital to get to Lisbon if it was possible at least I should be sorry to be ordered to joyn the army at this time, that I might not run the risk to be left behind with the sick at Portallegre or some cursed place among these Portuguese.'[76] At the very moment that Tomkins was attempting to save his own hide, Hunter was busy at Portalegre, near the Spanish border, treating the sick for whom Tomkins plainly had such little regard.

But if hostilities within the army's medical ranks were intense, at least the opposing nations had mended their differences. A truce was agreed between Britain and Spain in November, precursory to the Peace of Paris treaty which ultimately brought the Seven Years War to an end in February 1763. Under the agreement, Belle-Ile, which had been taken with such audacity and loss of life, was summarily handed back to France in exchange for Minorca. All that remained for the surgeons and their mates to do now was to evacuate the casualties in the front-line camps and the flying hospitals back to Lisbon and finally home. But given the considerable number and poor condition of many of the troops, along with the scarcity of transport, that process took many more months. By December there were still five hundred patients needing medical care at the hospital in Santarèm, and in January Hunter appealed for eighteen carts to transport eighty-four patients from three outlying hospitals. It was February, just days prior to the final treaty's declaration, before he managed to return to Lisbon.[77] He had been living on his wits, and variable army supplies, for more than six months.

As army activities finally wound down, there was at last time for Hunter to pursue his more abiding love – investigating the natural history of his adopted home. During his previous short stay in Lisbon, when he was barracked at the home of a local aristocrat, he had conducted an ingenious experiment to test whether fish could hear. Hunter had already discovered the inner organs of hearing in fish, which he had dissected and injected in Covent Garden, but their existence would still be disputed for many more years by fellow anatomists. Spotting an ornamental fish pond on the Lisbon estate where he was staying he persuaded his host to allow him to perform an experiment to demonstrate his earlier discovery. 'Whilst I lay on the bank observing the fish swimming about, I desired a gentleman who was with me to take a loaded gun and fire it from behind the bushes,' Hunter recorded. 'The moment the report was made the fish seemed to be all of one mind, for they vanished instantaneously, raising a cloud of mud from the bottom. In about five minutes afterwards they began to reappear, and were seen swimming about as before.'[78] With his usual tardiness, it would be twenty years before he reported his findings to the Royal Society, by which time a rival, the Dutch anatomist Peter Camper, had published the discovery.

Now at the end of the campaign, winding down the work of the scattered flying hospitals, he had time to stand back and survey the austerely beautiful landscape of the region he had traversed so many times. He captured more lizards for his growing collection, and he probably watched the eagles, vultures and kites soaring above the São Memede mountains along the frontier too. But when he stood on the edge of the vast Alentejo Plain, looking south as far as the eye could see across the expanse of open countryside studded with cork trees, olive groves and hilltop villages, he began to entertain thoughts that would one day lead him into territory almost as dangerous as his wartime escapades.

His strict religious education at the village school run by the Scottish Kirk would have taught him unequivocally not only that the world had been created by God in six days, but that its major geological features had been shaped by the great flood of Noah's time. But refusal to accept authorized beliefs was a way of life to Hunter: he had disputed the findings of fellow anatomists in London, he had challenged the accepted doctrines of his fellow surgeons in Belle-Ile, and now he stood in southern Portugal and dared to question the orthodoxy of the Church. Quite simply he could not accept that such an enormous plain had been created by a single flood lasting forty days; only an immense period of erosion by the sea could have produced such an expanse, he concluded.[79] The sight of peculiar natural stone structures, like 'inverted pyramids', convinced him the sea had not only covered the area for a long period of time, sufficient to wash away the lower strata of the stone columns, but had afterwards 'left it gradually'. Similarly heretical views had been expounded by Robert Hooke, the remarkable seventeenth-century scientist, but they had since been conveniently forgotten. For the time being Hunter kept his views to himself. It would be nearly thirty years before he committed his thoughts to paper.

Back in Lisbon by February 1763, Hunter wrote happily to William that he was at last acting as deputy director, although in reality this mattered little since officially no more appointments were being made.[80] Having briskly discharged most of the remaining troops left in the Lisbon general hospital, he was finally able to return home, with the remainder of the forces, in April. When he unloaded his army trunk onto the quay at Portsmouth, it contained more than two hundred specimens he had lovingly preserved from the ravages of war and continental heat during his two years' absence; army lifestyle had at least supplied the plentiful quantities of alcohol he needed for pickling his treasures. As well as fifty specimens of lizards and their tails – including his precious double-tailed lizards – he also repatriated several body parts belonging to unfortunate soldiers who had died during the campaigns. Among them were a shoulder blade, a piece of skull and a thigh bone, all showing the impressions of French musket balls, as well as a section of intestine taken from a soldier who had died in Portugal of dysentery.[81]

Back in his civilian clothes once more, John Hunter set out for London. Like his fellow demobilized army veterans he had no job, no prospects and only his army half-pay on which to survive.

7

The Chimney Sweep's Teeth

'It will be scarcely necessary to observe, that the new teeth should always be perfectly sound, and taken from a mouth which has the appearance of that of a person sound and healthy . . .'

John Hunter[1]

London, spring 1763

When the Norfolk country parson the Reverend James Woodforde passed a miserable night suffering toothache, he knew the consequences would be unpleasant. Developing toothache was no laughing matter in eighteenth-century Britain. As the slave trade brought cheaper sugar imports from the West Indies, and sugar became an inseparable addition to the copious amounts of tea consumed in salons and drawing rooms, wealthy Georgians developed a collective sweet tooth. The results were drastic: many an aristocratic debutante's smile was spoiled by black and rotting stumps, while the pain of tooth decay, abscesses and gum disease spelled misery for young and old alike. Although the young king, George III, surprised royal watchers by displaying a set of teeth that were 'extreamly fine', a more typical example of Georgian dental care could be seen in his financial adviser, the Duke of Newcastle: according to Horace Walpole, the tireless commentator on society, his 'teeth are jumbled out and his mouth tumbled in'.[2] Missing, blackened and diseased teeth were not confined to the upper classes; as a love of all things sweet spread throughout society, so did dental decay.

There was little effective remedy. While some optimists resorted to charms, amulets and far-fetched concoctions, there was often no alternative but to have a decaying tooth removed – usually painfully, ineptly and with much loss of blood. Both physicians and surgeons looked down on tooth-pulling as far beneath their status: the physicians were happy to administer enemas into a patient's backside but not to delve into their foul-breathed mouths, while the surgeons had decreed that alone among surgical acts tooth-drawing could be carried out by barbers. In consequence, most dental work was performed by a motley selection of unqualified and untrained opportunists, not only barbers but itinerant travellers, wig-makers and blacksmiths.[3] While some of the worst charlatans would offer to remove a painful tooth by the point of a sword – often on horseback, which if nothing else afforded them a quick get-away – at least the village blacksmith could fashion a more suitable instrument of torture. And torture it often was, as the Reverend Woodforde attested when he called his local blacksmith to despatch the cause of his agony:

My tooth pained me all night, got up a little after 5 this morning, & sent for one Reeves a man who draws teeth in this parish, and about 7 he came and drew my tooth, but shockingly bad indeed, he broke away a great piece of gum and broke one of the fangs of the tooth, it gave me exquisite pain all the day after, and my Face was swelled prodigiously in the evening and much pain. Very bad and in much pain the whole day long. Gave the old man that drew it however 0. 2. 6. He is too old, I think, to draw teeth, can't see very well.[4]

With blacksmiths and mounted swordsmen competing to mangle tooth-drawing, and scarcely any reputable medical practitioners prepared to take on the challenge, there was plainly room for improvement in dental care.

Returning to London in April 1763 at the age of thirty-five, John Hunter was homeless, jobless and without any obvious prospects. There was no place for him at his brother's anatomy school: William had found a new assistant to help run the lessons, which he had restarted in a warehouse in Piccadilly. And even if John had wanted to return to his fraternal partnership he soon wrecked that chance, quarrelling with William within two months of his return, most probably over the ownership of preparations John had left in his brother's care. The issue would become a perpetual source of friction. Smollett mentioned the row in a letter to William in June 1763, remarking, 'I cannot help expressing an eager Desire that your Brother's future conduct may entitle him to a revival of those favourable Sentiments in you, which he has indiscreetly forfeited.'[5] Although William, who had accrued a sizeable fortune, would help his brother financially several times after his return from the army, this was clearly not going to be one of them.[6] At the same time, John had scant hope of securing a hospital job without the patronage of several worthy governors, and little chance of finding a footing in private practice, since this was dominated by a handful of established surgeons. Struggling to make ends meet on his army half-pay of ten shillings a day and taking lodgings in seedy Covent Garden, he turned to one of the few occupations open to him and teamed up with one of London's best-known dentists, James Spence.[7]

It was a logical move. There was no shortage of wealthy clients requiring the attentions of a surgeon with the anatomical knowledge and skills to extract rotten teeth and treat gum disorders; Hunter could be assured of a steady flow of income. But it was not without its risks, since dentistry was held in singularly low esteem within the medical hierarchy. Hunter's bitter biographer, Jessé Foot, would describe his dalliance in dentistry in ornate detail, precisely because he hoped such an association would bring scorn on Hunter's head. In fact, the alliance Hunter forged with Spence, a fellow Scot, was simply ahead of its time. Attending Spence's premises to offer advice to his clients, Hunter had established nothing less than a modern system of professional consultation. As far as Foot was concerned, such a coalition was entirely disreputable; certainly Hunter's surgical rivals 'were above submitting to consultation with dentists', he sneered.[8]

Yet James Spence was no charlatan, as Foot himself patently knew. Only the year before Hunter returned from his army service, Foot had himself enjoyed Spence's talents. Then an impressionable eighteen-year-old surgeon's apprentice with a painful twinge in a troublesome tooth, Foot had visited the Gray's Inn Road shop in the knowledge that 'There was no one so high in fame for extracting teeth as the elder Spence.'[9] The premises were easily identified, Foot explained, by the painted hand that hung in the window, adorned at the wrist with lace ruffles and holding daintily between thumb and forefinger a large white replica tooth. Venturing inside he was pleasantly surprised, for the shop, which seemed to double as a barber's, was 'exquisitely neat'. 'The barber's blocks were as white as soap-suds could make them,' Foot recalled, 'and the blood basons were as shining as if they had been directly brought home from the scowerers. The teeth exhibited as specimens in the shop, were as white and polished as ivory.' When he met the shop's owner, Foot was even more impressed, recording that 'the civility of Spence was beyond all expression'. Swiftly passing over the 'dreaded process' of having his tooth yanked out, Foot was delighted when Spence refused, as one medical professional to another, to charge him a penny and then invited him into a back room to demonstrate a curious electrical machine that could make figures dance, bells ring and fire gunpowder. Others were equally admiring, for in 1766 Spence would be appointed 'operator for the teeth' to George III. Both his sons followed in their father's footsteps, becoming eminent dentists in their own right.

Given the high esteem in which Spence was obviously held, his popularity with patients and his apparent interest in scientific experimentation, it is easy to imagine how John Hunter was drawn towards an alliance with the plump and jovial dentist in 1763; indeed, Spence was one of the first 'tooth-drawers' in Britain to adopt the modern professional title, which originated from the French. Hunter made only one reference to working with Spence, significantly commenting on his professional amenability with the remark, 'he is the only operator I ever knew who would submit to be instructed, or even allow an equal in knowledge; and I must do the same justice to both his sons'.[10] And in the spirit of equals, Hunter worked profitably alongside the Spence family for at least five years, advising on every aspect of dental treatment.

The collaboration enabled him to put into practice the comprehensive knowledge of the human skull and jaws he had acquired from studying dead bodies in Covent Garden, as well as to draw on his more recent experience of treatment in the army. In addition to offering his expert opinion on extractions – and quite probably, since Hunter was known for his muscular strength, lending a judicious hand with a problematic molar – he also advised on inserting fillings, made of gold or lead, as well as scaling, filing, cleaning and treating gum disease. Children were frequent visitors to the joint practice. Unusually conforming to prevailing doctrine, Hunter recommended cutting through teething babies' gums with a blunted lancet to allow first teeth to emerge. Should the gums regrow, as they frequently did, the answer was to repeat the procedure on the howling infants, as Hunter later recorded: 'I have performed the operation above ten times upon the same teeth'.[11]

While the chief motive for Hunter's union with the Spences must have been financial, he treated his excursion into dentistry as he approached all experiences in medicine – with rigorous investigation in an attempt to improve understanding and practice. His surgical experience in the army was fresh in his mind, yet it was another memory from his service years which haunted him as he helped the Spences wrench out rotten teeth from fetid gums. While examining the extracted teeth with their long single or double roots, commonly known as 'fangs', his thoughts returned to his experiments on lizards in Belle-Ile and their strange ability to regenerate their tails. He had observed the same tendency in other animal tissue and had become fascinated by the ability of skin and bone to mend and grow. Determined to investigate further, he conducted a series of bizarre grafting experiments on living animals. First he cut off the spur from the foot of a cockerel and fixed it into the fowl's comb, where it appeared to continue growing. This, he noted, was 'an old and well-known experiment'.[12] Next he removed one of the testes from a rooster and implanted it in the bird's belly; it too seemed to flourish. In a variation on the same theme, he then transplanted the testis of another cockerel into the belly of a hen, with seemingly similar results.

Encouraged by his success so far, he now found a human volunteer – probably one of Georgian London's ubiquitous down-and-outs – who agreed to have a healthy tooth extracted, presumably for a generous fee. This Hunter transplanted into a cockerel's comb, as he excitedly recorded:

I took a sound tooth from a person's head; then made a pretty deep wound with a lancet into the thick part of a cock's comb, and pressed the fang of the tooth into this wound, and fastened it with threads passed through other parts of the comb. The cock was killed some months after, and I injected the head with a very minute injection; the comb was then taken off and put into a weak acid, and the tooth being softened by this means, I slit the comb and tooth into two halves, in the long direction of the tooth. I found the vessels of the tooth well injected, and also observed that the external surface of the tooth adhered everywhere to the comb by vessels, similar to the union of a tooth with the gum and sockets.

The carefully bisected specimen would become one of his most prized preparations. The specimen remains to this day in his museum – half a perfect canine tooth sticking incongruously out of a scarlet cockerel's comb.[13]

But although the tooth was indeed firmly fixed and seemed to be growing, it had not in reality bonded with the cock's comb, as he believed. In fact the tooth was dead – there was no connection of blood supply – and he admitted that other attempts failed, noting, 'I succeeded but once out of a great number of trials.'[14] By contrast, however, the testicle he had transferred to the hen's belly appeared to have been accepted, in a remarkable early organ transplant, and had even acquired blood vessels. Possibly the donated testicle was not rejected – as would be expected without modern medicines to encourage acceptance – because the hen and cockerel were closely matched genetically through inbreeding.[15]

Hunter evidently repeated his strange transplantation experiments, and others in a similar vein, on numerous occasions. Only a few years after he began his alliance with the Spences, a former pupil from his Covent Garden years wrote to a fellow ex-classmate to report 'many surprising things' being performed by their former tutor.[16] 'The cutting of spurs from the heel of a cock and making them grow in his head, J. Hunter has often performed and has such cocks at present,' wrote the incredulous ex-pupil, after spending the best part of a fortnight with Hunter. After describing Hunter's bizarre domestic flock, he went on to report that the surgeon planned the next day to perform a new experiment before 'several gentlemen' which would entail grafting a cow's horn onto the forehead of an ass.

Whether or not the horn grew on the donkey's head is unrecorded, but the early success of the testis implanting experiment and the apparent success of the tooth grafting soon prompted Hunter to attempt further transplanting trials, this time from human to human. By now he was convinced it was perfectly possible to transplant living human teeth. Already it was commonplace to buy false teeth in order to fill unsightly gaps – Samuel Pepys' wife Elizabeth had some teeth 'new done' as early as 1664 – but it was in the eighteenth century, as decay spread and vanity soared, that the market in replacement teeth really boomed.[17] Artificial teeth, fashioned from elephant or hippopotamus ivory, were widely advertised in newspapers but were usually expensive and ill-fitting. An alternative, cheaper and more lifelike, were real human teeth pulled from dead bodies, either from cadavers stolen from graves or from the corpses of soldiers killed on the battlefield. But these were not to everyone's taste, as one dentist noted when remarking that he rarely implanted human teeth 'because most people have a dread of teeth which have been obtained from a corpse'.[18]

There had already been attempts to transplant living human teeth from one person to another but these had rarely proved successful; most practitioners had simply abandoned the practice. Ambroise Paré, the French army surgeon, recorded one of the earliest known efforts in 1562, when a wealthy woman had a tooth extracted and replaced by another supplied by one of her ladies in waiting.[19] In a similar exchange, a French surgeon, Pierre Fauchard, reported the case in 1728 of an army captain who received a tooth pulled from a soldier in his company. By the middle of the eighteenth century tooth transplantation was being regularly performed in Paris by another dentist using young boys as his donors.[20] In Britain, too, transplantation was available before Hunter's time; it was regarded as commonplace in York in the late seventeenth century and was advertised in Norwich in 1762, a year before Hunter's return to England. Yet concerns about safety, efficacy and, for some at least, morality remained. It was Hunter, from 1763 onwards, who rejuvenated, popularized and legitimized tooth transplantation in Britain, initiating a fashion that would last well into the next century.

For Hunter, the principle of tooth transplantation presented an irresistible scientific challenge. It was the propensity of living tissue to grow, mend and adapt which fascinated him, for this was a key part of the puzzle of organic life, and regardless of ethical considerations he was determined to investigate this new possibility. Teeth mystified him, though: hard like bone, they did not continue to grow once erupted and his strenuous efforts to inject them failed to find any blood supply; in this case his instruments were simply too crude to trace the blood vessels and nerves in the living pulp. Still, he was certain that teeth possessed what he termed a 'living principle' – an ability to form and grow. The animal freaks he had created convinced him that successful tissue grafting was perfectly practical – indeed, he may have been the first to coin the term 'transplant' – and eager to put research into practice as always he set out to demonstrate the phenomenon on humans.

Advertising for donors, he soon attracted queues of impoverished girls and boys clamouring to earn a few pennies in return for their healthy teeth. While his well-to-do paying customers waited expectantly in a comfortable chair, Hunter yanked out a healthy front tooth from one of his ragged donors and promptly implanted it in the gaping mouth of his patient. Deftly he tied the new implant to its neighbours with silk thread, or sometimes seaweed, and the gappy youngsters were sent away with mouths bleeding and fingers clasped around their meagre earnings. Later describing the process, he recommended lining up several potential donors at once, remarking, 'The best remedy is to have several people ready whose teeth in appearance are fit, for if the first will not answer, the second may.'[21] Only the front teeth could be transplanted, since the double roots of molars made the procedure problematic, he explained, and the donors should be young and preferably female since their teeth were generally smaller. The operation should be performed as quickly as possible 'as delay will perpetually lessen the power upon which the union of the two parts depends', and he also recommended that the young female donors be inspected for signs of ill health.

How often Hunter performed live tooth transplants is unknown. He would refer to conducting the procedure only on a handful of occasions, although his involvement is described in case studies by others. Later writers would credit him with pioneering the operation – which he plainly did not – and suggested he performed it 'very frequently'; one early nineteenth-century editor described tooth transplanting as Hunter's 'favourite operation'.[22] But whether or not he practised the technique with regularity, Hunter certainly endowed tooth transplanting with a rationale and a scientific seal of approval which launched a veritable craze. The procedure was quickly adopted by other dentists in London and spread elsewhere until it reached a peak in the 1780s.

The operation was prohibitively expensive: one West End dentist would charge five guineas – almost the annual wages of a housemaid – to transplant a single live tooth at the height of the procedure's popularity.[23] And the transaction was always a one-way exchange within the social hierarchy, as a female dentist in York made abundantly clear when she offered to 'transplant teeth from the front jaws of poor lads into the heads of any Lady or Gentleman without putting both patients to any anguish'.[24] The artist Thomas Rowlandson made no bones about depicting such deplorable exploitation of poverty, as well as the anguish both parties plainly suffered, in his satirical painting *Transplanting of Teeth*, published in 1790.[25] The fashionable practitioner shown pulling a front tooth from the mouth of a grubby young chimney sweep could easily have been Hunter; in fact it is based on an Italian-born dentist, Bartholomew Ruspini, a disciple of Hunter's who practised in England from the 1750s onwards.[26] Yet despite some unease over the ethics of the operation towards the end of the century, transplanting continued to flourish, spreading across Europe and even to America. One New York dentist was prepared to pay as much as five guineas in 1782 for healthy front teeth – 'slaves teeth excepted'.[27] A young and impoverished Emma Hart, who became better known as Lady Hamilton, almost forfeited her renowned beauty – and quite possibly her future relationship with Lord Nelson – when tempted to sell her front teeth during the same period in London. On her way to the dentist a friend persuaded her to preserve her smile.[28]

Although transplantation became widely accepted, in

common with the general exploitation of the have-nots for the benefit of the haves in the eighteenth-century world, there were nevertheless isolated voices raised in protest within the profession. Thomas Berdmore, who was appointed George III's dentist in 1766 along with Hunter's partner James Spence, denounced the procedure in a treatise on teeth two years later. Not only was the operation 'precarious, ineffectual, and dangerous in general' it was also 'immoderately expensive', he argued, 'for it is not to be supposed that any young person will sell a handsome sound Tooth, to be torn out of his head, without being extremely well paid for his loss and pain'.[29] William Rae, another Scot who moved to London to practise dentistry in the 1770s, was an even more ardent critic, despite having been a pupil and remaining a close friend of John Hunter. Giving the first ever series of lectures on dental surgery in 1780, actually at Hunter's suggestion, he insisted that tooth transplanting was both unsuccessful and immoral. 'In the first place,' he warned, 'it is cruel to take the teeth of a poor creature, whose necessities may induce him to part with it as a means of procuring subsistence; and, in the second place, we are obliged to take them from poor people, who are very often diseased, and generally with the *lues venerea*.'[30] Although Hunter insisted that the lues venerea – syphilis – was not passed on through tooth transplants, Rae was invited to give his next series of lectures at Hunter's own lecture rooms. Hunter not only allowed but welcomed dissent from those whose opinions he respected.

Ultimately, however, the transplantation of live teeth would fall into disrepute. Although transplanted teeth could adhere for several years – one of Hunter's patients attested he had received three which stayed firm for six years – they never bonded permanently and could certainly pass on disease. Even Hunter's confidence was shaken when a wealthy female patient developed signs of venereal disease after he had given her teeth from a young donor. Explaining the case in 1771 to William Cullen, by then a professor at Edinburgh University, Hunter maintained that 'the girl from whom the teeth were taken had all the appearance of a sound person', but acknowledged that the recipient's own physician had confirmed his patient had contracted syphilis.[31] Despite the concerns, the operation would only finally be abandoned when aesthetically acceptable false teeth, fashioned from porcelain, appeared on the market in the early nineteenth century.

Although clinically a failure as far as teeth were concerned, the transplantation methods Hunter recommended laid down sound principles that would remain relevant in future human organ transplants. He had clearly understood the need for donor tissue to be as fresh as possible and was careful to match for size – both key factors in later transplants.[32] However, he had no notion of the need to match blood types or of the body's natural rejection, today countered through drugs, and he was obviously unconvinced that donor tissue could transfer disease. Although finally his tooth transplants were discredited, he remained fixated by the idea of regeneration, convinced that living tissue possessed an innate tendency to grow and unite. This notion – his 'living principle' – would continue to preoccupy him as a fundamental area of research.

Working with the Spences in the ignominious field of dentistry in the 1760s prompted Hunter to produce his first major work of research – a treatise on the teeth and jaws which he would publish in two parts in 1771 and 1778, *The Natural History of the Human Teeth* and *A Practical Treatise on the Diseases of the Teeth*.[33] For this he drew on the extensive study of human skulls, jaws and teeth he had conducted in the Covent Garden anatomy school – most of his observations had been made prior to 1755, he noted – and added the fruits of his experience as a consultant with the Spences, including his controversial advice on transplantation. The treatise aroused international interest and helped establish dentistry as a respectable profession in its own right. At a time when dental practice was so little regarded, scant attention had been paid by serious researchers to the topic; although Berdmore had published his own treatise in 1768, this was essentially a practical manual for dental practitioners. Hunter's work, by contrast, was the first to consider the teeth in a truly scientific manner, describing in detail the anatomy and physiology of the teeth and jaws. It would be considered one of the most important books in the history of dentistry.

At the same time, Hunter's steadily rising reputation for accuracy and sound judgement gave dentistry a major boost in status. His comprehensive descriptions of the anatomy of the teeth, facial muscles and bones of the jaws, with sixteen exquisite drawings by van Rymsdyk, are considered remarkable for their accuracy even today; some later practitioners would regard him as the father of scientific dentistry. Inevitably, he made errors: his reliance on stolen bodies misled him over the ages at which adult teeth emerged, and he was plainly misguided over the feasibility – and ethics – of transplanting live teeth. Yet he lucidly described several dental disorders, recognized the destructive nature of plaque and recommended its removal by cleaning or brushing, professed the benefits of eating fruits and salads, and gave teeth the names by which they are generally known today. Previously, teeth were known as incisors, canines and molars; Hunter established four classes of teeth – incisors, cuspids (canines), bicuspids (premolars) and molars – which were soon adopted and, although later superseded in Britain, remain the standard terms used by dentists in America.[34] Not surprisingly, his work rapidly became a bestseller, going through fifteen editions, including one in America, and translations into French, German, Dutch and Italian.[35]

The truanting schoolboy who had proved incapable of reading or writing until long after his classmates had apparently found his literary talent at last – or perhaps not. Jessé Foot was certainly incredulous. 'John Hunter never was the author of any production which has appeared under his name,' he alleged.[36] He maintained that Smollett had written Hunter's earliest publications, and possibly later works too. Yet Smollett left England for Europe in 1763 and although he returned briefly he moved permanently to Italy in 1768.[37] More believably, perhaps, another well-known Grub Street writer has been credited with helping Hunter shape his inexpert writing. William Combe, a young journalist struggling to make his name in London in the mid-eighteenth century, would later claim to have been the ghost writer of Hunter's treatise on teeth. According to an early nineteenth-century anecdote, the author who later found fame for his satirical poem *Dr Syntax's Three Tours*, claimed, 'Nay, John Hunter was the worst writer that ever took a pen in hand. I wrote his essay on the teeth for him, and it was a hard job too: for not only could I not understand him, but he evidently did not comprehend his own meaning. It was an Herculean labour to him to compose a sentence, and a week's work to make it intelligible and yet he was a most extraordinary man, and the most labourious one I ever knew.'[38] Perhaps the youthful creator of Dr Syntax did polish Hunter's 'Teeth', as he liked to called the treatise, although none of the handwriting on the original draft can be positively identified as Combe's. Indeed, the writer had a colourful reputation for invention.

There is no doubt, however, that Hunter did find putting his thoughts onto paper irksome and difficult. His writing, in letters and manuscripts, was not only erratic but sometimes hard to comprehend, and some of his pupils would later complain that his lectures were muddled and unclear. Yet often his obscurity was only because he was groping in the dark towards new ideas and theories; at times the terms to describe his far-sighted and visionary beliefs simply did not yet exist. Hunter was attempting to unravel the mysteries of organic life in an era long before an understanding of cell biology, immunology and evolutionary theory; often he was so far ahead of his contemporaries as to be dismissed as rambling and incoherent. Yet despite his obvious struggles he never shrank from writing, churning out vast amounts of manuscripts, letters, case notes and texts, both in his own hand and dictated to various amanuenses throughout his life. And when he did seek help in shaping his thoughts, as he freely admitted doing with his next treatise, it was purely for editing and tidying his grammar.

Despite the disdain some heaped on dentistry, Hunter's work with the Spences, and the treatise on teeth he later published, helped to establish the charismatic surgeon as a rising figure in the harshly competitive London medical world. With his reputation as a skilled anatomist well known, his expertise in surgery gaining respect, and his passion for curious experiments attracting interest, Hunter was fast becoming a familiar personality in medical circles. As well as extracting and transplanting teeth, he began to build up a small clientele of patients referred for other surgical problems – his spell as an army surgeon had given him an automatic right to practise on his return to civilian life – and he seemingly taught students at private classes in anatomy and surgery to eke out his income.[39] Although his blunt manners and refusal to conform to social niceties clearly offended some of his more stuffy contemporaries, he won firm friends and loyal supporters among other prominent surgeons and physicians, who were impressed by his immense energy, breadth of interest and ebullient manner.

Fellow enthusiasts in natural philosophy – as scientific studies were generally known – flocked to collaborate with him; life with John Hunter was nothing if not exciting. Whenever it became known on the medical grapevine that Hunter was planning to conduct a post-mortem or to attempt a new experiment, he attracted an audience of rapt medical men. Gradually, he was becoming a key figure in a small but growing band of professionals and amateur enthusiasts committed to pushing forward scientific boundaries. Many of these people were members of the Royal Society, Britain's most prestigious body devoted to scientific investigation. Founded in 1660, the society had been established under the auspices of Charles II with the help of such luminaries as Robert Boyle, Robert Hooke and Christopher Wren. By the mid-eighteenth century it had flourished into an eclectic grouping of professionals in a variety of fields liberally mixed with well-to-do and often aristocratic gentlemen professing a passing interest in experimental science; they met weekly to exchange ideas and published their findings in the *Philosophical Transactions*. Although he had not yet published sufficiently to warrant membership of this exclusive gathering, Hunter was nevertheless being fêted by some of its most illustrious fellows – and invited to play a prominent role in some of their more unusual occasions.

One such event took place on 16 December 1763 when a band of about half a dozen men assembled at the house of a Royal Society fellow, John Hadley.[40] Among the guests were John and William Hunter; whatever the nature of their row in the summer, the rift had plainly been mended. By the light of candles the men gathered round a wooden casket laid on the table. Inside it was an Egyptian mummy that had been gathering dust in the Royal Society's collection of curios for several decades. Working side by side as they had in Covent Garden, John and William carefully peeled away the layers of rotten brown linen covering the thin body. As the spectators peered forward to catch a first glimpse of the royal personage wrapped up thousands of years earlier, a murmur of disappointment must have rippled around the room. All that remained were shrivelled, brown bones, some of these even crumbled to dust, with the exception of the left foot where 'The toes being carefully laid bare, the nails were found perfect upon them all; some of them retaining a reddish hue, as if they had been painted.' Even the prints on the big toe could plainly be seen, and they were carefully reproduced in a sketch presented with notes of the findings to the next meeting of the Royal Society.

As the cold, dark days continued and Londoners shivered – only the previous winter the Thames had frozen over – Hunter was in his element: it was perfect dissection weather. After his army break from regular anatomy, he returned to his dissecting bench with gusto, and throughout the winter of 1763–4 he recorded in his case books details of numerous dissections. Some of the circumstances are vague: though he repeatedly refers to 'the dissecting room' it is not clear where this room was located in the early years after his return to civilian life. He may have set up dissecting facilities in his Covent Garden lodgings, or he could have used William's premises; certainly by autumn 1767 William had moved his lectures to purpose-built premises in Great Windmill Street, where he lived from 1768.[41] Equally, while Hunter's notes frequently refer to 'we', it is not always clear who he was working with, although at least some of these dissections must have been for the benefit of the pupils he had begun teaching. But the similarly vague details about his subjects leaves no doubt about the source of most of the corpses. With bodies still in short supply, the majority were obviously provided by his old friends, the body-snatchers. The lack of names, ages or histories for most of the men, women and children he cut open, and the cursory medical details sometimes recorded, plainly reveal their origins. A typical entry notes: 'In the Dissecting Room 1763/4. A very fat Woman was dissected ... I opened the Skull with a view to demonstrate the Brain, and there I found the cause of the Mortification and Death.' Another entry for the same period reads: 'Winter 1763/4. A Young Boy about four years was dissected.'[42]

So the anonymous corpses of London's poor continued

to find their way to Hunter's dissecting room, but increasingly now they were rubbing shoulders with the rather better-nourished bodies of some of Britain's richest and best-known individuals. Fellow surgeons, and especially physicians, who themselves did not possess the skills or training to conduct anatomy, began to seek out Hunter's expertise to open the bodies of patients who had died in unexplained circumstances. This was a momentous development. Although public dissections of criminals hanged at Tyburn still aroused widespread repulsion, there began a gradual movement towards general acceptance of autopsies conducted in private and with decorum in order to understand the causes of death.

Partly, this trend was prompted by the determination of a few enlightened surgeons and physicians who came to realize the significance of autopsies in determining how a patient had died; rather than simply dismissing all illness as a mysterious imbalance of humours, they grew to appreciate that signs in a body after death could be linked to symptoms in the living. Consequently, they persuaded certain more liberal-minded families to allow post-mortems on relatives who died. The Italian anatomist Giovanni Battista Morgagni had professed the importance of autopsy examinations when he published in 1761 the findings of some seven hundred post-mortems which demonstrated how certain diseases could be traced in organs after death; plainly at least some conditions had specific causes that might one day even be prevented.[43] This was a crucial first step towards a search for effective remedies for different diseases, although the real shift towards clinical medicine would not emerge until the following century. Morgagni's work was translated into English in 1769, reinforcing a trend that had been developing independently in Britain. Partly, too, the rise in post-mortems was driven by changing attitudes within society. The Georgians' avid fascination with their health encouraged people to seek answers when their loved ones died; since advancing knowledge in anatomy could sometimes now provide those answers, autopsies gradually became more acceptable. This was self-interest as much as familial concern: knowing the cause of a relative's death might help avert a similar fate for the survivors. Results of post-mortems were often sent to family members and occasionally reported in newspapers.

Since there was nobody in Britain more renowned for anatomical accuracy or who had conducted as many dissections, it was John Hunter who frequently performed the required autopsies. From the time he set up in London as an independent practitioner in 1763, his expertise in conducting post-mortems was in regular demand, and he became the central figure in the gradual acceptance of autopsy investigations. Nobody was more aware of the importance of post-mortems in improving medical care than Hunter. Indeed, when he was refused permission to perform an autopsy by the relative of one patient he had treated, despite his protestations that it would advance medical understanding, he was moved to lash out, 'Then I heartily hope that you yourself and all your family, nay all your friends, may die of the same disease and that no-one may be able to offer any assistance.'[44]

One of the physicians who regularly drew on Hunter's autopsy expertise was Sir John Pringle. Another member of the Scottish diaspora who had settled in London, Pringle was a learned scholar who had studied medicine at Edinburgh and Leiden. Having been appointed physician-in-ordinary to Queen Charlotte in 1761, he was a popular practitioner and a prominent figure in the Royal Society. As a fellow enthusiast for experimental zeal, he had quickly recognized Hunter's aptitude for investigation.

Pringle had first asked Hunter to conduct post-mortems on some of his patients when the young anatomist was working with William in Covent Garden. Possibly the earliest example was in April 1757, when Hunter's case books record that he opened the body of Major-General William Herbert in the presence of Dr Pringle.[45] His examination revealed a large stone in the major's gall bladder. A few years later, on 9 February 1760, Pringle had called on Hunter's skills again to open the body of another patient, a Mrs Johnston.[46] As one of the apparent spoils of his work, Hunter took a piece of the patient's liver home to perform a series of experiments. As he would frequently do from now on, he also kept a portion of Mrs Johnston's liver for his anatomical collection.[47]

Once Hunter had returned from his services to King and country abroad, his services to Pringle began in earnest. When one of Pringle's patients, a Mrs B. Campbell, died in 1763 from 'a very violent Nervous Disorder', Hunter was called to the house within twenty-four hours of her death to examine the corpse.[48] As rapidly became customary with such events, other interested practitioners were invited along for the show, in this case John's brother William and another physician, Dr George Baker. Hunter's investigations focused on opening Mrs Campbell's skull and dissecting her brain in an effort to find some physical explanation for her mental problems. Despite slicing her brain in two and even inverting the organ, no obvious reason for Mrs Campbell's psychiatric condition or her sudden demise could be found, he noted.

This did not deter Pringle from seeking Hunter's expertise again; indeed, Pringle's messages requesting John's attendance within days of the death of any of his patients only increased. And led by Pringle's example, other eminent physicians called on Hunter's investigative services too. Among his more notorious cases was the autopsy of William Chaworth, who was killed by his cousin, Lord Byron, in an argument in January 1765.[49] Byron, who was the fifth baron and great-uncle of the poet George Byron, had met Chaworth at the Star and Garter tavern in Pall Mall on 26 January. Here they pursued an ongoing petty quarrel over how best to deal with poachers; as the argument became heated they requested an empty room in which to settle their differences. In the scuffle that ensued, the baron stabbed his cousin in the stomach. While Chaworth clung to life, two of the most prominent surgeons of the day were called to the scene in an effort to save him. Neither Robert Adair, the army surgeon, nor Caesar Hawkins, the King's surgeon, could patch up the victim's deep wound and he was eventually carried to his apartments near Piccadilly with little hope of recovery. Hunter was called in the next morning to see the dying man, but it was too late even for his skills to make any difference. Twelve hours later, after 'violent vomitings and retchings', Chaworth expired.

Now Hunter's other expertise was pressed into action. His fellow surgeons asked him to open the body to inspect the site of the wound; perhaps the examination might reveal how death from such an injury could in future be averted. Recording both Chaworth's dying moments and his post-mortem in his case books, Hunter noted that the wound had led to widespread inflammation within the abdomen – much as he would have expected.[50] Given the clear evidence of his cousin's violent death, Byron was convicted of manslaughter before the House of Lords but, as a peer of the realm, escaped punishment with just a fine. The remorse he suffered over the fatal argument prompted him to live the rest of his life in seclusion.

Many of the autopsies Hunter recorded were being performed at the express request of families, anxious like any relative to understand the reasons for the loss of a loved one. One such case was an autopsy on a ten-month-old baby, 'a Son of Mr Abbott's', who had died suddenly from an unknown cause. 'This was the fourth Child that died in that way, and all about that Age,' he wrote in the case books; 'their parents were desirous of knowing if there could be any possible cause for it.'[51] Sadly, he could find no obvious reason to explain to the Abbotts why their son, and his three siblings, had all died before their first birthdays; possibly a congenital defect was the cause. In a similar tragic mission, he performed an autopsy on 'Sir William Lee's Child', an eighteen-month-old girl who died in the throes of a fever and convulsions; the family's physician had blamed her death on teething. He was again unable to confirm the cause of death, which could have been due to any one of the countless infectious diseases circulating in Georgian London, or indeed to the remedies prescribed by the family's physician. The infant had, after all, been dosed with magnesium and crabs' eyes.[52]

Before long, Hunter's popularity at houses of bereavement was bringing in much-needed extra income to supplement his fees from dental consultation and his army half-pay. By 1764 he considered himself sufficiently well off to contemplate getting married. Having taken up an invitation to the home of Lieutenant Robert Home, the former army colleague he had treated on Belle-Ile, he was smitten by the family's eldest daughter, Anne. It was not an obvious match. Well educated, elegant and poised, Anne inhabited a high-society world of fine manners and witty conversation which was largely alien to John.[53] While he had always baulked at books, even despised the written word, she had already shown literary flair and at twenty-two was considered an accomplished poet in the romantic style; some of her first poems would be published in an Edinburgh journal in 1765. Delighting in the company of other female intellectuals such as Elizabeth Montagu, Elizabeth Carter and Mary Delaney, she was numbered among the 'Bluestockings' who met at literary gatherings in emulation of the Parisian-style 'salons' or 'conversaziones' dedicated to the art of sparkling conversation. She was also regarded as some-thing of a beauty. Blonde-haired, blue-eyed Anne was described by one contemporary as 'very handsome, tall, singularly dignified and lady-like in appearance', while another pronounced her 'a very pretty woman and a very aggreeable one'.[54]

It is not hard to imagine what attracted John to Anne. It may be harder to appreciate what drew Anne to the thirty-six-year-old surgeon who was well known for his coarse language, disdain for etiquette, and casual dress, and who was more inclined to discuss curious exper-iments on live animals and dissections of dead bodies than lyrical poems on love and nature. Neither was John conventionally handsome, in the polished manner of his brother William, for example, whose fine and delicate features were captured in a painting in 1765 showing him in full grey wig and blue velvet frock coat decorated with gold brocade.[55] At five feet and two inches, short even for the Georgians, and with his stocky shoulders and short neck, John must have presented a somewhat incongruous contrast with the tall, elegant army officer's daughter. Yet when Anne's young brother Robert painted John at some point during their engagement, he revealed a debonair young man with an open and intelligent face, sensual mouth and dreaming eyes.[56] Eschewing a wig, as he generally would, his unruly hair was held in place by a black three-cornered hat while he sported a white cravat, a handsomely embroidered damson-red waistcoat, dark velvet breeches, white silk stockings and a dark blue jacket. A world away from the self-confident man of business shown in William's portrait, John was set in a wild woodland scene, his hand resting gently on the head of a large mastiff, entirely at one with the natural elements he worshipped and looking every inch the ideal prince for a romantically inclined young woman.

Admittedly, Anne might have been slightly alarmed had she known that the great brute resting its heavy jowls on John's knee was actually half-dog, half-wolf. Hunter was given the hybrid as a puppy in about 1766 by a well-known menagerie owner known as 'wild beast Brookes', who had bred a litter of nine puppies from a male wolf and female dog. While Hunter clearly adored his rather wild half-breed as much as it adored him, it scared the life out of passers-by; eventually it was stoned to death by a mob who mistook it for a rabid dog.[57]

A second portrait by Robert, painted at about the same time, shows a far more practical man, however.[58] Seated at a desk with a quill in one hand, the long, tapering fingers of his other hand resting on his knee, John is writing notes, perhaps about the skull of the small mammal placed in front of him. His coppery hair is curled simply at the sides, his eyes look confidently ahead, and this time his embroidered waistcoat is covered with a brown overall, presumably to protect his day clothes from the blood and grime of the dissecting table. In the background can be seen the painted casket of an Egyptian mummy.

It is possible that John first met Anne in earlier days, before he joined the army, for one of her closest friends, Alice Lee, had married the American surgeon William Shippen, who had lodged with John in the winter of 1759–60.[59] Lee and Shippen married in London in 1762, while John was in the army, and after returning home to Philadelphia they named their first child Anne Home Shippen, after Alice's friend. But perhaps the sparks were truly lit when John was called to see Anne as a patient in 1764. Her father was bewildered by the strange symptoms his daughter was displaying that summer: Anne complained of numbness down her left side and had developed bluish spots on her leg. Whether through respect for John's expertise or perhaps the notion that he might find a suitable partner for his twenty-two-year-old daughter, he called in his young army friend for a second opinion.

They were not the usual circumstances in which romance might be expected to flourish. With typical eighteenth-century attention to bodily functions, John noted in his case books that Anne passed a long roundworm in July, while in August 'She was much troubled with wind in her stomach especially at night.'[60] After consulting his friend Dr Pringle, Anne was put on a course of worming medicines and purgatives, supplemented by cold baths. After nine cold dousings she was pronounced recovered, or at least she had had her fill of the surgeon's medicine – although not, it seems, of the surgeon. The intimacy of the sickroom must have worked its magic – perhaps the aspiring young poet even read some of her verses to her attentive surgeon as she regained her health – and that year the pair became engaged.

Despite their divergent worlds, their contrasting interests and their different educational backgrounds, Anne and John forged a seemingly perfect partnership. In an era not noted for sexual equality, there was between them strong mutual respect; while neither ever truly engaged in the other's world, each allowed the other sufficient freedom to pursue their individual interests. Even the ever-critical Foot praised the union, remarking, 'To her he was directed, not only by personal attractions, but also mental endowments, which she possesses in a very eminent degree.'[61] Hunter quickly became a regular visitor to the Home household in Suffolk Street, off Pall Mall, and a favourite with all the family. Another of Anne's young brothers, Everard – who was an eight-year-old pupil at Westminster School when first John began to woo his sister – clearly admired the brilliant and exuberant surgeon; soon he was keen to follow in his footsteps. But it would be a long engagement. Hunter's financial circumstances were still too shaky a foundation for starting a family. Equally, his passion for experiment – particularly one highly risky self-experiment he was about to begin – may have provided another reason for the seven-year betrothal.

Fresh financial disappointment came in January 1765 when Hunter failed to secure a staff job at St George's Hospital that would have set him up with a lifelong surgical career. Having subscribed to the hospital for several years, he had become a governor in 1760, shortly before he sailed for Belle-Ile, and had dutifully attended board meetings since his return from the army. When one of the surgeons resigned in December 1764 John had high hopes of recouping his outlay. In the event, his former rival John Gunning, who had been assistant surgeon at the hospital for three years, secured the post – but not before Hunter had garnered a large share of the votes.[62]

Nevertheless, his finances were growing. In June 1765 he was able to buy a substantial piece of farmland at Earls Court, then a quiet village about two miles beyond the London sprawl, where he began building a sizeable house. At the point of making the purchase he was still lodging in Covent Garden, according to the deed of covenant, although by March the following year he had moved to a smart rented townhouse at 31 Golden Square in the heart of London's fashionable West End.[63] The villa and grounds Hunter began to develop at Earls Court would provide not only a welcome retreat from demanding city life but a dedicated biological research centre. Here he would keep his exotic animals, breed strange hybrids and perform his relentless experiments, free of interruption and interference from nosy neighbours.

Now that he possessed suitable premises and funds with which to finance his passion, he could indulge his obsession with experimentation to the full. In the grounds and laboratories he established at Earls Court, Hunter would range over his myriad interests, not only investigating the entire human body but every species of animal life. His experiments on regeneration and transplantation having fixed his interest on the so-called 'living principle', he began in 1766 to investigate durability of life and suspended states of animation. Deciding to test the commonly held notion that fish and reptiles could regain life after being frozen, Hunter devised a series of experiments that entailed freezing an assortment of animals.[64] Judging by the availability of ice and snow, he was evidently working in the depths of winter. Wrapped up against the cold, he persuaded the physician George Fordyce, a former pupil from the Covent Garden school who had remained a close friend, to help conduct the experiments. With the unexpected arrival of another friend, a Dr Erwin, who was a teacher in chemistry at Glasgow, their guest was roped in to help.

The three experimenters began by placing two carp in a glass vessel which they lowered into a tub, wrapped in woollen cloths for insulation and filled with ice and snow. To their consternation, the ice around the fish kept melting, leading Hunter to realize that animals generated heat; the discovery would prompt him to measure standard body heat in different life-forms in later experiments. As the carp continued to swim freely, the trio shovelled in more snow until, by now almost frozen themselves, they were forced to give up. While the three friends repaired inside to warm themselves before an open fire, their victims finally succumbed. 'They were frozen at last, after having exhausted the whole powers of life in the production of heat,' Hunter recorded. Now the real purpose of the experiment could begin. Full of anticipation, the enthusiasts thawed out the frozen fish in the hope they would regain their former vigour. Naturally enough, the carp remained as stiff and lifeless as ever.

Typically undeterred, Hunter repeated the experiment on a dormouse. The three friends settled down to watch as the little creature began to feel the drop in temperature. 'The atmosphere round the animal soon cooled,' noted Hunter, 'its breath froze as it came from the mouth; a hoar-frost gathered on its whiskers, and on all the inside of the vessel, and the external points of the hair became covered with the same.' Once again the threesome were defeated by natural body temperature: although the mouse's feet froze, it survived the extreme cold, living to preen its whiskers once more. A second dormouse was less lucky. This time working alone, Hunter soaked its fur in water, better to conduct the cold, and it was quickly overcome. 'The animal dying, soon became stiff,' he noted, 'and upon being thawed, was found quite dead.' With a miraculous resurrection now seeming increasingly unlikely, Hunter pressed on, taking a toad and then a snail as his deep-freeze victims.

Finally he had to admit defeat. The results were not just a blow for folklore – never one of Hunter's big considerations – but also to his naive ideas for making a fortune, as he later confided to his pupils:

Till this time, I had imagined that it might be possible to prolong life to any period by freezing a person in the frigid zone, as I thought all action and waste would cease until the body was thawed. I thought that if a man would give up the last ten years of his life to this kind of alternative oblivion and action, it might be prolonged to a thousand years; and by getting himself thawed every hundred years, he might learn what had happened during his frozen condition. Like other schemers, I thought I should make my fortune by it; but this experiment undeceived me.[65]

Successive freezing and thawing were plainly not the key to immortality, but Hunter was loath to surrender his fascination with reviving the dead.

Regeneration remained an interest in February that year

when the surgeon became his own patient. One morning at about 4 a.m., Hunter broke his Achilles tendon while jumping up and down on his toes; quite possibly he was dancing, partnering Anne at one of her musical soirées, or else simply trying to regain the feeling in numbed feet while working in his cold laboratory. Naturally he recorded the entire episode and his self-treatment, under the heading 'Mr Hunter's Case'.[66] He had been 'jumping and lighting upon my toes without allowing my heels to come to the ground' when his tendon suddenly snapped, he noted. 'I stood still, without being able to make another spring; and the sensation it gave me was as if something had struck the calf of my leg; and that the noise was the body which had struck me, falling on the floor, and I looked down to see what it was, but saw nothing.'

The accident provided a perfect case on which Hunter could practise his natural approach to treatment. Confident that nature would mend the break without human intervention, he declined any surgical aid or physicians' remedies, and after a brief rest with his leg bound he endeavoured to walk on the injured foot. For this purpose he adapted an old shoe by inserting pieces of leather to raise the heel, and as his movement gradually returned he reduced the height of the heel accordingly. Just as he expected, the tendon soon mended and he could walk perfectly normally. The lesson strengthened his conviction in nature's healing powers and, in a period when fascination with health commonly bred hypochondria, he would frequently exhort ailing patients to abandon their medicines and their beds in favour of exercise and fresh air.

In one instance, while staying with friends at a country house, he discovered the mistress of the family had been confined to a wheelchair since breaking her kneecap four years earlier. Hunter prescribed a series of intensive daily exercises – essentially early physiotherapy – in which the patient sat on the end of her dining table and attempted to move her toes. After one month she could wriggle her toes slightly, and after several more months of regular exercises she was finally able to walk again.[67] Regardless of the fact that his non-interventionist approach frequently meant forgoing a fee, many more sickly Georgians would be brought up sharp by Hunter's common-sense doctrine.

The tendon injury also afforded Hunter new inspiration for research. He experimented on several dogs by cutting their tendons, allowing them to heal naturally, then killing the hounds at various stages to examine the regrowth.[68] Already highly respected for his knowledge of the human body, Hunter was becoming widely esteemed for his understanding of animal anatomy too. In the early years after he had resettled in London, he began to compile the first catalogue detailing the specimens in his growing natural history collection.[69] Most of the pickled or dried preparations he recorded were parts belonging to animals, either dissected on his army campaigns – like the two-tailed lizards from Belle-Ile – or bought from circuses, menageries and auctions in England. They ranged from domestic creatures such as dogs, cats and donkeys, through native wild animals such as badgers, hedgehogs and deer, to exotic beasts from around the world, including leopards and monkeys. Already Hunter had obtained the liver, kidney and tongue from a lion in the Tower of London menagerie – possibly an elderly lion named Pompey which died there in 1758. He had also acquired the skeleton of an orca, or killer whale, which had beached itself at the mouth of the Thames in 1759;

Hunter had the twenty-four-foot-long carcass towed to Westminster by barge and probably dissected its huge hulk on the spot with the help of some of his pupils.[70] In addition he had obtained the body of a crocodile, the third he had dissected, which died in a London show during the winter of 1764–5. 'It was at the time of its death perhaps the largest ever seen in this country,' he wrote, 'having grown, to my own knowledge, above three feet in length, and was about five feet long when it died.'[71] With adventurers relentlessly exploring uncharted lands overseas, new species were regularly turning up on British shores. Increasingly, whenever a hitherto unknown animal came to the notice of amateur naturalists it was brought to Hunter for examination.

One such creature became the subject of Hunter's first paper to the prestigious Royal Society.[72] News of the slimy, olive-coloured aquatic animal that looked like a cross between a lizard and a large eel caused a stir when it first came to the notice of the scientific community in the 1760s. Possessing both a pair of legs and feathery gills at the front, and no hind legs at all, the creature of roughly two feet in length had been discovered in swamps in southern parts of North America; it was known by locals as the mud iguana. A Scottish physician and amateur naturalist, Alexander Garden, who lived in South Carolina, had captured several of the beasts and shipped their preserved bodies to a friend, John Ellis, who was one of Britain's most eminent naturalists. Aware the strange animal could be a newly discovered species, Ellis sent a specimen to another friend, the renowned Swedish naturalist Carl Linnaeus. Having established the modern categorization system of plants and animals, in which he described more than four thousand animal species,

Linnaeus was regarded as the chief authority on naming species. The professor wrote back excitedly to Ellis in 1765 from Uppsala, where he held the chair of botany, confirming that the animal represented not only a new species but also a new genus. He promptly named it the siren (Latin for 'mermaid') lacertina ('little lizard'). Assuming that the specimen Ellis had sent was the larva of an animal that would eventually develop four legs – in fact the *Siren lacertina*, or greater siren, continues in a permanent larval state, retaining just two legs – Linnaeus added, 'there is no creature that ever I saw that I long so much to be convinced of the truth as to what this will certainly turn out to be'. Ellis needed no further encouragement. A stalwart of the Royal Society, he immediately set about describing the external appearance of the new animal for fellow members. But Ellis had no anatomy skills; he needed an expert capable of investigating and describing the internal structure of the animal. For this he turned to John Hunter.

The greater siren was no stranger to Hunter: he had seen a specimen before, as well as its sister species the dwarf siren and lesser siren, when he purchased a job-lot of curiosities originating from South Carolina in 1758. At Ellis's behest he now dissected the new specimens to produce a full description of the creature. Bent over the peculiar animal with his knife, Hunter discovered that along with the siren's single pair of legs, it possessed both external gills like a fish and internal lungs like an amphibian. He sent his report to Ellis, who appended it to his own. Together they were read to the Royal Society on 5 June 1766.

In his first ever communication to the esteemed body of scientists, Hunter boldly suggested that the new creature represented a missing link in the chain of animals between fish and amphibians. 'This tribe of animals are widely different from all hitherto known,' he proclaimed. 'They are compounded of two grand divisions of the Animal Kingdom.' He added, 'They hold with respect to respiration a middle rank between Fish, which breath water and those immediately above them who breath air, viz, those call'd amphibia, placed in this respect between the two, filling up the scale.' He also noted that the siren's tiny eyes were well adapted to its environment, remarking, 'This smallness of the eye best suits an animal that lives so much in the mud.'

The 'Great Chain of Being' Hunter invoked was not a novel idea in mid-eighteenth-century scientific circles, for many naturalists subscribed to the idea of a ladder or scale ascending from the most primitive creatures to the most complex – humans. Rather than an early indication of evolutionary theory, the chain represented a fixed system, with every species having been designed by God in an immutable state. But for Hunter, the missing link he had described would come to mean something more than a mere rung in a ladder of creation designed by God. His deliberations set him on a trail that would eventually force him to clash even with his new-found friends in the society.

For now, though, he was warmly welcomed into the fold. Eight months later, on 5 February 1767, Hunter was elected a fellow of the Royal Society, recognized 'as a person well skilled in Natural History and Anatomy'.[73] Heading the list of seven proposers was John Ellis, while others included Daniel Solander, the Swedish botanist and disciple of Linnaeus who worked in the new British Museum, and Richard Warren, who was George III's physician. Hunter had become a fellow almost three months before his older brother, despite William having contributed a paper as far back as 1743.[74] Within a few years John Hunter would become one of the central figures within the Royal Society, not only the society's favourite anatomist but a lynchpin of scientific debate. In the meantime, he preserved the siren's heart in a jar.[75]

8

The Surgeon's Penis

'... these damned twinges, that scalding heat, and that deep-tinged loathsome matter are the strongest proofs of an infection.'

James Boswell[1]

London, May 1767

John Hunter had all before him. He was engaged to marry an accomplished society hostess, he was established as a rising surgeon with a growing private practice, he had just been accepted into the elite company of the Royal Society, and at thirty-nine he was an energetic, intelligent and healthy man in the prime of life. It seemed almost nothing could go wrong. And then one Friday in May 1767 he embarked on an astonishing and quite probably foolhardy experiment.

Never able to resist a puzzle, Hunter had determined to solve one of the foremost questions taxing medical practitioners of the day. Yet this riddle could not be examined in his usual way, using animals as subjects; only an experiment on a human being could provide the answers he sought. Accordingly, he took up his knife, dipped the blade into a festering venereal sore and deliberately jabbed the tip first into the end and then into the foreskin of a man's penis. Inevitably, he recorded the entire process: 'Two punctures were made on the penis with a lancet dipped in venereal matter from a gonorrhoea; one puncture was on the glans, the other on the prepuce. This was on a Friday; on the Sunday following there was a teasing itching in those parts, which lasted till the Tuesday following.'[2]

Hunter would never reveal the name of the human guinea pig whom he subjected to his reckless experiment on venereal disease in any of his written works. His identity would exercise his disciples, enemies and scholars for the next two centuries and beyond. Possibly, the man was a volunteer whom Hunter had plucked from his own household or local neighbourhood and persuaded to submit to his knife in return for a generous fee, just as his earlier victims had given up their teeth. Possibly, the person was a trusting but unwitting patient, for Hunter would certainly experiment on patients without their express permission in other cases. Or perhaps – and this is by far the most likely explanation – the victim of the bizarre experiment was Hunter himself.

Certainly, Hunter had good reason to focus his investigative skills on sexually transmitted diseases in the middle of the eighteenth century. Like any busy surgeon of the time, he quickly found that venereal complaints comprised a large proportion of his daily round. Syphilis, gonorrhoea and a host of other venereal infections were rampant in Georgian London, largely as a consequence of relatively liberal attitudes towards sexual freedom, along with widespread and broadly condoned use of prostitutes. Sex was big business in eighteenth-century London, little different to the thriving trades in tea, coffee and spices. As a commodity it was widely available, whether in dark alleys leading off the Strand, in the seedy brothels, 'bawdy houses' and slightly higher-class bagnios around Covent Garden, or by arrangement with any number of women prepared to offer sexual favours in return for a comfortable lifestyle. Customers eager to pay for illicit sexual relations spanned all walks of life, from the soldiers and sailors swarming the streets on leave to the dukes and dandies who gratified their physical desires after an evening's gambling in West End clubs. Prices varied hugely. According to James Boswell, a connoisseur of London prostitutes, a client could pay anything from the 'splendid Madam at fifty guineas a night, down to the civil nymph with white-thread stockings who tramps along the Strand and will resign her engaging person to your honour for a pint of wine and a shilling'.[3] And just as potential buyers of spices or tea would peruse catalogues describing the latest merchandise from overseas, so prospective clients for sex could flip through a handy pocket guide to select their preferred partner.

Published annually from 1771, *Harris's List of Covent-Garden Ladies, or Man of Pleasure's Kalendar* provided vivid particulars on London's many and varied prostitutes.[4] Potential customers were advised that Miss Brown of 7 Berwick Street, Soho, was 'constantly well dressed, and lives in very genteel lodgings at present'. At twenty-three, she could already boast eight years' experience. Like many of Covent Garden's 'women of the town' she had started work in her teens, possibly drawn to the metropolis by naive ideas of making her fortune. Alternatively, older clients were recommended to Mrs Hamblin, who lived, appropriately enough, at 1 Naked-boy-court, near the Strand. Although now approaching fifty-six and forced to enhance her charms with lavish makeup, she could offer her customers the benefit of thirty years' experience. At the same time, the directory provided essential details on different prostitutes' well-being. Formerly satisfied customers were cautioned to steer clear of Miss Young, who had 'very lately had the folly and wickedness to leave a certain hospital, before the cure for a certain distemper which she had was com-pleted, and has thrown her contaminated carcase on the town again'. Similarly, military gentlemen were warned to avoid Matilda Johnson since 'it is thought by some experienced officers, that her citadel is in danger, on account of a quantity of *fiery combustible matter* which is lodged in the *covered way*'.

One well-travelled tourist who quickly acquainted him-self with the brothels of Covent Garden when visiting London in 1763 was the renowned Italian lover Giacomo Casanova.[5] Infatuated by the charms of one unusually elusive young prostitute, who lured him into parting with large sums of money without once allowing him carnal pleasures, the libertine almost leapt into the Thames in despair. Although the object of his desires never relented, there were many more young women eager to satisfy Casanova's boundless lust. By the time he returned to the Continent the following year he took with him the sure symptoms of gonorrhoea as a souvenir of his London sojourn. It was one of many occasions on which he required treatment for venereal disease.

Boswell was another regular frequenter of London's brothels.[6] His first sexual experience, at the age of nineteen, took place shortly after his arrival in London in 1760, with a young prostitute who plied her trade at the Blue Perriwig in Southampton Street, off the Strand. His first encounter with 'Signor Gonorrhoea', as he later termed his recurring visitor, followed shortly after. Boswell duly visited a surgeon in Pall Mall to undergo the necessary treatment – a course of unspecified pills, a strict diet and the obligatory bloodletting.

His experience did not prove a salutary lesson. When he returned to London in 1762, following a brief spell back home in Scotland where he endured a second episode of venereal disease, he began to pay court to a young married actress, code-named 'Louisa' in his diary. After a cursory few weeks' wining and dining, Boswell persuaded her to spend a night with him in January 1763 in a room above a London tavern, where they gave their names as 'Mr and Mrs Digges'. Describing their night of passion with no doubt an eye on his future reputation, he boasted in his journal, 'A more voluptuous night I never enjoyed. Five times was I lost in supreme rapture.'[7] Louisa, for her part, declared his performance 'extraordinary', or so Boswell claimed.

But the by now familiar symptoms which soon ensued were by no means extraordinary. Just six days after his night of bliss Boswell dolefully admitted to his journal, 'I this day began to feel an unaccountable alarm of un-expected evil: a little heat in the members of my body sacred to Cupid, very like a symptom of that distemper with which Venus, when cross, takes it into her head to plague her votaries.'[8] The tell-tale signs of Boswell's condition were all too plain. After confirming the diagnosis with his surgeon, he confined himself to his lodgings, in Downing Street, to fulfil his course of treatment and escape the prying questions of his associates. After five weeks, and a fee of five guineas for the surgeon, he was sufficiently recovered to recommence his social life, as well as his sexual adventures with prostitutes.

Chastened for some time at least, Boswell now took precautions and donned a rudimentary condom when next he engaged in sexual activities, this time picking up a seventeen-year-old prostitute in St James's Park – a notorious haunt for casual sex. 'For the first time did I engage in armour', he noted in his journal for 25 March, adding that he found this a 'dull satisfaction'.[9] This was scarcely surprising since condoms of the time were ordinarily made from sheep's or pig's gut, secured with silk ribbon. Popularly held to have been invented by a certain Dr Condom, a physician to Charles II, they were reusable and had to be kept in water to maintain their suppleness.[10] Boswell dutifully washed and reused his condom – thinking of his own health of course rather than his partners' well-being – on several more occasions. At other times he threw caution, and condom, to the wind and further attacks of gonorrhoea inevitably ensued. Over a sexual career that would last more than thirty years, Boswell visited brothels throughout Europe, enjoyed numerous affairs and fathered illegitimate children after his marriage in 1769. As a result he suffered at least nineteen episodes of venereal disease, seemingly always gonorrhoea, which he recorded woefully in his diaries. His death in 1795 may even have been caused or accelerated by the various complications of his venereal complaints, exacerbated by excessive drinking.

As the frequency and severity of Boswell's attacks

increased he consulted many of London's top surgeons and physicians, including Percivall Pott and John Pringle. He may even, since his wife and son were certainly patients, have been seen by John Hunter, for the treatment of venereal diseases formed a major component of Hunter's work from his earliest days as a surgeon. His first recorded patient, the chimney sweep at St Bartholomew's, had been a victim of a stricture caused by gonorrhoea, and Hunter had since had plenty more opportunities to study sexual infections, on his ward rounds, in the army and in the dead bodies that turned up on his dissecting bench. Inevitably, he preserved some of the relevant parts: he pickled in spirits part of the penis of 'a man who died clap'd' and dried several bones and a skull bearing the long-term effects of syphilis.[11]

But now that Hunter was beginning seriously to build up his reputation and his clientele, the flow of victims of venereal complaints crossing the threshold of his new home in Golden Square grew steadily greater. Hunter would have undertaken house visits for his wealthier patients, but many may well have preferred to visit his surgery incognito, along with his clients of lesser means, rather than reveal their condition to family and servants.

Venereal disease was no respecter of class. Among the many patients Hunter treated for sexual infections were prostitutes and their married clients, servants and their masters, high-ranking army officers and rank-and-file soldiers, as well as a vicar, a surgeon and a Prussian count. It was not only Mr Anderson but Mr Anderson's servant who came under his care for venereal infections; both Lord and Lady 'L—' sought out his advice. Often Hunter discreetly concealed or coded his patients' names in his notes, but whatever their identity or background their intimate circumstances and unfortunate symptoms were dutifully recorded, along with some of their more elaborate stories intended to cover their indiscretions.[12]

Hunter knew all their secrets. One patient who consulted him with early symptoms of syphilis was Mr Maclean, who told Hunter that he 'lay with a Girl on Wednesday, and there appeared on the Friday a chancre on the inside of the lips of the urethra'. In reality it was unlikely syphilitic symptoms could have developed so soon after Mr Maclean's sexual encounter; as with many patients he simply blamed his attack on his last illicit liaison. With sexual diseases rife within military circles, many of Hunter's clients were army officers, such as 'Colonel MacDon . . .' who sought Hunter's advice when the long-term effects of syphilis persisted after his marriage. Along with many married men who frequented prostitutes, with or without their spouse's knowledge, 'Colonel MacDon . . .' had passed on his infection to 'Mrs MacDon . . .' who was now suffering from a swelling in her groin, an enlarged lymph gland, as a consequence.

Other patients were less candid. While society generally turned a blind eye to prostitution and its customers, some of Hunter's more embarrassed patients concocted far-fetched tales in an effort to disguise the true origin of their complaint. One 'Gentleman' claimed he had been sauntering innocently along the Haymarket – another popular prostitutes' haunt – when he was accosted by a woman who invited him to join her for a drink. 'He told her to be gone for a poxed Bitch. Soon after, he went aside to make water; she came behind him and took him by the Penis, saying, "If I am poxed, you shall be so too." After quitting him, he wiped the Glans and walked on, without further notice. Next morning, he found a disagreeable heat round the Glans, especially on the orifice of the Urethra, which alarmed him (he being a married man).' Hunter recorded the sorry tale without comment; he rarely took a moralistic standpoint. But he was somewhat incredulous at the claim by one patient to have abstained from sexual relations for almost two months before an attack of gonorrhoea. 'How came this Clap?' he queried. 'He gave his Word and Honour he had not lain with a Woman since; which is more than seven weeks.'

His own colleagues in the medical field were no less reckless in their extramarital relations, despite knowing the likely consequences of their actions. 'Mr Dawson, a surgeon had a Gonorrhoea two years ago,' recorded Hunter; 'he then took Mercury for it, but in vain.' And even men of the cloth were prone to stray. Reporting the case of the Reverend Mr Stevens, Hunter noted, 'He came to London, and one evening had connection with a Woman of the Town. Two or three days after, in the morning he observed a spot on his shirt, which alarmed him much, and he immediately applied to me for a Preventative.' To the errant cleric's dismay, Hunter informed him that no such medicine existed but advised him to steep his penis in warm water and to hold it over steam made by hot water and brandy, which if nothing else provided some comforting fumes.

In common with most surgeons and physicians of the day, Hunter was well aware that venereal diseases were transmitted by sexual contact. Sometimes, therefore, he would advise a patient to refrain from sexual relations with a spouse while symptoms persisted, while at other times he would give the all-clear for marital sex to be resumed. He realized too that venereal infections could be passed from a mother to her unborn child. Many infants born with syphilis were treated at the Lock Hospital, which specialized in venereal complaints after it opened in 1746. In some instances, infections were even transmitted to a child from its mother or a nursemaid while breastfeeding. In one family treated by Hunter, the wife contracted syphilis from her husband and passed it on to her newborn twins, who died soon after birth, as well as to the two-year-old daughter she was breastfeeding.[13]

Yet while methods of transmission were well accepted, understanding of venereal diseases largely ended there. Along with most practitioners of the day, Hunter believed that gonorrhoea and its more serious cousin, syphilis, were simply different forms of the same disease stemming from the same cause. The classic symptoms of gonorrhoea, commonly known as 'the clap', were widely regarded as the local manifestation of this one venereal infection, affecting only the genital parts. That these symptoms frequently disappeared of their own accord, without recourse to medical aid, helped confirm this view. When the less common but far more disastrous symptoms of syphilis, known as 'the pox', were observed in patients, these were attributed to the venereal 'poison' having circulated around the body, or having become 'constitutional' to use Hunter's term. The fact that such symptoms usually spread from the classic hard chancre on the genitals to a general rash, sore throat, swollen lymph glands (or 'buboes') and in some cases more serious complications again lent credence to the one-disease theory. So while Boswell somewhat miraculously managed to confine his many bouts of venereal disease to gonorrhoea, he expressed due anxiety that this infection might 'spread' to the rest of his body. 'I thought of applying to a quack who would cure me quickly and cheaply,' he remarked when another gonorrhoea attack appeared. 'But then the horrors of being imperfectly cured and having the distemper thrown into my blood terrified me exceedingly.'[14]

There was similar confusion over the origins of venereal disease, although this was rather more understandable since controversy continues today.[15] Symptoms of gonorrhoea had been recorded since ancient times, but it was only in 1495 that the first definite signs of syphilis were reported and it was then regarded as a new disease. Since the first cases were noted after French soldiers laid siege to Naples, the venereal epidemic which quickly took hold across Europe was initially termed 'the Neapolitan sickness'. It soon went through a long list of alternative names, according to the nationality of its sufferers and that of their closest enemies: thus it was called 'the French sickness' by the Italians, 'the Spanish disease' in Holland, 'the Polish disease' in Russia, and 'the Russian disease' in Turkey, while in Tahiti, where natives were introduced to syphilis by visiting eighteenth-century explorers, it was quickly dubbed 'the British disease'. For their part, the first British victims initially called the horrifying infection which reached English shores in about 1497 the 'Bordeaux sickness', since that was where it seemed to emanate from, but soon settled on the more general 'French pox', as it became widely known.

As the first European cases seemingly arose soon after Christopher Columbus had returned from the New World, it was generally reckoned that the new scourge had been imported from America. And this may well be true: in all probability the *Treponema pallidum* bacterium that causes syphilis was brought back by the first

European explorers, in a decidedly uneven exchange that resulted in the devastation of native American tribes by smallpox, measles, influenza and typhus. However, other theories include the possibilities that the infection had long been present in Europe but had not been distinguished from leprosy, or that syphilis developed in both continents from related diseases.

Although the term 'syphilis' was coined to describe the horrific symptoms of the highly virulent disease in the sixteenth century, the name would not fully catch on until the end of the eighteenth century – unlike the infection itself, which spread unchecked through European civilization. The intensity of the 'pox', or the 'Great Pox' as it was also known to distinguish it from smallpox, had somewhat abated by the middle of the eighteenth century, but the infection had become endemic and its ramifications could be severe. Though early symptoms of syphilis usually disappear of their own accord within a year or two, the infection can remain latent for decades. In some victims it re-emerges and in its final or tertiary stages can destroy bones, soft tissue, the heart, the brain, the eyes – indeed almost any part of the body. Allusions to miscreants having lost their noses – a fairly frequent long-term effect of untreated syphilis – were commonplace in eighteenth-century satirical cartoons and literature. In 1751, Henry Fielding referred in his novel *Amelia* to a woman whose nose had been destroyed, 'for Venus, envious perhaps of her former charms, had carried off the gristly part'.[16] Certainly by the mid-eighteenth century venereal disease in all its guises had become sufficiently widespread to provide unending employment for surgeons, physicians and the ubiquitous quacks claiming to offer miracle cures. One publication offering careers advice for young Georgian men in 1747 remarked that three out of four surgeons in London were reliant for their income on treating venereal infections.[17]

And if the origins of sexual infections remained obscure, even more confusion arose over the most appropriate treatment. Both orthodox practitioners and quack healers proffered an array of pills, potions, ointments and other remedies claimed to cure symptoms of 'the clap', although in reality most bouts of gonorrhoea resolved themselves after a few weeks. This was plainly good news for serial sufferers such as Boswell and Casanova, but it did little to dispel the muddle: every charlatan and over-ambitious surgeon could claim miraculous success for their singular approach. And it was little comfort for those, like Boswell again, who went on to develop the nastier complications untreated gonorrhoea could lead to, including inflammation of the prostate or testicles.

There was greater unanimity over treatment of 'the pox'. While the earliest known sufferers of syphilis were urged to press a cockerel 'plucked and flayed alive' to the affected parts, or failing that a 'live frog cut in two', treatment had become a little more straightforward by the eighteenth century, if no less unpleasant. Mercury was the universal remedy for classic signs of syphilis, probably on account of its earlier use in treating the similar symptoms of leprosy, and it would remain the standard treatment into the early twentieth century. As with most Georgian remedies, it had little if any effect, although it sometimes gave the appearance of success. The tendency of early symptoms of syphilis – the primary and secondary stages – to disappear without treatment after one or two years tended to grant mercury a seal of approval. After these early stages, however, the untreated syphilis bacterium could lie dormant for anything up to thirty years, and in roughly two-thirds of victims would never reappear. For those whose symptoms did recur, the ensuing damage could wreak severe and sometimes fatal destruction on internal organs.

According to the various surgeons' whims, mercury was administered as an ointment applied directly to the infected parts, by an injection or on a bougie – a cylindrical plug loaded with the mixture – into the penis or vagina, or orally as pills and potions. While lay healers pretended to offer patent remedies of their own, when analysed these secret recipes often comprised mainly mercury too. Unfortunately, the painful, unpleasant and noxious side-effects of mercury treatment were often indistinguishable from the condition itself. Mercury poisoning caused mouth ulcers, sore gums, loose teeth and copious production of black saliva, sometimes several pints a day, as well as leaving a tell-tale metallic taint on the breath. It was hardly surprising that many victims took themselves to the 'salivating' wards of the voluntary hospitals where they could at least suffer their treatment in relative privacy, safe from the prying eyes and in-quisitive noses of friends and neighbours.

With confusion obscuring the origins, nature and treat-ment of venereal disease, the field was plainly ripe for investigation. Although most surgeons preferred not to question the chief source of their sizeable fees, John Hunter could never resist a challenge. Not content merely to pocket his guineas and send his patients away in the full expectation of seeing them again before long, he made venereal diseases the next subject of his relentless research. It would be 1786 before he felt sufficiently confident to publish his investigations in his major work *A Treatise on the Venereal Disease*, but the experiments and observations that formed its basis were well underway by 1767.

There was little light Hunter could shed on the origins of the venereal 'poison', as he called it, and he confessed that 'we are still in doubt whether it arose in Europe or was imported from America'.[18] He was similarly honest about the dearth of understanding over the nature of the infection, in an age long before the existence of bacteria was discovered, confessing, 'We know nothing of the poison itself, but only its effects on the human body.' He had firm views, however, on the progress of sexual infections and the best mode of treatment. Drawing on his growing experience with the male patients who sought out his advice from the 1760s onwards, he fully delineated the unwelcome signs of itching, discharge, swelling, pain and unwanted erections his gentleman clients described. He was aware too that women could often contract gonorrhoea with few if any symptoms, which caused no little problem for those men seeking assurance that a prostitute or potential mistress was clear of the disease.[19] In such instances the only acceptable evidence that a woman was infected or 'clean' was the word of a gentleman – plainly a woman's word counted for little in such circumstances – as Hunter made clear: 'In such a case, the only thing we can depend upon is the testimony of those whom we look upon as men of veracity.'[20]

As to treatment of sexual diseases, Hunter was characteristically outspoken about the ineffectuality of the majority of medications claiming to cure gonorrhoea. His growing experience taught him that mercury, sometimes prescribed in cases of gonorrhoea as in syphilis, was useless for the former, but he likewise poured scorn on all other remedies for 'the clap' whether advertised by orthodox surgeons or untrained quacks. While syphilis required certain skills to treat, he asserted, gonorrhoea could be cured by 'the most ignorant'.[21] The reason, he explained, was obvious: 'gonorrhoea cures itself, whilst the other forms of the disease require the assistance of art'. He even questioned the benefit of medication at all, arguing, 'I am inclined to believe it is very seldom of any kind of use, perhaps not once in ten cases: but even this would be of some consequence, if we could distinguish the cases where it is of service from those where it is not.'[22]

With this motive in mind, Hunter performed an ingenious test, giving some of his unsuspecting patients pills made of nothing more effectual than bread. He recorded, 'The patients always got well; but some of them, I believe, not so soon as they would have done, had the artificial methods of cure been employed.'[23] The experiment must be one of the earliest examples of a controlled trial testing a placebo against an established medication. (He would later use the same deception on his wife, tricking her into believing she was enjoying the therapeutic benefits of the best spa water by sticking labels from the Bath pump room onto bottles containing ordinary water pumped from the Thames.[24] Plainly the veracity of the surgeon was sometimes no more to be trusted than that of his gentleman patients.) Hunter's bread-pills test provided solid proof that leaving gonorrhoea untreated was just as effective, or almost as effective, as offering the best that London's most eminent practitioners could prescribe. Not surprisingly, the conclusion did little to boost Hunter's popularity among his more mercenary colleagues when finally he published his treatise.

Syphilis was a trickier puzzle. Hunter described the symptoms of the 'lues venerea' in its various phases in colourful detail. Mercury offered patients the best chance of success, Hunter averred, although he was under no illusions that it provided a complete cure, aware that the disease could lurk in the body unnoticed for years before re-emerging to wreak more damage. But it was the enduring question of whether gonorrhoea and syphilis were really the same disease, one of the biggest medical enigmas of the eighteenth century, that truly concentrated his investigative energies. This was to form the central theme of his treatise and would prove the most controversial aspect of his research.

In common with the majority of Georgian practitioners, Hunter already subscribed to the thesis that gonorrhoea and syphilis were caused by the same agent or 'poison'. He based this belief on his view that no two diseases could occupy one body at the same time. With diagnosis still very much in its infancy – most infectious diseases were denoted simply as 'fever', for example – this was a relatively easy mistake to make. Hunter was well aware that the 'clap' and the 'pox' had quite distinct symptoms, and that one responded to mercury while the other did not, yet he was still certain that the two were simply different manifestations of the same infection. In common with most fellow practitioners he believed gonorrhoea represented the local stage of the disease while symptoms of lues venerea emerged when the disease spread throughout the body, or became 'constitutional'.[25] All his experience in consultations pointed to this sadly mistaken conclusion. Firstly, it was quite apparent that both conditions were contracted in the same way. More significantly, Hunter's case books clearly reveal that many of his patients were actually suffering from both infections at the same time; it was easy, therefore, to confuse the two. Captain Duncan, for example, who complained of a 'pain and running' followed by the appearance of a chancre, evidently had both gonorrhoea and syphilis.[26] But hypothesizing was one thing. In Hunter's regime there was only one way to solve any such mystery – by performing an experiment.

The plan was simple, and it should have been straightforward. In the spring of 1767 he resolved to inoculate a person with gonorrhoea and monitor the progress of the disease for signs of syphilis. If, as he expected, the signs of gonorrhoea were followed by symptoms of syphilis then he could prove that the two were one disease; if, as should have happened, no signs of syphilis emerged, plainly gonorrhoea was a separate disease. All Hunter needed was a compliant, willing and reliable human volunteer. Finding a donor with clear signs of gonorrhoea to provide the venereal matter he required was easy: there was no shortage of patients knocking on his door with the most virulent evidence of the clap. But obtaining a subject for his experiment was a more knotty problem. He needed someone he could be sure had previously been clear of venereal infection; someone who would be willing to undergo regular examination and treatment; someone he could observe on an almost daily basis over the long course of his trial. The obvious subject for the experiment on that fateful Friday in May was himself.

Taking pains to obscure the identity of the subject throughout, Hunter used neither the first person nor the third person in his notes of the trial. Accordingly after recording that the 'teasing itching' in the penis 'lasted till the Tuesday following', he continued, 'Upon the Tuesday morning the parts of the prepuce where the puncture had been made were redder, thickened, and had formed a speck; by the Tuesday following the speck had increased, and discharged some matter, and there seemed to be a little pouting of the lips of the urethra, also a sensation in it in making water, so that a discharge was expected from it.'[27] Classic symptoms of gonorrhoea had appeared, exactly as Hunter had expected. Examining the inflamed parts on an almost daily basis, he watched for the tell-tale signs of lues venerea. He was not disappointed: within ten days, to his evident satisfaction, an ulcer or chancre appeared on the foreskin and soon other signs of syphilis emerged. A gland in the right groin swelled, forming the classic bubo, then two months later 'a little sharp pricking pain was felt in one of the tonsils'. On examination this proved to be an ulcer, another common occurrence in the primary stage of syphilis. Seven months after the start of the experiment, 'copper-coloured blotches' broke out on the skin, clearly indicating that the syphilis had entered its secondary stage. Applying mercury to the festering sores on the genitals and tonsils, Hunter took care only to use sufficient quantities as he believed would control, not vanquish, the disease in order to carry on with his experiment, although in reality the symptoms probably disappeared of their own accord. For three long years he continued, anointing the sores with mercury and then letting them reappear, four times on the tonsils and three times on the skin, until at last he decided to administer enough of the poisonous ointment to eradicate the symptoms – or more likely the disease had simply lapsed into its latent and non-contagious phase.

The experiment, as far as Hunter was concerned, had been a resounding success: it proved to his satisfaction at least that gonorrhoea developed into lues venerea. In reality it was a complete disaster. The experiment had been doomed from the outset, since at the moment when Hunter plunged his lancet into the anonymous penis he had unknowingly used infected matter containing both syphilis and gonorrhoea bacteria; the person from whom he had taken the venereal pus had evidently, like so many of Hunter's patients, been a victim of both diseases. The results of the fated trial would set back medical progress in terms of the understanding of sexual diseases by half a century. It would be 1838 before the French-based physician Philippe Ricord categorically established that syphilis and gonorrhoea were two distinct infections after conducting his own series of inoculation experiments on a remarkable 2,500 unwitting patients.[28]

Hunter's error had been easy enough to make. Judged on the limited evidence of his flawed experiment there seemed no doubt that gonorrhoea produced the characteristic chancres of syphilis, although clearly he should have based his conclusions on a much larger sample. When he published the results in his treatise he was therefore adamant that 'a gonorrhoea will produce chancres'. He added, 'It proves many things, and opens a field for further conjectures.' Unfortunately the trial proved nothing, but it would indeed provide fertile ground for further conjecture – principally over the identity of its mystery subject.

Future biographers and scholars would argue vehemently over the question of whether or not Hunter inoculated himself with syphilis. Most early biographers made no reference to the experiment, but several later writers accepted unquestioningly that Hunter was its subject. To other writers, especially the surgeon's later devotees, the very idea that a man of Hunter's stature could have willingly inflicted on himself such a vile disease as syphilis was inconceivable – 'beyond belief' according to one, 'preposterous' in the words of another.[29] These disciples preferred to argue that their hero had infected a simple-minded youth dragged from the streets and kept a virtual prisoner in Hunter's house for the three-year experiment, rather than sully his image with the stigma of syphilis. Yet there is concrete evidence that Hunter did indeed inoculate himself with syphilis and may even have gone on to suffer the consequences.

Though Hunter never referred in writing to the subject of the controversial experiment, he did reveal his identity in his later lectures, according to the notes of some of his pupils. Notes taken by one pupil, a certain Mr Twigge, in 1787 are unequivocal. 'It has frequently been a subject of dispute whether the matter of a gonorrhoea and a Chancre essentially differ, or whether they are the same,' began Hunter, 'but as I have produced in myself a Chancre from the matter of a Gonorrhoea, that matter may now be easily settled.'[30] Almost exactly the same words are found in notes taken by another pupil, a certain Mr Brooks.[31] Hunter's devotees have attempted to argue that both references are errors and that Hunter really said 'I have produced myself a chancre . . .' This is difficult to believe without any evidence that Hunter ever said the latter – there are certainly no notes with this form of words – and since the alleged mistake appears in two sets of notes. By the time Hunter's collected works appeared in 1835, the surgeon who edited the venereal disease treatise, George Babington, would state matter-of-factly that Hunter had performed the experiment on himself. In the same work, Drewry Ottley, a physician trained at St George's, even reported Hunter joking about his self-experiment with the words, 'he repeated over so often, and in so peculiar a tone, "I knocked down the disease with mercury and I killed it" that the whole class at length burst into a loud fit of laughter'.[32]

Hunter's defenders have argued that he must have performed the experiment on another person, for the simple reason that he performed similar inoculations on unknowing victims. Certainly Hunter described several experiments he performed on patients at St George's Hospital to test out his theories on venereal disease.[33] And it is highly unlikely the patients freely gave permission for such trials or were fully aware of the consequences, for the notion of informed consent was a long way in the future. At other times, Hunter managed to procure or bribe 'volunteers' to participate in peculiar and unpleasant experiments. His tooth transplants were one example. An even more bizarre trial involved comparing the temperature of a penis in living and dead humans. For this experiment Hunter persuaded a volunteer to immerse his penis in water which was heated or cooled to different degrees while his temperature was checked.[34] Yet there is no evidence in the case of the venereal experiment that Hunter procured a volunteer. Indeed, in May 1767 he had no hospital patients on which to practise, and it is extremely unlikely that any of his private patients would have volunteered for such a reckless trial, or that he would have risked his reputation by hoodwinking them into one. The idea that he hid a homeless pauper in his new home in elegant Golden Square for three years seems equally implausible.

Yet Hunter certainly performed numerous other experiments on himself, in common with many of his contemporaries. In one instance he fed himself with madder, a root used to produce a crimson dye, in order to see whether it turned his urine red. (It did).[35] At another time he drank a potentially lethal poison, laurel water, to discern its effect.[36] Hunter even made a clear reference to self-experimentation, perhaps specifically to the venereal inoculation, in 1782 in an article in the *European Magazine*, which was sanctioned by himself. Describing his conservative approach to medical care, the article commented, 'Though an enemy to operations on others, he was regardless of himself, and exposed his person to all the active and artificial powers, by which he might ascertain the properties, and trace the effects of medicine on the human frame.'[37] Hunter was not alone in making such sacrifices in the pursuit of progress: many scientists through the centuries have resorted to using themselves as human guinea-pigs.[38] Indeed, the Scottish surgeon Benjamin Bell, a pupil of Hunter's, concluded that syphilis and gonorrhoea were separate diseases – although his conclusion in 1793 was never fully broadcast – following experiments by medical students at Edinburgh University. In these reckless trials students almost exactly, but rather more successfully, emulated Hunter's inoculation experiment by producing classic symptoms of syphilis from pus taken from a chancre.[39]

By the time Hunter's treatise did appear, in 1786, it was eagerly anticipated. According to Joseph Adams, one of Hunter's later pupils, 'It was no sooner known that Mr Hunter was engaged on such a subject than the expectation of the medical world was raised to the highest pitch.'[40] Still painfully aware of his inadequacies when it came to writing, Hunter this time met with a committee of three friends, the physicians Gilbert Blane, George Fordyce and David Pitcairn, who checked his script 'to render the language intelligible' before Hunter committed himself to print.[41] A fourth adviser, George Baker, who was one of George III's physicians and another of Hunter's medical friends, may well have helped in the editing process too, for Hunter dedicated the work to him.

The treatise would have a profound impact on the understanding and treatment of venereal disease for many decades. As far as most surgeons were concerned, the debate over the duality or unicity of syphilis and gonorrhoea was at an end: Hunter had proved to their satisfaction as much as his own that both emanated from the one poison. Only in Edinburgh did the arguments rumble on, prompting Benjamin Bell to publish the opposite conclusion in 1793, a view that was widely accepted only after Ricord's extensive experiments. Such was Hunter's influence that the use of mercury to treat gonorrhoea and its continued use for syphilis – for he argued that it only treated the symptoms and did not provide a cure – diminished substantially.[42] At the same time his detailed descriptions of the symptoms of venereal diseases increased general awareness. Certainly they had a profound effect on James Boswell, who sank into a deep depression for several weeks after reading Hunter's work in April 1786, although this did not last long enough to prevent him contracting two further bouts of gonorrhoea.[43]

Almost as controversial as Hunter's conclusions on the nature of venereal infections was his broadminded approval of masturbation – a highly contentious topic in eighteenth-century Europe. Ever since the Swiss physician Samuel Tissot had published his essay *Onanism or a Treatise upon the Disorders produced by Masturbation*, translated into English in 1766, masturbation had been condemned as the root cause of all manner of ailments, not least impotence. Hunter dismissed this nonsense peremptorily in his usual matter-of-fact style. To his mind, impotence was simply too rare a complaint to originate 'from a practice so general' while those he had treated for the problem did not seem to have resorted to masturbation 'more than usual'.[44] He went on, 'but this I can say with certainty, that many of those who are affected with the complaints in question are miserable from this idea; and it is some consolation for them to know that it is possible it may arise from other causes'. He declared, 'I am clear in my own mind that the books on this subject have done more harm than good.' Needless to say, nineteenth-century editors would feel compelled to add an apologetic footnote asserting that masturbation was indeed harmful.

Hunter also proffered eminently sensible sexual advice to one patient who was experiencing difficulties performing with a woman he particularly wished to impress: he should sleep beside her for six nights while doing all in his power to resist sexual intercourse – a remedy commonly suggested by modern sex therapists. By the end of the week the would-be lover had fully recovered his virility, 'for instead of going to bed with the fear of inability, he went with fears that he should be possessed with too much desire'.

But Hunter's liberal and outspoken views on sex and sexual diseases would bring him vehement enemies. Foremost among them was the young surgeon Jessé Foot, who dedicated much of his life to darkening Hunter's reputation seemingly on account of a chance remark Hunter made about a bougie Foot had invented to treat strictures caused by gonorrhoea, as the artist Joseph Farington would later confirm: 'Foot the surgeon, became rancorous against John Hunter because the latter had seemed to describe a Bougie which Foot had invented as not necessary. To revenge himself He wrote on Hunter with much malignancy & asserted many falsehoods.'[45]

Since his impressionable youth as a surgical apprentice, Foot had climbed the slippery medical career ladder to gain a post at the Middlesex Hospital and build a fledgling private practice. Having worked along the way in the West Indies and St Petersburg, Foot had returned to London determined to make his mark, especially in the lucrative field of venereal complaints. His first publication in 1774 would discuss diseases of the urethra, and he was soon specializing in genito-urinary conditions. At one point he even treated a patient who had somehow accidentally applied some gonorrhoeal discharge to his eye, in consultation with Hunter.[46] But travel had not broadened Foot's horizons: he remained firmly wedded to the dogma of traditional teachings, revered the classics and spent his evenings poring over the works of past masters. A full sixteen years Hunter's junior, he plainly aspired to knock the controversial surgeon off his pedestal.

No sooner did Hunter's treatise on venereal disease hit the streets than Foot responded with a venomous counterattack, ridiculing Hunter's comments in a three-part diatribe published the same year. Some of his criticisms were undoubtedly shrewd: Foot accused Hunter of generalizing from too few circumstances, failing to study his predecessors and contemporaries, and writing in obscure and long-winded language, although he did not doubt Hunter's conclusion that syphilis and gonorrhoea were one disease. But, preening and arrogant, he consistently over-egged his remarks with snobbish, petty and vicious cynicism. Facetiously referring to Hunter as 'the Professor', he sneered, 'I have before me many pages so loaded with rubbish, so many useless sets of distinctions, sections so narrative and inapplicable stand in my way, as Hercules himself would turn from'. Frequently employing sentences so meandering that even Hunter would have baulked at them, he confessed his 'pleasure' at attacking his supposed rival and pronounced himself Hunter's self-appointed 'voluntary watchman'.

The fact that Foot felt impelled to expend such immense time and energy attempting to undermine Hunter's considerable reputation probably says more about Hunter than about Foot. Few people were indifferent to John Hunter. As his iconoclastic views gathered notoriety, he drew around him a loosely bound coterie of devoted friends, like-minded experimenters and fascinated up-and-coming young medical men who were spellbound by the charismatic and innovative scientist. To be a part of this dynamic circle – challenging accepted dogma, debating pressing topics of the hour, performing astonishing experiments – was to live in the full, brilliant glare of the eighteenth-century Enlightenment. For those privileged enough to be admitted to the intoxicating atmosphere of this inner sanctum, there would be a constant flow of new ideas to stimulate the imagination, novel theories to shock contemporaries, startling discoveries with which to astound friends and family. This was life on the edge – daring, thrilling, sometimes frightening but always exciting. To be outside looking in could seem, in contrast, a dark, cold and lonely place. And Jessé Foot was decidedly on the outside. He had worked alongside the famed surgeon at least once, he had considered attending his lectures at one point but rejected the notion as too expensive, and perhaps he had even aspired to join the throng surrounding the fêted anatomist.[47] But the perceived slight about his bougie put paid to that and Foot turned away, cast out of the fold for ever, destined to become a bitter, peeved and unfulfilled young man whose only claim to fame would be his assaults on Hunter.

Sure enough, Hunter's devotees quickly charged to his defence when Foot launched his attack on the venereal disease treatise. One pupil, Charles Brandon Trye, quickly penned a carefully worded pamphlet in reply which chiefly took Foot to task for attacking Hunter without once offering any evidence to back up his claims. In true Hunterian style, it was facts, not wit, that counted, the results of tried and tested research that mattered, not the dubious merits of a classical education. 'Mr Hunter's Treatise may have its imperfections,' Trye patiently countered. 'Had Mr Foote attempted to have pointed them out in a manner agreeable to the true spirit and laws of criticism, his undertaking might have been praise-worthy.' Instead, he noted, Foot 'writes against Mr Hunter, rather than his opinions'. And he pointedly con-trasted Foot's pretentious aspirations to fame with Hunter's commitment to scientific progress by concluding, 'That there can be any thing in Surgery or in Science novel to Mr Foote, let those determine, who are better acquainted with his erudition and knowledge. But as there are many in the profession, who have no pretensions to omniscience, to them it is possible that Mr Hunter may teach something.'[48]

Hunter himself never stooped to respond to Foot's persistent jibes in public, but he wrote jocularly to Trye to thank him for 'the pains you have taken to laugh at Jesse Foot' and sanctioned the publication of the reply. 'Poor

Jesse Foot wanted a dinner, and he thought he saw a fine animal he could live on for a while,' Hunter explained, adding with typical dismissal, 'every animal has its Lice'.[49] And he had little time for Foot's sniping comments about his lack of a classical education, at one time commenting, 'Jessé Foot accuses me of not understanding the dead languages; but I could teach him that on the dead body which he never knew in any language dead or living.'[50]

Whether or not Hunter gave himself a potentially lifelong bout of syphilis in May 1767, his health certainly began a slow deterioration within a few years, displaying a variety of symptoms that could possibly have been early signs of tertiary syphilis. But in the months immediately following the controversial trial he seemed in the full bloom of vitality as he continued his extensive research programme, and, copper-coloured blotches or not, to court his romantic poet. Hunter was a perpetual guest in Anne Home's household according to her young brother Everard, who remembered the surgeon's visits during school holidays. Hunter, he later recalled, always treated him with 'particular kindness'.[51] This was not, however, a kindness Everard would seek to repay as he became increasingly jealous of the surgeon's reputation. In the meantime, his sister would have to remain patient.

As well as continuing to be a regular visitor to the Home family, Hunter was fast becoming an important figure at meetings of the Royal Society in Crane Court, off the Strand. Among kindred spirits – the leading naturalists, inventors, engineers and explorers of the age – Hunter flourished. While the wilder eccentricities of the society's activities were roundly ridiculed by contemporary satirists, it was natural territory for Hunter.

Never keen to confine his interests to medical matters, within the society he could range over the myriad scientific fields that took his whim. At society meetings and social events he could talk botany with Daniel Solander, the talented ex-pupil of Linnaeus, who had left his native Sweden for London in 1760 and joined the staff at the newly established British Museum shortly after. In between cataloguing the motley collection of items languishing on the museum shelves, the mild-mannered botanist had developed a warm comradeship with Hunter. John Ellis, the naturalist who first encouraged Hunter, was a mutual friend. Hunter also became a life-long friend of Joseph Banks, the well-connected aristocratic naturalist who had become a fellow of the society a year before Hunter at the age of twenty-three. Having just returned from a botanical expedition to Newfoundland and Labrador, Banks was busy classifying his flora and fauna samples at his home in New Burlington Street, a five-minute stroll from Hunter's house in Golden Square. Probably it was George Fordyce, Hunter's fellow collaborator in experiments, who introduced the pair.[52]

Eager to continue these stimulating scientific debates after meetings had ended, Hunter led a splinter group of fellow members and other amateur scientists he introduced to the company to a nearby coffee-house, initially Jack's in Dean Street and later Young Slaughter's in St Martin's Lane. At these boisterous weekly gatherings members dined on oysters and shared ideas for investigations or papers.[53] Hunter quickly became regarded as chairman of this elite club – in Dr Johnson's terms he was eminently 'clubbable' – which included not just Solander, Banks and Fordyce but a host of other luminaries of the eighteenth-century Enlightenment. Members of Hunter's circle numbered at one point or another Dr Nevil Maskelyne, the astronomer royal, who was bent on discovering the key to longitude; Robert Mylne, the architect of Blackfriars Bridge, who would later marry Anne Home's younger sister Mary; James Cook, the naval explorer; and James Watt, who was diligently working on his designs for improving steam engines. Other members, all household names in their fields, included the civil engineer James Smeaton, the royal instrument maker Jesse Ramsden, and the mathematician Sir George Shuckburgh.

Richard Lovell Edgeworth, the Irish inventor, was introduced to Hunter's circle when visiting London in the late 1760s by James Keir, the Scottish chemist and fellow member of the Midlands-based Lunar Club.[54] Describing Hunter's group as a 'society of literary and scientific men', Edgeworth noted in his memoirs, 'Without any formal name, its meetings continued for years to be frequented by men of real science, and of distinguished merit.' He added, 'John Hunter was our chairman.' According to Edgeworth, Hunter kept numbers strictly limited through a rigorous initiation rite which only the hardiest of candidates could hope to survive. It entailed subjecting each would-be member to a barrage of mockery and abuse. 'We practised every means in our power, except personal insult, to try the temper and understanding of each candidate for admission,' Edgeworth remembered. 'Every prejudice, which his profession or station in life might have led him to cherish, was attacked, exposed to argument and ridicule. The argument was always ingenious, and the ridicule sometimes coarse.' With Hunter's known reputation for foul language and plain speaking, some of the more sensitive applicants must have baulked at this outright assault in front of their friends and associates; it is certainly hard to conceive how the nervous James Watt ever passed muster. But once admitted, the heat of the coffee-house wrangles was easily matched by the warmth of its friendships. As Edgeworth recollected, 'I have felt, ever since I belonged to this society, the advantage of its conversation.'

As well as debating current enigmas of the day, club members shared ideas for papers they were considering presenting to the Royal Society and sometimes read these aloud to the gathered guests. One initiative Hunter may well have shared with fellow members in the club's earliest days, in the summer of 1767, concerned a set of experiments in which he hoped artificially to impregnate silkworms – a prototype attempt at creating test-tube babies.[55] Keeping a female moth in confinement until she laid some unfertilized eggs, Hunter carefully dissected a male moth to extract a sample of semen with a 'hair pencil', then combined the two in a covered box. The experiment proved a remarkable success: eight of the eggs hatched at the same time as others that had been naturally impregnated. 'Thus then I ascertained that the eggs could be impregnated by art, after they were laid,' Hunter recorded.

He would later apply the results to remarkable effect, helping a couple who were experiencing difficulties conceiving a child. Since the husband suffered a congenital abnormality called hypospadias, in which the urethral opening is at the base rather than the tip of the penis, he was unable to impregnate his wife naturally. Hunter recommended that the couple have intercourse as normal, ensuring the wife was sexually stimulated, then collect the husband's semen in a warmed syringe and inject this into the wife's vagina. Seemingly it worked: the couple had their first baby soon after. The case is the earliest known record of artificial insemination, although it was left to Everard Home to reveal the details to the Royal Society after Hunter's death.[56]

One Royal Society fellow who was never listed among the members of the coffee-house club, however, was Hunter's own brother, William. He had far more refined company to impress by this stage of his career. Having attended Queen Charlotte at all three of her births to date, William was heavily in demand at the childbeds of the nobility, delivering heirs to great fortunes as well as the unwanted offspring of illicit liaisons. In December 1767 he helped the Viscountess Bolingbroke, Lady Diana Spencer, to secure a divorce by confirming that he had attended the birth of a child born of her affair with Topham Beauclerk.[57] At other times William would take care of the illegitimate offspring of aristocrats' mistresses with gentlemanly discretion; he attended Martha Ray, the famous mistress of Lord Sandwich, who was later killed by a jealous rival.[58] But sometimes his vanity overcame his professional confidentiality: he would entertain friends with the story of secretly delivering the twin babies of the daughter of a famous peer in her family home without her parents suspecting a thing.[59]

Though the brothers inhabited overlapping but different worlds, they continued on friendly terms – for the time being. When William heard in 1767 of some curious animal bones and teeth, similar to those of an elephant but considerably larger, discovered near the River Ohio he enlisted John's aid to explain the phenomenon. William arranged for a warden at the Tower of London, which had somehow acquired a hoard of the bones, to send him one of the tusks and one of the teeth for examination. The eminent French naturalists Georges Louis Leclerc, better known as the Comte de Buffon, and his colleague Louis-Jean-Marie Daubenton had already inspected similar bones and tusks and concluded that they must belong to elephants. Religious dogma suggested that all animal life created by God still existed on earth, and William was ready to accept this view too. Just to be sure he showed the specimens to John, whose expertise in comparative anatomy was now widely recognized. John did not hesitate to disagree with the Frenchmen: 'at the first sight he told me that the grinder was certainly not an elephant's', William reported. After being shown two elephants' jaws, with distinctly different teeth, from John's growing collection, William had to concede that his brother was right. William went on to declare in a bold and important paper to the Royal Society in February 1768 that the mysterious teeth and bones must belong to a previously unknown animal – an 'incognitum' – which had probably become extinct.[60] The bones would later be identified as belonging to a mastodon, a relative of the mammoth. William delivered the eloquently argued paper, but it was John who had solved the riddle.

William's wealth was expanding as fast as his social standing. By 1768 he admitted to his old mentor William Cullen that he was 'sinking money so fast, that I am rather embarrassed'.[61] He had commissioned, at great expense, a new house with a purpose-built lecture theatre and museum in Great Windmill Street, which was ready for occupation that summer. On occasion, John would pass to his better-off brother needy cases he deemed worthy of William's charity. Once he sent an impoverished patient who needed a physician's help with the brusque note: 'The bearer is very desirous of having your opinion. I do not know his case. He has no money, but you don't want any, so that you are well met.'[62] Whether William's sympathy was sufficiently aroused to come to the aid of such cases went unrecorded, although he continued to help John financially on occasion. And when William moved to Great Windmill Street, he gave the lease of his former home, at 42 Jermyn Street, to John. It was a fit home in which a newly married couple could raise a family; but Anne would still have to bide her time.

That same summer, John finally won entry to another professional body, but this was one he cared far less about than his beloved Royal Society. On 7 July he passed the oral examination at Surgeons' Hall to obtain the diploma of the Company of Surgeons, before examiners who included his former tutor Percivall Pott.[63] It was a full fifteen years since he had first begun practising surgery but Hunter gave the moribund company such little credence that he would never actively participate in its business. At the height of summer in 1768 he was far more wrapped up in the preparations being made by three of his dearest friends to embark on a perilous journey, one he fervently hoped would bring him new treasures for his ever-growing collection.

9

The Kangaroo's Skull

'John Hunter was a great man – *that* any one might see
without the smallest skill in surgery ... He would set
about cutting up the carcase of a whale with the same
greatness of gusto that Michael Angelo would have hewn
a block of marble.'

William Hazlitt[1]

Plymouth, August 1768

After five days waiting apprehensively while summer
storms lashed the south coast, at last on 25 August the
clouds cleared and a fair wind coaxed the *Endeavour* out
of Plymouth harbour.[2] Crammed with a year's supply of
provisions, packed with scientific instruments, and
crewed by eighty-five sailors, including a drummer, the
little ship's destination was the other side of the world.
The voyage was the first dedicated scientific mission
of its kind. Inspired by the Royal Society, bankrolled by

George III, and victualled by the Royal Navy, the expedition had two important aims: to observe the transit of Venus across the sun from the South Pacific island of Tahiti and to search for a fabled hidden continent in the southern hemisphere.

In command was James Cook, the good-looking and good-natured lieutenant who had made his name during the Seven Years War. Like John Hunter, Cook was the son of a humble Scottish farmer, although his family had settled in Yorkshire; like Hunter he was forty this year. The two had almost certainly met through mutual friends in the Royal Society; although not yet a fellow, Cook had submitted a paper in 1766 on a solar eclipse. On board with him were two of Hunter's closest friends, Joseph Banks and Daniel Solander, both intent on discovering new varieties of flora and fauna with which to delight fellow naturalists. At just twenty-five, Banks displayed all the self-confidence of his privileged background and his education at Harrow, Eton and Oxford; having come into a fortune yielding £6,000 a year at the age of twenty-one, he could comfortably afford the £10,000 he had committed to the expedition. Along with a retinue of seven attendants and a pair of greyhounds, Banks had packed a welter of nets, hooks and containers for catching and preserving wildlife. Invited by Banks to join the trip, the plump, affable Solander had jumped at the chance, promptly obtaining leave from the British Museum to join the voyage.

With the holds already crammed full, there was little space for Banks and his entourage. But this was no deterrent to the botanizing aristocrat. 'No people ever went to sea better fitted out for the purpose of Natural History, nor more elegantly,' the naturalist John Ellis wrote excitedly to his pen-pal Linnaeus. 'They have got a fine library of Natural History; they have all sorts of machines for catching and preserving insects; all kinds of nets, trawls, drags and hooks for coral fishing; they have even a curious contrivance of a telescope by which, put into the water, you can see the bottom to a great depth where it is clear. They have many cases of bottles with ground stoppers of several sizes to preserve animals in spirits.'[3] With Cook forced to share his captain's cabin with Banks and Solander, it was a cramped but happy ship that headed for the open seas.

Back in London, Hunter waited eagerly for news of his friends' discoveries. Charting the stars and seeking lost continents were of little interest to him; as far as he was concerned the principal purpose of the expedition was to bring back new and exotic wildlife to boost his burgeoning collection. Now that he had built up his reputation as a private surgeon and an expert anatomist, his renown as a naturalist was spreading just as fast. Having first begun dissecting and preserving animals in the Covent Garden anatomy school, Hunter had since spread his net much wider. Before long he had become every bit as adept at procuring animal carcasses as he was at obtaining human cadavers. Only the suppliers were different. So Hunter had become a familiar figure at travelling shows and circuses, where he promised animal keepers a bounty if they saved him the bodies of their exhibits when they died. He was a frequent visitor too at London's markets, shops and animal dealers, where customers could buy all manner of creatures as pets, livestock or ingredients for the cooking pot. Having obtained his wolf-dog puppy from 'wild beast Brookes', who sold an assortment of exotic animals at his shop in the New Road, Hunter bought eels every month from a local fishmonger in an attempt to discover their method of generation. At the same time he cultivated friendships with various aristocrats who kept rare animals in their private menageries, pestering them for carcasses. But Hunter's appetite knew no bounds; the more he collected the more he desired.

Obtaining exotic animals was easier than might be imagined in eighteenth-century London; the capital was a cornucopia of wildlife.[4] The royal menagerie was the city's most popular tourist attraction; no day out was complete without a visit to the lions at the Tower. Officially established in 1235 with the gift of three leopards to Henry III, the menagerie had steadily expanded with successive royal acquisitions. By 1767, the year before the *Endeavour* left Plymouth, visitors could see five male lions, three lionesses, two lion cubs, a panther, a leopard, and four tigers with the genteel names of Sir Richard, Miss Groggery, Miss Jenny and Miss Nancy.[5] How many of these exhibits ended up on Hunter's dissection bench is unrecorded, although his catalogue of pickled animal parts from around the same period bears an uncanny resemblance to the menagerie's inventory. Later writings refer specifically to an ocelot, an antelope, two hyenas and a caracal, or desert lynx, all received from the Tower.[6]

For those who could not afford the menagerie's 6*d* admission fee, there was no shortage of opportunities to see rare animals. Fairs, novelty acts and freak shows featured dancing bears, performing monkeys and even trained bees, while travelling menageries displayed exotic creatures brought back from foreign explorations. Among the curiosities on show in the mid-eighteenth century were the first crocodile to be seen alive in England and a rhinoceros 'in a natural coat of mail or armour'.[7] Only a little later a guidebook to London's sights claimed that there were 'Lions, Tygers, Elephants, &c in every Street in Town'.[8] While this boast may have been an exaggeration, it certainly contained a kernel of truth. On one occasion Hunter burst into the bookshop belonging to his friend George Nicol and begged the loan of five guineas; it was needed, he explained, to buy 'a magnificent tiger which is now dying in Castle Street'.[9] Having won his friend's consent, Hunter had the tiger's corpse carted away to his dissecting table.

Though a tiger dying in a West End thoroughfare could still excite Hunter's enthusiasm, other animals were commonplace. With the livestock regularly driven through London's streets, the popular bear- and bull-baiting events, the ships bringing whale carcasses to the Port of London, and the many more animals unloaded at the docks for consumption – turtles were shipped in alive as dinner-table delicacies – and for entertainment – monkeys were popular pets – London was fairly overrun with exotic creatures.

This abundance of wildlife did little to enhance the populace's general knowledge of the animal kingdom, however. Many Georgians still believed in the existence of unicorns, dragons and mermen, while a 'wonderful centaur' was a popular London attraction in 1751.[10] Books offered little enlightenment. In his famous 1755 dictionary, Samuel Johnson described whales as 'fish' and made no mention of giraffes; although a giraffe-like beast came under the name 'camelopard' – it reputedly had extremely long legs, a long neck and a spotted brown and white hide – it was still doubted that such peculiar-sounding animals could exist.[11]

Making full use of London's myriad opportunities for studying wildlife, Hunter had voraciously enlarged his natural history collection. By the time Cook, Banks and Solander set sail, he had already accumulated assorted parts from a lion, a porpoise, a seal, a monkey, a leopard, an opossum, a mongoose, a flying squirrel and a mole from South Carolina, as well as his lizards from Portugal and Belle-Ile, numerous examples of native British species, and the two elephant jaws he had shown his brother. Many of the rarer animals were the first of their kind to be seen in Britain. Every new animal he obtained was transported back to his home and laid out on his dissecting bench, where Hunter wielded his knife and tweezers to explore its internal structure. Interesting organs were preserved in spirits and unusual characteristics meticulously noted in a catalogue.

When he moved from Golden Square to the new house at 42 Jermyn Street, his collection of dried bones, skulls, skins and pickled organs came too. And as the animal carcasses arrived at his back door with increasing regularity, the fledgling collection soon took over several of the best rooms of the house. William, with his love of fine furnishings and distaste for comparative anatomy, must have been appalled. Yet even he was ready to acknowledge that John was now Britain's foremost authority on animal anatomy. His brother, he would say, had 'dissected with great attention almost every known quadrupede'.[12] Just as John Ellis had sought Hunter's expertise in dissecting the greater siren, so other amateur naturalists now begged his help whenever they obtained previously unknown species. According to Everard Home, Hunter's future brother-in-law, 'no new animal was brought to this country which was not shewn to him; many were given to him; and of those that were for sale he commonly had the refusal'.[13]

Yet while the Jermyn Street house provided a spacious home for his anatomical collection, the heart of London's West End was not the ideal location for dissecting and experimenting on large and often noisy wild animals. For this his country retreat at Earls Court was perfect. Having bought the farmland in 1765, Hunter had begun building a house there shortly afterwards and had since added extensions to form a modest country villa with a variety of outbuildings.[14] Nobody who passed its iron gates, which fronted the east side of what would become Earls Court Road, could do so without stopping to stare. Though the two-storey house in itself was unremarkable, the crocodile's jaw that yawned wide over the front porch gave an early signal of its owner's unusual pre-occupations. But it was the scene surrounding the house that really drew gasps from passers-by. Its typically English lawns were grazed not only by sheep, horses and cattle but zebra, Asiatic buffaloes and mountain goats, while neighbours could hear the roars of lions and snarls of leopards emanating from a large grassy mound within the garden. Beneath this hillock Hunter had built three dens to house his collection of wild cats.

Visitors brave enough to walk through the grounds would first pass a fish pond, decorated with animal skulls. Nearing the house, the howls of dogs and jackals chained in the kennels mingled with the cacophony of noises from the pigs, donkeys and domestic fowl scrubbing for food in the yard. To one side, a large conservatory vibrated with the hum of bees entering and leaving glass observation hives, while surrounding the entire building ran a six-foot-deep trench which led at one end to a stout wooden door. Opening this door revealed an underground laboratory containing a large copper vat in which Hunter boiled down the bodies of animals, and at times even humans, to obtain their skeletons; the great cauldron would one day play a significant role in the most extraordinary of all his quests for specimens. A contemporary newspaper summed up the scene: 'In the garden of Mr John Hunter, surgeon at Earl's Court, are seen buffaloes, rams and sheep from Turkey, and a shawl goat from the East-Indies, all feeding together in the greatest harmony; besides a prodigious variety of other beasts and birds supposed to be naturally hostile to each other but among which, in this new paradise, the greatest friendship prevails.'[15]

Whether Hunter's country estate amounted to a Garden of Eden or a vision of hell depended much on the spectator's viewpoint. Jessé Foot, of course, took a negative stance. 'Nobody of common curiosity could have ever passed this original cottage, without being obliged to enquire, to whom it belonged,' he reported. The lawns were clipped by 'savage beasts, said to have been snared on the lofty and arborous mountains of Thibet, or on the dreary wilds of Boutan'; shipped to Britain for the yearly Bartholomew Fair, these 'were sure to be first shewn to John Hunter; – their cunning parasitical keeper'.[16]

How Hunter's neighbours regarded the curious resident in their midst is difficult to judge. Certainly the villagers must have hurried past the sight, and stench, of a large whale bone, left over from one of Hunter's dissections, which lay discarded for years in a gutter on the north side of his house.[17] But it is easy to imagine excited village children hanging on the iron railings to gawp at the extraordinary wild creatures in their incongruous pastoral setting. It has even been plausibly suggested that Hunter provided the model for the children's book character Dr

Dolittle, the eccentric country physician whose fascination for natural history inspired him to become an animal doctor.[18] In his fictional home of Puddleby, John Dolittle kept exotic animals and built up friendships with travelling circus owners, just like Hunter. Likewise, Hunter on occasion treated animals belonging to his patients and would ultimately be instrumental in founding the Royal Veterinary College.

For Hunter, his country menagerie fulfilled two essential purposes: it allowed him to observe living animals in natural surroundings and to perform investigations on animals both dead and alive. And as his growing London clientele brought him increasing income to indulge his passion for collecting, he would spend more and more time among the bizarre flocks and weird beasts at his rural hideaway. This was business mixed with pleasure: he enjoyed watching his wild creatures from the windows of his study and even played with some of them. Naturally he recorded his observations. After listening to the eerie calls of a pair of leopards mating, he noted, 'Their noise is a mew but not so loud & hoarse & have a gutteral or hollow sound when angry very strong.' On another occasion he was delighted to see a hawk and a pigeon living happily together in the same cage, and wrote, 'Thus Animals not chusing to devour or hurt those that they are acquainted with is of great service in the Animal System and the Effect is beautifull.'[19]

All his life, Hunter would retain the reverence for nature he had felt as a child. Despite performing many experiments on living dogs, he was particularly fond of his canine pets, and he admired the industry of the bees he studied for hours in the glass hives he had specially designed for the conservatory. He noted, obviously from painful experience, that a bee about to sting made a different noise 'from that of the wings when coming home of a fine evening loaded with farina of honey; it is then a soft contented noise'. He even went so far as to compare this hum with the notes of a pianoforte, remarking that 'it seemed to be the same sound with the lower A of the treble'.[20] On a balmy summer's evening, far from London's pungent, smoky air, listening to the bees returning to their hives, the cattle lowing in the fields and the pigs snuffling in the yard, the scene must indeed have seemed idyllic.

Life was not always so harmonious, however. His amorous leopards on one occasion broke free from their chains and ran into the yard where they attacked the dogs. The commotion was heard all around, and 'the howling this produced, alarmed the whole neighbourhood', Everard Home later related.[21] Without stopping to consider the risks, Hunter ran from the house and into the fray. Grabbing one leopard by the scruff of its neck as it was about to scale the wall into the village, with the other hand he yanked its mate from the middle of the dog pack. Then he carried both animals, struggling and squealing, back to their den before realizing how close he and the rest of the neighbourhood had come to peril. As soon as he had secured the beasts, Home recorded, 'he was so much agitated that he was in danger of fainting'. He would have his revenge in his customary manner: two leopard skulls later found a place in his collection. In another display of his muscular strength, Hunter enjoyed wrestling with a bull he kept. The animal, a 'beautiful small bull', was a present from Queen Charlotte in return for the donation of twenty-eight preparations Hunter had presented to create a miniature anatomical museum at the

Royal Observatory, Kew, for the edification of the young princes and princesses.[22] But he obviously underestimated his combatant, for one day the bull threw him and was about to gore him when a quick-thinking servant drove the beast off.[23]

Yet behind all the madcap antics with dangerous animals and the musical comparisons with the hum of bees lay a serious scientific intent. Hunter was one of a long line of anatomists who had studied animal bodies since earliest times. Aristotle had dissected numerous animals including whales, and since then many anatomists had used animals, dead and alive, to further their explorations. In his milestone anatomical works, Vesalius included a helpful drawing of a custom-made table on which live beasts could be secured during experiments.[24] Among Hunter's contemporaries, the Monros, father and son, in Edinburgh and Albrecht von Haller in Switzerland were all keen vivisectionists.[25] As with other anatomists of the time, their research was intended to illuminate human anatomy and physiology; there was little interest in the internal structure of animals for its own sake. As Monro I explained, comparative anatomy was useful in revealing when past anatomists had used 'brutes' to draw conclusions on human anatomy and to expose their errors in doing so. 'The third and great use we reap from this science,' he added, 'is the light it casts on several functions in the human oeconomy about which there have been so many disputes among anatomists.'[26]

Elsewhere in Europe, specific interest in animal anatomy was fostered by a few enthusiasts.[27] In the Netherlands, Peter Camper had devoted himself to animal dissections; like Hunter, he was interested in the hearing ability of fish as well as the air spaces in birds' bones. In

France, the continuing collaboration between Buffon and Daubenton resulted in an impressive thirty-six-volume work, the *Histoire Naturelle*, published between 1749 and 1804, outlining the anatomy of a plethora of animals. The pair's detailed descriptions ranged far more widely over animal nature than anatomists such as the Monros and Haller with their definite human focus; certainly they came closest to Hunter's single-minded mission to understand all natural life.

At the same time, many naturalists were busy collecting and cataloguing newly discovered forms of fauna and flora, either by risking their lives travelling to distant lands, like Solander and Banks, or by pottering around their own neighbourhoods, like Gilbert White, who collected his specimens in Selborne, Hampshire. Generally, however, this passion for natural history was confined to describing the external appearances of known or new species and categorizing them to fit into a particular system of classification, principally from the late 1760s the binomial system invented by Linnaeus. And though many amateur naturalists built up large stores of plants and animals, these tended to be either random selections of stuffed skins and dried flowers or highly specialized collections of a particular species. The huge hoard Sir Hans Sloane left to the nation in 1753 – it formed the foundations of the British Museum, which opened six years later – comprised a gigantic jumble of stuffed animals, birds' eggs, dried plants, fossils and precious stones, with little semblance of order. Other collectors owned 'cabinets of curiosities' containing a confusion of natural history exhibits, ethnic artefacts and antiquities. The Dowager Duchess of Portland recruited Solander to help bring order to her large collection at

Bulstrode Park in Buckinghamshire; Horace Walpole took bookings for visitors to his treasure trove of oddities at his Gothic villa, Strawberry Hill, in Twickenham.[28] Others, such as Hunter's friend Ellis, devoted their lives to illuminating a single group of animals. In the case of Ellis, it was corals; for John Walsh, the MP and Royal Society member, it was electric fish.

John Hunter's explorations in natural history were radically different.[29] Initially he had begun, like the Monros and Haller, examining animals largely to illuminate the human body. His early experiments injecting milk into dogs' intestines were aimed at understanding how the human lymphatic system worked; when he cracked open hens' eggs to examine the developing chick fetus he was keen to know how the human embryo grew. But his animal studies soon constituted an important pursuit in their own right. This was neither a cursory interest in random items of natural history nor a specialized focus on any particular species; nobody in Britain would range as widely across the study of animal life or with such unified purpose as Hunter. His relentless dissections of different species were a systematic exploration of the whole natural world; humans constituted an important part of this study but were never the sole interest. His chief aim was to discover general principles or rules governing all organic life. As he explained, 'All animals must have certain general principles, or they would not be an Animal; and it is from the different combination of these principles that produce different animals.'[30] It was always the big picture Hunter looked for; it was science on a large scale that drew him. His labours would make him a pioneer, though rarely recognized as such, in the discipline that would become established in the following century as biology.

Hunter made his mission emphatically clear when fellow enthusiasts pressed him for studies of particular animals. Urged by John Pringle, his faithful patron, to describe the anatomy of the turtle, Hunter declined because 'the publishing of the description of a single animal, more especially a common one, has never been my wish'.[31] A contemporary magazine article, which Hunter sanctioned, explained, 'He means to class the animal world according to their structure, in which he has made considerable advances.'[32]

The stirrings of this lifelong quest began early. When Hunter had tested the hearing of fish in Lisbon, it was not fish in particular that interested him but the sense of hearing in all animal life. Refusing to accept other anatomists' view that fish had no ears, he quickly established that they possess internal hearing organs, thereby confirming his beliefs about the function of hearing in general. He explained, 'I am still inclined to consider whatever is uncommon in the structure of this organ in fishes as only a link in the chain of varieties displayed in its formation in different animals, descending from the most perfect to the most imperfect, in a regular progression.'[33] Everything, he was certain, fitted logically into a pattern.

We may observe that in natural things nothing stands alone, every thing in Nature having a relation or connection to some other natural production or productions and that each is composed of parts common to most others but differently arranged, and therefore in every natural product there is an appearance of an affinity in some of its parts to some other natural production because it has some of its parts in its composition; and where there are the greatest number of those affinities or parts as also the closer the connection or affinity between those of one production with those of another, the nearer are those allied.[34]

But always a staunch believer in the power of visual evidence rather than the ephemeral quality of words, Hunter's aim was most clearly to be seen in his collection. The human and animal preparations which he had moved into the fine rooms in Jermyn Street were no haphazard medley of curiosities but an ordered display systematically exploring organic life. No other collection of its kind existed. His purpose is plain even from his earliest surviving catalogue, created soon after returning from Portugal in 1763. In it he grouped together similar or analogous parts of different animals and humans.[35] So the kidneys of a lion, a racoon, a seal and a man were recorded under one heading; the eyes of a leopard, a porpoise, a horse and a child under another. Without doubt his bottled and dried parts were organized in the same way: differently sized eyeballs bobbed in alcohol on one shelf while variously shaped kidneys floated in jars on another; digestive organs were displayed in one section and reproductive organs in another. Every time Hunter dissected an animal he had not seen before he was intent chiefly on discovering where it would fit into nature's system – precisely how its particular organs mirrored or differed from those of similar species, how its internal structure slotted into an overarching pattern. From the 1760s onwards he began actively to look for similarities and variations between species which he believed might explain the secrets of life itself.

No animal was too large or too small, too simple or too complex, for Hunter's knife. One day might find him stooped over his bench searching for the brain in an earth-worm, another would see him wrestling with the stomach of an elephant. He dissected the most basic animal forms, such as polyps, and the most sophisticated, the human body. Mostly working without the aid of a microscope – for fear that it might, quite reasonably in its early form, distort reality – he observed, 'The circulation of the insect is probably very slow, if we may judge of the whole class by the motion of the heart in the caterpillar. In the silk-worm, for instance, the heart beats only 34 in a minute.'[36] With scarcely credible patience and dexterity, he dissected brains in leeches, worms and centipedes, tongues in bees and reproductive organs in silkworms.

Large mammals, however, could be equally challenging and just as entrancing. After opening a huge sperm whale, probably on a barge on the Thames standing on top of its blubbery carcass, as he had in 1759, he noted, 'the tongue was almost like a feather-bed'. And he added with characteristic awe, 'The heart and aorta of the spermaceti whale appeared prodigious, being too large to be con-tained in a wide tub, the aorta measuring a foot in diameter. When we consider this as applied to the circu-lation and figure to ourselves that probably ten or fifteen gallons of blood are thrown out at one stroke, and moved with immense velocity through a tube of a foot diameter, the whole idea fills the mind with wonder.'[37] Hunter's poetical descriptions of whales would later be cited as inspiration for *Moby-Dick*.[38] And even if Dr Johnson informed the reading world that whales were fish, Hunter had no doubts about their position in the overall plan. After comparing their organs with those of other mammals in his collection, he remarked, 'I shall always keep in view their analogy to land animals'. Impressed as he was by the grandeur of cetaceans, Hunter was just as fascinated by the worms he found in the whale's intestines, for which he did resort to a magnifying glass, observing, 'The proboscis of the animal is protruded from its funnel-shaped receptacle ... and is armed with numerous minute recurved hooks, visible by the aid of a lens.'[39]

While similarities between normal species were a compelling interest, abnormalities were just as absorbing. Hunter was intrigued by deviations from the norm, or 'monsters' in contemporary language, and he avidly collected such peculiarities. Already by 1767 his collection included the brains of a calf with two heads, a pig with two bodies, a kitten with two mouths, and a creature he described as 'the Elephant-Pig or Cyclops'; these he grouped together with a child born without a skull and an infant with spina bifida. He was equally bent on obtaining living examples of such abnormalities: at one point he kept a lamb with three legs at his Earls Court farm.[40] Such oddities were a common obsession in eighteenth-century Britain; people flocked to see animals and human freaks at fairs and shows. But Hunter's interest was more than curiosity. He realized that all animal life possessed an innate ability to become altered or deformed – his double lizard tails were a clear example – and was gradually coming to believe that this propensity for change might explain how life first developed.

His interminable trials at Earls Court on living creatures investigated every bodily function, including temperature, circulation, respiration, generation and digestion, in every possible animal. In one series of experiments he measured the body temperature of dogs, a rabbit, hens, fish, slugs, a carp, a viper, an ox and 'sleeping' (hibernating) dormice, as well as humans.[41] Initially he used a standard mercury thermometer for these trials. Since its invention by Gabriel Fahrenheit in 1714, such instruments had been readily available from specialist instrument makers in London. But finding this too clumsy for his purposes he commissioned his friend Jesse Ramsden, the royal instrument maker, to make him a smaller, more accurate model, just six inches long and less than one-sixth of an inch wide, with a sliding scale made of ivory. With this he concluded that all warm-blooded animals have their own regular body heat, which varies when sleeping or awake.

Other experiments begun at Earls Court in the 1760s were designed to discover how bones grow. Having caught a chicken in the yard, he drilled two holes in one leg and fixed a piece of lead shot into each.[42] After a while, he killed the hen, cut off its leg and measured the distance between the two pieces of shot; while the leg had grown more than three inches, the gap was exactly the same. His trial suggested correctly that limb bones grew by accumulating material at the outer ends rather than universally throughout their structure. Next he repeated the experiment on a piglet. When it was slaughtered at full size, the results replicated those with the hen. Still this failed adequately to explain how bone tissue grew and developed. For this, Hunter selected two more pigs and fed them with madder root for a fortnight. He was not the first to use the plant, traditionally used as a vegetable dye, for such experiments. A surgeon called John Belchier had reported to the Royal Society in 1736 that eating madder stained pigs' bones red; a few years later a French researcher, Henri-Louis du Hamel du Monceau, had used this effect to establish that bones grew widthways like trees, by the addition of layer upon layer, as well as lengthways in layers added at the ends, although his conclusions were still hotly disputed. Hunter killed one of his two pigs at the end of the fortnight, while the other was fed for a further two weeks on a normal diet before being killed for comparison. Dissection of the bones of this second pig revealed red and white strata in certain parts, clearly confirming du Hamel's theory that bone grew layer upon layer. Other parts of the bone remained white, however, suggesting that old bone matter had been absorbed. Hunter named this simultaneous absorbing and depositing of matter the 'modelling process'.

Though the spacious grounds at Earls Court allowed Hunter to observe numerous animals over long periods, other people's creatures were equally rewarding to watch. Hunter described a zebra that had been imported to England by Lord Clive, the hero of conquests in India who had fallen from grace since returning to his stately home at Claremont in Surrey. After attempting in vain to persuade the female zebra to mate with an ass, Clive had ordered the donkey to be painted with black and white stripes; suitably embellished, 'she received him very readily', Hunter recorded.[43] His observations would later be cited by Charles Darwin as part of the explanation of his theory of sexual selection in *The Descent of Man* (1871).[44]

Generation was an abiding interest, not only in the pregnant human corpses Hunter had dissected in Covent Garden but in all manner of animals too. One winter in the late 1760s, Hunter caught six male house sparrows and compared the size of their testes as the mating season progressed. Preserving their tiny bodies to show the ten-fold increase in testicle size from the dimensions of a pinhead to those of a marble, he recorded with his typical admiration for nature, 'If we compare their size in January with what it is in April, it hardly appears possible that such a wonderful change could have taken place during so short a period.'[45] Before long he had repeated the experiment on frogs and skate, and proudly displayed the series to guests invited to see his collection.[46]

But in the late summer of 1768, with Cook, Banks and Solander heading for the South Pacific, Hunter was setting his sights on rather more exotic creatures than house sparrows. He would have to be patient, though: it would be three years before the adventurers returned to England with their treasures. At the same time his friends in the Royal Society waited eagerly for news of their celestial gazing and territorial searches. But for their president, James Douglas, the Earl of Morton, that news never came. On 12 October, as Cook neared the Equator, Morton died after suffering a stomach complaint for several years. Since the peer had been both a friend and a patient of John Pringle, it was only natural he should call in the society's favourite anatomist to dissect the body. 'I prevailed upon the family to have the body opened, & by the younger Hunter, an excellent hand for that business,' Pringle informed his friend Haller.[47] Unable himself to watch the post-mortem, since he suffered 'the weakness not to be able to see the dissection of a friend', Pringle nevertheless received a detailed report of the proceedings from Hunter, as well as a portion of his friend's diseased stomach. Whether or not the Earl of Morton's family shared Pringle's 'weakness' over the dissection of a loved one, they too were treated to a meticulous description of the autopsy. The diseased stomach, meanwhile, joined the exhibits in Hunter's home.

Hunter's collecting passion was proving an expensive habit. While some specimens, such as Morton's stomach and various animals, were gifts from well-meaning friends, Hunter was expending large sums to procure the anatomical curiosities he craved from dealers, circus owners and auctions. At the same time, of course, the flint glass jars and spirit for preserving his preparations were hugely expensive and heavily taxed, and his expanding Earls Court establishment required increasing numbers of staff to tend its animal population. There was his future wife to consider too: as an assiduous society hostess she would certainly expect generous household support in Jermyn Street. Although Hunter was making his way as an up-and-coming surgeon, his income from patients' fees was still insufficient to keep pace with his escalating outgoings. Indeed, it was this relative poverty – rather than Hunter's reckless self-experiment – that Everard Home later blamed for the delay to Hunter's long-awaited marriage. According to Foot, Hunter's income failed to match the 'perpetual expense' of his museum until 1780. Just as he had begged his friend George Nicol for five guineas to buy a dead tiger, Hunter would always be dependent on loans and handouts from friends and money lenders to make ends meet. On several occasions he mortgaged land at Earls Court to raise funds for his ventures.

Unlike William, who was rapidly building up a collection of coins, books and paintings as a solid investment, John had not the slightest inclination to generate a profit. All he earned, he spent. And he plainly regarded his routine work, pandering to the whims of malingering rich clients, largely as a way of fuelling his collecting habit. On one occasion he wearily told an assistant, 'Well . . . I must go and earn this damned guinea, or I shall be sure to want it tomorrow.'[48] When Hunter's friend the physician George Baker was asked by a mutual acquaintance whether or not the anatomist would appreciate some form of edible delicacy as a birthday present, Baker replied, 'He cares not what he eats or drinks and I am sure that a curious case or some anatomical curiosity would be more agreeable to him than all the wine and all the venison in the country.'[49] It was flesh for his dissecting table not meat for the dining table, alcohol for his preparation bottles not wine for his palate, that Hunter desired. Nevertheless, his expensive lifestyle and impending marriage made it imperative that he augment his earnings. And so, when a vacancy for a surgeon at St George's Hospital arose in November, it was an opportunity Hunter could not afford to miss.

On 9 December 1768, the boardroom of St George's Hospital was crammed full. More than 160 governors had turned up for the meeting to elect a new full-time surgeon. Bishops, lords, dukes and other pillars of Georgian society took their seats to cast their votes for one of the two candidates: the junior surgeon David Bayford, who had dutifully served his long apprenticeship to one of St George's most esteemed men, and John Hunter, the controversial anatomist and naturalist who had not treated a patient at St George's since his five-month stint as a house surgeon twelve years earlier.

There is little doubt which candidate the hospital's surgeons supported. The surgical staff comprised three powerful and ambitious men: Caesar Hawkins, William Bromfield and John Gunning, all of them prominent members of the backward-looking Company of Surgeons, all of them influential figures in London's medical establishment. Hawkins, who had worked at St George's since the year after its foundation in 1734, had served as George II's surgeon and now served George III in the same capacity.[50] Reputed to earn £1,000 a year – more than £70,000 in modern terms – from bloodletting alone, he was not the kind of man to question traditional doctrines. Bromfield, who had worked at St George's for twenty-four years, was not only a stalwart of the Company of Surgeons – the following year he was appointed its master – but a favourite with the royal household; he was soon to become surgeon to Queen Charlotte.[51] It was under Bromfield that Bayford, Hunter's rival for the vacancy, had completed his apprenticeship. So Bayford could almost certainly count on the backing of his former teacher, and most likely Hawkins too, and he would definitely have expected support from Gunning, the hospital's third surgeon, who had attained a staff post three years earlier.[52] Gunning had not forgotten Hunter's gall in snatching the house surgeon's post from under his nose in 1756, despite the fact that he had taken over the job himself later that year and had since won his staff position. As far as these three were concerned there was really no contest: Bayford was a St George's man, schooled in the St George's traditions, and having served his apprenticeship on the wards the vacancy was morally his. Furthermore, among the four physicians on the board, three may have been equivocal about Hunter's selection but there would have been no doubts in the mind of Donald Monro, second son of Alexander Monro I and older brother of the Hunters' bitter rival Alexander Monro II; indeed, it was probably Donald who had sparked the row between his brother and the Hunters by relating discoveries he had heard in William's lectures to his young sibling in Edinburgh.

But they had not reckoned with John Hunter, or rather with John's influential brother William. Since becoming governors themselves, both brothers had diligently attended board meetings during 1768.[53] Through these gatherings, and William's considerable contacts with the rich and powerful in Georgian society, the brothers had become friendly with fellow governors such as the actor David Garrick, whose wife was one of William's patients, and the artist Joshua Reynolds, another intimate of William who became a firm friend of John too. Whether he saw it as a favour for John or for William, Reynolds made sure he turned out for the St George's vote on 9 December. And this was no casual favour, for on the same day he had three crucial meetings with fellow artists in readiness for an audience with George III the next day to establish the Royal Academy of Arts.[54]

In truth, many of the high-ranking governors at St George's had probably never even heard of young Bayford, while almost all would have known of John Hunter. His reputation might have cut no ice with the staunch surgeons at St George's – only Bromfield was a Royal Society fellow – but it plainly swayed its all-important governors. The votes divided 42 for Bayford, 114 for Hunter.

At forty, having gained his surgical diploma only five months earlier and never having completed a traditional hospital training, but with more anatomical experience than the rest of the hospital's staff put together, Hunter had finally secured his first proper surgeon's job. It was the beginning of a steady rise in his prospects. A staff surgeon's job brought no salary – all hospital appointments were honorary – but it still promised a substantial boost in income: not only could hospital surgeons earn fees from teaching apprentices and house pupils, their private practice benefited from their leap in status. Moreover, Hunter now had access to a ready pool of patients on which to practise his art and perform his experiments. Just as he used the animals he kept at Earls Court as fodder for investigations, so his patients at St George's would become human guinea-pigs in his tireless research programme.

But it was the beginning, too, of bitter rivalry and pernicious infighting which ultimately would lead to disaster. Conflict was inevitable. Hunter's dogged determination to question accepted doctrines, his fascination with innovation and experiment, and his commitment to founding surgical practice on sound scientific principles were anathema to his fellow surgeons at St George's. But if Hunter's colleagues felt uneasy with their newest recruit, their qualms were not about to be assuaged by any efforts at tact or diplomacy on Hunter's part. Always outspoken and never one to suffer fools, Hunter was not the type of man to curb his language for the sake of harmony or to nurture change through gentle persuasion. When offered resistance, like the fierce little bull he kept at Earls Court he was more likely to put his head down and charge straight at his opponents.

For the moment, at least, an uneasy peace prevailed. Hunter duly attended the hospital to admit emergency patients on his allotted day, completed his ward rounds according to the agreed rota, and patched up casualties in the operating theatre as best he could. And if the surgeons at St George's kept their own counsel for the time being, Hunter's surgical skills were certainly in demand elsewhere in the capital. On 21 October the following year he was called out urgently to help perform an extremely rare and exceedingly risky emergency operation.[55] A twenty-three-year-old woman, Martha Rhodes, had gone into labour at her home in Holborn, but as she was just four feet four inches tall and had severe deformities in her spine and hips, the delivery was not going well. The midwife called to deliver the baby had quickly discerned that her patient's contorted frame would make a natural delivery exceptionally difficult, and in accordance with common practice when births were progressing poorly she had sent for a physician, William Cooper, for advice. Equally at a loss as to how to help, Cooper called in a bevy of colleagues for a bedside conference.

Altogether six physicians and five surgeons crowded around Martha's bed in the cramped and dark room. An examination confirmed what the midwife had already suspected: Martha's pelvis was too narrow for her to give birth naturally. Surgeons and physicians were unanimous: the only chance of survival for both mother and baby was a Caesarean section. Informed of their joint opinion, poor Martha 'cheerfully consented' to the operation. Henry Thomson, a surgeon at the London Hospital, was to perform the surgery; John Hunter, with his unsurpassed knowledge of the anatomy of the pregnant womb, would be his assistant. None of the medical men gathered around Martha's bed was in any doubt about the perilous nature of the operation and her slim chances of survival. None had ever performed or witnessed such a procedure before, and when Thomson hurriedly skimmed through the surgical texts he kept at home he found there 'very little satisfaction in regard to the manner of performing the operation'. All would have heard reports of successful Caesarean operations, but these were vague, unauthenticated stories, almost in the realms of folklore, and certainly lacked any useful technical advice.

Although the term Caesarean was widely believed to have emanated from the manner of Julius Caesar's birth, the Roman ruler had almost certainly not been born by this method, for his mother was still alive many years after his birth.[56] The operation was undoubtedly carried out in ancient times, but usually posthumously, when women died in labour. On the extremely rare occasions when the operation was performed on living women few, if any, survived. Since then accounts of Caesarean sections had circulated, with varying reports of success. In 1500, a Swiss farm labourer had reputedly performed a Caesarean on his own wife, who survived to give birth to five more children. In Ireland in 1738, a midwife had reportedly performed a successful operation on a woman who had been in labour for twelve days; the midwife had held the wound together with her hands while a neighbour ran to fetch needle and thread for the stitches. There were even stories of women who had in desperation cut open their own wombs during difficult labours. But there had been no accounts, not even folk tales, of surgeons performing successful Caesarean sections in Britain.

Thomson and Hunter were undeterred; in truth, they had little alternative. Dosed with opium, Martha Rhodes was placed on a table, her head on a pillow, as Thomson took up his knife. With physicians and surgeons craning to see, he made a six-inch-long incision in her belly, then opened the womb to reveal the baby curled inside. One of the physicians yanked the child out by its feet, upon which it 'cried as heartily as children commonly do'. Now Hunter pushed the woman's intestines out of the way while Thomson swiftly stitched the wound. Throughout the grisly procedure, Martha barely complained. As

Cooper later recorded, 'She behaved with surprizing fortitude during the whole process, lost very little blood, and seemed to be most of all sensible to pain when the needles were passing through the peritonaeum, especially on the right side of the wound.'

Afterwards, however, things took a turn for the worst: Martha declined and died five hours later, most probably from internal bleeding. Her child, who had seemed initially healthy, had severe brain damage; it died two days later. Hardly able to refuse the persuasive appeals of eleven eminent medical men, the grieving family consented to an autopsy and Martha was dissected in the presence of another large audience, this time including William Hunter, who reported details to the Royal Society. Although the name of the anatomist performing the autopsy went unrecorded, it was almost certainly his brother, John. It would be several more decades before a Caesarean section was performed by a surgeon in Britain – by James Barlow, in Blackburn in 1793, assisted by one of the Hunter brothers' early pupils, Charles White – after which the woman survived. Even then the operation was carried out without the aid of either pain relief or antiseptics.

Demand for Hunter's presence at post-mortems continued unabated; the practice was gaining wide acceptance within Georgian society. That December of 1769, it was Pringle again who called on Hunter's expertise to dissect a patient, a sixteen-year-old youth, who had died of a fever.[57] After watching Hunter saw open the skull of his former patient, Pringle was gratified to observe that the boy's brain appeared diseased, just as he had diagnosed. But as Hunter continued to remove and examine the youth's organs with his usual thoroughness,

THE KNIFE MAN

Pringle was baffled to see that the boy's stomach had a huge hole at one end. Convinced that his patient had not suffered any digestive complaint, Pringle questioned his friend on the organ's appearance. Hunter had seen the same effect many times in his twenty-one years of dissecting bodies. At first, he too had assumed the gaping holes in the stomach wall were connected to the cause of death, but having witnessed a similar phenomenon in bodies that had died a violent death – that is, in people who had previously been in good health – he had since surmised that the damage was due to the solvent power of the stomach itself. Naturally enough, he had confirmed his hypothesis in experiments on animals including a dog and 'a vast variety of fish'.

Pringle was fascinated, particularly since the process of digestion was a matter of intense debate among eighteenth-century anatomists. Although the French naturalist René Réaumur had discovered gastric acid in animals' intestines in 1752, confusion over how digestion occurred continued, rival anatomists arguing over whether the process was caused by heat, muscle pulverization or a chemical reaction. Not only did Pringle dash off a letter to his chief foreign correspondent, Haller, relating the news in excited detail, he persuaded Hunter to report his findings to the Royal Society. 'Where are we now!' Pringle declared to Haller. 'Must we return to a *menstruum* [solvent] for digestion; & a *menstruum* too that does not belong to the Laboratory of mortal Chemists? What a strange menstruum, to spare the living stomach, but to consume the dead one!'

But Hunter was in no such confusion. When he finally got round to putting his thoughts on paper for the Royal Society in 1772, his views were lucid and decisive.

312

Pointing out the clinical importance of distinguishing appearances in the dead body as a result of disease and those due to natural post-mortem changes, he explained that after death the digestive powers of the stomach acted on the body just as they had previously done on food. He had observed the effect on two men who had died from blows to the head and a soldier who had been hanged, he noted, as well as in many animals. 'These appearances throw considerable light on the principles of digestion,' he informed the fellows; 'they show that it is not mechanical power, nor contraction of the stomach, nor heat, but something secreted in the coats of the stomach, which is thrown into this cavity.'[58] This 'gastric juice', as he called it, was an acid, 'a little saltish or brackish to the taste', he added. How many of the fellows joined him for oysters at his usual coffee-house gathering that evening is unrecorded. In only his second paper to the society, Hunter had conclusively demonstrated the actions of the gastric juices, which contain hydrochloric acid, and settled the debate on digestion. He kept the youth's dis-integrated stomach, along with another from one of his own patients, a six-month-old boy, and preserved them in bottles.[59]

Hunter's shelves were filling up fast. Before long, the two stomachs were joined by the aorta of an old campaigner, Major-General Robert Armiger. At sixty-eight, the experienced soldier had married a woman of forty and after an evening's celebrations in March 1770 had brought her home to consummate the relationship. But the wedding-night excitement was all too much for the veteran of heavy battles and within half an hour of retiring to bed he suddenly died. Called in to dissect the body, Hunter confirmed the general had suffered a heart attack and confided to his case books, 'It is not known whether or not he was taken ill in the Act of Consummation.'[60] This was not prurient interest, it was simply that obtaining a dead body in the middle of copulation was a rare occurrence indeed and might feasibly shed light on the physiology of generation. Accordingly, Hunter also dissected the general's sexual organs, noting that his penis was 'very large, & almost half erected', his testicles 'fuller of blood than common', and that the sperm-carrying vessels were 'full of semen'.

While one day would see Hunter labouring over a naked corpse with a smile on its face, another would find him examining the carcasses of peculiar-looking beasts newly arrived on home shores. One such was the nilgai, or 'nyl-ghau', which had first been brought to Britain from India in 1767; a pair of the bull-like creatures with their distinctively blue coats had been sent to Lord Clive as a present. The following year a second pair was donated to Queen Charlotte, another enthusiastic menagerie owner, who was happy to oblige when her faithful male-midwife William Hunter asked to borrow the animals. Quite possibly cajoled by his younger brother, William kept the beasts in the stables at his new home in Great Windmill Street. He even had one of the curious animals, with its goatishly small head and tiny horns stuck incongruously on its robust, muscular body, painted by one of his artist friends, George Stubbs, who was fast becoming famous for his animal pictures.[61]

As he watched the gentle creatures, which licked his hand when he fed them, William suspected the nilgai might be a hitherto unknown species.[62] But he was aware this question could only satisfactorily be settled by one person, his brother John, and only then by dissecting the dead animal. So when, shortly afterwards and rather conveniently, one of the pair died, William obtained permission from Queen Charlotte for John to work on the beast. Just from examining its teeth and digestive system alone, John was convinced the nilgai was indeed a distinct species.[63] William, of course, reported the findings to the Royal Society, adding another paper to his name. John skipped home to Jermyn Street with his booty – the skeleton of the creature for his collection.[64]

Hunter now knew that before long even more exotic creatures would be in his hands, for news of the *Endeavour*'s arrival in Java in October 1770, after circling the islands of New Zealand and charting the western coast of New Holland, as Australia was known, had reached London. 'The Naturalists write with great spirits,' Pringle reported to Haller, '& say they are loaded with new plants & other natural productions.'[65] Waiting in eager anticipation of the new species he hoped to examine, that same month Hunter found a fellow enthusiast to share his passion for the animal kingdom.

Edward Jenner, a vicar's son from Berkeley in Gloucestershire, enrolled as a pupil at St George's Hospital that October and immediately took up residence as Hunter's first house pupil.[66] Well mannered, neatly dressed and gifted both in poetry and music, the twenty-one-year-old Jenner might have seemed more suitable a companion for Hunter's talented young fiancée than his brash, bombastic teacher; but in spite of the gap in ages and cultural interests, Hunter and Jenner were kindred spirits. Having lost his father, like Hunter, as a child, Jenner had spent his spare time at boarding school hunting, as Hunter had, for wildlife in the surrounding countryside. After having been apprenticed to a local surgeon since the age of thirteen, Jenner had come to London to complete his medical education. Enrolled at St George's, he now walked the wards alongside the hospital's most controversial surgeon, imbibed his iconoclastic views on treating patients, assisted as his 'dresser' in the operating theatre, and helped him in the dissecting room. When Hunter visited his wealthy clientele in their West End homes, or treated patients at his own house, Jenner was at his side, admiring the surgeon's no-nonsense advice delivered in his bluff manner. As if his days were not already busy enough, Jenner also enlisted for anatomy lectures at William's Great Windmill Street school, as well as attending lectures in chemistry and obstetrics. But his most productive and pleasurable hours were spent working side by side with Hunter at the Jermyn Street house they now shared, and at Hunter's Earls Court retreat, as they explored together the anatomy of the corpses delivered by the Resurrectionists, examined the bodies of rare creatures sent from the Tower, and conducted experiments on living creatures.

From the start, the lively young student revered and adored the charismatic mentor who fostered his interest in natural history, inspired a delight in experiment, and above all taught him to think for himself. It was Hunter's doctrine – of observation, experiment and application – Jenner would faithfully follow when, nearly thirty years later in 1796, he tested the smallpox vaccine. Not only would Jenner's innovation save millions of lives, it would become the only medical therapy ever to eradicate a disease completely from the face of the earth.[67] Hunter was equally enchanted by his industrious pupil, who shared his love of nature and novelty; Jenner would always be not just his first but his favourite disciple. So, as the

Endeavour finally approached the English Channel at the end of its three-year world tour both Jenner and Hunter were waiting impatiently to gain first sight of its haul of natural treasures.

They were not alone. Since hearing that Cook's ship was on its way home from Java, every naturalist in Europe had scanned the newspapers for details of the daring expedition's discoveries. When at last the ship anchored off Deal on 12 July 1771, nobody was disappointed. The *Endeavour* had almost been shipwrecked on the Great Barrier Reef and had lost thirty-eight of its crew to sickness, but its holds were crammed to bursting with a bounty of seeds, dried plants, bottled marine creatures and preserved animals of varieties never seen in Europe before. Chests of gold plundered from Spanish merchant ships could scarcely have aroused more excitement; it was a collector's dream. John Ellis wrote immediately to tell his friend Linnaeus that Banks and Solander had returned 'laden with the greatest treasure of Natural History that ever was brought into any country at one time by two persons'.[68] The two adventurers had indeed brought back no fewer than 1,400 new plant species, more than a thousand new species of animals, including a handful of mammals, more than a hundred birds, over 240 fish, and assorted molluscs, insects and marine creatures.[69] It would take the pair twelve years to classify their haul.

Hastening to welcome his friends, Hunter immediately recommended his talented new pupil to help them catalogue their finds. Most were destined for Banks's own collection, with a few choice items donated to the British Museum, but there were generous pickings for Hunter too. Among the new animals he added to his collection were a sea-pen, a simple aquatic animal, from Rio de Janeiro; sharks' eggs and eels from the South Seas; a mole-rat and a zorilla, or striped polecat, from the Cape of Good Hope; and part of a giant squid.[70] But most astonishing of all was the peculiar grey animal that Banks had named, with his limited understanding of native dialects, a 'kangooroo' or 'kangaru'. The ship's crew had first sighted the curious creature – 'an animal as large as a greyhound of a mouse colour and very swift' – while repairing their vessel on the east coast of New Holland on 22 June 1770; Banks saw the animal for the first time a few days later.[71] The following month the ship's second lieutenant, John Gore, shot a large male and Banks recorded in his journal, 'To compare it to any European animal would be impossible as it has not the least resemblance to any one I have seen.' The next day the kangaroo was served up for dinner and 'proved excellent meat', Banks wrote.[72] It was enough to make a comparative anatomist weep; the kangaroo was one of many exotic creatures the *Endeavour* crew devoured in their hunger for fresh meat. A second kangaroo fell victim to Gore's shotgun a few days later, and on 29 July one of Banks's greyhounds caught a small female. The flesh had been long since consumed, but Banks had brought back the skins and skulls of the extraordinary creatures. Back in London, he commissioned George Stubbs to paint a picture of the marsupial using a stuffed skin and a little imagination; it was the first portrayal of a kangaroo seen by Western eyes. He gave his friend, John Hunter, one of the skulls.[73]

It was not much to go on, but Hunter still hoped he could tell something about the strange animal Banks had described by examining its teeth and jaws and comparing them with species he had already dissected. He was confounded. 'The teeth of this animal are so singular that it is impossible from them to say what tribe it is of,' he recorded. There were similarities with the teeth of several animals with which he was familiar, yet he was forced to conclude that 'the teeth did not accord with those of any one single class of animals I was acquainted with, therefore I was obliged to wait with patience till I could get a whole'.

It would be almost two more decades before Hunter could fulfil his ambition, when John White, surgeon-general to the first British colony in New South Wales, sent back a treasure trove of preserved animals in 1788. As well as various birds, fish and insects, it included a dingo, a potoroo or kangaroo rat, several possums, and, finally, several complete kangaroos. The job of describing the mammals for White's subsequent book, *Journal of a Voyage to New South Wales*, published in 1790, fell to Hunter. As George Shaw, his collaborator, remarked, 'There was no person to whom these could be given with so much propriety as Mr Hunter, he perhaps being most capable of examining accurately their structure, and making out their place in the scale of animals.'[74]

At last Hunter was able to explore the entire anatomy of the kangaroo, to examine the female marsupial's unusual double reproductive organs, to appreciate its peculiar method of nurturing its young in pouches, and to describe other remarkable antipodean animals in detail. Hunter was plainly aware that the species Banks and Cook had discovered were unique to the antipodean islands, noting, 'they are, upon the whole, like no other that we yet know of', and that their anatomy showed particular adaptations to their environment. This realization, that there were species in parts of the world unlike those anywhere else, provided yet another piece to slot into the big puzzle of how life on earth had developed. His descriptions of kangaroos and other creatures from Cook's first voyage would eventually appear in his extensive work of comparative anatomy *Observations on the Animal Oeconomy* (1786); he dedicated the book to Banks. But he was not going to run the same risk again of waiting in eager anticipation for friends to bring new specimens for his collection only to find they had eaten the best bits. He drew up detailed notes, 'Directions for preserving animals, and parts of animals, for examination', expressly to enlighten well-meaning amateur explorers on how to preserve the specimens they brought home. They included instructions on the best way to preserve birds, by drowning them in spirits; small mammals, which should be pickled whole; insects, which should be 'wrapt up in very soft paper, and then packed up in cotton'; and large mammals, which should be cut into parts and brought back in several casks.[75]

The summer of 1771 was a busy one. Jenner and Solander were immersed in cataloguing the *Endeavour*'s haul and Hunter was finally going ahead with his marriage. The fact that his three-year experiment on venereal disease had ended the previous year may or may not have been the spur. No doubt his new hospital post and the £200 he received in 1771 for his treatise on teeth helped to boost his suitability for marriage.[76] And strangely, after waiting seven years, he was suddenly in a great hurry to arrange the wedding. A marriage licence was obtained on 21 July. That evening John dashed off a hurried note to his brother William: 'To morrow morning, at eight o clock at St

James's Church I enter into the Holy State of Matrimony. As that is a ceremony which you are not particularly fond of, I will not make a point of having your company there.'[77] William, who believed wedlock was incompatible with a career devoted to anatomy – he had dissolved his partnership with his assistant, William Hewson, the previous year chiefly on the grounds that he had married – did not attend the ceremony.

John Hunter and Anne Home were married on Monday, 22 July 1771, with her parents as witnesses; he was forty-three and she was twenty-nine.[78] Having returned to London just over a week earlier, Banks and Cook were home in time to attend the ceremony, as indeed one anecdote suggests they did. According to the tale, the travellers gave the couple a wedding present of some hickory wood which they had cut down in New South Wales; John had it made into a set of dining chairs for his 'Anny'.[79] Sparing a few days from Hunter's busy round of work, the couple spent a honeymoon 'out of Town', most probably at Earls Court.

One old family friend had been unable to attend the wedding. Tobias Smollett, the long-suffering writer, was ailing in his adopted home of Italy that summer, and on 17 September, two months after the publication of his most acclaimed novel, *The Expedition of Humphrey Clinker*, he died, aged fifty. Earlier in the year, in a moment of foreboding, he had promised John his body after death to display in his collection, declaring in a letter from Leghorn (Livorno), 'you shall receive my poor carcase in a box, after I am dead, to be placed among your rarities'.[80] By promising his body to Hunter, at least Smollett could make plain his consent to go under the knife in the knowledge he might end up on the

anatomists' slab in any case. His lifelong rival Laurence
Sterne had been buried in 1768 in St George's ground,
that popular grave-robbing haunt, only to reappear two
days later on a dissecting table at Cambridge University.[81]
Although the author of *Tristram Shandy* was recognized
by a friend, the dissection proceeded and Sterne's skeleton
was allegedly preserved at the university for several years.
Ironically, having expressly requested such an end,
Smollett escaped dissection. When he died his wife was
either unwilling or unable to ship his corpse from Italy.

There would be plenty more bodies, both human and
animal, to fill Smollett's place. As Anne enjoyed her first
days alone with her new husband and looked out from
their bedroom window at Earls Court on the rare and
varied creatures grazing her English country garden, she
could have been in no doubt of the extraordinary life that
lay ahead. After returning to their townhouse in Jermyn
Street, with its elegant rooms filled with preserved human
organs, heads, bones and fetuses, it would have been
abundantly clear that she had married an extraordinary
man.

10

The Electric Eel's Peculiar Organs

'The surgeons of Hunter's day thought of him as a mere imaginative speculator, and anyone who believed in him a blockhead and black sheep in the profession.'

Astley Cooper[1]

London, 1772

If London's West End was always bustling, then life at 42 Jermyn Street was frenetic. John Hunter's bachelorhood days, spent rattling around a large, empty house, were over. Now his home was constantly busy, his doors never closed, his neighbours' peace forever shattered. Throughout the day patients arrived for private consultations, pupils turned up for dissection practice, colleagues dropped in to discuss cases, visitors called for dinner, and servants scurried in and out on errands. In the evenings, coaches and sedan chairs drew up outside to disgorge guests for the musical and literary parties gregarious Anne hosted. And even in the middle of the night the neighbours might be woken by the bump of hampers being delivered to the basement. Every conceivable space in the house was pressed into use. As well as the Hunters' private rooms, there were servants' quarters, lodgings for the house pupils, a room for dissecting, and several rooms on the first floor dedicated to Hunter's anatomical collection.

In June 1772 came another addition to the household, for Anne gave birth to the couple's first child. The healthy, red-haired boy was named John Banks Hunter, in recognition of his father's explorer friend, although he was soon nicknamed 'Jock' or 'Jack', just as his father had been. As if the house was not already crammed to the rafters, in the autumn Hunter took in a young assistant, nineteen-year-old William Lynn, to help run the dissecting room, tend the collection and take dictation. At the same time, Anne's younger brother Everard moved in with the family. Having attended Westminster School, the sixteen-year-old gave up a place at Cambridge to accept Hunter's offer of an apprenticeship.[2] For the moment at least young Everard was grateful, declaring himself 'ambitious to tread the paths of science under so able a master'. But while Edward Jenner, Hunter's favourite pupil, would refer to his teacher as 'the dear man', and William Lynn later called his master 'Glorious John', Everard Home's lasting tribute to his mentor would be somewhat less noble.[3]

More than just a simple family home, the house in Jermyn Street was both a hive of domestic and social activity and a centre for intellectual and scientific discourse. Given Hunter's renowned stubbornness and blunt-speaking, this heady mixture could easily have proved a recipe for discord, but the intersecting businesses all ran concurrently with harmony and good humour. Anne managed the two households smoothly and hosted her soirées, which were acclaimed for their informal and jovial atmosphere.[4] Though she never published while her husband was alive, she continued to write poetry and shared her efforts with family and friends. Alongside the Bluestocking ladies, she could count among her male friends the prolific letter writer Horace Walpole and, later, the composer Joseph Haydn.

Although Hunter rarely participated in his wife's gatherings – literary debates were decidedly not his idea of fun – he usually took time out of his studies to greet her guests as they arrived.[5] The story that one evening he arrived home and exploded when he found his drawing room unexpectedly filled with dancing guests may well be apocryphal. Or perhaps he was just tired. According to the tale, he stormed into the room and announced, 'I knew nothing of this kick-up, and I ought to have been informed beforehand; but as I am now returned home to study, I hope the present company will retire.'[6] Sheepishly, Anne's friends shuffled out, or so the story went. Indeed, although he was certainly more comfortable in the company of his male, scientifically minded Royal Society chums, he did accompany Anne to the theatre, concerts and house parties. He might have lacked cultural accomplishment, but the inexhaustible anatomist could always be counted on for diverting conversation at dinner parties. Dr Johnson's close friend Hester Thrale was struck by one of Hunter's revelations at just such an event in the 1770s. She noted in her diary, 'The heart of a frog will not cease to beat *says John Hunter* for four hours after it has been torne from the Body of the Animal', adding dolefully, 'Poor Creature.'[7] Lord Holland, who was another member of the Hunters' social circle, remarked, 'John Hunter was neither polished in his manner nor refined in his expression, but from originality of thought and earnestness of mind he was extremely agreeable in conversation.'[8]

Just as John indulged Anne in her literary pursuits, so she made no attempt to curtail her husband's passion for experiment. Certainly it must have been irksome at times trying to ensure her guests did not accidentally bump into the Resurrectionists on the stairs or stumble into a room where a strange breed of animal was being dissected. It may well have been awkward, too, having friends to stay at their Earls Court country house – where she had introduced refinements such as painted panels on the doors[9] – only to be interrupted by the shrieks of animals suffering her husband's experiments. And in both homes she must have struggled to mask the smell of decay and alcoholic preservative clinging to the furnishings. Yet she plainly respected her husband's work and their relationship proved both a happy and successful alliance. Within the first five years of their marriage Anne gave birth to four children, although only two – John Banks and Agnes – would survive infancy. For all his surgical expertise there was little even Hunter could do to protect his offspring from the virulent childhood diseases that abounded.

With a young family to support, private patients to visit, house pupils to teach and hospital duties to fulfil, as well as his relentless programme of research, Hunter had more than enough to occupy his days. Yet inevitably, given his boundless zeal for novelty, he now embarked on a new project. So far his investigations had chiefly focused on enlarging his own knowledge and improving his own practice; he had published two papers for the Royal Society and a treatise on teeth, but his research work had largely served to satisfy his personal interests. Since his childhood days, when he had skipped lessons to explore country life, he had been bent on self-education. As an autodidact he excelled. And he clearly regarded this task of self-improvement as a lifelong project, for even in his late forties he would describe himself as 'following my business as a student'.[10] Now, however, in the autumn of 1772, he resolved to teach others what he had learned – or, more precisely, to teach them to learn for themselves too. The mission he embarked upon, to provide the foundations of a medical education for London's growing body of surgical pupils, might have seemed impossible to fault, yet it would set him on a headlong collision course with his colleagues at St George's.

Since he had taken up his staff surgeon's post at the hospital in 1768, young would-be surgeons had flocked to enrol as pupils under Hunter. Although William Bromfield and Caesar Hawkins boasted royal patronage and large private practices, Hunter outstripped both of them, and John Gunning too, when it came to attracting young surgeons to the hospital. Plainly, Hunter's growing reputation as a radical thinker was a magnet to the new generation of youngsters keen to enter surgery. In the 'age of experiments', when revelations in natural history, chemistry and anatomy were constant talking points in newspapers and coffee-houses, it was hardly surprising that upcoming surgeons sought out Hunter, not ageing, backward-looking Hawkins or Bromfield, as their role model and mentor. Equally, many of Hunter's growing circle of like-minded friends recommended relatives and acquaintances to his door. So while more than 120 youngsters signed the St George's register as pupils between 1768 and 1772, by far the majority enrolled with Hunter. In 1771 alone more than two-thirds of the pupils signed under Hunter's name, each of them staying at the hospital between six months and one year.[11] And the discrepancy continued, Hunter topping the student popularity polls year after year. Yet no matter how divergent the numbers, the pupils' fees were divided equally between the four surgeons. Since the sum total was relatively small – only £141 in 1772, for example – for the moment Hunter turned a blind eye to this incongruity.[12]

With his house pupils, his hospital students and his apprentice, a veritable posse trailed behind Hunter as he conducted his ward rounds, performed operations and undertook post-mortems. But though this was valuable practical experience in the traditional manner, it was not, in his view, an adequate medical education. It was never his aim to turn out passive replicas of himself, fit only to mimic his operating methods and copy his mistakes. Instead, Hunter wanted to nurture questioning, enquiring, sceptical young surgeons who were capable of thinking for themselves. For this he needed to convince them of his novel doctrine. At St Bartholomew's Hospital, Percivall Pott gave lectures on surgery free of charge to pupils enrolled there. Shortly after joining St George's, Hunter attempted to persuade his colleagues to do the same. A hospital, he later told the governors, should aim to be not just a charitable institution offering aid to the poor, nor even a place where surgeons gained experience before trying their luck on wealthier clients, but a centre for educating the surgeons of the future.[13]

At a time when none of London's six general hospitals offered an all-round medical education, and only Bart's provided any lectures at all, this was a futuristic vision. Hunter's proposal amounted effectively to creating at St George's both a medical school and a research centre. 'My motive,' he later explained, 'was in the first place to serve the Hospital and in the second to diffuse the knowledge of the art that all might be partakers of it.' And in a clear dig at his colleagues, he added, 'this indeed is the highest office in which a surgeon can be employed; for when considered as a man qualified only to dress a sore, or perform a common operation, and perhaps not all of those that may be reckoned common, he cannot be esteemed an ornament to his profession.'

His idea was given short shrift by his surgical colleagues. Despite several overtures – he even called a meeting with his three colleagues to discuss how the pupils' education might be improved – none would consent to his proposal. Although both Hawkins and Bromfield had staged anatomy lectures in their early careers, they were either too busy or too lethargic to bother now. Or, as Hunter would put it, 'their education had been prior to the period of improvement in this country'.[14] Eager for stimulation and disgruntled at the lack of attention, even those pupils signed to Bromfield, Hawkins and Gunning now turned to Hunter for extra-curricular direction. According to Hunter, 'they all wished to be dressers under me and at last complained to me and even threatened to recommend their young acquaintances to other hospitals if more general attention was not paid to them'. Although Hunter passed on their comments to the governors, and some of the students even complained anonymously to the board, it was to no avail.

No improvements were agreed because, according to Hunter, 'no one appeared desirous of doing anything but myself'.

Rebuffed by his colleagues but egged on by the students, Hunter resolved to go ahead alone. In the autumn of 1772 he invited pupils from St George's, regardless of which surgeon they had enrolled with, to a series of lectures at his own house free of charge.[15] A few years later, probably from 1775, he threw the lectures open to a wider audience, advertising his course in London newspapers and charging a modest four guineas for almost a hundred lectures running on alternate evenings from October until April.[16] The move split London's surgical fraternity down the middle: one half acclaimed Hunter as a genius and his lectures as inspired, the other half condemned him as a charlatan and his lectures as incomprehensible.

Jessé Foot, who stood naturally enough in the establishment camp, described the lectures as 'a sort of a skirmishing course – something new, and which could not be compared – consisting of surgical, physiological, and comparative anatomy branches, – and so mixing them together, as either to confound or illustrate each other'.[17] In fact, Foot had contemplated attending the course himself: he called at Jermyn Street for a syllabus, but changed his mind on the grounds that the 'terms were high' and the 'design was not liberal'. Hunter's St George's colleagues were equally dismissive. 'What his lectures were we cannot tell,' they later remarked snidely; 'we have understood that they were ingenious but physiological rather than chirurgical.'[18] Yet for Henry Cline, a twenty-four-year-old newly qualified surgeon at St Thomas' Hospital, as for many others, attending Hunter's lectures would prove cathartic. He would later say, 'having heard Mr Hunter's lectures on the subject of disease, I found them so far superior to every thing I had conceived or heard before, that there seemed no comparison between the mind of the man who delivered them, and all the individuals whether ancient or modern who had ever gone before him'.[19]

The schism was hardly surprising. As both his devotees and his enemies made plain, Hunter's lectures were unlike anything ever staged in London, or indeed Europe, before. And there were plenty of private lectures on offer. William Hunter's lectures in anatomy were immensely popular, Pott's course on surgery was highly regarded, and there were reputable lessons in midwifery and chemistry too. But though William's Great Windmill Street school provided an excellent grounding in human anatomy, and Pott's course described the common operations in step-by-step detail, these were essentially practical training. Hunter offered something fundamentally different. Although he titled his lectures 'The Principles and Practice of Surgery', he barely mentioned operations; indeed he encouraged his pupils to avoid performing surgery altogether unless absolutely necessary. And while he was undoubtedly London's most experienced anatomist, he scarcely discussed anatomy either. Instead, he offered his pupils a comprehensive introduction to the workings of the human body – its physiology – in order to teach them how the body works when healthy and how it reacts when diseased, along with many of his radical views on treatment along the way. His curriculum was designed in the belief that any surgeon wanting to treat disease and injury should first understand basic principles of health. 'They are to the surgeon what the first principles of the mathematics are to the practical geometrician, without the knowledge of which a man can neither be a philosopher nor a Surgeon,' he explained in a magazine article describing the course.[20]

It seemed logical enough, but this was a complete departure in a world where surgeons and physicians still based their practice largely on medical theories originating in Ancient Greece. Although few practitioners still seriously believed wholesale in the ideas of humoral balance, the language and the practices remained; the universally applied therapies of bloodletting, purging and vomiting emanated from the notion of letting out unwanted 'humours'. Hunter, in contrast, wanted to sweep away all past superstitions and unproven doctrines and begin from absolute basics. Most importantly, he aimed to provide his disciples with a grounding in life sciences – as inadequately as they were understood – in order that they should learn to reason for themselves. 'I do not intend to give my lectures as a regular course,' he explained, 'but rather to explain what appear to me to be the principles of the art, so as thereby to fit my pupils to act as occasion may require, from comparing and reasoning on known principles.'[21]

It was a revolutionary concept. At a time when surgical pupils were used to parroting the doctrines and copying the practices of their elders, the idea of thinking for themselves was shocking, uncomfortable, even distasteful to some, but liberating and inspirational to others. And so, as pupils made their way to Jermyn Street for the first lessons each October from 1772, there were wide variations in expectations. At twenty-four, having just gained his surgical diploma, Henry Cline considered he had learned pretty much all his elders could teach him on the human body. He enrolled for Hunter's lectures chiefly out of curiosity, or as he later explained, having heard 'so much talk of what was then rather sneeringly denominated "The New Opinions of John Hunter" which were generally pretended to be considered as Outre and Strange' he decided to go along and judge Hunter's views for himself.[22]

Squashed together, elbow to elbow, in one of the cramped rooms in Hunter's house, the students waited with their paper and quills at the ready for their rather nervous-looking teacher to begin. Hunter had never enjoyed public speaking. His aversion to lecturing had made him reject a partnership with William in 1758 and he had also declined an appeal – possibly from the Society of Artists – to stage anatomy lectures in 1768.[23] It would become his habit to take thirty drops of laudanum, opium mixed with alcohol, before starting each lecture.[24] As he shuffled his notes, the class would become impatient so that 'the more humorous and lively part of the audience would be tittering, the more sober and unexcitable quietly dosing into a nap', one pupil, John Abernethy, recalled.[25] William Cooper, the physician who had collaborated with Hunter in the recent Caesarean operation, was among those who commonly slept through lessons. He was unable, he told friends, to understand any of Hunter's views.[26]

Beginning slowly and hesitatingly in his gruff Scottish drawl, Hunter immediately confounded his audience by telling them not to take notes, or if they did to burn them later.[27] It was not that he was concerned they would produce pirate copies of his lectures, but that as a perpetual student himself his views were constantly changing. When one of the pupils, sufficiently intrigued to attend a second course, accused him of altering his views from one year to the next, Hunter calmly retorted, 'Very likely I did. I hope I grow wiser every year.'[28] When asked by another pupil whether he had put a particular viewpoint in writing, Hunter replied, 'Never ask me what I have said, or what I have written; but if you will ask me what my present opinions are, I will tell you.'[29]

To pupils used to meekly noting theories that had hardly changed for a few thousand years, this admonition was disturbing enough. But Hunter's faltering, meandering lecture style could hardly have helped matters. According to Foot, 'such was the natural confusion of his mind, that he would be frequently found incapable of explaining his own opinions from his notes'.[30] Of course, Foot had never actually attended one of Hunter's classes. But even among his most devoted pupils, Abernethy would admit that Hunter experienced 'great difficulty in communicating what he knew', while Joseph Adams agreed that most of his students 'acknowledged the difficulty they found in comprehending him'.[31] Yet Adams also added that 'his wit, or more particularly his archness, was always well directed' and that Hunter relished taking questions at the end of each session. Notes of Hunter's lectures, taken down by many students despite his exhortations, testify to his dry sense of humour and informal lecturing style, sprinkled with anecdotes and caustic asides, which must have proved a welcome antidote to the didactic, starched manner of other tutors. And while he could certainly seem 'a little abstruse', as he himself acknowledged, there was every reason why his views were sometimes difficult to elucidate, for as he always warned his pupils in the introductory lesson, 'many of my ideas, and the arrangement of my subject, are new, and consequently my terms become in part new'. Quite simply the language required to explain some of Hunter's doctrines did not yet exist. On one occasion, struggling to find the right word to explain an unfamiliar concept, he remarked, 'we have no language existing answerable to all my views of the animal œconomy, and to coin words would not answer the purpose, because then I must have a dictionary of my own'.[32]

Some of the novices, who reasonably enough had enrolled for the lectures to pick up some tips on surgery from the celebrated surgeon, were further bemused as he launched into his course. Far from initiating them into the secrets of successful surgery, as Pott endeavoured, Hunter began by discussing the very nature of organic life.[33] This was no easy task, since any useful studies in geology and biology were still many decades ahead. Nevertheless, Hunter began by outlining the differences between in-animate matter – rocks, minerals, earth – and living matter – animals, plants and vegetables – before moving on to grapple with the thorny issue of what distinguished living animals and humans from the dead. Still struggling to explain that particular puzzle himself, he proposed that life, or his 'living principle', was 'something superadded'.

Having discussed organic life in general, he moved on to humans. In a series of lectures stretching over the winter, he described the various functions of the human body in its natural or healthy state, ranging over muscle action, nutrition, respiration, circulation, bone growth and sleep. Understanding these normal functions was an essential grounding for any would-be surgeon, he insisted, telling his pupils, 'It is not only necessary for a Surgeon that he should know the different parts of an animal, but he should know their uses in the machine, and in what manner they act to produce their effect.'

Only after this lengthy foundation in physiology did Hunter discuss the effects of disease and injury, or pathology, in humans. First he explored the signs of disease, such as inflammation and fever, before describing specific illnesses. Ranging over cancer and scrofula, broken limbs and hernias, venereal disease and infectious fevers, he illustrated his opinions with beautifully prepared specimens from his collection as well as case histories gleaned from his twenty years' experience as a surgeon. When describing inflammation, he would pass among the students his preparation of a human tooth implanted in a cockerel's comb, as well as a maggot buried in the skin of a reindeer. The treatment of aneurysms, a pet topic, was illuminated by a preparation of a man's chest with a bulging aorta, while the bones of a lion were pressed into service for describing bone growth. There was no shortage of relevant specimens, for as he told his pupils, 'I have seen as much practice, and made a larger collection of diseased preparations than perhaps any man in Europe'. Meanwhile, his growing acclaim as a surgeon furnished him with entertaining anecdotes about aristocrats and celebrities with which to amuse his students. He could always raise a laugh with his tale of the recently deceased novelist Laurence Sterne, who believed a person only died because they had resolved not to live. When Sterne attempted to prove his conviction by leaping out of bed during his final illness, said Hunter, 'death, which soon followed, shewed his mistake'.[34]

But if the fidgeting, dozing, scribbling pupils now believed they were at last coming to the meaty topic of practical surgery, they were to be disappointed. Hunter's profound awe at the beauty of the human anatomy, coupled with his deep respect for the healing powers of nature, had of course taught him chiefly that surgery should only ever be considered as a last resort. 'Operations should never be introduced but in cases of absolute necessity,' he explained in a contemporary magazine.[35] For one of the city's top surgeons so power-fully to disdain surgery was unthinkable; Hunter described almost as many occasions when he had resolved not to operate as when he had gone ahead. But this was not to say that he avoided operations, even extremely risky ones, when convinced they were necessary, as he had recently proved by assisting at the attempted Caesarean delivery. Indeed, he outlined sufficient details of mastectomies, castrations, amputations and trepanning for even the most bloodthirsty young pupil, although even then it was theory rather than practice that dominated. In cases of cancer in particular he recommended radical surgery, knowing from post-mortems that 'leaving the least part of the cancer is equal to leaving the whole'. He even recommended examining the removed lump to ensure as much of the cancerous tissue as possible had been excised.[36] When patients died, which was a relatively regular occurrence given the primitive operating environ-ment, Hunter was disarmingly candid when it came to admitting his errors. While relating a trepanning oper-ation that had gone amiss he freely confessed, 'I think it is probable I killed him'.[37] Describing another operation, he declared, 'I acted like a blockhead'.[38] Medical error would always be a fact of life in surgery, but while other surgeons baulked at the very idea of confessing their blunders, for Hunter it was vital to learn from his mistakes.

His conservative approach extended to medical care in general, for Hunter did not allow traditional divisions between surgeons and physicians to stop him from pronouncing on physick as well as surgery. Many of his closest friends were physicians and his advice on general medical matters was increasingly in demand. Arguing that many minor ailments were best left for nature to cure, he related the story of a young boy who had been treated in vain by numerous physicians for a pimple on his leg. When the boy's father consulted Hunter on what should be done, he brusquely responded, 'Nothing.' Queried by the puzzled parent, Hunter added, 'Can anything be easier? I said, do nothing to the leg.' Free of the toxic potions and exposed to the air, the boy's leg soon recovered.[39]

For similar reasons, Hunter advised using the three favourite Georgian remedies – purging, vomiting and bloodletting – with caution. Warning that purgative medicines could severely weaken a patient, he advised, 'A single purge has been known to produce death in dropsy', and he recommended extreme care when administering medicines to induce vomiting.[40] Bloodletting too should be sparingly used: 'Bleeding, however, is a remedy of so much importance that it should be employed in all cases with great caution; yet not more than appears really necessary.'[41] In truth, however, bloodletting was impossible for surgeons to eschew completely, since Georgians routinely demanded the procedure as a universal panacea. Accordingly, Hunter did bleed many patients. In the summer of 1772, just before his first course began, he had bled the socialite Lady Mary Coke, on the recommendation of her physician.[42] 'Tis not that I am very ill,' she noted in her diary, 'but Mr Fox, who I now consult, advised me to be blooded in my foot.' Hunter, however, was one of the first to suggest that bloodletting was not only largely ineffectual but potentially dangerous. Even fifty years later his nineteenth-century editors would add a footnote to his works insisting that bloodletting and mercury, 'our chief curatives', were still valuable treatments.

As far as Hunter was concerned, the only treatments in the Georgian medical chest of any use were opium, for pain relief, and Peruvian bark, an effective remedy for the 'ague', or malaria, since it contained quinine. But as with his approach to all things, he believed medical remedies should be tried and tested. Just as he had compared bread-pills with mercury for gonorrhoea, he conducted a trial on a concoction of spider's web – a popular folklore remedy for various ailments. Having secretly given the mixture to a patient suffering from ague, he found the remedy 'had not the slightest effect'. Yet once his patient was informed of the treatment, 'the effect was produced, at least the disease did not return', he told his pupils.[43] He was well aware of the power of the human mind – the placebo effect – remarking of one macabre but commonplace therapy that 'Even tumours have yielded to the stroke of a dead man's hand.' On another occasion, at a loss as to how to treat a patient with boils on his back, he took experimental research to its extreme. In concert with one of his physician friends, David Pitcairn, Hunter proposed simply charging through the alphabet to try every remedy in the pharmacopoeia. Fortunately for their poor victim, the pair only got as far as 'F' – for 'fossil caustic alkali' – before the boils cleared up.

For all his iconoclastic views, Hunter was careful to shield his pupils from overt trouble. While expounding his controversial views on gunshot wounds, he warned, 'if you were examined at Surgeon's Hall how you would treat a gun shot wound, you would do well not to mention my doctrine, but to say according to the old plan, I would open the edges of the wound.' Ruefully, he added, 'They do not ask the reasons of things there.'[44] Hunter's aim was that the young surgeons attending his lectures would always 'ask the reasons of things'. He wanted them to take nothing for granted, to subject every common superstition and unproven therapy to scrutiny, to question every step they took. Essentially, he aimed to equip them to elevate surgery to the rank of a science. But not everybody was ready for such a dramatic change. The popularity of his lecture course would wax and wane over the next two decades. While sometimes fifty pupils crammed in to hear him speak, at other times only twelve turned up, according to Foot. Indeed, one lecture was reportedly so scantily attended that Hunter had a skeleton brought in so that he could begin his lesson with the customary address, 'Gentlemen'.[45]

Though some dozed, some left confused and others shunned the course altogether, there were many for whom Hunter's revolutionary view of medicine was life-changing. Henry Cline, the new surgeon who had strolled along to Jermyn Street out of curiosity, was one of them. He later recalled, 'When I heard this Man, I said to myself, *This is all day-light*. I felt that what I had previously been taught was comparatively nothing. I felt that I was now enabled to judge of what my experience and Observation had taught me; and thought I might, like Mr Hunter, venture to Think for myself.'[46] His eyes opened, his mind awakened, Cline urged fellow surgeons to attend the classes. They included Astley Cooper, a pupil at Guy's Hospital, who not only braved the scorn of other practitioners who denounced Hunter as a 'mere imaginative speculator' but was so impressed he continued going year after year. He would later call Hunter 'that immortal genius'.[47] John Abernethy, an apprentice from St Bartholomew's, was similarly affected. He declared, 'I believe him to be the author of a great and important revolution in medical science: of this I am certain, that his works produced a complete revolution in my mind.'[48]

Despite his faltering speech, his obscure language and his unfamiliar syllabus, John Hunter plainly won the minds and hearts of countless pupils who sat in his lecture room. No matter where they had trained or to whom they had been apprenticed, their allegiance was now to Hunter; they imbibed his doctrines, emulated his practices and preached his creed wherever they worked. Much more than his writings, it was Hunter's disciples who would spread his message to future generations of surgeons and apply his principles to future practice. In all, including almost five hundred young men who followed him at St George's, Hunter would teach an estimated one thousand pupils.[49] Many, such as Cline, Cooper and Abernethy, would become towering figures in the powerful nineteenth-century teaching hospitals; others would take his message overseas to Ireland, continental Europe and America. They formed an unstoppable army of evangelists. Their dedication to Hunter's standard was bound to broaden already wide divisions and stoke up already passionate jealousies. For Hunter's colleagues at St George's, this magnetic attraction to young surgeons from all over the globe, not least their own pupils and apprentices, would create an unbridgeable rift. According to Foot, Hunter was embroiled in 'continual war' at the hospital.[50] Hunter himself would say, 'I know, I am but a pigmy in knowledge, yet I feel as a giant, when compared with these men.'[51]

With excitable pupils tramping through the doors every other evening throughout the winter, traffic at 42 Jermyn Street had become heavily congested. Hunter's day was meticulously regimented to suit. Rising at dawn, in order to catch the first sunlight, he closeted himself in his dissecting room until his labours had given him sufficient appetite for breakfast at 8 a.m.[52] From 9.30 he saw patients who came to the house for consultations. Sometimes, however, this schedule would go awry since patients would occasionally arrive to find their surgeon in a blood-stained apron 'with his hands besmeared in the act of dissection'.[53] After tending the needs of the walking wounded, he set off at noon on house calls to his richer clients. On days when he was due at St George's, he would lead his pupils around the wards and work his shift in the operating theatre before returning home for dinner – always served promptly at 4 p.m. on Hunter's orders whether or not he was back in time. After eating, he snatched an hour's nap in his study before launching into an evening of further intense activity. As well as delivering lectures throughout the winter, he wrote letters, dictated notes to his assistants and catalogued his preparations until past midnight, finally retiring to bed in the early hours for a cursory four hours' sleep. Astley Cooper, who said Hunter generally worked from 6 a.m. until midnight or later, described Hunter as 'the most *industrious* man that ever lived'. Even the caustic Foot had to concede that 'perhaps there cannot be found his equal, who so completely filled up his time, in active industry'.[54]

Yet there was still time to entertain guests who dropped by for dinner or tea. Favoured pupils who showed particular merit were invited to join the family dinner table, as were fellow professionals – although not Hunter's colleagues at St George's – and there was room too for friends and associates visiting town. One such visitor was James Beattie, the Scottish poet and moral philosopher, who called at Jermyn Street with his wife Mary during a busy social schedule in May 1773. Having spent time chatting with Samuel Johnson the day before, the Beatties called at the Hunters' home, where they 'dined, drank tea and supped' until 11 p.m. 'Mr Hunter showed us his Anatomical curiosities, which are very numerous and well arranged,' Beattie recorded in his diary. 'He seems to be very profoundly skilled in Comparative anatomy.'[55]

Another party of guests visiting in early 1773 was rather less enamoured of Hunter's anatomical collection. George Cartwright, a trader and explorer, had brought back a group of Inuit people, some of the first 'eskimoes' ever to set foot in England, on his return from north-east Canada at the end of 1772.[56] As well as being presented at court, the family of five met with Banks, Solander and Boswell during their five-month stay. Keen to learn about their lives and environment, Hunter asked Cartwright to bring his party to dinner at Jermyn Street. After enjoying the meal, the head of the family, a priest called Attiock, wandered into a room within Hunter's backyard only to find himself face to face with a glass case full of human bones. Rushing back in a state of shock, he demanded to know whether these were the bones of other Inuit guests who had been killed and eaten by Hunter. Laughing at their confusion, and not a little economical with the truth, Hunter assured the party that the bones had belonged to executed criminals, who were dissected for the greater good of science. Still the visitors were in rather a hurry to leave for, according to Cartwright, 'Attiock's nerves had received too great a shock to enable him to resume his usual tranquillity until he found himself safe in my house again'. Plainly, the family recovered their confidence in Hunter sufficiently to allow him to commission portraits of all five members.

Amid the numerous arrivals there were departures too in 1773. Once the lecturing and dissecting season was over, Edward Jenner packed his bags to return to Berkeley. Having declined Cook's invitation to join his second round-the-world expedition as a naturalist on the *Resolution* the previous year, Jenner had opted for a quiet life as a country doctor in his native Gloucestershire. He would not be allowed to remain idle, however. From the moment he left London, Hunter besieged his beloved pupil with demands to send animal specimens and to conduct experiments in a stream of chatty letters. In return, Jenner pressed his teacher for advice on treating the various patients who sought his aid. The pair would exchange letters and gifts in an affectionate, lively correspondence spanning two decades; in one letter Hunter declared, 'I do not know anyone I wd sooner write to than you.'[57]

Perhaps more than anything else he was to write, Hunter's scrawled, misspelled, hurried but always fond letters to his favourite protégé reveal the tireless, erratic, ever-enquiring mind of the irrepressible anatomist and experimenter, always on the lookout for a fresh specimen to dissect or an investigation to launch. Jenner was often hard put to satisfy Hunter's voracious appetite, as letter after letter begged him to seek out local creatures and send them alive in boxes or preserved in spirits to his teacher's house. 'If you can pick me up anything that is curious, and prepare it for me do it; either in the flesh or fish way,' pleads the first surviving letter sent soon after

Jenner's departure.[58] 'I want a nest with the Egg in it also a nest with a young cuckow, and also an old cuckow,' Hunter demands in the next, adding apologetically, 'I hear you saying there is no end to your wants.'[59] Indeed, there was not. Succeeding letters included requests for bats, salmon spawn, hedgehogs, a live heron, a bustard and fossils. Sometimes Hunter's requests were specific, as when he appealed, 'cannot you get me a large Porpass for either Love or Money'.[60] Jenner duly sent a young dolphin netted from the Severn estuary. At other times the demands were all encompassing: 'I have but one order to send you which is send every thing you can get either animal vegetable or mineral, and the compound of the two viz either animal or vegetable mineralised'.[61] Generally Jenner obliged, scouring the Gloucestershire hedgerows for small mammals to send his mentor, along with occasional local delicacies such as Double Gloucester cheese, fresh fish and game. At times it was hard to determine which of Jenner's parcels was intended for the dissecting bench and which for the dinner table, especially as packages frequently arrived with vague or even no labels. 'Till yesterday we did not know from whom the hare came,' Hunter wrote in one letter, 'but the cook found it out; we thank you; it was a very fine one.'[62]

When he was not netting wildlife, Jenner was kept busy fulfilling Hunter's demands for experiments. Still investigating body heat, Hunter asked Jenner to test the temperature of hedgehogs and bats, sending him one of his custom-made thermometers for the purpose. At one point, when Jenner was in despair after being jilted by his fiancée, Hunter breezily countered, 'I shall imploy you with Hedge Hogs.'[63] But Hunter was keen to encourage his ex-pupil to pursue his own researches too, particularly his investigations on cuckoos which led in 1788 to Jenner's first paper to the Royal Society – revealing their unique mode of laying eggs in other birds' nests – as well as his landmark development of the smallpox vaccine. While Hunter's house-pupil, Jenner had explained how cowpox seemed to confer immunity to smallpox among milkmaids; before he left he had shown Hunter a sketch of a lesion left by cowpox on a milkmaid's finger.[64]

Jenner's leaving left a large dent in the Hunter household; he was missed by Anne, as he shared her passion for poetry and music, as well as by John. But for Anne's young brother Everard, who must at times have felt himself a cuckoo in the nest shared by the mutually adoring Hunter and Jenner, the departure presented a chance to fill the shoes of the favoured pupil. This was no easy task. Jenner understood his former teacher's blunt ways well enough not to take offence when Hunter criticized his 'damned clumsy fingers' for breaking one of his precious thermometers. The sensitive and self-important Everard bristled when Hunter snapped that he would never be able to make a decent preparation since 'his fingers were all thumbs', and he did not 'have sense enough to tie down a bottle'.[65] As Hunter's assistant, expected to attend his bidding according to his master's remorseless schedule, Home must often have felt the lash of his brother-in-law's sharp tongue. He would later complain bitterly that the surgeon indulged in violent rages and passions. 'His temper was very warm and impatient, readily provoked, and when irritated, not easily soothed,' he later recalled.[66] Others, too, would testify to Hunter's fiery disposition. Foot accused him of the 'bitterest utterings of swearing', and charged that 'he was ignorant of the rules of politeness'.[67] Even Lord Holland, who was a friend, admitted that 'his judgement was occasionally clouded by an irascible and tenacious temper' while he was 'apt to be positive, dogmatic and angry'.[68]

Without a doubt, Hunter could prove a formidable opponent to anyone who crossed him and his outspoken views often aroused strong passions in others. When in the army he had allegedly provoked Francis Tomkins to draw a sword on him. On one social occasion he took issue with a rival anatomist, Andrew Marshall, who insisted he could see differences during autopsies in the brains of people who had died of mental illness. Hunter, who from greater experience knew for a fact that this was false, immediately blasted, 'It's a damned lie.' In response, Marshall promptly tipped a jug of water over Hunter's head.[69] Yet it was his opponents, not Hunter, who were moved to violence in both instances. Perhaps more tellingly, one of Hunter's long-suffering assistants, the artist William Bell, would testify to his boss's foul temper although it was said that he 'absolutely idolised' Hunter.[70] At the same time, there were plenty of other assistants, pupils, friends and associates who would defend Hunter's conviviality, hospitality and kindness, and he undeniably evoked intense devotion in many who knew him. Plainly he prompted strong feelings both ways. But while some whom he had offended reacted instantly with drawn swords or jugs of water, Everard Home merely stored up the supposed slights for future revenge.

Now that he was forty-five, however, Hunter suddenly found himself the victim of his own irritability. One morning in 1773, soon after breakfast, he was struck by a violent abdominal pain which his usual thirty drops of laudanum did nothing to relieve. Scrupulously recording his own symptoms, just as he would for a patient, he found to his alarm that he could feel no pulse, his breathing had stopped and his countenance looked, in his expert opinion, 'like that of a corpse'.[71] Later describing the episode to his pupils, for no opportunity for learning was to be missed, he said, 'I cast my eyes on a looking-glass, and observed my countenance pale, my lips white, and I had the appearance of a dead man looking at himself.' Through sheer power of will, he told them, he forced himself to breathe. After taking brandy, madeira and ginger as stimulants, he was back at work by 2 p.m. Ironically, while Hunter seems not to have recognized his complaint at the time as an attack of angina, only the previous year he had himself dissected a man who had died from the condition. Hunter's notes of the post-mortem were included with a paper published in 1772 by the physician William Heberden which gave one of the first accurate descriptions of angina.[72]

Conceivably, Hunter's first angina attack was the result of the syphilis he had arguably given himself reaching the tertiary stage; during this final stage, which can begin anywhere from three to twenty-five years after initial infection, heart problems can occur. Equally, the angina, which would afflict him for the rest of his life, may well have been prompted by the continual strain of his hectic lifestyle. As well as completing his first private lecture course in 1773 in the teeth of opposition from his hospital colleagues, Hunter had the additional worry of knowing his dear Anny was pregnant with their second child. When Mary-Ann was born in December he was grieved to find her a 'weakly child'.[73] She seems to have developed curvature of the spine in infancy, for which she had to wear a back brace. Hunter referred in a note to a 'Miss Hunter' who suffered a 'preternatural curve of spine' and endorsed a back brace, invented by a certain Mr Jones, in his lectures.[74]

More additions to the already overflowing household soon followed. During 1774, Hunter employed John Andree, a young pupil who had shown particular aptitude for dissection, as another live-in assistant. Possibly one of his first jobs involved being on hand as Hunter participated in a second Caesarean section on 13 August that year.[75] This operation, performed by Hunter with the help of James Patch, a former pupil from the Covent Garden school, at least proved a little more successful than the first attempt. Once again, William Cooper had called a medical conference, inviting Hunter, Patch and twelve eminent male-midwives to the bedside of his patient, Elizabeth Foster, who was undergoing a difficult labour. As with their first patient, the woman suffered from severe distortion of the spine with an exceedingly narrow pelvis, although in this case it appeared to be due to a progressive bone disease. She had already given birth naturally several times but in her last three pregnancies her physicians had had to perform an 'embryotomy', crushing each child's skull in order to remove it from the womb. Even this drastic procedure seemed impossible this time, and on being informed that there was no other option, Elizabeth Foster consented to the Caesarean.

Laid out on a table in her lodgings with a handkerchief over her eyes, she was surrounded by at least fourteen medical men as Hunter made the first incision in her abdomen. William Hunter, who had a particular interest in the procedure since his classic work *The Anatomy of the Human Gravid Uterus* was at last being published that year, took notes. But though Cooper testified that the procedure was 'conducted with the utmost coolness, humanity, and skill', the operation on the woman's contorted body proved exceedingly tricky and Hunter severed a large artery in the process. As Patch pinched the artery together with his fingers, Cooper seized the baby by its feet and, after some difficulty, pulled the infant free. With the woman bleeding profusely and physicians pressing forward to watch in the hot and stuffy room, Hunter stitched up the wound. It came as little shock when Elizabeth Foster died the following day. What was surprising, given the traumatic birth and a delay in breathing, was that her baby survived; the child was still alive when Cooper wrote his description of the operation five months later. One life, at least, had been spared.

At the time, Hunter's wife was pregnant for a third time, and it must have been a substantial relief when Anny gave birth without complications to a healthy boy in November. The couple called the boy James, after John's favourite brother – there would never be a William – but at home he was known as 'Jemmy'. Regardless of the fact that his father pronounced him 'a fine boy', Jemmy was to live for only three months. Anne would later denote the month he died 'Black February' in a poem written seven years after his death.[76] Hunter was plainly fond of his children, enjoyed playing with them and was proud of their achievements. One of his pupils would later say, 'he has often told me, that if he had been allowed to bespeak a pair of children, they should have been those with which Providence had favoured him'.[77] Nevertheless, it is hard to discern whether he was more excited that November by the delivery of his second son or by the arrival of some particularly curious marine animals from South America.

Electricity was an absorbing preoccupation in eighteenth-century England, providing a lively talking point during Royal Society meetings and in salons and coffee-houses alike. Benjamin Franklin, the American politician and businessman, had helped stir up interest in the phenomenon in 1751 with a paper to the Royal Society arguing that lightning was an electrical force; the following year he demonstrated the fact with a perilous experiment which entailed conducting lightning down a kite string with a key attached.[78] The society's fellows initially scoffed at Franklin's conclusions, but they soon had to accept the veracity of his findings. The invention, in the 1740s, and rapid popularity of the Leyden jar – a metal-coated glass container that could store electricity to produce electrical charges on demand – made the properties of electricity the subject of both intense scientific speculation and wild fantasy. Physicians and quacks alike proclaimed the benefits of electrical therapy. The preacher John Wesley advertised his 'Electrical Machine' for curing all manner of ailments in 1772, and James Graham, the Scottish physician turned quack, would claim similar success for his electrical bath.[79] So when electric eels were shipped to London from Surinam in November 1774, the news created a sensation.

John Hunter was one of the first to hear. The strange fish – they are not really eels, as Hunter quickly observed – had first caused a stir when a showman had demonstrated their powerful electrical charges in South Carolina: a large eel can produce a charge of up to 600 volts, sufficient to injure or even kill an adult. It was witnessed by Alexander Garden, the naturalist who had sent the greater siren, and he had persuaded a British sailor to bring five of the creatures to England, principally for the interest of the Royal Society. Unfortunately, all five had died before reaching London, although one that remained alive when the ship docked at Falmouth had favoured several people with its famed shock, luckily without fatalities. Four of the eels, however, had been preserved in spirit and were brought immediately to Hunter. He was ecstatic. 'Mr John Hunter danced a jig when he saw them,' said his friend Solander in a letter to fellow enthusiast John Ellis, 'they are so compleat and well preserved.'[80]

Hunter was already familiar with the electrical powers of certain animals. Two years earlier he had dissected some torpedo fish – electric rays – at the request of John Walsh, a Royal Society fellow and MP, who had obtained several of the creatures off the coast of France near La Rochelle. Encouraged by Franklin, Walsh had become obsessed by the ability of the flat fish to produce weak electric shocks. At La Rochelle he performed a series of experiments linking circles of as many as eight people to the wings of the fish in order to form an electric circuit. Walsh wrote excitedly to Franklin, 'the effect of the Torpedo is absolutely electrical'. Having brought several dead specimens back to England, he asked 'the ingenious Mr John Hunter' to investigate their peculiar anatomy.

Peeling away the skin on each wing to reveal the two electrical organs, Hunter carefully investigated the hundreds of columns of tightly stacked discs, together concentrating naturally occurring electricity; the structure of the torpedo fish's electric organs would later inspire Alessandro Volta to create the first battery. At the same time, Hunter noted the extraordinary volume and size of the nerves connected to the electrical organs, and he presciently remarked, 'How far this may be connected with the power of the nerves in general, or how far it may lead to an explanation of their operations, time and future discoveries alone can fully determine.'[81] The Italian Luigi Galvani would demonstrate how electrical impulses prompt the nerves to generate muscle movement by electrifying frogs' legs in 1792, simultaneously inspiring literary fascination with electricity in people such as Mary Shelley, who went on to write *Frankenstein*.

Hunter's acutely observed anatomical observations were presented to the Royal Society on 1 July 1773. At the meeting Hunter passed around preserved specimens of a male and female torpedo with their organs dissected to reveal their remarkable structure. Yet the torpedo discoveries left much unexplained, and many doubted that their weak charge, which failed to produce a spark like the Leyden jar, was genuine electricity. As Walsh himself admitted to Franklin, his experiments had done 'little more than opening the door to inquiry' and 'much remained to be examined by the electrician as well as by the anatomist'.[82]

The electric eel, it was hoped, would provide the answers. Already the volunteers in Cornwall could testify to the powerful shock a single eel could deliver; the excitement that ran through the Royal Society was hardly less charged. Solander immediately began soliciting subscriptions for a scheme to bring back more live specimens from Surinam; he wrote to Banks to confirm the plan. Rushing to town to see the preserved eels for himself, John Walsh stumped up sixty guineas for three of the specimens 'so they may soon be examined and dissected by John Hunter'. Evidently Solander was having difficulties restraining Hunter and Walsh, for he warned Banks, 'If you don't come to town soon Walsh & Hunter seem to be bent upon beginning with opening one at least at the beginning of next week'. In the event, Banks did not make it in time. Unable to wait a moment longer, Hunter began dissecting the eels on 15 November, and quickly discovered their 'peculiar organs', exhibiting a similar structure to those of the torpedo but extending along much of the fish's body. Again noting the unusual size of the nerves supplying the electric organs, he furnished the Royal Society with a meticulous description the following May, while retaining two of the fish for his museum.[83]

That same summer of 1775 the first live electric eels arrived in London and parties to test how many people could feel their electrical charge at once became a popular craze. Walsh invited more than forty Royal Society members to his house to witness the experience first hand. He made the shock pass through a chain of twenty-seven people and even produced the elusive 'spark' which convinced remaining sceptics that the force was indeed authentic electricity. John Pringle, who had become president of the Royal Society in 1772, witnessed a second display with an even larger chain. 'The sparks were vivid & repeated,' he wrote to tell Haller, '& were seen, the last time I attended, by about 70 people at once; and in another experiment the shock was conveyed through the bodies of the same number of people, when they joined hands to hands to form a circle.'[84]

No doubt fired by so much popular excitement with animal anatomy, not to mention the almost symbolic circles of hands, Hunter now conceived a scheme to create a school devoted to the study of natural history. He asked Jenner to become a partner in the project but the country-loving doctor declined and the idea was soon forgotten in the flurry of continual industry. 'I own I suspected it would not do,' he wrote back dolefully to Jenner in August.[85]

Hunter had more than enough work to keep him

occupied. That same month saw Cook's return from his second voyage with a further haul of natural treasures. On 14 August, Solander visited the ship with a group of women friends. The party was shown a preserved Maori head, minus a portion which had been 'boiled and eat' on board the ship by two New Zealanders after the crew had purchased the head from a native hunting party.[86] Not surprisingly, the exhibit and its gory history had 'made the Ladies sick', Solander recorded. He knew exactly who would appreciate it. The next day, Solander took Hunter down to Deptford to claim the trophy, which was promptly added to his collection. So intense had his researches in anatomy and natural history now become that Hunter employed a young surgeon and talented artist, William Bell, on a ten-year contract to churn out drawings of the preparations he made as well as assisting in the dissecting room.

Despite the loss of young Jemmy, it had been a busy and fruitful year combining a happy family life with a successful work programme. Hunter reflected his satisfaction with his lot in a letter in November to his brother-in-law, the Reverend James Baillie, who had married his sister Dorothea in 1757 and had just been appointed professor of divinity at Glasgow.[87] 'As for my self,' said Hunter, after congratulating Baillie on his appointment, 'with respect to my family, I can only yet say, that I am happy in a wife; but my children are too young to form any judgement of.' He continued:

They consist of a stout red headed Boy, called Jock, three years and some months old; and a weakly girl called Mary-Ann, near two. We lost a fine boy call'd James, who would have been now about 12 months and Anny is near her time of a fourth. I am not anxious about my children but in their doing well in this world. I would rather make them feel one moral virtue, than read Librarys of all the dead and living languages. You know I am no Scholard, therefore do not feel the beauty of language when I do not see the use of it; but if that should be the line, which I meant they should follow, I should think myself happy in having such a Brother and in such a situation.

He ended the letter, 'it appears to be Anny's enjoyment, in seeing me please myself, while all these concurring circles go on, I must continue to be one of the happiest men living'.

His satisfaction must have been almost complete when, in the new year, London's most extraordinary surgeon was appointed Surgeon Extraordinary to George III. Although purely an honorary position, the post carried significant status. Though Hunter was not expected to treat the King, no doubt his no-nonsense manner would have appealed to the plain-living monarch far more than the preening surgeons and physicians who would torture him with bloodletting, blisters and purges during his incapacitating spells of illness. Hunter bought a new coach – 'the handsomest that was at court' – to receive his honour in January 1776.[88] Anny gave birth to their second daughter, Agnes, later that month, and it came as little surprise when 'weakly' Mary-Ann died the following month, at just two years old.[89]

Hunter was approaching the peak of his career. The King's seal of approval meant his professional opinion was increasingly in demand, and his advice was now being sought by more and more well-known Georgian figures. When David Hume, the Scottish philosopher and historian who had made an enemy of the Kirk with his sceptical writings, fell ill with abdominal pains in 1775 he was surrounded by the most eminent physicians of the day. In Edinburgh, William Cullen and Joseph Black rallied to his side; when he visited London a bevy of physicians attempted a diagnosis; and on travelling to Bath in the summer of 1776 the beleaguered patient was assured by a local physician, Dr Gusthart, that the spa waters would cure him.[90] None of them could offer a satisfactory explanation or any effective remedy for Hume's obvious decline. They were happy to posit elaborate theories and propose assorted therapies, but none was prepared actually to examine the patient in order to determine what might be causing his suffering. It was only when Hunter met the ailing philosopher and performed a physical examination that Hume finally discovered the true cause of his illness.

Hunter had arrived in Bath in June on a social visit and had immediately enquired after Hume; they were related by marriage, since Anne's father, Robert Home, was Hume's cousin – the spellings Home and Hume were interchangeable and both names were pronounced 'Hume'. On being invited by Gusthart to examine Hume, Hunter laid his hands on the suffering man's abdomen and could plainly feel a tumour, which he suspected was cancerous, in the liver. Since abdominal surgery was out of the question, there was no hope that an operation could save him. Although Hunter immediately conveyed his diagnosis to Gusthart, even then the philosopher was kept in the dark for several more days. Hume's relief when his physicians finally confessed Hunter's verdict, no matter how bleak, was palpable in the letters he wrote home. 'John Hunter ... coming accidentally to Town, and expressing a very friendly Concern about me, Dr Gusthart proposed that I should be inspected by him: He felt very sensibly, as he said, a Tumor or Swelling in my Liver,' he told his brother. Hume, who naturally preferred straight-forward scientific evidence over superstition, added, 'this Fact, not drawn by reasoning, but obvious to the Senses, and perceived by the greatest anatomist in Europe, must be admitted as unquestionable, and will alone account for my Situation'.[91] Relating the diagnosis to a friend, Hume added: 'You ask me how I know this; I answer, John Hunter, the greatest anatomist in Europe, felt it with his fingers.'[92] The verdict of Hunter's fingers, to Hume at least, carried more weight than the hypothetical musings of all the country's best physicians. And despite his physicians' dogged persistence with their meddling medication, the philosopher died in Scotland, of suspected liver cancer, two months later.

The outcome was more cheerful when Hunter treated another well-known writer, the diarist William Hickey, that same summer. Hickey had travelled to Margate on holiday in August but had burnt his foot when he fell asleep by the fire and one of his companions attached a burning taper to his boot as a prank.[93] By the time Hickey woke up, in extreme pain, the foot looked so badly injured that a local surgeon feared he would never walk again. A messenger was despatched urgently to London to summon Hunter for a second opinion. Racing to the coast in order to examine Hickey's foot, Hunter 'at once declared no ill consequence would arise'. And after taking Hunter's advice to keep his leg propped up, with a cold poultice applied to the burn, Hickey was back on his feet within days.

In the light of his royal honour, his controversial

lectures, his senior hospital post and the recognition of his skills among the country's top physicians, John Hunter had become a household name. In characteristic Georgian style his celebrity was acknowledged with a satirical poem, composed by a radical Scottish journalist, James Perry, who would later found the *European Magazine*. Entitled rather perversely 'The Torpedo: A poem to the electric eel' – plainly Perry was no naturalist – the lengthy piece of doggerel, published as a pamphlet in 1777, was addressed to 'Mr John Hunter, surgeon'.[94] Using the vogue for electric eels as an excuse to range over the various scandals concerning the country's nobility, the poem graphically captured many of Hunter's best-known ventures to date. It began:

> *O Thou! Whose microscopic eye*
> *Can every living thing descry,*
> *And search Dame Nature's womb!*
> *Whose power can raise the lifeless clay,*
> *Drag the pale spectres into day,*
> *And starve the hungry Tomb!*

Now John Hunter's powers to 'raise the lifeless clay' were about to be tested to the full.

11

The Chaplain's Neck

'Dr Dodd seemed to be willing to die, and full of hopes of happiness.'

James Boswell[1]

London, June 1777

On Sunday, 22 June 1777, the Reverend William Dodd was not delivering his customary sermon. Instead he sat in his dismal cell in Newgate prison composing a desperate appeal to Samuel Johnson in a last-minute effort to save his life. Dodd, a foolish and foolhardy clergyman who enjoyed the good life as much as good works, was sentenced to hang in five days' time. Since the beginning of the year, his predicament had become a *cause célèbre*; news of his legal battle filled the newspaper columns and his fate had gripped the nation.[2]

Having been ordained a priest some twenty years earlier, Dodd had devoted himself more to physical than spiritual pleasures. He threw himself into the social whirl of Georgian society, published a novel, and dressed in the dandiest of fashions, earning himself the nickname 'the Macaroni Parson'. He was a generous benefactor to numerous charities, not least the Magdalen House for 'fallen women', where he was made official chaplain. Although his sermons were popular – he had been appointed a chaplain to the King in 1763 – ultimately his extravagant lifestyle led to his downfall. With debts mounting, he staged an amateurish attempt to forge a bond for a hefty £4,200 – upwards of £250,000 in today's terms – in the name of his erstwhile patron, Lord Chesterfield. After the inevitable discovery of his fraud, he was found guilty of forgery at the Old Bailey in February 1777 and in May he was sentenced to hang.

Dodd's plight provoked an eruption of popular feeling demanding a reprieve. A petition with twenty-three thousand signatures pleading for a royal pardon was presented to George III, and Samuel Johnson, who had met Dodd once briefly, agreed to lend his powers of persuasion to the cause. The illustrious writer wrote an impassioned speech which Dodd addressed to the Old Bailey, as well as an eloquent sermon which he delivered to his fellow prisoners at Newgate, and after Dodd's last appeal for help on the Sunday before his expected execution Johnson came again to his aid by ghost-writing a poignant letter to the King.

Despite Johnson's well-chosen words, the media sympathy and the mass public support, all was in vain. No royal pardon arrived, and on 27 June crowds turned out to watch as Dodd was transported to Tyburn. 'On this occasion there was perhaps the greatest concourse of people ever drawn together by a like spectacle,' reported the *Gentleman's Magazine*. 'From Newgate to the place of execution the streets were thronged, and never were seen so many weeping eyes.'[3] Yet even as Dodd felt the noose around his neck, he had not lost hope of being saved. If Johnson's talents could not prevent him from dying, he fully believed John Hunter's skills would bring him back from the dead.

Not far from the sobbing crowds, at an undertaker's parlour in Goodge Street, Hunter was waiting with a number of medical friends to receive the curate's body. A bed had been prepared, a fire had been lit, medicines were lined up and a pair of bellows was placed at the ready. As the minutes ticked by after Dodd was presumed to have swung, the waiting men listened anxiously for the rattle of hooves signalling the arrival of the coach bearing his life-less body. So long as the delay could be kept to a minimum, Hunter was confident his plan to revive the unfortunate curate had every chance of success.

Hunter's optimism was by no means misplaced. He knew, from his numerous dissections of Tyburn Tree corpses, that most hanged convicts died from a long and slow process of asphyxiation rather than a swift and irredeemable broken neck. Accordingly, it was widely known that hanged convicts sometimes returned to life. In addition to the renowned cases of Anne Greene and William Duell, there had been several accounts of people returning from temporary unconsciousness after hanging at Tyburn.[4]

Aside from these well-publicized cases of recovery, Hunter was convinced from both his experiments and his theories that reviving a person after hanging was perfectly feasible. He had spent years attempting to understand precisely what constituted life, where life emanated from

362

and what caused life to end. Having initially proposed that blood contained a 'vital principle' that distinguished dead from living matter, more recently he had suggested that every particle of the body contained some kind of life force. But however imperfectly he was able to explain this 'living principle', Hunter's chief aim was to recreate it. The surgeons' equivalent of the philosophers' stone – defeating mortality, and even securing eternal life – was the goal that drove him.

Hunter's early efforts to freeze animals and bring them back to life had been one attempt to effect this power over death. While frustrated that this had failed to yield the fortune-making scheme of his dreams, he had not given up these pursuits; the exceptionally cold winter of 1775–6 had afforded him ample opportunities to return to his freezing experiments. When he observed that his cockerels at Earls Court had lost the jagged edges to their combs that winter, a servant explained that they often fell off during a hard frost. Needless to say, Hunter immediately replicated the situation by freezing the comb of a rooster; to his delight, the tissue grew back within a month.[5] In January 1777, a few months before Dodd's hanging, he was at work again with salt and ice, freezing a rabbit's ear for an hour before bringing it back to full-blooded life.[6]

At the same time, Hunter was busy investigating how long an animal's heart could beat after being removed from its body. It was in June, the very month that Dodd was transported to Tyburn, that he had chirpily informed Mrs Thrale of the ability of a frog's heart to continue beating for four hours after 'death'. And as he meddled with the boundaries between life and death, playing God to the animals on which he performed his experiments and rescuing a living child from the womb of a woman doomed to die, it must have seemed that the goal of immortality hovered tantalizingly within reach. Perhaps the enterprising surgeon really could 'raise the lifeless clay'.

Having devoted so much time and energy to such matters, Hunter was the obvious person to approach when a group of philanthropists determined to draw up advice designed to save people who drowned. William Hawes, an apothecary in the Strand, had raised the idea of a society dedicated to rescuing victims of drowning based on a similar body in Amsterdam.[7] He joined forces with a physician, Thomas Cogan, and the pair founded the Humane Society – later the Royal Humane Society – in 1774. The charity offered rewards of up to four guineas to anyone who succeeded in restoring life to any person 'taken out of the water for dead' within thirty miles of London. Well-meaning surgeons and physicians living near the Thames agreed to offer their aid free to help revive those who had drowned, but this was easier said than done. With their unerring lack of imagination physicians recommended bloodletting as the best method of reviving a victim; if this failed, ingesting tobacco vapours, usually by enema, was the fallback. Needless to say, neither method had met with much success. So in 1776, Hawes asked Hunter to develop a rather more factually based regime for resuscitation.

Hunter was happy to oblige, not only preparing detailed directions on attempted resuscitation for the charity but presenting his ideas to the Royal Society in March the same year.[8] It was a subject close to his heart, he explained, since inquiries into suspended animation had for many years 'been my business and favourite amusement'. Based on experiments he had performed and theories he had developed so far, Hunter advanced the view that a person who drowned should not automatically be considered dead but 'that only a suspension of the actions of life has taken place'. Indeed, this might be applied to anyone who suffered a violent death without irreparable injury to vital organs, he argued. And though he had so far had no opportunities to prove his views by experiment, he firmly believed it was possible to bring people back to life after drowning so long as their rescuers acted quickly – at least within an hour – and followed set guidelines.

Naturally enough, Hunter promptly dismissed bloodletting and tobacco enemas, along with purging or vomiting remedies, as more likely to 'depress life' than to restore it, insisting, 'I would by all means discourage bloodletting, which I think weakens the animal principle and life itself.' Instead, the first aim of any rescuer should be to throw air into the victim's lungs, for Hunter correctly believed that restoring breathing was the most effective route to revival. For this purpose he recommended a pair of double bellows, 'such as are commonly used in throwing fumes of tobacco up the anus' – though hopefully not the same ones – for pumping air into a person's mouth or nose. He cited the experiment he had performed back in 1755, in which he had kept a dog breathing artificially with a pair of bellows. Perhaps, he suggested, the newly discovered 'dephlogisticated air' – oxygen – which Joseph Priestley had described in 1775 might prove even more effective. In addition to inflating a victim's lungs, Hunter recommended holding stimulating vapours under the nose, warming the patient slowly in a bed and rubbing the body with essential oils.

If all else failed, Hunter suggested attempting to restart

the heart with electric shocks. 'Electricity has been known to be of service, and should be tried when other methods have failed,' he advised. 'It is probably the only method we have of immediately stimulating the heart.' In fact, Benjamin Franklin had first suggested that electricity might be used to revive people who were apparently dead, although he had never put his theory into practice. But Hunter may well have been referring to a case from 1774 when a three-year-old girl who fell from a first-storey window was revived with electric shocks to her chest, probably from a Leyden jar, in the first recorded example of successful defibrillation.[9] It would be nearly two centuries before this remarkable achievement became routine practice.

Finally, Hunter proposed that two people should work in tandem to effect resuscitation, and at every attempted rescue 'an accurate journal' should be kept of the methods used and degree of success. As ever, he believed that continual reassessment of practice was the route to improvement.

Hunter's recommendations to act quickly, concentrate on restoring breathing and apply artificial respiration would become the cornerstones of standard resuscitation practice, although simple mouth-to-mouth resuscitation would eventually be adopted from 1959 as the most successful method; his recommendation to use electric shock treatment, or defibrillation, to restart the heart or regulate its rhythm would only become widely adhered to in the 1950s. But though effective methods of rescue would take time to introduce, the society's laudable aims attracted numerous supporters. Among them was the Reverend Dodd, who made a donation in 1776, the same year in which Hunter produced his guidance; doubtless the two had met through their mutual interest. Now that his fortunes had turned, Dodd had the chance to make an even greater contribution to the charity's cause: in death, he represented the first opportunity for Hunter to test out his theories.

The events that ensued in the undertaker's parlour in Goodge Street would remain secret for nearly two decades; Hunter would never refer in writing to what may well have been his most remarkable experiment. Yet almost as soon as the hapless Dodd swung from the Tyburn gibbet, speculation about his fate began. 'Experiments were said to have been tried to bring Dr Dodd to life,' reported the *Gentleman's Magazine*, 'according to the instructions formerly published by Dr [*sic*] Hunter, but without effect. He hung an hour, and it was full forty minutes before he was put into a hearse.'[10] Fascination with Dodd's fate continued, and later that year a London magazine reported an Irishman's claim to have dined with Dodd in Dunkirk shortly after his supposed execution.[11] Another twenty years later, interest was revitalized in the *Gentleman's Magazine* with a reader's query about the reported revival. This elicited a flurry of replies repeating the stories of Hunter's experiment. According to one account, Hunter and his helpers tried to resuscitate the curate in a hot bath, and believed they would have succeeded had the crowd not delayed their efforts by half an hour too long. After it proved clear their plan had failed, the correspondent continued, the body was interred at St Laurence's Church in Cowley, west London.[12]

The obsession with Dodd did not end there. In 1794, a Scottish newspaper suggested Dodd was alive and well and living in Glasgow, seventeen years after being brought back to life by John Hunter. Relating an account of his dramatic resurrection, the anonymous writer revealed, 'When he was turned off, he felt a sudden impulse of pain at first, by his body whirling round very swiftly, he was soon deprived of all sensation, and afterwards remained totally senseless, until he found himself in bed, surrounded by Doctor C, Mr H, Mr D and Mr W, whom he perceived to be in tears, which may be considered as an effusion of joy at his recovery, of which they at one time despaired.'[13] According to this precise description, Dodd's body had been conveyed to the undertaker's house where Hunter and his three medical friends were waiting ('Mr H' was plainly Hunter; 'Dr C' could well have been the co-founder of the society, Thomas Cogan). As soon as Dodd's body was bundled out of the hearse and into the house, Hunter and 'Mr D' stripped the corpse and rubbed the skin vigorously for two hours before at last they saw a sign of breathing. Dodd's skin then broke out in a sweat, a groan emerged, and the curate sat up. Now fully restored to 'sound health' but in 'melancholy spirits' at his enforced absence from his native country, Dodd was living at the house of a friend, or so the writer claimed. So, did the life-loving curate breathe again after swinging at Tyburn? Had Hunter really defeated death?

Although Hunter never committed to paper the events that followed Dodd's hanging, he apparently did disclose details of the attempted revival in the relative privacy of his weekly coffee-house club. Charles Hutton, professor of mathematics at the Royal Military Academy, Woolwich, and a Royal Society fellow, later recalled the evening shortly after Dodd's execution when Hunter was persuaded by his friends to reveal the story.[14] It was true, Hunter told his rapt audience, that he and several other

Royal Society fellows had concocted a scheme to procure Dodd's body in order to attempt an experiment to bring him back to life. But the delays in obtaining his body meant that by the time it arrived at the undertaker's they had all but given up hope. Even so, they 'tried all the means in their power for the reanimation' but after labouring for a considerable time the chaplain's body remained cold and lifeless. The experiment, according to Hutton, had 'entirely failed'.

Certainly Hutton's account, published in a newspaper in 1822 after all the participants in the experiment were long dead, tallied with earlier descriptions of the attempted revival. No doubt, Hunter would have tried to inflate Dodd's lungs with bellows, as well as warming his body by the fire and rubbing his flesh, according to the guidelines he had submitted to the Humane Society. It is likely, too, that he would have employed electric shocks from a Leyden jar, in a scene evocative of the future *Frankenstein* novel. Yet all the evidence points to the conclusion that Hunter's ambitious experiment had indeed 'entirely failed'. Nevertheless, speculation about Dodd's whereabouts would continue down the centuries, fuelled partly by the fact that though a memorial stone attests to his burial in St Laurence's churchyard, no record of his interment can be found in the parish register.[15]

In truth, Hunter was not himself in the most robust state of health at the time he was labouring to restore life in Dodd. In April he had been struck down by a sudden dizziness that confined him to bed for ten days – a considerable period of enforced rest for someone used to working a nineteen-hour day – and he was still unwell in early May. Mentioning his illness in a letter to Jenner that month, he confessed 'it is still not perfectly recovered'.[16] In June, fewer than two weeks before Dodd was due to hang, Hunter's brother-in-law, the Revd James Baillie, wrote to William expressing considerable anxiety over John's health. Plainly, William had conveyed serious concerns, for Baillie commented, 'What you have wrote of your Brother's State of health sensibly affected us all. Dorry felt it strongly.'[17] Hunter was obviously sufficiently fit later in June to spend two hours furiously trying to engender life into Dodd's corpse, but he was persuaded in August, most probably by Anne, to repair to Bath for the quintessentially fashionable Georgian remedy of sampling the spa waters.

Considering his declared scepticism when it came to the efficacy of mineral waters, it is unlikely Hunter believed the Bath sojourn would confer any real benefit. In lectures, he cynically referred to physicians sending their patients 'to die at Bath or Bristol' once their patients could 'take no more physic or the physician can obtain no more fees'.[18] Hunter's late friend Smollett had described the typically unappealing scene in his novel *Humphrey Clinker* when his country squire Matthew Bramble described the communal bathing at Bath: 'we know not what sores may be running into the water while we are bathing, and what sort of matter we may thus imbibe'.[19] But for all the ridicule heaped on Bath in his fiction, Smollett had himself endorsed the healing powers of the waters, telling William 'I can feel a very sensible Effect from the waters' after visiting in 1762.[20]

Bath did little to help John Hunter, however, for he was 'extremely ill' in the autumn, according to Everard Home.[21] He was plainly suffering from angina again, and both Hunter and his friends believed that his life was in danger. It was Jenner, visiting his beloved ex-teacher in Bath, who was most alert to the signs; having read William Heberden's description of angina, Jenner could see the tell-tale symptoms in Hunter's malady. He said nothing to Hunter himself, and even held off writing on the topic for fear it would upset his mentor.[22] But he confessed his concerns to Heberden, adding, 'I am fearful if Mr H. should admit this, that it may deprive him of the hopes of a recovery'.[23]

Though Hunter himself may not have recognized the symptoms – or more likely deluded himself into dismissing them – he was all too aware of his own mortality by now. Such was his concern for the future that he decided to lose no time in putting his anatomy and natural history collection into better order; he knew it would provide the only source of income for his wife and two young children after his death. Before leaving for Bath, he instructed Everard Home and his assistant William Bell to start producing a catalogue of all the contents. But, according to Home, 'his impatience to return to town made him come back before he was well'.

No doubt Hunter was anxious to return in time for the winter season of lectures. This year he presented his course at his brother's lecture theatre in Great Windmill Street, as he had the previous year, beginning on 27 October 1777 and running every Monday, Wednesday and Friday through till April 1778. Seemingly happy to accommodate him, William gave his own lectures on anatomy on Tuesdays and Saturdays, while pupils of either course were encouraged to use the dissecting room for an additional fee. For those students who enrolled for both brothers' courses, this made for a punishing schedule, as young William Hamilton, who arrived in London in December 1777, could testify.

As the son of Thomas Hamilton – John's friend who had travelled with him from Lanarkshire in 1748, now a professor of anatomy in Glasgow – nineteen-year-old William was warmly welcomed. 'I waited on Mr J. Hunter today,' he wrote to tell his father on 22 December; 'he said he was vastly happy to see me and enquired very particularly about your health'.[24] Steadfastly refusing to take any fee from the youth, because he was 'happy to have it in his power to be of use' to his friend's son, John asked the novice anatomist to dine with him and Anne the following day. In his next letter, William reported, 'I dined on tuesday with Mr. Hunter, along with a friend of Dr Black's, his wife is a very pretty woman and a very aggreeable one'. He had met the twenty-one-year-old Everard Home, 'a very good young lad', too; Home was helping in William's dissecting room as an assistant.

Yet there was little industry in the dissecting room that December. 'Bodies are vastly scarce at present,' the new pupil informed his father; 'some of the men have been taken up and tried but I hope this will be soon over'. The men who had been 'taken up' were two of the brothers' regular suppliers, Williams and Holmes, who had been arrested when a grieving widower discovered his wife's body missing from St George's burial ground in Bloomsbury. Both gravediggers at the cemetery, Williams and Holmes were found guilty of stealing the corpse of Jane Sainsbury at Guildhall Court in Westminster on 6 December.[25] Although they were sentenced to a public whipping followed by six months' imprisonment, the former part of their punishment had to be remitted for fear that mass indignation at their crime would result in a public lynching.

The Great Windmill Street school was by now

notorious for its dealings with the Resurrectionists and William had become the butt of satirists in numerous cartoons exposing the deeds of the body-snatchers. In one sketch, published in 1773, a nightwatchman is shown arresting a grave-robber who has dropped the corpse of a young girl he was attempting to carry away in a hamper. The captured thief points decisively to a fashionably dressed man running away; the fleeing man is plainly identified as William by the notes he has dropped, entitled 'Hunter's lectures', and by the physician's cane he carries.[26]

John was undoubtedly a regular customer of the body-snatchers at the time for he still required fresh corpses for his own researches and for teaching, but he generally escaped the public humiliation and ridicule heaped on his brother. The fact that his lectures did not cover anatomy in the practical sense meant that he needed fewer stolen corpses for teaching purposes. At the same time, he had recourse to many more bodies than William through legal means. Well-heeled families increasingly requested him to perform legitimate post-mortems, while his hospital job allowed him free access to the 'dead house' at St George's to conduct autopsies on deceased patients.

Lack of bodies, however, meant lack of anatomical instruction. Not only were the school's regular suppliers now languishing in Newgate but the sudden vigilance of nightwatchmen and mourners made it extremely risky to scour the burial grounds in search of cadavers. 'I am afraid I shall not have much for my dissecting fee', moaned William Hamilton to his father, 'as bodies are not to be got and there are several before me'. Nevertheless, his fellow scholar George Reid had determined to venture out and 'lift one' himself and had promised to share his spoils with William, who added, 'If a Body be difficult to be got I will see if I can get a head or a leg or an arm or any thing to be doing with.'

In between the idle moments in the dissecting room, young William embarked on his course with John Hunter, taking a seat for his first lecture on 22 December. There was little chance of a seasonal holiday, however, since on Christmas Eve he was in the lecture room again listening to Hunter relate the 'application of his principles to practice'. Writing to his father on Christmas Day, William remarked with evident surprise that 'he does not describe any operations except the radical one for Hydrocele'. This procedure, which Hunter had pioneered to treat the usually benign condition in which fluid collects in the scrotum, entailed draining the liquid with a hollow needle. Hunter had discovered that preventing the wound from healing by introducing some lint or sponge would deter the fluid from collecting again.

The hectic pace of the student's life continued, and it was not until New Year's Day 1778 that William Hamilton wrote again. 'I have got a leg and thigh from the body the Dr. showed the operations upon and I had it injected', he told his father. He would have attempted this procedure himself except that the limb was 'rather putrid', he added; Everard Home had therefore performed the tricky manoeuvre for him. The dearth of fresh material persisted as 'all the burying ground is watched', William continued, 'so that I am afraid we shall have little dissecting for some time'.

In the meantime, despite the inconveniences, young William was enjoying his tuition. 'I am vastly pleased with both Mr. Hunters lectures,' he assured his mother; 'they are worth coming to London to attend, besides the benefit one derives from dissecting'. To his father he added, 'Mr Hunters course seems to be an exceedingly good one it principly treats the theory of Surgery and little or nothing of the practice.' Impressed by Hunter's novel views as well as his warm welcome, William was considering enrolling with him as a surgeon's pupil at St George's. In the event, he remained in London more than three years, eventually taking charge of William Hunter's dissecting room before returning to Glasgow to take over his father's chair in anatomy in 1781.

Once the lecturing season was over in April 1778, it was time for Everard Home to move on too. Now twenty-two, he had completed his six-year apprenticeship with John as well as gaining his diploma from Surgeons' Hall. And since his brother-in-law had neither the financial resources nor seemingly the inclination to continue supporting him, the young surgeon was forced to make his own way in the world. Quite possibly Home expected Hunter to take him on as an assistant or even partner, but there was never the kind of affection or admiration between the snobbish young man and his plain-dealing brother-in-law that existed between Hunter and Jenner, or indeed between Hunter and many other pupils. It was another slight Home would store up for the future. With barely disguised bitterness, he later remarked that since Hunter's expenses always exceeded his income, 'I had therefore no emolument to expect from remaining in his house, which made it necessary for me to take up some line for my own support'. Left to his own devices, Home joined the navy, finding a post as assistant surgeon to the naval hospital at Plymouth and soon after leaving for Jamaica to take a job as a staff surgeon in the colony. In the West Indies he busied himself conducting experiments on venom, pitting snakes, tarantulas and rats against one another.[27] John Andree departed the same year, so Hunter was left with only William Bell and William Lynn as his assistants and no let-up in workload.

It was that same spring, at the end of April, that Hunter's other brother-in-law, the Revd James Baillie, died suddenly leaving John's sister Dorothy distraught and destitute with three teenage children to support, no home and no income. Dorothy moved back to live in the family's old farmhouse at Long Calderwood, and William Hunter undertook to support the family. He adopted his new responsibilities with hard-headed efficiency – at least William had the resources to support his sister's family; John could barely look after his own household – but there was scant tenderness or sympathy. Although he paid the fees for seventeen-year-old Matthew to complete his education at Glasgow University, and the following year sent the youth to Oxford, frugal William kept his sister and her children perpetually impoverished.[28] Eventually following his uncle into the medical profession, and ultimately taking over his Great Windmill Street anatomy school, Matthew would remember William's help with gratitude but little fondness. 'His manner towards me was never familiar nor warm', he later wrote, 'but it was mild and kind'.[29] William expressed even less affection for his nieces, Agnes and Joanna, who were eighteen and sixteen when their father died. Although he undoubtedly fulfilled his duties towards his nephew, he would never meet his nieces. All three would become firm favourites in John Hunter's household.

Through shrewd investment, a circle of well-heeled patients and parsimonious living, William had accumulated substantial riches by the 1770s which he had carefully invested in bank savings, an extensive library, one of the largest coin collections in Europe, a spectacular collection of paintings and his anatomical museum. But though William collected art, and had been anatomist to the Royal Academy since 1770, it was John who treated artists, as well as authors and clergymen, without a fee. So when Samuel Johnson needed a surgeon who would treat a young artist friend in straitened circumstances without concern for payment it was to William he applied, seeking John's assistance.

Johnson was already acquainted with William through their mutual social circles; he had even asked William to present his latest book, *A Journey to the Western Isles of Scotland*, to George III.[30] But they never became warm friends, and it was William Cruikshank, William's partner in the anatomy school since 1774, who fondly tended Johnson through his many bouts of illness, refusing all payment for his services. Johnson similarly had several friends in common with John Hunter, but they probably never met. Certainly when writing to William in the summer of 1778 Johnson referred to 'not having ever seen' John, and it is possible the two would still not have met when Johnson died six years later. But already in early 1778 John had treated Johnson's faithful servant, the former slave Francis Barber, and doubtless for no fee, for Johnson told William in June, 'I am under great obligations to Mr. Hunter, your Brother, for the kind attention which he shows to my servant'.[31] It was in this same letter that Johnson craved William's help in securing John's assistance once more – to 'take the liberty of apply-ing to him again' – this time to offer surgical advice to an artist friend, Mauritius Lowe. Struggling to support a large family in abject poverty, Lowe was suffering some unnamed 'distemper', as Johnson explained: 'Mr. Lowe, an artist who gained the prize in the academy, has a disorder which Mr. Lockhart [presumably another surgeon] thinks very dangerous, and such as requires an operation which neither he nor the patient cares to venture without a consultation. It is therefore requested to Mr. Hunter that he will be pleased to appoint a time, as soon as possible to meet Mr. Lockhart, and inspect the malady.' Though Johnson did not reveal the nature of the 'malady', he plainly knew that Hunter would offer his services without payment. The case did not feature among Hunter's surviving notes, but since Lowe went on to live another fifteen years he evidently survived his appointment with the surgeon.

Johnson was fortunate in pressing his appeal to William when he did, for relations between the two brothers were about to slide dramatically downhill. That autumn, John moved his lecture course from William's school to a hired room in the Haymarket and he would never again return to his brother's premises. There was no explicit reason for the shift, but there were plenty of potential sources of conflict. The brothers had shared premises and pupils for two years with apparent amicability and mutual respect, but now, aged fifty and sixty, and both revered in their different spheres, their close proximity was inevitably a fragile arrangement. They may have shared the same roof for two winters, but they shared little in the way of temperament, interests and beliefs, and the balance of power had plainly shifted since the pliant young Jack had laboured to fulfil William's demanding work programme in Covent Garden. Now the younger brother had at least as strong a reputation in the London medical world as his older sibling, as well as a devoted following of pupils who acclaimed his novel philosophies; moreover, he was at the centre of a close-knit coterie of fellow enthusiasts and enjoyed even more of an exalted place within the scientific community. Both strongly opinionated and resolutely obstinate, although William certainly made his views known in a rather more genteel way than John, it was a wonder the pair had not clashed noisily already.

There had been rumblings of a brewing storm for many years. Smollett had hinted at a row in 1763 when he mentioned that John had 'indiscreetly forfeited' his brother's favours.[32] Horace Walpole is thought to have been referring to another argument between the brothers, whom he jokingly likened to the patron saints of medicine, when he told a friend in December 1776 that 'the quarrel between SS Cosmo and Damian, they say, is at an end'.[33] But if the brothers had argued at the end of 1776, during their first winter sharing lecture premises, this was a mere spat compared to the approaching conflict. For at the beginning of 1780 the London medical world was stunned and the normally cordial atmosphere of the scientific community shattered when John Hunter turned on his own brother at a meeting of the Royal Society.

More than twenty years had passed since John and his friend Colin Mackenzie had discovered the circulation of the placenta and excitedly told William of their findings. Since 1754 William had taught this discovery in his lectures, showed pupils the preparation John and Colin had made, and doubtless performed further research to confirm the finding himself. Six years earlier, in 1774, William had finally published his masterpiece, *The Anatomy of the Human Gravid Uterus*, in which he described the circulation of the placenta as well as reproducing exquisite illustrations of John's expert knife work, while making only grudging tribute to his younger brother's contribution. But having since then shared lecturing premises, conducted joint medical consultations and even performed animal dissections together – they jointly dissected one of the King's elephants which died in 1776[34] – there was no apparent reason for the supposed grievance to be revived now. So in January 1780 William could not have expected to be suddenly reproached over this age-old grudge, and certainly not with such ferocity.

The meeting of the Royal Society on 27 January began innocuously enough, and Banks, who had been elected president two years earlier when Pringle resigned, probably anticipated a quiet evening.[35] The usual recommendations for elections were made, followed by discussion of plans to strike a medal in memory of Captain Cook, who had been tragically killed the previous year by natives in Hawaii while on his third voyage. Then the business moved to the presentation of papers. The first was the conclusion of a paper started the previous week describing the birth of a child with congenital smallpox; it was read by John Hunter. There was little controversy there. But Hunter had a surprise up his sleeve. He now rose to deliver a second paper, 'On the Structure of the Placenta', which he nonchalantly announced would describe the separate blood supplies of the mother and fetus.

Within minutes of beginning in his usual stilted manner, it became startlingly apparent that Hunter was accusing his own brother – a fellow member of the society and the Queen's own physician – of outright plagiarism. Describing for the first time the discovery that he and Mackenzie had made in 1754, he now declared, 'I mean to exhibit my claim to a discovery of no small importance'.[36] For although his brother William had already outlined the circulation of the placenta in his classic book, he had done so, alleged John, 'without mentioning the mode of discovery'. This mode of discovery, by himself and Mackenzie – who had since died – was now meticulously detailed by John to the shock and embarrassment of the aghast members. He concluded by declaring that he now considered himself 'as having a just claim to the discovery of the structure of the placenta and its communication with the uterus'. Although the staid Royal Society minutes would record only that thanks were 'returned' for the paper, the atmosphere in the room as John sat down must have been as electric as one of John Walsh's eel parties.

Stung by this surprise ambush, William wrote to the society a peevish but characteristically sanctimonious letter which was read at the next meeting on 3 February.[37] In it, William blustered that the discovery in question had been published several years previously as his own, that he had long taught the discovery as his, and that he had always paid tribute to his brother's help as 'an excellent assistant'. Tellingly, at no point did he insist that he had actually made the discovery in question nor did he dispute his brother's right to priority, although he declared himself willing to let the Royal Society act as arbiter in deciding the merits of 'Mr Hunter's claim'. At the same time, William plaintively reminded the fellows that it was he who had first taught his upstart brother the skills of anatomy, 'and put him into the very best situation that I could for becoming what the society has, for some time, known him to be'.

As the dispute descended into the 'paper war' William

had so lamented in past arguments with rival anatomists, John now sent an impassioned and, for him, extremely eloquent letter to Banks, reiterating his claim with redoubled zeal. The response was accordingly read to the increasingly embarrassed fellows on 17 February.[38] In it, John explained that he had been impelled to reply for fear that 'silence on my part after his charge may be interpreted by my Enemies into an acknowledgement that I have intentionally claimed to myself a discovery in reality his due'. Restating the details of his discovery with Mackenzie, he proclaimed, 'I am as tenacious as he is to Anatomical discovery, and I flatter myself as tenacious also of truth.' And yet he was willing to forfeit this claim should his brother produce evidence to show he had himself made the discovery in question prior to 1754. Extending a somewhat prickly olive branch, he also declared himself ready to accept joint credit for the discovery – 'and abolish all remembrance of the succession of time' – should William refuse to accept his version of events.

Either battered into submission or infuriated into silence, William never responded. John had had the last word and thus set right twenty-six years of injustice – or so he thought, for neither brother was apparently aware that the crucial finding had really first been demonstrated by the Dutch anatomist Wilhelm Noortwyk in 1743. But if John could now regard himself as the victor in his wrangle with William, it was a heavy price to pay to permanently estrange his own brother. Wisely, the Royal Society declined to umpire the brothers' unseemly public dispute and John's paper was never published in the *Philosophical Transactions*, although he would later include a revised version in his *Observations on the Animal Oeconomy* in 1786.

Whether or not William's claim to priority over the placenta discovery had rankled with John for a full twenty-six years, it is unlikely that this was the true cause of their falling out. According to Jessé Foot, who often had a firm handle on the facts for all his malicious interpretation, the argument was about another matter entirely. Foot claimed that John had invited William to view a particularly interesting organ he had removed from a soldier at a post-mortem. Immediately coveting the part for his own collection, William took the preparation home and refused to give it up.[39] Quite conceivably, the quarrel over the soldier's organ had escalated into a full-blown wrangle raking over William's 'theft' of past preparations, as well as discoveries, in previous years. Certainly the dispute appeared to have arisen some months before John's outburst at the Royal Society, for when their nephew, Matthew Baillie, came to stay with William in 1779, he noted, 'At this time too I waited upon Mr and Mrs Hunter, and they received me kindly, although there was a disagreement between him and his brother, Dr Hunter.'[40] Indeed, the story of a tussle over a pound of flesh has more than a ring of truth to it, for not only were both brothers intensely avaricious when it came to their collections, William had only just emerged from an embittered dispute with his former partner, William Hewson.

It was Hewson, a pupil at the Covent Garden school when he had lodged with John in 1759, who had taken over John's role as William's assistant, and later became his partner, after the younger brother had joined the army. Perhaps because of this apparent usurping of his job John had always regarded Hewson with animosity, branding him a 'Plageerist' over certain anatomical discoveries, but this was nothing compared to the row that broke out between Hewson and William.[41] They first argued after Hewson got married in 1770 – to Mary Stevenson, the daughter of Benjamin Franklin's landlady – on the grounds that William believed marriage and a young family were incompatible with the relentless labours required of an anatomist. Explaining William's views to a colleague, Hewson joked, 'My friend Dr Hunter was much afraid it would spoil me as an anatomist'.[42] The row blew up into a full-scale dispute in which Hewson accused William of making him work too hard, refusing to let him use the library, making him pay for board and lodging, and reacting jealously to his achievements – complaints that might have sounded familiar to John too. In response, William charged Hewson with absenteeism, rudeness, using bodies bought by William for his own dissections, and that he 'employ'd a Man to pick Bones out of the Tubs & fit up a Skeleton for him' without permission. The wrangle led to William dissolving the partnership the following year, at which point he laid claim to all the work Hewson had produced under his roof. So intense was the dispute that Franklin, a mutual friend, had to negotiate a settlement. It was a process he described as an 'unpleasant Time'.[43]

William's argument with Hewson had been perhaps the most virulent before his breach with John, but it was by no means his only disagreement. As well as his rows with the Monros and Pott, he had fallen out with William Smellie, his first tutor in midwifery, and the artist van Rymsdyk, and he would continue to have arguments with his latest partner, William Cruikshank.[44]

Yet there were other, more fundamental reasons why William and John, who was no less argumentative, should have reached a cataclysmic rift by this stage in their careers. John's radical and outspoken views on the nature and even origins of life were increasingly at variance with William's more conventional and more God-fearing outlook, as William would certainly have discovered had he eavesdropped on John's lecture course in his amphitheatre. Indeed, the stark contrast for the brothers' various pupils, trekking from William's eloquent exposition on the divine creation of the human body on one evening to his younger brother's faltering and increasingly irreligious utterings on another, must have seemed decidedly comical at times. On a Tuesday evening, the pupils could pile in to hear William begin his lecture on the significance of anatomy with the pious declaration, 'Who can know and consider the thousand evident proofs of the astonishing art of the Creator, in forming and sustaining an animal body such as ours, without feeling the most pleasing enthusiasm?'[45] William's fulsome tribute to the mysterious works of God was entirely in keeping with the contemporary world view. Indeed, he may well have meant to caution the students expressly against imbibing the iconoclastic views of his less restrained brother when he went on to proclaim, 'The man who is really an Anatomist, yet does not see and feel what I have endeavoured to express in words, whatever he may be in other respects, must certainly labour under a dead palsy, in one part of his mind.'

Although William well knew that his brother's mind was far from dead, he was aware that his lectures on physiology were running perilously close to countering accepted religious dogma. For not only did John never once refer to the traditionally acknowledged role of 'the Creator' in forming all life – nature was always his preferred candidate for this wondrous achievement – he also suggested that life had originally appeared spontaneously out of inorganic material rather than over a six-day period in the Garden of Eden. He told his pupils, without equivocation, 'Animal and vegetable matter has certainly arisen out of the matter of the globe, for we find it returning to it again.'[46] Although John had married in church and enjoyed friendships with several clergymen, he certainly entertained views that bordered on heresy. In one unpublished manuscript he even wrote, 'All innovation on established systems that depend more on a belief, than real knowledge (such as Religion) arise rather from a weakness of mind than a fault in the system.'[47] Even the philosophy behind his lecture course – spurring on students to question established doctrines and daring them to think for themselves – was an encouragement to heterodoxy. William made no attempt to conceal his disapproval, condemning his brother's lecture course with the comment 'though it may strike weak, uncultivated minds, yet by men of finer intellects it is construed with great propriety as an indignity thrown out against the Great Author of All Things'.[48] William might have hoped still to protect his pupils from the anti-religious influence of his fraternal lecturer, but he had doubtless realized that he was unlikely to deter his brother from a course steering him directly towards a head-on collision with the Georgian establishment.

The brothers' breach would never be mended. Whether or not Benjamin Franklin could have healed their dispute, his diplomatic skills were now fully employed in negotiations between Britain and its American colonies. Shortly afterwards William complained bitterly to Dorothy that 'I have lived to have my affections much disturbed by ingratitude.'[49] But if John regretted his assault on William, he never once referred to their argument. When he later obtained a copy of a memoir on William published after his death, John scribbled numerous comments in the margins, possibly for a revised edition. Many of the remarks were laudatory, some of them dry, some of them comical, but none of them spiteful. He even defended William against Hewson's complaints, remarking, 'In this dispute Mr. Hewson showed great indelicacy, pursued it with great rancor and self conceit, and endeavoured to make a party affair of it.' Yet he made no mention of his own unresolved dispute and would only comment that 'He perhaps did not make sufficient allowance for the natural frailty of human nature'.[50]

Now veering closer and closer to sacrilegious theories, Hunter had already signalled his controversial views the previous year in a paper to the Royal Society on hermaphroditism, the rare condition in which male and female sexual organs occur in a single animal. His seemingly inoffensive paper, 'An Account of the Free-Martin', described three hermaphrodite cattle he had been invited to examine over a succession of years, both when alive and after death, by animal breeders he had befriended.[51] After dissecting the curious creatures, which looked to all intents and purposes like cows but always had a male twin, Hunter was the first to delineate their simultaneous male and female reproductive organs. He argued that not only did all species have a propensity to malformations but also every part in every species possessed this same ability; such a view steered perilously close to challenging the orthodox doctrine that all species had been created in a fixed and never-changing state. Even more significantly,

Hunter noted that different species tended to exhibit the same defects, and when these parts were malformed these were generally uniform deviations. This prefigured the idea that congenital malformations existed in some original form – or, as Hunter stated even more plainly in a paper in 1780, 'each part of each species seems to have its monstrous form originally impressed upon it'.[52] He even went so far as to ponder whether any natural hermaphrodites, such as snails and worms, had ever possessed distinct and separate sexual organs. 'Is there ever, in the genera of animals that are natural hermaphrodites, a separation of the two parts forming distinct sexes?' he asked. 'If there is, it may account for the distinction of sexes ever having happened.'[53] Not only did this remarkable query contradict accepted beliefs in fixed or immutable animals, it also suggested that one species had somehow gradually changed, effectively evolved, into another.

These startling observations may have passed by his colleagues at a sleepy meeting of the Royal Society without undue alarm, but their significance would later become dramatically clearer. Charles Darwin, too, would study natural hermaphrodites when developing his theory of evolution; the development of dual-sexed creatures into two opposite sexes represented a crucial part of the puzzle. Indeed, Darwin would turn to Hunter's work on the freemartin, and his 1780 paper on pheasants, when writing *The Descent of Man*, the book that described the place of humans in the evolutionary chain, almost a century later. In particular he was impressed by the anatomist's distinction between primary sexual differences, for the purposes of reproduction, and secondary sexual characteristics, to attract the opposite sex, quoting Hunter's definition at length.

Hunter's increasingly insistent appeals to Jenner to send him fossils from the rich oolitic limestone near his Gloucestershire home were another example of his growing obsession with understanding the origins of life. Hunter had long collected the curious formations that continued to present a puzzle to naturalists. It was still widely believed that fossils were the remains of animals that had died in the Flood, although a few radicals had daringly suggested these were actually the imprints of animals that had become extinct. Along with his bottled human and animal parts, Hunter was building up an extensive fossil collection; as well as pressing Jenner to send 'all the Fossels you find', he bought examples from sales. Ultimately, Hunter's fossil collection would become one of the largest in Europe but, unlike other collections of its kind, as early as the late 1770s he had placed his prize fossils side by side with modern examples of similar animals, for he told Jenner, 'I am matching my Fossill as far as I can with the resent'.[54] His researches were plainly headed for controversy.

Challenging authority had become a way of life to Hunter. In March 1781 he found himself ridiculed by one of the country's top judges for refusing to fall into line with considered medical opinion in one of the most notorious murder trials of the century.[55] Captain John Donellan was the prime suspect in the unexplained death of his brother-in-law, Sir Theodosius Boughton, in August the previous year. At twenty years old, Sir Theodosius had been a dashing, eligible bachelor in the full bloom of health. Within the year he was due to inherit a sizeable fortune from his guardian, but if he died before reaching twenty-one the money went instead to his sister, who was married to Captain Donellan. Sir Theodosius would never see his twenty-first birthday, for on 30 August he lapsed into convulsions from which he very soon died, just half an hour after taking medicine prescribed by the local apothecary for a venereal complaint. The medication was supposed to contain rhubarb, jalop, spirits of lavender, nutmeg water, syrup and water – a harmless if unpleasant laxative. On drinking the concoction, the young man had complained that it tasted nauseous; his mother, Lady Boughton, noted an aroma of almonds. Curiously, as Lady Boughton called for help and her son writhed in agony after taking the draught, Donellan came into the bedroom and carefully washed out the medicine bottle. Not surprisingly, as soon as Sir Theodosius uttered his last groan, the finger of suspicion fell firmly on Captain Donellan – the man who had most to gain from his death. When Donellan then ensured that his relative was hastily buried before a post-mortem could be performed, the coroner was promptly called in. Some ten days after Sir Theodosius had died, the coroner ordered his body exhumed. So decayed was the corpse in the height of summer that the post-mortem had to be performed in an open churchyard to reduce the stench. Statements by the two surgeons who performed the autopsy affirming that the body showed evidence of poisoning were sufficient to have Donellan arrested and put on trial for murder at Warwick Assizes in March 1781.

The circumstantial evidence stacked up against the accused was convincing, but the verdict finally hinged on the medical evidence relating to the apparent cause of death. Five medical witnesses – three physicians and two surgeons – testified to their sincere belief that Sir Theodosius had been poisoned, most probably with laurel water. Because laurel leaves produced prussic acid – a solution of hydrogen cyanide – water in which the leaves had been distilled could prove highly toxic, assuming a sufficiently strong concentration was consumed. The two surgeons who had opened the body were convinced they had discerned signs of poisoning, although crucially they had failed to examine either the bowels or the brain, blaming the 'offensiveness' of the decaying body. The physicians were similarly insistent that death had been caused by poisoning after conducting a few experiments on dogs, and had no hesitation in declaring laurel water, with its distinctive smell of almonds, as the mode of poison.

Only one medical witness was called for the defence: John Hunter. Having studied the account of the autopsy and the evidence given by his medical colleagues, Hunter took the stand. First he established his unrivalled experience in dissection – 'I have dissected some thousands during these thirty-three years' – then he demonstrated his unparalleled research work in comparative anatomy, specifically in poisons. Having 'poisoned some thousands of animals', Hunter told the counsel for the defence, he could attest that the effects of substances such as arsenic and opium were usually similar in both dogs and humans. But he dismissed the limited number of experiments conducted by his colleagues for the prosecution and had just as little regard for their cack-handed efforts at autopsy. As far as he was concerned, the details they described showed signs only of extensive decomposition. Without having dissected the victim's intestines it was impossible to aver that the man had died of poisoning; without examining his brain they could not discount a stroke or epileptic fit as the cause of death. Furthermore, Hunter's own experiments in forcing dogs to take laurel water had not produced the sudden death described in the case. Most importantly, though his medical colleagues had un-equivocally backed a verdict of poisoning based largely on circumstantial evidence, Hunter refused to entertain such speculation, confining his expert evidence to the medical facts alone. His defiant stance – a model of medico-legal professionalism – confounded the prosecution and infuriated the judge, Mr Justice Buller.

When cross-examined by the prosecution, Hunter admitted the circumstances were suspicious and conceded that 'If I knew the draught was poison, I should say, most probably, that the symptoms arose from that'. Nevertheless, he insisted, 'but when I don't know that that draught was poison, when I consider that a number of other things might occasion his death, I cannot answer positively to it'. Pressed by Buller to use his best judge-ment, he answered, 'I can give nothing decisive.' The judge was almost apoplectic with rage. He roundly con-demned Hunter for his reluctance to speculate, telling the jury, 'I can hardly say what his opinion is, for he does not seem to have formed any opinion at all of the matter.' Under Buller's forthright direction, backed by the testa-ment of five doctors, it took the jury all of nine minutes to find Donellan guilty. He was executed three days later and his body presented to local surgeons for dissection.

Whether or not Hunter believed Donellan was innocent, he was certainly convinced his trial had been unfair and his colleagues' testimony unprofessional. He told his pupils after the case, 'A poor devil was lately hanged at Warwick upon no other testimony than that of physical men whose first experiments were made on this occasion.'[56] Indeed, in similar circumstances, when he was sure of his facts, he was quite willing to offer decisive testimony. In an earlier murder trial in which a school-master was accused of killing a pupil by striking him on the head so that he fell against a chimney breast, Hunter's evidence was unequivocal. After performing a post-mortem on the boy Hunter found a fracture in his skull and concluded, 'From the above appearances it is my opinion that they were caused by some external violence, and that they were the immediate cause of his death.' Based on this testimony, an inquest recorded a verdict of manslaughter although the trial in October 1770 acquitted the offender after a spirited defence of his character.[57]

The Donellan trial was avidly followed by the press, and, just as with the attempted revival of Dodd, Hunter's central role inevitably came up in conversation soon after at his weekly coffee-house club. Egged on by his fellow enthusiasts to discuss the case, Hunter proclaimed that a man could drink as much laurel water as would kill a dog without any harmful effect. One of the gathering immediately took issue with this opinion and alleged that Hunter's experiments had been 'fabricated for the trial'. At this point, according to Richard Lovell Edgeworth, the Irish inventor who was a member of the club, 'a very unbecoming scene began'.[58] Whether or not Hunter and his unnamed opponent came to blows was left unsaid, although it seems plausible. But Edgeworth managed to calm inflamed tempers by leaping to the anatomist's defence, recalling that ten years earlier Hunter had informed the same group that he had himself swallowed enough laurel water to kill twenty dogs and lived to tell the tale. 'The assailant was quickly put down by my evidence,' he confided to his diary.

Relations within the coffee-house coterie must have

soon returned to their usual conviviality, for in February 1782 Hunter was enjoying a friendly social evening with his usual chums when Nevil Maskelyne, the astronomer royal, suddenly collapsed and fainted after eating tripe at their usual venue, Young Slaughter's coffee-house. Fortunately, Hunter was on hand to offer first aid. 'I immediately laid him along the floor,' he recorded in his case books. 'I sprinkled some cold water in his face: he began to recover and immediately vomited.'[59] After vomiting twice more the astronomer duly recovered.

With Hunter's many business interests forever escalating, at last even he had to admit that his house in Jermyn Street was far too small for his busy household, tireless research pursuits and burgeoning collection. Two remarkable and uncommonly large additions to his animal specimens in 1780 and 1781 had made continuing in the house just about intolerable. Even obliging Anne's patience must have been severely tested.

The first of these additions was a creature that had attained almost mythical status in eighteenth-century Europe. Giraffes, as the animals were sometimes known from the Italian term, seemed more fabulous even than unicorns and centaurs. But in 1779 the traveller William Paterson had journeyed into uncharted parts of southern Africa on an expedition funded by the keen amateur botanist Lady Strathmore. It was during this journey that he shot and killed a large male giraffe.[60] When the trophy was brought home in 1780 – it was the first giraffe ever seen in England – Lady Strathmore generously donated its skin and much of its skeleton to Hunter. Despite its lack of internal organs, Hunter was elated with his prize and made sure nothing was wasted. Having preserved several of the bones, he dissected the elastic ligaments in the neck in order to understand how its neck muscles worked, and then had the entire animal stuffed. A rather amateurish watercolour of the animal, as it might have looked alive, was probably painted by Hunter himself.[61] Unfortunately, the astonishing stature of the stuffed beast, estimated to have measured as much as eighteen feet (about six metres), made its accommodation rather difficult. With the rooms housing his collection already bursting at the seams, Hunter was forced to hack off the giraffe's legs and stand it in his entrance hall. The sight must have provided a dramatic welcome to visitors and patients.[62]

The following year another exciting find created further logistical problems for the household. In September 1781, fishermen captured a bottle-nosed whale that had ventured up the Thames beyond London Bridge. The carcass, measuring almost eight metres long, was bought by an 'oil-man' – presumably a dealer in whale oil – for the hefty sum of £70. According to Solander, relating the latest gossip to Banks, its buyer recouped at least his out-lay by exhibiting the 'stinking whale'.[63] Hunter was among the first to view the animal. He had already dissected an orca of about the same length in 1759, and a second in 1772, as well as the bottle-nosed dolphin which he had persuaded Jenner to send. (Having encouraged his ex-pupil to adopt his own distinctive methods of exploration, Hunter reported, 'the milk, which was tasted by Mr Jenner and Mr Ludlow, surgeon, at Sodbury, was rich, like cow's milk to which cream was added'.) Despite the buoyant whaling industry, whole whales in fresh condition were still a rarity and live ones impossible to transport. At some point Hunter had even paid a surgeon to board a whaler set for Greenland in the hope of obtaining useful specimens, 'but the only return I received for this expense was a piece of whale's skin, with some small animals sticking upon it', he lamented.[64] So the opportunity of investigating an entire whale of a new species was too good to miss and Hunter quickly persuaded its owner to let him dissect the creature. Helped by a crew of pupils and assistants, Hunter stood on top of the great animal wielding his largest knives. The scene created a stir in the press, one newspaper reporting that the whale's vena cava – the largest vein in the body – 'was capable of containing a child of a year old'. Hunter carefully noted its two tusk-like teeth in the lower jaw, while in its stomach he found 'the beaks of some hundreds of cuttle-fish'.

But finding a place to display its remarkable skeleton was a rather weightier problem. By now, not only was Hunter's home in Jermyn Street impossibly crowded, so that 'the whole suite of the best rooms in his house were occupied by his preparations', according to Home, the lease was fast running out too.[65] Hunter needed somewhere to display his extensive collection in its unique order and, in time, to be opened as a museum to public view. With this in mind, Hunter now searched not only for a fitting venue but for a dramatic new exhibit that could take its place as the crowning attraction of the museum. He was not to be disappointed on either score.

12

The Giant's Bones

'I lately got a tall man, but at the time could make no particular observations.'

John Hunter[1]

London, April 1782

News that the Irish giant was lumbering his way towards London reached the capital long before he did. Ever since making the short sea crossing from his home in Ireland to Scotland, Charles Byrne had become a national celebrity and his majestic-sounding stage name was on everybody's lips. So tall was Byrne, according to accounts that preceded him, that in Edinburgh he had lit his pipe from one of the lamps on North Bridge without even standing on tiptoes.[2] Variously reported to measure eight feet, eight feet two inches and even eight feet four inches tall, Byrne drew crowds wherever he went. As he crossed the border to journey south, appreciative audiences queued to witness his astonishing stature, hear his booming voice, and shake hands with the polite young man. Byrne was used to the attention, for he had caused a stir ever since he was an infant.

Born in a hamlet near the border of County Derry and County Tyrone in 1761, Byrne had soon achieved local acclaim. Although not an unusually large baby, he quickly outgrew his playmates and pretty soon towered over adults too. As news of the peculiarly tall boy spread through the countryside, wild myths developed, such as the tale that he owed his extraordinary height to his parents conceiving him on top of a haystack.[3] With the infant's growth showing no signs of slowing down, a sharp entrepreneur from a neighbouring village, Joe Vance, convinced Byrne's parents that the boy could prove to be their ticket to a fortune. Acting as his agent, Vance exhibited the youth at country fairs and village greens as a freak curiosity. The boy more than outdid his manager's expectations, attracting excited onlookers wherever he went, and Vance was soon convinced he could pull in even bigger crowds and more money by taking his charge to Britain and possibly even the Continent. After touring Scotland and northern England, the pair steadily journeyed south towards the capital in early 1782. They knew they would face stiff competition, for London had been a magnet for every manner of freak show for centuries.

John Hunter was not the only person with an interest in 'monsters' in eighteenth-century London. Each autumn, crowds flocked to Bartholomew Fair in London's East End to view the assortment of strange exhibits, both animal and human; in between times curiosities were shown at taverns and lodging houses. As well as wild beasts on show throughout the year, Londoners thronged to gape at unusual or deformed animals, such as a cow with two heads which was on show in early 1782. A young physician, Sylas Neville, was among the spectators in February. 'Saw a monster of the brute creation,' he recorded in his diary, 'a heifer with two heads, four horns, four eyes, four ears, four nostrils through all of which it breathes, eats & chews cud with both mouths.'[4] Neville revealed that 'an eminent surgeon & anatomist' had paid its owner to receive the carcass when the cow died. There can be little doubt that it was Hunter who had clinched this deal, despite already possessing parts of a calf with two heads which he had dissected in 1761.[5] Hunter was always in the market for more curious specimens for his prized collection.

More fascinating even than double-headed cows were the human freaks and oddities that had been exhibited in London for as long as anyone could remember. Incited by folk stories of men with tails, centaurs and mermen, Londoners paid to see people born with deformed or extra limbs or with appalling medical conditions. With no state help for vulnerable people, appearing in such shows was the only source of income for most; many travelled to London expressly for the purpose. One boy, born without legs, came from Austria to show himself at the Eagle and Child in Fleet Street in 1714, while a boy with one head and two bodies was exhibited at Bartholomew Fair at around the same time.[6] Conjoined twins were a regular sight in the capital; a man who was 'covered all over his body with large scales' – perhaps he suffered from the skin disorder icthyosis – was on show in 1758; and an albino negro girl drew similar interest.[7] And in case the novelty of watching static human exhibits should pall, many professional freaks learned tricks to keep their audiences entertained. One man without arms, described as 'the eighth great wonder of the world', could beat a drum, play a trumpet, fire a pistol and embroider with his feet.

Dwarfs were popular attractions in the capital too and often took pains to accentuate their almost mythological status. Corsican-born Madame Teresa, known as the 'Corsican Fairy', arrived in London in 1773 before travelling to Dublin, where she posed for a portrait immaculately fitted in a miniature suit to resemble a little mannequin. The painting was acquired by John Hunter, and he would follow her career with particular interest; details of her subsequent death, shortly after trying to deliver a normal-sized child, were later added to his case books.[8] Yet while dwarfs could generally pull a mesmerized crowd, Londoners always had a soft spot for giants.

Even more than dwarfs, giants were the stuff of legends.[9] They evoked wonder and fear at the same time, and exaggerated tales of their proportions and feats became mingled with folklore and fairy tales. Giants had always played a central role in London pageantry. The fabled Gogmagog, reputed to have lived in Cornwall in pre-Roman times, had somehow down the centuries become divided into twin giants, Gog and Magog, and their images fashioned in wicker were paraded through the city streets at the Lord Mayor's show every year. The threat of Gog and Magog visiting in the night was enough to make any fractious child promise to sleep, but it was difficult even for adults to separate fact from fiction. In the early seventeenth century John Middleton was said to have grown to the unlikely height of nine feet three inches. Even in the early eighteenth century it was widely supposed that extraordinarily large bones discovered in caves across Europe had belonged to gigantic human ancestors. Many believed the human race had been gradually shrinking since Creation; in 1718 a French academic calculated that Adam must have been 134 feet tall while Eve had measured 128 feet.[10]

By the middle of the eighteenth century, London streets echoed almost constantly to the thud of giants' feet. Among the most famous was Henry Blacker, known as the 'British Giant', who was shown in London in 1751. His fellow titans included Edward Bamford, dubbed the 'Staffordshire Giant', Daniel Cajanus, or the 'Swedish Giant', and Maximilian Miller, nicknamed the 'Saxon Giant', each claiming heights that ranged from the plausible to the incredible. There had even been an earlier 'Irish giant', Cornelius McGrath, who showed himself in Bristol and London in 1753. But when Charles Byrne arrived in London on 11 April 1782, everyone agreed he was the tallest giant ever to have walked the capital's streets.

Although he hardly needed to broadcast his presence, since he stood a full two feet taller than the average Londoner, an advertisement in the *Morning Herald* on 24 April proclaimed his arrival: 'IRISH GIANT. To be seen this, and every day this week, in his large elegant room, at the Cane-shop next door to late Cox's Museum, Spring Gdns, Mr. Byrne, the surprising Irish Giant, who is allowed to be the tallest man in the world, his height is eight feet two inche [*sic*], and in full proportion accordingly, only 21 years of age. His stay will not be long in London, as he proposes shortly to visit the Continent.'[11]

Although in reality Byrne probably measured an only slightly less remarkable seven feet eight inches, the undeniably surprising giant captivated London overnight.

Residing at an apartment in Spring Gardens, near Charing Cross, Byrne entertained audiences from 11 a.m. to 3 p.m. and 5 p.m. to 8 p.m. six days a week for a fee of 2s 6d per person. Overcoming any initial apprehension, audiences were soon bewitched by the gentle giant, who dressed in an elegant frockcoat, waistcoat, knee breeches, silk stockings, frilled cuffs and collar, topped by a three-cornered hat, and who spoke so politely and displayed such genteel manners. Byrne's large, square jaw, wide forehead and slightly stooped shoulders enhanced his placid demeanour.

He was soon the talk of the town. While newspapers published flattering reports of his physique, gossip columnists speculated on his love-life; one article suggested an assignation with a female dwarf, known as the 'Bird of Paradise', who was on show elsewhere in town.[12] The infamous quack physician James Graham even offered Byrne the first trial of his 'Celestial Bed', newly installed in his 'Temple of Health and Hymen' in Pall Mall; any couple spending a night on its curiously oscillating mattress was promised instant fertility. Wisely, Byrne declined, declaring himself 'a perfect stranger to the rites and mysteries of the Goddess Venus'.[13] Within weeks of his arrival, Byrne had met the King and Queen at Kew, had been fêted by members of the nobility and had been presented before the Royal Society, its members anxious to assess his prodigious stature and proffer theories for his peculiar condition. He even became the hero of the summer's pantomime, called 'Harlequin Teague or the Giant's Causeway', which ran for nearly a month at the Haymarket Theatre to rapturous applause.[14]

Among early visitors who paid to see Byrne was Sylas Neville, keen to view a curiosity to surpass the two-headed cow. 'Saw Byrne, the famous Irish giant, in whose person nature has exceeded her usual limits in a most astonishing degree,' he recorded in his diary. 'Even the great Patagonians are nothing to this – 8 feet 2 inches.'[15] But he was rather less complimentary about Byrne's natural attributes, observing that 'he stoops, is not well shaped, his flesh loose and his appearance far from wholesome'. One visitor who was particularly moved by viewing the giant was Count Joseph Boruwlaski, the diminutive 'Polish dwarf', who had arrived in London from the Continent only weeks before Byrne. He had been taken under the wing of the undisputed doyenne of fashionable Georgian society, Georgiana, the Duchess of Devonshire.[16] Having been patronized by royal families across Europe – although he had no true claim to his own assumed aristocratic title – Boruwlaski was disinclined to exhibit himself as simply another human freak. He had taken lodgings at 55 Jermyn Street, almost opposite Hunter's house, through the generosity of Georgiana, who had likewise paid a tailor to make him a suit 'embroidered with gems and silver'. Artfully, he managed to survive on the goodwill of benefactors, supplemented by giving occasional concerts.

Ever eager to observe deviations from the norm, whether in animal or human form, Hunter was quick to make Boruwlaski's acquaintance. Finding him a lively and intelligent man who lamented being forced to make a living out of his unusual condition, both John and Anne would become subscribers to the Count's memoirs when he published them in 1788. Naturally enough, Hunter was fascinated by Boruwlaski's medical condition; he introduced the Count to friends and invited him to meet his pupils at Sunday-evening scientific gatherings.

Describing the dwarf as a member of the human species 'in the compleatest miniature you ever beheld', one of the students reported, 'He has been much countenanced by John Hunter.'[17] By the end of 1782, Hunter had persuaded Boruwlaski to pose for a portrait by the artist Philip Reinagle. Smartly attired in a gold-braided uniform, waistcoat, breeches and buckle shoes, and sporting a miniature sword, the Count stands with dignity beside a chair, his shoulders reaching only just above the chair's arm.[18]

It was shortly after arriving in London that Boruwlaski was escorted by his patrons, the Duke and Duchess of Devonshire, to join the crowds at one of the Irish giant's shows. 'He was eight feet three or four inches high,' recorded Boruwlaski, repeating popular mythology. 'His shape was very well proportioned, his physiognomy agreeable; and what is very uncommon in men of this sort, his strength was equal to his size: he was at that time two-and-twenty.' As soon as the audience gawping at Byrne realized that the tiny dwarf was in the same room, all clamoured to see the two side by side. Boruwlaski was pushed to the front, and as the towering giant reached down to greet the miniature man, the delighted onlookers were no doubt reminded of Gulliver's encounter with the Lilliputians. 'Our surprise was, I think, equal,' Boruwlaski noted in his memoirs; 'the giant remained a moment speechless, viewing me with looks of astonishment; then stooping very low to present me his hand, which would easily have contained a dozen like mine, he made me a very polite compliment.'[19]

There can be no doubt that Hunter would have been among the first in the queue to view the Irish giant. It was but a brisk five-minute walk from Jermyn Street to the rooms in Spring Gardens where Byrne was on display.

Whether he joined the Royal Society party at their private viewing, or conceivably took along ten-year-old Jock and six-year-old Agnes with their half-crowns clasped in sweaty palms to one of the shows, or possibly both, is unknown. Certainly he developed an early fascination with the curiously tall young man which rapidly grew into an obsession. As the newspapers continued to report Byrne's real and imagined exploits, as well as carrying further tantalizing advertisements for his shows, it was easy to follow the movements of the 'Living Colossus'.[20] Whether or not Hunter ever got the chance to examine the giant – his name does not appear in his case books – it is highly probable that the Royal Society group that met Byrne was given leave to measure him, for an advertisement in July suggests they had checked his 'stupendous' height and affirmed his 'admirable symmetry'.[21]

An interest in giants had long been a feature of Royal Society inquiry. The early eighteenth-century president Sir Hans Sloane had examined some of the huge skeletons discovered across Europe, as well as a collection of large bones exhibited in London as a 'giant's hand'; he had concluded that the skeletons belonged to elephants and whales transported to Europe by the great Flood, and realized that the 'giant's hand' was a whale's fin.[22] But the existence of extraordinarily tall men like Byrne continued to flummox the natural philosophers. Some no doubt veered towards the popular mythology that Byrne's large size stemmed from his mode of conception; others would have regarded him as a throwback to the reputed giant human ancestors. Certainly, few could have failed to be curious about the youth as he towered over their heads during the private viewing. But none was more captivated than John Hunter.

With no time for superstitions or folklore, Hunter was intent on explaining the existence of giants. For him, as for his contemporaries, such human curiosities fitted into the category of 'monsters'; the modern term 'teratology', describing the study of anomalies in animal life, is a derivation from the Greek for monster. Hunter's fascination with 'monsters' went back, of course, to his earliest studies in anatomy. His collection of double-tailed lizards were classic examples of deviations from normal development, while the freemartins he had studied showed freak congenital abnormalities. Over the years he had observed, dissected and collected an extensive number of other human and animal oddities, and it was well known among the body-snatchers, animal breeders and even butchers he cultivated that he was always in the market for rare or unexpected finds. In the summer of 1782, not long after Byrne had arrived in town, Hunter petitioned a close acquaintance, the politician the Earl of Shelburne, to help find a job for a poor butcher who had frequently brought him 'curious parts of animals'.[23] Hunter's hoard of abnormalities now formed a separate section in its own right. This motley selection of bizarre finds was undoubtedly the stuff of nightmares. Along with his two-tailed lizards and two-headed cows, visitors granted the dubious privilege of looking around could witness malformed human fetuses, a duck with a foot on its head, a cow with an extra leg, a pig with two bodies and several double-headed snakes. But Hunter's penchant for peculiarities was not simply an obsession with collecting the grotesque, for he regarded such freaks of nature – they would similarly absorb Charles Darwin – as a key to the origins and development of life.

Given the general belief that nature was essentially

unchangeable and unchanging, human freaks such as Byrne presented something of a difficulty. If nature could produce such wild variations in certain beings, was it not conceivable such changes might occur in species too? As a consequence, even sensible men of science clutched at improbable explanations. To Hunter, however, the production of 'monsters' was clear proof of nature's ability to generate change. He had already suggested in his paper on the freemartins in 1779 that every animal, and every part of every animal, possessed an innate propensity to malformation.[24] In the following year, in a paper discussing some female pheasants that developed male plumage, he went further, arguing that this ability to produce abnormalities seemed to be present in the embryonic state and declaring that 'each part of each species seems to have its monstrous form originally impressed upon it'.[25] He spelled out this contentious idea with startling clarity for the time:

> Every deviation from that original form and structure which gives the distinguishing character to the productions of Nature, may not improperly be called monstrous. According to this acceptation of the term, the variety of monsters will be almost infinite; and, as far as my knowledge has extended, there is not a species of animal, nay, there is not a single part of an animal body, which is not subject to an extraordinary formation. Neither does this appear to be a matter of mere chance; for it may be observed that every species has a disposition to deviate from Nature in a manner peculiar to itself.[26]

So by 1780 at least, Hunter had established to his own satisfaction that nature could produce fluctuations in form and had speculated that this propensity existed in some inherent congenital state. He was aware, too, from his contacts with livestock breeders that such change was a regular and progressive process, noting that in eye pigmentation 'varieties are every day produced in colour, shape, size, and disposition' and adding unequivocally, 'It certainly may be laid down as one of the principles or laws of Nature to deviate under certain circumstances.'[27] It was but a small step from here to propose that not only individuals but even whole species could change their form, as Hunter was gradually coming to realize.

At the same time, Hunter appreciated that certain kinds of abnormality were inherited. 'I have seen three [cases of] Spina Bifida in the children of one family,' he noted in one unpublished paper; 'I have seen two hair lips in the children of the same parents.'[28] One patient, a certain Lady Hyde Parker, had a harelip; her brother and child had the same condition. This hereditary principle applied to animals too, as Hunter explained: 'A cow was brought to London for a show who had a supernumerary Leg upon the Shoulder which is a very common monstrosity but the curious circumstance was, she had a calf with the same Monstrosity.' And he concluded, 'How far an animal . . . which is a species of Monster, is endowed with the propagation of these peculiarities to its offspring is not yet determined but there are many circumstances which would make us suspect that such a principle often takes place.' The hereditary principle was clearly at work in producing exceptional stature too. Hunter's friend the physician Dr David Pitcairn had told him that the two tallest men he had ever seen were twins: one of them was six feet seven inches and his brother six feet five inches. These may well have been the Knipe twins, compatriots of

Byrne who were even reputed by some to be related to him. Yet while undoubtedly tall, the Knipe twins were hardly remarkable beside Charles Byrne. It was clear that Byrne was the living representation of one of the most dramatic examples of a congenital malformation Hunter was ever likely to see. He could barely contain his curiosity.

Hunter's reputation for paying top prices for unusual finds was famed throughout the country. As far afield as Cornwall, an angler who caught an unusual breed of fish off Penzance Pier in 1772 had promptly despatched his catch to Jermyn Street. His reward was no doubt generous.[29] Hunter had forged fond relations with the 'Polish dwarf' and followed the career of the Corsican Fairy with interest. Still his hunger for the unusual was unsated. Then, as if by magic, a simple country boy who proclaimed himself the 'Tallest man in the world' walked right into his neighbourhood and exhibited his freak form virtually on Hunter's doorstep. The opportunity was too good to resist. From the moment he set eyes upon Byrne's fabulous figure, Hunter knew that he had to possess his body.

In truth, there was another motivation for Hunter's determination to secure Byrne's body beyond the advancement of medicine. Although he was now earning an estimated £5,000 a year – around £300,000 in modern terms – from his private practice and students' fees, Hunter was still invariably strapped for cash.[30] Now fifty-four, his tawny hair touched with grey, forced to wear spectacles for close work and increasingly plagued with the symptoms of angina, Hunter must have been all too conscious of his own mortality. His only legacy, the sole future income for Anne and their two young children, would be his writings and his museum. He was keenly aware of his investment in the collection and eager in 1782 to promote its importance. In an article in the *European Magazine* detailing his ventures that year, Hunter revealed that he had already expended £10,000 on purchasing and maintaining his preparations, including more than £2,000 on buying dead animals alone.[31] He was still searching desperately for larger premises for the household and the collection; his quest to find the right accommodation 'harassed his mind', according to Home.[32] It was now becoming imperative to locate a new home for the cramped exhibits, to create a unique museum that would explain his lifetime's work. But he wanted a magnet to attract visitors too. The skeleton of a giant, who was even now drawing rapt crowds, would form the perfect centrepiece.

With his all-consuming conviction in the importance of his researches coupled with his success in collecting every manner of treasure from around the globe, Hunter naively believed his latest ambition should present little obstacle. He hardly expected the giant himself to pose any objection. In the same manner in which he regularly clinched deals with showmen, he assumed a transaction could be cordially agreed with Byrne. He took steps immediately to put an expert on the case. The man he recruited to help him in his mission was John Howison.

A shadowy figure about whom little is known, Howison had close links with both John and his brother William. In 1772 he had purchased some medals that William desired for his collection; three years later he took notes in William's lectures.[33] But he was plainly neither a coin dealer nor a surgeon, for long after William's death his nephew Matthew Baillie made provisions for Howison in recognition of services to the Great Windmill Street school. Howison also made notes of John's lectures, perhaps when John presented them at William's school in 1776 or 1777, but he was not one of John's pupils either.[34] Yet Howison was evidently of immense service to both brothers. He was, it seems, a general factotum, a jack-of-all-trades who was willing to perform whatever underhand and dirty tricks were necessary for the smooth running of the brothers' separate anatomy businesses. For it was not just coins that Howison was skilled at procuring, but bodies too. Quite possibly it was Howison whom the young William Hamilton meant when he mentioned 'John the servt who is a very necessary man to be great with', as he bemoaned the lack of bodies at William's school on Christmas Day in 1777.[35] Despite the brothers' irreconcilable rift, Howison was evidently still at the bidding of John Hunter in 1782; it was for him that Howison would help to pull off the most daring deception of all.[36]

He would not have long to wait. As he watched the giant parade in front of his delighted audiences, Hunter's astute observation skills told him that Byrne was not a well man. Sylas Neville, himself a physician, had of course pronounced Byrne's appearance 'far from wholesome'. Symptoms of Byrne's condition, the result of over-production of growth hormone caused by a benign tumour on the pituitary gland, now known as childhood-onset acromegaly or gigantism, would have been all too apparent.[37] As well as the sexual impotence Byrne himself had intimated, he would probably have suffered from painful joints, excessive sweating and headaches, while the placid nature noted by onlookers could well have been a sign of slowed intelligence. Although the true cause of

Byrne's extreme tallness would have been a mystery to Hunter – it would be many more years before the cause of his abnormality could be understood and treated – he was certainly aware that the untreated condition generally spelled an early death. Giants had a reputation for short lives: Bamford, the Staffordshire giant, had died at the age of thirty-six; McGrath, the earlier contender for Byrne's title, had died at twenty-four. Byrne, as he freely declared in his advertisements, was already twenty-two. Hunter knew he only had to bide his time.

There were plenty more bodies to keep Hunter busy while he kept his watch on the Irish giant that summer. In early May, a breathless messenger knocked at Jermyn Street to summon Hunter urgently to the bedside of his dear friend Daniel Solander. The good-natured botanist, who had lived at the home of Sir Joseph Banks since returning from the *Endeavour* voyage, had collapsed with a pain in his left arm that morning.[38] With Banks away at his country estate, the physician Charles Blagden had sent for Hunter, along with two more physicians. There was nothing any of them could do; Solander had suffered a stroke, and he died, aged forty-nine, a few days later, on 13 May. Hunter performed the autopsy, as no doubt Solander would have wished, the following day; far from suffering 'the weakness not to be able to see the dissection of a friend', like Pringle, Hunter had no qualms about taking a knife to his much-loved chum.[39] 'I found two ounces of coagulated blood in the right ventricle of the Brain,' he reported in a note to Blagden that bore no trace of the distress he must have felt at losing his affable friend.

It was the prime minister, Charles Watson Wentworth, the Marquis of Rockingham, who next fell under Hunter's knife. When Rockingham died suddenly on 1 July, just over a year after being appointed premier, the country was thrown into turmoil over who should replace him; in the event the King appointed the Earl of Shelburne, Hunter's friend. But at least there was no question as to who should perform his post-mortem. Throughout his long involvement with the volatile world of Georgian politics – he had earlier taken office as prime minister in 1765–6 before resuming the role in March 1782 – Rockingham had laboured with persistent abdominal pains which he dated to a fall from a horse in 1759. Hunter was one of innumerable doctors called in to essay a diagnosis over the years, and he recorded full details of the peer's medical history in his case books. 'Every Physician and Surgeon in Europ of any Note was consulted, and various were the opinions of the cause of this Pain,' he noted.[40] 'He probably visited every Bath in Europ as also every kind at Bath but nothing appeared to give any relief.' Assorted physicians and surgeons had variously blamed his liver and his gall bladder, and prescribed blisters, plasters, caustic medicines and opium, but the poor man had begged them to cut open his stomach and find the cause of his distress. Whether bravely or recklessly, Hunter had offered to perform this extremely risky operation in February 1768, when William wrote to Rockingham proposing that he and John undertake the procedure. Rockingham declined, lamenting that he would be unavailable at the appointed time – he may understandably have had cold feet – but declared that he 'would be glad of an inspection at some other time'.[41]

Saved from an examination that might well have proved fatal, Rockingham persevered with his frantic political and social life until he was struck down one last time at the height of an influenza epidemic at the end of

June 1782. Although Hunter was evidently among the doctors at Rockingham's bedside, judging from his detailed record of his last illness, even he was not now willing to perform the operation Rockingham desperately requested as the pain worsened on the morning of his death. When he expired a few hours later, it was promptly agreed that Hunter should perform an autopsy in a bid to unravel the mystery of the illness that had confounded so many. 'As this Case had call'd forth the attention of almost every Physical man in London and nothing had ever been made out,' Hunter recorded, 'the appearance after death became an object of inquiry, and many were anxious to be present at the examination.' Among the physicians gathered around Rockingham's corpse to observe Hunter's handiwork were the Prince of Wales's physician, Richard Warren, Hunter's St George's colleague William Bromfield, and John's brother William; even professional differences and family feuds could be forgotten in the excitement of an unusual medical case. But there was little enlightenment to be found inside Rockingham's body. Although Hunter noted that the valves to the arteries of the heart were partly furred, suggesting long-term heart disease, the post-mortem proved inconclusive.

As the summer faded, so too did London's mania over the Irish giant. Even the 'tallest man in the world' could hold the attention of fickle Londoners for only a few short months. By early autumn queues at Byrne's shows had dwindled, the curtain on 'Harlequin Teague' had dropped for the last time, and the city's residents were scouting for new diversions to excite their imaginations. And there was no shortage of amusements to rival Byrne for their attention and disposable income. Idle Londoners could, for example, witness acrobats, a camel and daring horse antics at Mr Astley's Amphitheatre Riding-School on Westminster Bridge.[42] In Piccadilly, the eccentric Mr Katterfelto offered the chance to see 'insects' in water, beer, milk and blood through his 'New Improved and greatly admired SOLAR MICROSCOPE'.[43] And in Spring Gardens, a stone's throw from Byrne's own show, the versatile Mr Breslaw thrilled crowds with his mind-reading and magic tricks, in which he commanded 'A FRESH EGG TO DANCE upon a Stick, in the middle of the Room, by itself' to the accompaniment of the violin and mandolin.[44]

Faced with such energetic competition, by early autumn Byrne was forced to move his show to another apartment, probably smaller and cheaper, above a sweet shop in Charing Cross. By November he had not only moved again, to a room at the Hampshire Hog in Piccadilly, but had dropped ticket prices for children and servants to one shilling.[45] More worryingly still, there were rival claims to his title. On display at his former haunt in Spring Gardens was the 'wonderful GIGANTIC CHILD', who at eighteen months old had already attained a height of three feet.[46] There were even rumours of another 'Irish giant', reputedly taller than Byrne, who was considering making his debut in London. Aged twenty-two, like Byrne, and like him sometimes adopting the stage name 'O'Brien' to suggest descent from the ancient king of Ireland Brian Boru, Patrick Cotter had arrived in England in 1779 and won acclaim in Bristol. Described in some advertisements as eight feet three and three-quarter inches tall, he plainly had his eye on Byrne's crown with the claim 'The Giant is upwards of Four Inches taller than the noted Burn'.[47]

With revenues falling, rival attractions stealing his audiences and his health now rapidly declining, Byrne turned to drink. Racked with pain and befuddled by alcohol, even now he considered leaving London for new audiences on the Continent. His failing health put paid to that. By spring 1783 it was all too clear that Byrne's brief life on earth, as transitory as his short spell as a national celebrity, was coming to an end. With no hope of treatment, the growing tumour in his brain was causing terminal damage; he may also have contracted consumption. Byrne plainly knew his days were numbered. But death itself was no longer his greatest fear; the Irish giant's worst dread was the anatomists, and especially the best-known anatomist of them all, John Hunter.

Having maintained his close watch on Byrne's health and whereabouts throughout the winter, with the aid of the giant's helpful advertisements relating each change of address, Hunter hoped that his vigilance was about to be rewarded. Like a leopard circling his prey, he closed in for the kill. Intent on beating any other anatomists to the prize, Hunter set his spy Howison to watch Byrne's every move. In truth, this was not the most challenging of tasks: Byrne towered head and shoulders above every other London pedestrian and it was simplicity itself for Howison to stalk his quarry through the West End streets as he stumbled from tavern to tavern. When Byrne made one last change of address, to an apartment at 12 Cockspur Street, and a final price reduction to one shilling for all-comers, Howison even took rooms a few doors away – he was listed in the parish rates books for part of 1783.[48]

It may well have been now that with characteristic audacity, Hunter made Byrne an offer he felt sure he could not refuse for the promise of his corpse after death. Whether Hunter himself proposed this Faustian pact to

Byrne or charged Howison with the unpopular task is unknown. If it was Hunter, at just five feet two inches tall and reaching only as high as the giant's waist, he would have needed to crane his neck to make his offer heard. It was an ill-judged mistake, for Byrne was understandably horrified at the proposal. Although members of well-to-do society were increasingly acceptant of the need for post-mortems to determine cause of death – after all, even the late prime minister had been dissected by Hunter – such enlightened attitudes had yet to permeate the general populace. To a poorly educated country boy, the notion of being cut open after death and quite possibly displayed for public humiliation like a common criminal, with the very real fear that this might deny him entry to the Promised Land on Judgement Day, was simply abhorrent. The idea that investigating his corpse might aid understanding of his medical condition and possibly help future victims would have meant little to Byrne. Fully cognizant of Hunter's quest, and knowing he was being stalked day and night by Hunter's accomplice, Byrne sought desperately for a way to outwit the anatomist. As Howison laid siege to the apartment in Cockspur Street and Hunter waited feverishly for news not five minutes away in Jermyn Street, Byrne made plans to foil them both.

When an urgent message arrived at Jermyn Street at the end of March 1783, however, it was not Byrne that was dying but Hunter's brother, William. Having been taken ill in early March, William had risen from his sickbed on the 20th to deliver the introductory lecture for his spring course.[49] Before he could reach the end of his lesson he collapsed and had to be carried to bed. His physician, Charles Combe, determined that William had suffered a stroke, for which the usual ineffectual therapies were applied. It was Matthew Baillie, the brothers' nephew, now working in the Great Windmill Street school, who summoned Uncle John. Although they had not exchanged friendly words since their bitter rift, and there was no deathbed reconciliation between the brothers, John eased William's last days by fitting a catheter. Visiting daily, he dispassionately recorded details of his brother's fading life in his case books.[50] William died, aged sixty-five, on 30 March. With his last breath, he told Combe, 'If I had strength enough to hold a pen I would write how easy and pleasant a thing it is to die.'[51] The intensely productive but ultimately destructive relationship of the Hunter brothers was at an end.

William's funeral was held on 5 April and he was buried in the vault of St James's Church, Piccadilly; having spent almost forty years dissecting corpses, there would be no autopsy or any risk his corpse might be stolen.[52] Led by Matthew, his mourners included the most eminent physicians and surgeons of the day, among them William Pitcairn, George Baker, George Fordyce, William Heberden and William Cruikshank. His own brother John was absent. In his will, William left a fortune in priceless books, coins, medals, paintings and anatomical preparations.[53] The entire collection, including the vast majority of John's painstaking work carried out at the Covent Garden school, was bequeathed to Matthew, on condition it revert after thirty years to Glasgow University; ultimately it would form the university's Hunterian Museum and the Hunterian Art Gallery. Matthew was also left £20,000, a half-share with Cruikshank in the Great Windmill Street school, and the family farmhouse – John Hunter's own birthplace – at Long Calderwood. To his sister Dorothy William left a measly £100, although his nieces, Agnes and Joanna, received £2,000 each, and there were token gifts of £20 for various friends and associates. To John, his only brother, his best pupil and his most illustrious collaborator, William left nothing. As his obituary in the *Gentleman's Magazine* flatly recorded, 'His brother, Mr. John Hunter, the surgeon, on account of some differences between them, is not named in the will.'

If John felt bitter at being so decisively and so publicly cut out of William's will, he did not show it, although there was no doubt that the money would have come in useful. But at the end of his last lecture of the spring term, without having mentioned his brother's death throughout the course, Hunter hesitated as the pupils made ready to leave. 'Here Mr Hunter seemed to finish,' remembered one of the students, Joseph Adams, 'yet to have more to say; at length endeavouring to appear as if he had just recollected something, he began "Ho! Gentlemen, one thing more: I need not remind you of the loss you all know anatomy has sustained!" He was obliged to pause, and turned his face from his hearers.'[54] Recovering his composure, but with eyes filled with tears, Hunter paid tribute to his brother's lasting contribution to anatomy. According to Adams, 'The scene was so truly pathetic, that a general sympathy pervaded the whole class; and every one, though all had been preparing to leave the place, stood or sat motionless and silent for some minutes.' The following year Matthew Baillie would hand the deeds for Long Calderwood to his Uncle John, having told his lawyer, 'I think I shall nearly feel as much satisfaction in delivering over the deeds to J. Hunter as if a sum of the same value was to be given to myself'.[55] Hunter gladly accepted the family home as his due, later remarking that 'the paternal estate of Long Calderwood came to his brother, the Dr. having no right to dispose of it'.[56]

Having obtained no help from William's fortune, and despite the fact that he was earning a sizeable annual income, in spring 1783 John was forced to raise a mortgage on his Earls Court land in order to buy a new home.[57] He had at last discovered a suitable house about to be vacated by the American artist John Singleton Copley in fashionable Leicester Fields, about to become known as Leicester Square. Having been laid out in the 1670s, the square had become a favourite residence for aristocrats, artists, writers and other professionals. It remained a popular address throughout the eighteenth century. William Hogarth had lived at number 30 until his death in 1764; Sir Joshua Reynolds worked from studios at number 47.[58]

The elegant and roomy four-storey townhouse at number 28 was an ideal new home for Hunter, his family and his large retinue of servants.[59] With its graceful front door opening into a large hall, there was ample accommodation for Hunter's study, an afternoon bedroom where he could take his naps, and a parlour to receive patients. From here the main staircase wound up to a spacious drawing room with four tall windows overlooking the square, providing a perfect venue for Anne's soirées. Above that there were two more floors of rooms, while beneath the house were subterranean stables for Hunter's coach and horses. Even so, there was still insufficient room for all Hunter's needs so he bought the house behind, 13 Castle Street – later Charing Cross Road – as well as the land between. Immediately he set builders to work erecting a huge two-storey structure bridging the two houses in order to create purpose-built premises for a lecture theatre, a grand parlour or 'conversazione room', and, of course, his treasured collection. With his usual lack of financial acumen, Hunter spent £3,000 for a lease of just twenty-four years on the Leicester Square house, while building work would cost a further £3,000.[60]

It was while he was in the throes of moving his household into Leicester Square at the end of May – the museum would have to wait another two years for the builders to finish their work – that Hunter finally received word from Howison. At his room in Cockspur Street, the Irish giant was dying. His thunderous voice no longer boomed and his enormous chest laboured over every breath. Only twenty-two years old but dependent on alcohol and almost destitute since his life's savings of £770 had been stolen in a Haymarket tavern in April, Byrne had gathered his few friends together to extract a binding last promise. Fully aware that the moment he died Hunter would come for his body, Byrne had concocted a plan designed to thwart him. As his friends leaned forward to hear his dying words, Byrne made them vow to seal his body in a lead coffin, ship it to the middle of the English Channel and plunge it to the bottom of the sea, far from the reach of even the most resourceful anatomist.

On Sunday, 1 June, Charles Byrne died. The event was immediately reported in the London newspapers:

Cockspur Street, Charing Cross, aged 22, Charles Byrne, the famous Irish giant, whose death is said to have been precipitated by excessive drinking, to which he was always addicted, but more particularly since his late loss of almost all of his property, which he had simply invested in a single bank note of £700 [*sic*]. In his last moments (it has been said) he requested that his ponderous remains might be thrown into the sea, in order that his bones might be placed far out of the reach of the chirurgical fraternity.[61]

Hunter's ambition was no secret; almost all of London knew of his obsession with obtaining the giant's corpse. And there were evidently others in the running too, for a few days later the *Morning Herald* reported that, 'The whole tribe of surgeons put in a claim for the poor departed Irish giant, and surround his house, just as Greenland harpooners would an enormous whale. One of them has gone so far as to have a niche made for himself in the giant's coffin, in order to his being ready at hand, on the "witching time of night, when church-yards yawn".'[62]

Though the idea of hiding within the giant's coffin was plainly fanciful, it was certainly true that any of the 'tribe' of London's anatomists would have been delighted to add the giant's corpse to their collections. William Cruikshank and Matthew Baillie, now jointly running the Great Windmill Street school, would hardly have turned down such a dramatic offer from any of their usual contacts. Joshua Brookes, a former pupil of William Hunter's, now running his own school in Great Marlborough Street, was another regular customer of the grave-robbers.[63] And John Sheldon, another of William's ex-pupils, who had opened an anatomy school in Great Queen Street, was undoubtedly a candidate. Having lived with the preserved body of a beautiful naked woman in a glass case in his bedroom for the past ten years – she was rumoured to be either a past patient or a lover – he would have had no hesitation in employing his embalming skills on Byrne.

Stories of the scramble to obtain the giant's corpse continued to fill the newspaper columns. A few days later, another report proclaimed, 'So anxious are the Surgeons to have possession of the Irish Giant, that they have offered a ransom of 800 g to the undertaker. The same being rejected, they are determined to approach the church-yard by regular works and terrier-like, unearth him!'[64] But while the anatomists vied for poor Byrne's body, his friends at least were true to their word. Having obtained an oversize coffin and secured their tall friend's body inside, they kept watch over the corpse for four days. In the interval they invited spectators to view the colossal casket, advertised as a remarkable eight feet four inches long, for a fee of 2s 6d – at least they would reap some profit for their pains.[65] On 5 June, in accordance with Byrne's wishes, they shouldered their heavy burden and transported their load to Margate, where they chartered a boat and tipped the great coffin into the sea. But whatever it was the grieving comrades consigned to the deep, it was not the body of the Irish giant.

No sooner had the newspapers reported Byrne's disposal than rumours began to circulate. First the *Gentleman's Magazine* described the report of the sea burial as 'a tub thrown out to the whale' – or, put plainly, a decoy. Then the *British Magazine* dismissed the burial as 'a pure fiction'. Finally, the *Annual Reporter Chronicle* charged, 'The giant expressed an earnest desire that his ponderous remains might be sunk out at sea; but if such were his wish, it was never fulfilled, as Mr Hunter obtained his body before interment of any kind had taken place.'[66] Terrified of reprisals from Byrne's bereaved friends, Hunter would never refer explicitly to his daring venture to seize the giant's corpse, but seize it he certainly did. Over the ensuing years details of his remarkable body hunt gradually surfaced, handed down by word of mouth.[67] The story that emerged was almost more remarkable than the tall tales dreamed up by the newspapers.

The truth was that as soon as Hunter heard from Howison that the giant had taken his last breath, he sprang into action and lost no time in seeking out the undertaker who was charged with carrying out Byrne's last request. It was a relatively simple matter to bribe the man, who may well have been one of Hunter's regular contacts, to procure the body. But Hunter was obviously not prepared for the colossal sum he would have to cough up to secure his prize. According to one version, the undertaker first agreed on £50 but quickly realized he could extract considerably more from the desperate anatomist. Step by step, he ratcheted up the price, until Hunter was forced to agree £500 for his booty. This was a colossal sum; Dr Johnson had advised Boswell that he could live well in London with a large family for a full year on twice this amount.[68] With no ready cash as usual, and already in debt over his house purchase, Hunter had to scrape together the money from one of his animal dealer friends, Pidcock, who owned a menagerie in the Strand. Clinching the deal was one thing; perpetrating the daring theft was quite another. With Byrne's friends watching the corpse day and night, it was plainly going to prove difficult to filch the body from under their noses. So together, the undertaker and Hunter cooked up an ingenious plot to hoodwink the mourners.

As Byrne's trusty companions bore his weighty coffin towards the Kent coast, accompanied by the duplicitous undertaker, inevitably they stopped at points along the way to partake of refreshment. With the nomadic wake becoming steadily merrier, no doubt encouraged by Hunter's accomplice, eventually the inebriated band were inveigled to call at a particular tavern where the crafty undertaker had made prior arrangements. Persuaded to deposit the coffin in a neighbouring barn, the revellers continued their boisterous wake. In blissful ignorance, they caroused inside while the undertaker's accomplices deftly unscrewed the coffin lid and swapped Byrne's body for a stash of paving stones. Byrne's friends took up their load once more, staggered on to the coast near Margate, and paid their last respects as they pitched a coffin full of stones into the brine.

Meanwhile, the giant's corpse was whisked back to London hidden under straw in a cart and delivered to Hunter's new house in Castle Street under cover of darkness. Hunter himself then drove the huge carcass, wrapped only in its funeral shroud, westwards to his Earls Court retreat before daybreak. Trundling the body into his underground laboratory, Hunter was still so afraid of discovery that he abandoned his usual meticulous dissection, his collector's zeal for possession of the spectacular specimen for once overcoming his surgeon's curiosity in investigating the rare condition. Instead, he hurriedly chopped the Goliath into pieces, threw the chunks into his immense copper vat, and boiled the lot down into a jumble of gigantic bones. After skimming the fat out of the cauldron, Hunter deftly reassembled the pile of bones to create Byrne's awesome skeleton.

Even then he was forced to shield his prize from public scrutiny, most likely keeping the towering skeleton secreted at his Earls Court house. As newspaper columnists had already pointed the finger at the notorious anatomist, he must also have kept the existence of the giant's skeleton concealed from even his closest friends and colleagues. That summer, however, he allowed a cryptic hint to emerge in a letter to Jenner: 'I hope to see you in London about two years hence, when I shall be able to show you something.'[69] It would be a full four years before Hunter confided his sinister secret to his dear friend Banks. 'I lately got a tall man,' he wrote in 1787, 'but at the time could make no particular observations. I hope next summer to be able to show you him.'[70]

For the time being, then, the giant's bones remained out of sight. But there were other human body parts, belonging to people just as famous in their time as the Irish giant, to keep Hunter satisfied. In September he was called out to tend the victim of a dramatic duel which pushed speculation about the giant out of the newspaper columns. Colonel Cosmo Gordon had been challenged to defend his honour according to the traditional rules of gentlemanly combat by an old army enemy, Colonel Frederick Thomas.[71] Duels were illegal in eighteenth-century Britain – participants could be charged with murder – but the practice was widely tolerated. Accordingly, the pair met at The Ring, a notorious duelling spot in Hyde Park, at daybreak on 4 September. Choosing pistols as their weapons, they marched eight yards in opposite directions, turned and fired. After initially missing, Thomas struck the first successful shot, wounding Gordon in the thigh. Returning fire, Gordon hit his opponent full square in the belly. Mortally wounded, Thomas fell to the ground.

Waiting in Gordon's coach nearby to treat the inevitable casualties, a young surgeon, Alexander Grant, now rushed to Thomas's aid; he extracted the lead ball from the veteran soldier's intestines at the scene. Realizing that the wound was serious, Grant called out his old tutor, John Hunter, for assistance as Thomas was carried to his own house nearby. There was nothing either of them could do to mend the fourteen-inch-deep wound in Thomas's guts, the bullet having passed right through the victim's intestines, and he died twenty-four hours later. At Gordon's trial for murder at the Old Bailey the following year, both Grant and Hunter testified that the pistol wound was undeniably the cause of death; there was no room for professional doubt in this instance. But given the nature of the quarrel and Thomas's role in his own fate, Gordon was cleared. A piece of the deceased duellist's jejunum – part of the small intestine – with a distinct bullet hole right through the middle, took its place among Hunter's anatomical specimens.[72]

Though Hunter still relied on the grave-robbers for regular supplies of body parts, more and more of the bottles containing diseased and damaged organs that wound up on his shelves were now clearly labelled with the names of respectable, wealthy and consenting Georgians. As demand for his services at post-mortems had increased, so the named body parts had grown. Privileged friends allowed to tour the collection could now peek at the internal organs of former pillars of Georgian society. Alongside Colonel Thomas's jejunum, the invited few could view the cancerous bladder once belonging to the Revd Mr Vivian, erstwhile vicar of St Martin's-in-the-Fields; the injected kidney of Lady Beauchamp, who had died of a fever; and the thickened arteries of Lieutenant General Thomas Desaguliers, who had been treated by Hunter at the siege of Belle-Ile and met him again on his deathbed. They could even examine the crumbling thigh bones that had once held aloft the Honourable Frederick Cornwallis, Archbishop of Canterbury, until his death in 1783.[73]

By now, Anne must have been well used to her husband's macabre collecting passion and the unappealing exhibits preserved in his collection. But quite how she felt about internal parts of her own family joining this melancholy hall of fame can only be conjectured. Robert Home, Hunter's former army mentor, had been ill since the previous summer after suffering a stroke and losing the use of one side of his body. Having almost recovered by July 1784, under the careful attention of his son-in-law, he was struck down again, becoming completely blind and entirely losing his reasoning. 'The total loss of sight, with almost the intire loss of Memory produced a very curious effect,' Hunter recorded in his case books; 'he lost entirely the rememberance of Light, and did not annex any Idea to Light'.[74] When Home died shortly after, Hunter performed an autopsy on the former surgeon; quite probably he was aided by Everard Home, helping to cut open his own father, having just returned from navy duties in the West Indies and resumed his role as Hunter's assistant. Having sawed open his father-in-law's skull, Hunter paid particular attention to the brain, looking for signs of the fatal stroke. A full report sparing little concern for relatives' feelings was filed in the case books and inevitably enough, a slice of Anne's father's kidney found its way into Hunter's collection.

13

The Poet's Foot

'. . . nothing is too good for our friend John.'

Adam Smith[1]

Leicester Square, London, April 1785

The genteel tranquillity that the residents of Leicester
Square had once enjoyed had been rudely shattered. For
two years, they had endured the continual din of builders,
carpenters and glaziers labouring in the south-east corner
of their fashionable square. But as the workmen finally
moved out of number 28 in the spring of 1785, the commotion only intensified. Carriages and pedestrians were
brought to an abrupt halt and the distinguished gentlefolk
arriving to sit for their portraits at Sir Joshua Reynolds'
famous studio could only stop and stare. Surrounded by
crates, the square's newest inhabitant supervised the
arrival of a seemingly interminable line of stuffed animals,
skeletons, skulls and bottles filled with dubious-looking

contents. Bearded and beginning to grey, the eccentric new neighbour directed his assistants as they carried a legless stuffed giraffe, two elephant jaws, bones belonging to lions, tigers and other exotic beasts, and the skull of a large whale through the door of his new home.

John Hunter had spent an anxious spring finalizing plans to transfer his anatomy and natural history collection into its new home. 'I am imployed as much as a thousand bees,' he told Jenner in a more than usually hurried letter that April. 'I am building moving xc. I wish this summer was well over.'[2] Meanwhile, he complained to his pupils that all the fees he earned from patients were immediately paid out in bills to carpenters and brick-layers.[3] But at last the work was finished and the remarkable building complete. Between the smart four-storey townhouse fronting Leicester Square and the inconspicuous, dowdy-looking house at its rear, facing Castle Street, stretched a spectacular brick and glass structure providing a lecture theatre, grand reception room and a purpose-built museum. Accommodating Hunter's myriad businesses as surgeon, anatomist, teacher and researcher while fostering his continuing connections with London's underworld, the dual-fronted house would later inspire Robert Louis Stevenson when he was writing his horror story *The Strange Case of Dr Jekyll and Mr Hyde*.[4] Although the plot for the story came to Stevenson in a dream, he is said to have based Dr Jekyll's house – the setting for the melodramatic transformation from good to evil – on Hunter's Leicester Square home. In the Gothic tale, written when the house was still a familiar London landmark in 1886, the honest Dr Jekyll had bought his house from 'the heirs of a celebrated surgeon'. Visitors entering the doctor's home were led across a yard towards a lecture theatre 'once crowded with eager students' and a dissecting room at the rear.[5] And it was from the 'old dissecting-room door', which opened on to a dingy thoroughfare at the rear of the house, that the grim-faced Mr Hyde emerged to commit his murderous deeds.

Visitors to John Hunter's new home were familiar with much the same layout.[6] The elegant front door of number 28 opened into a lobby where Mrs Hunter kept her sedan chair, and a parlour where patients could contemplate Hogarth's cautionary cartoons A Rake's Progress and A Harlot's Progress while waiting to see the surgeon. A corridor led to Hunter's study and his 'afternoon bedroom', where he took after-dinner naps. Reaching the back door, guests now crossed the gravel yard under a covered walkway to arrive at a great glass door, stretching more than twelve feet high, which opened into the remarkable new structure.

Three storeys high and measuring twenty-eight feet wide by fifty-one feet long, the ground floor accommodated a grand reception or 'conversazione' room, lined with paintings by fashionable artists. A door from the conversazione room led into a spacious amphitheatre where Hunter delivered his lectures and demonstrated his preparations on an oval slate table to pupils ranged on semi-circular benches. Ascending to the first floor, visitors emerged into a vast room spanning the entire top two storeys of the new structure. Lit by skylights and circled by a gallery, it was here, in his first purpose-built museum, that Hunter now anxiously directed the arrangement of his thousands of preparations.

Descending again, visitors passed a sunken basement yard protected by a glass roof; here Hunter would display his prized skull of a large bottle-nosed whale, which was too big even for the museum. For the intrepid few who ventured on, a door opened into the rear house, the dingy 13 Castle Street. In this cramped, comfortless accommodation, Hunter's four or five house pupils were squeezed into quarters, along with a housekeeper and a dissecting-room attendant. Most other rooms were given over to a printing press and overflow space for the collection, while the attic housed Hunter's dissecting room, as far as possible from the general household. Indeed, according to Everard Home, this house was 'entirely subservient' to the requirements of the museum.[7] Finally exiting by the plain street door, just as Mr Hyde would do in Stevenson's story, visitors emerged into the grimy and busy thoroughfare of Castle Street. Beside the door, a ramp led down to subterranean stables where both Hunter and his wife kept a coach and horses. And above this sloping drive hung a wooden drawbridge that could be lowered to allow mysterious cargoes to enter at dead of night and just as swiftly be raised to prevent entry, should that precaution prove necessary.

Welded skilfully together, these two contrasting houses suited Hunter's purposes admirably. Not only did the dual-fronted building present two very different faces to the world – just like the unfortunate Henry Jekyll – it would come to symbolize the mutually dependent but conflicting aspects of Hunter himself, at once the esteemed society surgeon pursuing a laudable quest for medical advancement and the obsessive collector immersed in illicit activities in order to enlarge his hoard of human and animal parts at whatever cost.

Most of the time the ingenious design of the building kept these two different worlds carefully apart. The family and their servants occupied number 28, and it was to this doorway that Hunter's patients arrived every morning and Anne's guests arrived by evening for her popular soirées. Meanwhile, the medical students lived, studied and dissected in number 13, and it was to this doorway that the usual sacks and hampers were delivered by night. Each Wednesday evening, Mrs Hunter welcomed the brightest talents of the Georgian cultural world through the graceful doorway of number 28 and up the marble staircase to the first-floor salon overlooking the square, where they recited, danced and gossiped into the early hours. At times, according to one assistant, Hunter would emerge from his study in the small hours and wearily climb the stairs to his bed just as his wife's guests were streaming down.[8] Then, the assistant rather romantically recalled, the surgeon would 'give a kindly greeting to the beauty of the year' or render a 'smart reply to the passing joke of the man of fashion'. But at the other end of the building, not long after the music had faded away, Hunter's pupils would be rudely awoken by the bump of a carcass being dragged up the back stairs and, as one house pupil put it, 'the Resurrection Men swearing most terribly'.[9] The unique layout allowed Hunter to range freely from one house, and one world, to the other. He was the Jekyll and Hyde of the Georgian period, offering his patients a dramatic cure one moment and dragging them off to his dissecting bench the next.

Now settled in the heart of London's West End and relieved to have found an appropriate home for his prized collection, it was here that Hunter embarked on his most industrious period yet. At the peak of his intellectual powers, at the height of his popularity with patients and pupils, he would treat many of the era's most famous personalities, contribute a stream of papers to the Royal

Society, publish his best-known works and receive international recognition. Yet the move to Leicester Square also marked the beginning of a serious decline in health. The smallest irritation could trigger another attack of angina, but, as uncompromising as ever, Hunter would indulge in increasingly bitter confrontations.

Overseeing the transfer of his collection to the new museum plainly took its toll. Having returned from his naval duties in Jamaica the year before, Home found his brother-in-law 'much altered in his looks' so that he 'gave the idea of having grown much older than could be accounted for from the number of years which had elapsed'.[10] At fifty-seven, Hunter's sandy hair was sprinkled with grey while his face looked pale under the straggly beard and moustache he now sported. Noting every symptom of his medical condition himself, or when too ill dictating to Home, he observed that the slightest exertion – 'as walking up a small ascent' – or the smallest anxiety – such as worrying about his 'Bees swarming' – could bring on the pain in his chest and left arm. Even so, he added, 'I could tell a story that called up the finer feelings, which I could not tell without crying, obliging me to stop several times in the Narration, yet the spasm did not in the least take place.'[11] Fully aware of the growing seriousness of his illness, Hunter told his friend Lord Holland that his heart would one day 'kill him going upstairs or in a passion'; his life, he told others, was 'in the hands of any rascal who chose to annoy and tease him'.[12] Yet even at the height of his illness he could be 'roused', he confided to Jenner, by the prospect of earning two guineas.[13]

Quite possibly it was the worry and exertion of the move that triggered a serious attack in April, when Hunter fainted away so completely that Home thought him dead.[14] Despite his scepticism about the efficacy of many contemporary remedies, Hunter resorted to the customary purges and emetics; submitted to being bled, cupped and blistered; bathed his feet in water mixed with mustard; wore worsted stockings in bed; and even applied electricity to his arm. After all, there were no effective alternatives. Much as he would have suspected, they provided no relief. The following month, on 20 May, he suffered another attack, prompted, he later confided, by the fear that he might have contracted rabies at a post-mortem. His friend the physician David Pitcairn was the first at Hunter's bedside; the surgeon's condition having failed to improve, the next day a whole troop of physicians arrived. David's uncle, William Pitcairn, George Baker, the King's physician, and Richard Warren, physician to the Prince of Wales, all marched through the Leicester Square door. The last two would shortly be summoned to treat George III for his mysterious bouts of mental illness. And in a practice run for the tortures they would perpetrate on the King, they now subjected Hunter to a battery of almost every therapy in their medicine bags over a period of nine days. After administering copious doses of rhubarb and senna as laxatives, aromatic spices as stimulants, and opium as a sedative, the physicians raised a large blister on Hunter's back in an effort to 'draw out' his illness. He may well have been thinking of his own treatment when he later jotted down the remark, 'There is nothing so vague as bleeding and giving Physic.'[15]

Although the frightening spasms continued, the patient was sufficiently 'roused' to resume his professional role in July, when his expert opinion was sought by one of his oldest friends. Benjamin Franklin had endured increasing discomfort from a bladder stone since 1782; in the midst of negotiating the American Treaty of Independence in France that autumn he had found travelling by carriage particularly painful. But desperate at the age of seventy-nine to avoid the agony and risk of a lithotomy, in July 1785 Franklin wrote from France to a friend, Benjamin Vaughan, in London asking him to seek the advice of the capital's most eminent medical men on the best course of action. Enclosing a full account of his ailment, in the third person, Franklin insisted that the pain was bearable most of the time and declared, 'Thus if it does not grow worse, it is a *tolerable* Malady, and may be supported for the short time he has the Chance of living. And he would chuse to bear with it rather than have Recourse to dangerous or nauseous Remedies.'[16]

Vaughan immediately submitted Franklin's case to five of London's best-known practitioners; of these, Hunter was the only surgeon – he was often now regarded on an equal level with his colleagues in physick. In a reply signed by Hunter, the consultants agreed that Franklin was wise to avoid surgery at his advanced age. 'What we shall advise therefore, will be such things as may either prevent an increase of the disease, or palliate the most pressing Symptoms,' they counselled.[17] Given the risks of the operation for anyone, let alone a man of Franklin's advanced years, it was eminently sensible advice. And if none of the medications would offer the politician much succour, at least the opium they recommended gave him some respite from the pain. Leaving France to return home that same month, Franklin continued to play a prominent role in American politics for several more years. Finally confined to bed, and almost completely dependent on opium, he died in 1790 at the age of eighty-four.

Still himself under doctors' orders in August 1785, Hunter repaired to Tunbridge Wells to take the waters for two weeks with Anne. Despite continuing spasms, he rallied sufficiently during his stay to tend Thomas Sheridan, the ailing father of the playwright Richard Brinsley Sheridan, for wind. 'Mr Hunter is here attending him,' Richard's sister, Betsy, noted in a letter. But it was the surgeon's wife, at forty-three still widely admired, who proved the patient's best tonic. She was 'in my Father's opinion the finest Woman here and I am pretty much of the same opinion,' Betsy confided. 'She has one of those countenances that I like, spirited good humour'd and free from affectation, at the same time that she possesses a considerable share of <u>real</u> beauty.'[18]

With the surgeon himself still far from well, however, the Hunters moved on to spend four weeks at Bath. A letter from Anne to Edward Jenner, informing their friend that they were staying in his neighbourhood, betrays the anxiety and tenderness she plainly felt for her husband. 'I take it for granted you will not be sorry to hear Mr. Hunter is so near you though you will lament that want of health is the occasion,' she wrote; 'he has been tormented with a flying gout since last March, and we are come here in hope of some favourable crisis before the winter.' Knowing that John was eager to see his dear friend, she had dashed off the letter to catch the evening post, explaining, 'as he is now asleep after dinner, I rather write myself than disturb his nap'.[19]

Although Hunter insisted he was sufficiently rested to return to London by the end of September for the winter lecturing season, his health would never completely recover. His output of work, however, only increased. Still surviving on four hours' sleep a night, and his usual hour's nap every afternoon, Hunter was invariably at his dissecting bench by daybreak. One young surgeon keen to become a pupil at St George's was told to present himself to the surgeon the following day at 5 a.m. Anxiously arriving at the unlikely hour, he discovered Hunter already hard at work. 'I found him in his Museum,' he recalled, 'busily engaged in the dissection of insects.'[20] Hunter had generally completed several hours' investigations before the first patients were shown in through the Leicester Square door at 9 a.m. By now the jam of carriages blocking the square and the clamour of waiting patients had created a veritable cacophony guaranteed to wake any late-rising neighbours. As the patients poured in, there was scarcely room to accommodate them all while they waited to present their ailments. Sometimes the drawing room had to be cleared of the children's French grammars to provide extra waiting room.[21]

Now regarded as one of the most fashionable surgeons in London – only Pott could boast greater popularity – Hunter treated people from every walk of life. But typically eschewing society etiquette, he had scant regard for their position in the social hierarchy. One of his reliable animal dealers was therefore encouraged to jump the queue ahead of the affronted nobility. 'When I called, if the house was full of patients, and carriages waited at the door, I was always admitted,' recalled Gough, who kept a menagerie in Holborn Hill. 'You (said Mr Hunter) have no time to spare, as you live by it. Most of these can wait, as they have little to do when they go home.'[22] Hunter could be equally dismissive of his rich and influential clients when he called at their town mansions. When asked by a fellow surgeon to examine a wealthy patient with a festering sore which refused to clear up,

Hunter impatiently listened to the case, folded his arms and briskly demanded, 'And so, sir, you have an obstinate running sore?' Assured this was indeed the problem, he continued, 'Why, then, sir, if I had your running sore, I should say, – Mr Sore, run and be damned.'[23] On another occasion he berated George Nicol, the King's bookseller, who was a good friend, over the harsh regime to which he subjected his children. Like many less enlightened Georgian parents, Nicol believed that exposing his youngsters to cold extremes in early life would harden them up; unfortunately his first five children had not survived this ordeal long enough to prove his case. Hearing that Mrs Nicol was pregnant for the sixth time, Hunter dropped by and asked Nicol whether he intended to 'kill this one' as he had 'killed the rest'. He went on to relate experiments measuring the temperature of nesting hens to convince Nicol that human offspring too needed to be kept warm. Duly rebuked, Nicol resolved to take better care of the forthcoming child.[24]

Similarly, the surgeon tendered little sympathy if he thought his patients were malingering. In one case he was called to treat Master Woodcock, the twelve-year-old son of well-to-do parents, for a supposedly painful right knee. Suspicious that the ailment was a ploy to avoid school – the former truant could plainly recognize a fellow miscreant – Hunter placed a bowl of fruit on the opposite side of the room, left the patient on a sofa, then spied from the door as Master Woodcock nipped nimbly across to help himself.[25]

Although Hunter might flippantly dismiss his patients with an oath and a scolding after a cursory glance told him little was amiss, he could be sympathetic and generous too. At times he would spend as much as an hour discussing a single patient's symptoms, according to one of his pupils, John Abernethy. 'I have heard many patients speak of Mr. Hunter, and none without a fond remembrance of his kindness and attention,' he later recalled.[26] And although Hunter was almost always desperate for money, he continued to treat artists, writers and curates for free, often taking pity on other impoverished patients too. When asked by one tradesman to perform a serious operation on his wife, Hunter fixed the fee at his usual twenty guineas; it was another two months before the couple asked him to go ahead with the procedure and presented the money. On learning that the delay had been due to the couple's difficulty in raising the not insignificant sum – equal to more than £1,000 today – Hunter promptly sent back nineteen guineas. 'I sent the husband nineteen guineas, and kept the twentieth,' he later explained, 'that they might not be hurt with the idea of too great obligation.'[27]

There was no relaxation in demand at the back door either. Enthusiastic young surgeons rushed to the Castle Street entrance to enrol for the autumn lectures, which began on 10 October in 1785.[28] After hanging their hats on the pegs ranged in the lobby they signed the pupils' register kept on a desk beside the door to the lecture theatre. James Parkinson, who would later publish the first description of the 'shaking palsy' that acquired his name, was one of the students in 1785; his notes would form one of the most comprehensive records of Hunter's lectures.[29] Wright Post, a young American surgeon, attended the course at about the same time; later appointed professor of surgery and then professor of anatomy at Columbia University in New York, he would import to America Hunter's method of operating for aneurysms. Over the next few years, many of Hunter's most famous pupils, destined to become eminent nineteenth-century surgeons, would attend his lectures. Among them were Astley Cooper, who emulated Hunter's close relations with the body-snatchers as well as his approach to surgery – he would boast that he could obtain any corpse he wished – and John Abernethy, who shared Hunter's brusque bedside manner but was similarly idolized by his students. Both pupils in 1786–7, they would become two of Hunter's most devoted disciples. Abernethy later declared that Hunter had made 'surgery a science'.[30] Cooper, who attended the course year after year, would fondly remember relieving the tedium of the walk back from Leicester Square 'by discussing Mr Hunter's opinions' with a fellow student. Fired by the ideas he heard, Cooper converted the sitting room at his lodgings into his own dissecting room and practised Hunter's experimental operations on stray dogs.[31]

As well as his controversial course on the principles of surgery, running on Monday, Wednesday and Friday evenings all winter, Hunter's purpose-built theatre and dissecting rooms allowed him in 1785 to add lessons in practical anatomy and operations in surgery. As if this was not enough to keep himself and his pupils perpetually busy, he now launched an institution devoted to furthering the students' education. Already, two years earlier, Hunter and his long-term friend the physician George Fordyce had founded the Society for the Improvement of Medical and Chirurgical Knowledge. Unusually drawing together both surgeons and physicians on an equal footing, this select band met fortnightly at Old Slaughter's coffee-house, a rival to Young Slaughter's, to report case histories and discuss advancements in the two spheres of medicine.[32] Details of important cases were published in its transactions; Hunter would himself contribute a total of six papers. Now Hunter and Fordyce wanted to extend this invaluable opportunity for mutual improvement to London's medical student community.

The Lyceum Medicum Londinense, which they jointly founded in 1785, would become a crucible for Hunterian thinking. Set up essentially as a students' forum, Hunter encouraged the pupils themselves to draw up its rules, organize its meetings and elect its presidents.[33] But with Hunter and Fordyce as its figureheads, keeping a fatherly watch over activities, inevitably its members were moulded in the unique Hunterian style of self-education, independent inquiry and experimental research. The society's weekly Friday-evening meetings were held in Hunter's lecture theatre, and each week he laid out novel or unusual preparations for the members' interest while allowing them to borrow books from his library.[34] Each member was expected to present a paper on a medical or surgical topic; failure to comply resulted in a fine, and ultimately expulsion. But there were carrots as well as sticks: every year Hunter and Fordyce awarded a gold medal, struck with their two noble profiles, for the best dissertation. At these exuberant, stimulating and noisy meetings, so different to the stultifying atmosphere at Surgeons' Hall, topical issues were hotly debated throughout the winter. Nothing else in London approached the Lyceum in either purpose or size; within two years the society could boast more than 250 members, and this number had almost doubled five years later. With such a large and dedicated fan club, Hunter could hardly fail to become the chief inspiration for the next generation of young surgeons.

Yet for all his unwavering popularity among medical students and moneyed patients, Hunter remained deeply disliked by his colleagues at St George's. Once Caesar Hawkins and William Bromfield had retired, in 1774 and 1780 respectively, Hunter had again raised his pet topic of providing free lectures at the hospital. He had even managed to persuade John Gunning, his steadfast rival, to join him in staging a few lectures in the winter of 1783 and again in 1785. None of their surgical colleagues – Caesar Hawkins's son Charles, and his nephew George, who was succeeded in 1783 by William Walker – could be persuaded to follow suit. But Hunter triumphantly broadcast his small victory in an addendum to the advertisement for his own lectures in autumn 1785, announcing: 'The Surgeons of St George's Hospital will in the course of the winter deliver some lectures in Surgery to the pupils.'[35]

One incentive, perhaps for Gunning as well as Hunter, may have been the establishment of the first hospital-based London medical school, at the London Hospital in the East End, by one of Hunter's early pupils, William Blizard, that same year. Inspired by his teacher's belief in medical education, Blizard had persuaded his hospital's governors to let him teach courses in anatomy and surgery, on condition he refrained from using any of the patients for demonstrations. Blizard even footed most of the bill for the lecture rooms built adjoining the hospital.[36] But while Blizard's fulfilment of Hunter's dream formed the solid foundations of the future London Hospital medical school, the initiative at St George's would prove short-lived. Gunning would abandon his efforts at medical education almost as quickly as he had begun them, in early 1786, lamenting that the lectures had cost him 'a great deal of time and trouble in composing them and reading them'.[37] Doubtless he was aware he had no chance of competing with Hunter's young fan club. If anything, his humiliating experience would sharpen his resolve to oppose the renegade surgeon.

Hunter's already shaky standing with his colleagues was further destabilized by his insistence on performing operations that they held controversial. Rarely varying the procedures they had learned as apprentices, Hunter's colleagues were loath to jeopardize their reputations among their private clients by attempting risky or novel operations. Accordingly, they unerringly continued the inept and sometimes unnecessary amputations, lithotomies and other procedures. Conversely, though Hunter generally professed a more conservative approach, shrewdly avoiding surgery whenever possible through his awareness of its dangerous consequences, he was still prepared to attempt unorthodox procedures when his anatomical knowledge and experimental investigations persuaded him they had a good chance of success. Often this meant he was prepared to undertake operations that none of his colleagues would contemplate. In one instance, he agreed to remove a swelling on the wrist of a woman who had injured her hand falling downstairs. Percivall Pott had declared that 'none but a Madman would do it', but Hunter adroitly cut away the lump, much to his patient's gratitude.[38]

It was luck, therefore, that brought John Burley, a thirty-seven-year-old man with a hideous deformity, to St George's door on Hunter's round rather than any of his three colleagues' in October 1785.[39] None of Hunter's fellows would have considered operating to remove the tumour, which had grown to an immense size, almost twice as large as the man's head, on the side of his face and below his jaw. Accepted by Hunter as a patient, Burley explained that the growth had first appeared when he had injured his cheek sixteen years earlier. Variously flesh-coloured and shiny purple, the hideous growth now weighed a staggering nine pounds. After a recent, second injury, the tumour had grown so fast that the poor patient had perceived it getting bigger every month. Having avoided the prospect of an operation until now, Burley was finally desperate for help.

Hunter carefully examined the immense growth, which was solid in parts and soft in others, and discerned that it was not connected to the patient's skull or lower jaw. Confident that cutting it away was therefore feasible, Hunter agreed to attempt its removal. Burley was duly prepared for theatre, and on 24 October, surrounded by his ever eager pupils, Hunter began the lengthy and highly delicate task of severing the mass. The procedure, he later noted in his case books, 'lasted twenty five minutes and the man did not cry out during the whole of the operation'. Finally freed from the unsightly and unwieldy burden he had carried for sixteen years, Burley walked out of St George's with only a long, neat scar to show for his ordeal. Naturally, Hunter made sure to preserve his handiwork for posterity, directing his artist, William Bell, to produce dramatic 'before and after' sketches. The tumour itself, inevitably, was cut into three sections and displayed prominently in Hunter's collection.

When Hunter followed this remarkable triumph with his even more controversial operation to bypass a popliteal aneurysm in the leg of the coach driver who arrived at St George's a few weeks later, his colleagues' scorn only increased. Not only would none of the other surgeons have entertained such an operation, they now openly opposed his methods. Despite the evident success of the procedure, as far as his rivals were concerned the episode merely confirmed Hunter's status as an experimentalist and a showman more interested in hoarding peculiarities for his strange collection and performing bizarre investigations on animal life than knuckling down to practical surgery. As Astley Cooper later put it, 'At this time none of the surgeons eminent for extensive practice placed any confidence in the surgical knowledge of John Hunter, who was chiefly known as a philosopher by means of his lectures and writings; they even contended against his views, as mystifying, if not inapplicable to the treatment of disease.'[40] But if his surgical colleagues could be stubborn and uncompromising, Hunter could be equally confrontational. His barely concealed contempt for his fellows ensured he remained isolated and despised, a perpetual outsider in his own workplace.

It mattered little to Hunter. His colleagues could only grind their teeth and mutter conspiratorially as accolades continued to be heaped on the maverick surgeon. Already honoured as Surgeon Extraordinary to George III, Hunter had won international acclaim for his experimental investigations with his election in 1781 to the Royal Society of Gothenberg and in 1783 to the Royal Society of Medicine and Royal Academy of Surgery of Paris. Recognition for his early military services came in January 1786 when he was appointed deputy surgeon-general of the army. The post, which was largely administrative, placed him second in command of the army's surgical services to his old friend and former boss Robert Adair.

These titles brought further prestige, but it was Hunter's new printing press that assured him lasting fame.

The long-awaited *Treatise on the Venereal Disease* became an overnight bestseller on its publication in March 1786, selling a thousand copies within the first twelve months, despite the malicious attack Jessé Foot immediately rushed to publish.[41] Certainly humoured by Hunter's enemies at St George's, if not actively encouraged by them, Foot had little impact on the success of the text: it was translated into French and German the following year, and a second English edition would be published in 1788. The printing press was kept busy. Collecting together the various papers he had submitted to the Royal Society on human and animal physiology, along with nine more previously unpublished tracts, Hunter published his wide-ranging book *Observations on Certain Parts of the Animal Oeconomy* later the same year. Dedicated to Banks, his friend and patron, it gathered together Hunter's myriad investigations on every aspect of life, from his dissections of beetles, bees and caterpillars to his discovery of the nerves of smell, the mode of descent of the testes, and his proposals for saving the drowned – all with exquisite illustrations by van Rymsdyk. Yet for all his success – he was now earning approximately £6,000 a year in fees – and professional recognition, the name on the plain enamelled plate beside the door of number 28 remained simply 'John Hunter'.[42]

Finally, in May 1786, Hunter's celebrity status was confirmed when the Royal Academy opened its doors for its annual summer exhibition. Alongside oils of the most famous personalities of the period, including the Prince of Wales and the actress Sarah Siddons, there hung Hunter's portrait, painted by the most fashionable society artist of the time, Sir Joshua Reynolds.[43] Seated at his desk, with a quill in one hand, his other hand supporting his chin in the customary pose of a philosopher, and elegantly clothed in the damson red velvet suit usually reserved for physicians, Hunter was surrounded by the anatomical paraphernalia that defined his life's work.

The highly revealing picture almost never made it to the summer exhibition, for Hunter was a reluctant subject who had only been persuaded to sit for Sir Joshua by a mutual friend, William Sharp, an engraver, keen to publish prints of the celebrated surgeon. Talked into the deal, Hunter had crossed the square to Reynolds' studio to sit for the preliminary sketches in 1785. But when Anne saw Reynolds' first drafts, faithfully portraying her husband with his straggly beard and untamed hair, she was not impressed. The wild-looking anatomist with his penetrating eyes may have been a familiar sight to Hunter's patients, friends and pupils, but the image certainly did not strike Anne as the statuesque figure she had in mind for public edification. The picture was allowed to gather dust; Anne later gave it away to an upholsterer in the Haymarket, John Weatherall, who had fitted out the museum.[44]

Persuading Hunter to shave off his tangled growth was the next step. According to stories passed down, either Anne or Reynolds convinced the surgeon to have a life mask made; naturally enough, before the wet clay could be applied to Hunter's face the beard had to go.[45] Hunter made further sittings in February and March 1786 for the second, more dignified, portrait which would grace the walls of the Royal Academy. Even then the business was far from straightforward, for Reynolds found his friend a restless and fidgety sitter; no doubt the anatomist had far more stimulating matters to attend to than sitting in Reynolds' studio striking a noble pose for hours on end. At length, Hunter apparently fell into a deep contemplation – he was probably puzzling out some enigma of natural history that was currently plaguing him – and Reynolds briskly sketched the thoughtful face which he unveiled at the summer exhibition.

If the intellectual gaze was Reynolds' choice, the symbolic objects surrounding the anatomist were entirely his own: each of the books and preparations in the painting were deliberately selected by Hunter to convey his most significant interests and contributions in all his various fields.[46] So the delicately injected preparation displaying the airways of the lungs – a bronchial tree – fixed upside down in a bell-jar, represented his unparalleled skills in anatomy and the art of making preparations. The specimen of a bone preserved in a cylindrical bottle, possibly a leg bone from an ass showing what appears to be a bone graft, demonstrated his skills as a surgeon and his knowledge of physiology. The sketch beneath his elbow appears to be a drawing of the fibres in muscles, probably in reference to a series of lectures on the topic he had staged for the Royal Society.[47] The two closed volumes on Hunter's desk, entitled *Natural History of Vegetables* and *Natural History of Fossils*, plainly indicated his passion for natural history; quite possibly Hunter intended to publish these manuscripts. The open book at his elbow, which seems to be the third in this series, displays sketches of human and animal skulls and bones, which no doubt most visitors to the Royal Academy that year regarded as signs of Hunter's renowned expertise in comparative anatomy. The fact that these drawings plainly depict a series of human and animal skulls in a striking gradation was doubtless lost on most visitors. Likewise the significance of the system of forelimbs or hands, ranging from the single hoof of a horse through the two-toed foot of a deer to the paw of a monkey and ultimately a human hand, would have eluded most viewers. But the curiously long feet, tantalizingly glimpsed in the top right-hand corner of the painting, would certainly have sent a shudder down the spines of most spectators that summer.

Having stealthily concealed from public gaze his prized skeleton of the Irish giant for three years, at last Hunter felt confident, or brazen, enough to allow a sly peek at the giant's destiny. What this told the idle viewer at the summer exhibition took no subtlety to unravel. The message was clear: here was a man whose zeal for collecting curious objects knew no bounds, who would evidently go to any lengths to obtain what he desired. Yet it would be two more years before Hunter unveiled more than the giant's unusually long feet to public view.

Hunter, at least, was in the public eye in more ways than one in early 1786, for it was now that the surgeon was called upon to wield his knife on the nation's leading statesman. Having performed a post-mortem on one prime minister, the Marquis of Rockingham in 1782, now Hunter was required to operate on a second, William Pitt the younger. After assuming the premiership three years earlier, at twenty-seven Pitt was now troubled by an encysted tumour on his cheek. Advised by his physicians that it should be removed, it was Hunter that Pitt chose to perform the delicate surgery. Hunter duly arrived at Downing Street with his pocket set of knives and proposed to tie the prime minister's hands in the customary fashion. But Pitt was having none of it. He inquired how long the operation would take, to which Hunter estimated six minutes, and insisted he would not move. Fixing his eyes on the Horse Guards' clock which he could see from the window, Pitt sat motionless until the surgery was completed, upon which he remarked: 'You have exceeded your time by half a minute.' Impressed by such stoicism, but doubtless also with an eye to future advancement, Hunter responded that he had never seen 'so much fortitude and courage in all his practice'.[48]

Reynolds' portrait was revealing in other ways too. The intelligent, new-shaven face that appeared in the engraving Sharp would print in 1788 from the 1786 portrait was changing rapidly; Reynolds had to rework his painting in 1789, probably in order to show the evidence of the strain induced by Hunter's continuing angina. Although by the summer of 1786 he was fit enough to visit his patients on foot, he could walk only slowly.[49] By October he was forced to travel everywhere in his carriage since he could not walk fast enough to keep warm, according to Home, who was deputed again to note down each symptom of the condition.

The prolonged illness afforded Home the chance he had been waiting for. Making himself indispensable to his former teacher, he moved into the Leicester Square house, adopted many of the surgeon's private clients when Hunter was too ill to visit them, and assumed control over much of his other day-to-day work. The heady experience of trying on the popular surgeon's mantle, directing his pupils and assistants, advising his patients, and generally preening himself in the reflected glory of the man portrayed in Reynolds' painting, proved all too tempting. Although he would never match pupils such as Jenner in Hunter's estimation, Home would do his utmost to remain the surgeon's right-hand man.

Though Hunter was now reduced to sitting impatiently

in London's chaotic traffic jams rather than sprinting along the pavements as he preferred, he was still performing exhausting operations lasting up to an hour, as well as post-mortems, without faltering. In November, his stamina was tested to the full when the elderly Princess Amelia, George III's aunt, died after a lengthy illness. It was Pott, Hunter's former teacher, who had treated the princess during her lifetime, but it was Hunter who was called to embalm her in death.

Inspired perhaps by interest in Egyptian mummies, the art of embalming had enjoyed something of a vogue in eighteenth-century England. Most famously, the eccentric dentist Martin van Butchell had directed William Hunter to embalm his wife when she died in 1775. A friend of both brothers, having attended both of their lecture courses, van Butchell subsequently kept his preserved spouse in his living room, where guests could view her by appointment.[50] Finally, the dentist's second wife insisted somewhat understandably that the shrivelled corpse be removed. It ended up in Surgeons' Hall, along with the body of the naked woman embalmed by anatomist John Sheldon. But it was Hunter's unequalled talents in preservation, as well as his experience in unwrapping Egyptian royalty, that made him the obvious candidate to preserve and wrap a Hanoverian princess. After all, even Foot acknowledged that 'If a body were to be embalmed John Hunter was sent for.'[51]

Hunter approached the delicate task with his usual precision, noting every step of the procedure, which took a gruelling three hours.[52] Assisted by Home, Hunter removed the abdominal organs, then sawed open the head and removed the brain from the body of the seventy-five-year-old woman. These were placed in a lead urn while the bodily cavities were packed with a mixture of aromatic herbs and flowers. The recipe for this concoction, described as 'Sweets', was meticulously noted; it included marjoram, cloves, musk and pulverized lemon. A second mixture, containing lavender, cloves, thyme and wormwood, was used to line the coffin. At least the atmosphere was more delicately fragranced than usual in the dissecting room. Perfectly perfumed, the princess was bound in green linen, which had been steeped in a mixture of beeswax, resin, powdered verdigris and mutton suet. There were precise measurements for the lengths of bandages required for each part of the body, and the method for waxing the fabric was similarly supplied. 'Put pack thread to the corners when you dip them,' Hunter explained, 'and stand on a table to draw them easily out of the pan.' Whether Hunter, now fifty-eight and pained with angina, scaled the table to perform this athletic feat, or whether the petulant Home had to carry out the task, went unrecorded.

Wrapping the corpse was an equally demanding job, as Hunter recorded: 'The body is wrapped up in two pieces & the face & head are covered with two pieces and afterwards rolled over with strips in every direction. The legs are then to be brought together and the two great toes tied & then all rolled up in one; the arms brought to the sides and the whole body is to be enveloped in two pieces each 7 feet long; the whole making one mass without any appearance of neck being retained.' Completely bound in green cloth, the princess's body was then wrapped in white and then purple silk, Hunter pointing out that 'The Purple is peculiar to the Royal family.' At last, mummified and cocooned, the royal aunt was laid in her coffin and the lid soldered down, but not before certain privileged visitors had viewed Hunter's handiwork. 'She is already embalmed, cered, and coffined,' Horace Walpole wrote to tell Lady Ossory, adding, 'her body is wrapped in I do not know how many yards of crimson silk, and she, they tell me, looks like a silkworm in its outward case.'[53]

Neither Hunter's royal performance nor his veneration at the Royal Academy did anything to lessen the jealousy among his St George's rivals. They notched up a small revenge when Hunter proposed his nephew, Matthew Baillie, for a physician's post at the hospital in the same year: his enemies closed ranks to ensure the alternative candidate won the position. Studious and talented, having been schooled by William Hunter in anatomy and by John in surgery and physiology, at twenty-five Baillie had been running the Great Windmill Street anatomy school with his partner, William Cruikshank, for three years. Already he was highly respected on the London medical scene, not least by his uncle John.

All of the Baillies – Dorothy and her daughters, Agnes and Joanna, had moved into the Great Windmill Street house the year after William Hunter's death – had become regular visitors at 28 Leicester Square. The Hunter household was nothing if not hospitable. Guests of all ages bustled through the busy doorway by day and night, but young people were always assured of a special welcome. So Matthew was quickly absorbed into the favoured set of bright young medical men whom his uncle fostered and encouraged; promising surgical pupils and young surgeons just starting out on their careers were often invited to Hunter's house for dinner and medical banter. Under his uncle's patronage, Matthew would eventually secure the coveted physician's post at St George's, and he would prove himself a true Hunterian disciple in 1793 when he published his landmark textbook, *The Morbid Anatomy of Some of the Most Important Parts of the Human Body*, outlining the pathological changes caused by various diseases.[54]

Hunter's nieces, Agnes and Joanna, now twenty-six and twenty-four, were equally welcome in the vibrant Hunter home; Anne encouraged Joanna to write her first serious poems and plays, while both sisters were regular guests at her weekly soirées. Agnes would later recall meeting some of the most admired literary figures of the day – including Horace Walpole, the young novelist Fanny Burney and the poet Elizabeth Carter – at her aunt's sparkling parties.[55] It was Agnes who later had the perspicacity to persuade her mother, Dorothy, to recite her childhood reminiscences of her youngest brother before they were lost to memory. The talented Joanna would likewise remember meeting the Italian poet Ippolito Pindemonte, 'a great Beau of those days', at Anne's literary evenings.[56] She would always remain a close confidante of Aunt Anne, but she had a particular affinity with Uncle John. 'My Uncle John Hunter I knew well and loved him very heartily,' she would write, '(for that was the kind of love that belonged to him) not tenderly.'[57]

For all the lively company and bright talents of the Baillie bunch, it was Anne's brother – wheedling, pompous, self-promoting Everard – who remained firmly at Hunter's side. In May 1787, Hunter persuaded the St George's governors to appoint Home as his assistant; Gunning was likewise allowed an assistant, Thomas Keate. Since Hunter had just received the Copley medal from the Royal Society – the society's highest accolade – as well as being welcomed into the American

Philosophical Society, it might have seemed churlish for the board to refuse. Ostensibly, Home's appointment was intended to ease the burden of hospital duties on the increasingly beleaguered surgeon. In reality, Hunter was busier than ever.

The case books Hunter maintained throughout his professional career attest to the immense number and variety of patients he treated at St George's, in his Leicester Square consulting room, and in clients' own homes during these most popular years. Although a large proportion of the notes have been lost, and many of those surviving are anonymous and undated, still Hunter's medical records provide a revealing social history of the time.[58] As well as unnamed ladies, gentlemen and peers, the range of tradespeople he treated included a lamplighter, coal porter, sailor, coachmaker, chairman, hairdresser, glover, fishmonger, house-painter, comb-maker and cowman. His services were often required below stairs as well as above. Among the service staff who benefited from his care were Lord Abercorn's butler, the Earl of Shelburne's maid, the Duke of Queensberry's cook, and Sir Gilbert Heathcote's porter, all of them identified only by their master's title. Yet while many of these patients' identities were either never recorded or quickly forgotten, Hunter's expertise was increasingly being sought by the Georgian personalities whose names would be forever remembered.

James Boswell had at last settled down to the hard graft of compiling his biography of Johnson when his eldest son, Alexander, fell ill in March 1787. Having moved back to live in his beloved London the previous year, he had initially lodged with his friend Pascal Paoli, the Corsican hero, before bringing his wife, Margaret, and their children down from Edinburgh to join him in a rented house in Great Queen Street.[59] The family's health was not in peak condition. After renewing his acquaintances with London prostitutes, as well as with Signor Gonorrhoea, Boswell had become depressed about his chronic condition after reading Hunter's venereal disease treatise within days of its publication. His wife had been ill with consumption for many years – the move to smoky London was far from beneficial – and now twelve-year-old 'Sandie' had a recurrent hernia condition. Hunter, who had first studied hernias more than thirty years earlier, was the obvious person to examine him; Boswell called the surgeon to the family home on 21 March.[60] 'Mr John Hunter visited him,' Boswell recorded in his journal, 'and found that Squires, the trussmaker, was right in his discovery that one of the testicles was not come down.' After examining Sandie, Hunter cast a professional eye over Mrs Boswell too, declaring 'she looked greatly better'.

Almost certainly Hunter and Boswell were already acquainted: the fact the surgeon considered Mrs Boswell 'better' suggested he had seen her previously, while the families had many mutual friends, including Reynolds, Paoli and Banks. An entry in Reynolds' appointment book just a week earlier, on 15 March 1787 – 'at home Mr B Dr King Mr Hunter' – may well have seen the pair dining together.[61] Just two months later, the Boswells were guests at one of Mrs Hunter's musical events, where their eldest daughter displayed her talents, for Boswell recorded in his diary for 19 May, 'went with my wife and two daughters to a Concert at Mrs Hunter's. Veronica played by General Paoli's intreaty.'[62] Most probably, Hunter was engrossed in his study during the evening's frivolities but on this occasion he was not allowed to retire quietly to bed. On returning home Mrs Boswell was seized with 'a severe fit of spitting blood' and Hunter was called to attend her. In truth, there was little he could do to ease Margaret Boswell's condition: nearly two centuries before the advent of antibiotics there was no effective treatment for her already advanced consumption. Hunter visited her three times more in the following year, prescribing a few medications, letting blood – although 'she had a horrour of that operation' it was still universally expected – and generally offering soothing words.[63] By then, she had only another year to live.

It was Boswell's tutor, the inspired economist Adam Smith, who next sought Hunter's help, travelling down from Edinburgh in April 1787 expressly to obtain the surgeon's aid.[64] Smith, perhaps the brightest star of the Scottish Enlightenment, had long held Hunter in affectionate regard. The two had probably met when Smith attended William Hunter's lectures in the 1770s, along with historian Edward Gibbon; no doubt the economist had also been impressed by Hunter's no-nonsense treatment of his friend David Hume in 1776. Two years later, Smith sent Hunter a copy of his epic work *The Wealth of Nations*, a year after its publication.[65] Now suffering cruelly with a bladder infection and haemorrhoids, the sixty-four-year-old professor travelled gingerly down from Scotland to stay with his friend the Scottish MP Henry Dundas in Wimbledon, where he was fêted by a bevy of politicians, including the prime minister, William Pitt. While physicians tended to Smith's bladder complaint, Hunter performed the delicate operation of removing the economist's piles. By mid-July one of his friends was informing another that Smith had 'been cut for the piles', while his bladder problem was 'much mended'.[66] A few days later, patently relieved of his former agony, Smith urged Dundas to recommend Hunter for two army appointments in the government's gift, one of them the post of surgeon at Chelsea Hospital, entreating that 'nothing is too good for our friend John'.[67] In the event, it was Thomas Keate, the latest conscript to the anti-Hunter faction at St George's, who secured the Chelsea job. Smith enjoyed a welcome reprieve from his ailments on his return to Scotland in July, but he would continue in declining health until his death in 1790.

There was little, however, to suggest the future fame, or notoriety, of the patient Hunter was called to visit in a shabby upstairs room off Oxford Street in early 1788. George Gordon Byron was born on 22 January after a long and difficult labour; when the baby emerged, his head was still enclosed in a 'caul', the birth sac, while his right foot appeared unnaturally twisted.[68] Just twenty-two and virtually penniless due to her absent husband's debts, his mother, Catherine, called Hunter to examine the baby's foot within days of his birth. Herself a Scot, and a stranger in London, she may have heard of Hunter's reputation from her Scottish relatives, or perhaps he was recommended by the male-midwives who attended her delivery. No details of Hunter's examination of the future poet's foot survive in his case books, but he did record that he 'inoculated Master Byron in both arms'.[69] The inoculation for smallpox, using the traditional method of jabbing the arm with some matter from another patient's pustules, appeared to work, after an anxious few days during which Hunter feared the reaction was too severe.

The infant's foot was another matter. Although Mrs Byron would later recall that Hunter declared her son's foot 'would be very well in time' so long as he was fitted with a special boot designed to straighten the deformed limb, she was seemingly either too hesitant or too impoverished to heed his advice. Three years later, having returned to Scotland, she asked her sister-in-law, Frances Leigh, in London to seek Hunter's help once again to obtain such a shoe. Lamenting that she could not get one made in Scotland, she remarked, 'as Mr Hunter saw George when he was born I am in hopes that he will be able to give you directions for a proper shoe to be made without seeing it [the foot] again', and she added plaintively, 'I am perfectly sure he would walk very well if he had a proper shoe'.

Whether or not Mrs Leigh ever sought Hunter's aid, the foot would never be completely cured. Byron's deformity – traditionally described as a 'club foot', or talipes, but possibly the result of mild spina bifida – would plague him all his life. He would successfully disguise the disability with a sliding walk, but he would remain forever self-conscious of his limp. Although he was later forced to wear an iron brace, made by a renowned quack in Nottinghamshire, this failed to mend the deformity. Many years later, the eleven-year-old boy, by then Lord Byron, would be examined by Hunter's nephew, Baillie; he concluded that the foot might have been mended had a corrective boot been used in infancy, just as his uncle had suggested.[70]

Hunter continued to offer his services free to artists, and it was Thomas Gainsborough, the portrait artist who longed to devote his time to landscapes, who requested the surgeon's aid in spring 1788. Gainsborough had spotted a lump in his neck three years earlier but since it caused no pain he had thought little of it; now it was so painful that he could not sleep comfortably at night and he anxiously sought the advice of both the physician William Heberden and John Hunter. They were equally dismissive of the lump, both assigning the pain and swelling to a cold that Gainsborough appeared to be suffering at the same time; Hunter prescribed a salt-water dressing while Heberden could throw no more light on the ailment. 'What this painfull swelling in my Neck will turn out, I am at a loss at present to guess,' the artist confided to a friend in April. 'Mr John Hunter found it nothing but [a] swell'd Gland, and has been most comfortable in persuading me that it will disperse by the continued application of a sea-water poultice.' He added, 'My neighbour Dr Heberden has no more notion of it'.[71] Uncharacteristically, and somewhat inexplicably, Hunter had failed to diagnose the cancerous tumour that would kill the artist that summer. Heberden, a respected physician, had been similarly remiss. Conceivably, Gainsborough truly had caught a cold which caused his glands to swell and mask the more serious complaint, or perhaps the pair colluded in concealing their patient's inevitable fate – though this was contrary to Hunter's usual candid style – in the knowledge there was little they could do to help.

For all the lionization of Hunter – the kindly, good-hearted Dr Jekyll of Leicester Square – by fellow scientists, grateful patients and Georgian high society, deeply seated suspicion and fear of the surgeon-anatomist – the secretive, sinister Mr Hyde who emerged from the Castle Street door – persisted among the general populace. The boom in private anatomy schools and the continual gravitation of medical students to the capital generated relentless demand for dissection material. As the Resurrectionists became more desperate, and more bold, in ransacking graveyards to supply the students' needs, so public vigilance and hostility were growing. Already this had reached such a fever pitch across the Atlantic, where former pupils of the Hunterian schools had imported the brothers' grave-robbing methods, that a fierce and bloody riot had erupted in New York. It began one Sunday in April 1788 when some boys playing behind the City Hospital had spotted a medical student dissecting an arm; their shouts quickly attracted an angry mob which rampaged through the building, destroyed anatomy preparations and seized several cadavers which were promptly reburied. But the fury did not abate, despite appeals from the city mayor, and the following day several surgeons and pupils had to take refuge in the jail. Full-scale battle ensued as the protesters attempted to storm the prison but they were rebuffed by a hurriedly raised armed guard. Pelted by stones, the soldiers were ordered to fire on the crowd, killing seven people and injuring several more.[72] Although the so-called Doctors' Riot forced the surgeons involved to swear affidavits denying they had stolen bodies for dissection, the clandestine grave-robbing and the protests would continue.

Medical students and professional body-snatchers were at least as busy, if generally more discreet, in London graveyards. At one point in 1788 two bodies were reported stolen from the burial ground of Chelsea Hospital, Hunter's old haunt, and a five-guinea reward offered for the capture of the perpetrators.[73] And now that Hunter had added anatomy classes to his lectures, his need for regular supplies of fresh bodies was greater than ever. Yet while it was widely known that corpses were delivered to the Castle Street door most nights throughout the winter, Hunter stealthily kept his involvement at arm's length. In November he was cited in a court case – the only time he would come anywhere near legal exposure – when an employee of Westminster General Dispensary, Edward Howe, was sent to prison for 'fraudulently obtaining a corpse from Mr Bradford, an apothecary of Grafton Street ... and stripping and selling it to Mr Hunter of Leicester Square'.[74] While Howe festered in jail, Hunter's legal record remained untarnished.

Fewer than two weeks later, William Lynn, Hunter's former assistant who had recently set up in practice on his own, became one of the first London surgeons arrested for body-snatching. Lynn's lawyer offered the traditional defence that it was no crime to steal a body since it had no owner, but the King's Bench made the historic judgement that no matter what the custom had been, grave-robbing offended common decency. Although Lynn escaped with a £10 fine, on the grounds that he might have committed his offence through 'ignorance', the judgement sent a clear signal to all the city's anatomists.[75] Though the nightly antics of the body-snatchers would only escalate, reaching epidemic proportions within the next few decades, London's surgeons would take care to avoid getting caught red-handed again.

Given this sinister world Hunter was forced through the nature of his calling to inhabit, it is little surprise that he provided inspiration not only for Robert Louis Stevenson but for the melancholy William Blake too. In his satirical piece of prose *An Island in the Moon*, written in the 1780s, the young Blake launched a scathing attack on intellectual society, ridiculing various members of the Royal Society but saving particular venom for surgery and anatomy. The villain of his piece, 'Jack Tearguts', was almost certainly John Hunter. Not only did Hunter have several acquaintances in common with the poet, but Blake spent most of his life living in the same neighbourhoods. His childhood home in the 1760s was minutes from Hunter's house in Golden Square; after marrying in 1782, Blake lived in Green Street, directly round the corner from Leicester Square, where he probably enjoyed a good view of both entrances to the anatomist's extraordinary home.[76] 'He understands Anatomy better than any of the Ancients,' Blake has his protagonist declare of Jack Tearguts. 'He'll plunge his knife up to the hilt in a single drive, and thrust his fist in, and all in the space of a Quarter of an hour. He does not mind the crying, tho' they cry ever so. He'll swear at them & keep them down with his fist, & tell them that he'll scrape their bones if they don't lay still & be quiet.'

But as Hunter now prepared to open the doors of his treasured museum to public view, even some of his friends in the scientific world feared he had gone too far this time.

14

The Monkey's Skull

'Does not the natural gradation of animals, from one to
another, lead to the original species?'

John Hunter[1]

Leicester Square, London, 1788

Anticipation among the distinguished visitors arriving at
28 Leicester Square was intense. Ushered through the
house and into the new extension, they pressed impatiently forwards. As well as members of the
Royal Society, the Royal Antiquaria Society and the Royal
College of Physicians, the guests included writers
and several important foreign visitors. Shepherded up to
the first floor, they arrived at the tall doors and stepped
into the great skylit room to gaze incredulously around.
All would have heard the rumours and speculation about
the famous anatomist's collection. Some of the stories
detailing exotic animals he had obtained sounded more

like the stuff of fiction, while the reports of human curiosities he had procured seemed equally fabulous. What they found, as they stared in wonder at the bottles filled with fleshy substances, the cases of dried organs, and the skeletons positioned around the large galleried room, and what they now heard from the lips of their illustrious host, was more surprising than any of them could have expected.

It was five years since Hunter and his young family had moved into Leicester Square, three years since he had supervised the transfer of his already large collection into its purpose-built accommodation. Only now, after he and his several assistants had spent many months sorting, arranging and cataloguing the ever-growing number of exhibits, was Hunter ready to reveal his museum to the outside world. But this was not just the happy conclusion of five years' planning, it was the culmination of his life's work. Ever since his boyhood days questioning country folk on the habits of field creatures, through the long winters exploring corpses in Covent Garden, and throughout the decades studying humans and animals, dead and alive, at his Earls Court research centre, Hunter had been struggling to understand the secrets of life itself. Each new species, each body part, each curiosity he had accrued in almost forty years' voracious acquisition represented another piece in this bewildering puzzle. At last, as he flung open the doors and welcomed the guests into his museum, he felt sure he had slotted together most of the pieces. A small figure in the lofty room, though recently grown a little more rotund through his enforced lack of exercise, Hunter waited as his guests perused the displays, preparing to deliver his opening words.

By anyone's standards, it was a remarkable scene. None

of the guests could fail to be amazed at the sight of the huge stuffed giraffe, captured in 1779, hacked in half to fit the Jermyn Street hall and now reunited with its legs, as it reared above their heads. One journalist, invited to record the opening, was plainly overwhelmed, noting that 'from the report of its size and other circumstances, it was hitherto much doubted by naturalists whether such an animal did really exist or not'.[2] Finally convinced that the giraffe was not a work of fiction, he continued, 'In point of size, it is above eighteen feet high, with an erect neck and long feet, and in many respects partaking of the species of the common camel. From the stiffness of its joints, it can neither stoop, nor lie down; but as nature is ever provident for its creatures, it receives its food from the leaves of trees, which from its extreme height it can readily do by putting his head in among the branches.'

There were more, equally remarkable, sights. Staring apprehensively around, the visitors could glimpse massive bones belonging to elephants, camels and whales; body parts from a zebra, a leopard, a pelican and a hyena; and entire preserved bodies of rare creatures such as an aardvark fetus, a Surinam toad carrying its young in pockets on its back, and a baby crocodile frozen at the point of emerging from its egg, the umbilical cord still intact. There were scarcely credible human curiosities too. Few could have failed to be moved by the five pitiful bodies of quins, lined up stiffly in a row. Born two years earlier, four months prematurely to a young mother in Lancashire, three had been stillborn and two born alive, though they survived only briefly. The physician who delivered the babies, all girls, had preserved their emaciated bodies in spirits, tied a label to each wrist indicating their order of birth, and sent them to the Royal

Society, which promptly gave them to its foremost anatomist.[3] Just as unusual was the skeleton of a man reduced to less than five feet tall by a rare disease, *myositis ossificans*, which had progressively turned his muscle into bone. Hunter had purchased the skeleton at an anatomical auction in 1783 for the considerable sum of eighty-five guineas.[4] But most stunning of all, as they raised their eyes the visitors came face to face with the magnificent skeleton of Charles Byrne, the acclaimed Irish giant, grinning down grotesquely in death at the spectators he had once enthralled in life. Revealing his prize trophy to London society for the first time, Hunter claimed he had paid 130 guineas for the body. Whether this was the genuine price, colossal in itself, or he was simply too embarrassed to reveal the true cost of 500 pounds he was reputed to have spent, would remain his secret.[5]

As they stared around, few of the spectators could disagree with the journalist's description of 'Mr Hunter's very curious, extensive, and valuable museum'.[6] By sheer volume alone, the collection was nothing less than spectacular. Ultimately it would total nearly 14,000 individual items, and it was not far off that number already; almost certainly it was the largest collection of its kind in Britain at the time. The range, too, was incredible: eventually it would encompass more than 1,400 animal and human parts preserved in spirits; over 1,200 dried bones, skulls and skeletons; more than 6,000 pathological preparations showing the effects of injury and disease; and more than 800 dried plants and invertebrates, as well as assorted stuffed animals, corals, minerals and shells.[7] In all, more than 500 different species were represented. In addition, there were nearly 3,000 fossils, which alone amounted to 'one of the largest and most select collections of extraneous fossils, that can be seen in this country', according to one contemporary.[8]

The accumulation of such a vast and varied hoard had cost Hunter a fortune – more than £20,000, according to the journalist attending the open day, 'beside a very accurate and industrious collection of near thirty years'.[9] But this too was probably a gross underestimate. Hunter at one point told his former assistant William Lynn that he had spent £70,000 on the collection; Hunter's will, written in 1793, would put the total outlay at more than 90,000 guineas.[10] Whatever the true cost, the continual expenditure explained why, despite earning upwards of £5,000 a year in the early 1780s and an estimated £6,000 thereafter – about £360,000 today – Hunter was invariably short of money. He was never out of debt to animal dealers, friends and money lenders, while his properties at Earls Court were forever being remortgaged in order to stump up more cash for new acquisitions. Lynn knew this better than most. Once, when he was ill after wounding his hand during a post-mortem, Hunter had offered to lend him £200. When Lynn recovered and called to thank his former boss for the offer, Hunter had completely forgotten the promise, exclaiming, 'I offer you money! That is droll, indeed; for I am the last person in this town to have money at command.'[11] With the considerable expense of running two large households, plus his wife's extravagant lifestyle, it was a wonder indeed that Hunter never ended up bankrupt. Nonetheless, he was quite prepared to stand by his offer to Lynn.

Hunter was himself the recipient of extraordinary generosity. The donors who had helped him to form his remarkable collection spanned every area of Georgian life.

He had received a hog deer from Lord Clive, and a gibbon, a baboon and an albino macaque from the former prime minister, the Earl of Shelburne. Queen Charlotte herself, of course, had donated the carcasses of two elephants which had died in her menagerie, as well as the little bull which had almost gored him. Explorer friends had been equally forthcoming. As well as the antipodean finds from Banks, Hunter had been given several animals by Captain Constantine Phipps, later Lord Mulgrave, from his voyage towards the North Pole in 1773. Julius Griffiths, a former pupil from St George's, had brought Hunter back an aquatic snail and the entrails of a pangolin from his expedition to Sumatra; sadly, Griffiths noted on his return to England, the entrails had been 'entirely spoiled from their long detention at the India House'.[12] Indeed, although Hunter never ventured beyond British shores after his brief military career, he managed to foster contacts around the globe to secure creatures from every corner of the world. In a typical letter to an acquaintance in Africa, he urged, 'If a foal camel was put into a tub of spirits I should be glad. Is it possible to get a young tame lion, or indeed any other beast or bird?'[13] He was never coy about his requirements. Even his servants were drawn into the mission. Hunter gave orders that when mowing the meadows his Earls Court staff should preserve every dormouse nest and beehive they stumbled upon.[14]

Now the fruits of this tireless quest were open to public scrutiny. As the last guests bustled in, Hunter began the first guided tour – 'a kind of peripatetic lecture', according to the newspaper columnist[15] – of his museum. It lasted between two and three hours. But this was scarcely surprising, for the museum encapsulated Hunter's entire career. As well as the handful of preparations he had held on to from his years in Covent Garden, there were bones displaying gunshot wounds from his spell in the army, the tooth grafted into the cockerel's comb from his period studying teeth, and tissues showing venereal infections from his research into sexual diseases. There were preparations demonstrating his surgical prowess in operations at St George's, organs harvested from innumerable autopsies, and cabinets showing results of experiments conducted at his Earls Court laboratory. It was nothing less than a record of John Hunter's life. More significantly, it was a representation of life itself. For, as Hunter made clear to his rapt entourage, the collection was no haphazard assortment of curiosities such as any number of eighteenth-century amateur enthusiasts had acquired, but a carefully ordered series of human and animal parts arranged expressly to investigate and illustrate fundamental principles about life on earth. Nothing else like Hunter's museum existed, or ever would exist. Even Jessé Foot had to admit, 'I know of no museum similar to this; it may be said to be, unique'.[16]

To most outsiders, this peculiar arrangement was simply perplexing; as far as Horace Walpole was concerned, the museum was just 'Mr Hunter's collection of human miseries'.[17] To Hunter, always scornful of the written word, its organization was entirely logical. His museum functioned both as a teaching aid, graphically displaying fundamental facts about anatomy and physiology to his pupils, and as a research tool, helping Hunter to investigate the general principles of life. As one contemporary report explained, 'The main object which he had in forming his Museum, was to illustrate as far as possible the whole subject of life, by preparations of the bodies in which these phenomena are presented.'[18] No static display of inanimate objects, such as Walpole's own magpie hoard, this was a dynamic and vibrant exposition of Hunter's theories on organic life.

Inevitably, given Hunter's lifelong commitment to rejecting traditional doctrines and stoking controversy, those beliefs were highly unconventional. Not only did the museum attempt to explore the physiology of all organic life, it also aimed – as he explained to visitors on his guided tour – to reveal the connections between all life. It was these unorthodox views that captivated his guests, as the newspaper report made plain: 'What principally attracted the attention of the *cognoscenti* was Mr Hunter's novel and curious system of natural philosophy running progressively from the lowest scale of vegetable up to animal nature.'[19]

The system was indeed novel, although entirely in keeping with all Hunter had taught and written. His collection was divided into three main sections. The first two – the greatest proportion – illustrated normal life: one part exhibited the anatomical structure of individual animals in order to display their physiology, the other elucidated the preservation or reproduction of entire species. The third section, the pathological series, showed examples of normal life gone wrong through disease or injury, although most of these preparations were stored in the lecture theatre, where they could be brought out during classes to underline Hunter's teachings. In the main museum, Hunter had organized the healthy human and animal parts according to bodily systems, as he had previously in Jermyn Street. So organs of digestion or parts of respiration were grouped together, running from the simplest animal structures to the most complex. But now he went further than ever, even placing vegetables and plants alongside analogous animal parts. The similarities between the tendrils of climbing plants and the prehensile tails of seahorses and chameleons were displayed in one series illustrating parts of locomotion; in the series demonstrating circulatory systems sap was compared to blood.[20] In all, fifteen series demonstrated the principal anatomical systems – digestion, bone structure, nervous systems, and so on – through a staggering range of species. Not only did the museum present uncompromising proof that humans, animals and even plants shared similar structures – a common make-up – which varied only in its complexity, it demonstrated precisely how each life-form was suited to its own particular circumstances.

If his guests were in any doubt of the potentially heretical implications of this arrangement, Hunter was quick to disabuse them. Drawing up in front of a row of skulls positioned in what he considered to be an ascending order of complexity, Hunter bracketed the human species along with monkeys. Betraying the classic eighteenth-century European belief in white superiority, which would prevail for at least the next century, he had placed the skulls of Europeans through to Africans in descending order. More significant, and more shocking to Georgian minds, was his inclusion of monkeys – most probably a chimpanzee – in this ordered series of skulls. Sparing no religious sentiments, Hunter explained, 'There is a regular and continued gradation of these from the most imperfect of the animal, to the most perfect of the human species. The most perfect human skull is the European; the most imperfect of this species is the Negro. The European, the Negro, and the Monkey form a regular series.'[21] Plainly unable to resist scandalizing his guests still further, Hunter then came out with his *pièce de résistance*: 'He also remarked, that our first parents, Adam and Eve, were indisputably black. This is quite a new idea; but Mr Hunter observed it might be proved without difficulty.'[22] The idea that the first humans were black – and since they were created in God's image, by implication God was therefore black – was startling. Whether or not he did indeed possess proof that human beings had originated in Africa, a notion that would be confirmed only in the latter half of the twentieth century, the radical ideas he expressed at this first public viewing of his extraordinary collection plainly demonstrated that he had moved far beyond conventional eighteenth-century dogma.

It was little wonder that Hunter's museum now attracted widespread interest from across the Continent. Keen to share his insights, Hunter decided to open the museum twice a year – in May to aristocrats and gentlemen, in October to fellow medical practitioners and natural philosophers.[23] Among its earliest visitors were the Dutch anatomist Petrus Camper and Johann Friedrich Blumenbach, a young professor of medicine at Göttingen; both were similarly absorbed with the place of humans in the pattern of life. Others included the anatomist Antonio Scarpa and the naturalist Giuseppe Poli from Italy.[24] The unique arrangement of the museum, the beliefs Hunter had proclaimed at its opening, and certain ideas he had already published, all went to suggest that he had formed views that would shock polite society, cause consternation among his contemporaries and even disturb some of his own pupils. For the time being it was enough to hint at these ideas by throwing open his museum; before long he would dare to spell them out.

*   *   *

These were not ideal times in which to challenge orthodoxy or convention. Over the winter of 1788 to 1789, Britain held its breath as George III descended into a mysterious madness and the country teetered between the government sustained by Pitt and the spectre of a regency under the irresponsible heir to the throne, the future George IV, who was in thrall to the opposition led by Charles Fox. Although Hunter was not among the surgeons and physicians who tortured the poor King, he evidently followed the daily medical reports, concluding that the illness was likely to resolve itself. 'It would probably come out to some sort of crisis, by which it would appear whether there was strength enough in the constitution to prevail over the disease,' he noted, estimating that the chances of recovery were '9 to 1' in the King's favour.[25] When the King was pronounced better in February 1789, Hunter joined in the celebrations by illuminating the windows of his Leicester Square house.[26]

But if the King had regained his sanity, within months it seemed the whole world had gone mad, as news of the storming of the Bastille on 14 July was met with both euphoria and revulsion in Britain. For William Wordsworth, an idealistic nineteen-year-old poet, the dawn of the French revolution spelled 'bliss';[27] for Hunter, at sixty-one a staunch conservative in politics if nothing else, it represented an unconscionable threat to the status quo. Replying to an acquaintance who wanted to bring a French friend to see the museum, he fumed, 'If your friend is in London in October (and not a Democrate), he is welcome to see it; but I would rather see it in a blaze, like the Bastile, than show it to a Democrate, let his country be what it may.'[28]

There had been other distractions to delay him putting his thoughts into writing. The death of Percivall Pott at the end of 1788 had left Hunter unassailably the premier surgeon in London, with a commensurate increase in clientele. Graciously, even Foot agreed, 'I think I may affirm – that his consultations were more in fashion, than any other surgeon's – and that his range of practice was more extensive: that we heard more of the name of John Hunter, than of any other surgeon.'[29] Hunter stepped into Pott's shoes within the Company of Surgeons too, filling his vacancy on the court of assistants, effectively its ruling council, in 1789. Having shown scant interest in, and even less regard for, the stultifying Company so far, he rarely bothered to attend. The fact that his chief opponent at St George's, John Gunning, became master of the Company the same year could not have encouraged his participation. Gunning's diatribe against the Company the following year, when he condemned its lack of books and lectures, must have struck Hunter as a trifle rich considering Gunning's own apathy towards giving lectures at St George's.[30]

Pott's demise also left Hunter as the undisputed figurehead of the capital's burgeoning community of medical students. Although in his sixties and often fatigued by his worsening angina, Hunter still inspired fierce devotion and enthusiasm in his youthful admirers. Among the newest recruits was a young Philadelphian, Philip Syng Physick, who had arrived in London under the wing of his father in January 1789.[31] When Physick's father asked the prospective tutor to list the books his son would read, Hunter had led the way to his dissecting room, where there were several open cadavers, and declared, 'These are the books your son will learn under my direction; the others are fit for very little.'[32] Plainly impressed, Physick moved his bags into the Castle Street quarters as a house pupil a month later. In May he enrolled as one of Hunter's pupils at St George's, and a year later he secured a job there, on Hunter's recommendation, as house surgeon.[33] Before heading north to take a medical degree at Edinburgh, Physick was persuaded to stay on as Hunter's assistant for several more months, helping in the museum. When Physick left for Scotland, Hunter praised his talents and industry to the extent that 'others', one of Hunter's last assistants recalled, felt disgruntled. Undoubtedly it was Everard Home who regarded Hunter's praises of the American 'as a reproof'. For his part, Physick viewed Hunter with an admiration that 'amounted to a species of veneration', according to a contemporary; after his return to America he 'never ceased to consider him as the greatest man that ever adorned the medical profession'. Physick would do more than any to import the Hunterian model to America. But it is easy to imagine how the mutual adoration of the charismatic elder surgeon and his talented, hard-working pupil should have so embittered Home, who considered himself natural heir to Hunter's regime.

He need not have panicked. With Hunter's activities increasing even as his health worsened, Home's assistance was constantly in demand. This was even more the case after Hunter was appointed surgeon-general of the army on Robert Adair's death in March 1790.[34] Thirty years after he had first enrolled as a young army surgeon, subject to the whims of his superiors and the scorn of his fellow practitioners, Hunter was now in supreme command of all the British army's surgical services at home and overseas. The appointment, by Pitt, with a salary of £1,200 a year, was not only recognition of his unparalleled prowess as a surgeon but a vindication of his controversial approach to treating gunshot wounds. But with hostilities between European powers rumbling on and fears growing as a result of the aggression of the revolutionary regime across the Channel, the job was no comfortable sinecure. Although Hunter would never leave his London home to inspect the military hospitals in the West Indies nor supervise his charges in their regiments, his army duties entailed a gruelling daily grind.[35] Working from his study in Leicester Square, or increasingly in the rural solitude of his Earls Court home, Hunter had a secretary, William DuPré, expressly to deal with the relentless army correspondence on pay, appointments and supplies.

He was determined to use the opportunity to set right the injustices that still rankled from his own military experience. Recalling his fury and humiliation at being denied promotion in Portugal, Hunter set about introducing a fair, consistent and progressive career ladder for all surgical appointments. With his characteristic disregard for custom and hierarchy, he refused to continue the system of patronage that permeated not only the services but all Georgian society. Conveying his intentions immediately to colonels of the regiments, he announced that all promotions to surgical jobs would be made strictly on merit and approved by him alone. According to the new system, which Hunter quickly had approved by the War Office, a lowly surgeon's mate with a regiment could progress by stages to become a hospital mate, a regimental surgeon, a staff surgeon or apothecary, and ultimately even to the grand position of physician or hospital purveyor. Any deviation from this clear path by colonels attempting to appoint their own surgical staff, often from among friends or relatives, was not to be tolerated, he made clear in an early circular.

With typical stubbornness, he refused to compromise these ideals no matter who might appeal to him. In one letter to Lord Amherst, the army's commander-in-chief, he expressed regret that a certain Colonel Whitelocke had been unable to appoint his brother to a vacant post, but insisted his new rules stipulated 'that I should have the Recommendation of Mates to Regiments, and with this view only, that proper Mates should be had, and that such should rise in Progression', adding pointedly, 'I think Colonel Whitelocke is not so ignorant of the Business of the W. O. as not to know this'.[36] In another letter, referring to a similar appeal from a General Mathew, just six days later, he noted that 'Recommendations from Officers . . . [have] no weight with me'.[37] And he was pre-pared to defend his meritocratic regime to the hilt, arguing, reasonably enough, 'I am engaging Young Men to enter as Mates to Regiments upon the Faith of future Promotion & if Gentlemen are admitted into the highest Ranks without having gone through the necessary previous Gradations, I shall lose the Confidence I have acquired'.[38] It was, he added, 'the Scene of Action' that he regarded as 'the School which is to fit Young Men for more important Stations'. He even wrote to two lowly surgeon's mates in the West Indies to enquire why they had languished in the same rank for ten and twenty-two years respectively; both were promoted to hospital posts the following year. The former country lad would never forget his humble roots. For all his opposition to the French revolution, Hunter had never been an upholder of class values; rewarding merit rather than bowing to privilege was the basic tenet of his lifelong ideology.

With Pitt studiously keeping Britain out of the various conflicts between European powers, most of Hunter's army business revolved around routine administration. Only in the last ten months of his command, after France declared war on Britain in February 1793, would Hunter have to equip his surgeons for battle; he would then organize surgical support for ten military expeditions. And when British forces faced Napoleon in 1815, much of their surgical back-up was still Hunter's legacy.

But if Hunter was leaning increasingly on his brother-in-law for assistance, even allowing Home to deliver his lectures from 1790, he was still a familiar face in Georgian sickrooms.[39] And he applied his usual experimental approach to the problems he encountered there. In one extraordinary case in early 1790, when called to treat a fifty-year-old man who was unable to eat as a result of a sudden paralysis of his oesophagus, Hunter devised a method of artificial feeding using a length of eel-skin stretched over a flexible tube. Pushing the tube down the patient's throat and into his stomach, Hunter was able to administer liquid food and medicines, saving the man from certain death by starvation, until the patient recovered his powers of swallowing. It was a method Hunter had used on numerous occasions when force-feeding animals for experiments, but it constituted the first recorded example of artificial feeding in humans. Reporting the details to his Society for the Improvement of Medical and Chirurgical Knowledge later the same year, Hunter noted that while eel-skins were particularly suited for the purpose, 'being smooth, pliable, and readily passed into the stomach', if these could not be procured 'a portion of the gut of any small animal, as a cat or lamb' would make a good substitute.[40]

Hunter was still happy to work with notorious quacks too. When Thomas Thurlow, the Bishop of Durham, grew seriously ill with a bowel complaint in the summer of 1790, Hunter was asked by leading physicians to conduct an examination. Immediately discerning from a rectal examination that the bishop had cancer of the rectum, Hunter realized there was no hope of recovery; as always it was Hunter's insistence on hands-on examination which put the physicians' dithering diagnoses to shame. Undeterred, the bishop's family called in a famous quack called Taylor in the forlorn hope his secret remedies might help, although hedging their bets they first asked Hunter and his colleagues to pronounce the potions harmless. Waiting for Hunter to arrive in the sickroom, Taylor was told to begin his demonstration but refused, saying he would 'do nothing till Jack Hunter came, for he had no opinion of any but him'.[41] Hunter breezed in and speedily agreed that Taylor's ointments were unlikely to do harm. But his inevitable curiosity in wanting to ascertain the ingredients of the mysterious lotions was sharply rebuffed, as Taylor exclaimed, 'No, no, Jack, I'll send you as much as you please, but I won't tell you what it's made of.' Despite the faith in quack remedies, Thurlow died the following year, as Hunter knew he would. The autopsy he conducted confirmed his diagnosis.[42]

Another prospective patient was rather less willing to submit to Hunter's probing fingers. The Austrian composer Joseph Haydn was a familiar visitor to the Hunter household during his stay in London in 1791 and 1792; but it was Anne, not John, who attracted him to Leicester Square.[43] Haydn became a regular guest at Anne's musical evenings, and he set six of her poems to music, his 'Six Original Canzonettas'. As their friendship grew, Anne would be regarded as Haydn's muse.

But the talented composer was not without his flaws: he suffered from painful polyps in his nose. Whether Hunter simply had an altruistic wish to ease Haydn's discomfort or conceivably he suspected the friendship with his wife went beyond purely professional interest, he determined to employ his surgical instruments on the composer. Initially, chatting in Hunter's study, Haydn seemed to consent to have the polyps removed, but a moment later, when he was roughly grabbed by Hunter's assistants, forced towards a chair and saw the surgeon bearing down on him with a pair of forceps glinting, he promptly changed his mind. 'I yelled and kicked and hit until I had freed myself,' Haydn later recalled, 'and made clear to Mr Hunter, who already had his instruments ready for the operation, that I did not want to undergo the operation.'[44] Finally, having convinced Hunter to put away his instruments, Haydn remembered, 'it seemed to me that he pitied me for not wanting to undergo the happy experience of enjoying his skill'. Returning to Austria, where his polyps continued to grow and cause pain, he would live to regret refusing the benefit of Hunter's skills.

Hunter's relentless workload, as well as his boundless energy for new projects – he was one of the founding members of the Veterinary College of London, forerunner to the Royal Veterinary College, when it was launched in 1791[45] – left little time for writing. Nevertheless, from about 1792 Hunter finally began to commit to paper his daring and potentially dangerous thoughts on the development of life on earth. As anti-revolutionary fervour spread to Britain, and sympathizers such as the chemist Joseph Priestley had to flee when their homes were gutted by furious mobs, John Hunter spent his evenings dictating blasphemous views that could potentially shake the world. For although he would never use the term 'evolution', he now set out to make plain that he believed all animals, including humans, were descended from common ancestors.

John Hunter was not the first to express controversial ideas about the origins of life, and he would certainly not be the last. But to challenge the traditional biblical story, that God had created the earth and all life over a period of six days, was still highly contentious towards the end of the eighteenth century, and would remain so for some time to come.[46] Many in Georgian society still accepted unquestioningly the precise calculation by James Ussher, the seventeenth-century Archbishop of Armagh, that the world had been created on the morning of 23 October 4004 BC. This prevailing doctrine denied the possibility of any significant time lapse between the creation of the earth and the appearance of human beings; it also supposed that all life had been formed in a state of perfection – no creatures had since changed or died out. Where contradictory evidence to this doctrine turned up, such as the discovery of bones belonging to animals that no longer appeared to exist, or fossils of marine creatures found on mountain tops, often convoluted theories were proposed to suit the traditional orthodoxy. The remains of unknown animals simply meant the creatures had not yet been discovered, while evidence of sea life in high places had been deposited there during Noah's flood. Such a fixed and hierarchical order was often expressed as the 'chain of being' – an idea developed in Ancient Greece but still widely supported in the eighteenth century – which imagined a single ladder leading neatly upwards from rocks, through plants, to the simplest animals and ultimately to humans.

Naturally there were notable rebels who wrestled with this religious straitjacket. In the seventeenth century, Robert Hooke, the eccentric stalwart of the fledgling Royal Society, had raised doubts that a single flood could have caused all the earth's diverse features or that the world could have existed for only six thousand years. Only a long period of continual change by natural forces – earthquakes, volcanoes and sea erosion – could have wrought such forms, he argued, while he maintained that fossils were the impressions of living organisms some of which had become extinct.[47] But Hooke's was an isolated voice. His contemporary, the naturalist John Ray, agreed that fossils bore images of living creatures, but he could not accept that the divine creator could have allowed any species to die out.

The pattern – lone mavericks contesting predominant theological opinion – was set. Although the spirit of scientific scrutiny fostered by the Enlightenment opened the door to further questions about the biblical world-view, there was no straight road of progress towards explaining the story of life on earth. Those daring to query the accepted ideology remained firmly on the fringes of intellectual society. Thus James Burnett, the Scottish judge known as Lord Monboddo, was mercilessly ridiculed for suggesting in 1774 that orang-utans were members of the human species. Boswell mischievously repeated Dr Johnson's jest about the judge's fondness for his tail in *The Journal of a Tour to the Hebrides*.[48] Another Scot, the pioneer geologist James Hutton, found himself the butt of society's scorn when he concluded that the earth had been formed over a vast period of time, through a gradual process of climate change, terrestrial movement and water erosion – just as Hooke had earlier proclaimed. Yet even while denying the biblical account of Creation and the Flood in his theories, presented to fellow members of the Royal Society of Edinburgh in 1785 and published in the society's transactions three years later, Hutton still insisted on God's role as a divine designer.[49]

On the Continent, the origins of the earth and humanity were just as hotly debated. Carl Linnaeus, the Swedish botanist who had developed the system of classifying plants and animals in the middle of the century, had gradually reformed his view that all species were fixed. Having grouped together similar species into what he termed a genus, he had come to believe that new species might occasionally be produced by interbreeding; perhaps God, for he was still in overall command, had simply created the head of each genus, which then produced local varieties – effectively new species. He even toyed with placing humans in the same genus as chimpanzees, but drew back for fear of outraging religious authorities.[50]

The Dutch anatomist Camper, an early visitor to Hunter's museum, had likewise been absorbed by the similarities between apes and humans. After dissecting several orang-utans, he concluded in treatises published in 1779 and 1782 that they displayed fundamental differences from humans, particularly an inability to form speech. But Camper took this research further, comparing monkeys' skulls with those of different ethnic groups to invent a cataloguing system of facial lines and angles by measuring the slant of the nose and forehead. Like Hunter, Camper ranked his skulls in a hierarchy ranging from monkey through African to European, although he insisted on a distinct gap between humans and animals. His conclusions had just been published, two years after his death, in 1791.[51] Skull comparisons were a pre-occupation too for Blumenbach, the physician who was another sightseer at Hunter's museum. Having accumulated an unparalleled collection of skulls from different ethnic groups, in the 1770s he proposed a hierarchy of human 'varieties', descending from the Caucasian down to the Ethiopian. According to Blumenbach, there had been a degeneration since the first humans, who had originated near the Caucasus mountains, as they migrated over time.[52] Yet even though the French polymath Pierre Louis de Maupertuis had proposed as far back as 1745 that life-forms had changed over time and that similar species shared common ancestors, both Blumenbach and Camper stuck resolutely to the idea of fixed, unchangeable species.

Taking a distinctly more daring view was the pre-eminent French naturalist Buffon, who like Hunter had accumulated a large collection of comparative anatomy and had developed some equally uncomfortable theories from his observations. Buffon had already enraged theological opinion by suggesting in 1749 that the earth was seventy-five thousand years old – a staggering increase on the orthodox six thousand years, if still considerably short of today's best estimate of about 4.5 billion years. After being censured by religious authorities, Buffon had recanted his heresy and instead proposed that the earth had developed over seven lengthy epochs, which correlated conveniently with the biblical days of creation.[53] But he remained undaunted, and in the 1760s and 1770s began to argue, as Maupertuis had done, that similar species shared common ancestors. Perversely, he stuck doggedly to the idea that species were fixed in form, suggesting that the different animals inhabiting the earth were varieties rather than species, all descended from thirty-eight original ancestors, akin to Linnaeus's genera. While still a long way from explaining how these different animals had emerged, Buffon's idea of a process of divergence – an original cat ancestor bringing forth lions, tigers and domestic cats, for example – represented a radical new approach, one that was still heavily resisted by theological interests as well as fellow naturalists.

Others, in Britain and in mainland Europe, were struggling with the same questions. Erasmus Darwin, who had attended the Hunter brothers' school back in 1753 and was now settled as a medical practitioner in Derby, was developing his views on the origins of life, unusually, in verse. His first poetic efforts had been published in 1789, although his theory that all life developed from a single ancestor – 'one living filament' – would only clearly be outlined in his two-volume work *Zoonomia*, in 1794 and 1796.[54] Likewise in France, the naturalist Jean Baptiste Pierre Antoine de Monet de Lamarck was studying the same issues; again it would be several more years before he published his similar belief in a primitive common ancestor, initially in 1802 and more fully in 1815.[55]

In 1792, therefore, as John Hunter prepared to outline his own views on such contentious issues, there had been isolated assaults on orthodox opinion but there was still no notion of a single common ancestor, no consensus that living beings had changed over time, and certainly no idea of how such a process might occur. Society in the main held firm to the biblical version of Creation and the Flood; any divergence from this view was regarded as blasphemous. Even the young Charles Darwin still adhered to this version when he set out on the *Beagle* in 1831; after his own faith had waned, his theories would be furiously attacked for their heretical stance throughout the nineteenth century.[56]

The extent to which Hunter was influenced by his contemporaries when considering the development of living beings, and in turn how he influenced others, is hard to discern. Although he always stressed his indifference to the written views of others, he did possess a reasonably sized library, containing works on natural history, geography, geology and natural philosophy, as well as anatomy and surgery.[57] On his bookshelves stood the voluminous works of Buffon and Linnaeus, as well as the *Transactions of the Royal Society of Edinburgh*, in which Hutton had just published his geological theories. Yet it was never Hunter's style to adopt the opinions of others without his own rigorous explorations. Moreover, the beliefs encapsulated in his museum, and those he now put down on paper, had been developed over a lifetime's inquiry.

From his earliest years, of course, Hunter had devoted his time to unravelling the puzzle of life on earth. His early investigations of embryo chicks had convinced him that new life developed from simple forms into more complex. Ranging over every animal species he could obtain, he had acutely observed the subtle variations in structure from the most simple life-forms to the most complicated, while noting how different creatures were best fitted to their particular environments. Always he had stressed the fundamental relationship between all living things; his lectures had progressed from considering inorganic material to plant life, animals and ultimately humans. And he evidently regarded humans as closely related to apes, judging from his opening-day address at the museum as well as comments he made to the poet and philosopher James Beattie when he visited in 1773, a full year before Lord Monboddo's shocking assertion. 'He is of opinion,' noted Beattie, 'that the Negroes are removed from us one degree in the scale of animals, and approach towards the monkey'.[58] That Hunter believed life-forms had changed over time – another heretical belief – was also clear. His investigation of the mastodon bones from Ohio, which he concluded belonged to an extinct relative of elephants, and his avid collection of fossils, in which he paired his trophies with 'the resent', demonstrated his fascination with how living beings had developed.

The process by which life-forms could change was also a vital question for him. He had been preoccupied with deviations from the norm and variations within species since the late 1770s. Writing on freemartins in 1779, he had argued that not only every species but every part in every species had a propensity to deviate from the norm.[59] In his article on pheasants the following year he had concluded that such deviations existed in an original, congenital form, remarking that 'each part of each species seems to have its monstrous form originally impressed upon it'.[60] He had even, of course, put forward the startling suggestion that animals with separate male and female genders might originally have developed from the accidental occurrence of a natural hermaphrodite with two distinct sexual organs.[61] This bold assertion makes plain that as far back as 1779 Hunter had abandoned the notion of a static, unchanging ladder of creation; he clearly believed that species were mutable and capable of developing into others. He was aware, too, from his connections with animal breeders, that variations in eye colour could become permanent 'with respect to the propagation of the animal, becoming so far a part of its nature, as to be continued in the offspring'.[62]

By the late 1780s Hunter had developed a fervent interest in artificial breeding – not only a vibrant eighteenth-century industry but a graphic demonstration of the way in which variations and deviations are passed down. As well as attempting to breed rare animals, including opossums, at Earls Court, he had tried to crossbreed different species; at one point he successfully mated one of his cows with a buffalo belonging to the late Marquis of Rockingham.[63] This interest had first been sparked by the wolf-dog hybrid he had owned as a young man; nearly thirty years later he was still enthralled by the notion of interbreeding dogs and wolves, only now it was not so much experimental curiosity as an attempt to pinpoint whether the wolf and dog belonged, in his words, to the same species.[64]

In the intervening years there had been several successful efforts by menagerie owners to mate dogs and wolves. In 1785, Hunter had been promised a puppy bred from a she-wolf and a male greyhound by the animal dealer Gough; to his chagrin a leopard in Gough's menagerie killed Hunter's pup along with two others. Two years later Hunter was more fortunate, obtaining a female puppy bred from the same wolf and another dog. Now attempting himself to mate his wolf hybrid with a dog, he pressed his friend Banks to procure testimonies from aristocrat acquaintances who had achieved the same end. In the meantime, Hunter had obtained a puppy born of a female jackal which had mated with a spaniel dog on a ship returning from the East Indies in 1786. He took his trophy to Earls Court where it mated with a terrier;

Hunter was like the delighted father when the jackal hybrid produced five puppies that November. One of its offspring was sent to Jenner, who wrote back, 'The little jackal-bitch you gave me is grown a fine handsome animal; but she certainly does not possess the understanding of common dogs. She is easily lost when I take her out, and is quite inattentive to a whistle.'[65]

Hunter's observations on interbreeding, published in a paper to the Royal Society in 1787, had led him to conclude that the wolf, dog, fox and jackal were indeed the same species. He based this assertion on the grounds that as well as sharing outward appearances, they could mate and produce offspring – a definition of species still commonly applied – although he overlooked the fact that most of the females had to be coerced or restrained in order to mate. Buffon, Hunter knew, had attempted the same trial – without success – in order to test his theory that wolves and dogs were only varieties of one species, related through a common ancestor. Hunter had plainly come to the same opinion, remarking, 'Here then being an absolute proof of the jackal being a dog, and the wolf being equally made out to be of the same species, it now therefore becomes a question whether the wolf is from the jackal, or the jackal from the wolf (supposing them but one origin)?' The fact that he suggested, like Buffon, that the animals were different varieties rather than species mattered little; what was significant was an appreciation that similar life-forms were descended from a common ancestor – 'one origin' – and had changed, considerably, over time. He shared too Buffon's belief that the different animals had migrated from an original population, in this case from the wolf, and had changed according to environmental and climatic conditions. Unequivocally outlining his belief that similar animals shared a common ancestor, Hunter proclaimed, 'To ascertain the original animal of a species, all the varieties of that species should be examined, to see how far they have the character of the genus, and what resemblance they bear to the other species of the genus.'

Within Europe, only Buffon had dared to venture such heretical views; within Britain, nobody had yet gone so far in challenging religious orthodoxy. Despite the very real risk that he could be condemned as a heretic, Hunter now determined to put into print his controversial theories. In particular, he began work on two documents speculating on the nature of fossils, while at the same time compiling a plethora of essays and notes which ranged over the entire animal kingdom.

Given his lengthy study and large collection of fossils, Hunter was the obvious person to be consulted when a hoard of fossilized bones was unearthed in a cave in Germany and sent for examination to the Royal Society in the early 1790s; he duly prepared a paper on his conclusions.[66] Studying the fossil bones, he found them curiously similar to those of a polar bear he possessed, yet almost twice the size, with the teeth in similar proportion. He concluded, as he had with the earlier mastodon bones, that the bones belonged to extinct animals akin to their modern-day counterparts. And he made plain that the process by which such life-forms had changed required 'a vast series of years'; indeed he repeated the phrase 'many thousand years' several times. Though this careful terminology might just fit the orthodox estimate of the age of the earth, Hunter cast doubt on the story of the deluge. The remains of marine animals buried under several strata of rock indicated that the sea must have invaded the land many times, he declared, and remained there, he repeated again, for 'thousands of years'.

If Hunter restrained his wildest calculations in the paper for the Royal Society, he felt no such constraints in the treatise he simultaneously produced to describe his own fossil collection.[67] In the slim two-part work, Hunter plainly allied himself with Hutton's uniformitarian theory – which he may well have read – which held that geological features had been formed by the same progressive forces seen in modern times acting over a vast period. Although Hunter's pioneering contributions to geology would never be fully recognized, he gave an expert explanation of the formation of the earth's key features, describing how rock strata had formed, how fossils had been made, and how the sea had produced gradual changes through erosion and deposition. He even speculated that the Thames valley had once been an arm of the 'German Ocean' – the North Sea – which had covered much of the Low Countries too. Having arranged each fossil in his collection alongside a portion of the rock strata in which it was found, Hunter observed that the same fossils were always discovered in the same strata, nearly two decades before William Smith, later dubbed 'the father of British geology', described rock sequences from fossil samples. Most contentiously, Hunter took these assertions to their logical conclusion and denounced the biblical version of the Flood, proclaiming that 'Forty days' water overflowing the dry land could not have brought such quantities of sea-productions on its surface'.[68] Supposing that the sea had changed places with the land on several occasions, he remarked, 'What number of thousand of years this would take, or how often this has happened, I will not pretend to say'.[69] But very little deterred John Hunter from speaking his mind. When speculating how long certain fossils might have existed in any singular state, he boldly proclaimed that 'many retain their form for many thousand centuries'.

Such a blunt denial of religious orthodoxy was too much for Hunter's Royal Society friends. In France, Buffon had been forced by the Church to recant a similar view on the age of the earth; even in 1823 William Buckland would attempt to 'prove' the veracity of the deluge. For Hunter to undermine the authority of the Church at a time when revolutionary fever threatened the country was unthinkable. Certainly that was the staunch reaction of Major James Rennell, a distinguished geographer and RS fellow, who had been asked, either by Hunter or by stalwarts of the society, to peruse the treatise. Writing to Hunter, after reading his document 'three times', Rennell urged him to change his timescale from 'many thousand centuries' to 'many thousand years'. Rennell himself had 'no quarrel with any opinions relating to the antiquity of the Globe', he insisted, yet he warned, 'there are a description of persons, very numerous and very respectable in every point but their pardonable superstitions, who will dislike any mention of a specific period that ascends beyond 6,000 years'. Evidently, while members of the Royal Society might entertain their doubts about the biblical story in the exalted seclusion of their cosy meetings, such heretical thoughts must not be aired in the public domain, especially at a time of social upheaval, as Rennell made plain. Questioning Hunter's denial of the Flood and emphasizing his concerns by underlining kcy phrases, Rennell insisted, 'again in page 8 you have rather questioned the Knowledge of a <u>Certain Person</u> [Moses];

that also is tender ground with some people, and at <u>this time</u> we must not let the Vulgar know how far we believe in the Books of Moses.'[70]

Whether or not Hunter bowed to Rennell's concerns is unclear. The fact that two surviving manuscripts, both versions of the same document, refer to 'thousands of years' rather than 'centuries' suggests that he did amend his treatise.[71] According to Home, not always a reliable commentator but working at Hunter's side at the time, Hunter refused to modify his comments and angrily withdrew the paper. Either way, Rennell's intervention effectively suppressed Hunter's unorthodox views – on the age of the earth and the deluge at least. The Royal Society never published the treatise and it would gather dust for almost seventy years before the Royal College of Surgeons finally hurried it into print, just a month after Darwin's *The Origin of Species* was published, at the end of 1859.

Even had he been induced to amend or withdraw his written views on fossils to suit the Royal Society's pious misgivings, there was no way Hunter could be persuaded to reform his radical beliefs. In voluminous notes and essays he furiously dictated, each evening he set out his controversial theories in all their full, unrepentant glory. Ranging over natural history, geology, fossils and anatomy, Hunter finally sought to lay down the overarching principles he believed governed all life on earth. Whether or not Hunter intended to publish these daring ideas is unclear, although given his disregard for convention it seems likely. Ultimately, they would be published in two lengthy volumes, entitled *Essays and Observations on Natural History, Anatomy, Physiology, Psychology and Geology*, more than sixty years later. Together they expounded the conclusions of a lifetime's research while classifying the thousands of animals Hunter had studied into families of related species.

Unequivocally, in these assorted notes Hunter outlined his views on the origins of life. First he made tacit acknowledgement of the biblical story of the Creation and the Flood; then he proceeded to demolish its veracity step by step. Beyond this perfunctory denial of the accepted ideology he would make no further reference to God, the Bible or any divine mode of creation. It is unlikely that Hunter saw himself as a crusading atheist, like his erstwhile patient David Hume, but he certainly displayed the opinions of a materialist, rejecting a divine plan of the world in line with his contemporary Erasmus Darwin. Although Hunter conformed to Church rituals – he had grudgingly consented to be godparent to Jenner's first son in 1789 with the comment, 'Rather than the brat should not be a christian I will stand Godfather' – he had of course declared that any belief system depending on faith rather than fact demonstrated 'a weakness of mind'.[72] Some of his disciples would later seek to downplay his irreligious beliefs.

Certainly Hunter was not held back by religious sensibilities, as Darwin would be. In the notes later published as *Essays and Observations*, he insisted not only that the earth was immensely old, but that its life-forms had changed substantially. This process of alteration had been so profound, producing so many variations in species, Hunter declared, that 'it becomes a doubt whether they were all original, or whether any one of them are original, or none of them; or, if any one be original, which that one is'.[73] He made plain too that he believed similar species had descended from common ancestors, asserting, 'To attempt to trace any natural production to its origin, or its

Hunter is shown in customary philosopher's pose, surrounded by symbols of his skill and knowledge – as well as a glimpse of the Irish giant's feet – in Sir Joshua Reynolds's portrait exhibited in the Royal Academy summer exhibition of 1786. His pocket set of knives (*below*) is preserved in the Hunterian Museum.

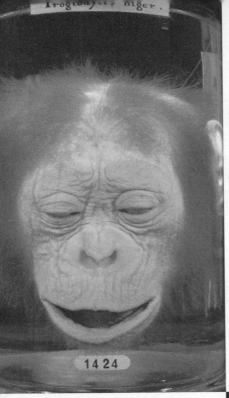

Troglodytes niger.

1424

Lacerta

2222

Hunter collected and preserved all kinds of animal and human specimens in his lifelong mission to understand the basic principles of organic life.

(*Clockwise from left*) A baby crocodile emerging from its egg with its umbilical cord still attached; the head of a chimpanzee caught in Sierra Leone in 1792 and shipped back for Hunter's collection; a double-tailed lizard, captured while Hunter was serving with the army on Belle-Ile; a coil of dried human intestine with its arteries injected.

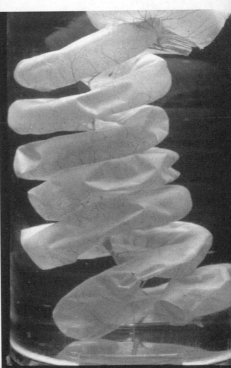

Hunter's country retreat at Earls Court provided the perfect environment for studying animals, both dead and alive. This watercolour, from Jessé Foot's malicious *The Life of John Hunter*, depicts wild beasts cropping the lawns, the den (underneath the central mound) which housed Hunter's leopards and lions, beehives for his beloved bees, and – improbably – a giraffe. Hunter also had lightning conductors, invented by his friend Benjamin Franklin, installed on the chimneys.

Studying freemartins, or hermaphrodite cattle, led Hunter to expound daring theories on the way in which species can deviate from the norm.

This study of a rhinoceros, probably an animal named 'Clara' which was touring England in the 1790s, was one of several Hunter commissioned from George Stubbs.

Brought back as a carcass from Captain Cook's first expedition to Australia, this kangaroo was the first to be seen in Britain. Hunter was given its skull.

This giraffe, or 'camelopard', was shipped from Africa after being shot in 1779 and donated to Hunter. Its legs were removed to fit his hallway. He is believed to have sketched this image himself.

(*Left to right*) From Jekyll to Hyde: John Hunter, the revered surgeon, by Sir Nathaniel Dance Holland, 1793; his wife, Anne Hunter, in later life; Hunter the eccentric maverick, with beard intact in the Reynolds portrait his wife rejected.

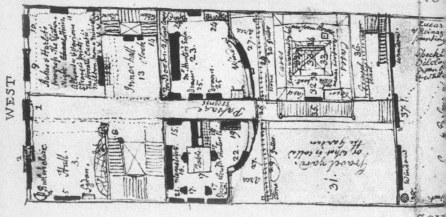

(*Above*) Ground plan of John Hunter's house in Leicester Square, which is believed to have provided the setting for the story of Dr Jekyll and Mr Hyde, based on the plan drawn from memory and annotated by William Clift in 1832. Clift's plan shows the elegant number 28, on the left – where patients queued for consultations with Hunter and guests arrived for Mrs Hunter's soirées – linked by a conversazione room, lecture theatre and museum to the dingy 13 Castle Street, where students rolled up for lectures and bodies were delivered for dissection.

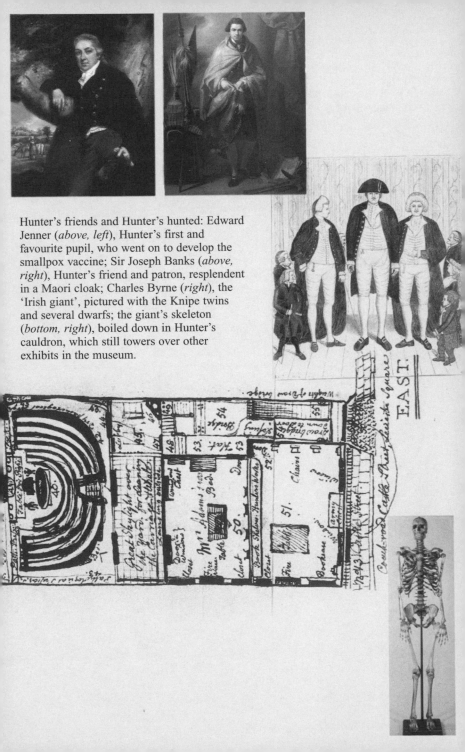

Hunter's friends and Hunter's hunted: Edward Jenner (*above, left*), Hunter's first and favourite pupil, who went on to develop the smallpox vaccine; Sir Joseph Banks (*above, right*), Hunter's friend and patron, resplendent in a Maori cloak; Charles Byrne (*right*), the 'Irish giant', pictured with the Knipe twins and several dwarfs; the giant's skeleton (*bottom, right*), boiled down in Hunter's cauldron, which still towers over other exhibits in the museum.

Hunter's museum (*right*), given to the custody of the Royal College of Surgeons after his death, proved a popular tourist attraction for Victorian gentlemen.

Intense jealousy drove Jessé Foot (*below*), a minor surgeon, to hound Hunter for most of his career. Upon Hunter's death Foot published a vindictive biography of him, funded by Hunter's enemies at St George's.

Although Hunter was aware of Foot's rancour, he never suspected that the ultimate betrayal would be perpetrated by his brother-in-law, Everard Home (*bottom*).

From humble origins and poorly educated, Hunter's last assistant, William Clift, would prove his most devoted disciple.

first production, is ridiculous; for it goes back to that period, if ever such existed, of which we can form no idea, viz. the beginning of time. But, I think, we have reason to suppose there was a period in time in which every species of natural production was the same; there then being no variety in any species.'[74] The suggestion that there had initially been 'no variety' in any species – in other words, only original species existed – pointed to a number of common ancestors, in line with Buffon's view. Yet the possibility that these early beings had first stemmed from a single common ancestor was certainly implied in his remark that 'it will be necessary to go back to the first or common matter of this globe, and give its general properties; then see how far these properties are introduced into the vegetable and animal operations'.[75] He did not hesitate either to suggest that new species had been produced – another heresy – for he remarked that tail-less, or Manx, cats probably first arose 'from a kitten being brought into the world without any tail'.[76] Equally he reiterated his understanding that artificial breeding showed how variations in species were passed down through generations.

Going further, Hunter was unequivocal that all living things were interrelated: 'We may observe that in Natural Things nothing stands alone; that everything in Nature has a relation to or connexion with some other natural production or productions; and that each is composed of parts common to most others but differently arranged.'[77] Unable to resist the logical summation of this fact, he declared that 'Every property in man is similar to some property, either in another animal, or probably in a vegetable, or even in inanimate matter.' This applied most clearly when comparing the early embryo states of humans – 'the most perfect animal' – and other creatures, as Hunter explained:

> If we were capable of following the progress of increase of the number of the parts of the most perfect animal, as they first formed in succession from the very first, to its state of full perfection, we should probably be able to compare it with some one of the incomplete animals themselves, of every order of animals in the creation, being at no stage different from some of those inferior orders. Or in other words, if we were to take a series of animals from the more imperfect to the perfect, we should probably find an imperfect animal corresponding with some stage of the most perfect.[78]

So, more complex animals mirrored the most simple forms in their embryonic stages, Hunter argued. Precisely the same observation, noting the similarities between the embryos of a dog and a human, would help Darwin to appreciate the common ancestry of all life.[79] But if Darwin held back from speculating on the place of humans until his *Descent of Man* in 1871, Hunter had no such qualms. 'The monkey in general may be said to be half beast and half man; it may be said to be the middle stage,' he declared.[80] Only the fact that the ape possessed toes shaped like fingers differentiated the two, he insisted. Most striking of all, Hunter laid out his views on the origins of different species, asking, 'Does not the natural gradation of animals, from one to another, lead to the original species? And does not that mode of investigation gradually lead to the knowledge of that species? Are we not led on to the wolf by the gradual affinity of the different varieties in the dog? Could we not trace out the gradation in the cat, horse, cow, sheep, fowl, etc, in a like manner?'[81]

Plainly Hunter had not taken that crucial extra step and proposed that all life had developed from a single original ancestor, nor worked out the method by which such change happened, but this was still a startling insight. Writing almost seventy years before the publication of *The Origin of Species*, Hunter traversed much of the territory Darwin would later explore to formulate his theory of evolution. Ahead of all his contemporaries, with the possible exception of Buffon, he had appreciated that diverse animals had developed over vast periods of time from common ancestors. And if Hunter's museum was not, as one devotee would later declare, a 'museum of evolution', certainly it displayed in the most graphic way how different life-forms were perfectly fitted to their environments.[82]

John Hunter's most controversial conclusions would never see the light of day in his own lifetime. Just as the Royal Society had successfully kept his radical views on the age of the earth under wraps, so his prescient theories on original species would be concealed from public view by someone he regarded as his ally. Because his far-sighted ideas languished unread for decades, Hunter's contribution to theories of the origins of life would never be recognized. Ironically, when his ideas were finally rediscovered and published in 1861, two years after Darwin's startling revelations shocked society, they were compiled and edited by Richard Owen, the man who had become Darwin's most vehement critic. It was scarcely any wonder that in his preface Owen dolefully remarked, 'Some may wish that the world had never known that Hunter thought so differently on some subjects from what they believed, and would have desired, him to think.'[83]

15

The Anatomist's Heart

'Well . . . there is only one more thing to do, and that is to burn the collection itself.'

William Clift[1]

Castle Street, London, 14 February 1792

To a penniless, orphaned Cornish lad, arriving in London for the first time in the winter of 1792, the clatter of horse-drawn traffic, the splendour of shop windows and the stench from uncollected refuse seemed overwhelming. Stepping over the threshold of 13 Castle Street, even more unlikely sights and smells awaited William Clift. Apprenticed to John Hunter for six years as anatomical assistant, artist and amanuensis, the slight youth was shown to his quarters in the rear house where he unpacked the four shirts and four neck cloths which were all his belongings before being set to work in the museum.[2] It was his seventeenth birthday, the same day as

Hunter's – or at least the day on which Hunter traditionally celebrated his birth – but there would be no
celebrations for Clift: he was too busy 'making little paper
boxes to hold little shells and such things' to party.

Born near Bodmin, the youngest in a large and desperately poor family, Clift briefly attended the village school,
by virtue of his mother almost starving herself, before
being orphaned at the age of eleven. Forced to fend for
himself, he found work in a plant nursery where he
demonstrated his talents for nurturing the blooms and for
drawing. His artistic skills were his undoing, however,
for he was peremptorily sacked after sketching a
mischievous caricature of the owner and was forced to
subsist by running errands, writing signs and finding odd
jobs. Among his regular haunts was the local priory,
where Clift became a favourite with Major Gilbert and his
wife, Nancy. It was the sight of Clift's striking chalk drawings, scratched onto her kitchen floor while he waited for
orders, which inspired Mrs Gilbert to recommend the
'very clever boy' to her childhood friend, Anne Hunter.
Knowing that John Hunter had been fervently seeking an
artist to replace William Bell since he had left in 1789,
Mrs Gilbert proposed young Clift. Expecting the poorly
educated, unsophisticated country youth to pass muster as
an anatomical artist was a gamble, but no more so than
the prospect of a Scottish farm boy rising to become
London's leading surgeon. Hunter agreed to take on Clift,
unseen, for a six-year apprenticeship without fee. The
position would bring no wages but at least Clift could rely
on board, lodging and, crucially, training.

It was a life of drudgery from the first – long hours,
cramped living quarters, no money and little thanks. But
after taking in his new surroundings – the peculiar

two-fronted house, the curious museum, the effervescent household of family, pupils and servants – young Clift was exhilarated. Sharp and perceptive for all his foreshortened education, he relayed his first impressions in excited letters to his siblings in Cornwall. 'We have a great family indeed', he wrote, listing the huge retinue of kitchen staff, maids, footmen and coach drivers squeezed into the two houses, along with the four house pupils and members of the family. Although John Banks Hunter, nearly twenty now, was away studying medicine at Cambridge, planning to follow in his father's footsteps, sixteen-year-old Agnes still lived at home, attracting suitors at her mother's musical evenings. In all, Clift reckoned there were never fewer than fifty people, including the staff running the house and farm at Earls Court and the regular workmen in both establishments, all dependent on Hunter's employment.[3] With the Leicester Square basement occupied by two coaches, one each for Mr and Mrs Hunter, and stabling for six horses, it made for a cramped existence. But after being shown the city sights by Robert Haynes, the dissecting-room attendant – even spotting the royal family promenading in St James's Park – Clift gushed, 'I like London very well.'

The chaotic city streets were enthralling; the shops selling 'ready made' clothes amazing; the glimpse of George III and the royal princesses astonishing. But most of all Clift was captivated by his new boss. At sixty-four, a stout figure with curling, white hair springing from either side of his face, Hunter had been laid low with another bout of angina – the spasms were increasingly common now. It was several days before he could meet his newest recruit. When he did, it was a moment Clift would remember all his life. 'He is a verry curious man,' he wrote to tell his sisters, 'and plain as well for he has hair as white as snow and has never got it drest, I think there is not a bit of Pride in him and all his clothes so plain (But very rich) and I am sure you would not think he was such a Grand Gentleman'.[4] Grand gentleman or not, Hunter treated his youngest, lowliest assistant with the same civility as his wealthiest patients. His master was 'mild and kind in his manner', Clift told his sister, and 'spoke as kindly and familiarly to his gardener or myself as to his equals or superiors'.[5] Like the assistants who had gone before and the pupils who still flocked around, Clift was smitten. The honest but steely Cornish lad would become Hunter's most devoted disciple.

If Hunter's health was failing, his energy was not. Every morning at six Clift met his master in the Castle Street dissecting room; Hunter would already be stooped over his bench examining minute creatures through a pair of spectacles modified to provide lenses of different magnifications. While Clift painstakingly learned the skills of dissecting, making preparations and illustrating his efforts, his boss would 'stand for hours motionless as a statue, except that with a pair of forceps in either hand he was picking asunder the connecting fibres of the vessels or parts, till he had unravelled the whole structure'.[6] Finding his teacher 'generally, though cheerfully, taciturn', several hours might pass without exchanging a word. At other times, slowly stretching and standing upright, Hunter would relax and entertain Clift with a 'shrewd and witty' remark.

Among Clift's first tasks was to help unpack and catalogue a treasure trove of antipodean species donated by Banks; his own house overflowing, the Royal Society president had split his animal collection between Hunter and the British Museum.[7] More building work was required to house the additional hoard: Hunter had a wall removed from the first floor in Castle Street to accommodate Banks's donation in its entirety. Not having had the benefit of Hunter's expert preservation techniques, however, many of the specimens were in poor condition. A black swan had rotted so much that Hunter decided it not worth stuffing; he gave the bird to Clift as a first exercise in preparation-making.

When Hunter reluctantly abandoned his dissecting bench to attend his patients, Clift was kept employed with errands and jobs in the museum. There were drawing classes too. Hunter initially enrolled Clift with a tutor at one of the local art schools but soon afterwards took in a French refugee, Monsieur St Aubin, who taught Clift at the house. The youth's artistic talents were quickly recognized; after Clift sketched an exotic bird from the collection, Hunter said 'he was in hopes I should do very well in a little time'.[8] After dinner at 4 p.m., when the entire household ate together, there was scant time for leisure. Each evening, except for Sunday, Clift sat with Hunter in his study copying out notes and taking dictation from eight until midnight.

It might be the end of a busy day but it was still a period of intense industry. As well as making clear copies from Hunter's scrawled notes of experiments, dissections, cases and autopsies, Clift took letters in dictation, replying to Hunter's friends, ex-pupils and acquaintances across the world, offering medical advice and begging specimens in return. By Clift's estimate Hunter received no fewer than three or four thousand letters in a year. Hunter tore strips from their edges as spare paper on which to scribble memos and Clift would copy these for inclusion in the correct places in the catalogues and other volumes. The discarded notes were used as spills to light candles or sent to the dissecting room as waste paper to mop up blood.[9] Clift was quick to observe how scrupulously Hunter looked after his manuscripts, updating the different volumes meticulously as new information came to light, whether on a particular disease or an interesting insect. 'Mr Hunter kept an account of the dissection of all animals that came under his inspection,' Clift noted, 'and whenever he re-examined any animal, he overlooked his previous account, corrected and added to it.'[10] Letters from favourite pupils such as Jenner and Physick were carefully preserved too and sometimes brought out to check over observations they had sent.

On Wednesday evenings, when the upper floors vibrated to the strains of Mrs Hunter's parties, Hunter would leave his studies briefly to put in an appearance and 'shake their mutual friends by the hand' before resuming his relentless work.[11] When Clift was finally released for the night, he left Hunter still engrossed in his papers. 'I never could understand how Mr Hunter obtained rest,' Clift mused; 'when I left him at midnight, it was with a lamp fresh trimmed for further study, and with the usual appointment to meet him again at six in the morning.'[12] As Hunter burned the midnight oil, Clift fumbled back to the Castle Street house in darkness – candles were too expensive and too risky to trust to a mere apprentice – feeling his way 'through the dead bones'.[13]

If Clift's day was closely structured, life in Hunter's household was anything but routine. On Sundays, which Hunter usually spent at Earls Court, Clift often went along; sometimes he was corralled into helping the farm staff catch insects. The tiniest, simplest forms of life were as much a fascination for Hunter as ever. On another occasion, in dramatic contrast, a young whale was caught in the Thames and transported to the basement dissecting room at Earls Court. Clift walked the pleasant two miles to the village every day for a week so he could help strip the blubber from the bones, accompanying Hunter back to London every evening in his carriage.

Hunter was spending more and more time at his country retreat, almost returning to his rural roots. He liked to sleep at Earls Court whenever he could, travelling to town for patients and pupils then returning every evening to potter in the orchards, hothouses and conservatory. Among his botanical experiments he was investigating the movement of plants, measuring how far the leaves of sensitive plants could unbend and planting beans in rotating baskets to check whether they would still grow upwards.[14] But his chief delight was still to watch his beloved bees humming in and out of their observation hives in the conservatory. He delivered the fruits of twenty years' study of bees in a paper to the Royal Society a week after Clift's arrival. Minutely describing their anatomy, even to the length of their tongues, Hunter outlined their intricately organized society, described their peculiar dance, explained their methods of generation, and even concluded, much to the incredulity of his contemporaries, that bees made the wax found in their hives. 'The wax is formed by the bees themselves,' he boldly asserted; 'it may be called an external secretion of oil, and I have found that it is formed between each scale of the under side of the belly.'[15]

New additions to the menagerie continued to arrive. Clift noted that Hunter maintained a 'large number of animals both tame and wild' not only at Earls Court but even at Leicester Square; some were presents, but many were 'considerably expensive purchases'.[16] The debts continued to mount. One animal, which seemed to be far from tame, was Hunter's favourite dog. Described as a Dane with smooth, bay-coloured fur by Clift, it may feasibly have been one of Hunter's crossbreeds; certainly he called it 'Lion', though whether for its size and wild nature or some other attribute, was unclear. And although Lion was Hunter's devoted 'playfellow and companion' he was obedient to nobody but his master. 'He was gentle as a Lamb,' remarked Clift, 'but alarmed every Stranger as he passed, by his great height and size, and romping disposition, when let loose.' Whenever he was let loose, Lion almost invariably broke a window with his wagging tail at his delight in being free; if any of the students took him off his chain Hunter made them pay for the ensuing glazier's bill. And if they tried to take him for a walk, Lion inevitably eloped and returned 'always without his Collar'.[17]

Almost as alarming for the villagers as seeing the unchained Lion loping towards them was the sight of Hunter himself driving off to town in a cart pulled by three Asian buffaloes, or zebus. For Londoners, the sight of their most senior surgeon, royally appointed to George III and head of the army's surgical services, clutching the reins of the three beasts with their huge curling horns as they ambled through the hectic streets was bizarre even by the city's eccentric standards. As far as Foot was concerned, Hunter's excursions by buffalo were just another example of his unseemly flamboyance, no less an advertisement than the 'showman's Dromedary' paraded through town.[18]

Certainly the zebus were a regular sight. According to Clift, they left Earls Court every Wednesday pulling a cart loaded with fruit and vegetables for the Leicester Square table and were usually led by one of the farm labourers. After the produce was unloaded in Castle Street, the cart was filled with manure from the underground stables and waste material from the dissecting room; both were used to fertilize the farm – nothing in Hunter's regime was wasted. On one Wednesday, however, the cart was driven to town by a simple-minded farmhand known as 'Scotch Willie'.[19] After lugging the usual hamper full of rotting flesh and bones down from the attic dissecting room, Willie led the buffaloes into the stables and repaired to the kitchen for 'beef and beer', leaving the foul-smelling basket uncovered in the cart outside. Before long some schoolboys spotted the load and, knowing it usually contained apples from the farm, jumped into the cart to investigate. Their disappointment was only matched by their horror. Clift recalled, 'The first object that struck their attention, instead of the Apples they expected, was the Putrid half dissected arms of a Man, green blue and yellow; – Livers, intestines and other parts'.

The boys' exclamations quickly drew a crowd, which grew bigger and more unruly as aghast passers-by took turns to view the contents of the cart. For many the grisly sight simply confirmed their suspicions about the notorious anatomist; the all too plain evidence of his nocturnal raids soon threatened to turn the curious crowd into a violent mob. At last the commotion reached Clift's ears in the house and he hurriedly summoned the house pupils, obliviously cutting up bodies in their blood-daubed aprons, to come down from the attic and help. Scotch Willie was likewise dragged from his lunch to fetch the buffaloes and attempt to harness them in order to steer away the cart. But by now the 'haloo-balloo' had grown so intense, and the beasts were becoming so agitated, that all that could be done was to shove the cart with its guilty load down the ramp to the basement and quickly batten the doors.

With the buffaloes trapped outside and the pupils barricaded behind the doors against the baying mob, a hairdresser in his white jacket and apron who had been lured out of his salon by the noise decided to make himself the hero of the hour. Egged on by the crowd, he stepped forward with his shears and cut one of the zebus free, only to find that it immediately turned on him and pinned him to the coach-house doors between its horns. As mob fury now turned to playhouse farce, the spectators whooped with delight when the buffalo charged for freedom, running down neighbouring Green Street and into Leicester Square, where it cantered around the genteel quadrangle with the luckless hairdresser 'holding on at the end of the long halter'. It was evening before the crowds had dispersed and the cart could be led discreetly from its subterranean hideaway in the dark. It was sent back to Earls Court, for once minus its haul of flesh.

With wild animals still a familiar sight on London streets, with or without Hunter's zebus, fear of catching rabies from feral dogs was a real concern. One day soon after Clift's arrival, two of Hunter's well-connected clients, Lord and Lady Erskine, knocked in panic at the Leicester Square door after being bitten by their pet dog in their carriage. Despite the fact that their pet was unlikely to harbour the deadly disease, Hunter dropped his work to deal with the emergency, smartly cutting away the flesh around their wounds – the usual remedy when rabies was suspected. The entire household, Clift recorded, could hear his lordship 'squeal out like a pig', while his wife 'did not utter a cry'. Both recovered from their ordeal with their pet pooch without ill effects.[20]

There seemed little hope, however, of saving Hunter's friend and neighbour Sir Joshua Reynolds, whose health was declining rapidly in early 1792. Reynolds had lost the sight in his left eye in 1789, three years after completing his portrait of Hunter. Having all but given up painting, the normally gregarious artist had become increasingly dejected and weak; by the end of 1791 the man whose dinners had been famed throughout London could scarcely bring himself to eat. With no outward reason for his degeneration, the physicians dismissed his condition as hypochondria. Only when his illness reached a crisis in early February 1792 did they realize that Reynolds' liver was unusually swollen. By then it was too late, even if they could have offered him any relief, and on 23 February Reynolds died.

The following day, Hunter crossed the square to perform the autopsy on his old friend. After opening the body, he found that Reynolds' liver was more than twice its normal size, its texture hard and fibrous, its colour strangely yellow. Most probably, although Hunter could not have realized it, Reynolds had died of cancer which had spread from his eye to his liver.[21] When Reynolds' funeral took place a week later in St Paul's, Hunter was asked to be one of the pallbearers but he reputedly refused, apparently lashing out that he 'wished Reynolds and his friends would go to the devil'.[22] In fact, Hunter was among the mourners at the ceremony, although quite possibly he declined to shoulder the coffin knowing it would have triggered another of his spasms.[23] Clift watched the funeral procession of forty-two carriages packed with mourners and forty-nine empty coaches signifying the respect of the nobility as it wound its way through the city just two weeks after his arrival in the capital. It was then, he recorded, 'the finest sight ever I saw in my life'.[24]

Another encounter that took place soon after Clift moved into Leicester Square, and one which would also reverberate all his life, was his first meeting with Everard Home. Strutting about the house as if he owned the place, and by now he almost felt as if he did, Home bumped into the new apprentice. Taking him for a naive country boy with a head full of superstitions, Home leered at him and asked if he was afraid of ghosts. 'I don't know, sir, I never saw one,' was Clift's logical reply. 'But I was never afraid of my school-fellows,' he added, 'though bigger boys than me.' It was a warning Home would fail to heed.

At the age of thirty-six, still living in his sister's house and still dependent on his brother-in-law's goodwill, Home was desperate to make a mark for himself. With his luxuriant, curling blond hair, thick sensual lips and large, doleful eyes, he cut a handsome figure striding in and out of Leicester Square, and he knew it: he revelled in fine clothes and preened himself in front of the students.[25] He was planning to marry the daughter of a vicar, a widow, later in the year, but ensuring a secure financial future remained elusive. Ever since moving back into the Hunter household in 1784, Home had worked hard to render himself indispensable to his former teacher. Talented and respected pupils had come and gone, some of them offered partnerships that they declined, but Home remained, clinging firmly to his position at the centre of Hunter's livelihood, biding his time. Having helped arrange

Hunter's celebrated collection, he had taken over much of the surgeon's routine work at St George's, inherited several of his wealthy clients, and since 1790 delivered most of the lectures each winter. When younger and cleverer surgeons such as the American Philip Syng Physick won Hunter's warmest praises, Home had to bite his tongue; when ex-students such as Astley Cooper, John Abernethy and Henry Cline – all now secure in their own hospital positions – clustered around Hunter's dinner table, idolizing their former tutor, Home kept his own counsel. Whether it was simply his constant proximity to Hunter or the growing strain of angina, which dealt Hunter painful spasms at the slightest exertion or annoyance, it seemed to Home at least that he bore the brunt of the ageing surgeon's bad temper. His brother-in-law 'spoke too freely' and 'sometimes too harshly to his contemporaries', Home would later complain, while his temper was 'readily provoked'.[26] Oddly, it appeared that Hunter's temper was rarely provoked by his other ex-pupils, who would remember their mentor's demeanour as 'extremely companionable', or by his assistants, such as Clift, who appreciated his boss's even-handed, generous nature. All the same, Home stayed put, ensuring that Hunter depended on him more and more for day-to-day support. Having delivered Hunter's lectures for two seasons, he had grown certain that he could match the acclaimed teacher and surgeon. Ambitious and vain, he was even beginning to believe that he could outshine his former master.

In spring 1792, Home's chance arrived when the post of senior surgeon became vacant at St George's. Having worked at the hospital as Hunter's assistant for five years, Home firmly believed the job should be his, assuring him a regular private clientele and a secure future. But he had not reckoned with the St George's medical mafia. More than twenty years of skirmishes and snubs had fermented into a seething, poisonous resentment directed against Hunter. All Hunter's acclaim within London society, his esteem in the scientific community and his popularity among the city's medical students counted for nothing with his fellow surgeons at St George's, who still clung to their antiquated practices and hierarchical education system. So when Hunter put forward his brother-in-law for the vacant position, John Gunning, his lifelong rival, immediately weighed in with his own candidate – his assistant, Thomas Keate.

With the date for the election by the board's governors fixed for 11 May, the scene was set for a major showdown. No doubt Home's obsequious manner and his plodding rather than brilliant skills did little to bolster his case with the governors or fellow surgeons. Keate, on the other hand, had not only served five years as Gunning's right-hand man, he had proved his worth as surgeon to Chelsea Hospital as well. Even so, Hunter was not giving up without a fight, and he made sure that his tame governors, Banks among them, turned up to cast their votes. In the end it was a close-run thing – 102 votes for Home and 134 for Keate. Bitter with humiliation, Home had no choice but to labour on in his junior position. Livid at his defeat, Hunter was determined to make his colleagues pay.

Hunter took the ballot result as a personal injustice. Decades of trying to introduce reforms in medical education, attempting to persuade his colleagues to present lectures for the students, and always shouldering the greatest responsibility for the hospital's pupils – not to mention the conflicts over Hunter's surgical techniques – finally boiled over. He could command every surgeon within the British army, he had the Royal Society at his feet, physicians bowed to his advice, but he could not win over his peers at St George's. Hunter resolved to teach his recalcitrant colleagues a lesson. He called them to a meeting at the hospital on 25 June and prepared to announce a climactic decision; but none of them deigned to turn up. Reduced to writing them a letter, he fired off a furious missive on 9 July addressed to all three senior surgeons, Gunning, Keate and William Walker.[27] Hunter announced he was no longer prepared to share out the pupils' fees as custom decreed; instead, he intended to pocket himself all the payments from the students enrolled with him, who numbered by far the majority. Throughout his hospital career he had trained more pupils than any of the other surgeons, yet while the accrued fees were being shared equally with the laziest on the staff his colleagues snubbed his efforts to improve medical education. It was not that he needed the money – less than £100 a year between four surgeons would make little impact on Hunter's debts; rather, he hoped the move would act as an 'incitement' to force his fellow surgeons to take their teaching duties seriously. There was no more room for diplomacy or coercion as Hunter fumed, 'I will not say it is a disgrace to be a surgeon to St George's Hospital; but I will say, that the surgeons have disgraced the Hospital.'

It was an uncompromising assault on the honour of the three other surgeons, an audacious challenge to their pockets and their pride, and they were suitably apoplectic. Gunning, assuming the role of chief retaliator, penned a brief acknowledgement while the trio met to discuss tactics. They would face Hunter down, call his bluff, they agreed. Outside St George's they knew Hunter could muster all the allies and admirers he wanted; inside the hospital he was isolated and alone. Writing back on 4 October, the three conspirators jointly declared their 'entire disapprobation' of Hunter's proposal and announced their intention to refer his conduct to a general board of governors planned for February 1793.[28] They knew they had him cornered. What Foot described as the 'continual war', for it had rumbled on behind the scenes at St George's for decades, had now burst out savagely into the open.

In truth, St George's had been languishing in the doldrums for several years. The hospital had attracted willing benefactors, generous endowments and eager pupils in its heyday, when Hunter's enthusiasm for training had helped bolster its reputation, but its position had slumped dramatically over the last decade. Falling income had forced the board to reduce beds from its original 250 to 150, while the number of students had declined in tandem. Hunter's waning interest, as his efforts to introduce lectures were repeatedly stonewalled and competing activities demanded his attention, plainly contributed to the slide. With his health now severely impaired he had all but withdrawn his commitment to the hospital; he still performed operations in front of the students but relinquished much of the routine work to Home. In the meantime, his passion for education had been directed to his own lectures, which were packed with students from St George's and elsewhere.

Indeed, by the late eighteenth century London had become a thriving centre for medical education, even eclipsing both Paris and Edinburgh, despite its lack of a university; but it was to the private schools, set up by entrepreneurs such as the Hunter brothers and their followers, that the future surgeons streamed. Belatedly attempting to meet the growing demand, St Bartholomew's Hospital and the combined St Thomas' and Guy's had followed the example of the London Hospital in founding medical schools. At St George's, where Hunter had proposed a rounded medical education before anyone else had conceived the notion, the trend went unheeded. Standing on the city's furthest edge, facing stubbornly away from its competitors, St George's remained on the extreme fringes of progress. Worn out with the effort of trying to bring his complacent colleagues into line with advancing practices, and worn down by his creeping heart condition, Hunter had stamina left for one last battle.

As the board meeting loomed, he spent an anxious and increasingly lonely winter. Philip Syng Physick, who had been helping in the museum since completing his degree in Edinburgh, had returned to Philadelphia in September 1792. He became a surgeon in Pennsylvania Hospital and later professor of surgery at the University of Pennsylvania, where he would instruct his students to 'observe, deduce and record' in true Hunterian fashion. Home had persuaded his fiancée to go ahead with their wedding in November, despite his failure to secure a senior hospital post; the couple moved into a new house nearby. As Hunter had now handed him complete charge of the lecture course he remained a regular visitor, but only Clift was left in permanent attendance, at Hunter's side from dawn until midnight, diligently improving his dissection, preparation and sketching skills while imbibing his master's teachings with a growing devotion. That autumn, Hunter gave him half a crown to see the freaks and oddities at Bartholomew Fair – always a good hunting ground for new acquisitions for the museum.[29] In reality, there was little the fair could offer to outdo the spectacles in the museum where Clift spent his days.

Although Hunter had relinquished the lectures, his workload, as ever, had scarcely diminished. Patients still queued for treatment at his Leicester Square surgery and Hunter still set off in his coach daily to call at the London villas of his moneyed clients. Among them in 1792 was the artist Joseph Farington, who had a troublesome cyst on his back. Hunter removed it – with appreciably more success than when he had treated Farington's rival Gainsborough four years earlier – and the forty-five-year-old painter returned to his landscapes. He would later remember Hunter's chance remark that the surgeon 'had some obstruction or complaint about his heart which he was well assured would cause his death suddenly at some period'.[30] Having dissected so many thousands of dead bodies and examined so many diseased hearts, Hunter could not have failed to realize that his increasingly frequent seizures were gradually strangling his circulation.

He distracted himself with more animal experiments in the comparative tranquillity of Earls Court, taking Clift along to help. Still intent on tracing the very first indications of life, Hunter had returned to the quest he had begun as a novice anatomist dissecting chick embryos, only now he was slaughtering sheep. Adopting the same method, he killed eight ewes at different stages, from a few hours to eight days after they had mated with the ram; there was mutton for the dinner table at Leicester Square every day for over a week. He made eighteen careful preparations of the different parts of the ewes' reproductive systems while Clift took notes, but was peeved to discover that the microscopic embryo still eluded him.[31]

As winter advanced, Hunter's army duties grew daily more onerous with revolutionary France harassing its European neighbours. When his elderly colleague Sir Clifton Wintringham could no longer cope with the pressures as physician-general to the army, Hunter took over his responsibilities too.[32] Despite his own dubious health, he was now in command not only of the army's surgeons but also all its physicians. And when France executed Louis XVI on 21 January 1793 and just over a week later declared war on Britain, it was Hunter who had to supervise both surgical and medical support for the armed forces heading for Holland, France and the West Indies.

Britain's naval supremacy would ultimately ensure victory against the French revolutionaries, but the revolutionary surgeon lacked such steadfast support when finally he faced his own adversaries at St George's on 28 February. It was a one-sided engagement from the start. Hunter set out his case in a long, impassioned and impeccably argued letter to the board, detailing the grudges and grievances that had plagued his entire hospital career.[33] His aim from the first had been to treat the sick and to educate the nation's future surgeons, he argued, yet he had met with opposition at every step, his early colleagues rejecting his moves to set up lectures and his later peers similarly blocking his efforts to improve the pupils' instruction. One surgeon who complacently dismissed Hunter's proposals with the retort that 'he did not see where the art could be improved' typified the prevailing view. Finally, finding 'all my efforts ineffectual', he had abandoned the cause, concentrating on his own lectures and leaning on Home as his health faltered. Reminding the board that he had taught more pupils than all three of his colleagues put together – a total of 449 since 1770 to their 284 – he had concluded it was no longer just to share the pupils' proceeds equally. He implored the governors not to regard the wrangle as 'a contested election between two men', even though 'I may appear to stand single'. Yet it was, and he did.

As Gunning, Keate and Walker delivered their response, Hunter knew he had been outflanked and out-manoeuvred. In a counterblast to the board, and plainly seeking to exploit the anti-Scottish feeling still prevalent in England, the three surgeons claimed that Hunter had attracted more pupils only because students had been recommended by his brother and his Scottish friends. They proceeded to launch a vicious assault on Hunter's character and reputation, not only accusing him of neglecting his responsibilities to St George's but ridiculing his lecture course. Insisting that 'the old practice of instruction' – the copycat method patronized since medieval times – was still the best form of educating young surgeons, they fired a snide shot at Hunter's pro-posed lectures: 'If they had been practical and contained principles and rules founded upon judgement and experience, with regard to the authority of others as well as our own, they would have been highly useful: if on the contrary they had leaned to Physiology and experiment with a contempt for all other opinion but their own they would have been pernicious.'[34] Even now, as Hunter's doctrines were being taught by his ex-pupils in hospitals throughout Britain and America, the term 'physiology' was a dirty word. But the insults and counter-insults were of no consequence. Knowing he could muster the board's support, Gunning persuaded the governors to set up a special committee to consider the future of medical education. John Hunter, the man who had done most to promote the cause of teaching at St George's, who had taught more students than any other surgeon in his day, was excluded.

The committee, which met in May, agreed in full a list of exacting rules drafted by Gunning and his allies outlining the expected conduct of surgeons and pupils.[35] Hunter was not even consulted. At first sight, the regulations appeared to represent victory for Hunter: at long last he had won his campaign for the surgeons to give lectures on surgery free of charge and in strict rotation. In reality, however, it was a calculated ruse to outwit him, for there were a string of onerous demands all the surgeons were required to fulfil. These included visiting their patients at least twice a week, supervising dressings once a week, and meeting in joint consultation every Friday. Any defaulters, the rules stipulated, would be reported to the weekly board for breach of duty. As Hunter was valiantly trying to supervise his army surgeons and his angina was frequently bringing him to his knees, these additional duties would plainly be ruinous. There seemed little doubt that his jealous rivals were attempting to force his resignation, or worse. And there was one further demand that would have profound reverberations for Hunter. The new rules directed that all future pupils must have certificates proving 'their having been bred up to the profession'. In other words, only those who had completed a full apprenticeship would now be admitted; no longer would clever, talented young men from modest backgrounds like Hunter, without the connections or the money to arrange a lengthy apprenticeship, be allowed to cross the threshold of St George's.

Hunter knew that his scheming opponents had won the

battle, even if they were the last of a dying breed. He had little choice but to comply with the punishing new regime. Throughout the summer months he dutifully attended the required meetings, delivered the requisite lectures and tended to his needy patients with good grace. Indeed, the hostile atmosphere at St George's seemed to pale into insignificance beside the inhospitable conditions his surgeons in the West Indies were battling. As the first casualties of the conflict filtered back to Britain, it was Hunter's job to find them suitable accommodation. Writing from his comfortable study in June, he attempted to find beds in London for 'Eighteen invalids now on board a ship in the River brought over from Jamaica, who appear to be in a very helpless Situation'. He found space for them in the Savoy, a dilapidated army hospital near the Thames, only to discover a week later that the beds were 'in a filthy state'.[36] He was even having to deal with such minutiae as the quantity of sheeting and the supply of medicines to the military hospitals, while doggedly imposing his appointments system. Yet all the time his failing energies were focused on the French foe overseas and on his declared adversaries plotting at St George's, the real enemy was always closer to home.

For all the conflict, in London and abroad, life at 28 Leicester Square seemed to carry on much as normal. Mid-October found Hunter making the final checks on his major new volume, the *Treatise on the Blood, Inflammation and Gun-shot Wounds*, which was ready to print. It summarized the fruits of his experiences as a young army surgeon during the Seven Years War; the sixty-five-year-old surgeon-general dedicated the work to George III in a fit of topical patriotic fervour. The introduction to his fossil collection, with its daring estimates of the age of the earth, was waiting for the press too, while his considered views on the German fossil bones he had recently examined were ready for delivery to the Royal Society.

In the meantime, three new house pupils had moved their belongings into the cramped bedrooms of Castle Street. Among them was an earnest young lad, James Williams, who was finding his new quarters rather comfortless after his home in rural Worcester. 'My room has two beds in it and in point of situation is not the most pleasant in the world,' he wrote to his sister Mary. 'The Dissecting Room with half a dozen dead bodies in it is immediately above and that in which Mr Hunter makes preparations is the next adjoining to it, so that you may conceive it to be a little perfumed.'[37]

Although the lectures Williams was now attending were being delivered by Home – 'never a very popular or diligent lecturer' according to one account[38] – Hunter had by no means surrendered all his tutorial duties. Encouraging rising new surgeons to see and think for themselves had always been among his greatest pleasures. So every morning at seven, Williams and his two fellow students met their white-haired teacher in his Castle Street workroom to assist in making preparations, 'and to see with what patience he does everything is astonishing', enthused Williams. Gradually he became accustomed to his eccentric mentor, telling Mary, 'Mr Hunter is a very good kind of man when you have been used to him a little tho' he has some oddities', and adding, 'but thank God he has none of that pompous haughtiness by which great men make themselves disgusting'. Odd, brash, outspoken and occasionally bad-tempered he may have been, but pomposity was never in Hunter's nature. Dissection practice was due to begin in a week's time, Williams wrote home, and by then he would need some funds to buy a corpse. The going rate was a guinea.

On Wednesday, 16 October, with the dissecting season poised to begin, John Hunter met his pupils in the preparations room at 7 a.m. as usual.[39] He appeared to be in a buoyant mood, regaling the pupils with whimsical anecdotes about children who feigned sickness to avoid school – rarely did they fool the wily old surgeon.[40] The start of the autumn term, with the prospect of an entire winter's dissecting ahead, had perhaps contributed to his jaunty manner. He was no doubt also looking forward to the return at the end of the week of Anne and his children, twenty-one-year-old John and seventeen-year-old Agnes, who had spent the past six weeks in Brighton.[41] Young John would be returning to his medical studies at Cambridge while Agnes would soon be entertaining guests again at her mother's soirées. Their father's anticipation at their impending return may well have been equalled by the thought of the pair of golden eagles that had been delivered to Earls Court that same morning by Gough, his reliable supplier.[42] Hunter would have been looking forward to observing their antics and devising some suitable experiments.

After helping the pupils make their preparations with his usual patience, Hunter joined them for breakfast; he sauntered into the room 'humming a Scotch air', remembered William Clift. 'He was in very good spirits,' noted James Williams, 'and eat hearty as usual.'[43] At noon, Hunter left the house with a full caseload of patients to visit and a meeting at the hospital to attend. Almost immediately, the butler realized he had forgotten his itinerary – the list of appointments the surgeon always carried with him – and Clift had to run after the carriage, which he overtook at Hunter's first appointment five minutes away near St James's Square.[44] After handing him the list, Clift stood and watched his master climb into his carriage 'as well as ever I saw him in my life'. His next stop was St George's Hospital.

In reality, Hunter's bluff humour, jokey anecdotes and Scottish melody were something of a front, for he knew that another conflict awaited him at the hospital. Two Scottish youths had recently written asking if they could enrol as pupils with him at St George's; like Hunter in his youth, they had not served the requisite apprenticeships. Hunter had informed them of the new requirement but had agreed, in his usual generous spirit, to press their case all the same. Accordingly, he had written to the board supporting their enrolment as pupils and his letter had been tabled for the forthcoming meeting. Hunter had hoped that Home would accompany him to the debate, or even go in his stead, but he had been called away urgently to treat wounded troops arriving at Deal from the battles in France. Preparing, then, to face his combatants alone, Hunter well knew the effect such an ordeal might have on his weakened heart, for only a few days earlier he had sunk wearily into a chair and told a colleague, 'One of these days, and not long first, you will hear that I have dropped down dead.'[45] As his carriage trundled west towards Hyde Park and dropped him at the entrance to St George's, Hunter was perfectly aware he was walking into a potentially deadly engagement.

The hospital staff had gathered in the ground-floor boardroom, directly beneath the operating theatre where Hunter had saved so many lives. Gunning and Keate were absent but William Walker, their fellow conspirator, was at his place, along with a junior surgeon, William Mathew, who had almost certainly been recruited to the opposing side.[46] Among the physicians, Hunter's only sure ally was his nephew Matthew Baillie. The hospital chaplain, Revd James Clarke, was in the chair. Before long the issue of the two Scottish youngsters came up and Hunter cleared his throat to speak in their favour.[47] But even as he began to argue their case he was immediately contradicted by one of his colleagues, most probably Walker. Unable to contain his temper, Hunter lashed back in fury. As the meeting threatened to erupt into an ugly debacle, Hunter suddenly stopped speaking, rose from his chair, staggered into an adjoining room and with a loud groan sank into the arms of one of the physicians. There was nothing the combined talents of the St George's staff could do to revive the hospital's renegade surgeon. Hunter had died, as he had lived, in rebellion, speaking his mind.

John Hunter's lifeless body was transported back from the hospital in a sedan chair, while his carriage trailed empty behind. Passing by at the time, Jessé Foot stood and watched the 'baystone horses returning through Piccadilly, home, without their master'.[48] The surgeon's corpse was delivered, like so many corpses before, to the doors of his Leicester Square home. Yet the demise of the man who had dealt daily with death seemed inconceivable, and the effect on the household was devastating. Servants and house pupils were stunned. Having known his master barely twenty months, Clift found himself 'at a loss for words'. Having met his teacher just weeks earlier, James Williams struggled to write a legible letter home; naively he told his sister, 'He will be universally regretted even by his most inveterate Enemies.'[49] With Home still patching up war wounds in Kent, Baillie rode through the night to fetch Anne and the children, who returned the following day. Like the rest of the household, they were speechless with grief. 'Mrs Hunter and Miss and Mr John are almost breaking their hearts,' wrote Clift. 'I did not see Mr John till today morning when he burst into tears and could hardly speak when I spoke to him.'[50]

Friends and acquaintances were equally shocked. 'I have just heard that Dr [sic] Hunter is dead suddenly at St George's Hospital in a fit,' Horace Walpole wrote to a friend. 'It is such a blow to his family, as he was in such repute.' His thoughts immediately turning to Anne, who was a dear friend, he told another acquaintance, 'I am exceedingly grieved for the great misfortune that has happened to Mrs Hunter, and I heartily regret the very amiable Doctor.'[51] Joseph Farington, who had been among Hunter's last patients, was moved to record in his diary, 'much concerned at an acct. in the newspaper of the death of John Hunter, the excellent surgeon, to whom I was greatly obliged in the course of last summer'.[52] Glowing epitaphs filled the press. Applauding Hunter's unparalleled skills, the *European Magazine* pronounced, 'He rose to a rank in his profession scarce ever remembered, that of an acknowledged superiority over the most eminent of his rivals.'[53] The *Gentleman's Magazine* declared Hunter 'an honour to his profession and to his country' and appended a poem by a physician friend eulogizing his achievements.[54] And the *Sun* charted Hunter's rise from a humble carpenter to quite simply 'the first Surgeon in the world'.[55] At St George's, however, the triumphant surgeons voted not to send their condolences to Hunter's widow.[56] Before long they would agree to pay Foot £400 to write his damning biography of their despised colleague.

On the day after Hunter's death, as his widow and children wept, the house pupils gathered in the attic dissecting room as if for their routine anatomy lesson – only this time the corpse laid out on the table in front of them belonged to the great anatomist himself. Unlike many of his fellow surgeons, who had decreed that their bodies be incarcerated in locked family vaults to escape the anatomist's knife, Hunter had expressly requested that an autopsy be performed after his death. With Baillie observing, Clift assisting, and the pupils craning to see, Everard Home, fetched back from Kent, picked up his knife and began to carve up his brother-in-law's body.

When he opened Hunter's chest, the tell-tale signs years of angina had wrought were plain to see in his heart and arteries.[57] If ghosts did indeed haunt the dissecting room, as Home had intimated to Clift, John Hunter would have enjoyed nothing better than to peer over the shoulders of his engrossed students and confirm his own prognosis. After recording his findings, Home sewed up the body for burial, flagrantly disregarding Hunter's request that his heart and Achilles tendon, which he had torn back in 1766, should be preserved.[58] To Hunter, it would have seemed perfectly natural that his damaged heart and his repaired tendon, pickled in spirits, should take their place on his museum shelves alongside the parts of his numerous patients to help teach generations of future surgeons fundamental facts about injury and disease. In life, Hunter's heart had always been in his museum; in death it would have been a fitting resting place. Yet this neglect would seem trifling compared to the outrage

Home would go on to perpetrate on his former tutor.

The funeral, on 22 October, was a small, quiet ceremony at St Martin's-in-the-Fields with only the family in attendance. Compared to Reynolds' extravagant sending-off a year previously, it was 'a very private burying', Clift recorded. Not possessing a black suit, the apprentice was unable to join the official mourners, but desperate to say a last farewell he persuaded the undertaker to let him inside the vault. There he took a final look at Hunter's black coffin. 'None of our people saw me there I believe,' he wrote to Elizabeth, 'and I did not want them to.'[59] For Clift, as for the family, life was now in turmoil. 'I am afraid our house will be turned quite upside down now the wall and support is gone,' he wrote.[60] He was right: both of the houses and all their occupants had been shaken to the foundations.

To his family, Hunter had left principally debts. They ranged from the £2 owed to George Bailey, the 'birdman' in Piccadilly, to the huge outstanding mortgage on Earls Court.[61] There was no money for mortgage payments, so Earl's Court House was sold, its fine furnishings auctioned, and its animals sent to Gough's menagerie. With only six years left on the Leicester Square lease, the house was rented out and the coaches, horses, paintings, library and furniture sold. Only Long Calderwood remained in the family, but the tiny farmhouse was far too humble to provide either home or income. The entire household was therefore homeless and penniless. All the servants were dismissed, with the exception of Clift, the housekeeper Mrs Adams, and the dissecting-room attendant Haynes, who remained in Castle Street. After the debts were settled there was nothing left. Hunter's entire lifetime's earnings – a veritable fortune – had been ploughed into his collection. Worth an estimated £70,000, he had intended the museum to be his family's inheritance, stipulating in his will that it be sold – to the nation in its entirety if possible – to provide his descendants with a livelihood. Unfortunately, the government was in no mood to invest in scientific heritage. When petitioned by Hunter's friends and pupils to stump up even £20,000, in the midst of war with France Pitt exclaimed, 'What! Buy preparations! Why, I have not got money enough to purchase gunpowder.'[62]

The prospects for the family were bleak. With no means of continuing his education at Cambridge, John Banks Hunter had to abandon all hope of a medical future; he joined the army where he would lead an ignominious career. With no form of support at home, Agnes had little option but to accept a marriage proposal, only seven months after her father's death; it would be a miserable union ending in an acrimonious separation, although she eventually found happiness in a second marriage. Neither would have children. The future was even less promising for Anne. Leaving her elegant home and servants and abandoning her circle of literary and musical friends, she was forced at fifty-one to take a job as a ladies' chaperone, catering to the whims of the daughters of an army surgeon.[63] Although she was allowed a temporary government pension, and published her collected poems in 1802, she would never again entertain.

While the government invested in gunpowder, Hunter's extraordinary museum remained in place, lovingly tended by eighteen-year-old Clift, who spent what was left of his meagre allowance from Home – co-executor with Baillie of Hunter's will – on replenishing the alcohol in the jars. Too poor to go out, he devoted his evenings to studying

Hunter's catalogues and manuscripts, feverishly working to understand his hero's radical theories and, because it was what he had been trained to do, copying as much as he could in his neat script. His art classes and anatomy training abruptly ended, Clift hoped that Home might find him dissection work, although he shrewdly acknowledged, 'I should never learn anatomy under him for he is quite a different man from Mr Hunter'.[64]

Certainly, Home appeared to be the only member of Hunter's household to escape the devastation left by his death, and even to derive some gain from his passing. Leaving his sister, nephew and niece impoverished, he stepped briskly into his brother-in-law's shoes, filling his vacant job at St George's, presenting his unread papers to the Royal Society, and cementing a friendship with Banks which helped him forge valuable connections among the aristocracy; ultimately he would become a close intimate and drinking companion of the future Prince Regent, later George IV. The long-suffering Clift, painstakingly preserving Hunter's priceless legacy year after year, was all but forgotten, until the government finally agreed to buy the museum in 1799 for the knockdown sum of £15,000.[65] The entire collection, some 13,687 preparations, was placed in the custody of the Company of Surgeons, renamed the following year the Royal College of Surgeons; in death, Hunter would bring the organization he had despised the status it had lacked during his lifetime. Clift was appointed its first curator.

Now that the fate of the museum was settled, Home suddenly demanded all Hunter's papers. Clift stalled as long as possible, 'having a kind of presentiment that if they were removed to his house some accident might befall them', while feverishly copying as much as he could.[66] When Home finally issued an ultimatum, Clift could resist no longer and all Hunter's writings – manuscripts, case books, lecture notes, catalogues and letters – were delivered to Home's house in a cart. With a proper salary at last, Clift married in 1801 and five years later moved into the college's new headquarters in Lincoln's Inn Fields, Hunter's unique collection safe in his capable hands.

For the next twenty years, while Home carved out a glittering reputation within the Royal Society, contributing a colossal ninety-two papers on anatomy and natural history, Clift and the trustees of the museum attempted in vain to recover Hunter's papers. Without the original catalogues it was impossible to produce a new guide to the museum. Without his unpublished manuscripts Hunter's most controversial ideas were kept in the dark, but requests for Home to return them were constantly rebuffed. For his voluminous contributions, Home was awarded the Royal Society's Copley medal, and he became vice-president in 1814. Rising fast in his profession, he was appointed sergeant surgeon to George III in 1808, first master of the Royal College of Surgeons in 1813 – the same year he was knighted by the Prince Regent – and first president of the college in 1822. But no appeal from the college nor from Clift, now an eminent naturalist in his own right, could persuade him to hand over the missing manuscripts.

Finally, on 26 July 1823, Home was riding in a chaise with Clift to a meeting at Kew when he mentioned there had been a fire at his house.[67] So fierce was the blaze that the flames had leapt out of the chimney and the fire brigade had had to be called. When Clift enquired how the fire had started, Home casually revealed that he had been burning Hunter's manuscripts. The loss was incalculable; Clift broke down in tears. There was, then, only one more thing to do, he lashed back at Home, 'and that is to burn the collection itself'. Although Clift had presciently copied many of Hunter's original documents, and a few more were later surrendered by Home and his family, having somehow escaped the blaze, the majority had gone up in smoke. Even the letters from Hunter's favourite pupils, Jenner and Physick, had perished – burnt, no doubt, in a fit of jealous rage.

Seeking repeatedly to justify his actions over the next decade, an arrogant Sir Everard insisted he had simply carried out Hunter's dying wishes. It was a lame excuse. Even if Hunter had requested that Home destroy his manuscripts – and Home had not even been present at his death – that did not explain why the act had taken him thirty years. The fact that he later surrendered several unharmed manuscripts, including some of Hunter's case books, further belied his plea. The truth was that Home had roundly plagiarized his master's unpublished works then brutally erased all evidence of his crime. The numerous papers he had read to the Royal Society and the collected lectures he had just finished proofreading would reveal identical passages to many in Hunter's surviving writings. Home would never atone for his wanton act of destruction. He died, 'a regular sot' according to the *Lancet*, in 1832.[68] Three years later, Hunter's surviving writings and lectures derived from pupils' notes were published in four volumes; after the rediscovery of his works on geology and the origins of life, these were published in 1859 and 1861.

Despite its lack of an explanatory catalogue, Hunter's museum had become a magnet worldwide. By 1833 Clift had conducted more than thirty-two thousand visitors around the collection, including Archduke Maximilian of Austria, Prince Christian of Denmark and Prince Louis Napoleon, as well as numerous foreign scientists.[69] Georges Cuvier, the French expert in comparative anatomy, was astounded when he visited, confiding that he had had no idea 'that there was such a collection as the Hunterian Museum'.[70] And in 1837, a year after returning from his five-year voyage in the *Beagle*, Darwin donated his fossil bones to the museum, asking Richard Owen, the talented assistant curator who had married Clift's daughter Caroline, to study them.[71] Over the next few years Darwin would become a regular visitor.

More than twenty years later, as Darwin anxiously put the finishing touches to *The Origin of Species*, John Hunter was set for a dramatic resurrection. Having read in January 1859 that the vaults of St Martin's church were about to be cleared, the naturalist Frank Buckland launched a frantic search to salvage Hunter's remains.[72] Equipped like a latter-day body-snatcher, Buckland examined more than three thousand coffins by lamplight in the foul-smelling vault. With only two coffins left on the eighth day of his quest, he at last located a black lead casket; the name on its brass plate read 'John Hunter'. Honoured with a second funeral – as befits someone who had two birthdays – Hunter was reinterred on 28 March in Westminster Abbey with full ceremony. A plaque placed above his new grave by the Royal College of Surgeons commemorated Hunter as the 'Founder of Scientific Surgery'.

More than his surviving writings, more even than his unique museum with its astonishing explication of life, Hunter's greatest legacy would remain his revolutionary impact on surgery. Having started out as a poorly educated, novice anatomist at a time when barbers still performed minor operations, Hunter had dedicated his life to applying the principles of science to surgery. By the time of his death, although his backward-looking colleagues at St George's still resisted, Hunter's scientific approach had already become widely accepted. After he died, his devoted disciples – the thousand or more pupils he had taught – spread his creed of scientific inquiry throughout Britain and America. Inspired by Hunter's example and teachings, determined young surgeons such as John Abernethy, Astley Cooper, William Blizard, Henry Cline and Anthony Carlisle headed the great nineteenth-century teaching hospitals and led their profession to a respected new status. Across the Atlantic, followers such as William Shippen, John Morgan, Wright Post and Philip Syng Physick promulgated Hunter's teachings in their new hospitals and established the foundations of American medical education. Progress was inevitably haphazard and Hunter's followers would sometimes forget his belief in the powers of nature and his conservative approach to surgery in their zeal to climb social ranks and establish glowing reputations, but through Hunter's pervasive influence the future practice of surgery would be based largely on the doctrine of observation, experimentation and application of scientific evidence. When Edward Jenner tested his smallpox vaccine on an eight-year-old boy in 1796, thus establishing the discipline of vaccination which would save millions of lives, he was studiously following his tutor's principles. When Joseph Lister tried out his carbolic-soaked lint on eleven patients in 1867, thus launching antiseptic practices that would prevent countless deaths, he was purposefully adopting his hero's methods. And numberless pioneering surgeons down the years would similarly follow Hunter's scientific principles in helping to render surgery safe and effective.

Yet of all the people who carried Hunter's torch, perhaps the one who understood him best was the poor, orphaned Cornish lad William Clift, who said, 'From the beginning, I fancied, without being able to account for it, that nobody about Mr Hunter seemed capable of appreciating him. He seemed to me to have lived before his time and to have died before he was sufficiently understood.'[73]

Chronology

National and international events

1727 George II crowned; Isaac Newton died.

1734 St George's Hospital opened.

1740 War of the Austrian Succession begins.

1745 Jacobite uprising.

1746 Jacobites defeated at Culloden.

1748 Peace treaty of Aix-la-Chapelle

1749 Royal fireworks celebrating peace.

1751 Gin Act introduced.

John Hunter's life

1728 John Hunter born 13/14 February at Long Calderwood, East Kilbride.

1746 William Hunter sets up Covent Garden anatomy school.

1748 John joins William in London.

1749 John trains with Cheselden at Chelsea Hospital; becomes instructor in Covent Garden anatomy school. Brothers move to house in Great Piazza.

1750 John spends second summer at Chelsea.

1751 John trains with Pott at St Bartholomew's Hospital; mother, Agnes, dies.

1752 Murder Act allows courts to direct that murderers be dissected.

1753 British Museum founded.

1755 Johnson's *Dictionary of the English Language* published.

1756 Seven Years War begins.

1760 George III crowned.

1761 George III marries Princess Charlotte of Mecklenburg-Strelitz.

1763 Treaty of Paris ends Seven Years War; Boswell meets Johnson.

1752 John treats first recorded patient, a chimney sweep.

1754 John becomes a pupil at St George's Hospital; discovers placental circulation.

1755 John at Oxford for a brief spell.

1756 John spends five months as house surgeon at St George's; William moves to Jermyn Street.

1757 Hunter brothers quarrel with Pott and the Monros.

1760 John ill and gives up anatomy; enlists as army surgeon.

1761 John takes part in capture of Belle-Ile.

1762 John sails for Portugal; William delivers Queen Charlotte's first son, the future George IV; John's first research paper, on the descent of the testes and congenital hernias, published in William's *Medical Commentaries*.

1763 John leaves army and returns to London; begins partnership with dentist James Spence.

1764 John becomes engaged to Anne Home.

1766 John's first paper, on the greater siren, read to the Royal Society.

1767 John elected fellow of the Royal Society; begins experiment on venereal disease;
Hunter brothers investigate large bones discovered near Ohio River.

1768 Royal Academy founded, with William Hunter as its first professor of anatomy; Cook's first voyage, with Joseph Banks and Daniel Solander, 1768–71.

1768 John moves to William's former house in Jermyn Street; gains diploma from Company of Surgeons; elected surgeon at St George's.

1769 John assists in Caesarean operation.

1770 Edward Jenner becomes John's first house pupil.

1771 Cook returns and Jenner helps classify specimens; Smollett dies.

1771 John publishes first major work, *The Natural History of the Human Teeth*; marries Anne Home.

1772 John Banks Hunter born; William Lynn becomes assistant; Everard Home becomes John's apprentice; John gives private lectures on surgery and physiology.

1773 Boston tea riots.

1773 Inuit visitors meet Hunter; Jenner returns home; John's first angina attack; Mary-Ann Hunter born.

1774 Humane Society (later Royal Humane Society) founded.

1774 John performs a Caesarean operation; John Andree becomes assistant; John dissects electric eels; James Hunter born. William Hunter publishes *The Anatomy of the Human Gravid Uterus*.

1775 American War of Independence begins.

1775 James dies; William Bell becomes assistant; John advertises lectures.

1776 Adam Smith's *Wealth of Nations* published; American Declaration of Independence; Gibbon's *Decline and Fall of the Roman Empire*.

1776 Agnes Hunter born; Mary-Ann dies; John appointed Surgeon Extraordinary to George III; treats David Hume; gives lectures at William's Great Windmill Street school, 1776–8.

1777 John attempts to revive Revd Dr William Dodd after hanging; second angina attack.

1778 Banks elected president of the Royal Society.

1778 Everard Home leaves to join navy; John publishes part two of his work on teeth, *A Practical Treatise on the Diseases of the Teeth*; John's brother-in-law, Revd James Baillie, dies and Dorothy moves to Long Calderwood with son and daughters; Johnson asks Hunter to treat artist friend.

1779 Cook killed in Hawaii.

1779 John's 'An Account of the Free-Martin' published in *Philosophical Transactions of the Royal Society*.

1780 Gordon riots in London.

1780 John accuses William of stealing his discovery of placental circulation; John given remains of first giraffe brought to Europe; 'An Account of an extraordinary pheasant' published in *Philosophical Transactions*.

1781 British surrender at Yorktown.

1781 John gives evidence in Donellan murder trial.

1782 Charles Byrne, the 'Irish giant', arrives in London; Hunter conducts autopsies on prime minister (Marquis of Rockingham) and Daniel Solander.

1783 American Treaty of Independence signed; Pitt the younger becomes prime minister.

1783 John moves to Leicester Square; William Hunter dies; John steals body of Irish giant; gives lectures in Leicester Square (Castle Street).

1784 Dr Johnson dies.

1784 Everard Home returns to London; John conducts autopsy on father-in-law, Robert Home; Matthew Baillie cedes Long Calderwood to John.

1785 *The Times* (originally *Daily Universal Register*) founded.

1785 Hunter moves collection to Leicester Square; consulted by Benjamin Franklin; visits Tunbridge Wells and Bath after further angina attacks; performs successful operation on popliteal aneurysm.

1786 Burn's *Poems*, chiefly in the Scottish dialect.

1786 John appointed deputy surgeon-general of the army; awarded Royal Society Copley medal; publishes *A Treatise on the Venereal Disease*; embalms George III's aunt, Princess Amelia; operates on William Pitt; Reynolds' portrait of Hunter unveiled at Royal Academy; Home moves in to Leicester Square.

1787 First convicts transported to New South Wales.

1787 John treats Adam Smith; Home appointed John's assistant at St George's; 'Observations tending to show that the wolf, jackal, and dog are all of the same species' published in *Philosophical Transactions*.

1788 George III ill winter 1788–9; riots against surgeons over body-snatching in New York.

1788 Museum opens twice a year; John treats Gainsborough and young Byron; William Lynn fined over body-snatching in London.

1789 Fall of the Bastille; William Blake's *Songs of Innocence*.

1789 John elected to Company of Surgeons' court of assistants; William Bell leaves; Philip Syng Physick becomes house pupil.

1790 John appointed surgeon-general of the army; invents method of artificial feeding; John's descriptions of antipodean mammals included in John White's *Journal of a Voyage to New South Wales*; Home takes over delivering lectures.

1791 Paine's *Rights of Man*, part one; Boswell's *Life of Johnson*.

1791 John helps found Veterinary College of London (later Royal Veterinary College); Haydn declines treatment.

1792 French republic declared; Paine's *Rights of Man*, part two.

1792 John writing *Observations and Reflections on Geology*; 'Observations on bees' published in *Philosophical Transactions*; William Clift taken on as apprentice; John performs autopsy on Reynolds; treats Farington; Home defeated in election for surgeon at St George's; row over hospital pupils' fees begins.

1793 Louis XVI executed; France declares war on Britain.

1793 John supervises medical provision for overseas expeditions; St George's adopts stringent rules on surgeons' duties and pupils' enrolment; Hunter dies, 16 October, at St George's.

1794 Erasmus Darwin publishes first volume of *Zoonomia*.

1794 Observations on fossil bones from Germany published posthumously in *Philosophical Transactions*.

1796 Edward Jenner successfully tests first smallpox vaccine.

1799 Pitt's government agrees to buy Hunter's museum and gives custody to Company of Surgeons; Clift appointed first curator.

1800 Company renamed Royal College of Surgeons.

1801 Home demands Hunter's manuscripts.

1803 War with France resumes.

1805 Nelson killed at Trafalgar.

1806 Museum moves into RCS's new headquarters in Lincoln's Inn Fields.

1815 Napoleon defeated at Waterloo.

1823 Home burns Hunter's manuscripts.

1832 Anatomy Act ends body-snatching.

1859 Darwin's *The Origin of Species*.

1859 Hunter reinterred in Westminster Abbey; *Observations and Reflections on Geology* published.

1861 *Essays and Observations on natural history, anatomy, physiology, psychology and geology* published.

1871 Darwin's *The Descent of Man*.

Key sources

Publications of John Hunter mentioned in the notes

The Natural History of the Human Teeth: explaining their structure, use, formation, growth, and diseases (London, printed for J. Johnson, 1771).

'On the descent of the testis', in William Hunter, *Medical Commentaries* (London, S. Baker and G. Leigh, 1762 and 1777).

A Practical Treatise on the Diseases of the Teeth; intended as a supplement to the natural history of those parts (London, printed for J. Johnson, 1778).

A Treatise on the Venereal Disease (London, the author, 1786).

A Treatise on the Blood, Inflammation and Gun-shot Wounds, by the late John Hunter (London, George Nicol, 1794).

The Works of John Hunter, ed. James Palmer (London, Longman, Rees, Orme, Brown, Breen, 1835), 4 vols.

Observations and Reflections on Geology (London, Taylor and Francis, 1859).

Essays and Observations on natural history, anatomy, physiology, psychology and geology, ed. Richard Owen (London, Van Voorst, 1861), 2 vols.

E. H. Cornelius and A. J. Harding Rains (eds), *Letters from the Past, from John Hunter to Edward Jenner* (London, Royal College of Surgeons of England, 1976).

E. Allen, J. L. Turk and R. Murley (eds), *The Case Books of*

John Hunter FRS (London, Royal Society of Medicine, 1993).

Biographies of Hunter mentioned in the notes

Adams, Joseph, *Memoirs of the Life and Doctrines of the late John Hunter* (London, J. Callow, 1818).

Dobson, Jessie, *John Hunter* (Edinburgh, E. & S. Livingstone, 1969).

Foot, Jessé, *The Life of John Hunter* (London, T. Becket, 1794).

Home, Everard, 'A short account of the life of the author', in *A Treatise on the Blood, Inflammation and Gun-shot Wounds, by the late John Hunter* (London, George Nicol, 1794).

Kobler, John, *The Reluctant Surgeon: The life of John Hunter* (London, Heinemann, 1960).

Ottley, Drewry, 'The Life of John Hunter, FRS', in *The Works of John Hunter*, vol. 1.

Paget, Stephen, *John Hunter, Man of Science and Surgeon* (London, Fischer Unwin, 1897).

Peachey, George C., *A Memoir of William & John Hunter* (Plymouth, Brendon, 1924).

Qvist, George, *John Hunter 1728–1793* (London, W. Heinemann, 1981).

Other sources, and abbreviations, used in notes

British Library – BL
The Hunter-Baillie Collection (at RCS) – HBC
The Hunter Album, RCS – HA
John Hunter – JH
Loudoun Papers (at RCS) – LP
Royal College of Surgeons of England – RCS
The Wellcome Library for the History and Understanding of Medicine – WL

Hunter sights

Scotland
John Hunter's birthplace at Long Calderwood is preserved as a

museum, the Hunter House, which tells the story of his life and the development of modern surgery. The Hunter House, 126 Maxwellton Road, East Kilbride, South Lanarkshire, G74 3LR, tel. 01355 261261.

In East Kilbride, the Hunter brothers are remembered in the Hunter Primary School, Hunter High School, Hunter Health Centre, Hunter Street in the old East Kilbride village, and The Hunters pub in Stewartfield.

London
John Hunter's collection of anatomical specimens and naturalist items is housed in the Hunterian Museum at the headquarters of the Royal College of Surgeons of England. Of the original 14,000 preparations, more than half were destroyed in an air-raid in 1941, while others have not withstood the ravages of time. Today about 3,500 survive, including the specimens displaying his successful popliteal aneurysm operations and the skeleton of the Irish giant, Charles Byrne. The museum is due to reopen after refurbishment in 2005. Hunterian Museum, Royal College of Surgeons, 35–43 Lincoln's Inn Fields, London WC2A 3PE, tel. 020 7405 3474.

A bust of John Hunter stands in Leicester Square, opposite the site of his former house at number 28, which is now a pub, The Moon Under Water. A blue plaque denotes his former house at 31 Golden Square. William Hunter's Great Windmill Street school is now the rear of the Lyric Theatre, Shaftesbury Avenue.

A note on money

Making direct financial comparisons between the eighteenth century and modern times is not straightforward. As a rough guide, the Bank of England estimates that:

£1 in 1750 would be worth £81.63 today.
£1 in 1760 would be worth £71.69 today.
£1 in 1770 would be worth £61.05 today.

£1 in 1780 would be worth £60.24 today.
£1 in 1790 would be worth £53.70 today.

(Source: Retail Price Index October 2003, Bank of England)

A guinea was equivalent to 21 shillings, so that for example 5 guineas was worth £5 5s.

Notes

Chapter 1

1   JH, *A Treatise on the Blood*, p. 397.
2   Everard Home, 'An account of Mr Hunter's method of performing the operation for the cure of the popliteal aneurysm from materials furnished by Mr Hunter' in *Transactions of a Society for the Improvement of Medical and Chirurgical Knowledge*, 1 (1793), pp. 138–81. All details about the coach driver and his operation are taken from the above, unless indicated. Details are also given in Home, 'An account of Mr Hunter's method of performing the operation for the cure of the popliteal aneurysm communicated in a letter to Dr Simmons' in the *London Medical Journal*, 7 (1786), pp. 391–406, and in Home, 'Supplement to an account . . . etc', 8 (1787), pp. 126–36.
3   My thanks for advice to Sir Peter Bell, professor of surgery at Leicester Royal Infirmary; Professor Harold Ellis, clinical anatomist at Guy's, King's and St Thomas' School of Biomedical Sciences; and Alan Scott, honorary consultant in vascular surgery and director of the multi-centre aneurysm screening study. The causes of aneurysms are still unclear but they occur when the elastin in an artery loses its elasticity, causing the walls to bulge outwards. It is possible, according to Professor Bell and Professor Ellis, that the top of a coach-man's boots or the seat of his coach could injure the artery walls at the back of the knee if already weakened by the underlying condition.

4   Dorothy Porter and Roy Porter, *Patient's Progress: doctors and doctoring in eighteenth-century England* (Oxford, Polity Press in association with Blackwell, 1989), p. 59.

5   JH, *Case Books*, p. 97.

6   George W. Corner and Willard E. Goodwin, 'Benjamin Franklin's bladder stone' in *Journal of the History of Medicine*, 8 (1953), pp. 359–77.

7   JH, *Case Books*, pp. 450–1.

8   The figures are cited by John Gunning, William Walker and Thomas Keate in a letter to the governors, n.d. (1793), transcribed in Peachey, *A Memoir*, pp. 282–96.

9   Bransby Blake Cooper, *The Life of Sir Astley Cooper* (London, J. W. Parker, 1843), vol. 1, p. 152; and Adams, *Memoirs*, p. 109.

10   Henry Cline, Hunterian Oration at the RCS (1824); John Baron, *The Life of Edward Jenner* (London, Henry Colburn, 1827), p. 10.

11   John Abernethy, *Physiological Lectures* (London, Longman, 1825), p. 51.

12   Foot, *The Life*, p. 280.

13   Anon., 'John Hunter at Earl's Court, Kensington 1764–93', leaflet reprinted from the *Atheneum* of 1870, HA, p. 5.

14   Foot, *The Life*, p. 242.

15   E. H. Cornelius, 'John Hunter as an expert witness', *Annals of the Royal College of Surgeons of England*, 60 (1978), pp. 412–18.

16   Percivall Pott, *The Chirurgical Works of Percivall Pott* (London, printed for T. Lowndes, 1779), vol. 3, p. 202.

17   JH, *The Works*, vol. 1, 'Lectures on the principles of surgery', p. 536.

18   JH to Edward Jenner, 2 August (no year), *Letters from the Past*, p. 9.

19   JH, *Case Books*, pp. 338–41.

20   JH, *The Works*, vol. 1, 'Lectures on the principles of surgery', p. 536.

21   JH, *Hunterian Reminiscences, being the substance of a course of lectures in the principles and practices of surgery delivered by Mr John Hunter in the year 1785, Taken in shorthand and afterwards fairly transcribed by the Late Mr*

James Parkinson, ed. J. W. K. Parkinson (London, Sherwood, Gilbert and Piper, 1833), pp. 130–1.

22   Steven G. Friedman, *A History of Vascular Surgery* (New York, Futura, 1989), *passim*.

23   Everard Home, 'An account' (1793).

24   Details of the stag experiment were reputedly handed down from William Bell, Hunter's assistant of the time, to a later assistant, William Clift, who retold the story to the Victorian naturalist Richard Owen. See Lloyd G. Stevenson, 'The stag of Richmond Park' in *Bulletin of the History of Medicine*, 22 (1948), pp. 467–75; Stevenson, 'A further note on John Hunter and aneurysm' in *Bulletin of the History of Medicine*, 26 (1952), pp. 162–7; anon. (ed.), *British Medical Journal*, 1 (1879), pp. 284–5; Jessie Dobson (ed.), *Descriptive Catalogue of the Physiological Series in the Hunterian Museum* (Edinburgh and London, E. & S. Livingstone, 1970), part 1, pp. 4–8.

25   JH, *The Works*, vol. 1, 'Lectures on the principles of surgery', p. 210.

26   JH, 'Lectures on the principles of surgery by John Hunter, taken in notes by Joseph Pearce' (1791), RCS ms 49 c 10.

27   JH, *The Works*, vol. 1, 'Lectures on the principles of surgery', p. 536.

28   Paolo Assalini, *Manuale di Chirurgia del Cavaliere Assalini* (Milan, Pirola, 1812), p. 86. My thanks to Robinetta Gaze for her translation from the Italian.

29   Everard Home, 'An account' (1793). Particular thanks to Professor Harold Ellis for explaining Hunter's operation, and to Alan Scott and Sir Peter Bell (see note 3) for describing modern treatment. Today, the problem is commonly tackled with bypass surgery, using either a synthetic vessel or a section of vein taken from the thigh, although smaller aneurysms are still occasionally treated by tying the artery above and below and relying on collateral circulation, as in Hunter's day.

30   David C. Schechter and John J. Bergan, 'Popliteal aneurysm: a celebration of the bicentennial of John Hunter's operation' in *Annals of Vascular Surgery*, 1 (1986), pp. 118–26; Paolo Assalini, *Manuale di Chirurgia*, p. 86.

31   The leg of the first coach driver can still be seen in the Hunterian Museum, specimen P 275, alongside the limb of the fourth patient, specimen P 279, which was obtained by a Hunter disciple, Thomas Wormald, from the man's widow in 1837.

Chapter 2

1   Samuel Johnson to Revd Dr Taylor, 21 September 1782, in Bruce Redford (ed.), *Letters of Samuel Johnson* (Princeton University Press, 1992–4), vol. 4, p. 74.

2   Home, 'A short account', p. xv.

3   William Hunter to James Hunter, 17 September 1743, HBC, vol. 2, p. 5.

4   There are several biographies and studies detailing William's life. The most useful include C. Helen Brock, 'The happiness of riches' in William Bynum and Roy Porter (eds), *William Hunter and the Eighteenth-century Medical World* (Cambridge University Press, 1985), pp. 35–54; Brock (ed.), *William Hunter 1718–1783: a memoir by Samuel Foart Simmons and John Hunter* (University of Glasgow Press, 1983); Brock, 'The early years of James, William and John Hunter', unpublished PhD thesis (1977), East Kilbride public library; Sir Charles Illingworth, *The Story of William Hunter* (Edinburgh and London, E. & S. Livingstone, 1967).

5   Martin Kemp and Marina Wallace, *Spectacular Bodies* (London, Hayward Gallery, 2000), p. 29.

6   HA, p. 21. A note by William Ferguson records a villager saying that his father-in-law stated John had been born in the room above the kitchen.

7   Old parish register of East Kilbride, copy in East Kilbride public library; the Hunter Family Bible, RCS; a commonplace book belonging to an uncle of William and John Hunter, RCS. Even today the Hunterian Society celebrates Hunter's birthday on 13 February while the RCS honours him on 14 February.

8   Hunter's parents' date of marriage, and his siblings' dates of birth and death, are recorded in the Hunter Family Bible, RCS. All of the children's dates of birth are also given in the

old parish register of East Kilbride.

9 For details of the history of East Kilbride and the Hunter brothers' early lives, see David Ure, *The History of Rutherglen and East Kilbride* (Glasgow, David Niven, 1793) and T. E. Niven, *East Kilbride, the History of Parish and Village* (Glasgow, Gavin Watson, 1965). Many thanks for advice and clarification to Bill Niven, local historian and former provost (mayor) of East Kilbride, whose father Eric (T. E.) Niven previously charted the history of the village.

10 The house where John Hunter was born at Long Calderwood is preserved as a museum, the Hunter House (see Hunter sights above). Contrary to popular belief, William Hunter was born in the village, before the family moved to Long Calderwood, according to the old parish register. Thanks to Bill Niven for pointing this out.

11 Paget, *John Hunter*, p. 27.

12 Reminiscences of Dorothea Baillie, told to her daughters Agnes and Joanna Baillie, HBC, vol. 2, p. 1 and vol. 6, p. 18.

13 Hunter's pupils Astley Cooper and John Abernethy both said that Hunter had men read for him: R. C. Brock, *The Life and Work of Astley Cooper* (Edinburgh and London, E. & S. Livingstone, 1952), p. 47; and John Abernethy, *Physiological Lectures* (London, Longman, 1825), p. 202. Hunter displayed classic symptoms of dyslexia, according to the British Dyslexia Association, personal communication, August 2003.

14 Anon., article from *European Magazine* in 1782, reprinted in John Abernethy, *Physiological Lectures*, pp. 341–52.

15 Foot, *The Life*, p. 60.

16 JH, *The Works*, vol. 4, pp. 165–75.

17 W. R. Le Fanu, *A Bibliography of Edward Jenner* (Winchester, St Paul's Bibliographies, 1985), p. 101. The comment is recorded by Benjamin Waterhouse in a letter to Jenner, 24 April 1801.

18 JH, *The Works*, vol. 1, 'Lectures on the principles of surgery', p. 217; Richard Owen (ed.), *Descriptive and Illustrated Catalogue of the Physiological Series of Comparative Anatomy* (London, RCS, 1840), vol. 5, p. xiii.

19 Arthur Herman, *The Scottish Enlightenment* (London,

Fourth Estate, 2003), pp. 60–2.

20   C. Helen Brock (ed.), *William Hunter 1718–1783*, p. 1. In annotations in the original Simmons biography, John Hunter says his brother James co-wrote a comedy with Smollett and the two attempted to have it staged in Edinburgh.

21   James Hunter to William Hunter, 24 March 1741, HBC, vol. 2, p. 13.

22   William Hunter to Agnes Hunter, 3 June 1742, HBC, vol. 2, p. 3.

23   Peter Laslett, *The World We Have Lost – Further Explored* (London, Methuen, 1983), 3rd edition, p. 108. The figure for life expectancy at birth in England in 1751 is given as 36.6 years.

24   M. Dorothy George, *London Life in the Eighteenth Century* (London, Peregrine, 1966), p. 399.

25   Roy Porter, *The Greatest Benefit to Mankind* (London, HarperCollins, 1997), p. 296.

26   Samuel Johnson to Hill Boothby, 31 December 1755, in Bruce Redford (ed.), *The Letters of Samuel Johnson*, vol. 1, p. 120.

27   Roy Porter, *The Greatest Benefit to Mankind*, pp. 245–303. For more discussion of medicine in the age of enlightenment see Roy Porter, *Enlightenment: Britain and the creation of the modern world* (London, Penguin, 2000).

28   Samuel Johnson to Hester Thrale, 24 August 1780, in Bruce Redford (ed.), *The Letters of Samuel Johnson*, vol. 3, p. 304.

29   William Hogarth, *The Company of Undertakers* (1735), discussed in Fiona Haslam, *From Hogarth to Rowlandson: Medicine in art in eighteenth-century Britain* (Liverpool University Press, 1996), pp. 52–66.

30   Tobias Smollett, *The Adventures of Roderick Random* (Oxford University Press, 1999; first published 1748), p. 27.

31   *Gentleman's Magazine*, August 1748.

32   T. Jock Murray, 'The Medical History of Dr Samuel Johnson' in *The Nova Scotia Medical Bulletin* (June–August 1982), pp. 71–8.

33   *The New Dispensatory of the Royal College of Physicians of London, faithfully translated from the Latin of the*

Pharmacopoeia Londinensis (London, W. Owen, 1746).

34   Guy Williams, *The Age of Agony* (London, Constable, 1975), pp. 184–5. The sum would be worth about £400,000 today.

35   Ibid., p. 182.

36   Reminiscences of Dorothea Baillie, told to her daughters Agnes and Joanna Baillie, HBC, vol. 6, p. 18.

37   Foot, *The Life*, p. 10.

38   M. Dorothy George, *London Life in the Eighteenth Century*, p. 37.

39   Christopher Hibbert and Ben Weinreb (eds), *The London Encyclopaedia* (London, Macmillan, 1983), p. 369.

40   Hogarth published his etching *Gin Lane* on 1 February 1753.

41   C. Helen Brock (ed.), *William Hunter 1718–1783*, p. 5. In his annotations on p. 8, John Hunter states that William rented apartments belonging to the Society of Naval Surgeons.

42   Susan C. Lawrence, *Charitable Knowledge: hospital pupils and practitioners in eighteenth-century London* (Cambridge University Press, 1996), p. 85.

43   John P. Blandy and John S. P. Lumley (eds), *The Royal College of Surgeons of England: 200 years of history at the millennium* (London and Oxford, Royal College of Surgeons of England, Blackwell Science, 2000), pp. 6–7.

44   William Hunter, *Two Introductory Lectures* (London, printed by order of the trustees for J. Johnson, 1784), p. 88.

45   Ibid., pp. 88–9.

46   Ernest Finch, 'The influence of the Hunters on medical education' in *Annals of the Royal College of Surgeons of England*, 20 (1957), pp. 205–48.

47   Home, 'A short account', p. xv.

48   William Hunter, *Two Introductory Lectures*, p. 102.

Chapter 3

1   William Hunter, *Two Introductory Lectures* (London, printed by order of the trustees for J. Johnson, 1784), p. 113.

2   Middlesex Sessions Rolls, December 1747 (ms 2889), London Metropolitan Archives. The case was also reported

in the *Gentleman's Magazine*, December 1747, and the *Westminster Journal*, 26 December 1747, BL.

3   William Hunter, *Two Introductory Lectures*, p. 67.

4   Ibid., p. 87 (William's italics).

5   William Hunter, *Medical Commentaries* (London, A. Hamilton, 1762), p. 20.

6   Christopher Lawrence, 'Alexander Monro primus and the Edinburgh manner of anatomy' in *Bulletin of the History of Medicine*, 62 (1988), pp. 193–214. With thanks to Andrew Cunningham for drawing my attention to this paper, and for discussion.

7   William Hunter, *Two Introductory Lectures*, p. 87.

8   William Hunter, *Medical Commentaries*, p. 8.

9   Joan Lane, 'The role of apprenticeship in eighteenth-century medical education in England' in William Bynum and Roy Porter (eds), *William Hunter and the Eighteenth-century Medical World* (Cambridge University Press, 1985), pp. 57–105, especially p. 88.

10   Dorothy Porter and Roy Porter, *In Sickness and in Health* (London, Fourth Estate, 1988), p. 53.

11   Alan F. Guttmacher, 'Bootlegging bodies: a history of body-snatching' in *Bulletin of the Society of Medical History of Chicago*, 4 (1935), pp. 352–402.

12   Robert Latham (ed.), *The Shorter Pepys* (London, Penguin, 1985), p. 261.

13   Toby Gelfand, 'The "Paris manner" of dissection: student anatomical dissection in early eighteenth-century Paris' in *Bulletin of the History of Medicine*, 16 (1972), pp. 99–130; and Alan F. Guttmacher, 'Bootlegging bodies'. The legal situation would remain unchanged until the Anatomy Act of 1832 provided a source of unclaimed bodies from workhouses.

14   Andrew Langley, *Georgian Britain 1714 to 1837* (London, Hamlyn, 1994), p. 9. For more details on hanging in Georgian London see Peter Linebaugh, *The London Hanged: crime and civil society in the eighteenth century* (London, Allen Lane, 1991) and Linebaugh, 'The Tyburn riot against the surgeons' in Douglas Hay (ed.), *Albion's Fatal Tree: crime and society in eighteenth-century England* (London, Allen Lane, 1975), pp. 65–117.

15   Ralph Hyde (ed.), *The A to Z of Georgian London* (Lympne Castle, Kent, Harry Margary in association with Guildhall Library, London, 1981). The site of Tyburn Tree is shown on John Rocque's map at the junctions of Tiburn Lane and Tiburn Road (today Park Lane and Oxford Street) near to where Marble Arch now stands.

16   Samuel Richardson, *Familiar Letters on Important Occasions*, cited in Linebaugh, 'The Tyburn riot'.

17   Cecil Howard Turner, *The Inhumanists* (London, A. Ouseley, 1932), p. 41.

18   Peter Linebaugh, *The London Hanged*, pp. 38–9.

19   Martin Fido, *Bodysnatchers: a history of the resurrectionists, 1742–1832* (London, Weidenfeld and Nicolson, 1988), pp. 4–5. The skeleton of Jonathan Wild remains at RCS headquarters in Lincoln's Inn Fields.

20   Ruth Richardson, *Death, Dissection and the Destitute* (London, Phoenix Press, 2001). Richardson's book provides a detailed analysis of body-snatching practices and public opinion towards them.

21   Cecil Howard Turner, *The Inhumanists*, p. 50.

22   William Hogarth, *The Reward of Cruelty* (1751), from *The Four Stages of Cruelty*. See Roy Porter, *Bodies Politic: Disease, Death and Doctors in Britain, 1650–1900* (London, Reaktion Books, 2001) for discussion.

23   Cecil Howard Turner, *The Inhumanists*, p. 67.

24   Peter Linebaugh, 'The Tyburn riot', p. 103.

25   *Gentleman's Magazine*, October 1748; their crimes are listed on The Proceedings of the Old Bailey website, www.oldbaileyonline.org

26   JH, *The Works*, vol. 2, 'A treatise on the venereal disease', p. 159.

27   C. Helen Brock (ed.), *William Hunter 1718–1783: a memoir by Samuel Foart Simmons and John Hunter* (University of Glasgow Press, 1983), p. 9. John called the artists' group the Society of Painters.

28   The case of John Walker, 20 April 1748, is detailed on The Proceedings of the Old Bailey website www.oldbaileyonline.org, reference ti7480420-1.

29   Ruth Richardson, *Death, Dissection and the Destitute*, p. 31.

30 Report from the Select Committee of the House of Commons on Anatomy, 22 July 1828, BL. Evidence to the select committee was given by two of John Hunter's pupils, Sir Astley Cooper and John Abernethy, and by Abernethy's assistant, Dr James Macartney, as well as by two anonymous body-snatchers, A. B. and C. D.

31 Cecil Howard Turner, *The Inhumanists*, p. 107.

32 Report from the Select Committee. Granville Sharp Pattison, a leading anatomy teacher in America, described his student days at Glasgow stealing bodies from graveyards. He helped export the practice to America.

33 Peachey, *A Memoir*, p. 42.

34 Peter Linebaugh, 'The Tyburn riot'.

35 Bransby Blake Cooper, *The Life of Sir Astley Cooper* (London, J. W. Parker, 1843), *passim*. Astley Cooper's nephew, Bransby Cooper, outlined the body-snatchers' methods in his biography of the surgeon. Rigor mortis – the process in which the dead body stiffens – usually begins a few hours after death and is complete by about twelve hours. It then wears off and the body becomes limp again within twenty-four to thirty-six hours of death, although the process takes longer in colder temperatures. My thanks to Dr Alistair Hunter, academic manager of the dissecting rooms at Guy's, King's and St Thomas' School of Biomedical Sciences, for advice.

36 Alan F. Guttmacher, 'Bootlegging bodies'.

37 James Blake Bailey (ed.), *The Diary of a Resurrectionist 1811–1812* (London, Swan Sonnenschein, 1896), p. 140; and Report from the Select Committee, *passim*.

38 Report from the Select Committee, evidence from C. D.

39 Report from the Select Committee, evidence from A. B.

40 Report from the Select Committee, summary.

41 Liza Picard, *Dr Johnson's London* (London, Weidenfeld and Nicolson, 2000), p. 297. Picard gives the monthly wage of a seaman with the East India Company as £1 15s in 1762; Report from the Select Committee, evidence from A. B.

42 Report from the Select Committee, evidence from Sir Astley Cooper.

43   Report from the Select Committee, evidence from Dr James Macartney.

44   James Blake Bailey (ed.), *The Diary of a Resurrectionist*, p. 145.

45   JH, *Case Books*, pp. 308–9.

46   JH, *Case Books*, pp. 313–14.

47   Anon., 'The Hunters and the Hamiltons: some unpublished letters' in *Lancet*, 214 (1928), no. 1, pp. 354–60. The letter is from the future Professor William Hamilton to his father, Professor Thomas Hamilton, 25 December 1777.

48   Ottley, 'The Life', p. 10.

49   Paget, *John Hunter*, p. 47.

50   JH, *The Works*, vol. 2, p. 158.

51   JH, *The Works*, Atlas, pp. 5–6.

52   William Hunter, *The Anatomy of the Human Gravid Uterus exhibited in figures* (Birmingham, J. Baskerville, S. Baker and G. Leigh, 1774).

53   Anon., *European Magazine* (1782), reprinted in John Abernethy, *Physiological Lectures* (London, Longman, 1825), pp. 341–52.

54   Thomas Rowlandson, *The Dissecting Room*, c. 1770.

55   William Hunter, *Two Introductory Lectures*, p. 113.

56   C. Helen Brock (ed.), *William Hunter 1718–1783*, p. 5. The description is given in John Hunter's annotations.

57   William Hunter, 'Lectures Anatomical and Chirurgical by Dr William Hunter' (1775), RCS ms 42 c 42–4.

58   Jane M. Oppenheimer, 'John and William Hunter and some contemporaries in literature and art' in *Bulletin of the History of Medicine*, 23 (1949), pp. 21–47.

59   Notes to the Hunterian Museum, RCS.

60   Adams, *Memoirs*, p. 37; John Abernethy, Hunterian Oration (1819), in John Abernethy, *Physiological Lectures*, p. 54.

61   Foot, *The Life*, p. 12.

62   Ottley, 'The Life', p. 10.

63   Foot, *The Life*, pp. 81–2.

64   Bransby Blake Cooper, *The Life of Sir Astley Cooper*, vol. 1, p. 103; Ottley, 'The Life', p. 10; Home, 'A short account', p. lxv.

65 C. Helen Brock (ed.), *The Correspondence of Dr William Hunter 1740–83* (Glasgow University Library, Special Collections, 1993), ms Hunt Add q65–7. Janet's death is mentioned in a letter from William Cullen to William Hunter, 29 May 1749: John Thomson, *An Account of the Life, Lectures and Writings of William Cullen, MD* (Edinburgh, W. Blackwood and Sons, 1859), pp. 539–40.

Chapter 4

1 JH, *The Works*, vol. 4, 'An account of the organ of hearing in fishes', p. 294.

2 C. G. T. Dean, *The Royal Hospital Chelsea* (London, Hutchinson, 1950), *passim*. The Royal Hospital Chelsea still provides a home for army pensioners today while the grounds are the venue for the annual Chelsea Flower Show. For more information see the hospital's website at www.chelsea-pensioners.org.uk

3 Biographical detail about William Cheselden can be found in Sir Zachary Cope, *William Cheselden 1688–1752* (Edinburgh and London, E. & S. Livingstone, 1953); Knut Haeger, *The Illustrated History of Surgery*, revised update edited by Sir Roy Calne (London, Harold Starke; Chicago, Fitzroy Dearborn; 2000); Sidney Lee and Leslie Stephen (eds), *Dictionary of National Biography* (London, Smith, Elder and Co., 1908–9); John P. Blandy and John S. P. Lumley (eds), *The Royal College of Surgeons of England: 200 years of history at the millennium* (London and Oxford, Royal College of Surgeons of England and Blackwell Science, 2000); Sir Zachary Cope, *The Royal College of Surgeons of England: a history* (London, Anthony Blond, 1959).

4 Details of the lithotomy operation and ancient surgery in general can be found in Ghislaine Lawrence, 'Surgery (Traditional)' in William Bynum and Roy Porter (eds), *Companion Encyclopaedia of the History of Medicine* (London and New York, Routledge, 1993), pp. 961–83. Today, bladder stones are much less common, although doctors are not certain why they should have declined; different diets may be the reason. Surgeons today normally

remove bladder stones in an operation which involves opening the bladder through the abdomen, or by using a special instrument, a lithotrope, which is inserted through the urethra into the bladder to crush a stone; in either case the patient would be under general anaesthetic. Occasionally lasers or ultrasound are used to destroy a stone. The lithotomy position, as used by Cheselden, survives in operations for haemorrhoids and similar conditions. (Personal communication, Professor David Kirk, consultant urologist, Gartnavel General Hospital, Glasgow, November 2003.)

5   Robert Latham (ed.), *The Shorter Pepys* (London, Penguin, 1985), p. 32; Roy Porter, *The Greatest Benefit to Mankind* (London, HarperCollins, 1997), p. 235.

6   Cheselden's lithotomy operations are described in detail in Sir Zachary Cope, *The Royal College of Surgeons of England*. Other aspects are discussed in Ira M. Rutkow, *Surgery: An Illustrated History* (St Louis, Mosby-Year Book Inc. in collaboration with Norman Pub, 1993), pp. 263–7; Toby Gelfand, 'The "Paris manner" of dissection: student anatomical dissection in early eighteenth-century Paris' in *Bulletin of the History of Medicine*, 16 (1972), pp. 99–130. Dr James Douglas, who witnessed many of Cheselden's lithotomies, recorded that 'he seldom exceeds half a Minute' (quoted in Sir Zachary Cope, *William Cheselden 1688–1752*, p. 29).

7   Sir Zachary Cope, *William Cheselden 1688–1752*, pp. 29–30 quoting from the fourth edition of Cheselden's *The Anatomy of the Humane Body*.

8   William Hunter, *Two Introductory Lectures* (London, printed by order of the trustees for J. Johnson, 1784), p. 73.

9   Sir Zachary Cope, *William Cheselden 1688–1752*, p. 91, quoting from Le Dran, *The Operations in Surgery of Mons. Le Dran, translated by Thomas Gataker with remarks, plates of the operations, and a sett of instruments by William Cheselden* (London, C. Hitch and R. Dodsley, 1749).

10   Home, 'A short account', p. xvi.

11   Joan Lane, 'The role of apprenticeship in eighteenth-century medical education in England', and Toby Gelfand,

' "Invite the philosopher, as well as the charitable": hospital training as private enterprise in Hunterian London', both in William Bynum and Roy Porter (eds), *William Hunter and the Eighteenth-century Medical World* (Cambridge University Press, 1985), pp. 57–103 and 129–51; Susan C. Lawrence, *Charitable Knowledge* (Cambridge University Press, 1996), *passim*.

12   Joan Lane, 'The role of apprenticeship'.

13   Tobias Smollett, *The Adventures of Roderick Random* (Oxford University Press, 1999; first published 1748), pp. 86–7.

14   Guy Williams, *The Age of Agony* (London, Constable, 1975), *passim*; David J. Warren, *Old Medical and Dental Instruments* (Princes Risborough, Bucks, Shire Publications Ltd, 1994), *passim*.

15   Ira M. Rutkow, *Surgery: An Illustrated History*, pp. 266–7.

16   Le Dran, *The Operations in Surgery of Mons. Le Dran*, *passim*. Details of Cheselden's methods of amputation, trepanning and the operation for a harelip are all taken from his comments on Le Dran's surgery. General details are also taken from Lorenz Heister, *A General System of Surgery* (London, W. Innys, 1745), 2nd edition. Information about the instruments used can be found in David J. Warren, *Old Medical and Dental Instruments*.

17   William Wadd, *Mems. Maxims, and Memoirs* (London, Callow and Wilson, 1827), p. 20. Dropsy or oedema would usually have been a symptom of heart failure or kidney disease. Today, fluid retention is easily treated with medication.

18   Sir Zachary Cope, *William Cheselden 1688–1752*, pp. 75–9. Today, cataract surgery entails a similar technique in removing the hard, opaque part of the lens, although nowadays this is replaced with an artificial implant and, naturally, the operation is performed under anaesthetic.

19   Agnes Baillie to Matthew Baillie, RCS, relating the memories of her mother Dorothea, William and John's sister, described the dissecting room as being behind their house in Covent Garden (HBC, vol. 2, p. 1). Detail on Covent Garden

can be found in *Survey of London* (London Survey Committee, 1970), vol. 36 and Sheila O'Connell, *London 1753*, catalogue to accompany exhibition of the same name at the British Museum 23 May to 23 November 2003 (London, British Museum Press, 2003).

20   William Hunter, *Medical Commentaries* (London, S. Baker and G. Leigh, 1777), 2nd edition, details several of the pupils who attended William's early lectures and their later posts. Lecture notes made by Charles White, dated 1752, have recently been discovered although it is believed he attended the school a year or two before that date. See William Hunter, *Hunter's Lectures of Anatomy*, notes by Charles White (Amsterdam, London and New York, Elsevier, 1972).

21   Desmond King-Hele, *Erasmus Darwin: A Life of Unequalled Achievement* (London, Giles de la Mare, 1999), p. 14.

22   For help in understanding the process of dissection in Hunter's day, as well as the privilege of witnessing modern medical students undertaking a dissection class, I am indebted to Dr Alistair Hunter, academic manager of the dissecting rooms, and Professor Harold Ellis, clinical anatomist, at Guy's, King's and St Thomas' School of Biomedical Sciences, as well as all the staff in the dissecting rooms at Guy's.

23   Hunter recommended a north-facing dissecting room in an unpublished manuscript, 'Injections etc', n.d., ms 49 d 11, RCS.

24   JH, *Case Books*, pp. 401–2.

25   JH, *Case Books*, p. 405.

26   John M. T. Ford (ed.), *A medical student at St Thomas's Hospital, 1801–1802: The Weekes family letters* (London, Wellcome Institute for the History of Medicine, 1987), p. 78.

27   JH, *The Works*, vol. 4, 'Some observations on digestion', pp. 81–116, describes the gastric juices; JH, *Essays and Observations*, vol. 1, p. 189, describes the taste of mucus in the urethra and semen.

28   William Hunter, *Two Introductory Lectures*, p. 89.

29   JH, *Essays and Observations*, vol. 1, 'On making Anatomical Preparations by Injections, etc.', pp. 385–98. All

quotations on Hunter's methods of making preparations are taken from this essay unless otherwise stated.

30 Notes to the Hunterian Museum, RCS.

31 F. J. Cole, *A History of Comparative Anatomy from Aristotle to the Eighteenth Century* (London, Macmillan, 1944), pp. 458–9; Martin Kemp and Marina Wallace, *Spectacular Bodies* (London Hayward Gallery, 2000), p. 62.

32 T. V. N. Persaud, *A History of Anatomy: the post-Vesalian era* (Springfield, Charles C. Thomas, 1997), pp. 43–4.

33 JH, *Essays and Observations*, p. 124.

34 Ottley, 'The Life', pp. 75–6.

35 C. Helen Brock, *Calendar of the Correspondence of Dr William Hunter, 1740–83* (Cambridge, Wellcome Unit for the History of Medicine, 1996), p. i.

36 John H. Teacher, *Catalogue of the Anatomical and Pathological Preparations of Dr William Hunter in the Hunterian Museum, University of Glasgow* (Glasgow, James MacLehose and Sons, 1900). Teacher estimated that the original collection Hunter bequeathed to the university totalled 3,384. Maggie Riley, at the Hunterian Museum, Glasgow, estimated that William's original collection numbered 3,755 (personal communication, 2002).

37 William Hunter, *The Anatomy of the Human Gravid Uterus exhibited in figures* (Birmingham, J. Baskerville, S. Baker and G. Leigh, 1774). William Hunter gives the date of the arrival of the body as 1751 in the preface of his *Gravid Uterus* but in the text he refers to the winter of 1750. In fact, the drawings by van Rymsdyk are dated 1750, as confirmed by staff at Glasgow University Library, Special Collections (personal communication, 2003).

38 Ibid., preface. Later quotes from William are all from the preface unless otherwise stated.

39 C. Helen Brock (ed.), *William Hunter 1718–1783: a memoir by Samuel Foart Simmons and John Hunter* (University of Glasgow Press, 1983), p. 17. In annotations, John says William 'would have his brother dissect the parts for him'.

40 John L. Thornton and Patricia C. Want, 'Jan van Rymsdyk's illustrations of the gravid uterus drawn for

Hunter, Smellie, Jenty and Denman' in *Journal of Audiovisual Media in Medicine*, 2 (1979), pp. 11–15.

41   John H. Teacher, *Catalogue of the Anatomical and Pathological Preparations of Dr William Hunter in the Hunterian Museum*, vol. 1, pp. xlix–l; William Hunter, *The Anatomy of the Human Gravid Uterus*, preface. Teacher has shown that twelve plates are dated – I to X in 1750, XV and XXVI in 1754 – and that four more undated plates – XIII, XXI, XXII and XXXII – are probably from the years 1750–4. The plates depict six women. William refers to the second and third 'subjects' arriving before the first ten plates were completed.

42   John H. Teacher, *Catalogue of the Anatomical and Pathological Preparations of Dr William Hunter in the Hunterian Museum*. Thanks to Anne Delau, curator of the Hunterian Art Gallery at the University of Glasgow, for checking details of the portrait. The portrait was commissioned by Glasgow University in 1787 and completed in 1789; it can still be seen at the Hunterian Art Gallery.

43   JH, *The Works*, vol. 4, p. 62.

44   Notes to the Hunterian Museum, RCS.

45   John H. Teacher, *Catalogue of the Anatomical and Pathological Preparations of Dr William Hunter in the Hunterian Museum*, pp. 326, 396–404, 509, 571–3, 589–90.

46   JH, 'A Copy of the Oldest Portion of Catalogue, in Mr Hunter's handwriting', n.d., ms 49 e 53, RCS. This catalogue dates four items as having been dissected between 1754 and 1760. Others may have stemmed from this period but cannot be identified.

47   Home, 'A short account', p. xvi.

48   Betsy Copping Corner (ed.), *William Shippen, Jr, pioneer in American medical education* (Philadelphia, American Philosophical Society, 1951), from William Shippen's diary, p. 28.

49   Sir D'Arcy Power, *A Short History of St Bartholomew's Hospital, 1123–1923* (London, St Bartholomew's Hospital, 1923), *passim*.

50   JH, *The Works*, vol. 1, 'Lectures on the principles of surgery', p. 210.

51   JH, *A Treatise on the Venereal Disease*, pp. 128–9.
52   C. Helen Brock (ed.), *William Hunter 1718–1783*, p. 7, annotations by John Hunter.
53   C. Helen Brock, *Calendar of the Correspondence of Dr William Hunter, 1740–83*, p. 7.
54   John Thomson, *An Account of the Life, Lectures and Writings of William Cullen, MD* (Edinburgh, W. Blackwood and Sons, 1859), vol. 1, appendix, correspondence with William Hunter, pp. 540–3.

Chapter 5

1   William Hunter, *Medical Commentaries* (London, A. Hamilton, 1762), supplement to the first part of *Medical Commentaries*, p. iii.
2   Biographical details of Alexander Monro II and the Monro dynasty in general can be found in T. V. N. Persaud, *A History of Anatomy: the post-Vesalian era* (Springfield, Charles C. Thomas, 1997), and Malcolm Nicolson, 'Medicine' in P. H. Scott (ed.), *Scotland: A Concise Cultural History* (Edinburgh, Mainstream, 1993), pp. 327–42.
3   William Hunter, *Medical Commentaries*, p. 19. The dates, details and comments regarding the arguments between the Hunters and the Monros, and the Hunters with Pott, are all taken from William's *Medical Commentaries* unless otherwise stated.
4   Roy Porter, *The Greatest Benefit to Mankind* (London, HarperCollins, 1997), pp. 182, 183, 242.
5   C. Helen Brock (ed.), *William Hunter 1718–1783: a memoir by Samuel Foart Simmons and John Hunter* (University of Glasgow Press, 1983), stated in annotations by John Hunter, p. 28.
6   Ibid., p. 8.
7   Ibid., p. 41.
8   Anon., 'Reviews and Notices' in *British Medical Journal* (1861), pp. 303–5.
9   Reminiscences of Dorothea Baillie, told to her daughters Agnes and Joanna Baillie, HBC, vol. 6, p. 18; C. Helen Brock, 'The happiness of riches', in William Bynum and Roy

Porter (eds.), *William Hunter and the Eighteenth-century Medical World* (Cambridge University Press, 1985), pp. 35–54.

10   C. Helen Brock, *Calendar of the Correspondence of Dr William Hunter, 1740–83* (Cambridge, Wellcome Unit for the History of Medicine, 1996), p. 8. Brock states that William opened an account at Drummonds in 1755.

11   C. Helen Brock (ed.), *William Hunter 1718–1783*, p. 8, annotations by John Hunter.

12   Copy of John's signature, written as Johannes Hunter, in the enrolment register at Oxford University, 5 June 1755, preserved in the HA, RCS.

13   Simon Schama, *A History of Britain: The British wars 1603–1776* (London, BBC Worldwide Ltd, 2001), p. 393.

14   Ottley, 'The Life', p. 14, quoting Hunter speaking to his pupil, Sir Anthony Carlisle.

15   Letter from Minson Hales to John Hunter, 11 April 1753, quoted in C. Helen Brock (ed.), *The Correspondence of Dr William Hunter 1740–83* (Glasgow University Library, Special Collections, 1993), refers to William having been 'dangerously ill'. Ottley, 'The Life', p. 16, states that John took over a portion of lectures in 1754.

16   Home, 'A short account', p. xxiv.

17   Useful sources on the history of anatomy include T. V. N. Persaud, *A History of Anatomy*; Roger French, 'The Anatomical Tradition' in William Bynum and Roy Porter (eds), *Companion Encyclopaedia of the History of Medicine* (London and New York, Routledge, 1993), pp. 81–101; and Roy Porter, *The Greatest Benefit to Mankind*. William Hunter provided his students with a summary in the first lecture of each course. See William Hunter, *Two Introductory Lectures* (London, printed by order of the trustees for J. Johnson, 1784).

18   The history of discoveries of the lymphatic system is explained in Nellie B. Eales, 'The history of the lymphatic system, with special reference to the Hunter-Monro controversy' in *Journal of the History of Medicine*, 29 (1974), pp. 280–94, as well as in sources mentioned above on the general history of anatomy.

19   Nellie B. Eales, 'The history of the lymphatic system', quoting Alexander Monro, Jr, *De testibus et de semine in variis animalibus* (Edinburgh, 1755), p. 55; other details of the Hunters' row with the Monros are taken from William Hunter, *Medical Commentaries*.

20   William Hunter, *Medical Commentaries*, p. 7. William's italics.

21   Home, 'A short account', p. xviii.

22   JH, 'A Copy of the Oldest Portion of Catalogue in Mr Hunter's own handwriting', RCS ms 49 e 53. The specimens listed in this first catalogue were all collected before 1764, and since Hunter spent most of the latter period in the army, most of these animals were probably obtained before 1760 while he worked with William.

23   John Abernethy, *Physiological Lectures* (London, Longman, 1825), p. 5.

24   JH, *The Works*, vol. 3, pp. 76–7.

25   Stephen Inwood, *The Man Who Knew Too Much: the strange and inventive life of Robert Hooke 1635–1703* (London, Macmillan, 2002), p. 47.

26   Andrew Cunningham, 'The pen and the sword: recovering the disciplinary identity of physiology and anatomy before 1800, I: Old physiology – the pen' in *Studies in History and Philosophy of Biological and Biomedical Sciences*, 33 (2002), pp. 631–65. Details of eighteenth-century embryology research can also be found in Brian Cook, *Contributions of the Hunter brothers to our understanding of reproduction, an exhibition from the University Library's collections* (leaflet, Special Collections Department, Glasgow University Library, 1992).

27   Laurence Sterne, *The Life and Opinions of Tristram Shandy* (London, Penguin, 1967; first published in 1759–67), p. 36.

28   JH, 'Of the different methods to be taken to examine the progress of the chick in incubated eggs', RCS ms 49 d 11 (n.d.); also reprinted in Richard Owen (ed.), *Descriptive and Illustrated Catalogue of the Physiological Series of Comparative Anatomy*, vol. 5, Products of Generation (London, RCS, 1840). Hunter's experiments on embryology were published in JH, *Essays and Observations*.

29   JH, *The Works*, vol. 3, p. 106.

30   JH, *The Works*, vol. 4, 'The animal oeconomy', pp. 187–92.

31   JH, 'A Copy of the Oldest Portion of Catalogue', p. 16. Specimen C4, showing the first pair of cranial nerves, is dated 1754 and was therefore in Hunter's original collection. The specimen can no longer be located.

32   Fenwick Beekman, 'Teacher and pupil: the brothers William and John Hunter from 1748 to 1760' in *Bulletin of the History of Medicine*, 27 (1954), pp. 501–14, quoting, on p. 511, an advertisement for Hunter's *The Natural History of the Human Teeth*; John H. Teacher, *Catalogue of the Anatomical and Pathological Preparations of Dr William Hunter in the Hunterian Museum, University of Glasgow* (Glasgow, James MacLehose and Sons, 1900), identifies seven specimens of teeth in William's museum which were probably prepared by John.

33   William Hunter, *Medical Commentaries*, p. 1.

34   Ibid., pp. 2–4.

35   Ibid., p. 34.

36   The pupils' register of St George's Hospital, transcript at RCS, 3 vols. Vol. 1, p. 1, records that John Hunter was appointed a house surgeon on 5 May 1756.

37   Information on the hospital's history is taken from George C. Peachey, *History of St George's Hospital* (London, J. Bale, 1910–14).

38   Foot, *The Life*, pp. 75–6. Foot describes the duties of a house surgeon as well as the post-holder's responsibility for the 'keys of the dead house'.

39   JH, *Case Books*, pp. 292–3.

40   Ibid., pp. 294–5.

41   Foot, *The Life*, p. 75.

42   C. Helen Brock, *Calendar of the Correspondence of Dr William Hunter*, p. 10. According to Brock, William took a lease on the house in Jermyn Street in the summer of 1756.

43   William Hunter, *Medical Commentaries*, p. 89.

44   JH, 'Observations on the state of the testis in the fetus, and on the hernia congenita' in William Hunter, *Medical Commentaries*, pp. 75–89.

45 William Hunter, *Medical Commentaries*, p. 89.

46 JH, 'Observations on the state of the testis'.

47 The argument with Pott is described fully in William Hunter, *Medical Commentaries*, supplement pp. 12–27, and is also discussed in Fenwick Beekman, 'The "Hernia Congenita" and an account of the controversy it provoked between William Hunter and Percivall Pott' in *Bulletin of the New York Academy of Medicine*, 22 (1946), pp. 486–500.

48 Fenwick Beekman, 'The "Hernia Congenita"', quoting Pott's second edition of *A Treatise on Ruptures*, 1763, p. 139.

49 William Hunter, *Medical Commentaries*.

50 Anon., article in the *European Magazine* (1782), reprinted in John Abernethy, *Physiological Lectures* (London, Longman, 1825), pp. 341–52.

51 Nellie B. Eales, 'The history of the lymphatic system'.

52 JH, 'The modern history of the absorbing system', RCS ms 49 e 5. These notes, in the handwriting of Hunter's later assistant and brother-in-law Everard Home, were apparently part of an original catalogue to Hunter's museum.

53 The details of the experiments on the five animals are described by John Hunter in his brother's pamphlet, William Hunter, *Medical Commentaries*, pp. 42–8. Technically, certain fats can enter the veins but only in minute quantities.

54 Joseph Wright, *An Experiment on a Bird in the Air Pump*, exhibited 1768, National Gallery.

55 John Wiltshire, *Samuel Johnson in the Medical World, the doctor and the patient* (Cambridge University Press, 1991), pp. 128–38, quoting Samuel Johnson, *The Idler*, 17, 1758.

56 Haller's experiments are discussed in Andrew Cunningham, 'The pen and the sword', p. 653; John Wiltshire, *Samuel Johnson in the Medical World*, argues persuasively that Haller and not Hunter was the target of Johnson's attack.

57 JH, *The Works*, vol. 4, 'Some observations on digestion', pp. 81–116.

58 Betsy Copping Corner (ed.), *William Shippen, Jr, pioneer in American medical education* (Philadelphia, American Philosophical Society, 1951), quoting a letter from William

Shippen senior to his brother, Edward Shippen, 1 September 1758, p. 7.

59   Ibid., p. 25.

60   *Dictionary of American Biography* (Oxford University Press and New York, Charles Scribner's Sons, 1928–58), vol. 42, pp. 117–18.

61   The period from 1760 to March 1761 is fairly obscure in Hunter's life. Various biographers refer to his falling ill in 1759 or 1760, but the latter seems most likely since he was clearly in fine form while Shippen lodged in his house up until January 1760. He does not himself refer to being ill, but early biographers, Foot and Home, both say his health suffered in 1760 while Ottley states he suffered from an inflammation of the lungs. William refers to his brother's ill health in his *Medical Commentaries* without being specific about the date. John himself says unequivocally that he 'quitted' anatomy in 1760 in his 'The animal oeconomy', and in an unpublished ms he says this was in the 'early summer' of 1760. Yet he records two post-mortems and one case of treatment in his case books that summer. An article on his lectures in the *European Magazine* in 1782, apparently approved by Hunter, attributes his decision to quit to his desire 'for a more enlarged field of observation'. He was living in Covent Garden again in the winter of 1760–1, when Morgan stayed, according to Bell's biography of Morgan. Foot, *The Life*, p. 74; Home, 'A short account', p. xviii; Ottley, 'The Life', p. 20; William Hunter, *Medical Commentaries*, p. 35; JH, *The Works*, vol. 4, 'The animal oeconomy', p. 292; JH, RCS ms 49 e 5 (n.d.); JH, *Case Books*, p. 317 (two post-mortems) and pp. 111–12 (surgical care); anon., article in the *European Magazine* (1782); Whitfield J. Bell, *John Morgan, Continental Doctor* (Philadelphia, University of Pennsylvania Press, 1965), p. 48.

Chapter 6

1   JH, *The Works*, vol. 3, 'A treatise on the blood, inflammation and gun-shot wounds', p. 575.

2   T. Keppel, *The Life of Augustus Viscount Keppel* (London,

Henry Colburn, 1842), pp. 293–320. Keppel's misgivings about the troops are related in letters from Major-General Studholme Hodgson to the Earl of Albemarle. His 'secret instructions' are also detailed here.

3   Details of the Seven Years War and the Battle for Belle-Ile are related in Tom Pocock, *Battle for Empire, the very first world war 1756–63* (London, Michael O'Mara Ltd, 1998); J. Fortescue, *A History of the British Army* (London, Macmillan and Co., 1899), vol. 2, pp. 521–38; W. Clowes, *The Royal Navy, a history* (New York, AMS Press, 1966), vol. 3, pp. 234–6.

4   Anon., article in the *European Magazine* (1782), reprinted in John Abernethy, *Physiological Lectures* (London, Longman, 1825), pp. 341–52.

5   Roy Porter, *Blood and Guts: a short history of medicine* (London, Penguin, 2003), p. 109.

6   A. Peterkin, William Johnston and R. Drew, *Commissioned Officers in the Medical Services of the British Army 1660–1960* (London, Wellcome Historical Medical Library, 1968), vol. 1, p. 33.

7   JH, RCS ms 49 e 5 (n.d.). Hunter says he embarked from Portsmouth in the year that he was commissioned for an expedition which was abandoned.

8   JH to William Hunter, 11 July 1761, HBC, vol. 2, p. 14.

9   Jeremy Lewis, *Tobias Smollett* (London, Jonathan Cape, 2003), p. 28.

10   Tobias Smollett, *The Adventures of Roderick Random* (Oxford University Press, 1999; first published 1748), p. 187.

11   T. Keppel, *The Life of Augustus Viscount Keppel*, p. 309, quoting a letter from Hodgson to the Earl of Albemarle, 12 April 1761.

12   Guy Williams, *The Age of Agony* (London, Constable, 1975), p. 212, quoting Edward Ward in his *Voyage from England to India*.

13   Tobias Smollett, *The Adventures of Roderick Random*, p. 149.

14   *Gentleman's Magazine*, April 1761, p. 229, quoting a letter from Hodgson reporting the victory, 23 April.

15   T. Keppel, *The Life of Augustus Viscount Keppel*, quoting a letter from Hodgson to the Earl of Albemarle, 17 May 1761.

16   JH, *The Works*, vol. 3, p. 575.

17   Ibid., p. 559.

18   JH, *Case Books*, p. 65; Dobson, *John Hunter*, p. 55.

19   Sir Neil Cantlie, *A History of the Army Medical Department* (Edinburgh and London, Churchill Livingstone, 1974), vol. 1, p. 133.

20   Ibid., p. 107.

21   Dobson, *John Hunter*, p. 51.

22   JH to William Hunter, 28 May 1762, published in the *Medical Times and Gazette* 1867, pp. 515–16. Four of John's letters to William from Belle-Ile are preserved in the RCS Library, HBC, vol. 2, while two more – cited above and 23 March 1762 – were discovered later and published in the *Medical Times and Gazette*.

23   G. E. Gask, 'John Hunter in the campaign in Portugal, 1762–3' in *British Journal of Surgery*, 24 (1936–37), pp. 640–67. Page 664 cites pay rates of different medical staff.

24   JH to William Hunter, 28 September 1761, HBC, vol. 2, p. 18.

25   Many thanks to Mick Crumplin, honorary consultant surgeon and honorary curator at the Royal College of Surgeons, for advice on Hunter's treatment of gunshot wounds compared to his contemporaries', as well as for general advice on army surgery. Debridement – cutting away deadened tissue – is the accepted practice today.

26   Roy Porter, *The Greatest Benefit to Mankind* (London, HarperCollins, 1997), p. 188.

27   JH, *The Works*, vol. 3, p. 549.

28   Sir Robert Drew, 'John Hunter and the Army', reprinted from the *Journal of the Royal Army Medical Corps*, 113 (1967), no. 1, p. 11.

29   JH, *Case Books*, pp. 274–5.

30   JH, *The Works*, vol. 3, pp. 549–50; JH, *Case Books*, p. 275.

31   JH, *The Works*, vol. 3, p. 555.

32   Ibid., pp. 574–5.

33 Sir Anthony A. Bowlby, *British Military Surgery in the Time of Hunter and in the Great War*, Hunterian Oration 1919 (London, Adlard & Son, 1919), p. 25, quoting G. J. Guthrie.

34 JH, *The Works*, vol. 3, pp. 574–5.

35 Ibid., p. 572.

36 Many thanks to Mick Crumplin again for his advice on Hunter's policy towards amputations. Early amputations are today considered to lead to better outcomes.

37 JH to William Hunter, 23 March 1762, printed in the *Medical Times and Gazette* 1867, p. 516, refers to his appointment as director of the hospital, the titles he was awarded and his need to keep a horse for the job.

38 JH to William Hunter, 11 July 1761, HBC, vol. 2, p. 14.

39 JH to William Hunter, 12 April 1762, HBC, vol. 2, p. 15.

40 JH to William Hunter, 11 July 1761, HBC, vol. 2; and 14 and 28 September 1761, p. 18.

41 C. Helen Brock, *Calendar of the Correspondence of Dr William Hunter 1740–83* (Cambridge, Wellcome Unit for the History of Medicine, 1996), p. 23.

42 JH, *Case Books*. The cases are featured on pp. 275 (Thruber) and 67–8 (Home/Hume).

43 Alexandre Dumas, *The Man in the Iron Mask* (Oxford University Press, 1991), p. 517. Porthos dies in Belle-Ile after the island is attacked by Louis XIV's forces.

44 JH, *The Works*, vol. 3, p. 21; Richard Owen (ed.), *Descriptive and Illustrated Catalogue of the Physiological Series of Comparative Anatomy*, vol. 5, Products of Generation (London, RCS, 1840), p. 61.

45 JH, *Essays and Observations*, p. 245.

46 Jessie Dobson (ed.), *Descriptive Catalogue of the Physiological Series in the Hunterian Museum* (Edinburgh and London, E. & S. Livingstone, 1970), part 1, p. 265.

47 Details of Hunter's time in Portugal are fully described in the Loudoun Papers (LP), a set of letters, records and sick returns archived at the RCS Library. His spell in Portugal is also described in G. E. Gask, 'John Hunter in the campaign in Portugal', pp. 640–67; Fenwick Beekman, 'John Hunter in Portugal' in *Annals of Medical History* (1936), n.d., vol. 8,

pp. 288–96; and Sir Robert Drew, 'John Hunter and the Army'.

48 LP, vol. 1, ms 23, return of invalids by JH, 26 June 1762.

49 Ibid., ms 22, n.d.

50 Ibid., ms 37, n.d.

51 Ibid., ms 59, 9 August 1762.

52 Ibid., ms 27, 1 July 1762.

53 JH to William Hunter, 25 July 1762, Lisbon, HBC, vol. 2, p. 2.

54 LP, vol. 1, ms 8, 9 May 1762.

55 Ibid., ms 45, W. Young to Lord Loudoun, 19 July 1762; and ms 47, W. Maddox to Colonel Cosnan, received by Lord Loudoun, 22 July 1762.

56 JH, Case Books, p. 278.

57 LP, vol. 1, ms 56, report by Major Biddulph, 31 July 1762.

58 Ibid., ms 55, report by Peter Bernard, 31 July 1762.

59 Ibid., ms 77, letter P. Bernard to Lord Loudoun, 30 August 1762.

60 Ibid., ms 61, H. Smith to W. Young, 13 August 1762.

61 Ibid., ms 74, W. Young to Lord Loudoun, 28 August 1762.

62 Ibid., ms 98, William Wiseman to General Armstrong, 20 September 1762.

63 Ibid., ms 114, JH to Lord Loudoun, 7 October 1762.

64 Ibid., ms 74, W. Young to Lord Loudoun, 28 August 1762.

65 Ibid., ms 86, W. Young to Lord Loudoun, 8 September 1762.

66 Ibid., ms 87, W. Young to Lord Loudoun, distribution of the physical gentlemen, 14 September 1762; and ms 91, W. Young to Lord Loudoun, 13 September 1762.

67 Ibid., ms 86, W. Young to Lord Loudoun, 8 September 1762.

68 JH, Case Books, p. 38.

69 LP, vol. 2, ms 115, return of the sick from Macao, JH to Lord Loudoun, 7 October 1762; and ms 128, JH to Lord Loudoun, return of the sick from St Domingo, 10 October 1762.

70 LP, vol. 1, ms 91, W. Young to Lord Loudoun, 13 September 1762; and vol. 2, ms 137, William Cadogan to Lord Loudoun, 21 October 1762.

71 JH to Lord Loudoun, 28 October 1762, copy cited in Fenwick Beekman, 'John Hunter in Portugal', pp. 288–96.

72 JH to William Hunter, 16 November 1762, HBC, vol. 2, p. 7.

73 Foot, *The Life*, p. 80.

74 A. Peterkin et al, *Commissioned Officers in the Medical Services of the British Army*, vol. 1, p. 22, gives Francis Tomkins as having joined as a regimental surgeon on 3 September 1751.

75 LP, vol. 2, ms 169, Samuel Hayes to Loudoun, 8 November 1762.

76 Ibid., ms 207, Francis Tomkins to Colonel Cosnan, 6 December 1762; and ms 205, 5 December 1762.

77 Ibid., ms 197, W. Young to Lord Loudoun, 2 December 1762; and ms 246, JH, return of the sick, 2 January 1763.

78 JH, *The Works*, vol. 4, p. 293.

79 JH, *Observations and Reflections on Geology*, p. xvi.

80 JH to William Hunter, 22 February 1763, cited in C. Helen Brock, *Calendar of the Correspondence of Dr William Hunter*, p. 25.

81 R. Craig, 'Gunshot wounds then and now: how did John Hunter get away with it?' in *Papers presented at the Hunterian Bicentenary Commemorative Meeting* (London, Royal College of Surgeons of England, 1995), pp. 15–19, describes the three gunshot wound specimens with impressions of French musket balls. JH, 'A Copy of the Oldest Portion of Catalogue, in Mr Hunter's handwriting', ms 49 e 53, RCS, n.d., lists fifty specimens of lizards and the soldier's intestine.

Chapter 7

1 JH, *The Works*, vol. 2, 'Treatise on the natural history and diseases of the human teeth', p. 99.

2 Anne S. Hargreaves, *White as Whales Bone: dental services in early modern England* (Leeds, W. S. Maney and Son Ltd, 1998), p. 9, citing the Duchess of Northumberland describing George III, and p. 11, citing Horace Walpole describing the Duke of Newcastle.

3   Details about the history of dentistry can be found in Anne S. Hargreaves, *White as Whales Bone*; Malvin E. Ring, *Dentistry: an illustrated history* (New York, Abrams, 1985); John Woodforde, *The Strange Story of False Teeth* (London, Routledge and Kegan Paul, 1968).

4   James Woodforde, *The Diary of a Country Parson*, ed. J. Beresforde (Oxford University Press, 1981), vol. 1, p. 183.

5   Tobias Smollett to William Hunter, 14 June 1763, HBC, vol. 1, p. 91.

6   C. Helen Brock, 'The Happiness of Riches', in William Bynum and Roy Porter (eds.), *William Hunter and the Eighteenth-century Medical World* (Cambridge University Press, 1985), p. 41. Brock says William's bank account shows several payments to John.

7   Dobson, *John Hunter*, p. 108. Hunter gave his address as Covent Garden in June 1765 when purchasing land at Earls Court so it is reasonable to assume he had settled there on returning from Portugal. Foot, *The Life*, p. 132. Foot is the only source stating Hunter embarked on dentistry in an alliance with James Spence at this time, although Hunter himself refers to working with Spence in his treatise on teeth.

8   Foot, *The Life*, p. 131.

9   Sidney Lee and Leslie Stephen (eds.), *Dictionary of National Biography* (London, Smith, Elder and Co., 1908–9), vol. 7, pp. 367–8; Foot, *The Life*, pp. 133–4.

10   JH, 'Treatise on the natural history and diseases of the human teeth', p. 95n.

11   Ibid., p. 108.

12   Ibid., p. 104.

13   The specimen showing a human tooth transplanted into a cock's comb is P 56 in the Hunterian Museum. The cockerel's testicle in the hen's abdomen is P 53.

14   JH, 'Treatise on the natural history and diseases of the human teeth', p. 104.

15   Sir Roy Calne, 'Replacement surgery and transplantation' in *Papers presented at the Hunterian Bicentenary Commemorative Meeting* (London, Royal College of Surgeons of England, 1995), pp. 12–14.

16   Dr William Irvine to Professor Thomas Hamilton, 17 June

1771, cited in 'The Hunters and the Hamiltons: some unpublished letters', *Lancet*, 18 February 1928, pp. 354–60.

17 John Woodforde, *The Strange Story of False Teeth*, p. 24.

18 Henry W. Noble, 'Tooth transplantation: a controversial story', shortened version of a lecture given to the Scottish Society for the History of Medicine, 15 June 2002, available on the History of Dentistry Research Group website www.rcpsglasg.ac.uk/hdrg/home.html

19 Ibid., p. 1.

20 Ibid., p. 2.

21 JH, 'Treatise on the natural history and diseases of the human teeth', p. 100.

22 Ibid., p. 104, note by Thomas Bell, lecturer in comparative anatomy at Guy's Hospital, writing in 1835.

23 Fiona Haslam, *From Hogarth to Rowlandson: medicine in art in eighteenth-century Britain* (Liverpool University Press, 1996), p. 253.

24 Henry W. Noble, 'Tooth transplantation: a controversial story', p. 2.

25 Fiona Haslam, *From Hogarth to Rowlandson*, pp. 252–3; Ruth Richardson, 'Transplanting Teeth: reflections on Thomas Rowlandson's *Transplanting Teeth*' in *Lancet*, 354 (1999), p. 1740.

26 J. Menzies Campbell, *Dentistry Then and Now* (Glasgow, Pickering and Inglis, 1963), p. 64.

27 John Woodforde, *The Strange Story of False Teeth*, p. 84.

28 Ibid., p. 81.

29 Thomas Berdmore, *A treatise on the disorders and deformities of the teeth and gums* (London, the author, 1768), p. 102.

30 William Rae, 'Lectures on the Teeth' in *British Journal of Dental Science* (1857), pp. 517–21, taken from a verbatim manuscript note of lectures beginning 12 April 1782 by Mr Tomes; Christine Hillam, 'New notes on the lectures of William Rae' in *Dental Historian*, 33 (1998), pp. 50–72.

31 JH to William Cullen, 24 September 1777, transcript of letter, ms Cullen 204, Glasgow University Library, Special Collections.

32 Thanks for advice to Bob Corfield of UK Transplant.

33   JH, *The Natural History of the Human Teeth* and *A Practical Treatise on the Diseases of the Teeth*.

34   Hunter's contribution to dentistry is discussed in Jerry J. Herschfeld, 'John Hunter and his practical treatise on diseases of the teeth' in *Bulletin of the History of Dentistry*, 29, 1 (1981) pp. 32–6; J. Menzies Campbell, *Dentistry Then and Now*, pp. 88–106; Irwin D. Mandel, 'Revisiting John Hunter' in *Journal of the History of Dentistry*, 48, 2 (2000), pp. 57–60; and David E. Poswillo, 'John Hunter's contribution to dentistry' in *Dental Historian*, 38 (2001), pp. 13–17. Many thanks to Malcolm Bishop, dental surgeon, for his help in explaining Hunter's contribution to dentistry and its significance today.

35   Irwin D. Mandel, 'Revisiting John Hunter', p. 57.

36   Foot, *The Life*, pp. 62–3.

37   Jeremy Lewis, *Tobias Smollett* (London, Jonathan Cape, 2003), *passim*.

38   Lloyd G. Stevenson, 'The Elder Spence, William Combe, and John Hunter' in *Journal of the History of Medicine*, 10 (1955), pp. 182–96; Harlan W. Hamilton, 'William Combe and John Hunter's essay on teeth' in *Journal of the History of Medicine*, 14 (1959), pp. 169–78.

39   Home, 'A short account', p. xviii. Home says Hunter taught practical anatomy and operational surgery for several winters at this time.

40   John Hadley, 'An account of a mummy, inspected at London 1763, in a letter to William Heberden, MD FRS, from John Hadley, MD FRS' in *Philosophical Transactions of the Royal Society*, 54, 1764 (New York, Johnson Reprint Co., 1965), pp. 1–14.

41   C. Helen Brock, *Calendar of the Correspondence of Dr William Hunter 1740–83* (Cambridge, Wellcome Unit for the History of Medicine, 1996), p. 38.

42   JH, *Case Books*, pp. 323 and 324.

43   Roy Porter, *The Greatest Benefit to Mankind* (London, HarperCollins, 1997), pp. 263–4. The gradual acceptance of post-mortems in Georgian society and Hunter's role in this trend has been described by Simon Chaplin in a lecture, ' "An Excellent Hand for the Business": John Hunter and the art of

dissection in Johnson's London', given at Dr Johnson's House, London, 20 November 2003.

44 John Abernethy, *Physiological Lectures* (London, Longman, 1825), Hunterian Oration 1819, pp. 40–1.

45 JH, *Case Books*, p. 300.

46 Ibid., pp. 316–17.

47 The specimen of Mrs Johnston's liver is thought to be P 1103 in the Hunterian Museum.

48 JH, *Case Books*, p. 359.

49 Sidney Lee and Leslie Stephen (eds.), *Dictionary of National Biography*, vol. 3, p. 584; Jessie Dobson, 'John Hunter and the Byron family' in *Journal of the History of Medicine*, 10 (1955), pp. 333–5.

50 JH, *Case Books*, pp. 213 and 347.

51 Ibid., p. 332.

52 Ibid., pp. 356–7.

53 Biographical details about Anne Home Hunter can be found in Aileen K. Adams, ' "I am happy in a wife": a study of Mrs John Hunter (1742–1821)' in *Papers presented at the Hunterian Bicentenary Commemorative Meeting*, pp. 32–7; Jane M. Oppenheimer, 'Anne Home Hunter and her friends' in *Journal of the History of Medicine*, 1 (1946), pp. 434–45; and Sir Arthur Porritt, 'John Hunter's Women' in *Transactions of the Hunterian Society*, 17 (1958–9), pp. 81–111.

54 'Reminiscences of Mrs John Hunter' by her great-niece, Mrs E. Milligan, in 1866, HBC, vol. 2, p. 58; Professor William Hamilton to his father, 25 December 1777, cited in 'The Hunters and the Hamiltons: some unpublished letters', *Lancet*, 18 February 1928, pp. 354–60.

55 *Dr William Hunter* by Allan Ramsay, c. 1765, Hunterian Art Gallery, University of Glasgow.

56 *John Hunter FRS* by Robert Home, c. 1770, Royal Society. Although dated at around 1770, this shows a younger man than in the second Home portrait.

57 JH, *The Works*, vol. 4, p. 320.

58 *John Hunter* by Robert Home, Royal College of Surgeons, c. 1775–8. An engraving taken from this painting by H. Cook, at the Royal Society, dates the painting to c. 1765 and also shows the mummy more clearly.

59   A. Home Shippen (Nancy Shippen), *Nancy Shippen, Her Journal Book*, ed. E. Armes (Philadelphia, J. B. Lippencott Co., 1935), pp. 52–5, BL.

60   Jessie Dobson, 'Some of John Hunter's patients' in *Annals of the Royal College of Surgeons of England*, 42 (1968), pp. 124–33.

61   Foot, *The Life*, p. 240.

62   Dobson, *John Hunter*, pp. 114–15.

63   Peachey, *A Memoir*, pp. 144–5, cites the details of Hunter's purchase of land at Earls Court; W. W. Hutchings, *London Town – Past and Present* (London, Cassell, 1909), p. 674, re. Hunter living at 31 Golden Square. A blue plaque denotes the house.

64   JH, *The Works*, vol. 4, pp. 131–55. The experiments were first related in two papers to the Royal Society, 'Experiments on animals and vegetables with respect of the power of producing heat', read 22 June 1775, and 'On the heat etc of animals and vegetables', read 19 June and 13 November 1777.

65   JH, *The Works*, vol. 1, p. 284.

66   JH, *Case Books*, p. 233.

67   JH, *The Works*, vol. 1, 'Lectures on the principles of surgery', p. 512.

68   JH, *Case Books*, p. 233. Two specimens of dogs' tendons survive as P 109 and P 110.

69   JH, 'A Copy of the Oldest Portion of Catalogue in Mr Hunter's own handwriting', RCS ms 49 e 53.

70   Museum notes, Hunterian Museum, RCS.

71   JH, 'The modern history of the absorbing system', RCS ms 49 e 5. These notes, in the handwriting of Hunter's later assistant and brother-in-law Everard Home, were apparently part of an original catalogue to Hunter's collection.

72   JH, *The Works*, vol. 4, 'Anatomical description of the amphibious bipes of Ellis (Siren Lacertina)', pp. 394–7, first published in the *Philosophical Transactions of the Royal Society*, 56 (1767), pp. 307–10; JH, 'General observations on the Pnumobrankes', miscellaneous papers, ms 49 d 11, RCS.

73   Royal Society Journal Book Copy, vol. 26, 1767–70, 5 February 1767 (no page numbers).

74   William was elected FRS on 30 April 1767.

75   There are two specimens showing the heart of the greater siren in the Hunterian Museum, 912 and 913.

Chapter 8

1   James Boswell, *Boswell's London Journal, 1762–1763*, ed. Frederick A. Pottle (Yale University Press, 2000), 20 January 1763, p. 156.

2   JH, *The Works*, vol. 2, 'A treatise on the venereal disease', p. 417. The treatise was first published in 1786.

3   James Boswell, *Boswell's London Journal*, 14 December 1762, pp. 83–4.

4   Anon., *Harris's List of Covent-Garden Ladies, or Man of Pleasure's Kalendar for the year 1779*, from excerpts at Dr Johnson's House, Gough Square, London.

5   Derek Parker, *Casanova* (Stroud, Sutton Publishing, 2003), pp. 156–64.

6   William B. Ober, *Boswell's Clap and Other Essays: medical analyses of literary men's afflictions* (Southern Illinois University Press, 1979), pp. 1–42.

7   James Boswell, *Boswell's London Journal*, 12 January 1763, p. 139.

8   Ibid., 18 January 1763, p. 149.

9   Ibid., 25 March 1763, p. 227.

10   Sheila O'Connell, *London 1753*, catalogue to accompany exhibition of the same name at the British Museum 23 May to 23 November 2003 (London, British Museum Press, 2003) p. 144.

11   *Descriptive Catalogue of the Pathological Series in the Hunterian Museum*, vol. 1, (London, E. & S. Livingstone, 1966), p. 15, describes the penis as specimen P 30; *A Guide to the Hunterian Museum, bicentenary edition* (London, Royal College of Surgeons, 1993), p. 21, details the bone and skull specimens, series P 714 to 746.

12   JH, *Case Books*. The cases cited are respectively on pp. 252, 252, 267, 266, 260–1 and 269. Hunter gives no dates for his consultations with venereal patients.

13   JH, *The Works*, vol. 2, 'A treatise on the venereal disease', p. 387. The case referred to happened in 1782.

14 James Boswell, *Boswell's London Journal*, 20 January 1763, p. 156.

15 Information on the history of venereal disease is given in Claude Quétel, *History of Syphilis* (Cambridge, Polity Press, 1990); William Bynum, 'Treating the wages of sin: venereal disease and specialism in eighteenth-century Britain' in William Bynum and Roy Porter (eds), *Medical Fringe and Medical Orthodoxy 1750–1850* (London and Sydney, Wolfeboro, N.H., Croom Helm, c. 1987), pp. 5–28; Allan M. Brandt, 'Sexually transmitted diseases' in William Bynum and Roy Porter (eds), *Companion Encyclopedia of the History of Medicine* (London, Routledge, 1993), vol. 1, pp. 562–84. I am grateful for the advice of Dr Michael Waugh, consultant genito-urinary physician at Leeds General Infirmary, on the nature and treatment of venereal diseases.

16 Fiona Haslam, *From Hogarth to Rowlandson: medicine in art in eighteenth-century Britain* (Liverpool University Press, 1996), pp. 117–18.

17 William Bynum, 'Treating the wages of sin', pp. 8–9.

18 JH, *The Works*, vol. 2, 'A treatise on the venereal disease', p. 138.

19 Ibid., p. 187.

20 Ibid., p. 190.

21 Ibid., pp. 163–4.

22 Ibid., p. 193.

23 Ibid.

24 Lord Holland (Henry Richard Vassall Fox), *Further Memoirs of the Whig Party 1807–1821* (London, John Murray, 1905), pp. 343–4.

25 JH, *The Works*, vol. 2, 'A treatise on the venereal disease', p. 425.

26 JH, *Case Books*, p. 259.

27 JH, *The Works*, vol. 2, 'A treatise on the venereal disease', pp. 417–19. It is not true, as the extract shows, that he described the subject in the third person. Hunter's defenders have argued that he always described his own health in the first person, but this is not the case either. Writing about his own angina in *The Works*, vol. 3,

'A treatise on the blood, inflammation and gun-shot wounds', p. 150, he begins 'A gentleman was attacked with a pain in the situation of the pylorus' and continues in the same vein.

28   Deborah Hayden, *Pox: genius, madness and the mysteries of syphilis* (New York, Basic Books, 2003), pp. 29–31; Diane Beyer Perett, *Ethics and Error: the dispute between Ricord and Auzias-Turenne over syphilization 1845–70* (Stanford University, 1977), pp. 13–29.

29   W. J. Dempster, 'Towards a new understanding of John Hunter' in *Lancet* (1978), vol. 1, pp. 316–18; George Qvist, 'John Hunter's alleged syphilis' in *Annals of the Royal College of Surgeons of England*, 59 (1977), pp. 205–9; Qvist, 'Some controversial aspects of John Hunter's life and work' in *Annals of the Royal College of Surgeons of England*, 61 (1979), pp. 138–41; Qvist, *John Hunter*, pp. 47–50. Qvist described the notion that Hunter inoculated himself as 'preposterous' while Dempster called it 'beyond belief'.

30   JH, 'Lectures on the principles of surgery by John Hunter 1787', transcription of notes by Mr Twigge, RCS ms 49 e 28, p. 390.

31   Philip J. Weimerskirch and Goetz W. Richter, 'Hunter and venereal disease' in *Lancet* (1979), vol. 1, pp. 503–4. The notes cited are in the Edward G. Miner Library of the University of Rochester Medical Center, New York: JH, 'Lectures on venereal diseases', ms c. 1800. Other surviving notes of Hunter's lectures either fail to mention the experiment or do not cover venereal disease at all.

32   Ottley, 'The Life', p. 47.

33   JH, *The Works*, vol. 2, 'A treatise on the venereal disease', p. 387.

34   JH, *The Works*, vol. 4, 'The animal oeconomy', pp. 139–41.

35   John Sheldon, *The History of the Absorbent System* (London, the author, 1784), p. 31. Sheldon states that Hunter 'informed me that he had fed himself with madder' and that it had turned his urine red.

36   Richard Lovell Edgeworth, *Memoirs of Richard Lovell*

Edgeworth Esq (London, R. Hunter, 1820), vol. 1, pp. 190–1. The circumstances are described more fully in Chapter 11.

37   Anon., *European Magazine* (1782), reprinted in John Abernethy, *Physiological Lectures* (London, Longman, 1825), pp. 341–52.

38   Examples include Robert Hooke, sitting in an airtight box to test air pressure, and the Italian Lazarro Spallanzani, who swallowed and regurgitated linen bags to examine the solvent effect of saliva. See Stephen Inwood, *The Man Who Knew Too Much: the strange and inventive life of Robert Hooke 1635–1703* (London, Macmillan, 2002), p. 107; Roy Porter, *The Greatest Benefit to Mankind* (London, HarperCollins, 1997), p. 253.

39   Benjamin Bell, *A Treatise on Gonorrhoea Virulenta, and Lues Venerea* (Edinburgh, James Watson and Co., 1793).

40   Adams, *Memoirs*, p. 235.

41   JH, *The Works*, vol. 2, 'A treatise on the venereal disease', preface, p. 123.

42   H. Clutterbuck to Joseph Adams, 1799, RCS ms 27 c 5, p. 18. Clutterbuck complained that Hunter's views led to reduced use of mercury.

43   William B. Ober, *Boswell's Clap and Other Essays*, p. 23.

44   JH, *The Works*, vol. 2, 'A treatise on the venereal disease', pp. 304–7.

45   Joseph Farington, *The Farington Diary*, ed. J. Greig (London, Hutchinson and Co., 1922–8), vol. 3, p. 660, entry for 13 September 1796.

46   Jessé Foot, *Observations upon the New Opinions of John Hunter, in his late treatise on the venereal disease* (London, T. Becket, 1786), in three parts, RCS, p. 28.

47   Foot, *The Life*, p. 243. Foot said he called for a syllabus for Hunter's lectures in 1773.

48   Charles Brandon Trye, *A review of Jesse Foote's observations on the new opinions of John Hunter in his late treatise on the venereal disease* (London, John Murray, 1788), pp. 55, 1 and 57.

49   JH to Charles Brandon Trye, copy of letter, 24 February (no year), Hunterian Society Catalogue, ms 5610, 29/5, WL.

50 Ottley, 'The Life', p. 22. The remark was found on a scrap of paper among Hunter's manuscripts after his death.

51 Home, 'A short account', pp. xxi–xxii.

52 Sir Arthur Porritt, 'John Hunter: distant echoes' in *Annals of the Royal College of Surgeons of England*, 41 (1967), pp. 1–24.

53 Home, 'A short account', p. xx. Home suggests Hunter set up the group shortly after joining the RS, although Joseph Adams later argued it was unlikely such a novice member could have organized the club so soon. However, Richard Lovell Edgeworth (see next note) appears to confirm that the club did begin in the late 1760s. Edgeworth said that the club met at Young Slaughter's.

54 Richard Lovell Edgeworth, *Memoirs of Richard Lovell Edgeworth Esq*, vol. 1, pp. 188–9; Jenny Uglow, *The Lunar Men* (London, Faber and Faber, 2002), pp. 124–5.

55 JH, *The Works*, vol. 4, pp. 461–3.

56 Everard Home, 'An Account of a Hermaphrodite Dog', first read to the Royal Society 7 March 1799, tracts RCS. In this paper, Home refers to Hunter's apparently successful experiment in artificial insemination, although he does not give a date. The experiment is also discussed in Brian Cook, *Contributions of the Hunter brothers to our understanding of reproduction, an exhibition from the University Library's collections* (leaflet, Special Collections Department, Glasgow University Library, 1992).

57 C. Helen Brock, *Calendar of the Correspondence of Dr William Hunter 1740–83* (Cambridge, Wellcome Unit for the History of Medicine, 1996), p. 39.

58 C. Helen Brock (ed.), *William Hunter 1718–1783: a memoir by Samuel Foart Simmons and John Hunter* (University of Glasgow Press, 1983), p. 59.

59 William Wadd, *Mems. Maxims and Memoirs* (London, Callow and Wilson, 1827), p. 283.

60 William Hunter, 'Observations on the bones, commonly supposed to be Elephants Bones, which have been found near the River Ohio in America' in *Philosophical Transactions of the Royal Society*, 58 (New York, Johnson Reprint Co., 1965), pp. 34–45.

61   C. Helen Brock, *Calendar of the Correspondence of Dr William Hunter*, letter William Hunter to William Cullen, 1768, p. 40.

62   Ibid., letter John Hunter to William Hunter, p. 106.

63   Company of Surgeons Examination Book, 1745–1800, 7 July 1768, facsimile at RCS.

Chapter 9

1   William Hazlitt, 'The Indian Jugglers' in *The Fight and Other Writings* (London, Penguin, 2000) p. 123. The essay was first published in 1821.

2   Details of the *Endeavour*'s voyage are taken from a variety of sources, principally Ernest Rhys (ed.), *The Voyages of Captain Cook* (Ware, Hertfordshire, Wordsworth Editions Ltd, 1999), which is based on Cook's journals; J. C. Beaglehole, *The Life of Captain James Cook* (London, Adam and Charles Black, 1974); and Patrick O'Brian, *Joseph Banks* (London, Harvill Press, 1997).

3   Ray Desmond, *Kew: The History of the Royal Botanic Gardens* (London, Harvill Press, 1995), p. 87, citing letter J. Ellis to C. Linnaeus, 19 August 1768.

4   Information about London's animal collections is taken from Julia Allen, *Samuel Johnson's Menagerie* (Norwich, The Erskine Press, 2002); Geoffrey Parnell, *The Royal Menagerie at the Tower of London* (pamphlet, Leeds, Royal Armouries Museum, 1999); and Daniel Hahn, *The Tower Menagerie* (London, Simon and Schuster, 2003). Grateful thanks for further information to Geoffrey Parnell of the Royal Armouries Library.

5   Anon., *An Historical Account of the Curiosities of London and Westminster* (London, J. Newbury, 1767), pp. 12–27, BL.

6   Jessie Dobson, 'John Hunter's animals' in *Annals of the Royal College of Surgeons of England*, 17 (1962), pp. 379–486.

7   *Gentleman's Magazine*, December 1751, p. 571.

8   Richard D. Altick, *The Shows of London* (Cambridge, Mass., Belknap Press, 1978), p. 35.

9   Ottley, 'The Life', p. 30. Castle Street later became Charing Cross Road.

10   *Gentleman's Magazine*, 1751, p. 153, describes the 'wonderful centaur' on show in Charing Cross.

11   Julia Allen, *Samuel Johnson's Menagerie*, p. 15.

12   William Hunter, 'An account of the nyl-ghau, an Indian animal, not hitherto described' in *Philosophical Transactions of the Royal Society*, 61 (New York, Johnson Reprint Co., 1965), pp. 170–81.

13   Home, 'A short account', p. xxxi.

14   Details of Hunter's Earls Court home, known as Earl's Court House, are taken from various cuttings in the HA. It was demolished in 1886.

15   *Morning Post*, 30 August 1793, excerpt in HA, p. 14.

16   Foot, *The Life*, pp. 240–2.

17   'John Hunter at Earl's Court, Kensington 1764–93', leaflet reprinted from the *Atheneum* of 1870, HA, p. 5.

18   Laszlo A. Magyar, *John Hunter and John Dolittle* at www.geocities.com/tapir32hu/hunter.html. This theory is also supported, I believe, by a letter from Hunter when asked for his view by Edward Jenner on a patient. In typical conservative style his reply was, 'I believe the best thing you can do is to do little' (JH, *Letters from the Past*, p. 10).

19   JH, miscellaneous notes and extracts, ms 49 e 19, RCS, n.d.

20   JH, *The Works*, vol. 4, 'Observations on bees', pp. 422–66.

21   Home, 'A short account', p. xix.

22   Jessie Dobson, 'The Hunter specimens at Kew Observatory' in *Annals of the Royal College of Surgeons of England,* 8 (1951), pp. 457–62.

23   Home, 'A short account', p. xxxviii.

24   Andrew Cunningham, 'The pen and the sword: recovering the disciplinary identity of physiology and anatomy before 1800, II: Old anatomy – the sword' in *Studies in History and Philosophy of Biological and Biomedical Sciences*, 34 (2003), pp. 51–76.

25   Andrew Cunningham, 'The pen and the sword: recovering the disciplinary identity of physiology and anatomy before

1800, I: Old physiology – the pen' in *Studies in History and Philosophy of Biological and Biomedical Sciences*, 33 (2002), pp. 631–65.

26 F. J. Cole, *A History of Comparative Anatomy* (London, Macmillan and Co. Ltd, 1944), p. 20, quoting Alexander Monro I, in his work edited by Monro II, published in 1783.

27 The work of Camper, Buffon, Daubenton and others is described in Charles Coulston Gillispie (ed.), *Dictionary of Scientific Biography* (New York, Charles Scribner's Sons, 1970), various entries; John Gribben, *Science: a history 1543–2001* (London, Allen Lane, 2002), pp. 221–9; F. J. Cole, *A History of Comparative Anatomy*, p. 20 and appendix. For a comprehensive discussion of the pursuit of comparative anatomy, see Andrew Cunningham, *The Anatomist Anatomis'd: An experimental discipline in eighteenth-century Europe* (Aldershot, Ashgate Publishing, 2006).

28 Richard D. Altick, *The Shows of London*, pp. 20 and 24.

29 Stephen J. Cross, 'John Hunter, the animal oeconomy, and late eighteenth-century physiological discourse' in *Studies in the History of Biology*, 5 (1981), pp. 1–110, provides a good explanation of Hunter's purpose.

30 JH, miscellaneous notes and extracts, ms 49 e 19, RCS, n.d.

31 JH, *The Works*, vol. 4, 'The animal oeconomy', preface by Owen.

32 Anon., article in the *European Magazine* (1782), reprinted in John Abernethy, *Physiological Lectures* (London, Longman, 1825), pp. 341–52.

33 JH, *The Works*, vol. 4, pp. 292–8.

34 JH, miscellaneous notes and extracts, ms 49 e 19, RCS, n.d.

35 JH, 'A Copy of the Oldest Portion of Catalogue in Mr Hunter's own handwriting', RCS ms 49 e 53. The specimens listed in this earliest surviving catalogue were all considered to have been collected before 1764.

36 JH, *Essays and Observations*, vol. 1, p. 107.

37 JH, *The Works*, vol. 4, 'Observations on the structure and oeconomy of whales', pp. 331–92. The paper was first published in *Philosophical Transactions of the Royal Society* in 1787.

38   Herman Melville, *Moby-Dick* (London, Penguin, 1972), p. 85. First published as *The Whale* in 1851.

39   Jessie Dobson (ed.), *Descriptive Catalogue of the Physiological Series in the Hunterian Museum* (Edinburgh and London, E. & S. Livingstone, 1970), part 1, p. 19.

40   JH, *Essays and Observations*, p. 52.

41   JH, *The Works*, vol. 4, 'Experiments and observations on animals with respect to the power of producing heat', pp. 131–55.

42   JH, *The Works*, vol. 4, 'Experiments and observations on the growth of bones', pp. 315–18; Jessie Dobson (ed.), *Descriptive Catalogue of the Physiological Series in the Hunterian Museum*, pp. 8–12. The bone growth experiments are also discussed in G. Bentley, 'John Hunter's studies of the musculoskeletal system' in *Papers presented at the Hunterian Bicentenary Commemorative Meeting* (London, Royal College of Surgeons of England, 1995), pp. 20–5.

43   JH, *Essays and Observations*, vol. 1, p. 194.

44   Charles Darwin, *The Descent of Man*, ed. Richard Dawkins (London, Gibson Square Books, 2003), p. 540.

45   JH, *The Works*, Atlas, p. 18. The six sparrows are still in a perfect state in the Hunterian Museum, specimens 2457–62.

46   Dr William Irvine to Professor Thomas Hamilton, 17 June 1771, cited in 'The Hunters and the Hamiltons: some unpublished letters', *Lancet*, 18 February 1928, pp. 354–60.

47   Otto Sonntag (ed.), *John Pringle's Correspondence with Albrecht von Haller* (Basel, Schwabe, 1999), Pringle to Haller, 14 October 1768, pp. 116–24. The earl's stomach is preparation P 1019 in Hunter's museum.

48   Ottley, 'The Life', p. 28.

49   David Morris, 'John Hunter – myth or legend?' in *Hunterian Society Transactions* (1974–6), pp. 43–55.

50   Sidney Lee and Leslie Stephen (eds.), *Dictionary of National Biography* (London, Smith, Elder and Co., 1908–9), vol. 9, p. 206.

51   George C. Peachey, 'William Bromfield 1713–1792' in *Proceedings of the Royal Society of Medicine*, 8 (1915), pp. 103–26. Peachey says Bayford was an apprentice to Bromfield.

52 Sidney Lee and Leslie Stephen (eds.), *Dictionary of National Biography*, vol. 8, p. 788.

53 Dobson, *John Hunter*, p. 113.

54 Jane M. Oppenheimer, 'John and William Hunter and some contemporaries' in *Bulletin of the History of Medicine*, 23 (1949), pp. 41–2.

55 The Caesarean operation is described by William Cooper, the physician initially called in by the midwife, and by Henry Thomson, the surgeon who performed the operation, in *Medical Observations and Inquiries*, 4 (1771), pp. 261–71 and 272–9.

56 J. H. Young, *The History of the Caesarean Section* (London, H. K. Lewis and Co. Ltd, 1944), pp. 1–54.

57 Otto Sonntag (ed.), *John Pringle's Correspondence with Albrecht von Haller*, Pringle to Haller, 3 April 1770, pp. 135–6; JH, *The Works*, vol. 4, pp. 81–121; JH, *Case Books*, pp. 374–5.

58 JH, 'On the digestion of the stomach after death' in *Philosophical Transactions of the Royal Society*, 62 (New York, Johnson Reprint Co., 1965), pp. 447–54.

59 The youth's stomach is specimen 592; a similar preparation of human stomach destroyed by gastric acid after death, dating from about 1755, is specimen 591.

60 JH, *Case Books*, pp. 370–1.

61 Martin Myrone, *George Stubbs* (London, Tate Publishing, 2002), p. 46.

62 William Hunter, 'An account of the nyl-ghau, an Indian animal, not hitherto described', pp. 170–81.

63 JH, 'Note on teeth and colon of Nyl-ghau and goat', n.d., ms H 147, Glasgow University Library, Special Collections.

64 The nilgai skeleton is specimen no. RCSHC/CO 1347 in the Hunterian Museum.

65 Otto Sonntag (ed.), *John Pringle's Correspondence with Albrecht von Haller*, Pringle to Haller, 13 June 1771, p. 165.

66 For details on Jenner's life, see Richard B. Fisher, *Edward Jenner 1749–1823* (London, André Deutsch, 1991); John Baron, *The Life of Edward Jenner* (London, Henry Colburn, 1827).

67 Jenner's vaccine, using a small dose of cowpox to protect

against the deadly and disfiguring smallpox, eventually led to the complete eradication of the disease, declared by the World Health Organization in 1978.

68 Edward Duyker and Per Tingbrand, *Daniel Solander, Collected Correspondence 1753–82* (Melbourne University Press, 1995), p. ix.

69 Harold B. Carter, *Sir Joseph Banks 1743–1820* (London, British Museum (Natural History), 1988), pp. 95–6.

70 It is exceedingly difficult to identify the animals Hunter obtained from Cook's first voyage since records are incomplete. There are numerous antipodean animals in the Hunterian Museum, but it is not always clear whether they were brought back on Cook's first voyage or by later explorers, such as John White, who donated many animals to Hunter after his journey to New South Wales in 1790. The sources for animals named in the text are the sea-pen (preparation 2925); Richard Owen (ed.), *Descriptive and Illustrated Catalogue of the Physiological Series of Comparative Anatomy*, vol. 5, Products of Generation (London, RCS, 1840), p. 61 (sharks' eggs and eels); JH, *Essays and Observations*, vol. 2, pp. 235–6 and 69–70 (mole-rat and zorilla); giant squid (preparation 308).

71 Harold B. Carter, *Sir Joseph Banks 1743–1820*, pp. 89–91.

72 Joseph Banks, *The Endeavour Journal of Joseph Banks 1768–1771*, ed. J. C. Beaglehole (Sydney, Trustees of the Public Library of New South Wales in association with Angus and Robertson, 1962), vol. 2, pp. 93–4.

73 Much debate has centred on the identity of the kangaroos seen by Banks and Cook. T. C. S. Morrison-Scott and F. C. Sawyer argue convincingly that the skull given to Hunter came from a Great Grey Kangaroo, most probably the second one shot by Gore, based on a photograph of the skull; see Morrison-Scott and Sawyer, 'The identity of Captain Cook's kangaroo' in *Bulletin of British Museum (Natural History)*, 1 (1950), part 3, pp. 45–50. Hunter refers to Banks giving him a skull from Cook's first voyage in JH, *The Works*, vol. 4, p. 485. Hunter's description of the teeth, which follows, is from the same source. The skull was destroyed during the Second World War in 1941. Many

thanks to the staff of the Natural History Museum for help.

74   John White, *Journal of a Voyage to New South Wales*, ed. A. Chisholm (Sydney, London, etc., Angus and Robertson, 1962), first published 1790.

75   JH, 'Directions for preserving animals, and parts of animals, for examination', n.d., RCS ms HUN:J 37.

76   A letter from Dr William Irvine to Professor Thomas Hamilton, 17 June 1771, cited in 'The Hunters and the Hamiltons: some unpublished letters', *Lancet*, 18 February 1928, pp. 354–60, states that Hunter received £200 for his teeth treatise.

77   JH to William Hunter, Saturday [*sic*] evening, n.d. (21 July 1771), HBC, vol. 2, p. 10. The day was in fact Sunday.

78   Copy of Register of Marriage at St James's Westminster, 1771, HA, p. 21.

79   Kobler, *The Reluctant Surgeon*, p. 157, states that Cook and Banks attended the wedding but without any reference. The story of the travellers presenting hickory-wood logs to the couple is contained in a curious pamphlet by DRAGM (believed to be a pseudonym for Robert Anstruther Goodsir), *Only An Old Chair* (Edinburgh, David Douglas, 1884).

80   Tobias Smollett, *The Letters of Tobias Smollett*, ed. Lewis M. Knapp (Oxford, Clarendon Press, 1970), extract from a letter to John Hunter, Leghorn, 9 January 1771, p. 140; Jeremy Lewis, *Tobias Smollett* (London, Jonathan Cape, 2003), pp. 270 and 278–9. Other writers have suggested Smollett promised his corpse to William Hunter, but Knapp, who is regarded as the authority on the writer, and Lewis, his most recent biographer, both state his offer was made to John. The letter extract has no addressee.

81   Sidney Lee and Leslie Stephen (eds.), *Dictionary of National Biography*, vol. 18, p. 1101.

Chapter 10

1   R. C. Brock, *The Life and Work of Astley Cooper* (Edinburgh and London, E. & S. Livingstone, 1952), p. 145.

2   Home, 'A short account', p. xxii.

3   John Baron, *The Life of Edward Jenner* (London, Henry

Colburn, 1827), p. 10, says Jenner called Hunter 'the dear man'; in Jessie Dobson, *William Clift FRS* (London, William Heinemann, 1954), p. 109, Clift says Lynn called Hunter 'Glorious John'.

4 For details about Anne Hunter see Janet Todd (ed.), *A Dictionary of British and American Women Writers* (London, Methuen and Co., 1987), pp. 169–70; Aileen K. Adams, ' "I am happy in a wife": a study of Mrs John Hunter (1742–1821)' in *Papers presented at the Hunterian Bicentenary Commemorative Meeting* (London, Royal College of Surgeons of England, 1995), pp. 32–7.

5 Jessie Dobson, *William Clift FRS*, p. 109.

6 Ottley, 'The Life', p. 41.

7 Hester Thrale, *Thraliana: The Diary of Mrs Hester Lynch Thrale 1776–1809*, ed. Katherine C. Balderston (Oxford, Clarendon Press, 1951), vol. 1, p. 67.

8 Lord Holland (Henry Richard Vassall Fox), *Further Memoirs of the Whig Party 1807–1821* (London, John Murray, 1905), p. 345.

9 *Kensington Express*, 20 February 1886, cutting in the HA, p. 9.

10 Letter JH to James Baillie, 23 November 1775, HBC, vol. 7, p. 17.

11 These figures are cited by John Gunning, William Walker and Thomas Keate, Hunter's enemies at St George's, in a letter to the governors, n.d. (1793), printed verbatim in Peachey, *A Memoir*, pp. 282–96.

12 Figures for the fees are quoted in JH, letter to his colleagues, 9 July 1792, cited in Peachey, *A Memoir*, p. 272.

13 JH, letter to the governors, 28 February 1793, cited in Peachey, *A Memoir*, pp. 275–82.

14 JH, letter to his colleagues, 9 July 1792, and JH, letter to the governors, 28 February 1793, cited in Peachey, *A Memoir*, pp. 273 and 275.

15 Hunter states that he began lecturing privately, inviting pupils from St George's free of charge, in 1772 in both his lecture notes and an article, which he sanctioned, in the *European Magazine*. JH, *The Works*, vol. 1, 'Lectures on the principles of surgery', p. 210; Anon., article in the

European Magazine (1782), reprinted in John Abernethy, *Physiological Lectures* (London, Longman, 1825), pp. 341–52.

16 Peachey, *A Memoir*, p. 162. There has been debate about when Hunter opened his lectures to the public, different biographers giving 1773 or 1774 as the year, but Peachey makes a convincing case for 1775, when the first known advertisement was placed. The *European Magazine* article refers to Hunter lecturing privately in 1772, 1773 and 1774. Further evidence for the lectures not being given publicly until after 1774 is given in a paper signed by Hunter in May 1774, certifying that a pupil attended lectures 'which I gave several of the pupils of St George's hospital', RCS ms 49 e 59.

17 Foot, *The Life*, pp. 243–4.

18 Reply from John Gunning, William Walker and Thomas Keate to the governors, n.d. (1793), in Peachey, *A Memoir*, p. 289.

19 Henry Cline, Hunterian Oration at the RCS, 1824.

20 Anon., article in the *European Magazine* (1782), reprinted in John Abernethy, *Physiological Lectures*, pp. 341–52.

21 JH, 'Lectures on the principles of surgery', p. 208. Hunter's idea of educating medical students so that they can educate themselves has been revived only recently by the General Medical Council.

22 William Clift, relating details told to him by Henry Cline, in a note on the inside cover of JH, 'Lectures on the principles of surgery', notes taken by Hopkinson, probably between 1781 and 1785, ms RCS. Cline attended in 1774 or 1775.

23 Hunter stated in his lectures that he declined an invitation to become an anatomy teacher in 1768. Kemp says he was asked in 1769 by the Society of Artists to read lectures and dissect a cadaver. He accepted the latter. JH, 'Lectures on the principles of surgery', p. 210; Ruth Vincent-Kemp, 'George Stubbs and his Eighteenth-Century Patrons' in *Veterinary History*, 3 (1983), 1, pp. 1–10.

24 Adams, *Memoirs*, p. 75.

25 George Macilwain, *Memoirs of John Abernethy* (London, Hurst and Blackett, 1854), vol. 1, p. 253.

26 R. C. Brock, *The Life and Work of Astley Cooper*, pp. 4–5.

27 Foot, *The Life*, p. 245.

28 Ottley, 'The Life', p. 48.

29 Ibid.

30 Foot, *The Life*, p. 245.

31 John Abernethy, *Physiological Lectures*, p. 6; Adams, *Memoirs*, p. 73.

32 JH, 'Lectures on the principles of surgery', pp. 207 and 235.

33 The contents of Hunter's lectures are taken from JH, 'Lectures on the principles of surgery' in *The Works*, vol. 1, unless otherwise specified. These are transcribed from short-hand notes taken by Nathaniel Rumsey in 1786 and 1787, although they follow very much the pattern of notes taken by other pupils at various times.

34 JH, 'Lectures on the principles of surgery', p. 20.

35 Anon., article in the *European Magazine* (1782), reprinted in John Abernethy, *Physiological Lectures*, pp. 341–52.

36 JH, 'Lectures on the principles of surgery', pp. 625–8.

37 Ibid., p. 495.

38 Stephen Jacyna, 'Physiological principles in the surgical writings of John Hunter' in Christopher Lawrence (ed.), *Medical Theory, Surgical Practice* (London and New York, Routledge, 1992), p. 145, citing notes of Hunter's lectures, RCS ms 49 e 23.

39 JH, 'Lectures on the principles of surgery', p. 429.

40 Ibid., p. 406.

41 Ibid., p. 405.

42 Mary Coke, *The Letters and Journals of Lady Mary Coke*, ed. J. A. Home (Edinburgh, David Douglas, 1889–96), 23 July 1772, vol. 4, p. 102.

43 JH, 'Lectures on the principles of surgery', p. 360.

44 Quoted in Stephen Jacyna, 'Physiological principles in the surgical writings of John Hunter', citing JH, 'Surgical lectures', notes at the Royal College of Physicians of Edinburgh, ms M8 47, pp. 208–9.

45 Sir D'Arcy Power, *Hunterian Oration 1925* (Bristol, John Wright and Sons Ltd, 1925), p. 9.

46   William Clift, relating details told to him by Henry Cline (see note 22).

47   R. C. Brock, *The Life and Work of Astley Cooper*, p. 147.

48   John Abernethy, *Physiological Lectures*, introductory lecture 1815, p. 126.

49   Sir Arthur Porritt, 'John Hunter: distant echoes' in *Annals of the Royal College of Surgeons of England*, 41 (1967), p. 10.

50   Foot, *The Life*, p. 280.

51   John Abernethy, *Physiological Lectures*, p. 199.

52   Ottley, 'The Life', p. 52.

53   Foot, *The Life*, p. 248.

54   R. C. Brock, *The Life and Work of Astley Cooper*, p. 147; Foot, *The Life*, p. 239.

55   James Beattie, *James Beattie's London Diary*, ed. Ralph C. Walker (Aberdeen University Press, 1946), 25 May 1773, p. 40.

56   George Cartwright, *A Journal of transactions and events, during a residence of nearly sixteen years on the Coast of Labrador* (Newark, Allin and Ridge, 1792), vol. 1, p. 271; Anthony A. Pearson, 'John Hunter and the woman from Labrador' in *Annals of the Royal College of Surgeons of England*, 60 (1978), pp. 7–13. The portraits are in the Hunter drawing books at the RCS.

57   JH, *Letters from the Past*, p. 10. The booklet reprints thirty-three of Hunter's letters. There are known to be fifty-one in all, of which thirty-two are kept at the RCS library. Others are also given in John Baron, *The Life of Edward Jenner*. Many are undated. The letters quoted here are all cited in the RCS booklet.

58   JH, *Letters from the Past*, p. 7.

59   Ibid., p. 8.

60   Ibid., p. 13.

61   Ibid., p. 11.

62   John Baron, *The Life of Edward Jenner*, pp. 31 and 40–1.

63   JH, *Letters from the Past*, p. 23.

64   Richard B. Fisher, *Edward Jenner 1749–1823* (London, André Deutsch, 1991), p. 26.

65   Ottley, 'The Life', p. 36.

66　Home, 'A short account', p. lxv.

67　Foot, *The Life*, p. 250; Adams, *Memoirs*, 1st edition, annotations made by Jessé Foot in a copy at the RCS, p. 52.

68　Lord Holland (Henry Richard Vassall Fox), *Further Memoirs of the Whig Party 1807–1821*, pp. 341–2.

69　Jessé Foot, annotations in Adams, *Memoirs*, p. 219.

70　Jessie Dobson, *William Clift FRS*, p. 11.

71　JH, 'Lectures on the principles of surgery', p. 244.

72　F. Dudley Hart, 'William Heberden, Edward Jenner, John Hunter and angina pectoris' in *Journal of Medical Biography* (1995), vol. 3, pp. 56–8.

73　Letter JH to Revd James Baillie, 23 November 1775, HBC, vol. 7, p. 17.

74　JH, miscellaneous notes and extracts, RCS ms 49 e 19; JH, 'Lectures on the principles of surgery', p. 344.

75　William Hunter, ms notes H 56, 13 August 1774, Glasgow University Library, Special Collections; William Cooper, 'An account of the Caesarean operation' in *Medical Observations and Inquiries* (1776), vol. 5, pp. 217–32.

76　Anne Hunter, 'To the Memory of a Lovely Infant', *Poems* (London, T. Payne, 1802).

77　Adams, *Memoirs*, p. 110.

78　Benjamin Franklin, 'The kite experiment', *The Autobiography and other Writings* (Penguin Classics, 1986), pp. 214–15.

79　Fiona Haslam, *From Hogarth to Rowlandson: medicine in art in eighteenth-century Britain* (Liverpool University Press, 1996), pp. 196–8.

80　Edward Duyker and Per Tingbrand, *Daniel Solander, Collected Correspondence 1753–82* (Melbourne University Press, 1995), letter Solander to J. Ellis, 7 November 1774, pp. 340–1. More detail on Walsh and his electric fish experiments can be found in Marco Piccolino and Marco Bresadola, 'Drawing a spark from darkness: John Walsh and electric fish' in *Trends in Neurosciences*, 25, 1 (2002), pp. 51–7.

81　JH, 'Anatomical observations on the torpedo' in *Philosophical Transactions of the Royal Society*, 63 (New

York, Johnson Reprint Co., 1965), pp. 481–9. Several preparations of the electric organs of the torpedo fish survive in Hunter's museum as specimens 2168 to 2179.

82   JH, *The Works*, vol. 4, p. 402.

83   JH, 'An account of the Gymnotus Electricus' in *Philosophical Transactions of the Royal Society*, 65 (New York, Johnson Reprint Co., 1965), pp. 395–407. The specimens are 2185 and 2186.

84   Otto Sonntag (ed.), *John Pringle's Correspondence with Albrecht von Haller* (Basel, Schwabe, 1999), Pringle to Haller, 13 December 1776, pp. 348–9.

85   JH, *Letters from the Past*, Hunter to Jenner, 2 August (1775), p. 9.

86   Edward Duyker and Per Tingbrand, *Daniel Solander, Collected Correspondence 1753-82*, Solander to Banks, 14 August 1775, pp. 354–5.

87   Letter JH to Revd James Baillie, 23 November 1775, HBC, vol. 7, letter 17.

88   Jessie Dobson, *William Clift FRS*, p. 13, citing Clift referring to Hunter's new coach.

89   JH, RCS ms 49 e 19, p. 470.

90   David Hume, *The Letters of David Hume*, ed. J. Greig (Oxford, Clarendon Press, 1932), vol. 2, pp. 324–5.

91   Ibid., to his brother John Home (Hume), 10 June 1776.

92   Ibid., to John Crawford, 15 June 1776.

93   William Hickey, *Memoirs of William Hickey*, ed. A. Spencer (London, Hurst and Blackett, 1913), vol. 2, pp. 86–7.

94   Anon. (attributed to James Perry), 'The Torpedo: A poem to the electric eel', 1777, RCS.

Chapter 11

1   James Boswell, *The Life of Samuel Johnson* (London, Everyman's Library, 1992), p. 739.

2   Details of Dodd's life and even more famous death are taken principally from Jessie Dobson, 'John Hunter and the unfortunate Doctor Dodd' in *Journal of the History of Medicine*, 10 (1955), pp. 369–78; Revd W. Foster, *Samuel Johnson and the Dodd Affair* (Lichfield, Johnson

Society, 1951); as well as accounts in the *Gentleman's Magazine*, as listed, and in Boswell's *Life of Samuel Johnson*, as cited.

3 *Gentleman's Magazine*, 47 (1777), 27 June, pp. 293–4.

4 Early nineteenth-century records reveal that out of thirty-six bodies dissected after hanging between 1812 and 1830, the heart was still beating in ten, although the dissection still went ahead. See Jessie Dobson, 'Cardiac action after "Death" by hanging' in *Lancet*, 261 (1951), pp. 1222–4.

5 JH, *The Works*, vol. 4, p. 153.

6 Ibid., p. 152.

7 P. J. Bishop, *A Short History of the Royal Humane Society* (London, RHS, 1974). I am grateful for the help of Janet Smith at the RHS.

8 JH, 'Proposals for the recovery of persons apparently drowned', read to the Royal Society 21 March 1776, in *The Works*, vol. 4, pp. 165–75.

9 D. Duda, L. Brandt and M. El Gindi, 'The history of defibrillation' in R. Atkinson and T. Boulton (eds), *The History of Anaesthesia: proceedings of the second international symposium on the history of anaesthesia held in London 20–23 April 1987* (London and New York, Royal Society of Medicine, 1987), pp. 464–8. I am grateful for the help of Peter Baskett, retired anaesthetist and editor of the journal *Resuscitation*, and to John Zorab, retired consultant anaesthetist, for advice on resuscitation.

10 *Gentleman's Magazine*, 47 (1777), 27 June, p. 346.

11 Jessie Dobson, 'John Hunter and the unfortunate Doctor Dodd', citing the *London Review of English and Foreign Literature* of September 1777.

12 *Gentleman's Magazine*, 60 (1790), pp. 1010, 1066 and 1077–8.

13 Jessie Dobson, 'John Hunter and the unfortunate Doctor Dodd', citing the *Aberdeen Journal*, 19 August 1794.

14 Ibid., citing a letter from Charles Hutton in the *Newcastle Magazine*, March 1822.

15 Ibid., p. 376.

16 JH to Edward Jenner, 11 May 1777, Glasgow University Library, Special Collections.

17 Revd James Baillie to William Hunter, 16 June 1777, HBC, vol. 1, no. 89.

18 JH, *Hunterian Reminiscences, being the substance of a course of lectures in the principles and practices of surgery delivered by Mr John Hunter in the year 1785, Taken in shorthand and afterwards fairly transcribed by the Late Mr James Parkinson*, ed. J. W. K. Parkinson (London, Sherwood, Gilbert and Piper, 1833), p. 149.

19 Tobias Smollett, *The Expedition of Humphrey Clinker* (London, Penguin Classics, 1967; first published 1771), p. 75.

20 Tobias Smollett, *The Letters of Tobias Smollett*, ed. L. Knapp (Oxford, Clarendon Press, 1970), Smollett to William Hunter, 2 October 1762, p. 109.

21 Home, 'A short account', p. xxvii. Home refers to the episode in 1776 but it is understood to have been 1777.

22 F. Hart, 'William Heberden, Edward Jenner, John Hunter and angina' in *Journal of Medical Biography*, 3 (1995), no. 1, pp. 56–8, citing a letter Edward Jenner to Caleb Parry, 1799.

23 William Le Fanu, *A Bibliography of Edward Jenner* (London, St Paul's Bibliographies, 1985), p. 25, citing a letter from Edward Jenner to W. Heberden, n.d., possibly 1778 or 1786.

24 Anon., 'The Hunters and the Hamiltons: some unpublished letters' in *Lancet*, 214 (1928), no. 1, pp. 354–60. The article reprints several letters sent by William Hamilton to his father Thomas Hamilton in 1777–8, from which quotes here are taken.

25 *Gentleman's Magazine*, 6 December 1777, p. 608.

26 W. Austin, *The anatomist overtaken by the watch in carrying off Miss W—ts in a hamper* (London, William Austin, 1773).

27 Sidney Lee and Leslie Stephen (eds), *Dictionary of National Biography* (London, Smith, Elder and Co., 1908–9) vol. 9, pp. 1121–2. The experiments are described by Home in miscellaneous manuscripts, RCS ms 49 e 5, referring to 1782.

28 Sir Arthur Porritt, 'John Hunter's women', reprinted from *Transactions of the Hunterian Society*, 17 (1958–9), WL.

29 Matthew Baillie, *A Short Memoir of My Life* (1818), reprinted in the *Practitioner* (1896), RCS.

30 Samuel Johnson to William Hunter, 29 December 1774, HBC, vol. 1, p. 53.

31 Samuel Johnson to William Hunter, 2 June 1778, cited in Bruce Redford (ed.), *The Letters of Samuel Johnson* (Oxford, Clarendon Press, 1992), vol. 3, pp. 117–18.

32 Tobias Smollett to William Hunter, 14 June 1763, HBC, vol. 1, p. 91.

33 W. S. Lewis et al (eds), *The Yale Edition of Horace Walpole's Correspondence* (Yale University Press, 1937–61), Horace Walpole to Lady Ossory, 4 December 1776, vol. 32, p. 334.

34 Cutting from *St James's Chronicle*, n.d. (1776), in HA, p. 10, refers to the elephant dissection.

35 *Royal Society Journal Book Copy*, 1777–80, vol. 29, 27 January 1780, pp. 573–84.

36 JH, 'On the Structure of the Placenta', *Royal Society Letters and Papers* (1780), vol. 65, p. 138. The paper was later published in a revised form in JH, *The Works*, vol. 4, pp. 60–71.

37 William Hunter to RS, 3 February 1780, *Royal Society Letters and Papers* (1780), vol. 65, p. 138.

38 JH to Joseph Banks, 17 February 1780, *Royal Society Letters and Papers* (1780), vol. 65, p. 140.

39 Foot, *The Life*, p. 250.

40 Matthew Baillie, *A Short Memoir of My Life*, RCS mss Baillie, p. 7.

41 Lloyd G. Stevenson, 'William Hewson, the Hunters and Benjamin Franklin' in *Journal of the History of Medicine*, 8 (1953), pp. 324–8.

42 C. Helen Brock (ed.), *William Hunter 1718–1783: a memoir by Samuel Foart Simmons and John Hunter* (University of Glasgow Press, 1983), pp. 17–19.

43 Benjamin Franklin to William Hunter, 30 October 1772, HBC, vol. 1, p. 89.

44 C. Helen Brock, *William Hunter 1718–1783*, p. 50.

45 William Hunter, *Two Introductory Lectures* (London, printed by order of the trustees for J. Johnson, 1784), p. 64.

46   JH, *The Works*, vol. 1, 'Lectures on the principles of surgery', p. 214.

47   JH, miscellaneous notes and extracts, RCS unpublished ms 49 e 19.

48   C. Helen Brock, *Calendar of the Correspondence of Dr William Hunter 1740–83* (Cambridge, Wellcome Unit for the History of Medicine, 1996), pp. 75–6.

49   Ibid., p. 89.

50   C. Helen Brock (ed.), *William Hunter 1718–1783*, p. 28.

51   JH, *The Works*, vol. 4, 'An Account of the Free-Martin', pp. 34–43.

52   JH, *The Works*, vol. 4, 'An Account of an extraordinary pheasant', pp. 44–9, first presented to the Royal Society in 1780. See also Brian Cook, *Contributions of the Hunter brothers to our understanding of reproduction, an exhibition from the University Library's collections* (leaflet, Special Collections Department, Glasgow University Library, 1992). As well as discussing Hunter's discoveries and Darwin's comments, this paper also notes that one of the three freemartins was not in fact a true example – although this makes little difference to Hunter's conclusions.

53   JH, 'An Account of the Free-Martin', p. 36.

54   JH to Edward Jenner, 6 July 1777 and 29 March 1778, in *Letters from the Past*, pp. 17 and 20.

55   E. H. Cornelius, 'John Hunter as an expert witness' in *Annals of the Royal College of Surgeons of England*, 60 (1978), pp. 412–18; *Gentleman's Magazine* (1781), pp. 156 and 209–11.

56   JH, 'Lectures on the principles of surgery', p. 350.

57   Thomas R. Forbes, 'Two new John Hunter manuscripts' in *Guildhall Studies in London History*, 1 (1973), pp. 24–7.

58   Richard Lovell Edgeworth, *Memoirs of Richard Lovell Edgeworth Esq* (London, R. Hunter, 1820), vol. 1, pp. 190–1.

59   JH, *Case Books*, p. 97.

60   Jessie Dobson, 'John Hunter's giraffe' in *Annals of the Royal College of Surgeons of England*, 24 (1959), pp. 124–8; Sidney Lee and Leslie Stephen (eds), *Dictionary of National Biography*, vol. 15, pp. 471–3.

61   John Hunter's drawing books, RCS.

62   Foot, *The Life*, p. 246.

63   Daniel Solander to Joseph Banks, 6 September 1781, in Edward Duyker and Per Tingbrand, *Daniel Solander, Collected Correspondence 1753–82* (Melbourne University Press, 1995), pp. 394–5. Hunter says he obtained the bottle-nosed whale in 1783 in the atlas accompanying 'The animal oeconomy', but he must be mistaken for Solander refers to the same animal in his letter of 1781, while a newspaper cutting of the same year is plainly the same whale. JH, *The Works*, vol. 4, 'Observations on the structure and oeconomy of whales', pp. 331–92; newspaper cutting (untitled and undated, but handwritten note says 1781), HA, facing p. 14.

64   JH, *The Works*, vol. 4, 'Observations on the structure and oeconomy of whales', pp. 331–92.

65   Home, 'A short account', p. xxii.

Chapter 12

1   JH to Joseph Banks, 1787, transcribed in the *Atheneum* (1869), copy in the HA, p. 5. The letter is understood to have been destroyed in the bombing of the museum in 1941.

2   Sidney Lee and Leslie Stephen (eds), *Dictionary of National Biography* (London, Smith, Elder and Co., 1908–9), vol. 3, p. 579.

3   Jessie Dobson, *William Clift FRS* (London, Heinemann, 1954), pp. 118–19, citing research in the 1840s by a retired naval surgeon, Mr Gough, in Ireland.

4   Sylas Neville, *The Diary of Sylas Neville 1767–1788*, ed. Basil Cozens-Hardy (Oxford University Press, 1950), 22 February 1782, p. 290.

5   JH, *Case Books*, p. 329.

6   C. J. S. Thompson, *The Mystery and Lore of Monsters* (London, Williams and Norgate, 1930), pp. 63 and 66.

7   Liza Picard, *Dr Johnson's London* (London, Weidenfeld and Nicolson, 2000), p. 251. Thanks to James Munro for suggesting that the man covered with scales suffered from icthyosis.

8   William Le Fanu, 'Hunter's Dwarfs' in *Annals of the Royal College of Surgeons of England*, 6 (1950), pp. 446–9; JH, *Case Books*, pp. 477–8. The portrait *Teresa, the Corsican Fairy* was painted by William Hincks in 1774. The entry in the case books appears to be a letter sent to Hunter by another practitioner.

9   Edward J. Wood, *Giants and Dwarfs* (London, Bentley, 1868). Details about the giants exhibited in London and folklore are from Wood and C. J. S. Thompson, *The Mystery and Love of Monsters, passim.*

10   Jan Bondeson, *A Cabinet of Medical Curiosities* (Ithaca, Cornell University Press, 1997) p. 74.

11   *Morning Herald*, 24 April 1782, BL.

12   Ibid., 30 April 1782, BL.

13   *Parker's General Advertiser*, 24 August 1782, HA, p. 14.

14   *London Chronicle*, 17–20 August 1782, Guildhall Library.

15   Sylas Neville, *The Diary of Sylas Neville 1767–1788*, 4 July 1782, p. 293.

16   Joseph Boruwlaski, *Memoirs of the Celebrated Dwarf Joseph Boruwlaski, a Polish Gentleman* (London, 1788), pp. 199–200; Edward J. Wood, *Giants and Dwarfs*, pp. 33–43.

17   Dr William Blackburne to Professor William Hamilton, 1789, Glasgow University Library, Special Collections MS Gen 1356/78.

18   Philip Reinagle, *Joseph Boruwlaski* (1782), Royal College of Surgeons of England.

19   Joseph Boruwlaski, *Memoirs of the Celebrated Dwarf*, pp. 199–201.

20   *Morning Herald*, 12 August 1782, BL.

21   Ibid., 22 July 1782, BL.

22   Jan Bondeson, *A Cabinet of Medical Curiosities*, pp. 85–6.

23   JH to William Petty (Earl of Shelburne), 29 July 1782, cited in S. Wood, 'Two further letters of John Hunter and notes on Rockingham's last illness from Hunter's Case Book' in *Annals of the Royal College of Surgeons of England*, 5 (1949), pp. 347–50.

24   JH, *The Works*, vol. 4, 'An Account of the Free-Martin', pp. 34–43.

25   JH, *The Works*, vol. 4, 'An Account of an extraordinary pheasant', pp. 44–9, first presented to the Royal Society 1780.

26 Ibid., pp. 44–5.

27 JH, *The Works*, vol. 4, 'On the colour of the pigmentum of the eye in different animals', pp. 277–8.

28 JH, RCS ms 49 e 19.

29 Jessie Dobson, 'John Hunter's animals' in *Annals of the Royal College of Surgeons of England*, 17 (1962), pp. 379–486. Dobson refers to a 'powter fish' caught in 1772, and sketched in Hunter's drawing books.

30 Home, 'A short account', p. lxvi.

31 Anon., article in the *European Magazine* (1782), reprinted in John Abernethy, *Physiological Lectures* (London, Longman, 1825), pp. 341–52. The £10,000 expenditure would be equivalent to about £600,000 today.

32 Home, 'A short account', p. xxix.

33 C. Helen Brock, *Dr William Hunter's Papers and Drawings in the Hunterian Collection of Glasgow University Library: a handlist* (Cambridge, Wellcome Unit for the History of Medicine, 1980), H 363, p. 42. Brock details a receipt for medals from John Howison in 1772. Howison, 'Lectures anatomical and chirurgical by William Hunter', ms, 2 vols, 1775, Newcastle University Library, Pybus Collection. An inscription on these notes states that they were purchased from the executor of the late Mr Howison, who had long been an assistant, probably 'in a manual capacity', to William Hunter and Matthew Baillie, and records that Baillie made provision for Howison (personal communication, Alan Callender, special collections assistant).

34 JH, *The Works*, vol. 1, 'Lectures on the principles of surgery', p. 202. The preface refers to notes of Hunter's lectures owned by Benjamin Brodie, which are ascribed to Mr Howison.

35 William Hamilton to Thomas Hamilton, 25 December 1777, reproduced in Anon., 'The Hunters and the Hamiltons: some unpublished letters' in *Lancet*, 214 (1928), no. 1, pp. 354–60.

36 Ottley, 'The Life', pp. 106–7. Ottley refers to Howison as 'his [Hunter's] man' and describes how he was set to follow Byrne.

37 A. M. Landolt and M. Zachmann, 'The Irish giant: new

observations concerning the nature of his ailment' in *Lancet* (1980), no. 1, pp. 1311–12. Thanks to Professor John Wass, professor of endocrinology at the Radcliffe Infirmary, Oxford, and to the Pituitary Foundation, for medical advice. Childhood-onset acromegaly, or gigantism, is the term for overproduction of a growth hormone in childhood. Acromegaly is the same condition, after normal growth has stopped, in adults. Both usually have the same cause: a benign tumour on the pituitary gland. Today the tumour would be removed by surgery.

38   Harold B. Carter, *Sir Joseph Banks 1743–1820* (London, British Museum (Natural History), 1988), p. 181.

39   Ibid.

40   JH, *Case Books*, pp. 126–7 and 405–6; S. Wood, 'Two further letters of John Hunter and notes on Rockingham's last illness from Hunter's Case Book'.

41   Charles Watson Wentworth, Marquis of Rockingham, to William Hunter, 18 February 1768, RCS.

42   Mr Astley's show is advertised in the *Morning Herald*, 11 April 1782 (and various other dates), Guildhall Library.

43   Ibid., 1 August 1782 (and other dates).

44   Ibid., 29 October 1782 (and other dates).

45   Cited in Jessie Dobson (ed.), *Descriptive Catalogue of the Physiological Series in the Hunterian Museum* (Edinburgh and London, E. & S. Livingstone, 1970), part 2, p. 201.

46   *Morning Herald*, 18 November 1782, Guildhall Library.

47   G. Frankcom and J. H. Musgrave, *The Irish Giant* (London, Duckworth, 1976), pp. 17 and 26. Cotter eventually arrived in London in 1785. He was variously described as measuring between seven feet eight inches and eight feet seven inches.

48   *Morning Herald*, 23 April 1783, Guildhall Library; Poor Rate Collector Books 1783, St Mary's in the Fields Parish Records, Guildhall Library – John Howison is listed as a house occupier.

49   C. Helen Brock (ed.), *William Hunter 1718–1783: a memoir by Samuel Foart Simmons and John Hunter* (University of Glasgow Press, 1983), p. 27.

50   JH, *Case Books*, p. 98.

51   C. Helen Brock (ed.), *William Hunter 1718–1783*, p. 71.
52   Anon., obituary of William Hunter in *Gentleman's Magazine* (1783), p. 364.
53   C. Helen Brock (ed.), *William Hunter 1718–1783*, p. 27.
54   Adams, *Memoirs*, pp. 133–4.
55   Matthew Baillie to R. Barclay, cited in Paget, *John Hunter*, p. 238.
56   C. Helen Brock (ed.), *William Hunter 1718–1783*, p. 27, annotation by JH.
57   Adams, *Memoirs*, p. 92.
58   Tom Taylor, *Leicester Square: its associates and its worthies* (London, Bickers and Son, 1874), pp. 281 and 341.
59   The house at 28 Leicester Square was later demolished and a pub currently stands on its site. A tatty bust of John Hunter stands in the square opposite. Details of the house interior are shown in a plan sketched by Hunter's last assistant, William Clift, in HA, p. 39.
60   Home, 'A short account', p. xxix. The lease and works cost £180,000 each at today's prices.
61   *Gentleman's Magazine* (and others with the same notice), June 1783, p. 541. Although the article states Byrne lost £700, a later court case attests to the theft of £770 in two bank notes.
62   *Morning Herald*, 5 June 1783, BL.
63   Jessie Dobson, 'Eighteenth century anatomists', *Practitioner*, 169 (1952), pp. 180–4; Stewart Craig Thomson, 'The Surgeon-Anatomists of Great Windmill Street School' in *Bulletin of the Society of Medical History of Chicago*, 5 (1937–46), pp. 301–21.
64   *Morning Herald*, 16 June 1783, BL.
65   *Parker's General Advertiser*, 5 June 1783, BL.
66   *Gentleman's Magazine*, 5 June 1783, p. 541; *British Magazine*, n.d. (1783), in HA; *Annual Reporter Chronicle*, June 1783, cited in 'The Demolition of Earl's Court House', *West London Observer*, 6 February 1886, HA, facing p. 10.
67   Details of Hunter's theft of the giant's body are given in Ottley, 'The Life', pp. 106–7, and Tom Taylor, *Leicester Square*, pp. 403–7. Both relate basically the same story. The latter description, which includes details of the barn swap, is

told by Richard Owen based on the story handed down from Hunter's last assistant, William Clift. Hunter would later claim he had paid 130 guineas.

68 Adam Sisman, *Boswell's Presumptuous Task* (London, Hamish Hamilton, 2000), p. 68. Hunter's outlay would be worth about £30,000 today.

69 JH to Edward Jenner, n.d. (1783), in John Baron, *The Life of Edward Jenner* (London, Henry Colburn, 1827), p. 65.

70 JH to Joseph Banks, n.d. (1787), transcribed in a leaflet, 'John Hunter at Earl's Court Kensington 1764–93' reprinted in the *Atheneum* (1869–70), HA. The original letter is said to have been destroyed when a bomb fell on the Hunterian Museum in 1941.

71 Cosmo Gordon, murder trial, 17 September 1784, on The Proceedings of the Old Bailey website, www.oldbaileyonline.org, ref. t17840917-1.

72 The specimen is P 140 in the Hunterian Museum.

73 JH, *Case Books*, p. 382 (Revd Vivian, specimen P 205), p. 9 (Lady Beauchamp, P 389) and p. 393 (Lieutenant General Desaguliers, P 292); Jessie Dobson, 'Some of John Hunter's patients' in *Annals of the Royal College of Surgeons*, 42 (1968), pp. 124–33 (Hon. Frederick Cornwallis, P 378 and 379).

74 JH, *Case Books*, pp. 548–50.

Chapter 13

1 Adam Smith to Henry Dundas, 18 July 1787, in Adam Smith, *The Correspondence of Adam Smith*, ed. Ernest Campbell Mossner and Ian Simpson Ross (Oxford, Clarendon Press, 1977), pp. 306–7.

2 JH to Edward Jenner, 22 April 1785, *Letters from the Past*, p. 36.

3 Adams, *Memoirs*, p. 93.

4 *The Sketch*, 24 February 1897, excerpt in HA, facing p. 39. This article, reporting the planned demolition of Hunter's home at 28 Leicester Square in 1897, relates that Stevenson 'is said to have chosen' the house as the scene for *Dr Jekyll and Mr Hyde*.

NOTES

5   Robert Louis Stevenson, *The Strange Case of Dr Jekyll and Mr Hyde* (London and Glasgow, Collins, 1953; first published 1886), pp. 37–8.

6   William Clift, 'Ground plan of John Hunter's House based on the plan drawn from memory and annotated by William Clift in 1832', HA, p. 39. Everard Home gives the dimensions of the extension in Home, 'A short account', p. xxx.

7   Home, 'A short account', p. xxx.

8   Tom Taylor, *Leicester Square: its associates and its worthies* (London, Bickers and Son, 1874), pp. 429–30. Taylor is quoting Hunter's last assistant, William Clift.

9   James Williams to Mary Williams, 8 October 1793, in G. Edwards, 'John Hunter's last pupil' in *Annals of the Royal College of Surgeons of England*, 42 (1968), pp. 68–70.

10   Home, 'A short account', pp. l–li.

11   JH, *Essays and Observations*, vol. 1, p. 266.

12   Lord Holland (Henry Richard Vassall Fox), *Further Memoirs of the Whig Party 1807–1821* (London, John Murray, 1905), p. 344; Ottley, 'The Life', p. 121.

13   JH to Edward Jenner, May 1788, cited in Ottley, 'The Life', p. 110.

14   Home, 'A short account', pp. l–li. Home describes Hunter's various episodes of illness and treatment in detail.

15   JH, loose memo, RCS ms 49 e 19.

16   Benjamin Franklin to Benjamin Vaughan, July 1785, cited in George Corner and Willard E. Goodwin, 'Benjamin Franklin's bladder stone' in *Journal of the History of Medicine*, 8 (1953), pp. 359–77.

17   JH et al to Benjamin Vaughan, n.d. (1785), cited in George Corner and Willard E. Goodwin, 'Benjamin Franklin's bladder stone', p. 366. One of the physicians was also named John Hunter, here latinized as Ionnes Hunter, who is occasionally confused with the surgeon.

18   Elizabeth Sheridan, *Betsy Sheridan's Journal: letters from Sheridan's sister 1784–86 and 1788–90*, ed. William Le Fanu (London, Eyre and Spottiswoode, 1960), p. 68.

19   Anne Hunter to Edward Jenner, 13 September 1785, cited in Ottley, 'The Life', p. 96.

20   H. Leigh Thomas, Hunterian Oration 1827, WL.

21   Adams, *Memoirs*, p. 111.

22   Ibid., p. 199.

23   James G. Mumford, *Surgical Memoirs and Other Essays* (New York, Moffat, Yard and Company, 1908), p. 157.

24   Ottley, 'The Life', p. 29.

25   JH, *Essays and Observations*, vol. 1, p. 270.

26   John Abernethy, Hunterian Oration 1819, published in *Physiological Lectures* (London, Longman, 1825), p. 55.

27   Anon., 'John Hunter', newspaper cutting, no title, n.d., HA, p. 13.

28   Peachey, *A Memoir*, pp. 164–5, citing an advertisement in the *Gazetteer and New Daily Advertiser*, 1 October 1785. Clift's plan shows the hat pegs and pupils' register.

29   JH, *Hunterian Reminiscences, being the substance of a course of lectures in the principles and practices of surgery delivered by Mr John Hunter in the year 1785, Taken in shorthand and afterwards fairly transcribed by the Late Mr James Parkinson*, ed. J. W. K. Parkinson (London, Sherwood, Gilbert and Piper, 1833).

30   John Abernethy, *Physiological Lectures*, introductory lecture 1815, p. 134, WL.

31   Bransby Blake Cooper, *The Life of Sir Astley Cooper* (London, J. W. Parker, 1843), vol. 1, p. 142.

32   Cuthbert E. Dukes, 'London Medical Societies in the Eighteenth Century' in *Proceedings of the Royal Society of Medicine*, 53 (1960), pp. 699–706.

33   Dobson, *John Hunter*, pp. 241–2.

34   Thomas Chevalier, Hunterian Oration 1821, WL. Chevalier was one of Hunter's pupils.

35   Peachey, *A Memoir*, pp. 164–5, advertisement in the *Gazetteer and New Daily Advertiser*, 1 October 1785.

36   Rita R. Auden, 'A Hunterian pupil: Sir William Blizard and the London Hospital' in *Annals of the Royal College of Surgeons of England*, 60 (1978), pp. 345–9.

37   Letter from John Gunning, William Walker and Thomas Keate to the governors of St George's, n.d. (1793), printed verbatim in Peachey, *A Memoir*, pp. 282–96.

38   JH, *Case Books*, pp. 239–40.

39   Ibid., pp. 450–1. Three sections of the tumour, P216, 217 and 218, survive in the museum.

40   Bransby Blake Cooper, *The Life of Sir Astley Cooper*, p. 232.

41   JH, *Treatise on the Venereal Disease*; Adams, *Memoirs*, p. 101.

42   Home, 'A short account', p. lxvi; William Clift, 'Ground plan of John Hunter's House'. The plan shows Hunter's name by the door.

43   David Mannings, *Sir Joshua Reynolds: a complete catalogue of his paintings* (Yale University Press, 2000), pp. 271–2. Hunter's portrait was no. 223, entitled *Portrait of a gentleman, half length*, in the customary style of many portrait titles, in the original catalogue. Thanks to Elizabeth King, research assistant at the Royal Academy Library, for information on the portrait and exhibition. Thanks also to Andrew Cunningham for explaining the archetypal philosopher's pose.

44   Selwyn Taylor, *John Hunter and his Painters* (London, Royal College of Surgeons of England, 1993), p. 1. Reynolds' first portrait now hangs in the Court Room at the Society of Apothecaries' headquarters, Apothecaries' Hall. It is understood to have been donated by Weatherall's nephew, Thomas Knight. Many thanks to Dee Cook, archivist of the Society of Apothecaries.

45   The life mask is preserved at the RCS.

46   The items displayed in the Reynolds portrait are discussed in Selwyn Taylor, *John Hunter and his Painters*; Sir Arthur Keith, 'The portraits and personality of John Hunter' in *British Medical Journal* (1928), pp. 205–9; Lord Brock, 'Background details in Reynolds's portrait of John Hunter' in *Annals of the Royal College of Surgeons of England*, 48 (1971), pp. 219–26; and Qvist, *John Hunter*, pp. 188–9.

47   The sketch of angled lines has been variously considered to show facial angles and branching arteries. My thanks to Dr Alistair Hunter, academic manager of the dissecting rooms at Guy's, King's and St Thomas' School of Biomedical Sciences, who convincingly suggests they depict muscle fibres. This

could be a reference to the Croonian lectures on the muscles which Hunter delivered to the RS.

48   John Ehrman, *The Younger Pitt* (London, Constable, 1969), vol. 1, p. 594. My thanks to Cyrus Kerawala, maxillofacial surgeon at the Royal Surrey County Hospital, Guildford, for advice on the likely form of the cyst.

49   Home, 'A short account', pp. lvii–lviii.

50   John Richardson, *The Annals of London* (London, Cassell and Co., 2000), p. 218.

51   Foot, *The Life*, p. 247.

52   JH, *Essays and Observations*, vol. 1, 'Of Embalming', pp. 398–400.

53   W. S. Lewis et al (eds), *The Yale Edition of Horace Walpole's Correspondence* (Yale University Press, 1937–61), Horace Walpole to Lady Ossory, 4 November 1786, vol. 33, p. 535.

54   Matthew Baillie, 'A Short Memoir of my Life' (1818), reproduced in the *Practitioner* (1896); Matthew Baillie, *The Morbid Anatomy of Some of the Most Important Parts of the Human Body* (London, J. Johnson and G. Nicol, 1793).

55   Dobson, *John Hunter*, p. 238.

56   Joanna Baillie, *The Collected Letters of Joanna Baillie*, ed. Judith Bailey Slagle (Madison, Fairleigh Dickinson University Press; London, Associated University Presses, 1999), vol. 1, p. 387.

57   Ibid., p. 923.

58   JH, *Case Books*.

59   Adam Sisman, *Boswell's Presumptuous Task* (London, Hamish Hamilton, 2000), pp. 156–7.

60   James Boswell, *Private Papers of James Boswell from Malahide Castle*, ed. G. Scott and F. Pottle (1933), BL, vol. 17, p. 17, 21 March 1787.

61   David Mannings, *Sir Joshua Reynolds*, p. 272.

62   James Boswell, *Private Papers of James Boswell from Malahide Castle,* vol. 17, p. 31, 19 May 1787.

63   Ibid., pp. 74–5, 77 and 83 – entries for 7, 12 and 18 March 1788.

64   R. H. Campbell and A. S. Skinner, *Adam Smith* (London

and Canberra, Croom Helm, 1982), p. 202; John Rae, *Life of Adam Smith* (London, Macmillan and Co., 1895), p. 402.

65   Adam Smith to William Strahan, 20 December 1777, in Adam Smith, *The Correspondence of Adam Smith*, pp. 229–30.

66   John Rae, *Life of Adam Smith*, p. 406.

67   Adam Smith to Henry Dundas, 18 July 1787, in Adam Smith, *The Correspondence of Adam Smith*, pp. 306–7.

68   B. Eisler, *Byron: Child of Passion, Fool of Fame* (London, Hamish Hamilton, 1999), pp. 12–13; A. B. Morrison, 'Byron's lameness' in *The Byron Journal* (1975), pp. 24–31.

69   JH, *Case Books*, p. 148.

70   B. Eisler, *Byron: Child of Passion, Fool of Fame*, pp. 42–3.

71   Thomas Gainsborough to anon., n.d. (but dated to April 1788), Hunterian Society collection at WL, ms 5610.

72   James Joseph Walsh, *History of Medicine in New York: three centuries of medical progress* (New York, National Americana Society, 1919), vol. 2, pp. 382–9.

73   C. G. T. Dean, *The Royal Hospital Chelsea* (London, Hutchinson, 1950), p. 88.

74   Dobson, *John Hunter*, p. 179.

75   Report from the Select Committee of the House of Commons on Anatomy, 22 July 1828, appendix 21, Rex v. Lynn, BL.

76   Jane M. Oppenheimer, 'A note on William Blake and John Hunter' in *Journal of the History of Medicine*, 1 (1946), pp. 41–5; W. Blake, *Poetry and Prose of William Blake*, ed. G. Keynes (London, Nonesuch Press, 1927), pp. 865–87; Peter Ackroyd, *Blake* (London, Sinclair-Stevenson, 1995), pp. 30 and 81.

Chapter 14

1   JH, *Essays and Observations*, vol. 1, p. 37.

2   Anon., newspaper cutting (no title), n.d. (pencilled 1788), HA, p. 13.

3   Richard Owen (ed.), *Descriptive and Illustrated Catalogue of the Physiological Series of Comparative Anatomy* (London, RCS, 1840), vol. 5, Products of Generation, pp. 177–8.

4   Anon., *A Guide to the Hunterian Museum* (London, RCS, 1993), p. 21.

5   Anon., newspaper cutting (no title), n.d. (pencilled 1788), HA, p. 13.

6   Ibid.

7   Dobson, *John Hunter*, p. 190.

8   Benjamin Hutchinson, *Biographia Medica, or historical and critical memoirs of the lives and writings of the most eminent medical characters that have existed from the earliest account of time to the present period* (London, J. Johnson, 1799), vol. 1, pp. 495–6. The total number of fossils is given as 2,773 by Richard Owen in JH, *Essays and Observations*, vol. 1, p. 293. Frederic Wood Jones ('John Hunter as a geologist' in *Annals of the Royal College of Surgeons of England*, 12 (1953), pp. 219–45, especially p. 233) calculated the collection at 2,957. Editors of the 1859 publication of *Observations and Reflections on Geology* erroneously gave the total as 415.

9   Anon., newspaper cutting (no title), n.d. (pencilled 1788), HA, p. 13.

10   Ottley, 'The Life', p. 72; Anon., *Gentleman's Magazine* (1793), in Hunterian Society Collection, WL MS 5610.

11   Ottley, 'The Life', p. 116.

12   Jessie Dobson, 'John Hunter's animals', in *Annals of the Royal College of Surgeons of England*, 17 (1962), pp. 379–486.

13   JH to an unknown correspondent, 15 January 1793, Hunterian Letters RCS 49b 18a, Grey-Turner Bequest.

14   Richard Owen (ed.), *Descriptive and Illustrated Catalogue of the Physiological Series of Comparative Anatomy*, p. 41.

15   Anon., newspaper cutting (no title), n.d. (pencilled 1788), HA, p. 13.

16   Foot, *The Life*, p. 266.

17   W. S. Lewis et al (eds), *The Yale Edition of Horace Walpole's Correspondence* (Yale University Press, 1937–61), vol. 15, Horace Walpole to Revd Robert Nares, 5 October 1793, p. 241.

18   Article, 'Penny Cyclopaedia', cited in Tom Taylor,

Leicester Square: its associates and its worthies (London, Bickers and Son, 1874), pp. 418–19.

19 Anon., newspaper cutting (no title), n.d. (pencilled 1788), HA, p. 13.

20 Jessie Dobson, *A Guide to the Hunterian Museum (Physiological Series)* (London, E. & S. Livingstone, 1958), *passim*.

21 Anon., newspaper cutting (no title), n.d. (pencilled 1788), HA, p. 13.

22 Ibid.

23 Home, 'A short account', p. xxxv.

24 Richard Owen, preface to 'The animal oeconomy' in JH, *The Works*, vol. 4, p. xxxviii. Scarpa had visited the collection in 1781 and Camper in 1785. Blumenbach visited in the early 1790s. My thanks to Simon Chaplin for additional information.

25 David Morris, 'John Hunter – myth or legend?', Hunterian Oration 1975, *Hunterian Society Transactions* (1974–6), pp. 43–55.

26 J. Menzies Campbell, *Dentistry Then and Now* (Glasgow, Pickering and Inglis, 1963), p. 61.

27 William Wordsworth, 'The Prelude', book XI, *Poetical Works*, ed. Thomas Hutchinson (Oxford University Press, 1975), p. 570.

28 Paget, *John Hunter*, p. 230.

29 Foot, *The Life*, p. 274.

30 John P. Blandy and John S. P. Lumley (eds), *The Royal College of Surgeons of England: 200 years of history at the millennium* (London, Oxford, Royal College of Surgeons of England, Blackwell Science, 2000), p. 16.

31 Jessie Dobson, 'William Clift to Philip Syng Physick' in *Annals of the Royal College of Surgeons of England*, 34 (1964), pp. 197–203. The article includes the full transcript of a letter from Clift to Physick which is given two dates, 8 May 1835 and 25 April 1836.

32 Sir Ernest Finch, 'The influence of the Hunters on medical education' in *Annals of the Royal College of Surgeons of England*, 20 (1957), pp. 205–48.

33 St George's Pupil Register, transcript RCS, vol. 1, May 1789.

34   A. Peterkin, William Johnston and R. Drew, *Commissioned Officers in the Medical Services of the British Army 1660–1960* (London, Wellcome Historical Medical Library, 1968), vol. 1, p. 33.

35   Lloyd G. Stevenson, 'John Hunter, Surgeon-General 1790–1793' in *Journal of the History of Medicine*, 19 (1964), pp. 239–66. Stevenson cites Hunter's correspondence collected at the Public Record Office. Thanks to Andrew Cunningham for helping me put Hunter's approach into an eighteenth-century context.

36   JH to Lord Amherst, 5 May 1791, cited in Lloyd G. Stevenson, 'John Hunter, Surgeon-General 1790–1793', p. 246.

37   JH to Matthew Lewis, 11 May 1791, cited in Lloyd G. Stevenson, 'John Hunter, Surgeon-General 1790–1793', p. 246.

38   JH to Lord Amherst, 29 August 1793, cited in Lloyd G. Stevenson, 'John Hunter, Surgeon-General 1790–1793', p. 263.

39   Home, 'A short account', p. xxxvi.

40   JH, 'A case of paralysis in the muscles of deglutition, cured by an artificial mode of conveying food and medicines into the stomach', *Transactions of a SIMCK*, 1 (1793), pp. 182–8. The paper was read on 21 September 1790.

41   Ottley, 'The Life', p. 87.

42   JH, *Case Books*, pp. 589–91.

43   Aileen K. Adams, ' "I am happy in a wife": a study of Mrs John Hunter (1742–1821)' in *Papers presented at the Hunterian Bicentenary Commemorative Meeting* (London, Royal College of Surgeons of England, 1995), pp. 32–7.

44   B. Bugyi, 'J. Haydn and the Hunters' in *Proceedings of the XXIII International Congress of the History of Medicine, London 2–9 September 1972* (London, Wellcome Institute of the History of Medicine, 1974), vol. 2, pp. 904–7. In JH, *The Works*, vol. 1, 'Lectures on the principles of surgery', pp. 568–9, Hunter says of nasal polyps that 'the best mode of removing them is with a forceps'.

45   Ottley, 'The Life', p. 125.

46   For a comprehensive overview of the development of ideas on evolution see Peter J. Bowler, *Evolution: the history of an*

idea (University of California Press, 2003), 3rd edition. Other useful summaries include John C. Greene, *The Death of Adam: evolution and its impact on Western thought* (Iowa State University Press, 1981), 5th edition; and Roy Porter, *The Making of Geology: earth sciences in Britain 1660–1815* (Cambridge University Press, 1977). Very many thanks to Andrew Cunningham for helping me to understand Hunter's contribution to this field.

47   Stephen Inwood, *The Man Who Knew Too Much: the strange and inventive life of Robert Hooke 1635–1703* (London, Macmillan, 2002), pp. 125–6.

48   Peter J. Bowler, *Evolution: the history of an idea*, p. 51; Adam Sisman, *Boswell's Presumptuous Task* (London, Hamish Hamilton, 2000), pp. 114–15.

49   Peter J. Bowler, *Evolution: the history of an idea*, pp. 61–2; John C. Greene, *The Death of Adam*, p. 76; Roy Porter, *The Making of Geology*, p. 159.

50   Peter J. Bowler, *Evolution: the history of an idea*, pp. 69–70; John Gribben, *Science: a history 1543–2001* (London, Allen Lane, 2002), pp. 218–19.

51   John C. Greene, *The Death of Adam*, pp. 189–91; Peter J. Bowler, *Evolution: the history of an idea*, p. 52.

52   Peter J. Bowler, *Evolution: the history of an idea*, pp. 52–3.

53   John Gribben, *Science: a history 1543–2001*, pp. 221–6; Charles Coulston Gillispie (ed.), *Dictionary of Scientific Biography* (New York, Charles Scribner's Sons, 1970), vol. 2, pp. 576–82.

54   Charles Coulston Gillispie (ed.), *Dictionary of Scientific Biography*, vol. 3, pp. 577–80.

55   Ibid., vol. 7, pp. 584–93; John Gribben, *Science: a history 1543–2001*, pp. 335–8; Peter J. Bowler, *Evolution: the history of an idea*, pp. 86–95.

56   For details on Charles Darwin, see Adrian Desmond and James Moore, *Darwin* (London, Penguin, 1991). A useful short summary of Darwin and his ideas can be found in Patrick Tort, *Charles Darwin: the scholar who changed human history* (London, Thames & Hudson, 2001).

57   Qvist, *John Hunter*, p. 35. Qvist cites a list of Hunter's books later sold by auction.

58   James Beattie, *James Beattie's London Diary*, ed. Ralph C. Walker (Aberdeen University Press, 1946), 25 May 1773, p. 40.

59   JH, *The Works*, vol. 4, 'An Account of the Free-Martin', pp. 34–43.

60   JH, *The Works*, vol. 4, 'An Account of an extraordinary pheasant', pp. 44–9, first presented to the Royal Society 1780. See also Brian Cook, *Contributions of the Hunter brothers to our understanding of reproduction, an exhibition from the University Library's collections* (leaflet, Special Collections Department, Glasgow University Library, 1992).

61   JH, 'An Account of the Free-Martin', p. 36.

62   JH, *The Works*, vol. 4, 'On the colour of the pigmentum of the eye in different animals', pp. 277–85.

63   JH, *Essays and Observations*, vol. 1, p. 228.

64   JH, *The Works*, vol. 4, 'Observations tending to show that the wolf, jackal, and dog are all of the same species', pp. 319–30, first published in *Philosophical Transactions of the Royal Society* in 1787.

65   Edward Jenner to JH (n.d.), cited in JH, 'Observations tending to show that the wolf, jackal, and dog are all of the same species'.

66   JH, *The Works*, vol. 4, 'Observations on the fossil bones presented to the Royal Society by his most serene highness the Margrave of Anspach by the late John Hunter', pp. 470–80. This was read to the RS by Everard Home on 8 May 1794.

67   JH, *Observations and Reflections on Geology*. Two copies of the ms version of this paper exist. One is believed to have been taken in dictation by William Bell and William Clift (ms 49 c 1), the other to have been copied by Clift between 1793 and 1800 (ms 49 c 2). Both are preserved at the RCS Library.

68   JH, *Observations and Reflections on Geology*, p. x. Hunter's contribution to geology is discussed in Frederic Wood Jones, 'John Hunter as a geologist', pp. 219–45; and in George Qvist, 'Some controversial aspects of John Hunter's life and work: Part 5, geology and palaeontology' in *Annals of the Royal College of Surgeons of England*, 61 (1979), pp. 381–4.

69   JH, *Observations and Reflections on Geology*, p. xlvi.

70   J. Rennell to JH (n.d.), transcript in RCS ms 49 c 2, pp. 102–5.

71   JH, RCS ms 49 c 1 and ms 49 c 2. It has always been assumed that Rennell was commenting on the *Observations and Reflections on Geology* treatise, partly because later editors changed 'thousands of years' to 'thousands of centuries' in this, and partly because Rennell's letter is attached to the two ms from which it was published. It is conceivable that he was really commenting on Hunter's 'Observations on the fossil bones', which also contains the phrase 'many thousands of years'. In some ways this would make more sense as the paper was intended for the RS, while it is unclear why Hunter would seek Rennell's views on his other treatise. Home read the fossils paper to the RS in 1794 after Hunter's death and either he or Hunter might have made the amendment.

72   JH to Edward Jenner, 17 August (no year, but identified as 1789), *Letters from the Past*, p. 39; JH, miscellaneous notes and extracts, RCS unpublished ms 49 e 19. Joseph Adams, a former pupil, stated that Hunter had been described as a materialist (Adams, *Memoirs*, p. 233).

73   JH, *Essays and Observations*, vol. 1, p. 3. It was Richard Owen who compiled Hunter's various notes into the two volumes.

74   Ibid., p. 4.

75   Ibid.

76   Ibid., p. 246.

77   Ibid., p. 9.

78   Ibid., p. 203.

79   Charles Darwin, *The Descent of Man*, ed. Richard Dawkins (London, Gibson Square Books Ltd, 2003; first published 1871), pp. 9–10.

80   JH, *Essays and Observations*, vol. 1, p. 43.

81   Ibid., p. 37. This section is headed 'On the Origin of Species', although the title was probably added by Richard Owen while editing the original manuscript. My thanks to Simon Chaplin for elucidating this point and other advice on these notes.

82 George Qvist, 'Some controversial aspects of John Hunter's life and work: Part 6, evolution' in *Annals of the Royal College of Surgeons of England*, 61 (1979), pp. 478–83. Qvist calls the collection 'a museum of evolution'. Thanks to Andrew Cunningham for explaining that it was not.

83 JH, *Essays and Observations*, vol. 1, preface.

Chapter 15

1 William Clift, quoted in Paget, *John Hunter*, p. 253.

2 Details of Clift's early life are taken from William Clift, 'On his condition as Hunter's clerk', RCS ms 49 e 45; William Clift, 'A short account of my life' (1840), RCS ms 49 e 45; Richard Owen, biography of William Clift, RCS ms 49 e 45; Jessie Dobson, *William Clift FRS* (London, Heinemann, 1954); Frances Austin (ed.), *The Clift Family Correspondence 1792–1846* (University of Sheffield, 1991). My thanks to Dr Frances Austin-Jones for further advice on Clift's life.

3 William Clift, 'List of John Hunter's household' (1792), RCS ms 49 e 68.

4 William Clift to Elizabeth Clift, 5 March 1792, *The Clift Family Correspondence*, p. 30.

5 Jessie Dobson, *William Clift FRS*, pp. 10–11.

6 John Abernethy, *Physiological Lectures* (London, Longman, 1825), quoting William Clift, p. 209.

7 Benjamin Hutchinson, *Biographia Medica, or Historical and critical memoirs of the lives and writings of the most eminent medical characters that have existed from the earliest account of time to the present period* (London, J. Johnson, 1799), vol. 1, p. 483.

8 William Clift to Elizabeth Clift, 24 December 1792, *The Clift Family Correspondence*, pp. 49–50.

9 William Clift to John Clift, 11 October 1792, *The Clift Family Correspondence*, pp. 47–8; Jessie Dobson, 'A note on John Hunter' in *Annals of the Royal College of Surgeons of England* (1954), vol. 15, pp. 345–6.

10 Jessie Dobson, 'A note on John Hunter', quoting William Clift.

11   Jessie Dobson, *William Clift FRS*, p. 109.

12   R. H. Franklin, 'John Hunter and his relevance in 1977' in *Annals of the Royal College of Surgeons of England* (1978), vol. 60, pp. 266–73.

13   William Clift, 'A short account of my life', RCS ms 49 e 45.

14   Richard Owen (ed.), *Descriptive and Illustrated Catalogue of the Physiological Series of Comparative Anatomy* (London, RCS, 1840), vol. 5, Products of Generation, pp. 359 and 11–12.

15   JH, *The Works*, vol. 4, 'Observations on bees', pp. 422–66, first read to the Royal Society on 23 February 1792.

16   William Clift, 'List of John Hunter's household' (1792), RCS ms 49 e 68.

17   Jessie Dobson, *William Clift FRS*, p. 10.

18   Foot, *The Life*, p. 242.

19   W. R. Le Fanu, 'John Hunter's buffaloes' in *British Medical Journal* (1931), vol. 2, p. 574.

20   Jessie Dobson, *William Clift FRS*, p. 9.

21   Ottley, 'The Life', p. 121; Ernest E. Irons, 'The last illness of Sir Joshua Reynolds' in *Bulletin of the Society of Medical History of Chicago*, 5 (1939), no. 2, pp. 119–42.

22   Ottley, 'The Life', p. 121.

23   Jane M. Oppenheimer, 'John and William Hunter and some contemporaries in literature and art' in *Bulletin of the History of Medicine*, 23 (1949), pp. 21–47.

24   William Clift to Elizabeth Clift, 5 March 1792, *The Clift Family Correspondence*, pp. 30–1.

25   Details of Home's life can be found in A. W. Beasley, *Home Away from Home* (Wellington, Central Institute of Technology, 2000).

26   Home, 'A short account', p. lxv.

27   JH to his colleagues, 9 July 1792, in Peachey, *A Memoir*, pp. 272–3. The complete correspondence between Hunter and his colleagues in their row of 1792–3 is printed verbatim in Peachey's biography.

28   John Gunning, William Walker, Thomas Keate to JH, 4 October 1792, in Peachey, *A Memoir*, pp. 274–5.

29   William Clift to J. Clift, 11 October 1792, *The Clift Family Correspondence*, pp. 47–8.

30 Joseph Farington, *The Farington Diary*, ed. J. Greig (London, Hutchinson & Co., 1922–8), vol. 1, pp. 6–7, 17 and 18 October 1793.

31 Richard Owen (ed.), *Descriptive and Illustrated Catalogue of the Physiological Series of Comparative Anatomy*, vol. 5, pp. 120–6.

32 Lloyd G. Stevenson, 'John Hunter, Surgeon-General 1790–1793' in *Journal of the History of Medicine*, 19 (1964), pp. 254–5.

33 JH to the governors of St George's Hospital, 28 February 1793, in Peachey, *A Memoir*, pp. 275–82.

34 The surgeons' reply, (n.d.), in Peachey, *A Memoir*, pp. 282–96.

35 Surgeons' letter to the committee appointed to examine the laws relative to the surgeons' pupils and to consider the best method of improving their education, 27 May 1793, in Peachey, *A Memoir*, pp. 297–303.

36 JH to Matthew Lewis, 6 and 12 June 1793, in Lloyd G. Stevenson, 'John Hunter, Surgeon-General 1790–1793', p. 257.

37 James Williams to Mary Williams, 8 October 1793, in G. Edwards, 'John Hunter's last pupil', *Annals of the Royal College of Surgeons of England*, 42 (1968), pp. 68–70.

38 Ottley, 'The Life', p. 123.

39 James Williams to Mary Williams, 16 October 1793, in G. Edwards, 'John Hunter's last pupil'.

40 William Clift, note added in JH, RCS ms 49 e 19.

41 William Clift to Elizabeth Clift, 18 October 1793, *The Clift Family Correspondence*, p. 79.

42 Jessie Dobson, 'John Hunter's animals' in *Annals of the Royal College of Surgeons of England*, 17 (1962), pp. 379–486.

43 James Williams to Mary Williams, 16 October 1793, in G. Edwards, 'John Hunter's last pupil'.

44 William Clift to Elizabeth Clift, 18 October 1793, *The Clift Family Correspondence*, p. 79.

45 Dobson, *John Hunter*, p. 344.

46 Peachey, *A Memoir*, pp. 219–21.

47 Ottley, 'The Life', pp. 131–2. Details of Hunter's last

minutes are also related in James Williams to Mary Williams, 16 October 1793, in G. Edwards, 'John Hunter's last pupil'; William Clift to Elizabeth Clift, 18 October 1793, *The Clift Family Correspondence*, p. 79; and Home, 'A short account', p. lxi.

48 Foot, *The Life*, p. 182.

49 William Clift to Elizabeth Clift, 18 October 1793, *The Clift Family Correspondence*, p. 79; James Williams to Mary Williams, 16 October 1793, in G. Edwards, 'John Hunter's last pupil'.

50 William Clift to Elizabeth Clift, 18 October 1793, *The Clift Family Correspondence*, p. 79.

51 W. S. Lewis et al (eds), *The Yale Edition of Horace Walpole's Correspondence* (Yale University Press, 1937–61), Horace Walpole to M. Berry, 19 October 1793, vol. 12, p. 38, and Horace Walpole to Revd Robert Nares, 20 October 1793, vol. 15, p. 244.

52 Joseph Farington, *The Farington Diary*, vol. 1, pp. 6–7, 17 October 1793.

53 *European Magazine*, November 1793, HA, p. 11.

54 *Gentleman's Magazine*, 63 (1793), pp. 964–5.

55 The *Sun*, October 1793, cutting in the HA, p. 16.

56 Lloyd Allan Wells, 'Aneurysm and physiological surgery' in *Bulletin of the History of Medicine*, 44 (1970), p. 422.

57 Home, 'A short account', pp. lxii–lxv.

58 Dobson, *John Hunter*, p. 349.

59 William Clift to Elizabeth Clift, 20 November 1793, *The Clift Family Correspondence*, p. 81.

60 William Clift to Elizabeth Clift, 18 October 1793, *The Clift Family Correspondence*, p. 79.

61 William Clift, 'List of John Hunter's household' (1792), RCS ms 49 e 68.

62 Ottley, 'The Life', p. 137.

63 Sir Arthur Porritt, 'John Hunter's Women' in *Transactions of the Hunterian Society*, 17 (1958–9), pp. 81–111.

64 William Clift to Elizabeth Clift, 18 October 1793, *The Clift Family Correspondence*, p. 79.

65 Ottley, 'The Life', p. 142.

66 William Clift, 'Note on the preservation of the Hunterian

Observations before their destruction by Sir Everard Home', RCS ms 49 e 45.

67   William Clift, evidence to the parliamentary committee on medical education (1834): appendix in JH, *Essays and Observations*, vol. 2, pp. 493–500; and in Paget, *John Hunter*, pp. 252–6.

68   *Lancet* (1832), cited in A. W. Beasley, *Home Away from Home*, p. 83.

69   Qvist, *John Hunter*, p. 72.

70   John Abernethy, *Physiological Lectures*, p. 5.

71   Sir Arthur Keith, 'Memorable visits of Charles Darwin to the museum of the Royal College of Surgeons' in *Annals of the Royal College of Surgeons of England*, 11 (1952), pp. 362–3.

72   Anon., newspaper cutting, HA, p. 24; *Illustrated London News of the World*, 2 April 1859, HA, p. 27.

73   Richard Owen, biography of William Clift, RCS ms 49 e 45, quoting William Clift.

Wendy Moore is a writer and journalist. After working as a reporter for local newspapers she has specialized in health and medical topics for more than twenty years. As a freelance journalist her work has been pubished in a range of newspapers and magazines, including the *Guardian*, the *Observer* and the *British Medical Journal*, and has won several awards. Having written extensively on medical history, she obtained the Diploma in the History of Medicine from the Society of Apothecaries (DHMSA) in 1999 and won the Maccabean prize for best dissertation that year. She lives in south London with her partner, Peter, also a journalist, and two children, Sam and Susannah. *The Knife Man* is her first book.

Index

NOTE: this index is in alphabetical order except for the subheadings under Hunter, John, life milestones, which are chronological. Initials JH refer to John Hunter, WH to William Hunter.

INDEX

A SELECTION OF NON-FICTION TITLES
AVAILABLE FROM BANTAM AND CORGI BOOKS

THE PRICES SHOWN BELOW WERE CORRECT AT THE TIME OF GOING TO PRESS. HOWEVER
TRANSWORLD PUBLISHERS RESERVE THE RIGHT TO SHOW NEW RETAIL PRICES ON COVERS WHICH
MAY DIFFER FROM THOSE PREVIOUSLY ADVERTISED IN THE TEXT OR ELSEWHERE.

40664 7	CHE GUEVARA	Jon Lee Anderson £14.99
81442 7	A POUND OF PAPER	John Baxter £7.99
81672 1	GWEILO: MEMORIES OF A HONG KONG CHILDHOOD	Martin Booth £7.99
81506 7	GALLIPOLI	L.A. Carlyon £9.99
81447 8	INTO AFRICA	Martin Dugard £8.99
81194 0	GENESIS OF THE GRAIL KINGS	Laurence Gardner £7.99
50692 7	THE ARCANUM	Janet Gleeson £6.99
81247 5	THE MONEYMAKER	Janet Gleeson £6.99
81521 0	ARBELLA: ENGLAND'S LOST QUEEN	Sarah Gristwood £9.99
81445 1	HIMMLER'S CRUSADE	Christopher Hale £7.99
14789 3	THE DREADFUL JUDGEMENT	Neil Hanson £7.99
14975 6	CONFIDENT HOPE OF A MIRACLE: THE TRUE STORY OF THE SPANISH ARMADA	Neil Hanson £8.99
81485 0	THE AIR LOOM GANG	Mike Jay £7.99
81608 X	THE UNFORTUNATE COLONEL DESPARD	Mike Jay £7.99
81628 4	THE PRESTER QUEST	Nicholas Jubber £7.99
81353 6	THE DEVIL IN THE WHITE CITY	Erik Larson £7.99
81493 1	FATAL PASSAGE	Ken McGoogan £7.99
81642 X	ANCIENT MARINER	Ken McGoogan £7.99
81498 2	GENGHIS KHAN	John Man £7.99
81658 6	ATTILA THE HUN	John Man £7.99
81522 9	1421: THE YEAR CHINA DISCOVERED THE WORLD	Gavin Menzies £9.99
81657 8	ONE FOURTEENTH OF AN ELEPHANT	Ian Denys Peek £9.99
99886 9	WILFUL MURDER	Diana Preston £7.99
77210 0	A PIRATE OF EXQUISITE MIND: THE LIFE OF WILLIAM DAMPIER	Diana and Michael Preston £8.99
77100 7	TO THE HEART OF THE NILE	Pat Shipman £8.99
99982 2	THE ISLAND AT THE CENTRE OF THE WORLD	Russell Shorto £7.99
81539 3	THE MAPMAKER'S WIFE: A TRUE TALE OF LOVE, MURDER AND SURVIVAL IN THE AMAZON	Robert Whitaker £7.99

All Transworld titles are available by post from:
Bookpost, PO Box 29, Douglas, Isle of Man, IM99 1BQ
Credit cards accepted. Please telephone +44 (0) 1624 677237,
fax +44 (0) 1624 670923, Internet http://www.bookpost.co.uk
or e-mail: bookshop@enterprise.net for details.
Free postage and packing in the UK. Overseas customers: allow
£2 per book (paperbacks) and £3 per book (hardbacks).